"Consequently this country is at war with Germany"

War, Life and the BBC

The Day by Day War Diary of Marjorie Redman MBE

This book is published by Propagator Press, an imprint of:

AMS Educational Ltd
38 Parkside Road
Leeds
LS6 4NB

ISBN   978 1 86029 817 2

Designed by Propagator Press
Printed in Great Britain

Cover design: Roger Shapley, BAA

Marjorie Redman MBE
1907 – 1976
Portrait by Peggy Scott 21.7.37

FOREWORD

Published wartime diaries can offer not just a privileged entry into the heart of the writer's everyday circumstance amidst the turmoil of great events, but, on occasion, a reflection of a wider response to the challenges demanded from a people at war.

If the diarist were in a key position in an opinion-forming agency, or had an influential role on a Home Front, highly patriotic publication, then there is the distinct likelihood of stimulating, and even revelatory, reading. As the Sub-Editor of the BBC magazine, *The Listener*, this diarist, Marjorie Redman, writes well, observes sharply and is uninhibited in recording an unauthorised viewpoint. She has, indeed, created a gem.

Long being familiar with the genre of First and Second World War contemporary accounts, I automatically set high standards before judging a document to be of exceptional significance, and it was when I read Marjorie's entry for Tuesday September 17th 1940, that I saw that this was no ordinary writer, concerned only to record that which brings comfort. She describes a colleague coming into the office at 10 am, having tried to cheer himself up with a pint or two and succeeding only in depressing himself even further. He declares to one and all that we are 'beaten to a frazzle. People can't stand it. We might as well give in'. Marjorie is obviously determined to record events as they are......not to paint a chocolate box picture of everyone smiling through adversity.

There may be a vein of pessimism in Marjorie herself, but perhaps realism would be a fairer assessment. She writes on the day of truly calamitous news from the Far East, February 15th 1942:

"Singapore has fallen and the Japanese have overrun the whole of Malaya. This dismal news was announced by the Prime Minister in a broadcast at 9 o'clock. He introduced the information into the middle of his talk and tho' it was expected, I felt it as a blow. (At any rate he has kindly provided *The Listener* with a first article for its next issue). He tells us also of the advantages of having America, Russia and China as our allies: and gets in a hit at the people who by their criticism make the running of the war-machine difficult."

I am attracted by such dispassionate reportage. It brings the reader out of the warm cocoon of assurance that the public never believed the war could be lost, comforting though it is to read this so often expressed in memoirs.

There is no need to deduce from the above that Marjorie subsumes herself into being merely a barometer indicating national morale. Not at all – she worries about the fate of a dress she has bought and is having altered at the department store, D. H. Evans, during the height of the 1940 Blitz. The shop is closed and there is devastation all around the Regent Street area. Will she be able to pick the dress up? Then she indulges herself with the purchase of blue silk pyjamas, thinking, 'If I am blown up the extravagance cannot matter and if I am not they will be very useful.' This phrase nicely encapsulates Marjorie's sense of humour and her practical nature.

It is abundantly clear that music was an important part of her life, with attendance at recitals and concerts regularly recorded. She even, when describing the air raids, compares the sounds of various calibre anti-aircraft guns to the sounds produced by particular orchestral instruments.

If the final entry published in this spell-binding document, May 9th 1945, is in the nature of a grouse about getting *The Listener* out a day late, when 'all the news we have sweated to get in will be out of date', this is unsurprising given the circumstances. As she went on to record, 'Am very tired and dispirited'. She was not alone. It had been a long haul and how valuable for anyone filled with images of untrammelled rejoicing over victory in Europe, that Marjorie Redman's words, true to the end, command a more thoughtful response from the reader.

We are fortunate in having her diary in print.

Dr Peter H. Liddle F.R.Hist.S.
Life President, The Second World War Experience Centre, Horsforth, Leeds
March 2009

INTRODUCTION

I cannot remember the War. While I was growing up there was a dearth of real information about those years that many older folk wanted to forget. I did not read Marjorie's diaries until after her death and, when I was first privileged to do so, I could not put them down until I had got to the last page. Only then did I begin to comprehend in some small way what it must have been like for a cultured and gentle young woman with a quietly determined spirit and a liberal-minded and compassionate view, even of the enemy, to live and work through those years in London.

The diaries were not initially meant for publication and until now few people have read them. The vivid descriptions of daily life at that time, finely observed and written with characteristic wit and charm are a unique record that deserves a wider audience.

Marjorie was born in 1907 in Stroud, a small country town in Gloucestershire nestling between the surrounding hills and set in glorious countryside. She was the second of four children, having an older brother Roy, and two younger sisters, Phyllida and Hilary.

Despite the religious observances required on Sundays and the fact that the Baptist Chapel and its affairs certainly dominated the lives of her parents, Marjorie's family life was secure, happy and quite liberal for the times. Children in those days enjoyed a freedom almost unknown today, to roam at will through the countryside, cycling, having picnics, playing games of cricket with their friends or picking wildflowers or blackberries. Unless they were late home their parents did not need to worry about them.

Marjorie grew into a cultured young woman with strong literary tastes. She did not play an instrument herself, but had many friends who did and she loved to listen to classical music. She enjoyed reading and poetry. After her schooling she attended a secretarial college in Kensington and, at the end of her training, she went to work at the BBC for Children's Hour. In those years of the Depression you had few choices, so if a job was offered you accepted it gratefully. Marjorie had fallen on her feet though, as working at the BBC was deemed glamorous! The pay, however, was minimal and Marjorie soon found a way of increasing her earnings by writing plays, stories and rhymes to be broadcast on the programme. Over the years she went on to write poems and articles – some very funny – for such publications as *Woman's Journal*, the *Evening News* and *Punch*. Her friend, Joyce Johnson, who was a professional artist and illustrator, produced line drawings for some of them.

Later Marjorie got a transfer within the BBC to become secretary to the Editor of *The Listener*, a BBC publication that had only started two years previously. Later still she was promoted to Sub-Editor when someone else left, and it was in this position that she worked throughout the war years and until her retirement.

After the war was over, Marjorie continued to share a London flat with her two friends, Tina and Greta. In 1957 she was awarded the MBE, something that frequently happened to loyal and long-serving BBC staff. A further ten years later she began to suffer ill health, and in 1969 she retired and returned home to Stroud to live with her widowed mother and her sister, Phyllida, at the house where she had been born. Following a long battle with an obscure and devastating form of cancer, fought with quiet courage and immense dignity, Marjorie died in 1976.

Throughout her life, Marjorie retained those principles she learned at home and in the Baptist Church. She had many friends, both men and women. She never married. Perhaps she lost someone special in the war years. I once heard my mother say that there was a particular young airman whose death Marjorie found devastating. Certainly Marjorie's poem potently expresses the feelings of loss that so many people suffered so often during those years.

Death Overseas

Glanced at by light of the morning
You came in a careless glory,
And out of the spring you were taken,
Ravished away in the spring-time
Like buttercups' brief-burned story.
Sun through the quickening treetops
Flared on the scattering hawthorn.
Two of us walked by the hedgerow,
And the wheatblades were singing together,
The blackbird shouted for joy,
Assured of the coming of summer.

The golden bowl in the breaking
Is perfect in beauty for ever,
With tales for the generations,
For women to tell their children,
Of the passionate heart's endeavour.
Rain-rocked wind of the autumn
Hurries the leaves down-twisting.
One of us goes by the hedgerow
Through fields that are bare and older.
Silent birds in the bushes
Speak the oncoming of winter.

Marjorie was intelligent, cultured and witty with a wonderful ability to see the incongruous side of life. She was kind, generous, gentle, and although known for a calm and equable temperament, she had a mind of her own that brooked no compromise on matters of conscience. She was highly valued by her Listener colleagues, much liked by her many acquaintances and truly beloved by her friends and all her family. She was my aunt.

Christine Shapley
March 2009

Marjorie with
family, friends
and
colleagues

Marjorie's mother looks on as Marjorie, Joyce Johnson and John and Peter Beavan race to complete jigsaw puzzles.

Joyce Johnson & Marjorie on the lawn at home in Stroud

Marjorie and her father in the garden at home

Marjorie as a bridesmaid for her sister,
Hilary, August 1939

Marjorie, with her nephew, Martin, 1943

Marjorie and an editorial colleague visit the printer. *(BBC Copyright P13.685)*

1939 - 1945

The Day by Day

WAR DIARY
of
Marjorie Redman MBE

The war that everyone has been talking about for
so long seems to be upon us.   I think the past eighteen
months have been the happiest I have ever had.   In February
of this year Joyce and I had a fortnight in Switzerland: we
went by air with John, and joined five others who had gone
by boat.   I fell off a bob-sleigh and hurt my knee and
couldn't ski the second week, but lay in the sun and looked
at the pine-trees with snow on them.   When we came back, the
aeroplane was above white clouds, shining and beautiful.

There was a warm spell in early summer when Joyce
and I had lunch on Regent's Park Lake, and sometimes breakfast.
We often went to the Beavans at weekends to hear music and
play Scramble.   We have both ~~often~~ thought what a pleasant
life we led.   I say this because I expect the war will change
our lives pretty completely.   Should like to put on record a
golden weekend we had cycling in Berkshire last autumn.

An eventful year for the family.   Spent my last
weekend at Cambridge on January 6, and on February 24 Roy, Babe,
David and Phyllida sailed for South Africa.   On June 4 Babe
had a daughter.   Phyllida is now on her way home.   Then in
January Hillary announced unexpectedly that she was engaged to
Leonard Evans, and on August 5 they were married.

After the wedding I had some holiday at home, and
Joyce came for a week, Peter for five days, Buddy for three,

and John for a weekend.   Joyce, Peter and I cycled to Joyce
Green's cottage at Bould, Oxon., for a night.   Except for
the thought of war we were all very carefree and happy, and
the sun shone all day.

When war seemed very near, Joyce left London (rather
unwillingly) for a weekend with Joyce Green, which was to be
prolonged indefinitely if war were declared.   I then went to
stay at the Beavans where John was almost alone.   Duque and
Arthur were on holiday in Switzerland, Peter and Buddy at music
camp.   Frank was there - he worked all day and practised his
violin for four hours every evening - and Max was sometimes
there and sometimes not: and there were two girls in a flat at
the top of the house.   We went to several Proms, one on August
31 - a mixed programme, with Strauss and Vaughan Williams, and
altogether a terrific amount of brass.   This was the last evening before London was blacked out.   There was a newspaper man
outside Queen's Hall calling: "More 'opeful news: America
takes an 'and" - referring to Rossevelt's plea for peace.
Felt slightly comforted by his optimism.

Friday, September 1, 1939.

Hitler invades Poland.   Evacuation of children from London
begins.   We wonder if war will be declared at once.   Go into
music room to hear broadcast news at 11 p.m.   Dare not put on
lights because windows and skylights are undarkened, so sit in
dark and hear bulletins in several languages.   Finally John
tunes down wireless and begins to play softly on piano - Brahms,
I think.   Contrast between it and the news we are fearing makes
me weep into sofa.   When J. speaks, am unable to answer, and
he thinks I am asleep.   English news finally comes on at 12.15
and contains nothing that we do not already know.

Saturday, September 2.

Buy dark coverings for windows, from Kilburn High Road.   In
afternoon go out on Hampstead Heath with John and look at balloon
barrage.   Effect very pretty.   One balloon is actually being
launched from the heath.   We also see sandpits where they are
digging out sand for sand-bags, with extraordinary-looking con-
traptions like prehistoric animals.

We have a late tea at Oxford Road, in the middle of
which Arthur rings up from Victoria to say that he and Déuque
have got back safely.   They arrive at 7.30 or so.   Much talk,
and a game of Scramble which makes everything seem more normal.
During the night there is an abnormally fierce thunderstorm,
like a warning from an Old Testament Jehovah.   Hear afterwards

that the Cabinet was meeting while the storm raged.   Wish
they, and all the statesmen in Europe, had fallen on their
faces together at the heavenly portent, and decided to live
peaceably.

<u>Sunday, September 3</u>
Listen to wireless at 10 a.m.   It says that the British Ambassador has informed Hitler that unless a reply is received
by 11 a.m. to the Note demanding withdrawal of German troops
from Poland, war will be declared by Britain.   The P.M. to
speak at 11.15.   After this dreadful announcement they put
on a record of a beautiful string trio.   Duque and I weep.
Listen again at 11.15, and Mr. Chamberlain says that no reply
has been received and we are therefore at war with Germany.
There follow certain broadcast instructions, in the middle of
which our wireless set dwindles out.   Almost at once we hear
the air-raid warning signal.   Look at each other incredulously,
then get gas-masks and go into Frank's room, which is the safest
in the house.   There are Arthur, Duque, Frank and his girl
Ethel who spent the night here, John, two girls from the flat
at the top of the house, and me.   We keep thinking of things
we ought to have, like shovels and spades to dig ourselves out
with, and have to go out and get them while the weird warning
signals go on and on.   My mouth is dry and my knees tottery,
and I feel I am no heroine.   John goes up to the top of the

house with one of the girls to put out an oil-stove they left
burning.   They look out of the window at the balloon barrage
and get so interested they hardly get back before the All
Clear is sounded.

Go into Hyde Park in afternoon, with Arthur and
Duque and a young man called Victor who comes to see Peter.
A nice afternoon with blowy white clouds and sun.   People in
Park all carry gasmasks in cardboard boxes.

Great air-raid preparations in the house during out
absence, which are continued on our return.   John starts playing something soft on piano in evening which sets me weeping
again.   We go for walk down a darkened Kilburn High Road and
I feel nightmare-ish.

All go to bed early.   I take some time to go to
sleep.   At 3 a.m. am having dream that it is all a mistake
and there is no war, when am awakened by the sirens.   All go
downstairs.   Frank and Ethel have gone to the latter's home,
so there are only six of us.   Duque suggests Scramble.   Feel
it will kill me, but make an effort and find myself winning,
and even the All Clear doesn't stop us from finishing our
round, rather sleepily.   Find it difficult to get to sleep
again.

<u>Monday, September 4</u>

To work this morning, to new offices in communication with
B.B.C. main building, so that we can take shelter if necessary.
Work of the paper very behindhand, but staff pretty cheerful.
Go into park in lunch-time.   Very deserted.   Everyone feels
this war is a bad dream from which they will presently wake
up.   People give it anything from 3 weeks to 10 years.   To-
day France starts military operations.   The Germans torpedo¢
a liner off the coast of Scotland - the <u>Athenia</u> - with many
Americans on board.   Wonder if this will shake American neutrality.   Egypt breaks off diplomatic relations with Germany.
Feel newspaper news is so censored we shall never know what is
the truth.   A fine day, with the balloons shining silverly in
the sky.

          Have p.c. from Daddy sent from Llandudno, where he
and Mother are on holiday.   They heard of invasion of Poland
while on tram at Great Orme and are very worried about me.
Also note from Aunt Nina who is preparing to evacuate with her
old lady to Notts.   Evacuation (official) of schoolchildren
finished today.

          Hilary has undertaken work as ambulance driver.
Phyllida is on her way back from S.Africa in the <u>Warwick Castle</u>.
Glad Roy, wife and two children are safely in Pretoria, and wish
P. had stayed with them.   Mother and Daddy should be home by
now.

Tuesday, September 5

South Africa decides to join rest of Empire in supporting
Britain.

Listener very late going to press.   Leave office
at 7.30 and eat at B.B.C.   Get to Beavans at 8.30.   Meet
Arthur going up to the pillar-box.   He says they have all
decided to go out to their cottage at Aldbury for the night.
Set off before I have time even to read three letters which
are waiting for me: Duque, Arthur, John, two girls from flat,
and me.   We take completely dark electric train for miles:
then steam train with dim blue light in carriage, and after
arriving at Tring walk two miles through the dark to Aldbury.
Very warm and pleasant and smelling beautifully of the country.
Seems remote from anything like war.   Peter, at music camp,
has key of cottage, so Arthur knocks up the landlord (it is
10.45) to see if he has another.   He hasn't, but lends us
screwdriver and chisel, with which John scrapes away mortar
and prises pane from window.   Declares it is breaking his
heart to destroy such good work.

He is able to unbolt back door and lets us all in,
and we make tea.   Cottage minute but charming.   Arthur and
Duque have double bed in one of the two bedrooms, John has "li-
lo" on floor downstairs, and the two girls and I have the second
bedroom - they have a bed each and I have mattress on floor.

Sleep well in spite of hardness.   It is so nice to be away
from air-raid sirens.

                 September
Wednesday, ~~August~~ 6

Get up at six, and John, Joan and I walk to station, accompanied by Arthur.   Very lovely walk through early morning
sun, with a band of mist lying in valley.   As the three of
us wait for the 7.56 on Tring platform, a porter comes along
and says there is an air-raid on and we'd better come further
down; so we walk twenty yards down platform to shelter of
wooden roof, which he seems to consider safe.

          Train arrives and about a dozen passengers get in.
We lean out but can neither see nor hear signs of raid: only
people gazing with interest at sky from upper windows of houses,
making no attempt to take cover.   At Hatfield a man leans
against the carriage door and says there is a battle raging
over the North Sea and three German planes are unaccounted for
- hence lack of any All Clear.

          John leaves us at Harrow, to get connection to Tedding-
ton.   He is disappointed that there is nothing to see in the
heavens.   We feel a little lost without his moral support.

          At Willesden, where five members of the British Army
are learning to do right turns on the platform (why?), we are
bustled out of train because 'there is a raid on', and forthwith

bundled into another (presumably bomb-proof).   In carriage
is fat lady who, when I admire aesthetic effect of balloon
barrage, says earnestly: "About how many men would be on
board each?"

Just before Euston hear the All Clear.   Am relieved
to find shall not be approaching big railway terminus with the
bombs falling.

Make arrangements with B.B.C. to billet me for the
night, and am fixed up at Clifton Hotel, Welbeck Street.

Get home to find Beavans determined on cottage again.
Reject invitation to join them.   Joan and her companion also
elect to stay in London.   Part sadly from Duque and Arthur and
John, who go in to Kilburn Bridge station as I take 31 bus to
Fitzjohn's Avenue.   There see David, going to bed early after
stretcher duty last night.   See Mr. and Mrs. Davison, who are
in great state of perturbation.   Take bus to Baker Street and
get to hotel soon after 8.30.   Everything blacked out to such
an extent it is very gloomy.   Settle down for night at 10 and
sleep undisturbed till 6 or so.

Thursday, September 7

Beautiful day.   Sit in park at lunchtime.   Leave soon after
5.30 and get 6.35 home from Paddington.   It has been rescheduled
so that it stops much longer than usual at Reading and also
makes a stop at Didcot.   It is very late even on its new time

and gets to Stroud about 9.45, where Daddy is waiting patiently in the darkness.   No light of any sort in carriage.   At
end of journey talk to man who is getting out at Chalford to
go to Far Oakridge.   He is a lawyer and works at the Treasury
and is interesting and has nice voice.   What he looks like I
have no idea.   We are two disembodied voices speaking into
darkness.

No one attempts to collect my ticket.   Glad to be so
far from London and sleep long and well.

Friday, September 8
Am sitting on lawn with Mother about 4 p.m. when Joyce walks
along side of house with bicycle, having come from Bould.
Very pleased to see her again.   She is extremely brown.   Says
I look white.   Much gossip re. War, Beavans, etc.   She says
she nearly wept along the way Peter and she and I cycled the
other week.   They had warning at Bould too, on Wednesday morning.   She requests bath, since Bould has none, and soaks for
some time before going to bed.   I sleep very beautifully again.
Such a relief not to have to place, torch, respirator, etc., to
hand before getting into bed.

Saturday, September 9
I hire bicycle from Taylors and set out with Joyce over common
at 11.   At Cirencester we send p.c. to Buddy and Peter, and

another to Duque, Arthur and John.   Have lunch in field about
two miles along the Bibury Road.   Very sultry and thundry.
After meal, lie and rest, and at 2.15 Joyce rises, says adieu
and oozes out of field with bicycle.   I lie on for half-an-
hour more, then return at leisure through a lazy afternoon,
arriving back about 4.30.   Return bicycle after tea and do
shopping.   Go walk on common with Mother.   On return, about
8.30, telegraph boy arrives with wire from Southampton:
"Arrived safely home 12.10 tonight Phyllida".   Very relieved.
Rush down to tell Daddy and meet him in Wallbridge.   Go on to
find if train is indeed expected at that hour.   At 10.45 Daddy
and I set off down hill to station in starlight.   Learn from
porter who is sweeping up platform (do they always do this at
midnight?) that train will be 35 minutes late.   Sit in dark
waiting-room.   Train when it comes is pitch black and full of
soldiers.   Pop finds P., after first nearly kissing a stranger
in the darkness.   She is a bit tired after a very trying four
or five days in expectation of being torpedoed.   We bear
luggage to shop and then walk home, where there is much talk
before we go to bed at about 2 a.m.

Sunday, September 10
All get up very late and Daddy gives S.S. a miss.   He is the
only one to go to chapel.   Phyllida has harrowing talk to tell

of four days without taking off her clothes, keeping lifebelt always at hand, battened down portholes, no cigarette light allowed on deck, etc.   They heard the broadcast news of the sinking of the Athenia.   Ship had less than 100 passengers instead of the 1,000 it holds, but contained lots of gold from South Africa, and so was probably marked down by the enemy. For forty-eight hours the captain did not leave the bridge. At Southampton he made a little speech to the passengers, nearly weeping with tiredness.   Thanked them all for being so calm, apologised for the inconveniences they had undergone, but said that if they'd known the deadly peril they were in, coming round into the Channel with submarines on every hand, they'd have seen the necessity.   They all cheered him.   Southampton is surrounded by balloon barrage: they saw two troopships going out.   P. looks the same as ever in spite of all these harrowing adventures.   On the 12 o'clock news we hear that the Warwick Castle, chased by submarines, "gallantly eluded its pursuers". Daddy expresses the hope that he'll live another five years just to see the outcome of this war.

P. and I walk to Tom Long's Post in afternoon and are picked up by parents in returning car.   I get the 4.52 to Paddington, in company with Olive Brown's husband, Bill Burnett, who seems a very nice person.   He gets me tea and biscuits at Swindon where we have to change and wait for half-an-hour. Travel with a lot of workmen, one of whom describes an effort

by his pals to build an air-raid shelter in Bethnal Green.
Apparently with connivance of a friendly policeman they commandeered a lorry, took it to a place where sandbags were
being filled, and were regarded as an official car and given
tons of sand, in two separate loads.

I arrive at Fitzjohns and find note from David to
say he and J X - I don't know which one - are gone out to get
a meal and will be back later.   Unpack and undress by candle-
light, since I have nothing to black out my windows.   Go downstairs about 10 and find it is David's Joyce who is here - felt
she couldn't bear cottage alone and has had two nights in London
and is staying tonight.   So my Joyce got back to empty house.
Hope she didn't mind.

To bed and sleep very well.

Monday, September 11.

Beautiful day, as it has been ever since this war
started, but colder.   Get to office and find they have put
black paper over all the windows so that only when they are
opened - fortunately possible to-day, but what about mid-winter?
- does any light come in.   Feel very annoyed with Hitler about
this.

Printers seem very slow and work is all held up.
Go out and try to buy electric battery for torch in lunch-hour.
Unavailing.   But get two lbs. sugar for mother, who cannot get

any in Stroud.   Find in middle of Woolworths, where I
come face to face with a mirror, that I am wearing my hat
back to front, with bright row of flowers at back.   "This
is War", I think gloomily, as I reverse it.   Find the same
thing again when in dairy buying milk on way home.   Must
pull myself together.

     The Warwick Castle in in all the headlines to-day
as the liner which eluded two U-boats.   Feel very famous
at having had a sister on board.   Hilary rings up to hear
news.   Invites me to go and live with them, and I make lame
excuses because I don't think Shirley is very safe and don't
want the journey every day.   She has a husband so doesn't
need my company.

     Dinner with David, who has to go out immediately
afterwards to the Blind School at Swiss Cottage, on A.R.P.
duty till midnight.   Joyce went back this morning.

     Am lent horrible pair of plush curtains by the house,
to dim my lights.   Feel grateful but cross with Hitler.   Go
out on lawn to see result.   Chink of light at top, but feel
any aeroplane able to see it from above will be superhuman.

     Write to Arnold Foster to know about madrigal choir.
Suppose it won't meet.   No room for gracious things like
music in a world at war.   Suppose room will be made again
some day?

Tuesday, September 12

Much colder. Go to printers to pass formes, because though
arrangements have been made for us to pass them at Broadcasting
House while war is on, to avoid being bombed in the unsheltered
retreats of Fetter Lane, everyone is convinced that there will
be no air-raid to-day, and it may hurry printers if Mr. Abraham
and I are on the spot. A forlorn hope, as I do not leave till
7.30, and he stays till 8 for last forme. He treats me to
lunch at Gamages, and in afternoon Editor appears, followed
almost immediately by Edgar Holt, who comes to see me, stays
and chats and plays a game of "Hanging". Has come for holiday
to London, which he says feels much safer than Liverpool.
Windows of Speaights all blacked out so that we work by electric
lights all day, and do not leave till after dusk.

Get home in gathering darkness soon after 8. Bus
conductor tells me there is an awful slaughter going on on the
roads in consequence of black-out. "They're overdoing it", he
says.

At Fitzjohns find Joyce, who has come up to sort out
and remove her belongings. I take supper tray into David's
room and talk to them both. Afterwards she and I grope through
darkness down the Avenue and on to a 31 bus to Oxford Road, where
I want to collect some clothes left at Beavans. Cheered to
find Duque and Arthur returned from cottage and Peter and Buddy

from camp.   Two last as cheerful as ever, though their
livelihood has deserted them and they are pacifists and re-
solved not to fight.   I say "I believe Buddy would be cheerful if a bomb was coming through the roof", to which Peter
replies: "Oh yes.   He'd say 'Ignore it, boys, ignore it'."
Peter walks home with us, while we bump into everyone.   Comes
in and drinks lemonade.   I have been asked by John to go and
hear string quartets at the Edric Cundells tomorrow evening,
and Peter says he'll ask if Joyce can come too.

Anthony Eden, in a broadcast talk, says: "We have
decided to fight to show that aggression does not pay, and the
German people must realise that this country means to go on
fighting until that goal has been reached".   This seems to me
a quite lunatic statement.

Wednesday, September 13.
In lunch-hour manage to buy eight electric batteries from Woolworths, 6 for Miss Wearing and 2 for me; and 2 lbs. of sugar
from Selfridges for Mother.   Feel I have done well, and all
with my hat the right way round.   Get to Hampstead Tube Station
at 6 and meet Joyce and Peter, whence we go to Flask Walk to the
Edric Cundells - a nice square house on the corner of Well Walk,
rather pleasantly untidy inside, with piles of MS. music of
Edric's and sculptured heads of Helena's.   They are trying to
buy in a few tins of petrol before it is rationed, because the

allowance will only let them motor down to see their two small
children, now at cottage in Essex, once a fortnight.

John arrives, and youth called David, and Edric
comes in full of glee because he has persuaded the authorities
to allow the reopening of the Guildhall School of Music (of
which he is Principal) after the holidays.   We hear records
of camp music, and have pleasant meal in what is their air-raid
room.   Then hear quartets.   Sit in room one side of hall with
doors open, while the men play in room on other side of hall.
Feel normal for the first time since war started.

Tell Helena I shall be living alone, and she asks
casually why I don't go and live there.   So staggered by this
proposal can give no reply, but want to accept.

More quartets, and records of part of Edric's Mass
performed at camp.   Then Helena goes off on Ambulance duty, and
Joyce, I and two Beavans walk down Fitzjohn's Avenue in the dark.
A kind air-raid warden helps us with torch along Flask Walk.
John disdainful; says he can see quite well.   They ask us to
Oxford Road for night, but we stop at our own domain and say
goodbye, Peter arranging to help Joyce to Paddington tomorrow,
and I arranging to see her if possible at weekend.   "Makes me
feel very isolated", says John, who doesn't care for his new
abode at Teddington.   I say he can come for weekend too, but
he is determined to be sorrowful and says he has to work Sat.

morn and play tennis match Sat. aft.

I scrabble inadvertently against David's door in the dark and he emerges expecting to see the mad German lady who wanders about the house going into wrong rooms. Last night she went in to his. "Is anyone there?" asked D. No reply. "Who's that?" No reply. He thereupon flashed his torch full in her face and said severely: "You're in the wrong room!" "Of _course_!" she said, as if that was what she'd intended all along; and went out.

We talk a little and go to bed at 12.30.

Thursday, September 14

Hear from Joyce at breakfast that mad German lady came fumbling at her door last night. "Is anyone there?" asked J. "No", said m.G.l. in surprised voice. She also appeared round J's door this morning, and then just went out and shut it again.

I buy Mother 2 more lbs sugar. This means I take home 7 lbs and my case (which Pop insists on helping carry up hill) is extremely heavy. They give us blue lights in train. There is talk of slackening black-out regulations a bit, because of accidents. People are to be allowed to use torches if they are dimmed.

Very little war news of any note. We are not told much.

Friday, September 15

Russia, according to newspapers, preparing to attack Poland and agreeing with Germany to partition the country between them.

I go down to Frome Park Road and call on Mrs. Matthews, wife of Speaights' foreman, who is staying there with her mother, sister and small son. She turns out to be a mild, gentle little person with a soft voice. She, her mother and sister all declare they know me well by repute. I do not see small boy. They appear to be about to lunch on a minute mound of tinned salmon and some tomatoes.

Towards 4 o'clock go up to see Aunt H., who is resting. Till she appears I talk to Elsie, who, when she breaks a dish now, says: "Damn Hitler". Stay to tea and talk to several visitors, among them old man of 85 from Tufnell Park, who is a cousin of Grandpa's. Appears to be in fine fettle, though gets rather confused between my grandfather and great-grandfather, so that when I assert that "I remember him quite well: I was eight when he died", he is staggered.

Walk home through rain: meet Olive by farm. Her husband coming down from London tomorrow and she is going back with him. Can't stand it without him any more. Get home about 6. Find Joyce arrived by bicycle about 5, rather tired after windy journey during which she came through aerodrome where at intervals barbed wire was across part of the road, and there were soldiers with fixed bayonets who, however, let her pass.

After tea write to Mrs. Davison to announce my intention of leaving 20 Fitzjohns. Go down to P.O., find Mother who has been shopping, and we walk up fields and to first seat on common before returning home. View from hill very strange with no lights - we might be looking at uninhabited Welsh valley.

Play Rummy when Daddy comes home. Mother wins.

Saturday, September 16

A ton of coal arrives before I get up - great relief, as the weather is colder and we are very low. Daddy gets notification that he will have petrol allowance for business - about half what he asked for, but he was advised to ask for a lot, and thinks he can make do with this. They apportion it in "units"; at present the unit is a gallon, but this may be reduced later. Meantime, rationing of petrol, which was to have begun to-day, postponed for a week because coupons not ready. Papers say there were enormous queues at petrol stations in London yesterday. Cinemas, which have been closed since outbreak of war, to reopen till 10 p.m., except in Central London, where they will close at 6.

Joyce and I go into town and buy her skirt and jumper

at Clark's, which makes us late for dinner.   I enquire at
station about trains tomorrow, and emerge from conversation
with porter to find J. talking to clergyman whom she says is
Paul Gliddon, minister at Kings Weigh House, London, who is
member of Peace Pledge Union and is holding meetings here for
the Fellowship of Reconciliation.   He expresses hope that some
of P.P.U. members will be put in prison - otherwise it will
show that Government thinks them of no account.   Joyce suggests it may show a change of heart in the Government, but I
snort at this, and he says she is too charitable.

Daddy does not turn up for tea.   I go down and find
him very busy, out on roof trying to black out a glass venti-
lator.   He reports that people have gone crazy and are buying
up stuff like mad fearing prices will rise - which of course
they will, since compulsory war risks insurance has already
made many wholesale firms raise their prices by as much as 15
per cent.   Meantime it is almost impossible to get any goods
from warehouse.

Short walk on common with mother.   Joyce reports
that Florence and her husband called in our absence.   We play
Rockaby and Rummy.

Sunday, September 17

Hitler issues ultimatum to Warsaw that unless they surrender
he will bomb the city without mercy.   Russian troops cross the

Polish frontier: the Russian Ambassador says they have not
violated their non-aggression pact with Poland because Poland
does not now exist.   After morning service, during which we
sing a hymn saying

> This is the day of peace,
> Let there be peace to-day,

I have discussion on Pacifism with Mr. Hitchings (minister)
and Mr. Millard.   Former is Pacifist personally but doesn't
know that he agrees with it nationally.   Latter is complete
Pacifist.   Mother enquires what right we have to praise the
Lord for our safety, when the poor Poles are being bombed.

Daddy, at dinner, expresses the pious hope that God
will blast Hitler to hell; and damn him eternally; and burn
him up for ever.   Afterwards reduces sentence to 300 years.

It turns out sunny, fresh day - nice for Joyce who is
~~Monday, September 18~~
On cycling back to Bould.   After dinner I walk as far as the
Bear, where Daddy and Mother pick me up in car and we go through
Nympsfield to Frocester and back.   At tea, we hear again the
broadcast announcement that Russia has invaded Poland.   After
long silence, Daddy, feeling he must blame somebody for something, says explosively: "I thought the children's address
this morning was too feeble for words".   "What was it about?"
I enquire.   "Can't remember.   I only know it was feeble in
the extreme".   "I know: it was about miracles".   Furious
snort.   "It'd have been a miracle if any of the children had

understood a word of it".

Catch 4.52 from Stroud. Stand to Kemple. Wait
¾ hour at Swindon, then stand in conditions like tube in rush-
hour. And no light. Had been reading Clive Bell's "Civilisa-
tion" on Swindon platform and already come to conclusion that
we were as uncivilised as could be. Opinion confirmed. And
all people within view very unprepossessing except one girl
with bright grey eyes who gets out at Didcot (she has been saying goodbye at Swindon to youth in Air Force uniform also with
shining grey eyes). Despise them all, though they are so cheerful in adversity and I daresay they'd be as brave as lions in an
air-raid, while I might cower in corner and whimper with fright.

At 20 Fitzjohns, find my room almost obliterated by
Joyce's leavings transferred from her room, which has been let.
Everything cluttered together, wanted and unwanted: drawings,
books, jigsaw puzzles, half-empty pots of jam, china, cups with
broken handles, pictures, dirty cushions. Sit on edge of bed
and eat two beef sandwiches very savagely and am angry. Put
up velvet curtains in dark. Find on putting on light that one
is inside out. Aware that there must be large chinks of light
showing at top. Don't care. Pack two cases with books, drawings, etc., drink some lemonade and go to bed.

Find I am very fond of this room and shall be sorry
to leave it.

Monday, September 18

Arise at 10 to 8. On looking out of window at first think
that all the balloons in the barrage have got loose and are
flying north-east, to Ely perhaps. Very beautiful. But
see after staring that it is white clouds driving south-west
behind them that make them look so.

. Pack more cases with Joyce's goods and some of my
own. Take taxi to her studio at 39 South Hill Park with 2
big cases, 2 small cases, 1 hat-box, 1 basket full of books, 1
cardboard box full of drawings, 1 bookcase, 1 stool. Stagger
with these to studio at extreme top of house and get very hot.
Am late to office. Everyone very gloomy because Russians are
advancing into Poland. After lunch comes news of sinking of
aircraft carrier Courageous.

Mr. Abraham and I go to printers. After dinner David
helps me take rest of stuff to studio. Two cases, 1 hatbox, 1
cardboard case of crockery, 1 hockey bag with china, 3 large
pictures, 5 cushions, 1 roll of drawings, 2 box files, 1 parcel
containing sleeping-bag. And Joyce had said blithely that I
could do it all in one. On return spend rest of evening packing clothes in suitcase and rucksack.

Tuesday, September 19

Uneventfully busy day. Mr. Abraham and I at printers till 6.30.
Mr. Matthews tells me he's "very grateful" to me for going to see

his wife.   This makes me feel a worm.   Why shouldn't I be
the grateful one?

At lunchtime go into Wallis's snack-bar and see a
familiar-looking face smiling.   Say: "Who _are_ you? ... I
know ... Beavans ... _Queenie_".   Have never heard her surname
so cannot identify further.   Says she saw Peter at Didcot on
Thursday going back to camp, after parting from Joyce en route
for Bould.   Cannot get anything to eat quickly, so go out and
have two extremely dry sandwiches at milk-bar.   The Editor
comes down after lunch, but says this will not be a regular
thing.

In evening pack bags and turn out hundreds of letters,
among them one from Cora Hazard.   Read it and try to imagine
her as not alive, but cannot.   Or as being at any rate disembodied.   Find the idea conveys nothing to me.   Like saying
space is curved.   Try half-a-dozen times to ring up Cundells,
but they are out.   To bed at 10.30, and watch very bright star
through window.   Could never have seen it but for Hitler, I
suppose.   Love the London night sky all dark.

Papers say British Expeditionary Force is now in
comfortable billets in France, eating bacon and eggs and singing
"Boomps-a-Daisy".   Hope the Poles are gratified.

<u>Wednesday, September 20.</u>

At breakfast watch balloon going higher and higher.   Can
never stop admiring morning sun on them.

   About 10 ring up Edric Cundell and ask if I may
leave some bags in at lunch-time.   Leave B.B.C. at 12.30 and
after quick lunch go to Fitzjohn's and thence transport 2 suitcases, 1 rucksack and 1 typewriter to 75 Flask Walk.   Empty
cases and rucksack and return them to No.20, where I partly re-
pack them.   Am then accompanied to bus by Mr. Marchant, who
talks in depressed voice and smells very strongly of alcohol.
He says goodbye and I feel a pig that I didn't shake hands with
him.   Complete packing after work in afternoon, and arrive at
Cundells with 3 cases, gasmask, rucksack, 2 coats and an umbrella
- alas, leave last in taxi.   Miss Meagher says goodbye very
nicely and tells me to come back soon.   John, Peter, Bernard
Robinson, David someone, and girl Trixie somebody all there
already.   I have nursery to sleep in.   Nurse's things not
cleared from cupboard and drawers, so put my goods on bed I am
not going to sleep in.   John says am I going home for weekend,
and remarks pensively that he is doing nothing this weekend; so
invite him down.

   During dinner learn that George Mathieson is engaged,
to very nice girl, Mary something.   Also that Frank and Ethel
are married.

   Mozart quintet followed by Brhams, followed by Mozart

piano quartet; followed by Beethoven Trio, Op 1, followed by
Beethoven quartet in E minor. Helena comes in at 11.30 from
Ambulance duty, and reports that tomorrow morning's papers say
Czechs are in revolt against Hitler and hundreds are being
executed.

To bed very late.

Thursday, September 21

Have nice breakfast nearly alone; Helena appears in dressing-
gown towards end of meal. Papers confirm news about Czech
rising. Mr. Pringle, who comes into office later in day, from
Ministry of Information, says there have been risings which
have been suppressed, but it is expected that there will be
recurring outbursts from time to time, probably not on very big
scale - at any rate not yet.

Try to get preserving sugar in lunch-time, with idea
of making blackberry jam at weekend. Can only get 2 lbs. gran-
ulated from Selfridges.

Roosevelt trying to get Congress to repeal Neutrality
Laws.

Meet John at Paddington, and we travel with most entertaining Welshman called Bob Owen, who is full of fierce
patriotic fervour and of much information on every conceivable
subject. Sometimes waves arm and declaims as at public meeting;
then leans over and confides in one's ear - doesn't mind whether

mine or John's, but bounces from one side of carriage to the
other, proving that all good things come from Wales.   Tries
rather forlornly to prove that I also have Welsh blood, and
rather than abandon hope promises to look up my pedigree.
On arriving home find Mother and Daddy have been to tea with
two Joyces at Bould, returning with beans, plums and fragrant
herbs.   Mother says cottage feels so safe, like harvest-home
where all is safely gathered in ere the winter storms begin -
preserves and jams and stored fruit and drying vegetables.

Friday, September 22
Rumanian Prime Minister assassinated.   Germany says English
are responsible because of annoyance at Rumanian neutrality.
Roosevelt asking U.S. Congress to allow sale of arms to belligerents while not coming in as combatants.

        Cloudy morning, which turns fine later.   Address, with
J's help, lot of circulars to Madrigal Choir members, asking
about possibility of starting session this winter.   Play gramophone as we peel potatoes; then sit in sun and do mathematical
puzzles out of magazine.

        After dinner, Daddy takes us to the crossroads between
Edge and Whiteshill, and we pick blackberries.   Go to indicator
on National Trust part of beacon, and think we can see Steep
Holme miles away in Bristol Channel.

        Walk home: half expect Joyce to be there, but she is

not.   Play Rummy and Monopoly.   I am soon knocked out, but
at 11.30 Daddy and John are still at it, and finally have to
count assets before Daddy is adjudged victor.

Saturday, September 23.
Russia planning to have much bigger piece of Poland than
Germany.   Wonder if they will fall out about it.

Letter from Joyce: she is not coming this weekend.
John disappointed; so am I.

Go shopping in morning.   I buy Mother oven-proof
dish: John buys her chocolates and Fullers cake.   Coming up
fields meet Florence and husband; also see Bob on motor-bicycle
looking very handsome and foreign with moustache.

After dinner Daddy takes John and me to top of Selsley.
Rather cold, but go through wood where it is warmer.   Too misty
for good view.   I walk with Mother on common in evening, while
J. reads and nobly washes up tea things.   Meet Florence and Ken
again.   Play Rummy, and more Monopoly which I win.

Sunday, September 24
Sigmund Freud, Psychologist, dies in Hampstead.   Was refugee
Jew from Vienna.

Harvest Festival with Mother in morning.   Cabbages
behind me on window-sill throw out horrid smell, but general
smell of nice greengrocers.   John wraps himself in motor-rug

and reads in garden.   After dinner, Letter-bags.   Daddy
rouses himself from slumber and takes us all to Sheepscombe
and Painswick Castles, where J and I climb up to beacon.
Come back quickly because parents want to go to evening service (at 5.45 on account of blackout).   J and I play Monopoly
and he wins.   Catch 7.35.   Eat sandwiches in corridor with
only blue light.   After Didcot both have seats and play not
finishing words very pleasantly to Paddington, which we reach
at 11.15.   Buses scarce, and I go circuitous route to Hampstead via Kilburn and Chalk Farm.   Station at Chalk Farm so
sandbagged can only find small slit to admit me.   No ticket
office working and no lifts.   Very tired.

Monday, September 25
Bright morning, much better than weekend weather.   ~~Great-(-~~
Greta (maid) says to me severely in broken English: "You must
not make your bed.   No.   I must make it".   So I don't.

        Warsaw being bombed to bitts by the Germans because it
won't surrender.

        Reduce chaos in my room very slightly.   Edric and
young man (name forgotten) to dinner.   Spend evening listening
to them talking about war, and Cedric about some of his experiences in Serbia during last war.   To bed about 11.30.   Very
tired.

<u>Tuesday, September 26</u>

Warsaw still holding out, though in ruins.

At printers till 4 o'clock.   On return to Broadcasting House John rings up to say he and Duque and Arthur
are going to film.   Will I meet them at 6.15 at Piccadilly
Circus.   Do so, and we feed at Corner House, which is dark
without and light within.   Then to cinema at Sloane Square,
where we see end of "South Riding" (seen it before) and whole
of "Bluebeard's Eighth Wife".   Latter very funny.   J. laughs
till he cries.   I laugh, but somehow not wholeheartedly.
Feel amused but rather miserable, and cannot bring myself to
look at news-reel, which is nothing but war and jingo-ism.
Find it very interesting that the end of "South Riding", which
is a King George V's Jubilee Fete with everyone singing "Land
of Hope and Glory" rouses not a flicker of enthusiasm in the
audience.   Neither do pictures of our defences.   The only
thing that stirs them is a picture of the Duke of Windsor in
uniform, about to undertake war work.   That brings a clap.

We emerge to dark streets but moonlight is beautiful
and makes London look unreal.   Tube to Victoria and then have
grand walk across Hyde Park to Marble Arch, which I enjoy very
much though being silent and miserable at same time.   Feel I
am perverse and foolish.   Am invited to Oxford Road for night
and go hoping to see Buddy, who sails for a job in Canada on

Saturday.   Find he is spending night in Surbiton: this
rather convenient, however, as I have his bed.

At 11.30 am rash enough to suggest game of Scramble
and I win, in spite of almost complete numbness of tired
brain.   Peter comes in at 12.15, being finally home from
prolonged music camp.   Stands behind and gives me poke when
I am missing something.   John stops him, as I am getting on
too well anyway.   Bed at 12.30 and feel I am too tired to
sleep, but manage it all right.

Wednesday, September 26
New War Budget.   Income Tax up to 7/6 in the £.   Hitler
and Stalin making peace plan with (so they say) Mussolini's
help.   It is stated that we have sunk one quarter of the
German U-boats.   Find this hard to believe.   Persistent
rumours that a raid practice, or else a genuine raid, is
imminent.

Buy 4 lbs. of sugar for Mother in lunch-hour: also
camel-hair coat for myself which I feel is the sort of plain
useful thing for a war.

Can't imagine what will go in next week's Listener,
since nothing but news and gramophone records seem to have
been broadcast.   Spend most of day in abortive attempt to
make up a crossword puzzle based on nursery rhymes.

Home to Cundells and succeed in tidying up my room.

Edric has been making kite to take to his three-year-old
at the weekend. Shows it with pride. It is of cane and
black-out paper. John, Peter, David and girl called Beryl
(who goes early) come for music, which is again very pleasant.
I write letters meantime. Later Katharine Lawson comes.
Knits beside me; then sings most beautifully some Schubert,
Brahms and Purcell. Greta, who brings in some tea, has been
sitting on stairs listening to songs in her native German.
She is Jewish refugee and has small boy of 4 in Jewish children's home at Hatfield. Her husband was Aryan so the marriage
was dissolved. Has to get police permit to visit child.

Thursday, September 27

Warsaw surrenders. Germans say they have hit our Aircraft
Carrier <u>Ark Royal</u>. Admiralty denies this, and a lot more
news broadcast by Germany. Russian Ambassador and Von
Ribbentrop have 4-hour conversation. Everyone rather gloomy
about probable German-Russian military alliance, in which it
is thought Turkey will join.

Buy 2 more lbs sugar for Mother. Now $4\frac{1}{2}^d$ per lb.

Feel rather unwell and resolve to go to bed early.
Eat alone while Edric behind me tries unsuccessfully to mend
a lamp. He, Helena and I go for very pleasant moonlight
stroll on heath. Then Edric plays piano which I enjoy very
much. He tells me about Katharine, who came yesterday. He

found her behind the counter in a music shop in Dundee,
where he went to judge a musical competition. Heard her
singing Brahms songs to herself in the waiting-room. She
came up to the Royal College and for two years lived with
the Cundells in St. John's Wood.

Joyce's poster for Punch Autumn Number in the Underground. Tube so crowded on homeward journey, I almost
overflow every time door opens.

Buy little red penny notebook and press it into
Helena's hand, saying it is my rent-book, but nothing more
happens and I haven't paid anything for my keep.

Cannot go to Stroud tonight because Miss P. is
moving her flat and wants tomorrow off to see to it.

Friday, September 29

Germany and Russia to make military alliance unless we agree
to peace terms. And ~~German~~ Russian-Turkish pact being negotiated.
Very depressed, but as soon as I leave London behind me feel
more cheerful. Travel with Miss Evans, Mr. Thomas's secretary, who lives at Painswick and whom I like very much. Moonlight without illuminates every house, while within we have
only dim blue light. War seems remote bad dream. Daddy
meets me. They have had two letters from S.Africa sent by
air-mail at 1/3 per oz., one since they heard broadcast of
Warwick Castle's safe arrival. Also letter from Hilary say-

ing she may give up ambulance driving and take up organisation of juvenile centres.

Saturday, September 30

Beautiful day.   Shopping in morning.   Get tin of Ovaltine
for A.R.P. stock, bribed thereto by 2 free samples of the
extract and one of rusks.   After dinner walk to Auntie
Tuttie's across common.   Feel very uplifted; run across
grass; and compose following not-very-good verse, which at
time I think of such merit I nearly burst into tears:-

> The bombing aeroplanes were swooping down
>   And in despair I said that God was dead.
> I came where golden fields had turned to
>   brown
>   Because the grain had all been harvested,
>   And faint against the brown I saw the sheen
>   Of next year's corn, already showing green.

Show Aunt T. photos of S. Africa and of wedding, while I
have tea with her.   Leave her two of the wedding pictures
and also 10/- note.   She spreads the three bits of paper on
table before her and says: "I don't know which is most precious".   Then adds: "Yes, I do" - taking up and fondling
photographs.   "Because I've got to have _that_" (indicating
filthy lucre).   She is 84, but wants to live a little longer
yet in spite of war.   Hedges covered with old man's beard and
hips and blackberries.   Joyce at home when I get back, having
very much enjoyed her 40-minutmile cycle from Bould.   Says
conditions in her private life, at any rate, couldn't be

pleasanter.   After I've eaten a second tea we stroll round
common with Mother, Joyce in Daddy's grey overcoat.

Mr. Franklin comes in during evening to take
details for National Register.   Play Rummy; and so to bed.

Sunday, October 1

Germany sinking or seizing a great many neutral ships.   She
and Russia still formulating peace plan.

To chapel in morn, while Joyce stays at home.
Very tired, and after dinner sun myself in deck-chair, and
when sun vanishes, go indoors and snooze in armchair.   Prepare to depart by 4.52, but Daddy comes in from service at 3
and says train has been taken off.   So play Letter-bags with
Joyce and we tie at 43, and then catch 7.15.   Should not have
got seat, but kind and beautiful member of R.A.F. gives me his
corner.   At Swindon my neighbour gets out, and am joined by
R.A.F., who talks incessantly, shares my sandwiches, and at
Reading fetches 3 bars of chocolate.   He then strikes match
to show me photograph of girl, in profile, and asks if it conveys anything to me.   Study it till match burns his fingers
and say it reminds me of someone, can't remember whom.
Apparently it is like my own profile, and it is to this like-
ness to a young lady he was once engaged to, that I owe my seat.

Bright moonlight without.   Presently R.A.F. tires
and goes to sleep, very nearly on my shoulder.   Almost go to

sleep myself in corner, wondering if it is my National Duty
to allow my person to become resting-place for heads of hitherto unknown, if handsome, members of H.M. Forces.   Just before
Paddington, rouse the recumbent figure and say if he is quick
and lucky he may get his Uxbridge connection at Piccadilly.
He springs to life, hopes he may "run across me" again, and
vanishes into the dimness of the station.

By bus to Warren Street.   London very quiet and empty.
To Hampstead by tube, and go to bed without seeing anyone.

Monday, October 2
Still glorious weather, with silver balloons against clear blue
sky.   Very irked by B.B.C.'s blacked-out windows.   At printers,
light is even worse.

Archbishop of York gives very clever broadcast on our
attitude to the war: proves that we are fighting in a noble
cause for noble reasons.   Cannot agree.   But he does say that
when we have turned out Hitler and his gang we must see to it
that we do not impose a peace, but get the Germans and the Poles
and the Czechs and everyone together, and make a peace.   Do
agree.   But why in the world slaughter each other first?
Edric thinks we are all uncivilised and have no conception of
beauty.   He shows me his photograph album of last war.   Most
of the photographs very faded.   Produces smudge and tells me
it is marvellous picture of range of mountains; another smudge

is remarkable aerial view of Turkish trenches.   But see
quite clear picture of Helena as nurse.

Tuesday, October 3

Swedish Government said to be "taking action" about sinking
of their ships by U-boats.   Stalin, having over-ridden
Estonia, bullying several more Baltic States.   Petrol up to 60
2/- a gallon.

Weather continues fresh and sunny.

Everywhere you go there are posters: "Freedom is
in peril.   Defend it with All Your Might".   We can't buy
sugar, or petrol, and they're going to ration our food.   And
you can't switch on a light without darkening the windows.
And they can billet people on you at will, and search your
house without a warrant.

Wednesday, October 4

Reports that Turkey refuses to recognise the partition of
Poland.   And Italy reaffirms her neutrality.

Cold.   I spend lunch-hour shopping, and don't get
back to work till 3.30.   Feel conscience-stricken, but we
went to press yesterday and there is very little to do.

In evening, music.   John comes, but not Peter, who
is on tour with the Philharmonic.   But lots of others: total
of 14.   Very much enjoy it.   By 12.15 most of them have gone,

but a string quartet persists. When I hear them begin on
another Haydn at this hour, am overcome with weariness and
go to bed. It is pouring with rain, and they do not leave
till it has abated somewhat: at 1 a.m. I hear voices on the
doorstep saying goodbye.

   During evening I put light on on top landing and
then open my bedroom door, where curtains are not drawn.
Result: thundrous knock on door from A.R.P. warden, whom I
suspect of standing on pavement without and listening to music.

Thursday, October 5

Hitler makes triumphant entry into Warsaw.

   Have day off, because I worked on Friday last week.
Get up early and catch 9.15 from Paddington in pouring rain.
Travel with man just back from India, whose boat took five
weeks on journey that usual takes a little over a fortnight.
Tells me they had a cruise round Indian Ocean; then were instructed to go via Capetown and up West Coast of Africa; but
4 days from Cape received wireless instructions that Mediterranean was now safe, so turned round and recrossed Equator
(thereby confounding a passenger who had booked for S. Africa).

   Mother worried at instructions from Gas Co. that
only 75 per cent. of last year's consumption is to be used.
Does not know how to cut down, as she is always careful, and
we have no gas-fires to economise on.

In afternoon drive to Stinchcombe Hill (excuse
being fetching of parcel from Miss Luker's at Cainscross!)
where I have never been before.   Walk across nice soft grass
to summit and look down on Severn, very clear.   Blowy day;
sun and white clouds.

Send long letter to Roy.   Rummy in evening.   Tell
Daddy I will teach him a Patience called Idiot's Delight, the
idea of which is to get 4 aces in a row.   Instruct him to
put out 4 cards from top of his pack, which he does, and they
turn out miraculously to be the four aces.   We look at them
stunned, then laugh and laugh, and between gasps he enquires
if he has now finished the game.

Letter from Joyce, who is going up to town to Colour
Class and to meet Mrs. Witten, and may spend night either at
Bexley with White Rolls Royce and Roland Hunt; or at Oxford
Road with Scramble and John.

Friday, October 6
Get up so late, breakfast at 11.   Have been lying in bed
wondering what the idea of creating a lot of human beings really
was (if any); and what the humans ought to do about it (if
anything); and what relation, for example, washing up and
shopping, have to Ultimate Reality (if there is such a thing).
Also reflect for some time on fact that my friends are scattered,
that very likely I shan't be able to come home for weekends if

conditions get very bad, and that therefore I shall have to
rely on my own resources for enjoyment. Have relied for so
long on Joyce, Beavans, visits to Cambridge and to Fuchs's,
etc., feel arid and resourceless. Come to conclusion I have
no individual life and do not know how to set about having
one. In fact, rather doubt my own existence.

After these abstractions, rise and go down to Stroud
and buy myself nice solid pair comfortable walking shoes with
very square toes, with which I am pleased. Also get Mother
2 lbs sugar by looking winningly at man in Strange's.

Miserable letter from Phyllida. Children have
whooping-cough and Miss Haskins has retired and is at home, and
is so fussy F. feels she can't bear it.

Daddy brings forth theory that we have to have a war
now and then to buck us up and keep us from being decadent.
Then contradicts himself by quoting Longfellow's "Arsenal" at
enormous length, to effect that if half the energy put into
war were applied to "redeeming the human mind from error", it
would be a Good Thing. I have a theory wars happen because
we are all pagans and feel we have done wrong, and have to offer
up a tremendous human sacrifice now and then to feel we have
expiated our sins.

Daddy has to deliver parcels and takes Mother for
ride. I walk over Selsley, through woods to Surprise Point -
very fast, to make myself feel real. Clear and lovely on top

of hill.   To tea at Aunt H's and home via Jacob'sLadder.
Aunt H. has about 2 cwt. of sugar laid by, and 7 tons of
coal.

        Hitler makes speech: so clever and convincing,
if any of our statesmen had made it we should applaud every
word.   And if he backed up his words by deeds he would be
a Good Thing and not a Bad Thing.   He says Germany is
celebrating the greatest victory in her history ... "I can
only thank God at this moment that He has so marvellously
and wonderfully blessed us in our first hard struggle for our
right and pray to Him that He will guide us and all others in
the right path along which not only the German people but the
whole of Europe will find a new happiness and peace".   At
same time Anthony Eden broadcasts that ... "All human progress
is a record of man's endeavour to outlaw the rule of force.
This is a war to redeem hope, to give the peoples of the
world a chance to live and breathe, to free our children from
the haunting dread that shadows our own time, to create for
them a future where moral and spiritual values shall prevail.
Twenty years ago we thought we had won such a victory.   This
time - God willing - we shall not fail".   And the Archbishop
of York, in his broadcast of October 2, said: "Over against
the deified nation of the Nazis our people have taken their
stand as a dedicated nation ... In that spirit we enter the

conflict".

It all seems rather difficult for God.

Saturday, October 7

Charles Trevelyan, in The New Statesman, says: "Safety can
only come through universal disarmament ... Soviet Russia
proposed disarmament to the world while Germany was still
disarmed and democratic, but she was contemptuously disregarded".   Bernard Shaw, in the same paper, says: "We are enduring all the vagaries, from mere discomfort to financial ruin,
ef-the-ine and the breaking up of our homes, of the ineptest
Military Communism.   Powers which no Plantagenet king or
Fascist Dictator would dream of claiming have been granted to
any unqualified person who offered to assume them, including
an enterprising burglar".   He adds: "The primitive instinct
that is at the bottom of all this mischief" is "sheer pugnacity
for its own sake".   I incline to agree.

Another beautiful day.   In afternoon try to take
2.25 bus to Painswick to see Molly Evans.   So full, cannot
get on, but Daddy takes me by car.   She lives in very pleasant
Cotswold house beside golf links, with marvellous views.
Find there also her sister Kathleen, a girl from B.B.C. called
Margaret, and four hefty young men called Martin, Michael,
Hubert and I forget the fourth.   We all set forth with Mrs.
Evans and walk to Sheepscombe.   Go to head of combe through

woods and then have tea at Fortune's Well.   Would have had
it in garden but get bitten by midges.   Arty-crafty sort of
meal, but a very merry party.

Back to the Cheltenham road in time to see 6.5 bus
go past.   My handbag at house, so have to go back.   Next bus
7.25.   Thundery clouds roll up suddenly and it rains heavily.
The party leaves in instalments, and Molly walks down to Painswick with me, by which time it is fine again.   Find Mother
has been trying to meet me with mackintoshes and is worn out.
Rummy and supper.   Sky now clear and stars bright.

Sunday, October 8

Walk on common with Mother in afternoon.   Meet Hilda and Mrs.
Franklin with Florence's baby, who smiles at me engagingly and
kicks.

Get seat in crowded 7.15.   Forget there is no moon
now, and stumble blindly out of Hampstead tube into pitch black
night.   Stump noisily along middle of Flask Walk, under no
doubt erroneous impression that this makes for safety.   Creep
about house very quietly not to disturb Cundells, and 20 minutes
later they drive up to front door, having just returned from
cottage with Katharine Lawson, who spends night in my room.
Like her very much, but cannot sleep with strange influence
about.

India is saying she'll support Britain, if Britain

will show she is really fighting for democracy (as she says
she is), by giving home rule to India.   Most of the papers
have not mentioned this awkwardness.

Monday, October 9

C. R. Attlee, Leader of the Opposition, in broadcast:- "We
are fighting to get security for ordinary men and women in all
countries, including Germany ... If Herr Hitler wants peace,
he must show it by deeds ... The fate of the Czechs shows what
happens to those who rely on his word".   R. A. Scott James,
also in broadcast:- "We went into the war ... primarily to
preserve the freedom of the mind upon which all other freedoms
depend".

Joyce rings up in morning to say what she has had is
Roland Hunt and White Rolls Royce, and has now missed train
from Paddington.   What Shall She Do?   I say lunch with me,
and she arrives at B.B.C. at noon and we eat, talk hard, and I
put her into Regent's Park tube, I hope in time to catch her
next train.

To supper at Heimann's.   Get to Kensington High St.
in dark and realise I am lost.   Ring them up, and Ernest says
take bus to West Kensington and he will meet me with torch:
which he does.   Very pleased with himself that he has been
elected F.R.P.S.   He and Elfie try to persuade me to send
telegram to P.M. to the effect that they might as well have

conference now without war, as afterwards.   Thousands have
already been sent.   Ask me to stay night, but I feel I ought
to turn up at Flask Walk occasionally and return in darkness.

Tuesday, October 10

Hectic day at printers till 6.30.   At 6 am receiving telephone corrections from Evensham and breaking up formes.

John rings up and I go to Beavans and have late
supper alone, while he and Peter do grand black-out of music
room with green shiny stuff to match cushions.   They then
perform Dvorak's cello concerto while I wrap up in rugs and
eiderdown and listen with great enjoyment.   John very cheerful because he has left Teddington and is living at home again.
Duque and Arthur both have bad colds.

Scramble: then Monopoly, which goes on till nearly
1 a.m.   So I stay for night and have Buddy's bed and all the
bedclothes keep insisting on being in heap on floor.   Feel
unable to cope with them in black-out.

Wednesday, October 11

Russia grabbing Estonia.   Finns getting nervous and all reported to be massing on frontier.   Surprised to find there
are hundreds of thousands of Finns, not a couple of dozen or so.

Appalling discovery made that Listener has described
poisonous toadstool - giving picture - as edible mushroom.

Feel frightful all afternoon: not, as I should, at thought
that people may die; but at thought of gross inefficiency.

Arnold rings up from Manchester to say Marjorie had
a son yesterday morning. Richard. Both well. Wants me
to go up and see them.

Music in evening. Brahms sextet. Also quintet
and sextet of Edric's. Edric at dinner describes mysterious
people he and Helena met, who say war is due to the "Black
Hand" and to the Grand Orient Order of Masons, and whom he
suspects of being German agents. A Mrs. Williams who has come
to dinner interjects at every pause: "Oh Edric, and did/you to
give them the plans of the Guildhall?"

they want

Thursday, October 12
Cundells off to cottage early. I get lift to B.B.C. from
Mr. and Mrs. Williams, who stayed last night. Editor, re-
turning from country, very kind about our wickednesses re.
fungi: broadcast announcement to be made on dangers of Fly
Agaric.

Lunch with Arnold Foster and Joan Western at M.M.
Club, to discuss Madrigal Choir plans. A.F's livelihood
badly hit by war.

Busy day. Then to Greens at Bould for weekend.
Train appallingly slow. Met by Joyce (Johnson) who has
waited nearly an hour. Walk two miles to cottage. David

here: has boil and stye and therefore week's leave.   He
and Joyce (Green) both have bad colds.

To bed: and after initial fright, when I complain
a maybug is buzzing in my hair and squeal to Joyce, who kindly rises and says it is only fly crawling on wall - I sleep
beautifully.   This cottage very friendly and reposeful.

Mr. Chamberlain makes important speech in House in
reply to Hitler's speech.   Do not know yet what he said.

Friday, October 13

Get up pleasantly late, and lazily read Oxford Book of English
Verse by fire.   Later sit in sun at door.   Polly, wife of
Pruett, ex-Assistant Editor of Countryman, to lunch.   Joyce
and I walk with David and he saws wood and we come home with
logs and sticks.   Only bad thing is the aeroplanes, which
are very active and noisy.   Those woods near Bould very heal-
ing to the mind, and mine often seems bruised when I go into
them.   Luscious blackberries everywhere, and rusting harvest
hedgerows all over the place.

Saturday, October 14

Cloudy.   Joyce and I go to Idbury to see two girls, Mervyne
and Diana, who are building cottage.   They are making road to
it themselves, and we help by transferring lots of stones from
one place to another.   After a bit feel no wonder that road-

men spend so much time gazing at traffic, talking to each
other, and eating bread-and-cheese.   Mervyne and I heaving
enormous stone up a bank when she says, out of nothing: "Not
much need for Vitamin B for the bowels if you do this sort of
thing".

After lunch David and his Joyce go for walk, and I
go out on bicycle while Joyce J. stays in to draw.   I go
through Westcote all among yellow leaves, while about 15 aeroplanes, monoplanes and biplanes of every sort, circle above me
as if I am their bombing objective.   Suddenly all decide I am
not worth it and take themselves home to tea, while I go on,
get on to Burford Road, and sing loudly to myself as I go.
Rains and I get very wet on way home.   May is here, explaining
why she can't stay to tea.   She used to be on Countryman, and
is now Uncle Herbert of the Children's Corner of an Oxford newspaper, and writes about her pipe and flannel trousers.

Sit on windowseat reading, wondering at some fantastic-
ally yellow chestnut leaves Joyce and David bring in.   They
look like painting by Van Gogh, or artificial decoration for
very modern flat.   A bemused wasp stings my leg and J. cures
it with iodine.

Two partridges, expected for supper, turn out to be
one pheasant.   David suggests they have pooled the game birds
like petrol and butter.

- 50 -

See newspaper report of Chamberlain's speech. He
says no reliance at all can be placed in Hitler's word and
we cannot make terms with German people while he and his gang
are in power. Germans submarines very daringly enter Scapa
Flow and blow up Royal Oak, and escape.

Sunday, October 15

Rain all day. This keeps aeroplanes away. Sit on windowseat
and read "Tortilla Flat" by John Steinbeck, which I enjoy very
much. Also feel grateful to my friends, and comfortable and
happy, and write following not-very-good sonnet:

All these my friends are living flame
   And I am but their looking-glass:
Their love and hatred, pride and shame,
   In bright procession crowd and pass.
Their gladness kindles all my fire,
   Their sorrow quenches every spark;
I have no hope but their desire,
   And no despair except their dark.

O friends, keep bright the glowing coal,
   Nor let the gathering ashes lie.
I know no soul except your soul,
   And if it fail, I too must die.
      Reviving, you shall always see
      The spirit dancing still in me.

Even at time of its birth, have no illusions about ~~these~~ this
effort.

After tea walk up to village with David and Joyce
(Green), and am scarcely home before the car comes to take me
to station. At first I sit on bag in corridor, and afterwards
kind-hearted guard finds me seat.

Monday, October 16

About 12 German aeroplanes over Edinburgh.   Bombs aimed
at Forth Bridge and at warships in the Firth.   Some men
killed on one boat.   Four German aeroplanes brought down.
Germans sink 1 British and 2 French boats in Atlantic.

Colder.   Foggy.   Get up by accident rather early
and fetch madrigals from J's studio.   Usual busy Monday.
Pay Helena two week's rent.   She produces my little red book.
At one end she has made list of things she must buy for the
children;   in the middle are household accounts;   and at the
other end she enters that I have paid 3 week's rent, because
she says I am there so little, 35/- is ridiculous sum to pay.

Tuesday, October 17

Germans attacking on Western Front.   French reported retreating "according to plan".   Air-raid warnings on East Coast but
no ~~raid~~.   Yesterday in Scotland, raid but no warning.   Feeling is that war has now begun.

Very busy at printers.   Am presented with beautiful
apple and flowery speech by man on "The Schoolmaster".   Editor
(Listener, not Schoolmaster) comes down after lunch.   Argue
with him re. Pacifism and am subjected to a good deal of
teasing.   Too tired to combat it and nearly burst into tears.

Tell Ed. his opinion doesn't matter, and he withdraws into
hurt silence, but afterwards takes Mr. Abraham and me to
Hennekey's and gives us sherry.   We lean across counter and
agree that Music is the same thing as Religion, and that
people who understand either project themselves into a kind
of Fourth Dimension.   I recite to myself a new Beatitude:-
"Blessed are they who are not bounded by three dimensions, for
theirs is the Kingdom of Heaven".   Our differences melt into
a pleasant haze of alcohol.   Cannot cope with 2nd glass sherry
~~preferred~~ proffered by Mr. A., and secretly eat as many biscuits
as I can decently arrange to gather up from dish on counter,
to counteract increasing dizziness.   Go on to Mervyn Horder's,
where Madrigal Choir is meeting.   Am nearly an hour late, and
the business part cannot go forward till I, the Secretary,
arrive.   Share a copy of Weelkes with frightfully prim fellow
alto and breathe alcohol all over her.

Get home at 8.30 and find J.D.Solomon and Major
Glendinning to supper, which they are all having very late.
J.D., as A.R.P. Warden, dons tin helmet in which he looks very
extraordinary, and goes forth into night, returning later with
duty done.   At Helen's suggestion he and Major G. going to
share flat.

Letter from M.III.

Wednesday, October 18

Music in evening: John, Peter, Hardy Lee, Alan and Loveday
Richards (A. very grand in blue uniform with shiny buttons
because he is Lieutenant-Surgeon), Katharine, David, Peter
Latham and wife, an A.R.P. colleague of Helena's name unknown,
and a young man who shows us sets and costumes he has just designed for production at the Mercury. I read "Queer Street"
(Edward Shanks) and listen to Brhams Piano Quintet and to K.
singing Purcell's "When I am Laid in Earth", and am very happy.
To bed at 1 a.m. and as usual am too stimulated to sleep. At
what I judge to be 2.30, great noise without as of heavy lorry
running into impenetrable object. Sound of breaking glass:
men emerge from Warden's sandbag shelter: woman's voice says
"Are you still alive in there?" After a bit lorry starts up
engine and backs protestingly. Wonder if front fence is in
ruins and go to sleep.

Thursday, October 19

Pouring rain all day. Joyce rings from Paddington, en route
for White Rolls Royce again. I meet her for lunch at Dutch
Oven. She is wearing sprig of hips and borrows £2 before going off to Charing Cross.

　　　　　Am exceedingly depressed by news that if air-raids
get bad Listener may move to Wembley, where no one, I feel,
will ever be able to lunch with me again.

Britain concludes pact with Turkey, in which Turkey promises to help Allies if Germany attacks Rumania. ~~German-~~ Turkish pact comes to nothing.

Carriage to myself from Paddington to Stroud. Take advantage of this to make affirmations aloud and to say poetry to myself. Noise of train allays some of my self-consciousness. My voice very monotonous. Interested to discover its pitch varies from doh to soh above. Try varying this and stretching to, say, lah above or below, but result very odd. Resolve to listen to other people's pitch.

Near Swindon two beautiful searchlights raking the sky. Surprised to find all clouds gone: moon and stars. One stars detaches itself from heaven and moves. Searchlight follows. Feel if I were managing searchlight could do it much better: but perhaps they work by faith and not by sight.

Friday, October 20
Clear sunshine. Go into Stroud with Mother and decide on coat and hat for her, navy blue. Then at 12.45 gallop up fields and we find pears, put in oven in new casserole, burnt to cinder.

After dinner we wash up 3 meals' crockery. I then depart via fields for Mrs. Hawkins', with whom I have tea. Elderly admirer of Mrs. H's present. Miss Churchman and I agree that the war is a senseless and criminal affair. Walk

back over fields in dusk.   Play Rummy.   Rationing of gas
and electricity revised to allow 100 per cent of power used
in corresponding quarter last year.   Mother feels less conscience-stricken therefore about this morning's pears.   Air-
raid warnings in Scotland: enemy planes off coast.

Saturday, October 21

This rationing business going too far.   Paper even talks of
rationing of water, of which God, war or no war, has sent
such quantities that in Bedfordshire and Northamptonshire
towns have been flooded, cattle washed away, and bridges destroyed.

Another beautiful day here.   Set out to walk to
Auntie Tuttie's, but instead sit on seat with Mother, and returning, climb apple tree and gather about four-fifths of the
crop of cookers.   They smell heavenly, but earwigs are everywhere.

Letter from Roy, asking news of war.   They hear
German broadcasts in English, which are contradicted entirely
by our own broadcasts in English.   Anti-British feeling very
high among Dutch population, and being fanned by Germans.
Knox-Shaw writing to Radcliffe Trustees about telescope mirror.
Also letter from P., who is in bed with bad cold.

Sunday, October 22

Very misty till lunch-time, when it becomes fine again.
C.E. Anniversary.   Daddy enjoys himself leading tenors in
"All Ye that Cried Unto the Lord" in morning, and in afternoon, while Mother and I go on common, helps in "I Waited
for the Lord".   We sit near where we were yesterday, but
mist in valley makes view mysterious and different.   Train
held up on journey back to London, probably by fog.

Monday, October 23

Florence Horsbrugh, M.P., in broadcast: "We are fighting that
the boys and girls of today may have a better world to live
in as the men and women of tomorrow".   Facile nobility.

          Lunch with Joyce, on her return journey from White
Rolls Royce.   Last see her backing into heap of concreted
sandbags declaring that not for anyone will she miss her train
from Paddington.

          At printers till 6.40, when go to Beavans, have
solitary meal while John, Peter and Victor Smith play in music-
room, then join them.   J. and V. play Brahms' Fourth Symphony
on two pianos, while Peter shows me photographs.   Later we
play Monopoly till 12.30, and I stay for night.

Tuesday, October 24

Ribbentrop makes very fiery speech at Danzig, saying that
England was determined to have war with Germany and had been
planning it for years.   R.A.F. in reconnaissance flights
over Berlin and Hamburg.

At printers till 7.30.   New route home, devised
by Mr. A., not a success, because King's Cross station shut,
and we go by Met., change Euston Square, walk to Warren Street
and at last get on to Hampstead line.   Find Cundells, returned from day at cottage, just going out to supper at 8.30.
Greta brings me nice meal which I eat alone.   Beautiful
concert on wireless from French station.   Brahms' Violin
Concerto.   Very tired.

Wednesday, October 25

Five British merchant ships sunk.

Quiet day at office.   Mr. A. gives me sherry on
way home.   I then encounter Miss Dorothy Pearse-Gould in
Hampstead lift.   She says she has just come from Drummond
Street Mission.   I say what I hope are right things, breathe
sherry inher face, and wonder if she has just given a
Temperance Address.

Music, including beautiful Schubert Sextet.   Leave
a small remnant still playing César Franck at midnight, and

go to bed beneath a bright moon.

Thursday, October 26

Goebbels says it's time Germany began bombing Britain.   So
tremendous clap of thunder during morning causes Miss Playle
to clutch at her gas-mask.   Two German U-boats sunk.

        Catch 5.30 from Euston to Manchester.   Get about
last seat in restaurant car,which has blinds and proper
lights.   Sit beside two pillars of Wesleyan Church, whose
conversation consists of: "What did you think of Brown's appointment at Yeovil?"... "Of course I laid it before the
General Purposes Committee".   The older gave account of
George Lansbury's interview with King Leopold of the Belgians
just before war, which caused Leopold to broadcast his appeal
for peace.   Listen hard to them in intervals of reading
Osbert Sitwell's "Before the Bombardment".

        Arnold meets me at Wilmslow and we drive to Hale
in moonlight.   M. feeding fortnight-old Richard: both look
very healthy.   Mrs. Funchs Senr. here, but her husband away
for night.   I have camp bed in lounge.

Friday, October 27
American Senate ~~repeals~~ alters A... d.... f Neutrality Bill and agrees to sell
arms on "Cash and Carry" principle.   This means that buyers
fetch goods in their own ships and pay before having them,

and rather excludes Germany.

I rise from my camp bed like a mummy, my bed-
clothes being wound above and below me.   Watch bathing of
Richard, who is very much like Christopher was at that age;
play ball with C.; write letters.   Father Fuchs returns.
In afternoon go shopping in Altrincham with Christopher,
Mother Fuchs and Aunt Daisy, who turns up for afternoon.
In evening read by fire: Winifred Holtby's "South Riding" -
book much better than the film: and listen to Dvorak's
Nigger Quartet on wireless.

Saturday, October 28
Christopher's third birthday.   He has three red woollen
suits, a drawing-book, a ball, and from me an ingenious toy
consisting of a clown with an umbrella and basket, and when
wound up the umbrella twirls and up a little spiral go two
balls which fall into the basket before they start mounting
again.   M. has made iced cake with seven candles - three for
Christopher, and four for Arnold who was forty on Thursday.
In afternoon C. takes me for walk, directing me to playground
where he goes down a chute and swings, then leading me unerr-
ingly down a footpath to a lake where we see men fishing.
Various rituals have to be observed: we have to call "Cuckoo
Mamma" down a grating; look into all wastepaper baskets to

see what is inside; and walk on extreme edge of one section
of kerbstone.

Reni, refugee maid, had mother and brother in
Warsaw and has had no news of them since war began.

Mining disaster in Dunfermline.   German aeroplane
brought down in Scotland.

Sunday, October 29
Cold.   Have cello recital from Carl Fuchs - the broadcast
he would have made if war had not broken out.   Enjoy seeing
him play almost as much as hearing him, and think of Peter
and the way he looks when he's playing.

Arnold takes me to Altrincham in car with C., and I
go by electric train to Manchester.   "Good-evening, Miss
Radman", says voice behind me on Manchester station, and find
Miss Mills, head of B.B.C. Registry.   Travel with her in
dark train and get home at about 11.30.

Monday, October 30
While in B.B.C.-bound bus in Great Portland Street, deep in
book, see people running and am told there has been an air-
raid warning.   Proceed to Broadcasting House.   Find offices
deserted; hear siren, see editor coming in and say tentatáve-
ly "I think there's an air-raid warning".   "No, that's the
All Clear", he says, and the staff returns from the Concert

Hall where it has taken shelter.

At printers till 7.20.   Supper with Edric, who
has bad cold and goes to bed early, while I read "Queer Street".

Tuesday, October 31

Mussolini reconstructing Cabinet, Army and Air Force - a
regular business, but reports say that he's getting rid of
the pro-German element.

Very busy at printers: Mr. A. and I have bought
pocket chess for slack moments, but have scarcely time to
look at it.   Finish at 6.45, and take dismal journey to
Hilary's at Shirley, which I reach at 8.30.   Beautiful meal
of what I eat under the impression that it is beef, but
learn afterwards that it is lamb.   Read and chat and listen
to wireless.   Get German station in English saying Poles
used poison gas supplied to them by Britain.   Sleep on
mattress on floor of spare room.   H. has letter from Mother
saying Phyllida has visited Tunbridge Wells to see if it
still stands, since German wireless reports it in ruins.
Same source states Stroud has been razed to ground.

Wednesday, November 1

Have day off in lieu of Friday this week.   Wakened by wireless in next room at 8 a.m. reporting speech by Molotov,

Soviet Foreign Minister, which says again that Russia is
neutral but blames England and France for continuing war.
The so-called neutral Russia is trying to get some islands
from Finland.

H. and I go to West Wickham shopping, taking next-
door fifteen-months-old Cynthia, very plump, in her pram.
H. gardens and I write diary, knit, etc. Return to Hampstead for dinner and music in evening. J.D. and another man
play chess, and I try to knit jersey for Christopher, follow
chess and listen to Trout Quintet, all at once. Have to un-
knit quite a lot afterwards. After Brahms Horn Trio I go to
bed, but leave Beethoven still going strong. Peter says he'd
like to come to Stroud for weekend, but on looking up diary
finds the one before Christmas the only time free. Books it
provisionally.

Thursday, November 2

Busy day. To Beavans in evening: Gladys and Marcelle, nice
couple, there. Scramble, three stories by Arthur, violin by
John. Then Peter comes in and he, John and I play Monopoly
till 1 a.m. My fault, and very silly of us. I take Bitter-
mints, which are not appreciated, J. saying frankly he'd rather
have Woolworth's sweets. He also enjoys sweetened condensed
milk on bread-and-butter, tin marked "Not for Babies".

Friday, November 3

Duque says at breakfast that John does not get enough sleep,
so I feel remorseful that I suggested Monopoly last night.

Very busy day.   Catch 6.55 home and travel with
fretful baby.   Weather has become mild and unsettled.   Knit
in dimness of railway carriage, occasionally putting on torch
to pick up dropped stitches.

Saturday, November 4

Ration cards received, but rationing not yet in force.
Letter from Roy.   Suggestion that mirror may be completed in
America.   The Williams' native boy, who has left them, has
sent following letter:-

> "With your regards and your words I get it.
> I did understand all you Explain me,
> please.   I am sorry.   I am still bessy
> with my work at home please.   I will try
> and come at end October please.   Please
> give regards to your child.   Is that all.
> What I answer.   With greetings to you.
> I am still alive.   Yours faithfully
>   Joe Mothari Mawewe".

American House of Representatives has also lifted embargo on
sale of arms.   Germany cross.

Russia says Finland trying to provoke a war, because Finland has been laying mines in harbours of places
Russia demands.

Walk on common in afternoon.   Meet Florence, whose
baby smiles at me very coyly, and Miss Blanche and Agnes

Clutterbuck.   Miss B. says they have 30 evacuated children
at her school and no extra teachers.   Many evacuated children have returned to their homes, where no schools are open.
Half expect Joyce to be at home when I return, but unsettled
weather no doubt kept her away.

Sunday, November 5

No fireworks by order of the Government.

Finnish Prime Minister has been making speech in
which he says that Finland has no quarrel with anybody and
wishes to have peace, but she must try to defend what is her
own.   News also reports that enormous orders for arms have
already been placed with America by this country.

Beautiful morning which turns to dull afternoon and
wet evening.   Go on to common, and there am staggered to
see Mr. Mellor, sub-editor of "World Radio" also taking a
solitary walk.   He is spending long weekend at the Bear,
having come away from London first because he has been run
down and unwell, and second to get away from three refugee
Germans for whom he gave guarantees of maintenance and who, he
feels, may never get to America as planned, under the new law.
He pours out his troubles, walks with me round the common, and
gives me a message to his Editor to say he'll be back on Tuesday afternoon.

Monday, November 6

Wild, wet day. Busy at printers. Bernard Robinson to
supper. Bridge, during which I am instructed in the
"forcing two". Long letter from Mrs. Morris, in Devonshire.
She refers to "that utterly damnable Hitler and his gang",
and says (Quaker as she may be): "I am sorry for the pacifists in a way - but principally I think because they seem
to look on the shedding of blood (awful though it is) as
worse than any other deed however vile. It appears that
they put a higher value on the life of the body than of the
spirit". Letter also from Aunt Nina requesting me to write
a parody on "Then you'll remember me" (which I don't know)
to accompany the gift of a dictionary which she is making to
a friend.

Tuesday, November 7

Mild and damp. Molotov says Russia will _not_ be dragged into
this war.

At printers till 5.30. Alarmed by enormous black
rat which drops from ceiling of lavatory nearly on top of me
- looking for water in the cistern, Mr. Morgan says.

Manage to get to the Madrigal Choir (being held at
Mervyn Horder's) and enjoy it very much.

Wednesday, November 8

Germans massing on Dutch frontier.   Queen Wilhelmina of
the Netherlands, and King Leopold of the Belgians make peace
appeal to belligerents.   Germans said not to have been told
by their leaders.   British submarine sunk.

Discover "Then you'll remember me" is song from "The
Bohemian Girl" beginning "When other lips".   Get vocal score
from Music Library and send off not-very-good parody to Aunt
Nina.

Lunch with Mr. Abraham at Chinese restaurant.
Fried chicken and pineapple with rice and little rolled pancakes with something savoury and oniony in them;   and China
tea.   Also sherry with him in pub. on way home, when we play
bagatelle on a set which tinkles bells and twinkles electric
lights and records the most astounding score in a very short
time.

Music at Cundells.   Schubert piano trio;   Smetana
quartet;   Mozart quartet.   I knit.   Weather very close, and
everybody rather sleepy and tired, especially Peter, who returned at 4 a.m. from Bristol, where Boyd Neel Orchestra was
giving broadcast last night.   Nevertheless he is last to
leave, and when I go to bed is still playing cello and piano
sonata with Edric.

Thursday, November 9

Bomb explodes in attic of Munich building where Hitler is
making speech, but alas he left a quarter of an hour sooner
than was expected, and so escaped.   Six people killed and a
number injured.   Germany blames (jointly) the British nation
and German Jews for this outrage, and regard it as sign from
heaven and mark of providence's favour that Hitler was spared.
The English regard it otherwise.   It is suggested that Hitler
arranged the whole thing himself, to make good excuse for
further hatred.   He now threatens to begin the war in earnest,
just to show us.

          Wet in London, but travel to Stroud by usual train
(empty and late) and find they have it beautiful day.

Friday, November 10

Many arrests in Germany in connection with bomb explosion.
Belgium and Holland mobilising, and Dutch prepared to cut
dykes.   Talks between Finland and Russia said to have broken
down.

          Go to Stroud in morning and try to exchange my
"regular" food ration card for a "travellers" one, so that I
can get food both here and in London.   Am asked my occupation,
and after saying "Sub-Editor", find myself object of great
interest to three females in same room as my questioner.

They gaze at me fixedly, trying to look as indifferent to
my appearance and fate as possible; until a young man comes
in, when they simultaneously shift their gaze to him.   After
some time it is discovered that I am in the Rural District
Office, and that now Rodborough is part of Greater Stroud I
ought to be in the Urban building at the bottom of High St.
So I go out, but have no time left for further activity, but
have to rush home with the fish for dinner.

Walk oncommon in afternoon.   Autumn colours still
beautiful and weather very mild and pleasant.

At 9.30 we are playing 3-hamded bridge and Daddy
is about to make a grand slam, when Joyce appears at back door,
carrying 45-year-old black hat in one hand and horse's nosebag
from Morocco in other, and says she has walked from Bisley,
whither she had a lift from a girl who works on the Countryman.
So after much questioning as to How and Why and When and (rudely)
How she would Get Back, we abandon game which Mother and I were
on point of losing, and have supper.

Saturday, November 11

Armistice Day, which Stroud does not appear to observe.   We
hear service from Westminster, with choir singing "sufficient
is Thine arm alone and our defence is sure", and wonder why,
if they believe this, they do not cast their anti-air-craft
guns into the ocean.   The Queen broadcasts message to women

of the Empire.

Joyce and I walk to Selsley and through woods to
Surprise Point: colours beautiful, especially yellow of elms.

Sunday, November 12

Daddy had funny turn last night - made strange noises and sat
bolt upright in bed and frightened Mother.   Seems all right
this morning.

Hitler sends reply to Wilhelmina and Leopold to say
Germany will carefully consider peace suggestions.   George VI
has also sent reply, saying we can't negotiate with Germany
till they withdraw from Austria, Czechoslovakia and Poland.

Armistice Day service at Chapel: very pleasant and
not jingoistic at all.   Mr. Clark, at home on two days leave
from Air Force somewhere in Yorkshire, says war will be over
before Christmas for lack of support - "everybody thinks so".
Hope he is right, but am not so sanguine myself.   He promises
to let us have leaflet/dropped by British over Germany.

J. and I set out for walk on common after dinner,
but meet Miss Ashton, who is on her way to Bryans with the information that last Tuesday Aunt Hermie fell down some steps
and broke a collar-bone.   So we turn Selsley-wards and visit
her, and while we are there Daddy and Mother arrive.   So we
return by car.

Joyce sees me off on 7.15 train.   Very dim light.

Talk to doctor, also in carriage. At Kemble man gets in
(turns out also to be doctor) and says he is reading French
novel and must have light so intends to scrape some of blue
from bulb. I lend him nail-file with which to do the deed,
and he takes off a lot. When I ask does he think he has
used my nail-file in the National Interest, he points out
that the Armed Forces of the Crown in next carriage have removed almost every vestige of blue from their light. Run-
down battery means that while train is stopped, our light
goes out altogether, so our crime is not discovered in any of
the numberous stations at which we halt.

Monday, November 13

Learn that on Friday a French Announcer threw himself from a
second-floor window of Broadcasting House and has since died.
He was under notice.

Letter from Edgar Holt beseeching me to write to
him soon and asking whether Hilary did get married after all.
Have already given him this information on more than one occasion, and feel if he doesn't remember it, must love me for
Myself Alone and not my Little Sister.

Busy at printers. Leave spectacles at Hampstead
and my eyes ache. To Beavans, where Pauline Jones and Irene
Richards also are. Like both of them very much. We play
pingpong, scramole and monopoly with great enjoyment, and

I get so hot feel shall explode.   But cool down during
pleasant walk home from Swiss Cottage up Fitzjohn's Avenue.

<u>Tuesday, November 14</u>
Income Tax form assuring me that I have to pay £26.19s. for
each coming <u>half</u>-year.   Feel I must be immensely rich if
state can expect so much of me.   Also letter from Aunt Nina
thanking me for verse but pointing out that I spell 2 words
wrongly.   As I racked my brains for some time first to think
of words people always do make mistakes in and then ingeniously
to work them in to the poem, feel she has no sense of humour.
And there were at least 4 of them anyhow.

To-day's best newspaper placard: "BUG BOMB BOGEY
DEBUNKED".

British destroyer sunk.

Germans drop bombs on Shetlands, and according to
our news kill one rabbit; according to theirs destroy two
aeroplanes.

To madrigals which I enjoy but am rather tired.
Greta gets me nice dinner which I eat alone, and afterwards
hear German broadcast in English, about our Secret Service -
a catalogue of murders committed (to prove that we were responsible for the Munich bomb too).   Most sinister voice,
which makes my flesh creep, and when a car revs up outside am
sure the noise is an air-raid siren and tremble accordingly.

To-day read Churchill's broadcast of Sunday, and do not feel
proud of our own boasts, threats and sneers.

Wednesday, November 15
Receive from Mr. Clark, via Mother, copy of leaflet as dropped
by British aeroplanes over Germany: quotations from Hitler's
speeches saying the Russians are blood-stained criminals and
Germany will have nothing to do with them: and that they will
never risk their young men in a war for the sake of the Polish
Corridor, but have made non-aggression pact with Poles.

      Music in evening: Schubert Trout Quintet again, and
Edric's Sextet. Also two Beethoven Cello Sonatas by Peter -
in A and C major. Beautiful.

Thursday, November 16
Pouring wet day. Train to Stroud only 10 minutes late - best
since war started. Talk to two women in carriage. One tells
me about her London house being burgled while she is at Gloucester; the other tells me about her daughter who is in a play by
Ian Hay at Stratford-on-Avon. Neither of them speaks to the
other, however. Since the war people are prepared to tell me
their life histories: feel must be because my face is blacked
out, as they didn't do it before.

Friday, November 17
Wireless reports internal dissension in Germany. General Von

Blomberg said to have been shot, and many others arrested.
Meeting of the Supreme War Council at Downing Street, during
which agreement is reached between French and British about
economic warfare.

Misty mild day.   Walk with Mother on common in
afternoon.   Gales during last week have blown off almost all
remaining leaves from trees, so that the landscape has stopped
being autumnal and become wintry.

Do my best to persuade Stroud's Food Controller to
let me have traveller's ration card, but though Mr. Franklin,
who is working there, would let me have my way, the mighty one
insists that I am neither a commercial traveller, member of a
theatrical company nor travelling lecturer, and therefore I
must take bits of food to and fro between Stroud and London
in my suitcase.   Friendly-disposed young woman tries to persuade him that my connection with the B.B.C. might put me in
the theatrical category, but he thinks not.   Hope they won't
take to rationing milk.

Saturday, November 18

More reports of unrest in Greater Germany.   Prague under
martial law.   Several students arrested, and schools and
colleges closed for three years.

Pouring wet day.   Go to visit Aunt H. and have tea

with Mish Colesh and three others.   Aunt's black eye looks
better.   Cards with parents in evening.   P.c. from John
saying is his map here: it is a green book, 6 inches by 10
inches.   Feel, from a scientist, this description very in-
adequate.

Daddy and Mother read detective thrillers nowadays
to make them forget war.

End of prolonged summer time.

Sunday, November 19

Dutch passenger ship sunk by mine off East Coast of England
and many passengers drowned: also Flemish ship off coast of
Belgium.   Germany said to be encountering difficulties in
trade negotiations with Rumania, since Germany has no money
and wants to do everything on a basis of barter.   Four bomb
explosions in London, two in Piccadilly, one in Upper Regent
Street: I.R.A. suspected.

Much finer day, but colder.   Walk with Mother in
afternoon.

Uneventful journey to London.   Letter from Aunt N.
She has re-read my poem and apologises for not seeing point
before.

Monday, November 20

On way downstairs to breakfast meet Alice Robinson.   She
and Bernard have been spending night here.   Also another
Camp person, who has been cooking breakfast - Greta being
unwell and staying with her sister.

At printers alone, because Mr. A. just completing
last summer's holiday.

German aeroplanes over Scotland and Thames Estuary:
no bombs dropped.   Driven off by anti-aircraft guns.   Four
ships sunk.   For third day in succession German planes over
neutral Holland.   Dutch planes go up and fight them.

Come home to empty house.   Cundells gone to cottage
and Greta still at her sister's.   Peer into many cupboards
hoping to find an egg, but cannot.   Drink large amount of
Ovaltine and eat bread and cheese and marmite and two apples.
Knit and listen to wireless - something I take to be by very
modern composer, but decide like it very much: learn at end
it is Sibelius' First Symphony.   Announcer says we must
register for food rationing before Thursday.   Rouse myself
sufficiently to write to Stroud and ask for my ration card to
be transferred to Hampstead.   Letter from Joyce.

Tuesday, November 21

German reconnaissance plane brought down off Kentish coast.
Several more of our ships sunk.

Slept very long and well in empty house.   Meet
Raymond Baldwin in Willow Road, and he presses me to call
in and visit him at No.17.   Mendaciously promise to do so.
Very heavy day at printers.   Have raging headache all morn-
ing.   Make myself eat lunch I don't want, and it goes.
Leave at 6.20 and creep humbly into madrigals an hour late.
Mr. Foster makes me feel better by saying "Good! Here's Miss
Redman", and I struggle with something in Latin alleged to be
by Handel, but cannot believe he ever wrote anything so fright-
ful.

Get to Flask Walk at 8.   Find house still empty
and feel cannot face immediate future without hearty meal.
So walk down to Belsize Park and find with difficulty very dim
sign saying "Restaurant. Open".   Seat myself inside door,
which has huge light-trap looking like "Another Part of the
Battle.   The King's Tent", but the only creatures who come
through are obviously second-rate seene-shifters or bankrupt
deputy business managers.   Eat large meal and feel able to
cope with life once more.   Wish I were a man with a wife to
get meals and talk to me, a function which I should not fulfil
myself nearly as well as earning living.

On return try to wind wool by draping it round chair
and get it into dreadful tangle.   Cundells arrive and we
drink Ovaltine together.   They tell me of shortcomings of one
of their domestics at cottage.   Have horrible feeling I should

be just as incompetent myself. Then Helena holds my wool
and I remember how she derided some woman who wound her wool
badly. Feel humbler and humbler.

. Returning from bathroom to bedroom, find fire
glowing in darkness, and remember Phyllida when she was little
girl, standing naked before a fire after her bath, with two
little thick dark pigtails down her back. At this recollec-
tion of a safer and happier world, find myself bursting into
tears.

Wednesday, November 22

Germans dropping "magnetic" mines into sea by parachute from aeroplanes.
Ten ships sunk. On other hand, 11 of their planes brought
down.

Seventeen people to music in evening. Never know whether
this house will be empty and foodless, or full of people and
macaroni cheese. Very good pianist, Franz Osborn, plays
the chromatic fugue and then Prokofiev's "Three Oranges" piece.
Think something wrong with piano, but find (he is pupil of
Schnabel, who snorts dreadfully when playing) it is F.O. making
extraordinary noises. Ends the Prokofiev with regular shout.
We have Brahms' sextet in G, and Peter and Franz O. play
Beethoven Cello Sonata in A. Renie Richards here, and stays
for night. John says I ought to come back earlier on Sundays
in order to join in Fun and Games at OxfordRoad.

Thursday, November 23

Very wet day.   In lunchtime, Mollie Evans and I go to one
of the National Gallery lunch-hour concerts, armed with sandwiches.   This principally because Boyd Neel playing.   (Renie
had to get to rehearsal for it at 9.30 this morning.)   Enjoy
programme beyond words.   Myra Hess in the Fifth Brandenburg
Concerto.   Also Elgar's Introduction and Allegro for strings.
Peter has to rush off afterwards to Philharmonic concert at
Queen's Hall - for which Edric offered me tickets, but cannot
easily leave work all afternoon.

To Hilary's for night.   Long and trying journey.
Am cast out of Trafalgar Square tube into I know not what side
of the Square.   "Oh, where is CharingCross Station?" I ask
of the void, and a kind man says "You come along O' me, Lady",
and I follow him trustfully across a dozen streams of traffic.
At Shirley am cheered to find Leonard on same bus.   Hilary
produces enormous meal, looking very fetching in little apron
with red hearts for pockets.   Phyllis and Fred come in for
coffee and we play Coon Can and I lose 1d.   Hear theGerman
broadcast in English still decrying British Secret Service.
Germans have been arresting two Englishman in Holland (or
rather kidnapping them) for, they say, arranging the Munich
bomb explosion.

Friday, November 24

English say if Germans drop bombs about the sea in this un-
called for way, they will stop all neutral shipping going to
Germany.   The newspapers state that Hitler had ordered invasion of Holland for November 12 at 6 a.m., and only countermanded order for attack four hours before it was due, because
he found (a) that Belgium would not remain neutral; (b) that
this would rouse U.S.A. opinion against him too much.

Pack and send Christmas presents to South Africa,
at postage cost of 3/9.   Have to declare price and nature of
contents.   It is all pasted on outside of parcel. Find this
embarrassing: like undressing in public.

By 6.35 to Stroud.   Knit vigorously and have to pick
up stitches by light of torch.   Brilliant moonlight for walk
home from station.

Saturday, November 25

My food card returned to me here.   Told to call at Hampstead
Food Office with it.   Feel shall be lucky if get any food at all
Ships going down like anything.
Cold.   Short walk with Mother in rain and wind.   Finish
jersey for Christopher, which intend to give M. for her birth-
day.tomorrow.

German liner sunk.   Passengers saved.

Sunday, November 26

Great winds last night.   On way to church, hear fire-brigade
going down Bath Road.   It is met, at bottom of hill, by police
car, out of which leaps officer, stops fire-engine, and issues
instructions to proceed to Brimscombe.   "How's that, then?"
slowly enquires leader of Stroud's A.F.S., and when it has
seeped in that for sake of practice Brimscombe-wards they must
indeed wend, the engine starts again with terrific jerk, nearly
precipitating tin-hats into road.   They cling on, trying to
look used to this sort of thing, and at last, with great explosion and clouds of black smoke, they are off.

Come in from afternoon walk with Mother and find Daddy
in armchair and gnome-like little urchin sitting on tumpty by
fire, a large apple bulging from each pocket and a large grin
on his face.   Daddy says "Have you got a cake for him, Mother?"
and he goes off with his grin wider than ever.

At Paddington wait 20 minutes for bus: then cannot
get on.   One woman who pushes through, leaves large handbag behind in gutter, which I pick up.   Comes back for it, and rewards
me with full story of death by heart-failure of her husband who
for 27 years drove one of the 2 trams which went underground at
Kingsway.

Monday, November 27

Ships still being sunk.   At printers alone till 6.30.   Beautiful walk from Fond Street up Willow Road in brilliant moonlight.

After dinner, Helena, Edric and I walk on heath.   See searchlight being manipulated from beside Ken Wood House.   When we
get back, Edric puts on records of his "Serbia", a Symphonic
Poem he composed in dugout in Salonika in 1917-18;   also his
String Quartet which 4 or 5 years ago won Daily Telegraph prize
of £100.   I follow score with terrific concentration.   Then
am shown little dirty music MS. books in which, in trenches, he
made notes for Symphonic Poem.

Tuesday, November 28

After waking in night and finding watch stopped and trying to
put it right by striking clock, get up at 7.45, under frightful
strain of thinking it is 9.30.   Letter from Joyce, on back of
which, in trolley-bus, I clothe poem which was born (decently)
in bed last night.   Seem to know it by heart, and am afraid it
may not be my own new child after all:-

Ought to be
called "On
looking at
Moon and re-
flecting that
Hitler cannot
black it out
or bid it stay".

Be still, my heart: remember that the sun
  Goes unperturbed upon his ordered way,
Progressing calmly till his course is run.
  For all days end and so too must to-day.

Be still, my heart: remember that the moon
  Serenely gives her regulated light,
And punctually knows no "late" or "soon".
  All nights must end and so too must tonight.
          do

O heart, be still: the silent stars above
  Go surely down to the impersonal west,
Knowing no fear or anger, hate or love.
  All things must end and thou too shalt have rest.

Finish at printers at 5.15 and get early to madrigals, which
enjoy very much.   Find extraordinary but nice "Hodie Christus

Natus Est" is by Jacobus Han<u>dl</u>, 1586, not G.F. Han<u>del</u>.   Home
soon after 8.   Lathams in for bridge, so I do many Useful Jobs
amd write, and when Helena goes on duty, take her hand, partner-
ing Peter Latham.   He plays brilliantly - can tell exactly how
many tricks every player could have made on any sort of trumps
- but is very patient and kind with me .

<u>Wed∅nesday</u>, ~~December~~ <u>November 29</u>

Dentist at 10 a.m.   He reports 2 fillings needed.   Had just
planned new surgery when war began, and now many patients have
gone away and all his students (he had 90 % of London's dental
students under him) evacuated.   Can't get into army dental work
because over 45.   From him go to Food Office at Marie Curie
Hospital, Fitzjohn's Av., and get ration card transferred to
Hampstead.

      Depleted party for music at night: Marie (girl from
Guildhall School), Hardy, David, Peter (who comes late, in tails,
straight from Beecham concert and reports that audience hissed
B. because he wouldn't let them have encore from favourite tenor),
and young man called Bell who says Lathams said he could come.
I let him in and introduce him to Helena.   Edric lets him out
later, murmuring "Well, any time ... ", and then turns to me and
says "Who <u>was</u> that young man? ... Oh, I thought perhaps he was
just passing and heard music and came in".

      Major Glendinning also comes.   Is at War Office, and

says last January the Govt. knew all about German "magnetic"
mines and had plans for an antidote.   Ships to cope with them
are now ready.

Russia repudiates Non-Aggression Pact with Finland.

Thursday, November 30
Russia bombing Helsinki.   Feel much worse about invasion of
peaceful little Finland than about Poland.

Very mild wet day.   In lunch-hour go with Molly Evans
to National Gallery concert.   Kamaran Trio: three of plainest
women I ever saw, but playing not too bad.   Ireland, Loeillet,
and Brahms.

To tea with Beavans: only Peter, John and their Uncle
Cheeno.   Play Monopoly, and J. and I make duplicate set of
Properties and we play double game: Peter and I v. John and
Cheeno.   Draw.   Don't finish till 12, and they press me to
stay for night.   P. very sweetly gets me hot-water bottle while
J. searches for suitable pyjamas and after rejecting many,
supplies enormous pair blue-and-white striped ones, trousers
of which dangle over ankles while in coat I am lost.

Friday, December 1
Finnish Government resigns.   Armistice called with advancing
Russians.

Very tired, but rise at 7.30 and after early breakfast

with John, Cheeno and silent Peter in dressing-gown, go to
Hampstead to collect bag for weekend.   Pack it full to brim
in great hurry, and find later have forgotten pyjamas, hairbrush and face-flannel.   Another lunch-time National Gallery
concert, with Misses Playle and Scott-Johnston.   Large, cheerful, friendly crowd.   See authoritative-looking man standing
beneath archway eating sandwiches out of paper-bag.   Brahms
programme by Elena Gerhardt, Myra Hess and Lionel Tertis.   Very
beautiful.

Meet David on 6.5 for Kingham and are met by Wells
in rain.   Insist must get to bed early, and after going at what
I think is 11.15, find it is only 10.15 and am very pleased.

Saturday, December 2

Oh, How I slept.   And this morning is not only sunny and clear,
but warm too.   Joyce and I go walk in woods.   Polly comes to
lunch, bringing a meat-pie for herself because we have only 4
herrings.   Halfway through her husband turns up.   He'd sent
telegram from town but she hadn't had it.   May comes after
lunch and we all take tea to a woodcutter's hut in middle of
woods.   Stuff sacks with bracken for seats, make wood-fire in
stone fireplace, and boil billycan and toast crumpets.   Have
forgotten cups and drink out of vessels in which tea and sugar
were packed.   Joyce (J) whittles pieces of stick to make two
long-handled toasting-forks and 1 prehistoric but useful spoon.

Sit and talk in firelight while light from window (no glass)
wanes.   Storm blows up, but is gone before we leave, and walk
away from clouds towards the bright west where there is a rim
of orange across the horizon

Sunday, December 3

Get up late and am in disgrace, so go and polish shoes in wash-
house and sing O Worship the Lord in the Beauty of Holiness into
brightness of morning.   We go to woodcutter's hut again, make
gorgeous fire and cook lunch.   Have each, 7 cocktail sausages
and several mushrooms and tomatoes and raw apple chunks and
bread and roasted chestnuts and bread fried in black mushroomy
pan and Cox's Orange Pippins.   On walk home, J. and D. get a
great branch of gorse and I walk along with it like Birnam Woods.
After we come in it pours with rain and D. says if I stay tonight
shan't be later than 10.30 in morn., so I read all through Aldous
Huxley's latest novel, "After Many a Year", an extraordinary book
which is just a vehicle for expressing philosophy already ex-
pounded in "Ends and Means".   He says: "Individuals ... are
under no necessity to remain exclusively on the human level of
existence.   It is in their power to pass from the level of the
absence of God to that of God's presence ... Peace is the serene
activity which springs from the knowledge that our 'souls' are
illusory and their creations insane, that all beings are poten-
tially united in eternity".

        Joyce (David's one), in middle of getting tea and

discussing T. E. Brown, suddenly produces following gem:-

> O Cosmo, what a Cant-u-ar,
> How you do go it,
> Hitching your wagon to the
>   star of war.
> How do you do it?

- following it by sturdy defence of half-rhymes. Her husband,
in midst of making toast, with no warning bursts into following:-

> I dreamt that I dwelt in Fortnum and Mason's:
> I ate myself sick and then I was sad.
> So I joined the department for buckets and basins:
> And then I felt better and then I was glad.

Go on and on with reading, in midst of smell of gorse and of
violets David picked in garden this morning. J. going to have baby

Monday, December 4.

R.A.F. raid on German naval base in Heligoland. Russians try
to come over Finland in planes and land in parachutes, but are
surrounded and taken prisoner. King in France with troops.

After suffering from Aldous Indigestion - could not
sleep: his book going round and round in my head all night -
rise at 6.30 and travel to London with David through cold morning. Mr. A. back from holiday, so printers not so hectic.
My left eye inflamed, I fear from strain through reading Huxley
so concentratedly by lamplight without glasses.

In evening Edric nearly goes mad at broadcast of Brhams'
Fourth Symphony conducted by Adrian Boult. Says it's too slow,
tears his hair, conducts it himself as it should be, says 'Oh
my God!' and switches off.

Very tired. To bed early.

Tuesday, December 5

Russia planning invasion in north of Finland. Halifax defines
war aims. Says has had many enquiries as to why we can't have
conference now instead of fighting first. Answer is that the
present German Government cannot be conferred with because when
it does make agreements (i.e.Munich), it breaks them.

Printers and madrigals as usual. Alone in house for
night: Edric and Helena gone to cottage for birthday party.
Cannot find any means of securing door leading from sitting-room
to side of house, and have to go to bed with it unlocked.

Wednesday, December 6

Did not sleep for imagining burglars on stairs. Discover Mrs.
MacDonald (char) took away key in order to be able to get in
this morning, and thought she had locked door first.

National Gallery concert with Mr.A. and Miss M. Rosé
String Quartet: Schubert and Beethoven (6 major). Very good.
Hugh Walpole in crowded audience.

Man comes into office about 5; says our light shows
and we must shut windows. Protest that B.B.C. staff will shortly
die of suffocation if denied air, but he doesn't mind.

Music at night. Mrs. Rosenberg tells me Rosé is 80
years old and was for 60 years in Vienna Philharmonic Orchestra.
Is now refugee. We have glorious Brahms Quintet. I read third
of "Hornblower" books (C.S.Forester), "Flying Colours". Grand.
Edric, who has to go by train to Worthing tomorrow to conduct
his Symphony, finds

he has no money for the fare and borrows £3.   Helena also
borrows 2/- to get to A.R.P. centre.   Fortunately, cashed
cheque to-day, or should be penniless myself.

Thursday, December 7

News is madder thane ver.   We are sending arms to Finland;
so is Germany, so is Italy - but Italy days this doesn't mean
she is any more friendly with the democracies.

Very cold misty morning.   In train to Stroud we
have blinds and fairly good lights.   Sorry I have neither a
book with me nor enough wool to go on with knitting.   Talk to
North Country commercial traveller who is going to Stroud to
visit Daniels's iron-works.   Says he is glad I spoke first,
since a lot of women think if they're in a compartment with a
man and no one else and he begins to talk, he has designs on
her.   Hope he didn't think I had designs on him.

Friday, December 8

Three cargo ships sunk.   German submarine sunk.   German aeroplanes driven off coast of Scotland in aerial battle.

Hilary and Leonard expected for weekend, but telegram
announces they cannot come.   It pours with rain all day till
the evening.   About 11 a.m. I go over common to see Auntie
Tuttie and arrive soaked.   She is very distressed at my wetness
and does not believe my assurances that I shall take no cold.
Have cup of tea before I start back - along Butterrow to avoid

gale on top of hill.   Margaret to be married on Saturday week.

Hilda brings up Florence's baby to say Goodbye.   F. returning to Birmingham.

Saturday, December 9

Still mild and rainy.   Manage triumphantly to get 1 torch battery from Woolworth's.   Sugar and butter, authorities say, are not rationed yet, but people can get only 1 lb. sugar and $\frac{1}{2}$ lb. butter each per week.   For myself, I call this rationing.

P.c. from Hilary.   Leonard's colleague has jaundice; hence postponed visit.   Two letters from S.Africa.   David so obstreperous they think of sending him to Nursery School, mornings 8.30 - 11.30.   Can't let him run in garden because of snakes, and Babe not allowed out alone to take him long walks: hence he is full of surplus energy.

Mother told, owing to military camps plus black-out it is unsafe for girl to walk in streets of Gloucester after dark.   Daddy (who from time to time has firms trying to get him to sell birth-control appliances on the sly), has now received literature about some tablets for the "cold" wife or husband. Very expensive, too.   But if the inhabitants of Gloucester begin to be stimulated further, Where shall we Be?

British cruiser torpedoed.   League of Nations considering case of Russia and Finland.

Wireless programme of Edwardian songs.   Much gayer
and happier than ours.   But they lived in an age which was
able to believe in the inevitability of progress.

Sunday, December 10

Wake at 4 - 5 a.m. and hear extraordinary noise going on apparently just other side of garden fence.   Knocking sounds: and
old rotten wood being broken.   Get up and lean a yard from
open window but can see nothing.   After about 5 minutes noises
stop and I go back to bed.   Cogitate as to cause.   Reject
theory that Mr. Clutterbuck (aged 80) has murdered his wife and
is disposing of remains: also idea that Mrs. C. (younger but
tubercular) has been doing the same for her husband on a dank
December night..   Cannot be cow, since none are at large this
time of year.   Perhaps someone burying box of gold for duration
of war?   Or hoard of petrol?   Think criminal probably saw
white face, streaming hair and light blue pyjamas protruding
from window, and will climb up water-pipe and do me in for spying.   Shall be too scared to utter cry.   Fall into sleep in
which Mrs. Clutterbuck points out real cause - A.R.P. shelter
which over-worked authorities have built jointly for our two
gardens during night.   Wake from this and have another dream
that our garden is music-camp and the Beavans arrive, to explain
All.   Parents in morning suggest it is petty thief after rotting
wood of our fence, which appears to be the case.

Travel back to London with Molly Evans and Diana Boddy. Train 1¼ hours late. Take taxi. First one I try says he hasn't enough petrol to get to Hampstead.

Monday, December 10

Greta back. Helena at cottage for week, while German nurse, Dora, here for holiday. Edric on week's examination tour. At printers till 6.50.

Good broadcast by Noel Baker, pro League of Nations. Quotes Nansen as saying once: "The difficult is what takes a little time. The impossible is what takes a little longer".

Placards say 5 British ships sunk. Broadcast news says at least 5 U-boats sunk last week.

Tuesday, December 12

League of Nations' appeal to Russia re. Finland receives no reply. Russians massing troops for attack on Korelian Isthmus. Germany, who was supporting Finland, finds Britain sending help and therefore sympathies veer round to Russia. England and France make financial agreement stabilising exchange between pound and franc for duration of war. Von Ribbentrop says Britain alone caused war. It was he who told Hitler he could go ahead because Britain would not fight.

Printers and madrigals. Collect subscriptions in Mrs. Western's absence and spend rest of evening doing sums.

Greta comes in and talks: Christmas in England is No Good and not what it is in Germany, where Christmas trees reach the ceiling and though everyone has goose, nobody overeats and feels ill.

Wednesday, December 13

In Cundells' absence, no music for first Wednesday since war began.

Cold day. Dentist 9.30: another filling, much pleasanter than last one. Usual alloy for fillings came from Sweden and is unobtainable. Mr. C. now uses English stuff, not as good. Hilary comes for lunch and we buy her bag for my Christmas present, to match hood of her new coat. In evening, go to Everyman with Greta: "100 Men and a Girl". Very good, in spite of failure of sound recording in middle, and my erroneous impression at first that it is new film effects stunt to have gesticulating characters and no sound ("speechless with rage" à la cinema). Greta's conversation difficult to contend with: "What I mean ... It is not like dis ... What I mean, it goes not so, isn't it? I tink how is it when dey go so ... What I mean".

R.A.F. said to have been over Heligoland all last night. No bombing mentioned.

Thursday, December 14

Russians bombing two towns in North of Finland, which Fins are

said to be abandoning.   League expels Russia.   British destroyer sunk through collision in darkness with another warship.
139 feared lost.   German pocket-battleship, "Admiral Graf
Spee",driven into harbour at Montevideo (Uruguay) by three
British cruisers.   International law says she can stay there
for 24 hours, and longer to complete necessary repairs.   Meantime British ships wait for her outside harbour.   "Britain's
first naval victory in the war at sea" (wireless).

R.A.F. fight over Heligoland.   4 German and 3 British
planes down.   War seems to be starting up.

Shopping in lunch-time: go on till 2.45 without food,
by which time am telling myself in mournful numbers life is but
an empty dream.   So eat 3 ephemeral sandwiches and 1 glass exquisite tomatoe-juice at Green Lizard , at cost of 1/8, and feel
better.

Cold: Greta says she will bring my dinner up to lounge
because "dis moch varmer for you, what you mean?"

Broadcast in German from Germany which we pick up by
accident is telling Germans that food is very scarce in France.
Apparently same story being circulated about England, since
Miss Sprott's refuggee has letter from his Mother in Germany
(which comes via friends in Switzerland) asking shall she try
to send him chocolate or food of any kind. Greta's brother-in-
law has done diagram in this week's Picture Post, showing pro-

portion of various kindsof food to be bought by 1 day's
 in 1929 and in 1939
wages/in Germany, Italy, Gt.Britain and U.S.A.   Italy much

the lowest.   U.S.A. about 3 times anybody else.   Not such a

terrific difference between Germany and England, though Germany

less in 1939 than in 1929.

<u>Friday,December 15</u>

Shopping.   Go to Fortnum and Mason's, where many millionaires

are buying caskets of caviare and rafters of turkey (collective

noun just learned), and having it all put down in little black

books by obsequious assistants.   Do not see why I should not

get something at F. and M.s and buy tin of shortbread to give

Beavans for Christmas, and soap for Joyce.

   , To Stroud.   Train very late.   Met by Daddy, who has

walked into post in darkness and bumped his nose.   Also is very

grieved with himself because he spoke sharply to his small boy

and made' him cry.   Broods on fact that he is Bully (same man

who cheered all through Churchill's blustering speech).

Saturday, December 16

Cold.   Shopping.   All shops say cannot get things ordered
so not much choice.   Daddy could sell masses of khaki pull-
overs, mufflers, shirts, etc., but can't get any.

Get news from Rome in English which alleges sister-
ship of "Graf Spee" en route for Montevideo with escort to
rescue her.   Also British "Ark Royal" and escort on way to
prevent rescue.   English news less definite.   Russians claim
victories in Finland.   Finns deny any advance.

Sunday, December 17

Mr. Clark, at chapel this morn, promises more R.A.F. leaflets.
Says we're still dropping them over Germany in great numbers,
but no one supposed to know, and when leaflets moved from one
aerodrome to another, cargo has to be entered as "nickel".

"Graf Spee" said to have to leave Montevideo at 9.30
G.M.T. tonight.   "Ark Royal", our wireless news says, is at
Rio refuelling with other ships.   Inhabitants of Uruguay ex-
pecting spectacular sea battle and all trying to get front seats.

Very cold.

Monday, December 18

"Graf Spee" last night weighed anchor, and when 5 miles from
Montevideo was "scuttled" by crew: i.e. they blew it up, after
first taking off in boats.   Men being interned at Buenos Aires.
Broadcast by Churchill at night, in which he extols our naval

exploits (about which Announcer has been talking in voice too smug for words: pleased as I am, I cannot out say it). British submarine sinks German cruiser. Fight over Heligoland. 12 German planes, 12 British planes down. 2 British trawlers sunk.

Big Russian attack in Carelian Isthmus repulsed with heavy losses. *Canadian troops arrive in England.*

Printers. Sherry with Mr. A. on way home. He urges me to a second which I decline: says I am drunk anyway. Tells me stories of his nonconformist forbears and his wife's Plymouth Brethren relations all the way home.

Cundells back. Edric has had 2 teeth out and is very sorry for himself. Shows me picture of himself conducting his symphony at Worthing. Helena packing presents for innumerable nephews and nieces and sitting-room a wilderness of brown paper. Greta cooking Christmas fare: brings us hot mincepies at 11 p.m.

Tuesday, December 19

Helsinki being bombed by about 200 Russian planes.

Printers. John rings up: says he has day off: can I lunch? Mr. A. kindly takes quick and early lunch to let me out at 1.30. J. shows cards and invites me in tonight. So I go along after madrigals, carrying 3 camp-stools left at Mervyn Horder's by careless singer. Table at No.14 covered with cards which John tries to pair up with list of people. I play Monopoly with Peter. At 11.30 have not finished, though both

have reached starvation level several times.   So count assets
and I am winner.   At Flask Walk find Cundells gone for Christmas.   Greta still here.

Wednesday, December 20
Third largest German liner, "Columbus", "scuttled" by crew.
Captain of "Graf Spee" shoots himself at Buenos Aires.   Germans
attacking ships from air, including fishing vessels.   Cold and
snow stop fighting in N. Finland.   Himmler, head of German
Gestapo, in Rome.

       Wake very late.   Late to work.   Have shampoo and set
in lunch-hour and feel horribly tidy.   Work late.   Get home
8 p.m.   Greta shows with pride large scarlet tin engine she
has bought for her Tommy at enormous cost to her of 2/6.

Thursday, December 21
Lunch with Peter at Bertorelli's.   Have luscious minestrone
soup and zabbaglione.   See Stephen Spender.   Working till 7
o'clock.   Cold.   A few balloons up (they haven't been up lately)
Seems to be expectation of air attack soon.   Wireless programme
about Poland and German atrocities.   Fear Hate campaign beginning.   Unfortunately Greta says such tales of horror true.
Gerneral Sir Ernest Swinton, in broadcast, deprecates sending
of presents by English people to German prisoners of war.
"Sentimental hysteria".   Another name for loving one's enemies?

Says they may be the men - at any rate are comrades of them -
who bombed defenceless fishermen.   Hitherto we've been told
to hate only Hitler.

Rationing of coal, gas and electricity to stop.
Russians bombing Helsinki.   In N.E., Finns say Russians driven
back.

Receive R.A.F. leaflet, via Mother.

Friday, December 22

Very cold.   At printers all day till 8.15 when go by moonlight
to Hilary's.   Mother already there.   H. mistook time of train
and arrived late at Paddington and meantime Mother got to Victoria
alone, where H. found her in corner seat of Croydon-bound train.
Mother very pleased with herself at this achievement and thinks
herself experienced traveller.

Letter from the Beals in Victoria, British Columbia.
About the war, Carl says: "I have yet to meet anyone in this
country who has the foggiest idea of what should be done afterwards (assuming our side wins, of course)".

Big railway accident in Germany.

Song of the war seems to be soulful ballad "There'll
always be an England".

Saturday, December 23

Another German rail accident.   Eighth since war began.

Very cold and foggy. Hoar frost on everything.
Mother complains didn't sleep. "But you couldn't be cold
with all those blankets", says H. "It isn't blankets I want",
shudders Mother, "it's a ma-an". Wonders how Pop is getting on.

We go shopping in Wickham and nearly freeze. ~~Come~~
Spend afternoon and evening by big fire.

Pile of presents under Christmas tree in corner grows
mysteriously from time to time.

Reports of snow and frost on Western Front.

Sunday, December 24

Not quite so cold. Hear from bed Leonard complaining "Well,
I've used a whole 'Telegraph' and a whole 'News Chronicle' and
a whole ~~pi~~ bundle of wood. There must be a starling's news up
the chimney".

We go to church: arrive 10.30, find Communion in progress and return at 11.15 for Matins. No Christmas hymns, except "O Come O Come Emmanuel". On way back L. and I get 4
blankets and 1 pillow from flat of Miss Slack, which we bear away
in our arms.

Billy Walton (girl from S.Africa now taking Ph.D in
Economics at Oxford) and Peter (medical student) call in.
Listen to carols from King's, Cambridge, at at about 5,30 Daddy
arrives. Mother rushes at him, saying: "Are you all right?
Did you miss me?" L. precipitates 3 plates of Irish stew at

Mother's feet.   H. loses her engagement ring and drops and
smashes clock.   Mother upsets tea on carpet.   But black kitten
has adopted us and sleeps in armchair, which heartens us.
Parcels under tree still increasing.

I.R.A. raid on the magazine of the Eire Army in
Phoenix Park, Dublin.   Take masses of ammunition.

Pope makes Peach speech.

M. Daladier says "We are fighting against war itself".
Silly.

Monday, December 25.   Christmas Day.
Little warmer but still foggy.   Late breakfast and then much
opening of presents.   Visits from neighbours, Mr. and Mrs.
Johnson, 7-year-old Tony, 17-month-old Cynthia.   Leonard has
model aeroplane for Tony, over which he and Mr. J. pore for considerable time before launching with much excitement in the
Close - by which time Tony has gone off on scooter.

H. cooks her first Christmas dinner (chicken, cauliflower, potato, etc.) with much success.   At 3 the King broadcasts: we hold our breaths because he is so nervous and stutters.
Phyllis and Fred to tea.   Billy Walton comes in evening.   Games
and much enjoyment till midnight.   Peaceful Christmas Day in
spite of war and news that Russians still bombing Finland.

Tuesday, December 26
All go to Orpington to lunch and tea with Mr. and Mrs. Evans.
Mrs. E. looks very ill.   Husbands firm has evacuated and he is

home only for weekends, and concocted following advertisement
for his wife:- "Elderly lady requires someone to sleep with her
4 nights a week in absence of husband", and was surprised when
she rejected it.   Ronald and wife (Lily) and her parents join
us for tea.   Lily's father a bus-driver.   First Christmas he
has had free for 17 years.   We sing carols, and songs - new
("Run, Adolf, Run") - and old ("Excelsior") with great gusto.
Daddy, after minute quantity of port, begins to declaim Tennyson
in sonorous voice and is silenced by undutiful offspring.   Ring
still lost.

Finns were bombed by Russians on Christmas Day from 9
a.m. to 3 p.m. *Australian troops arrive in England,
Indian troops in France.*

Wednesday, December 27

Wakened by squeal of excitement from H., who has found in daily
paper that unknown quotation with which King closed Christmas
Day speech was by Miss M.L. Haskins (i.e. Phyllida's Miss London
Haskins).   It was:-

> "And I said to the man who stood at the gate of
> the year, 'Give me a light that I may tread
> safely into the unknown'.   And he replied,
> 'Go out into the darkness and put your hand
> into the Hand of God.   That shall be to you
> better than light, and safer than a known way'."

Colder.   Mother and I see Daddy on to train at East
Croydon.   Dustmen come and kindly sieve our rubbish for ring:
also char-lady comes and hunts.   But no ring found.

To tea with Phyllis, where Leonard joins us at 5.45.

Russians driven back 20 miles by Finns, but still
bombing civilians.   Many very bad earthquakes in divers places,
especially in Turkey.

<u>Thursday, December 28</u>
Finns say they've taken several thousand Russian prisoners.
What on earth can they do with them?

Arise earlier than of late and return to work.   Snow
during day.   Very busy.   To supper with Mr. and Mrs. Abraham
at their house in Frognal, and enjoy lazy evening just talking
by big fire.   Like them both very much.   Walk home through
snow in brilliant moonlight.   Greáta back but not Cundells.

<u>Friday, December 29</u>
Germans say they have sunk battleship.   We say they have only
hit it, not badly, and killed three men.

Still snowy.   Very busy day.   Miss Scott-Johnstone
has German meables.   To Paddington to catch 6.35 to Stroud.
On platform a dark girl with spectacles peers in my face and
says "Hello" in very friendly way.   "I say "Hello" and add
politely "I'm afraid I don't know who I am speaking to".   She
gives bounce of surprise and says "I'm your sister".   Can't
imagine why I didn't recognise her, except that I thought she
and Mother had gone down earlier in day.   Mother has flu or
some bilious affliction and is in bed.   P. tells of excitement
about King's broadcast quotation: telephone going all day and

nearly all night, reporters, photographers, pathé gazette, requests to put lines on illuminated panels and Christmas cards. We have dinner ont rain, which is an hour late.   Met by Pop who is glad to see us.   Bitterly cold.

Saturday, December 30

Finns say Russian troops in revolt.   Severe weather on all fronts.   Thousands dead in recent earthquakes. *in Turkey.*

    P. cooks dinner.   We go to tea with Mrs. Hawkins, who is in bed and looks very thin.

    Milder in evening, and snow melting.

Sunday, December 31

More dreadful reports of earthquake havoc.

    Hill slippery.   Pop plays at morning service and has to take young people's service at 6.30.   We go to lunch at Aunt Hermie's.   Aunt N. and Miss Vivian (school-teacher from Bristol) there.   Mish Colesh in bed with cold.

    Train to London $\frac{3}{4}$ hour late starting and $1\frac{1}{2}$ hours late at Paddington.   Taxi home and arrive just in time to wish driver Happy New Year.   Greta has put on fire for me.   Am just ready to leap into hot bath when Helena and Edric come.   Have been to local pub with J.D. to drink in New Year.   Children here for week: drains in cottage being overhauled.

- 104 -

New Year's Day, 1940

Wonder fearfully what year will bring forth.   Letter from
Mother who is getting better.   Norman (4) and Harriet (2) at
breakfast with nurse: four eyes stare at me in unembarrassed
curiosity.   By evening, sitting-room is full of toys and nurse
has bronchitis.

Finns claim great victories.   Tacoma, which was fuel
ship of Graf Spee, has outrun time limit and has to leave Montevideo harbour, but sails back in again and is interned, with
crew, for duration of war.

Tuesday, January 2, 1940

Russians suffering heavy losses.   Stalin asks Hitler for help.
Two German planes brought down over Shetlands.   "Daily Telegraph"
suggests we shall have severe raids in March - incendiary bombs
on railways, ports, etc.

Buy new frock and jumper.
                                        with Edric and Helena:
In evening to "Who'll Take Liberty", a politically-
minded pantomime, at Whitehall Theatre, for which Guy Sheppard,
youth who came in one evening and showed us designs, did costumes
and scenery.   Both very good, and show good in parts.   Anyway,
enjoyed it.

Wednesday, January 3, 1940

Roosevelt makes speech: "I hope that we shall not have American

ostriches in our midst.   It is not good for the health of the
ostriches to continue to bury their heads in the sand".   Seems
to infer that though America neutral, she could not afford to
let Germany win.

Two Swedish ships sunk by U-boats.

Russians said to be calling up more men.   Report of
accident to Russian troop-train with big loss of life.   According to Rome, much discontent in Leningrad.

Ten more villages destroyed by earthquake in Turkey.

Thursday, January 4, 1940

A little warmer.   Has been so cold all week have had to sleep
in d ressing-gown.   Snow from week ago still on ground.   But
am spoilt by Greta who comes in and shuts window and puts on
fire before I get up.

Was to have been music tonight, but John/in bed with
and David
flu and Peter has job.   Sole arrival woman with unlikely name
of Miss Sugars who plays viola.

America to make loan of £25 millions to Finland.
Finns bomb Russian air base, headed, papers say, by Italian.
Goering to take full charge of German war economy.   Sir Ernest
Swinton gives harrowing broadcast announcing that we are fight-
ing for our very existence.

So we may be, but I spend whole day reading and checking proofs of Listener index, since no other way of saving the

situation occurs to me. Am slightly better than John Butterworth, who cannot bring himself to return from Music Camp, but has gone to live at cottage where he gets up at about 11.30, reads detective novels, goes to pub., and goes to bed again. Was offered job at Sadler's Wells but would not come back for it.

Friday, January 5, 1940

Government to take over complete control of shipping.

Work in morning and then take 1.55 to Stroud. Train full of soldiers. Change at Swindon, where talk to Red Cross nurse stationed at military hospital at Marlborough. Says no wounded yet, but lost of militia from camps, who have got septic feet because are not used to wearing boots. A Major has told her war will last 5-6 years.

About 6.45 Mother reports light in sky over Stroud. F. and I go to entrance of fields and see large building ablaze. Steele's Garage. Go down to town, but by then it has died down. Find Daddy and staff shut up shop to go and see interesting spectacle, which at height of fire was most terrifying. Our wireless accumulators among the things burnt. P. hears some far-fetched person suggesting sabotage - "to show Hitler the way".

Saturday, January 6, 1940

Hore Belisha (Minister of War) resigns. No reasons given for resignation. Was apparently offered alternative job in Cabinet but refused. Oliver Stanley succeeds him. Lord Macmillan also resigns from Ministry of Information (second resignation from this post since war began) first was Sir Archibald Sinclair

Succeeded by Sir John Reith.

Buy cardigan in Stroud.   Walk on common in afternoon.
Very misty, but warmer.   Feel depressed.   Had dream last night
had to pilot fighter aeroplane to attack German bomber (there
was no way of getting out of it).   Knew should be killed and
very frightened.   Surprised to wake and find myself safe in
bed.   Stayed there all morning.

Italian and Hungarian Foreign Ministers having talks,
presumably about Balkans and Russia.

Sunday, January 7, 1940
Misty and mild.   Chapel and walk.   Return to London by usual
train.   Carriage to myself with curtains and lights, but at
each station lights go out and I sit in darkness.   Train nearly
an hour late.   Children staying at Flask Walk another week.

Monday, January 8, 1940
Finnish troops defeat whole Russian division of 15,000 men.
Tanks, arms, cars and field-kitchens captured.   Report that
Hungary and Italy have concluded military alliance "to protect
and maintain peace in the Balkans and South-Eastern Europe".
Hoping that Yugoslavia will enter into Triple Friendship Pact,
to allow Italy to move troops through Y. to help Hungary if
necessary.

Rationing of butter ($\frac{1}{4}$ lb.), sugar (12 oz) and bacon
($3\frac{1}{2}$ oz) begins to-day.

Chief Censor (Usborne) retires to take up work of
"naval construction".

Commercial and Financial agreement signed between
Britain, France and Turkey.

Bomb thrown into headquarters of Londonderry Constabulary.

Earth tremors in Turkey, Switzerland and Belgium.

Beautiful day, mild and fine, and balloons all up.
Feel unwell and depressed.

Tuesday, January 9

Wonder when I wake up why there are no sounds from children.
At 8.30, Greta comes and tells me baby has eaten 20-30 green
tablets (iron and copper) from box belonging to Dora, and 2 or
3 large white 'headache' tablets (1 is normal dose for adult).
She is lying grey and limp in her cot when I see her. Emetics
are administered and Doctor comes. Norman, subdued and wondering, has breakfast with me alone. I go off very late, and am
not cheered by sight, in Willow Road, of about 8 corpses (?)
stretched on grass at edge of heath, while stretcher-bearers in
tin-hats bustle about importantly.

Upset by allthis, and can scarcely keep from weeping
while I take telephoned corrections in what seems to me completely idiotic talk by Brierly on International Law and contraband.
Ring up at lunch-time and Helena says baby a little better, but
when I get home after madrigals, find she is having oxygen every

quarter-of-an-hour and has had haemorrhage.   However, Doctor,
who has come every 2 hours, says at 10 p.m. there is an improvement, and she looks more natural, though still very white.

Chamberlain makes speech saying worst of war is still
to come, air-raids included, and probably clothes will be rationed.

Wednesday, January 10, 1940

Baby a little better.   Her cheeks have some pink, she moves
her legs a little too, but does not smile.   Lies looking up with
enormous eyes, most heart-rendingly.

British liner, Dunbar Castle, 10,000 tons, sunk by mine
off S.E. coast.   48 passengers all saved.   2 of crew believed
missing.   All balloons up, and general air of expectation about.
Music at Beavans.   John still at home with remains of flu.
Peter, David, Trixie, Hardy and Arnold Cooke.   Brahms, Purcell,
which enjoy very much.   P. seems bit depressed.   Invites me
to lunch-time concert tomorrow.

Arnold Fuchs rings up: here for few days and wants to
do theatre.

Thursday, January 11, 1940

Baby has bad day, being fed through rectum.   All Edric can say
when I come in late and meet him on stairs is that she is alive.

At lunch-time go to hear Bourdon (Flute) Trio, with
Peter as cellist, at Mary Ward Settlement.   Eat sandwiches and
enjoy programme.   But too many of these concerts now running,

and they're stopping this series at end of week.

At 6 meet Arnold and we go forth with my suitcase, looking rather like elopement, especially as I have to cling on to his arm in blackout. Eat at Chinese restaurant off Piccadilly, and then go to "The Corn is Green"; very enjoyable (saw it once before, with John). We then have Horlicks at S.F. snackbar and I promise to go to Manchester when summer-time begins. Amusing tales of Christmas broadcast from Sandringham. Eddie Woods (B.B.C. engineer in charge), when King said "This chair isn't in the right place", replied simply "It is". After King's try-out, Woods says "You can't say 'aggression' and 'suppression' next to each other like that", to which King replies "I can and I'm going to".

Big air-battle over North Sea. 1 German plane down in sea, 1 down in Denmark, 1 British plane down. Russia making another big attack in Finland (N.B. says she is not at war with F. but is trying to liberate the workers).

Friday, January 12, 1940

Baby seems bit better: is being fractious - good sign.

Beautiful day but very cold. Get 9.15 a.m. train to Stroud, and enjoy journey in daylight. P.C. and letter from Joyce to say not coming. Mother and I visit Mrs. Hawkins who is in bed. Miss Churchman goes out to grocer's. Reports assistants very harassed by ration coupons.

Crescent moon with one very bright star close to it against orange horizon. Looks like "At the Oasis", or "The Trackless Desert".

Everything frozen.   Mrs. Cope observed fetching
water from Stores in large toilet jug.

Saturday, January 13, 1940
Still bitterly cold.   Get up late and go down to town and buy
pair black shoes.   After dinner to Aunt Hermie's with magazines,
and for walk on Selsley, calling back at Enderley for tea.

        Meat ration announced as 1/6-worth per head per week.
German aeroplane brought down over N.East coast of Scotland.
Reconnaissance planes over Eastern Germany and Austria.
Russians in Carelian Isthmus said to be telling Finns through
loudspeakers to surrender - "or else the Germans will come".

Sunday, January 14, 1940
Still very cold.   Chrysanthemums which Mrs. Franklin has put
on Communion Table at chapel look frost-bitten, and it is found
she has given the poor things no water.   Mr. Evan Thomas dead.

        Germany concentrating troops on Belgium and Dutch
frontiers.   Holland and Belgium mobilising men.

Monday, January 15, 1940
Baby crying when I wake: able to protest, smile and talk once
more and threatens to be very trying.   Weather still fine and
cold.   After duty at printers, go to Mrs. Morris's for night.
She has returned from evacuation into country, being unable to
bear sitting about and making polite conversation interminably.

All B.E.F. and R.A.F. leave from France stopped,
owing to tension in Holland and Belgium.

Tuesday, January 16, 1940

Three British submarines lost - Undine, Starfish and Seahorse.
First British submarine losses of the war.   Believed to have
been trying to attack German Fleet in Heligoland Bight.   100
men missing, but some said to have been picked up by Germans.

Hore Belisha speaks in House on his resignation.
Says nothing, except that his first concern is to win the war.
Seems to imply that his democratic reforms in the Army had some-
thing to do with it.

Terribly cold: snow in the afternoon.   Edric has 7
teeth out.   Baby better and inclined to be peevish.

Tension in Holland and Belgium a little eased. (This
phrase taken from paper.   Imagine all Belgians and Dutch, who
have been standing stiffly to attention, now shifting their
position, but not yet able to sit down.)

Wednesday, January 17, 1940

Still bitterly cold.   Write protesting memo. to Editor asking
for more heat in our room, since I am so frozen my brain is numb.
Expect to be told there is a war so we must all be as uncomfortable as possible.

At lunchtime go with Miss Hearing to National Gallery
concert.   Kutcher String Quartet (Mozart), and Quartet plus

Malcolm Sargent at piano in Dvorak Quintet.   Very enjoyable.

Suppose no one but Cundells would in present circumstances - baby inclined to yell inconsolably and Edric minus front teeth - have 10 people to supper and play clarinet quintets.   Pauline Juler with Clarinet.   John, Peter, David, Pauline Jones, Helen somebody (nice), Hardy, Arnold Cooke.   J. has not been back to work yet.   Wears villainous cap to keep his head warm (not indoors).   Helena shows recovering baby, with pride.   J., after gazing at her in cot for some moments, remarks: "She has an expression just like our cat".   Peter in good form.   Brahms and Mozart clarinet quintets: both heavenly.

Thursday, January 18, 1940
Last night at 12.30 could hear guns in distance.   In middle of morning, am certain can hear them again, and people in building on other side of street go up to roof and gaze heavenwards. At lunchtime papers announce trouble as two terrific explosions at Waltham Abbey munitions factory, Essex, which blew out windows for miles round.   Five killed and many injured.

B.E.F. leave granted again, since situation on Netherlands frontiers seems better.

Home by usual train and arrive in snowstorm.

Friday, January 19, 1940
Pipe bursts in bathroom.   Almost everyone in Stroud has frozen water supply.   Accompany Mother to town to get her woollen

suit and frock.   She stands stiffly with her arms held out
one each side, like small child, and looks miserable at each
one, but we do choose dark blue suit with light blue jumper,
and plum-coloured frock.   Try to persuade Daddy to abandon
dreadful suit he is wearing - which is thinnest he has got -
but he says he always was fond of it; and when I point out
that it shines on every part of it, stands in doorway and sings
at top of voice "Then shall the righteous shine forth as the
sun".   Implore Mother to give trousers to Turkish earthquake
while he is in bed, which is what she has done to his old rain-
coat, to his great chagrin.

      Chilly walk on common after dinner.   Meet Mrs.
Franklin, who says husband has been in bed for fortnight with
bronchial catarrh and she has to fetch all water from next door.

      Russians in retreat.   Goering makes speech blaming
England for war, saying Germany hasn't attacked so far because
she never wanted war anyway, and the only thing to do with the
English is to annihilate them.   Says inhabitants of Britain
will soon discover what the Führer's plans are.

      All Europe having Arctic weather.   Berlin said to
be ̷s̷o̷f̷t̷ short of coal.   Poor things.   We are thankful here
that coal is not rationed as at first threatened.

<u>Saturday, January 20, 1940</u>

Lord Halifax makes speech saying he would ten times rather be
dead than bealive in a world under the Nazi regime.   Mr. Churchill broadcasts.   More or less tells neutrals they'd better join
with Allies before it's too late or they'll all be swallowed up
by Germany.

        Very cold.   People sledging on common.

~~Saturday,~~ <u>Sunday, January 21, 1940</u>

Terrible bombing in Finland.   News broadcast, followed by talk
by Rev. J.S. Whale on the Fact of Evil.   Says we can't blame
Hitler, or Stalin, or Protection, or any one thing, for the state
of the world; we are all guilty.   Mrs. Kenred Smith says she
doesn't believe we shall have peace yet because we're not ready
for peace in our hearts.

        Destroyer "Grenville" sunk in Atlantic.

        Bitterly cold.   Edgar (milkman) says his handkerchief
freezes in his pocket.   Daddy rushing about till nearly 11 a.m.
trying to unfreeze things.   Drinking tap running, though sink
and bed bathroom basin frozen up.   In afternoon he goes to Pagan-
hill to take service, with Hilary's Bristol University scarf
round his neck.   The plum-coloured stripe quite the worst colour
for his complexion but he is very pleased with himself.

        Train at night unheated, late and crowded.

Monday, January 22, 1940

Archbishop of York broadcasts ... "We have no right to be engaged
in war at all except so far as we believe that to be God's will
for us at this time".   Well, I don't.   So what?

Am very upset by Editor's insisting on my having on
Letters page reproduction of a leaflet, dropped by Germans in
France.   Shows two soldiers, one French, one English, preparing
to dive together into a lake of blood.   The English soldier
pushes the French one in, and as he struggles and drowns walks
nonchalantly away.   Everyone but me thinks this a "scoop" and Mr.
T. very scathing when I tell him it is horrible.

Work late at printers.   Get food at Marble Arch Corner
House in very depressed state.   Feel better after eating.   Hear
full performance of maudlin popular song: chorus -

> "There'll always be an England
> And England shall be free,
> If England means as much to you
> As England means (tiddly-pom) TO ME".

No one rises and cheers, but the waitress hums the tune as she
removes pile of plates.   Decide England Means to Me Cotswold
Hills anda stone wall, and perhaps Parliament Square anda red bus.
This no doubt very superficial view to take.

Go on to Beavans, where J. still not back at work after
flu.   Is very extra nice to me.   Beats me at Monopoly, invites
me in tomorrow night, and on Sunday week if I can bring myself to
return early from country to hear octets.   Arthur has copy of

"The Week" (Communist paper circulated by post), which says tales
of Finnish victories have been exaggerated beyond all truth.
Duque reads Arthur's story going into Penguin Parade.   Ski-ing
tale: recognise various touches from Lech.   Duque says I look
ill. Walk home from Swiss Cottage by moonlight and enjoy it.

        Italian liner burnt out, but passengers saved.   Neutrals
annoyed by Churchill's speech.

Tuesday, January 23, 1940
Russians said to be launching biggest attack yet.

        Nice madrigals.   En route for Beavans go into same
Lyon's as yesterday and have hardly sat down before leader of
orchestra announces special request item "There'll always be an
England".   At Beavans play Monopoly with John and Nan Heatherly
(girl who ski-red with last Easter's party), and win.

        Home by full moon very late.   Cannot sleep for some time

Wednesday, January 24, 1940
Snow still on ground, though temperature higher than of late.

        Morning news exceedingly depressing.   Destroyer "Exmouth"
lost: all crew believed dead.   General Hertzog, speaking in South
African Parliament, not only attacks war but seems to support
Hitler and to want S.A. to conclude separate peace with Germany.
Rumania letting Germany have oil.   Japan protesting because British
have seized and searched some of her ships.   Mr Ackerley says we
ought to stop the war at once and call conference of all Powers,

neutrals included.   No good saying we can't deal with Hitler, because there he is and he'll have to be dealt with along with everyone else.

Feel depressed and unwell (ought to go to bed earlier), and when Miss P. makes caustic remark, start shedding floods of tears.   No one observes my shame (I hope) but Mr. Abraham, when everyone else gone out.   He is so nice I weep still harder, while he pats me soothingly and insists I have lunch with him - at Mrs. Cook's off Piccadilly, because he has to have fitting for suit at Austin Reeds.   Am very grateful to him and feel a bit better.

Nice music in evening.   Franz Osborn (pianist): they do first two movements of Dvorak's PianoQuintet (request from me, backed up by Peter).   Leave them still playing when I go to bed wearily at 11.45.   My thumb going septic under nail, where I must have pricked it: very painful.   Feel ill and cannot sleep.

Thursday, January 25, 1940
Milder.   Matron puts poultices on my thumb, morning and after-noon, and gives me three spare ones for weekend.   Home by usual train.   Hilda Franklin engaged to Joe, who wanted her to marry him 12 years ago when she was 18.   Have both been otherwise en-gaged since them.   Romantic Reunion happened over Florence's baby which she was taking for walk on common.

Friday, January 26, 1940
Lloyd George has had much to say in Parliament about need to plough

up all possible land for food-growing.   Blames Government for
not laying in supplies of animal feeding-stuffs.   Says pigs,
poultry, etc., being killed for lack of food.   (Quite true that
no one round Stroud can get Indian corn for hens.)

      Also this morning announcement that bacon ration is to
be doubled, which argues that many pigs have been killed already.

      Cold thaw.   On common mud lies on top of ground which
is still frozen solid.   Mr. Keen's pipes burst, water coming
through bathroom floor into larder, and while it pours with rain
and his stop-tap is burst there is no way of stopping water.

      I stay in bed till 1 o'clock and in evening feed hoggish-
ly on $\frac{1}{4}$-lb. very gummy gums and wish I hadn't.   If everyone behaved like me, how should we win the war?

Saturday, January 27, 1940
Germans have forbidden anyone at all, even neutrals in Germany, to
listen to foreign broadcasts.   And have taken away wireless sets
from Poles.   Finns said still to be holding back big Russian
attack.   We hear meat will be short this weekend, but get our
usual joint.

      To Aunt H's to tea in rain.   Mother has neuralgia and
does not go out in cold.   Feel better. Have slept well for two
nights.

      Two airmen killed at aerodrome on common.   This will
not be announced in papers.

Sunday, January 28, 1940, and Monday the 29th.

Extraordinary weather conditions continue: a layer of ice over
everything. Instead of hoar-frost outlining every twig and
branch, which would be usual, there is a line of ice along every
smallest protuberance. Paynes' poplars are all splayed out at
the top because of the weight of ice. Roof gutters solid with
ice; the hill a smooth glassy surface. Daddy bravely puts
socks over shoes and goes forther, largely because he didn't have
the key of the shop last night to lock up. Wireless now reveals
that recent temperatures have been lowest since 1894.

I catch usual train after groping down hill with Daddy
at snail's pace. It leaves fairly punctually but arrives at
Paddington at 4.30 a.m. Soldier in carriage, who shares my sandwiches, remarks that "after you've been in the Army a bit you can
eat anything" (and they were very nice ones), and adds: "You might
have many a worse place to spend the night than a nice warm railway carriage", then snores loudly. But I cannot sleep. Outside it snows. At Swindon, a few yards from which station we
halt for $2\frac{3}{4}$ or $3\frac{3}{4}$ hours - I lose count - one railwayman says we
have to wait for the Westbury Local: another than we cannot move
because everything - points, signals, etc. - is frozen. Paddington full of stranded passengers. Wait an hour or more for first
Underground train. Bakerloo to Baker Street; change on to Met.,
where snow intunnels makes green and blue firework display every
time wheels touch it, lighting up coaches where light inside has

been dimmed.   Walk from Finchley Road through steeps of un-
spoiled whiteness, sometimes quite deep, and arrive home at
6.30.   Yearn for hot bath, but water cold.   Greta brings me
tea at 7.30, and I go to work, rather wearily, at usual time.

Meet Joyce for lunch.   She has been to Bexley for
weekend.   Very pleased to see her: fear her journey to Kingham
will be slow.

Letter from Roy, who says Astronomer Royal is dealing
with telescope mirror in England, and Mount Wilson Observatory
has promised to try to get it finished if possibleit can be sent
to America.

My thumb still swollen and painful.   Was to have gone
to H's for night but weariness and dislocation of all traffic
decides me to wire postponing visit.   Also John invites me for
evening (it is his birthday), but do not go.

Worst raids of war on Finland.   Red Cross hospital
bombed.   Also many attacks on ships round our coasts.   Real
extent of damage not announced.   News of frightful Nazi atrocities in Poland: 18,000 said to have been put to death.   Mr. A.
says tales probably exaggerated very much - in Russian literature
the Poles appear as Irish do in ours, as colossal liars.

Tuesday, January 30, 1940

My thumb burst last night and feels much better.
                    Traffic chaos gradually clearing.
            Snow quite deep. / Printers. Madrigals.
                Light-ship bombed.   Hitler makes speech.   The mixture,

as before.

Wednesday, January 31, 1940

Cold, snowy and raw.   Only David, Hardy and John to eat macaroni.
(Peter rehearsing).   They play quartets with Edric.

Thursday, February 1, 1940

National Gallery concert: Boyd Neel Orchestra.   Go down through
snowy streets.   Handel, Abel, Bach, Delius, Warloch.   Very
beautiful, especially Handel.

In evening to Hilary's.   Slow journey.

Friday, February 2, 1940

½ Russians bombing about 20 towns in Finland.   Balkans in process of making Entente, to keep the peace in S.E.Europe, they say.

Very cold.   Snow crisp and icy underfoot.   Get up
very late and knock bottle of milk all over dining room table
and floor.   Phyllis and Fred to dinner.   Poptatoes do not come
and I go forth to find them in darkness, and Fred carries 10 lbs.
of them along with him.

Saturday, February 3, 1940.

Again get up late, and this time scorch bottom of Leonard's
beautiful dressing-gown as I stand in front of electric fire.
Feel I am not Perfect Guest.   We go to Phyllis for elevenses and
stay till 12.45.   L. does not come home for lunch till 3.30.
We go to cinema at West Wickham and see "Blackmail", in which
hero tries to push villain into blazing oil-well.

Three German bombers brought down off East coast and Scottish coast. One, which crashed at Whitby, is first to come down on English soil in this war.

Sunday, February 4, 1940

"Blackmail" film so excited me, I dream am pursued by relentless mad female (wife of schoolmaster) who wishes my blood. Wake in terror and hear through darkness steps coming up to front door. No knock. Steps appear to retreat. Get up, and find it is 6 o'clock and morning paper has been pushed through letter-box. Go back to bed, and we none of us rise till about 11.15, and at noon have breakfast-cum-lunch, after which I wash up an incredible amount of crockery while H. and L. shovel and sweep slush in garden. Rapid thaw has now set in and snow is disappearing.

Leave about 4.45 and travel to Kilburn. Greatly dislike manner of young man with whom I am alone in corridorless carriage of Victoria-bound train, and get out at Clapham Junction and get in again further down. It is not my wont to take fright at strangers, and hope I am not becoming a Suspicious Spinster who always thinks she is Being Followed by A Man. No Beavans yet returned from Bernard's music-making. Let myself in with key I had at beginning of war, and read E.H. Young's "William" with much enjoyment. Someone ought to have told me to read it before. Vanguard arrives - Peter, Ann Joseph and Arnold Cooke. No surprising at finding me there reading. John, Marian Gregg,

Linda, and several others follow; and later Arthur and Duque
and young man, cousin of Beavans, who vows he knows me because
he lives near Music Camp and remembers seeing me there 2 years
ago. Schubert Octet, very nice. On return to Cundells, find
Bernard Robinson here. Edric showed him into my room by mistake
last night, and he slept in my dirty sheets and used my dirty
towel. Tonight he sleeps in Greta's room: she has left, having got job as cook in home where small son is. Helena says she
thinks she has got new girl - with six-months'-old baby. Upon
my asking whether she has husband as well, or has acquired a
baby more or less by accident, H. says she really forgot to ask,
but anyway the girl has been highly recommended. Greatly admire
this careless attitude to life.

Monday, February 5, 1940
Finns reported to have destroyed another Russian Division.
But bad bombing on Finnish towns and a lot of damage done.

Printers as usual. Am depressed and tired. Weather
has become mild and a bit foggy. In evening A.R.P. warden calls:
but light he has seen found to be not ours. Dora (German nurse)
impressed by his politeness. Says it would not be so in Germany.
When she came to London first, was very impressed by gentleness
and kindness of our policeman.

Greta made apricot tart specially for me before she went,
and we have it for dinner. (Shall miss hearing her saying "Yes
yes, I komm; ein moment, yes yes" as she rushes to answer telephone. Or no, she never rushed, she lumbered).

Tuesday, February 6, 1940

Pandake Day, but don't have pancakes.

   Unwell and depressed, but Mr. Abraham helps to keep
me cheerful at printers.

   I.R.A. leave bombs about (one at Euston) as protest
against execution tomorrow of two Irishmen found guilty of the
bomb explosion at Coventry where 5(?) people were killed.

   Meat rationing to begin on March 11.

Wednesday, February 7, 1940

- Though really it is Thursday, being 12.35 a.m., and why I write
now I don't know, for have felt run down and tired all day.
Lunch with Angela, who looks thin: has been having festered leg
and thumb ever since September when she was in Sark and a wave
dashed her on to a rock.

   Write lament for my King (about 6 stanzas) which Mr.
Abraham always checks when we play chess. Have given it to him:
he laughs and puts it in his leather case and I hope he'll make
some music for it.

   In afternoon we have air-raid practice - i.e. at 5 p.m.
go down to basement with gas-masks and sit in a dull dark dock
in which I should hate to die; it is too cold already.

   Music in evening, to which many people come. Raymond
somebody plays trumpet. David's last Wednesday: he sails for
his native Australia on Tuesday. And Hardy can come no more,
but is being sent away on a Government job. John asks me to

film on Monday: arrangements complete when Peter reminds him
they are rehearsing quartet then.   So invites me back early on
Sunday instead, but do not think I want to leave at 11 a.m.
Peter mentions that he and Pauline might like to cycle at Easter
- perhaps in Cotswolds?   He is rather pale: has been to doctor
who says he is nervy and gives him tonic.   Everyone is looking
years older than they looked a few months ago.

Have been reading Winifred Holtby's letters to a friend
who was a headmistress in S.Africa.   W.H. was so full of desire
to help everyone and better the world, it seems foolish that God
allowed her to die at age of 36.   Norman asks to-day: "Daddy,
why does God die people?"

Weather mild and rather unsettled.

Thursday, February 8, 1940
At breakfast say goodbye to children, who are returning to cottage
When I come down, Norman is grappling with rather over-cooked
sausage, and says: "It isn't ripe; it's too hard".

Mild, misty morning.   At lunch time go with Lesley Coad
to concert by three men on staff - 2 pianos (Bach) and songs.
Don't know their names, but enjoy it.   Wish our office was one
which had its air-raid shelter in concert-hall - a quite pleasant
place in which to be bombed.   Have lunch with Lesley afterwards.

Feel 90 years old and inclined to weep all the time, and

am glad am going home for weekend this evening.

Russians appear to be having more success than hitherto.

Friday, February 9, 1940

Attacks on shipping round the East coast; not much success reported. One German bomber brought down.

Lord Tweedsmuir (John Buchan), Gov. Gen. of Canada, ill.

Roosevelt sending representative to Europe to see
neutrals and discuss possible peace.   Britain doesn't seem to
receive his efforts very well - says Britain and France have made
quite clear the only terms on which a settlement can be reached.

Man giving broadcast talk on Hitler, who has heard him
speak, says a kind of inspiration - what his Lieutenant described
as the Holy Ghost - enters into him as he speaks, so that the
influence which he exercises over his audience is irresistible.

Stay in bed till midday, being very tired.   Go in
afternoon to Stroud and then by fields to common, where meet
Mother in King's Count.   Weather cold again: water freezing.
There is a new moon, and it may be it will be cold again till the
moon changes.   Our bathroom leak still unmended.   Meat has been
scarce in Stroud.   Our butcher says before the war he would have
been prosecuted for having in his shop the carcases now delivered
to him for sale.   He is not getting nearly enough for the customers who have registered with him, although rationing has not
officially started yet.

Mother knitting scarf for troops. Daddy, inspired, brings home wool at lunch-time and starts knitting too. After 2 rows he says he shall sell the scarf in the shop; after 3, decides to charge 7/11 for it, since it is hand-knitted; after 4, finds he unaccountably has 2 extra stitches and I have to undo it and cast on again for him. I start sock, and hope war will be over before it is finished.

Saturday, February 10, 1940

Feel better. Go for two hours' walk in morn, over common, then via Woodchester to Selsley, up the path Joyce and I went with bicycles in the summer when we lost the bicycle-pump. Back home by Jacob's Ladder. Rather cold, but sunshine with promise of spring. Many people have said to Mother that the extraordinary weather we've been having lately "seemed as if it was Meant", or "seemed as if it Had to Be". Mother did not dare enquire import of this, but supposed it to mean that Heaven was giving us a sign of its displeasure. This weekend we have our usual joint of meat.

Sunday, February 11, 1940

Cold. We sing in chapel remarkable hymn to trilly tune, one verse of which ends "though He was charged wi-ith madness here". Daddy, walking up hill afterwards, remarks that all hymns by Isaac Watts, except about two, should be expurgated from book. Spend considerable part of sermon time in mental comparison between Hitler and Jesus, and find many points in common. Both made extraordinary

claims for themselves; both possessed of some supernatural
power whereby they exercised great influence upon their hearers;
both followed to the death by some and considered mad by others.
But whereas Hitler has now concluded plan for dividing up Europe,
Jesus said his kingdom was not of this world.

Travel to London by new train leaving at 6.23.   No
lights except very intermittently.   No one at Hampstead - all gone
to cottage with children.   Find side door won't lock and put
chair against my bedroom door.   Cold: do not sleep very well.

Monday, February 12, 1940

German decree placing all workers not of German origin in "second-
rate" category so that they are treated like coolies.   (N.B. We
treat S. African natives in same way on their own territory.)
Russians attacking vigorously in Carelian Isthmus.

John Buchan (Lord Tweedsmuir, Governor-General of Canada)
dies at age of 64.

Feel better and much more cheerful, though discouraged
by news from returning Cundells that they may shut up house at
Easter and go to cottage for summer.   Water frozen and when I
let out bath water on second floor, plug of bath on first floor,
in which Cundells are disporting, pops up and a flood of icy black
water pours in.

Tuesday, February 13, 1940

Very cold and inclined to snow.   Edric spends hour or so unfreezing water pipes.   At printers till 7.50, so miss madrigals.

Wednesday, February 14, 1940

Two U-boats sunk.   Weather still very wintry: a sprinkling of
snow on ground.   Feel much better and enjoy music in evening.
Sydney Harrison, pianist and author of "Music for the Multitude"
comes.   Our new maid, Irma, has arrived, with baby.   Father of
of child (a girl) is an Englishman who promised to marry her and
she found out too late that he was already married.

Thursday, February 15, 1940

Russians capture some outposts of Mannerheim Line.

To Stroud by 6.55 and have carriage to myself all the way.
 Have bought myself frivolous hat, and winter woolies for next year.

Friday, February 16, 1940

Russians have penetrated Finnish defences at three points.
Sweden refuses Finns military aid, but British subjects may now
volunteer for service in Finland.

          Three Danish ships sunk.   Neutrals angry with Germany.

          Am giddy and faint when I get up, and spend most of day
knitting my Sock for the Troops.   Turn heel in fine style.

Saturday, February 17, 1940

Feel better.   Several inches of snow fell last night.

          British cruiser takes German "Altmark" (spelling?), which
was supply ship to "Graf Spee", in territorial waters (~~Danish~~) Norwegian, and
removes several hundred prisoners taken from British merchant ships

sunk by Graf Spee in S. Atlantic.   Germany describes this action
as "swinish" and "piratical" and protests to ~~Denmark~~ Norway who protests
to Britain.   Britain says she was within international law, because ~~Danish~~ Norwegian territorial waters were being used to transport prisoners to Germany.   Germans scuttle a ship attacked by English.

Sunday, February 18, 1940

Reactions on Altmark incident reported.   Most countries lean to
British point of view, except Hungary.

        Lot of snow last night, and at 11 a.m. it is still snow-
ing, so get 11.16 to London.   Arrive at Hampstead between half-
past 3 and 4, and find Cundells are not having music as they said
but are at Beavans.   After walking on heath for half-an-hour to
see it under snow (but last night's fall appearsto have been confined to the West Country);   eating 2 scrambled eggs and drinking
some Ovaltine;   finishing off my sock;   and admiring Irma's baby
whose name is Margaret Rose - with a German surname that sounds
something likeHopple-popple - go to Oxford Road too.   Ann Joseph,
Nan, two men there besides Cundells.   Pingpong and bridge.   Raining when we leave.   Taxi to Hampstead.   Sleep rather badly.

Monday, February 19, 1940

Everyone very pleased about "Altmark" business, but pleasure modi-
fied by German sinking of British destroyer with loss of nearly
all men.   British capture 2 more German ships.   Finns retreating.
Twenty French ambushed and killed on Western Front.

Miss Mearing has German measles.   There is a great
epidemic of it, as well as of influenza.

Thaw has set in: weather much milder, which is pleasant
but rather tiring.   Feel cheerful again.   In evening to Beavans.
Win Scramble.   John plays piano: then Nan comes.   She is only
19 but seems much older and is very fond of John and her face fell
quite visibly when she saw me there.   Felt inclined to say she
had Nothing to Fear from me, but confined myself to reading Cold
Comfort Farm and leaving her free to make admiring remarks to J.
if she chooses.   Duque, who almost has no voice because of a cold,
says (but not when anyone is there):   "Isn't it time you got yourself a Man?"   Does this mean she wants me to have a go at John?
Or that she wants me not to?

Listen to broadcast news, which says that Norwegian
Foreign Minister states Altmark did not call at any Norwegian port,
but naval authorities at Bergen did not think everything was as it
ought to be.   (Don't quite know what this means).

Eighteenth Soviet division destroyed.   Russians say
they've captured over 300 Finnish fortifications.

Greek steamer torpedoed;   crew saved.

Tuesday, February 20, 1940

Helena reads extract from Sunday Times which says that neutral
observers think the war will end this year, and that there is great
difference of opinion about carrying on the war, between Hitler

and his Ge/nerals.

Edric gone to Shrewsbury with orchestra.

Printers and madrigals.

Wednesday, February 21, 1940

Still much fuss about Altmark, and a great deal of talk on International Law, which always strikes me as very odd when we're all
trying to kill one/#/y another.   Anyone would think God had en-
graved an International Law on Moses' tables of stone.

Swedish town bombed by Russian planes - just over Finnish border, so may be a mistake.

Music at night.   Jean ~~Stewart~~ Henderson, secretary to Low, the
cartoonist, comes.   Low has German measles.   The Penguin edition
of his cartoons has already run to 100,000 copies.   (N.B. Best-
seller among Penguins is Shaw's "Intelligent Woman's Guide to
Socialism" which sold half-a-million.)   Beaverbrook (newspaper
owner) did not expect war in September - took a 5/- bet with Low
against it.   At time of Italian invasion of Abyssinia, Low did
cartoon of Chamberlain washing his hands of the business (when
Britain ought to have been fulfilling her obligations under the
League of Nations Covenant).   The caption read: "And he took
water ..."   Beaverbrook refused to publish: Low refused to do
another cartoon till it went in.   After more than a fortnight,
Beaverbook capitulated.   Incidentally, am interested to learn
that one cartoon had to be omitted from book - one about Poland,

which apparently in 1920, with full connivance of Britain, made
war on Russia and took from her all the land Russia has now taken
back.   This has not been mentioned in the English newspapers
lately.

Franz Osborn also at music.   Schubert piano trio (beautiful) while I knit furioso.

Weather
~~Heather~~ very mild.   Go into park in lunch-hour and feel
Spring about.

Thursday, February 22, 1940

Two German planes brought down on East Coast.   In lunch-time to
National Gallery concert by myself - Menges String Quartet playing
Beethoven.   Programme too long, and am late back.   Weather still
mild and spring-like.   To Stroud by 6.35 in moonlight.   They
have photographs of David and Miriam: also letter reporting this
conversation:

Babe: "David, are you an Englishman?"

David: "No".

Babe: "Are you Afrikaander?"

David: "No".

Babe: "What are you, then?"

David: "Granpa's".

At report of this, Daddy nearly wept with pleasure.

Friday, February 23, 1940

Hear broadcast speeches from Guildhall, where men of Ajax and

Exeter, who defeated Graf Spee, are being entertained to lunch.
Mother very upset at news that billets for 800 more evacuated
children are to be found in Stroud. I try in vain to get aluminium double saucepan in Stroud. Suppose aluminium all used for
aeroplanes. Hear Daddy ordering underwear from traveller, who
seems to think none will be forthcoming. Firm expects about 25%
of last year's supplies.

Mr. Turner, who comes to door with vegetables, etc.,
is asking customers to save scraps for him, since he can get no
food for his hens.

In afternoon to Auntie Tutties, and give her £2 Roy sent.
She places notes carefully inside book called "The Glory in the
Grey" and says she wants a new world. Home by Butterrow in rain.
Daddy and I go by full moon to meet Hilary and Leonard who come on
9.10 for weekend.

Paper criticises Peace Pledge Union which, it says, has
been picketing men outside Labour Exchanges to get men to abstain
from military service. If this is so, I think it wrong. People
have a right to their own opinion.

Saturday, February 24, 1940
Summer time begins tonight, to cheer our blackout.

Walk on common in morning and go by car to Cirencester
in afternoon. See lots of planes at aerodrome over common: also
small anti-aircraft guns. Mother's charwoman (Mrs. Knight) has

husband working at aircraft factory at Gloucester, which King
and Queen visited the other day.   (Wives all wanted to know what
Queen wore. Men said grey coat, green frock and blue hat. Wives
refused to believe it).   At this factory, the men know nothing
of what is going on in any workshop but their own.   One workshop
was empty, which they seemed to think Wouldn't Do, and hustled
men into it, to stand about with tools, so that when the King asked
one of them what he was doing, he hadn't the slightest idea.
In the Manager's office a man was found who had no business there,
and the police escort knocked him down and handcuffed him.   They
have had several men suspected of spying, and when police go to
arrest them they have vanished.   One man ran confectioner's and
baker's shop: had 2 ovens and never used one.   Girl in his employ
got suspicious and told police.   They found a transmitting set in
one oven - but two men in charge of shop had disappeared meantime.

Paragraph found in yesterday's "Telegraph":-
~~Sunday, February 25, 1940~~
        "Dr. Little (Conservative) asked the Prime Minister to
approach the leaders of Churches to fix a day of prayer beseeching
God 'to bring the war to a speedy end by the overthrow of the enemy
and promote such a spirit of brotherhood and goodwill among the
nations of the earth that they will seek war no more'.

        "Mr. Chamberlain said that consideration would be given to
the suggestion at the appropriate time.   'I do not think that time
has yet arrived', he added." \\

Sunday, February 25, 1940

Chapel.   Begin with hymn

> "I thank Thee Lord that Thou has made
> The earth so bright",

which I do not sing but Mrs. Kenred Smith bellows.   Follow with

chant:
> "The Lord thundered in the heavens
> And the Most High uttered his voice:
> Hailstones and coals of fire ..."

which I shout joyfully but Mrs. K. despises.   In long prayer hot

water pipes make fearful noises, leading Mother to suppose that

the whole system, and particularly the part which runs beneath our

pew, is about to blow up.   I think irreverent thoughts to effect

that the Lord is thundering in the hot water pipes.

In afternoon we go to Beacon Tump.   Hilary, Leonard and

I walk through woods from Edge.   Trees on beacon torn by ice of

a few weeks ago.   Plenty of wood lying about and we take some

home in car.   To London by 6.23 with Molly Evans.

Monday, February 26, 1940

Finns lose important posts in Mannerheim Line.   Sumner Welles,

on mission to Europe to discuss Roosevelt's suggested peace terms

with various countries, sees Mussolini.

Hilary, who comes from Stroud with L. this morn, rings

up at lunchtime from Dickens & Jones and implores me to go at once

and save her from buying 5½ guinea suit.   Do so: but find what

she really wanted was moral support in buying it.   We get her blue

suit at 4½ guineas which I think suits her better, and have lunch
together before I go on to printers.

At night John and Peter come in for bridge and I am
instructed in the finer points of the game. Get good cards and
win 1/2 from Edric but afterwards lose it all to Helena.   Am
haunted all night by hands of cards which I cannot sort into suits.

Tuesday, February 27, 1940
Finns still losing positions.

Very hectic day at printers.   Edric has given me ticket
for Philharmonic Concert which starts at 7 p.m.   Mr. Abraham kindly lets me go at 6.45 (find later he works on till 7.30), and I
taxi to Queen's Hall, where am in fourth row of stalls, next to
Major Glendinning - shy but nice.   Weingartner conducts Mozart's
Symphony in E flat, Brahms' Variations on Theme by Haydn, and
Beethoven's Seventh Symphony.   First Symphony Concert I've been to
since war started and enjoy it to the full.   Peter, on back bench
of cellos, sees me and waves.   Grimaces to say I am to meet him
afterwards.   So at t̸h̸e̸ end, when we have risen to our feet and
cheered this German who has conducted an English orchestra through
three German works and has then given us the National Anthem, so
that I nearly burst into tears - Major G. and I progress slowly up
to foyer.   P. invites Major G. to come and play Scramble but he
declines.   We see woman knocked down in blackout as we cross
Oxford Street into Underground.   Many people rush to her aid so

we go on.   At Oxford Road are John and Pauline.   I win Scramble.
Peter says now all the proposed cycling party for Easter is met
together and we will discuss plans.   Pauline, surprised, says
she has no holiday at Easter, so plans, it seems, have already
gone astray.   Arthur shows nice story about King Lear which he
has had published in magazine called "English".

Wednesday, February 28, 1940

Horrible discovery made that ~~prin~~ photograph in Listener which
purports to be Anthony Eden inspecting Indian troops in Egypt is
really ~~fex~~-Kaiser, before the war, reviewing Prussian Guards in
Germany.   Printers have used wrong block, same size as right one.
Editor takes news very well, because his dog has just eaten hole
in bedroom carpet, which seems worse evil.

Peter Latham and wife come in.   Also John, Pauline,
Helen, fair unknown girl and husband, Trixie and friend.   Peter
making records.   Helena invites Beavans and me to cottage for
Easter.

Weather mild and dull.   Buy silk frock which do not like

Thursday, February 29, 1940

Vibourg seems on point of surrender to Russians.

E. F. Benson, biographer and novelist, dies aged 72.

Travel to Bould by 6.5 and talk to young airman in train
who went to France day before war was declared and is home for
first leave of 10 days.   He looks not more than 19, and is a gunner

who sits one end of plane and machine-guns enemy.   Says they
have spies who tell Germans when our planes are going up.   Six
of the nine planes in his squadron went up one day and met forty
Messerschmitts who must have been told they were coming.   None
of our planes returned and all the men were killed.   This is the
sort of thing that doesn't get into our newspapers.   He denies
stories current in London that German planes are made of inferior
metal: says they have a metal lighter than, and twice as strong
as, anything we use.   But skill of pilots is about equal to ours.
Says they are expecting big offensive any time now and are all
ready to run away!   Expresses opinion that our Navy is no good
(jealousy of Senior Service?), and says what we have been told
about sinking of U-boats is not true.

Very pleased to see Joyce, and the Other Joyce, whose
baby is beginning to make its presence known.

Friday, March 1, 1940

First of the month when large-scale bombing on this country is
expected.

Beautiful morning, sunny but rather cold.   Walk with
Joyce, and on return we all eat lunch in porch.   In afternoon to
Idbury for Joyce to have bath at Mervyn and Diana's cottage.   Call
at Mrs. Dix's for cream.   She says Vibourg falling.   While J.
baths I write and read in long room looking over wold.

Folly to tea, and David comes in evening.

Saturday, March 2, 1940

Slept better last night, and not such a headache this morning.
Another beautiful day of bright sunshine but cold wind. Letter
from Ruth who has settled so heartily into being Congregational
minister's wife, can hardly believe she is same person as before.
Walk in woods. May to tea. Discussion in front of fire with
two J's on Wives, Mistresses, Suicide, Buddhism and the Salvation
Army.

Sunday, March 3, 1940

Another perfect day, full of contrasts: snowdrops in garden,
bare trees in woods; ice crackling underfoot, sun so warm that we
lie and bask, looking up through silver-birch boughs to unbelievably blue sky. Picnic beside hut. Trees are waiting for spring,
to burst into leaf: already there are catkins on all the hazels
and poplars. Everything else is waiting for something too -
invasion by Hitler perhaps, or perhaps by the spirit of God. I
never saw anything so expectant and lovely.

        In middle of supper David calls us to look at green and
red sky, and while we are admiring Mr. Bond comes with car and J.
and I go to station. "What is this train called?" J. asks porter.
He looks surprised. "Seven-fifteen?" prompts J. "No, seven-
twenty-eight", he replies. We are confounded, as didn't know of
existence of such a train, but it takes me safely to Paddington.

        String quartets in progress at Cundell's. Alice and
Bernard for night. Edric has bought recorder, on which he plays

wobbly scale while I try to help by (very infuriatingly) humming
the next note and pointing it out at same time in the Beginners'
Manual, as if he didn't know what F was.

Monday, March 4, 1940

A little irritated by everyone after yesterday's glories.   Italy
also is irritated, by Britain's stopping her coal imports from
Germany, under the law of contraband.   A note of protest is received, and Britain is obviously unwilling to offend such a powerful neutral.   Finns in retreat.   Sumner Welles has left Germany
and is now coming to England.

Edric plays me Bach on piano - just right, because he
sounds so sane and ordered and dependable and safe.   Then Brahms
concerto which I follow with score.   Then Mozart piano concerto,
in which he puts in various orchestral bits with 'tum-ti-tums' and
shouts.

Tuesday, March 4, 1940

Terribly hectic day at printers, during which get very depressed
because outside there is bright sunshine and we have black paper
all over the window.   Work till 7.15, so miss madrigals.   Gundelb
have Theodore Holland and wife to supper.   Go in unobtrusively
while they are eating and find water hot, so bath, and when I let
out water, Irma goes into dining-room and says water is rushing
away somewhere and flood is imminent.

Join visitors for coffee, and Mr. Holland holds forth on

Mozart, who is a "blackmailer", because ... well, I was too
tired to take in the reason, but was very entertained.

Wednesday, March 6, 1940

Britain takes six German coal ships bound for Italy.   Eighteen
men of B.E.F. captured.   I.R.A. bomb explodes in Park Lane.

I buy Mother aluminium double saucepan.   Man in Lewis's
says there will be no more aluminium goods when stock is exhausted.

Leave work at 4.45 and go to students' concert at Guildhall.   Come out of Blackfriar's Station into unexpected openness
with sunshine on river.   Guildhall is shabby and dingy.   I sit
in row of staff next to Principal's wife, feeling very distinguished.
Very good violinist, tenor singer and 17-year-old girl pianist.
Edric (addressed by porter as Mr. Principal) shows me theatre.

Only quartet expected inevening, but people keep coming
- 3 Majors of British Army, 1 German and 1 Hungarian refugee, 2
ladies of German-Jewish origin, Arnold Cooke, and finally Peter in
evening dress straight from Beethoven Mass at Queen's Hall.
German refugee thinks he must not speak to anyone till he has been
introduced.   "Wolff", he mutters to Arnold Cooke, who leaps to
it nobly and murmurs "Cooke".   Cannot then distinguish that they
make another remark to each other for entire evening.

Road accidents since blackout have caused 10,000 deaths
- four times the number of men killed during the war itself.

Thursday, March 7, 1940

Britain takes more of Italy's coal ships.   We are all being
urged to save money and buy War Loan and Savings Certificates.
Feel if I do this shall be making money out of war and do not like
idea.

To Beavans, where play Scramble and Monopoly.   Ken
there - J's friend from Cardiff.   Also young boy from Sheffield
who came up to appear to-day before Conscientious Objectors'
tribunal and who asked for hospitality through "Peace News". His
Tribunal at home put him down for non-combatant service, and he
appealed against this decision.   Tribunal to-day did not uphold
his appeal.   He says he cannot do non-combatant service, because
that helps on the war and he thinks war is wrong.   Will therefore
have to go to prison.

Friday, March 8, 1940
Home by midday train.   At Swindon see Molly Evans' mother and
travel down with her - beautiful sunshiny day.

Saturday, March 8, 1940
Crocuses coming up in garden.   Still sunshine.   Walk to Selsley
with Aunt H's bag which she left at home.   Go over hill to Kings
Stanley and back to Enderley to tea.   Oncommon with Mother afterwards, and Rummy at night.   Russia making Peace overtures to
Finland - demanding much more from her than she demanded before war
began.   Meantime fighting continues.

<u>Sunday, March 9, 1940</u>

To London by 6.23.   Read Mr. Abraham's life of Tolstoy, in
which am extremely interested.   Near Slough, sky is lit up
by light from burning building looking like large factory,
which is blazing as if it was full of petrol.

<u>Monday, March 10, 1940</u>

Meat rationing begins.   Everyone allowed 1/10-worth of meat
a week, but this does not include fish, poultry, or 'offal' -
i.e. tripe, liver, kidney, sweetbreads, etc. And no coupon
needed for meal in restaurant.

      Children home from cottage, because Cundells think
there will no bombing while Sumner Welles is in Europe.

      To Beavans.   Lot of people, including young German
composer called Hans Gellhorn, whose quartet is performed.
Lift home from Gordon Smith through inky blackness.

<u>Tuesday, March 11, 1940</u>

Finnish-Russian negotiations still in progress.

      In evening, Dora (German-Jewish nurse) and Helena
argue on Finland.   Dora thinks English are hypocrites: that
they say they want to help poor Finland but really are swayed
by quite different considerations, and why don't they admit it?
Helena's view typically (and completely honestly) upper-middle-
class British, which Dora cannot understand.   She thinks we are
animated by purely altruistic motives, though admits that it

is to our advantage not to allow Russia to win.

Wednesday, March 12, 1940

Finnish hostilities cease at noon.   Terms of the peace with
Russia are hard.   Finland loses Vilpuri, islands in the
Karelian Isthmus, and all its Mannerheim line of fortifications:
also a lot of its industrial districts.   France and England had
promised force of 50,000 to help Finns, but Sweden would not let
troops go through her territory - Germany had threatened that if
she did, German troops would invade Sweden.   I discuss non-
resistance with Mr. Abraham, from which all that emerges is that
I am a Worm suffering from Mental Confusion.

        Go in lunch-hour to look at Bedford College in Regent's
Park.   Students have been evacuated to Cambridge and the rooms
they lived in are being let to the public.   Decide to go and
live there after Easter.

        Lovely music at night.   Franz Osborn (pianist) in the
Trout Quintet (Schubert), and later Beethoven Trio.   But by that
time I have gone to bed, being extremely tired, perhaps because
of the mild weather.

Thursday, March 13, 1940

At meeting of the East India Company at Caxton Hall, Westminster,
last night, an Indian shot dead Sir Michael O'Dwyer, and wounded
Lord Zetland, Lord Lamington and Sir Louis Dane.   Sir M.O. was
Governor of the Punjab at the time of the Amritsar rising in 1919,

when 5,000 Indians were ~~pied~~ fired on by British troops, and
400 natives were killed and 1,200 injured.   Lord Haw-Haw has
lately been making great capital out of the Amritsar Massacre
on the Hamburg wireless, and will have much to say on this ass-
assination.

      Finland planning defensive alliance with Norway and
Sweden.   Everyone tells me that England had done everything
she could for Finland, but the Dutch paper "Handelsblad" says,
according to the News-Chronicle: "Hard and bitter words must
be spoken of the Allies who left Finland in the lurch ... The
entire world expected that the British Government at the moment
the Red armies violated Finnish territory would openly, unconditionally and fully support Finland, not hesitating to fulfil
the promise ... The Allies pride themselves upon ruling the
waves and could reach Finland via Petsamo.   They have furnished
Hitler with a new and great diplomatic success.   Their morale
and credit have sustained a new shock.   Europe cannot build a
future upon their policy".   The last sentence is significant,
since all our talk just now is of the new Europe we will make
when we have won the war.

      Cold again: snow storms in morning.   Home by 6.55.

Friday, March 15, 1940
The day when everyone expected Hitler's Blitzkreig to begin,
but all that is reported on the 6 o'clock news is that the

butter ration is to be doubled (8oz) on March 25, that another
German ship has been scuttled, that the Russians have entered
Vilpuri, and that there have been arrests in Prague.

It is thought that the Russians will now try to make
an agreement with Turkey, with the object no doubt of breaking
up the alliance between Turkey and Great Britain.

Beautiful sunshine, with a few sharp storms: rather
cold. Walk over common. The beech-trees are beginning to
show some signs of life but not much yet - Spring very late because of cold weather.

Saturday, March 16, 1940
King Carol of Rumania has let the Black Guards, a Nazi organisation, back into his country.

Sunday, March 17, 1940
Rainy. German raid on Scapa Flow: 14 planes. Warship
damaged, 8 men killed, 1 civilian killed. (First civilian to
be killed in Britain in this war). In my carriage on way back
to London is woman whose son is on ship in Scapa Flow: she has
heard broadcast about raid, but it did not say which ship was
hit. I read Tolstoy's "Gospel in Brief", and knit.

Monday, March 18, 1940
Hitler and Mussolini meet in Brenner Pass early this morning.
Some people think meeting called by Mussolini to discuss Sumner

Welles' visit.

To Beavans, where are Nan and Gordon.   Scramble,
Monopoly and Pingpong.   Enjoy it all, but feel I have out-
grown the Beaven era, though have not entered another.   Depressed.

Tuesday, March 19, 1940

Showery.   Everyone in state of great gloom, because Germany
says result of Brenner Pass conversation is to be a three-power
pact between Italy, Germany and Russia.   This looks bad for
Allies.

R.A.F. bombs German naval base in Sylt - retaliation
for Scapa Flow bombing.

My face covered with Spring blotches.   Feel unwell,
tired and depressed.   Even the other-worldliness of Tolstoy's
"New Testament in Brief" fails to cheer me.   '"I was thinking
about this world", said Mr. Salteena sadly'.

Wednesday, March 20, 1940

Blowy, fine day.   Papers full of our raid on Island of Sylt.
Germans say they sank 6 warships at Scapa Flow, but Admiralty
denies this.

Take suitcase of clothes to Bedford College in lunch-
hour.   Return through park where yellow, purple and white
crocuses are growing through the grass, and a barrage balloon,
like a huge silver amphibian, is moored to the ground.   Music
in evening.   Last of our macaroni cheese Wednesdays, alas.

Thursday, March 21, 1940

New French Government formed, under premiership of M.Reynaud.
At work at printers till 7.0.   At Flask Walk is Edric only,
all the others having gone to cottage.   We cook chops and
warm up vegetables and have quite a good meal.   E. shows me
elaborate route he has worked out, with landmarks all the way -
"Raspberry Canes", "Cricket Field", etc., for use tomorrow.

Good Friday, March 22, 1940

Up betimes and at 10 o'clock Edric and John depart on bicycles
- Edric on Helena's, wearing beret. I am left in charge of
fearfully overloaded car.   Helen Bartrum arrives with still
more luggage, and Guy Pertwee, elocution teacher from G.S.M.D.,
with yet another suitcase.   I travel at back, so hemmed in I
get quite numb, trying to save from destruction 2 suitcases and
1 enormous and ancient lampshade with fringe.   Hood of car
down or lampshade would never get in.   At Much Hadham, where
we meet cyclists, I am revived with sherry and coffee.   Continue
with John, on bicycles.   Enjoy ride over undulating country
lanes.   Half-a-mile of watersplash, in which we get very wet
and muddy.   Have to climb into field with bicycles and walk.

Cottage among half-a-dozen others.   Yellow, with
blue paint.   Crocuses on grass in garden.   Three clocks on
kitchen mantelpiece say variously 4.10., 8.35 and 2.20.   Last
is approximately right.

Recorder trio, wood-gathering, bridge, string trio.

Saturday, March 23, 1940

Walk, during which Edric, John, Helen and I stand in middle
of wood and sing Tallis's Canon. Finish with drinks at The
Woodman and darts for an hour. I am much the worst. Edward
Elliot and 2 daughters, Margaret and Susan, both red-haired
and beautiful, to tea and supper. Music, including duet between Edward (bassoon) and Helen (recorder): and Margaret in
oboe quartet.

Easter Day, March 24, 1940

Never had an Easter Sunday without church before. Walk in
morning, then John departs for London until tomorrow, and after
lunch I go for 1½ hours on bicycle alone, which I enjoy very
much. Open country something like Berkshire Downs.

Day began musically with Helen playing recorder in bed,
while Baby sits on top of me listening. Gradually an audience
accumulates, so that Helena comes up and finds Edric and three
children sitting on two beds. Slippery Ann in evening.

Monday, March 25, 1940

Beautiful day. Digging in morning, not for Victory but for
Beauty, taking earth from one part of garden to another. Then
I cycle to station on chance of meeting John, but he has come
early and gone for round on his bicycle. Basking in garden
in afternoon and Edric teaches us to play Poker. Parry and

Mildred Williams to tea.   Up to pub, on step of which John,
Helen and I give our Round, "There was an old man of Calcutta".
I depart for London by 8 o'clock train, standing in crowded
corridor all the way.   Cannot find way into Bedford College
in dark - get into deserted lecture-rooms and interminable
corridors where lights do not work, and my torch fails.   After
much peregrination find Night Porter who leads me to Room 60,
and after bath I go gratefully to bed.

Tuesday, March 26, 1940
Pouring wet day.   Roused by maid at 7.30 and at breakfast see
Miss Hope-Simpson (also of B.B.C.) who helps me forage for food.
Printers till 6.30.   At dinner learn there is creche on top
floor of college, for babies who are being evacuated.   Sit next
to night nurse.   Miscellaneous collection of people at dinner,
including Dorothy Sayers, detective writer, here on visit.
To Hampstead to collect clothes.   In tube lift is notice requesting us to pray for Victory and for a Just Peace, with never a
doubt that they are synonymous.

Wednesday, March 27, 1940
Mackenzie King (Liberal) who wants greater war effort, wins in
Canadian elections.   Editor, in conversation, says you cannot
tell the truth in war time, or keep to any standards of morality.
This apropos very good letter which I may not publish in case it
offers help to Lord Haw-Haw.

To Beavans, with Helen.   Pingpong, Poker and
Scramble.

Thursday, March 28, 1940

Last night got home at 12 and found hot-water-bottle in bed
and vase of daffodils on table, both put there by Miss Hope-
Simpson, who is in next room.   Very touched by this kindness.
Brilliantly fine day, but cold.   Dutch bring down British
bomber.   Archbishop of Canterbury, in to-day's Listener, says:
"Let us set ourselves to carry through the task of liberating
the world from evil forces, which is laid upon us in this grim
war".   This is from his Easter Day broadcast sermon.   In view
of his office, feel he might preach "Be not overcome of evil,
but overcome evil with good", instead of "overcome evil with a
bigger and better evil".   At the beginning of the war everyone
told us we had no quarrel with the German people, only with
Hitler.   Now they broadcast talks all tending to the view that
the German people are so corrupt by the teaching of Nazism that
there is no truth in them and that one cannot negotiate a peace
with any of them.   Even Mr. Abraham says the only thing to do
is to exterminate them.   What rubbish.

Friday, March 29, 1940

To Stroud by 6.35.   Man in carriage rails against Jews.   Young
soldier remarks, apropos Western Front, that he thinks it is a
wrong idea to have 2 lines of defence built by 2 nations against
each other.

Opinions on Hore-Belisha: young soldier that he was
'for the ranks' and was turned out by the big-wigs because he
wanted to democratise the Army: railer against Jews that he
was fired for his connection with fraudulent companies. Railer against Jews has on rack 2 dozen rose-bushes to plant in his
garden, so probably has his good points.

At Bryans, learn that last weekend Leonard had flu
and Daddy had slight heart attack on Easter Sunday morning,
after busy day on Saturday. Is now better.

Saturday, March 30, 1940

We have our usual joint, in spite of official rationing: the
only thing we don't get plenty of is sugar. I am allowed to
bring home 3 oz. from Bedford College.

Winston Churchill, in broadcast, warns us that we must
expect intensification of war.

Sunday, March 31, 1940

Rainy. Last day of month in which most people expected big
air attacks, and Joyce's Man in Front said we'd have peace.
Both wrong.

Take Ruby play of hers which I typed yesterday. Mr.
Clark, at chapel, gives me 2 more R.A.F. leaflets, one in German
and one in Czech. The latter tells them not to revolt - yet.

Monday, April 1, 1940

Beautiful day. Shining yellow forsythia bushes all over park.

Write letters at my desk with pigeon-holes in evening and feel
very grand.   R.A.F. over Germany again.

Tuesday, April 2, 1940

P.M. says economic war will be prosecuted without mercy (doesn't
put it as baldly as that).   Several air-battles.   Listen to
9 o'clock news in common room at Bedford College, where are
several foreign students (men) - a Swede, Lithuanian, Spaniard,
etc.   They do not appear to think much of our news, especially
the Lithuanian - and when I tried to listen from a foreigner's
point of view, it did sound smug: Germans had attacked a convoy,
quite unsuccessfully; we had engaged in air fights, always out-
numbered and always getting away scot free but with damage to
our opponents; all the neutrals ought to sympathise with us because we are fighting their battles as well as our own (this provoked a snort).   All in Stuart Hibberd's most self-complacent
tones.

       Extract from the "New Yorker":-

      "Asked to set aski aside a suitable day for general
prayer throughout the United Kingdom for the speedy end
of the war, P.M. Chamberlain replied that the question
would be considered at the proper time.   'I do not think
that time has yet arrived', he said.   This remark, we
feel, represents about the ultimate in British caution.
The P.M. apparently has an uneasy faith in the power of
prayer, combined with a lack of faith in the divine grasp
of the situation.   Pray for the end of the war, and
there's just a chance that that's what you'll get; peace
right on the dot, with all the issues still up in the air
and the balance of power yet to be determined.   The P.M.,
it seems, has no doubt that God can put a stop to hostilities any time He feels like it, but he would rather not

trust Him with the details.   The time for peace will
be decided at No.10 Downing Street.   Until the Cabinet gives the word, the people will kindly refrain
from stirring up the Almighty.   Until the Empire has
things under better control, God can just count
sparrows".

Wednesday, April 3, 1940

To National Gallery concert in lunch-time.   Three Mozart
sonatas (violin and piano).   Buy pen for Daddy's birthday
and hairbrush for Aunt M.   At 5.30 take suitcase to Flask
Walk to collect belongings, and there find Edric and Helena
who have come up for a day's shopping.   Go out with E. and
buy kipper for my supper which I eat with them.

New pound notes, blue and brown, just issued.   The
bank clerk says there was some talk of Germany dropping bogus
pound notes to upset our currency, hence the new ones.   Ten
shilling new ones still to come.

Thursday, April 4, 1940

Daddy's 64th birthday.   Many changes in the Cabinet.   Sir
Samuel Hoare made Air Minister in place of Sir Kingsley Wood,
who becomes Lord Privy Seal.   Mr. Churchill still First Lord
of Admiralty, and is now also head of the Committee of Service
Ministers.

Americans warned to leave Belgium.

To Beavans, where are Han and Arnold.   Talk to Duque
who tells me all about the boys' youth and collects 10/- from

me for down-and-out Pacifist costermonger she has befriended.
She is always giving her last halfpenny to the needy, half of
them bogus, and doesn't even call herself a Christian.

Friday, April 5, 1940
Aunt N's 60th birthday.   She is eligible for a pension.   To
Stroud by 6.55.

Saturday, April 6, 1940
Lovely spring day: walk on common.   Still have plenty of meat
for weekend joint.

      Meet woman who sells me 7 bunches of wild daffodils
for 1/-.   She assures me they will bring me luck.   "You need
luck, don't you?"   "We all need that nowadays" I say evasive-
ly.   "It's faith we all need, lady, can't do anything without
that", she says.   Have so many daffodils, have to put them in
pastry bowl.

Sunday, April 7, 1940
Britain is sending Notes to Scandinavia; it is not clear yet
to me about what.   The Nazis say the neutrals had better Look
out because of British Menace.

Monday, April 8, 1940

Allies mine three areas in Norwegian territorial waters, which
are vital to German shipping, and receive protest from Norway
on "the most severe and most unwarranted violation of neutrality since war started".   Foreign student at dinner gives
opinion that in a few days we shall be at war with Norway.

Meantime all the daffodils are coming up in the
grounds here and in Regent's Park.   Phyllida's birthday.

Tuesday, April 9, 1940

Germany invades Denmark and Norway in early morning. Denmark
offers no resistance and by night is entirely in German hands.
Occupation carried out very efficiently: one report says thousands of armed troops were landed by plane and marines from
merchant ships.   Norway resisting.   So far from our being at
war with Norway, it seems she is our new Ally.   Her government
moves from Oslo, which surrenders during afternoon.   Rumours
afloat all day: one says Oslo and other towns bombed, but later
news says planes over the city for two hours dropped leaflets.
Half population of Oslo evacuated, but ordered by Germans to
return.   Germans mine west coast of Norway.   Germany says she
has taken Norway and Denmark under her protection because of
threat of invasion from Allies.   Reports also says she has
told Sweden that she must accept Germany's "protection" or be
invaded.   Telephone communication between Norway and England
is cut off, so all news comes via America.

After being so depressed over this news that I can
scarcely speak all day, I listen to 9 o'clock bulletin in company of one Turk, one Lithuanian, one Italian and one German
refugee.   They are none of them sneering at the news now.
All anti-Nazi except Italian, who gives no opinion.

In midst of all this stir, which rouses many people
to more enthusiasm for the war than has yet been apparent, the
English Madrigal Choir gives a concert at S. Kensington to the
Geological Survey.   The man who thanks us at close of performance says it is good to be taken into another world for an hour.

Wednesday, April 10, 1940
Meet Mother, and Daddy at Paddington at 12.45.   We lunch at
Victoria and I leave them waiting for Croydon-bound train.

Eight o'clock morning news says Norway is coming to
terms with Germany.   This denied later.   Reports of naval
battles, sinking of two German ships, one British ship, and that
oneBritish ship is aground.   Also report that Iceland has
declared war on Germany.   But all news is obscure.

At night to film with Peter: "It's love I'm After" -
very entertaining.   When we come out the sky is filled with
searchlights, and porter on Kilburn station says he supposes
since Churchill took over he's making them all practice.

Thursday, April 11, 1940
Sea and air battles off coast of Norway.   Reports say Bergen

recaptured by British and Nazis in Oslo receive ultimatum that
unless they surrender they will be bombed.   But in statement
in H.of C., reported in evening bulletins, Churchill denies
this.   Says we have occupied the Faroe Islands: that since
Monday Germany has lost several U-boats, four cruisers, two or
more destroyers, considerable number of battleships, ten troopships, twenty planes.   British have lost four destroyers and
two or three ships have been damaged, six planes.   France says
there are clear preparations for big German offensive on the
Western Front.

Mr. Ackerley expresses to Miss Playle opinions so like
my own that I can scarce forbear to cheer, but hold my peace.
She is very angry, and her arguments in favour of war contra-
dict each other to such an extent am left with conclusion that
at bottom of her heart, unbeknown to herself, she likes war, as
I am convinced many people do.   It provides a little excitement
in their otherwise monotonous existences.

It is revealed within the portals of the B.B.C. that
Lord Haw-Haw is man called Joyce, who had two brothers working
at B.B.C. - one was Clerk of Works, the other a studio assistant.   They have both been sacked - latter was found stealing
light bulbs, wire, etc.

Beautiful day of sunshine.   Everyone much more cheerful after hearing of British successes.   Daddy rings to say he
and Mother, Hilary and Leonard are going to Eastbourne, because,

if I hear aright, L. has been given £20 by his employer to
recuperate from flu.   I arrange to join them for weekend.

Friday, April 12, 1940
Get 5.45 from London Bridge to Eastbourne and at 7.20 or so
join the family at Warriston House.

Much news, confused for me by unfamiliarity with
Norwegian names.   British have laid an enormous minefield in
North Sea and have sunk more ships.   In reconnaissance flights
and attacks on two warships, five of our planes lost.   At end
of news "Onlooker" (Norman Birkett) goes to a lot of trouble to
try to justify a blockade which starves civilians.

Saturday, April 13, 1940
Fine but cold.   In morning call on Gorricks.   Play golf on
cold miniature course.   In afternoon I walk alone to Beachy
Head where see parents who have come by bus.

At hotel, lady boarder who has disappeared for forty-
eight hours, returns almost dead drunk.   Is finally removed,
protesting, in Black Maria, and nervous new arrival decides
house is disorderly and leave immediately.

Nine o'clock news promises important announcement at
10.15.   It comes through finally at 10.45, after half-an-hour
during which Hibberd puts on records with apologies between each.
He then says Admiralty announce that at noon today (while we

played golf) the <u>Warspite</u>, with destroyers of the Second
Flotilla including the <u>Cossack</u>, sailed into Narvik Fjord and
sank four German destroyers.   Three others fled up an adjacent
inlet and were followed and sunk.   Three of our ships were
damaged but no seriously.   Earlier in the week an attempt on
the Fjord had been made when two British ships were sunk, two
German ones left in flames and one was thought to be sinking,
and the rest of our ships had to withdraw.   Everyone thinks
this must now mean the British have landed in Norway, but no
statement to that effect is made.

Sunday, April 14, 1940

British have laid mines enough to shut up the Baltic altogether.
Papers full of yesterday's naval victory.

Fine but coldish.   Parents to chapel - Presbyterian,
preacher Dr. Reid, very crowded, chairs in aisle.   H. and L.
listen to band.   I walk to Beachy Head and back.   In afternoon
to putting course at end of Parade.   Mother and I sit in shelter
while others play.   Tea out of doors.   Mother, Daddy and I
catch 6.36 to Croydon, where key L. has given us won't fit door,
and I rush to Phyllis's and get key she has.

Monday, April 15, 1940

British forces land in Norway, it is not announced where.

Phyllida, en route for Stroud, for night.   We go to
Stewart's for dinner, and to "Rebecca" by ~~Pamela~~ Daphne du

Maurier (Celia Johnson and Owen Nares) which we enjoy.   Home
by moonlight.

Mr. Lambert's wife is going to divorce him and he is
going to marry Miss Morgan.

Tuesday, April 16, 1940
Meet P. for lunch.   Working too late to go to madrigals.   John
invites me to ballet tomorrow, but have arranged to go to Mrs.
Morris's$\frac{1}{2}$

British have recaptured Narvik, the Norwegian iron ore
port, which Goebbels says now is anyway of no importance whatever!   Reports says our troops have landed in seven places.

Wednesday, April 17, 1940
Stavanger aerodrome bombed by Navy: Trondheim aerodrome, 150
miles north of Stavanger, bombed by R.A.F.   Fighting in Narvik
Town.   Norwegians says their troops in north have made contact
with British.   H.M. submarine Thistle lost.   Minefield laid
across entrnace of Firth of Clyde.   Railways fares to be increased by 10% from May 1.

To Mrs. Morris's for supper.   At 8 o'clock or so
David comes, following confused telephone call in which Mrs M.
thinks he is her cousin.   I stay for night, since, in spite of
bright moon, Mrs. M. thinks I ought not to go through Regent's
Park alone.   Sleep in enormous nightdress of Mrs. M's, with
long sleeves which come over my hands, and torchon lace everywhere.

Thursday, April 18, 1940

Extract from broadcast discussion in the series "Under Nazi Rule": "You can say that the standard of living of the British workers is 150% higher than that of the German worker under this so-called German Socialism".   This is intended as anti-German propaganda, but strikes me as providing reason for the war.   (Though N.B., standard might have been higher if Germans had spent less on armaments.)

Mr. Thomas comes back from lunch in Fleet Street and says Mussolini is expected to march into Yugoslavia this week-end.   The world is mad.   Sir John Reith (Minister of Information) says "There is too much neutrality at home", adding that we all want a set purpose and high resolve.   But the Germans have high resolve too.   I feel we are being called upon to fight to preserve the status quo, which for millions of people is not worth preserving.

Friday, April 19, 1940

Paper has been rationed and size of newspapers greatly reduced. Size of Listener to be reduced a little, but not greatly since we are regarded as an organ of propaganda because we reproduce all the broadcast ministerial utterances.   Feel therefore I am taking part in the general stirring up of hatred and wish I had job which did not do this.   People are now beginning to say that if we win a lenient peace with Germany will be impossible.

Lunch with Mr. Abraham, rather by accident.

Travel to Stroud with soldiers who have 24 hours
embarkation leave before sailing tomorrow for some destination
unknown.

Saturday, April 20, 1940

French troops land in Norway.

Walk to Selsley with P. Coming down Jacob's Ladder
observe that roof of Daniels' steel works is camouflaged so that
it looks like ploughed fields. Shops in town which sell vegetables now tip them straight into basket with no paper round them.

Sunday, April 21, 1940

Very warm and fine. To Beacon Tump. P. and I walk through
woods from Edge, meeting Mother and Daddy on beacon. Travel
back at night with Carey Kenred Smith. I read Tolstoy and he
studies.

Monday, April 22, 1940

Still mild and sunny. Glorious walk through park to B.B.C.
Helmann to supper. We explore grounds of college. She is so
belligerently Pacifist, makes me feel quite pro-war. News reports
successes in Norway. Mussolini had not yet invaded Yugoslavia.

Tuesday, April 23, 1940

Budget Day. Tobacco, beer, spirits, matches, to be taxed.
Postage to be increased to 2½d. for letters, 2d. for postcards.
Phone calls to be dearer.

Work too late to go to choir. To Beavans. Music,
Scramble. Tentative suggestion that Joyce's and my holiday in
lakes should become cycling in Cornwall with John and Gordon
Smith. Peter comes in from concert looking very white and
tired. Weather very mild. In late evening, heavy rain.
Taxi home, which costs 5/6.

Wednesday, April 24, 1940

Sleep late, feel unable to hurry, and arrive at office at 10.15.
Still mild and wet. Successes reported in Norway.

In lunchtime to National Gallery concert. Mozart
(E major) and Brahms (B major) trios. Kathleen Long (piano),
Eda Kersey (violin), James Whitehead (cello). Very enjoyable,
especially ~~Sezereke~~ Scherzo in Brahms. In evening to Beavans where we
have music, including works on four cellos (Beethoven's First
Symphony, slow movement, transcribed). Edric among the company.

Thursday, April 25, 1940

News says Navy still bombarding Narvik, which the other day was
reported captured by British. R.A.F. yesterday bombed 7 or 8
German air bases, and the Germans have now bombed Scapa Flow.
Each side claims to have done great damage, but each side says
the other did none. News from Norway very obscure. Successes
reported recently seem largely to have been in the imagination
of journalists.

Fine and lovely. Lunch with Aunt N., who has come
up for day from Tunbridge Wells. I walk home with Editor. Take

him through grounds of Bedford College and show him nice way
to Baker Street.   He talks about friends of his who take no
interest at all in the war and says he can't understand their
attitude.   I can.

Friday, April 26, 1940
British troops apparently retreating in Norway.   Mr. Thomas
says we have no strategists in high places.

I buy, in lunch-hour, gloves, blouse, slacks, and
then feel I have wantonly disobeyed injunctions of Chancellor
of Exchequer to save money.

To Stroud by 6.35 with Molly Evans.   Met by Daddy
and by Joyce who has cycled from Bould.

Saturday, April 27, 1940
British seem to be doing not too well in Norway.

Cauliflowers in Stroud are 1/6 each, however small.
I get one big one.   Joyce and I do lawn, I mowing, she shearing.
Heavy thunderstorm at 6 o'clock, when we are just wanting to go
for walk... (insertion of new ribbon in typewriter) ... We do
go for walk later.   Everything vivid green after rain, and blue
mist in valleys.   Daddy comes home very worn out (Leslie away
with sprained ankle).   He says a woman tells him three German
aeroplanes were over Stroud on Friday!

Sunday, April 28, 1940

News from Norway none too good.   Daddy stays in bed resting
till afternoon.   Has pain round his heart and is rather breathless.   Joyce starts back as Mother and I go to chapel.   Not as
warm as yesterday.   I return by 6.23 with Molly Evans.

Monday, April 29, 1940

Am typing in single spacing to save paper, since supplies have
to be cut down to 30 per cent of normal.   Three German trans-
port ships sunk.   This makes 27 since invasion of Norway.
Admiralty says German claims about ships they've sunk are untrue.
Nazis are saying we've bombed open towns in Germany.   This is
denied, but is considered prelude to bombing by Germans.   Mr.
Abraham prophesies that within a month Italy, Switzerland, Sweden,
Turkey, Rumania - in fact the whole of Erope - will be fighting.
Pres

Tuesday, April 30, 1940

Two British submarines lost, and Germans take important base in
Norway.   Everyone very depressed.
     Very tired after strenuous day at printers, followed by
madrigals.   A murky mist has arisen, blotting out the spring.
Everything appears to me hopeless - the state of the world, the
weather, and myself.   But enjoyed the singing, or as much as I
was able to concentrate on.

Wednesday, May 1, 1940

Everyone fearfully gloomy about reverses in Norway, where in some
parts Allied troops have had to withdraw.   Raids by R.A.F. on
Stavanger aerodrome, where it is said great damage was done and
7 of our planes were lost.   Staff of Listener discusses war all
day without respite, till I feel thoroughly ill.   Haven't even
anyone to exchange thoughts with when I get home.   All the same,
have pleasant, if melancholy, walk in park.   At dinner a nice
girl who works at the N.U.S. has bought a recorder: I show her
how to play a scale and she lends it to me for evening.   And in
lunchhour I hear three Brandenburg Concertos (3,4 and 6) at the
National Gallery - part of Boyd Neel Orchestra with Peter's shock
of hair waving furiously just in front of me.

Thursday, May 2, 1940

Donald Tyerman, in broadcast: "The men and the materials and the
trade are there - if we put them to the proper use, which is wag-
ing the war".   Thus, he admits will depreciate the standard of
living.   Dreamt last night, among other things, that I was making
an impassioned speech in defence of Communism.   Am inclined to

think it is the only way to cure the world's ills.

British troops have to withdraw from Norway in several places.

Read beginnings of several books I have written at various times and try to work out development, but my mind refuses to be stimulated.

Friday, May 3, 1940

Gloom very thick on a bright spring day. Sweden says we have betrayed Norway. Italy says we're No Good. America thinks we Did Try. More Allied withdrawals. There seem to be British troops now only at Narvik.

Feel intensely depressed. Try to cheer myself at lunch-time by buying 6 pairs stockings. Do my best to conceal this purchase from Miss Playle, who thinks we should buy nothing, but darn and darn (what about the shopkeepers?).

Listener to be reduced to 44 pages, with further drastic cuts in view, because of paper shortage. To Stroud by 6.35.

Saturday, May 4, 1940

Leslie still laid up with bad ankle, but Daddy not so done up as last week. We have plenty of meat and butter, and are only short of sugar.

Beautiful day. I shop for Mother, mow and trim two lawns, walk round Apperly's and to cowslip field where I pick large bunch, then climb over wall and exit by way of Butterrow school yard, and so home. In evening walk again on common with Mother. Rather tired by these exertions.

Sunday, May 5, 1940

Daddy takes morning off, and sunbathes on cement, meeting Mother and me in fields on way home from chapel. In afternoon we go to Beacon Tump and I walk through woods. Very warm, and country looking lovely. Do not want to return to the depression of London.

Dreamt last night was in place like the British Museum, with
Mother.   An evil-looking man came up and showed a paper he had
obviously stolen from Daddy's pocket,because it was a permit
without which D. would be arrested.   He aaid: "It would be very
awkward for Mr. Redman, wouldn't it, if he couldn't show this when
he was asked for it ... How much is it worth to you?"   Mother
fumbled in her handbag to see what she had, and said fearfully
"I'll give you a pound for it".   "Certainly not", said I, very
angry, "it's blackmail".   I then arose and shouted imperatively
through the long halls of the museum: "God! Send a policeman at
once - this man is blackmailing us".   The Lord did not reply immediately, so I repeated the order.   No policeman arrived, but a
little attendant came quietly through a door behind me, and I
take it the situation was saved, since I was quite happy when I
woke up.

Monday, May 6, 1940

Several of our ships have been sunk.   People are calling the
Norway business "a second Gallipoli" and saying that Chamberlain
must go for not managing to get us a victory.
          Joyce at Bedford for a few nights, which is very pleas-
ant.   We walk in park, play letter-bags, and talk about Her Life.
J. regards this spring as a Nice Present, a Small Compensation
before the Balloon Goes Up and the Bombs Come Down.

Tuesday, May 7, 1940

Debate in House on Norway.   All British Fleet seems to have
gathered in the Mediterranean, and we are seeing Italian Envoys
(I suppose to tell them we mean no harm if they'll be good).
Butter ration to be cut to 4 oz again.
          At printers: after which make effort to reach our new
meeting-place for madrigals, which is, I am told, near headquarters of London Fire Brigade.   After walking for an hour, and being directed from one wrong headquarters to another, I arrive exhausted as meeting is breaking up.   To Beavans, where Joyce is.
Scramble, and talk of proposed cycling holiday in Cornwall.
          Peter's conscientious objections rather wobbling.   He
says he'll break his mother's heart if he gives in now.

Wednesday, May 8, 1940

George Lansbury, M.P., Socialist M.P. and ardent Pacifist, died
last night aged 81.   In debate in House on Norway, Admiral Keyes
says he wanted to force Trondheim Fjord, and could easily have
done it, but the Admiralty wouldn't let him.   Accuses it of in-
eptitude.
          To National Gallery concert.   Beethoven Quintet in C
major and Mendelssohn Octet in E flat major.   See Betty Hartley
for first time in about 3 years - she up from Cornwall for 3 days
only.   In evening, J. and I too tired to do anything but amble
round lake and flop in two armchairs.

<u>Thursday, May 9, 1940</u>

In House of Commons, Chamberlain gets majority of only 81 on
Norway question.   Late evening papers say he will probably re-
sign and Winston Churchill may take his place.   Lloyd George
makes speech saying we had not carried out undertakings given to
the Democratic gov. of Germany at time of Treaty of Versailles -
solemn promise that if Germany disarmed we would follow her
example.   We are now, he says, faced with the most terrible
answer ever given to people who have broken faith and broken cov-
enants.   Beverley Baxter calls LL.G. "brilliantly mischeivous".
        Death sentence now to be enforced for spying and other
offences.   Evening Standard says "If the Home Secretary was satisfied that a person or organisation was concerned in systematic
publication of matter calculated to foment opposition to successful opera prosecution of the war and serious mischief might be
caused thereby, he could cause a formal warning to be given.   If
any person or organisation so warned subsequently published matter
to foment such opposition, those responsible were liable to penal
servitude for s even years or a fine of £500, or both".   This is
probably directed against "Peace News", several officers of P.P.U.
being now summoned for showing poster saying "Wars will end when
men refuse to fight.   What are you going to do about it?"
        To Tchaikovsy Centenary Concert at Q.H. with Joyce.
Complimentary tickets from Mr. Abraham.   Romeo and Juliet Overture, 1st Piano Concerto (Cyril Smith) and Fifth Symphony.   Very
enjoyable.   Peter playing.   He waves bow at us and we have
coffee with him afterwards.

<u>Friday, May 10, 1940</u>

Lying in bath at 8 a.m. I hear through open window someone's loudspeaker proclaiming that Hitler has invaded Holland and Belgium.
Later I walk down corridor and hear conversation between two char-
women: "E've invaded Olland".   "Oo ave?"   "Itler".   E haven't!"
Great excitement everywhere.   Feeling of relief that things have
come to a head.   Rumours afloat all day.   One says five incendiary bombs dropped from German plane on village near Canterbury,
but as it further appears that they were dropped in the middle of
a wood and have not yet been discovered, feel this probably inaccurate.   Govt. cancels Bank Holiday on Monday, and B.B.C. says
staff must work, but as the printers are closing down anyway, it
is decided to run the Listener on a skeleton staff composed of its
two plumpest members, Miss Playle and the Editor.   Arrive home by
usual train and learn that wireless has just given news of Mr.
Church- Chamberlain's resignation and Mr. Churchill's assumption
of office as Prime Minister.

<u>Saturday, May 11, 1940</u>

Mother gets up on kitchen table to take down last night's blackout
and falls in getting down.   I leap out of bed on hearing her cry
out, which makes me so faint, I am the one who has to be revived.

I beseech her to have doctor to see if anything is broken, but
she steadfastly refuses. I shop, go to cowslip field and return
laden, and mow and roll lawn.

Germans dropping troops by parachute on to Holland.
100 of their planes brought down. Our troops advancing through
Holland and Belgium to meet Germans.

Cabinet changes announced: P.M., Winston Churchill;
Lord President of Council, Chamberlain; Lord Privy Seal, Attlee;
1st Lord of the Admiralty, A.V. Alexander; Secretary of State
for War, Anthony Eden; Secretary of State for Air, Archibald
Sinclair; Minister without Portfolio, Arthur Greenwood. It is
therefore a Coalition Govt. with members from all parties.

Sunday, May 12, 1940

Rise with frightful headache to hear news at 9, and feel more and
more as it proceeds that cannot bear this war; end by being sick
and retire to bed again, rising to bath and wash hair after parents
have gone to chapel. In afternoon have recovered, and walk from
Edge to Beacon Tump in beautiful sunshine.

Germans have crossed Albert Bridge into Belgium. Para-
chute troops are being dropped in various disguises - e.g. as
workmen or clergymen. Activity on Franco-German frontier. Sub-
marine "Seal" lost. More Cabinet changes: Lord Chancellor, Sir
John Simon; Chancellor of Exchequer, Sir Kingsley Wood; Home
Secretary, Anderson; Secretary of State for Colonies, Lord Lloyd;
Minister of Supply, Herbert Morrison; Minister of Information,
Duff Cooper (so what about Sir John Reith?)

Mother's ribs seem no worse. She still refuses to see
doctor. Is verydepressed at news that 400 more Civil Servants
are coming to Stroud, and looks for the billeting officer every
minute.

Monday, May 13, 1940

Bombing on large scale continuing in Holland and Belgium. All
male Germans and Austrians between ages of 16 and 60 who live on
East Coast of England, have been interned. We are warned that if
we see parachute troops we are to inform police. (N.B. Sight of
man in dog-collar descending from heaven with bible in one hand and
revolver in other, should be regarded with suspicion. Especially
if he is singing Rule Britannia with slightly foreign accent).

Beautiful day. In morning we go to garden near Painswick which is open to public. Nice Cotswold manor house which
has been taken over by some duchess with money, who has laid out
grounds in very pleasant informal way.

In afternoon to Stanley Park, and en route we pick up
Mrs. Franklin. She, Mother and I browse in beautiful gardens of
which we are almost sole occupants, while Daddy enjoys himself
with field glasses on side of Selsley Hill. We picnic at
Surprise Point and I am put on to train at Kemble, after we have
had to change wheel for puncture. Stand in corridor all the way
and talk to woman whose husband was killed in lastwar, and whose

baby died because of the nervous state of the mother. Now she
says she has another husband, of military age, and another little
girl: is she to go through it all again? Adds that almost worse
than the men being killed in France is the breakingup of homes,
where the wife has gone to the country with the children, and the
husband, with no ill intentions, has taken up with another woman,
while his wife, lonely in the country, has takenup with another
man. If peace came tomorrow, she says, their home would never
be the same again.

Tuesday, May 14, 1940

Another beautiful day. At printers till 8.30, with only sandwich
lunch. Rumour that Maginot Line has been broken causes great
gloom, but it is only Sedan, in the advance posts of the Maginot,
which has been evacuated by the French. Forces taking up positions in front of Brussels. Liége not fallen, as reported.
Main forces of the Dutch Army retire behind Holland's chief water-
line defence, width of which is 3 - 5 miles. Rotterdam threatened. Dutch Government arrives in London. More changes in British
Government. Sir John Reith to be Minister of Transport, Lord
Beaverbrook to be Minister of Aircraft Production.

Wednesday, May 15, 1940

Holland surrenders. Fighting still going on in Zeeland, but
otherwise country is being taken over by Germans. The High
Command says that in their falt,crowded country, civil evacuation
isimpossible, and to avoid further massacre they must give in. A
quarter of the Army and most of the Air Force has beendestroyed.
Miss Playle and Mr. Abraham very bitter against the Dutch for what
seems to have been their only course if they did not want to be
annihilated. Deep gloom everywhere all day. We have been 8
months at war and Hitler has taken four countries.
        In lunchtime to National Gallery, where Peter, whom I
see outside, directs me to seat labelled "Artistes Only". Bach,
2nd and 5th Brandenburgs. Very sane and comforting. At end of
concert, complete stranger asks me, do I know of a bassoon player.
I say: "Ann Joseph". "I've tried her - she can't do it". I
suggest: "Edward Elliot", and young man decides to try him: so
we part.
        In evening to Beavans, where are clarinet quintets to
which I listen and knit, rather depressed the while.

Thursday, May 16, 1940

R.A.F. makes biggest raid of war. Was all last night East of
Rhine bombing roads and other communications by which Germans are
getting reinforcements into Holland. Terrific battle going on
near Brussels. More warnings against possible parachute landings.
Owners of cars asked to make sure that they cannot be taken away

easily.   English warned to leave Italy, Italians warned to leave
Turkey, Americans warned to leave Europe!   (Human race warned to
leave the Earth).
      Miss Playle to supper.   Still glorious weather.

Friday, May 17, 1940

Sentry with fixed bayonet standing in entrance of Broadcasting
House when we arrive.   But wide-open window looking almost on to
street at back is unguarded.   Miss P. suspects traitors and spies
on every hand and talks of them incessantly, till at end of afternoon, feel can bear it no longer and dissolve into secret tears.
      R.A.F. has been bombing again.   There is a bulge in the
Maginot Line, which gets bigger and bigger: everyone thinks if we
can hold the Germans for the next few weeks, we shall win, but they
are sending half of their entire army into the battle, and the
question is, will the line break?
      To Hilary's for weekend.   She suspects she may be going
to have a baby: is so sick, has seen doctor, who has given her
medicine.   Seems a terrible time to start a baby, but she says if
she waits till the end of the war, she may not even have a husband

Saturday, May 18, 1940

The "bulge" bigger.   General Gamelin calls upon his men to conquer or die.   France says situation is grave but not catastrophic.
Germans have a new kind of heavy tank which is very effective.
R.A.F. have bombed oil stores and other military objectives at
Bremen and Hamburg.   Germans say we have wantonly attacked
civilians.   This is taken as preliminary to bombing over here.
      I shop, mow four lawns and cut edges of three.   Hilary
spends most of day in deck-chair in sun, with bad backache and cold.

Sunday, May 19, 1940

Leonard gets us breakfast in bed: then Mr. and Mrs. Evans call at
11 and have coffee.   H's cold slightly better.
      Battle of the Bulge still raging.   Winston Churchill
broadcasts, warning us to expect air bombardment, and it seems to
me saying that the whole of France may be overrun.   Assures us he
is certain of final victory.   Heartening, if serious: a good
leader for war-time.

Monday, May 20, 1940

General Weygand has succeeded General Gamelin as Commander-in-Chief
of the Allied Arm Forces.   The Bulge is widening.   America says
Russia is getting alarmed at fury of German attack, in case it
should turn East, and that if we can hold the line, Russia may come
in with the Allies.   Italy sending out anti-Ally propaganda and
expected to come in to war at any moment.
      In evening, to Beavans to discuss holiday.   Peter taking
course to turn himself into wireless telegraphist in Merchant Navy
(non-combatant duties), so can't come.

Tuesday, May 21, 1940

H.M.S. "Effingham" (light cruiser) sunk.   Arras and Amiens have
fallen to Germans.   I go to madrigals and afterwards get food in
Strand Corner House.   The orchestra still plays cheerfully.   It
is colder and is clouding up for first time for weeks, and I wonder
if Germans will take advantage of clouds to come and bomb us.
        Afterwards to Beavans, where family quartets are in pro-
gress and I am entire audience while John enjoys himself leading
Haydn No.43, and Duque plays second fiddle with great seriousness
and concentration, and Peter manages to grin and bite his bottom
lip at same time over the viola, and Pauline pulls agonised faces
over her cello.   Feel much more cheerful although news is so bad.

Wednesday, May 22, 1940

French Prime Minister makes speech saying unbelievable blunders
have been committed by Army - bridges not blown up, etc.   Weygand
says if we can hold Germans for a month, war is $\frac{3}{4}$ won (so how long
will it take us to win whole war?)   Rumour that General Gamelin
has shot himself.   Am afraid the bulge has burst.
        I anger Mr. Abraham by saying we ought not to fight
(must learn to hold my tongue), and he says England is full of
crawling lice like me and that's why we're in the state we are in
today.   In middle of argument I burst into tears, and he is sorry
and gives me lunch.   In spite of this, and general gloom, feel
much cheerfuller than of late.   Everyone very pessimistic, and
Miss P. works off her feelings by spy-hunting with great vigour.
        The British Government takes over everything - all
property, businesses, etc.   Firms like armament manufacturers to
work 7-day week till further notice.   This revolution - I cannot
decide whether it is Communist or Facist - has been carried out
in a few hours in the true British way, i.e. constitutionally by
Act of Parliament.   But if anyone had proposed such a thing in
peace-time, he would have been laughed to scorn.
        David to supper: he cheers us both first with sherry at
Sherrifs.

Thursday, May 23, 1940

Office enlivened by Miss Mearing, who tells of one of her father's
church workers who has asked Mr. Mearing to shoot her, if Hitler
should win war.   The Mearings have decided she ought to undertake
her own destruction.
        To Sacha Guitry film with John.   Before it we walk in
St. James's Park, and see Admiralty offices with barbed wire en-
tanglements around them, and - so a policeman tells me - a lot of
guns hidden. *A Conservative M.P. imprisoned under new Treason Act.*

Friday, May 24, 1940

Boulogne
~~Bordeaux~~ captured by Germans, who, we hope, will not by some "un-

leaders arrested.

beKievable blunder" be given tickets for Folkestone. Deep.
gloom descends on everyone. *Sir Oswald Mosley & other Fascist*
          To Stroud by 6.35, with Heimann, who is staying with
Mildred Humpidge.   Tell Mother news about Hilary and she is very
upset.

Saturday, May 25, 1940

News from France very obscure.   We are warned that nothing may be
known for some days.   Road from Minchinhampton to Cirencester is
closed at the Ragged Cot, where it runs beside the aerodrome.
Planes have been sabotaged there lately, and eight or more crashes
have happened in a week.   Also tale is current of two ladies who
were travelling on top of bus to Cheltenham and saw man making
notes as they passed Brockhurst munitions factory.   They informed
conductor, who phoned during one of the bus's halts, and detectives
met bus at Cheltenham, where man was found to have on him complete
plans of both Brockhurst and Quedgeley.
          Walk with Heimann on common in morn.   Buy rather heavy
second-hand bicycle for £2.

Sunday, May 26, 1940

Still very little news of fighting.   There has been an air-raid
in East Kent (yesterday there was one off East coast of Yorkshire).
Extent of damage not stated.   Fifteen French generals have been
deprived of their posts.   (Treachery?   or incompetence?)
          Sunday School Anniversary.   Preacher quotes from Psalms
~~"Be not afraid of evil tidings~~ "He shall not be afraid of evil
tidings: his heart is fixed, trusting in the Lord".   But if
people's hearts are not fixed, what must they do?   He does not
tell us.   This is day of National Prayer, and we are asked to
pray for victory, which should like to do, but feel cannot, since
though the Germans are bad, and I feel worse than us, to God we
must all look pretty black.   Last Sunday Daddy suddenly produced
the Old Testament and read from Deuteronomy:
     "Beware that thou forget not the Lord thy God, in not
  keeping his commandments, and his judgments, and his statutes,
  which I command thee this day: lest when thou hast eaten and
  art full, and hast built goodly houses, and dwelt therein; and
  when thy herds and thy flocks multiply, and thy silver and thy
  gold is multiplied, and all that thou hast is multiplied; then
  thy heart be lifted up, and thou forget the Lord thy God ...
  and thou say in thine heart, My power, and the might of mine
  hand hath gotten me this wealth ... And it shall be, if thou do
  at all forget the Lord thy God, and walk after other gods, and
  serve them, and worship them, I testify against you this day
  that ye shall surely perish.   As the nations which the Lord
  destroyeth before your face, so shall ye perish; because ye
  would not be obedient unto the voice of the Lord your God".
          Which he said meant the British Empire.

Monday, May 27, 1940

Not much news.   R.A.F. continues to do exploits, but Peter says
they can get no more volunteers for rear gunners (expectation of
of life of a rear gunner is six weeks).   Allied Armies are cut
off in France and may not be able to get supplies.
        To Beavans: talk holiday and play monopoly with John.

Tuesday, May 28, 1940

King Leopold of the Belgians, against the advice of his ministers,
surrenders.   This means B.E.F. in Belgium is in almost hopeless
plight and situation becomes increasingly black.   Evening Standard
has leader "King Quisling".   Rumour later that Belgian Army is
continuing to fight.   America waking up to danger to her of Nazi
victory.
        I go to madrigals, and try to forget quobbles of my
stomach, which always goes back on me in a crisis, in fa-la-las.
Afterwards walk along embankment (south of river) and look across
at Houses of Parliament, where lights are showing - not yet black-
out time - and Churchill may still be giving his statement on the
situation in Belgium.   The river is at full tide, and everything
looks peaceful enough except for barbed wire round L.C.C. headquarters and heaps of sandbags on Embankment.   Cross Westminster
Bridge and continue by river to Charing Cross, trying to make myself accept idea that reality is neither Good nor Bad: it just Is,
and the thing to do is to accept it willingly, since it has to be
accepted anyway.

Wednesday, May 29, 1940

B.E.F. trying to fight their way to the coast.   It is said that
they have only one day's food left.   British have captured Narvik,
which now seems very unimportant.   Sir Stafford Cripps on his way
to Moscow to try to make trade pact with Russia.

        Germans said to have planes which can carry tanks.
Terrible story told in talk broadcast to Empire of plight of refugees in Belgium, who are dying beside the road in thousands,
pressed on by Germans, who are using them as screen against the
enemy.
        Nice dinner with David at the Isobar, Hampstead.   I then
go to Beavans where we decide to cancel holiday (evening papers
have said workers in industry to have none), but instead arrange
weekend cycling in Berkshire.   We play scramble late and I stay
for night.

Thursday, May 30, 1940

The Russians say they won't deal with Sir Stafford Cripps but only
with an Ambassador, as any other country would.   So Cripps may be
made an ambassador.   B.E.F. still retreating to coast, but no one
knows how they can embark when they get there.

Several members of Dutch Government staying at Bedford
College, and with them a reporter for the paper which is the Dutch
equivalent of The Times.   He is very devout - crosses himself and
says a long grace before every meal.

Friday, May 31, 1940

Many more of B.E.F. getting away than expected.   But four destroyers sunk in the doing of it.

        By the grace of God only, since buses, ticket-queues and
the fact that my bicycle has to be fetched by lift from some secret
storehouse, all work against me, I catch 7.40 to Didcot with half-
minute to spare, and travel with John and Peter.   At Didcot we
meet Joyce, who has that second arrived by another train, and who
immediately mounts her bicycle and rides away into the evening with
Peter without a word, my one attempt at conversation - "What time
did you have to leave Bould?" being met with a curt "Does it matter?"
Get to Abingdon, which is full of soldiers, and stay night at Crown
and Thistle - 17th century, with courtyard full of wistaria,
garden full of roses, bar full of R.A.F. and picture of stagecoach
with four horses in gloomy atmosphere and title "All Right!", and
no supper because staff have gone home.

Saturday, June 1, 1940

Did not sleep for noise of aeroplanes - bombers start from aerodrome here.   Friendly soldier in market-square asks for our
identity cards as soon as we appear on bicycles.   Lorry of returning B.E.F. shrilly cheered by children, small crowd, and themselves.
Lunch in field near Eynsham.   Peter in rather a sulk, because he
wanted big meal at restaurant, not "one banana, one apple, one bun".
But he turns out a much more considerate companion than John -
pushes me up hills, and gets off and walks with me when they are
too steep, and purposely goes slow when I cannot keep up with the
others - none of which John makes any attempt to do, though he is
willing to perform running repairs on bicycles.
        Joyce finds lovely house to stay in, on outskirts of
Burford, with honeysuckle outside window and cool green garden.
Bous sleep in nearby house.   Very tired, and go to bed early after
listening to news: more B.E.F. coming across from France.   Our
trade negotiations with Italy broken down.

Sunday, June 2, 1940

My 33rd birthday.   Feels no different from 32, but the idea makes
me droop.   Peter presents me with pennyworth of aniseed balls in
recognition of the day.   Very warm and fine.   We go through
Burton-on-Water, the Slaughters and the Swells, to Stow-on-the-Wold,
where we have very good lunch.   There is not a sign-post left in

England, all having been removed in case parachute troops land.
(N.B. at Burford they were very jittery about parachutists, because
they are surrounded by aerodromes.)

After lying in field, we go through Moreton-in-the-Marsh
to Chipping Campden, where Peter and I take train for London - Joyce
and John having one day more. In train meet B.E.F. Sergeant who
came back last Wednesday. Lay for three hours in sand on Dunkirk
beach waiting for boat to take him off. They had to swim to small
rowing boat, which took them to fishing smack, in which they crossed
Channel to Dover, all the time being bombed. Dunkirk completely
devastated. B.E.F. in good spirits and most of them brought out
safely. "Honest, I don't know how we did it". Says the Germans
would never have got into Belgium if one bridge which the Belgians
had to blow up, and could easily have done so, had not been left
open. Germans "are like sheep. They come up, wave after wave,
and are mown down by machine-guns and they still come". They have
first-class equipment, incredible numbers, tremendous number of
planes, but their infantry is "just trash". And in order to prevent the British blowing up a bridge they had dynamited, they drove
a crowd of refugees on to it and stood behind them. Obviously
they have a higher regard for our decency than we have for theirs.
The Sergeant's chief comment on his adventures was: "Honest, I
couldn't 'elp laughing!"

Monday, June 3, 1940

Pity not to be on holiday on such a fine day.

One or two bombs on Ashdown forest. Paris bombed -
about 200 dead. 887 craft took part in evacuation of B.E.F. Of
222 naval vessels used, 6 destroyers and 24 minor boats lost.

Mussolini has evacuated barracks in Rome, so that the
city is an "open" town and not a military target. He is expected
to come into the war this week.

Tuesday, June 4, 1940

Very busy at printers. Nowadays almost everything has to be done
on Mondays and Tuesdays, or the paper is entirely out of date.

Churchill, in speech in House on evacuation of B.E.F.
from Belgium, says he expected 20,000-30,000 men might be re-
embarked. Actually 335,000 got away, and losses were about
30,000. Losses in material were enormous - nearly 1,000 guns and
all our transport, all armoured vehicles which were with our Army
in the North. What had happened to us in France and Belgium was
a colossal military disaster.

Narvik, which British had recaptured, mostly destroyed
by German bombers.

Italy put on war basis.

It is not true that General Gamelin has committed
suicide. Newspaper says he is in Paris - free, but deprived of
all office.

Wednesday, June 5

On way to dentist's, realise have brought wrong handbag, with
nothing in it.   Dismount from bus and take taxi, and borrow 2/6
from Mr. Course to pay for it.

Germans launch tremendous attack on Somme.   French
said to be holding the line.   We are warned, in wireless talk,
that when bombing starts here, or if we are invaded, not to crowd
on to roads and impede troop movements, but to stay put as long
as possible unless told to move by some responsible authority.

Children may be sent to Canada and Australia for safety.

Thursday, June 6, 1940

Bombs on many East Coast towns and villages.   They say only six
people injured and do not mention any killed.   Our bombers over
Germany, however, reported to have done great injury to oil depots.
Rather distrust these two pieces of news in conjunction with each
other.

Attack on Somme still very great.   A few German tanks
have penetrated, but again they say it is unimportant.   Distrust
this too.   These German tanks seem invincible.

Italy taking more war measures, and U.S.A. telling her
she will cut off all trade connections with Italy if Italy extends
war area.

Hilary rings up - has been home for two days and is
worried about mother, who seems ill and very nervy - was quite
knocked sideways by news of Belgium's surrender.

Buy sandals and immediately see pair exactly what I
wanted, so buy them too.   Feel very wicked after doing this.

Friday, June 7, 1940

French have to fall back a little on Somme.   More bombs on East
Coast.   I come to Stroud - 6.35 taken off, so have to travel by 6.30
and change at Swindon.

Saturday, June 8, 1940

Still very hot, and all the week have felt very tired.   Mow lawn
in evening.

French have been over Berlin, bombing - retaliation for
bombing of Paris.

Sunday, June 9, 1940

Fear Germans still advancing.   Archbishop asks us to have day of
thanksgiving for rescue of B.E.F., which followed day of prayer a
fortnight ago.   Rev.George McLeod, in broadcast sermon, reminds
us that two days after our prayers, Belgium surrendered, and we
must be prepared to thank God for that too.   Feel many people will
find this difficult to stomach.

<u>Monday, June 10, 1940</u>

A day of oppressive gloom, which looks as if a thunderstorm, or
the end of the world, is imminent. I feel it is a portent of
impending doom, and the doom makes itself known at 6 o'clock,
when the broadcast news announces that Italy has declared war on
the Allies. Mr. Duff Cooper, in the 9 o'clock news, tries to
prove that this is almost a help to us, and I cannot help remem-
bering the old Dutchman who at dinner said the B.B.C. told many
lies, and that there was something amiss with a people which had
to be buyed up with untruths. (He further called someone - I
think and hope the Italians - "hee-ay-nas".) The news also announces German advances in France, the sinking of four British
ships including an aircraft carrier in a naval engagement off
Norway, the withdrawal of British troops from Norway, the arrival
in England of the Norwegian King and Government, and the laying
down of their arms by the Norwegians. Although exploits by the
British and French Air Forces are described at length, cannot
help wishing a French advance could have been announced instead.
Roosevelt to speak at 12.15 a.m., but don't think I shall stay up
to hear him.

<u>Tuesday, June 11, 1940</u>

Mother's birthday. At printers till 6.20, when Editor gives Mr.
A. and me sherry. I proceed, half drunk, to Baker Street, where
I get a sandwich before going on for Madrigal concert at Swiss
Cottage. Find Hampstead Music School deserted. Puzzled: take
out announcement of concert and look at it, and find it was yes-
terday evening. Depressed, because coulde asily have gone.
Walk in Park instead, with three more Bedfordites.
        Roosevelt last night promised all material aid to Allies.
Question seems to be: will it be quick enough? André Maurois,
in broadcast, implores us to send aid to France immediately.
Italians now fighting with Germans.
        Princess Wilhelmina and her two children land in Nova
Scotia. Other English people, including some men at the B.B.C.,
are sending wives and children to Canada.

<u>Wednesday, June 12, 1940</u>

Egypt breaks off diplomatic relations with Italy. We have bombed
Libya and Italy has bombed Malta. Paris getting ready for siege.
        Get up with fearful headache and am sick - probably the
result of feeding on only two sandwiches yesterday. Lunch with
Joyce. We part rather miserably, wondering if we shall ever see
each other again, since today B.B.C. circulated memo. cancelling
all Saturday mornings after June 15, and extending hours of work
to 6.30 in evening. Feel exceedingly depressed as I walk home
through beautiful roses in Regent's Park. To film with three girls
from Bedford. One I like - secretary to Sir Richard Acland.

Thursday, June 13, 1940

Germans within fifteen miles of Paris, which French Government
left several days ago. Hitler said once he'd be there by June 15,
and he has horrible way of doing what he says. Germans have been
throwing a smoke screen over Paris and getting tanks across Seine
under its cover. British division cut off in Flanders. Germans
claim 30,000 prisoners: War Office says 6,000 - this apparently
happened at end of May but is only just announced because of vast
German claims to prisoners. The division tried to embark from
rocky coast in fog - suggested it ~~was aritifial one~~ artificial one
manufactured by Germans. Turkey breaks off commercial relations
with Italy. Reynaud appeals to Roosevelt, saying France is desperate
        Ring up Joyce at Bexley, because last evening between
11.45 and 12 had feeling she was in dire peril. If she was, she
has been delivered from it unbeknown to herself. But she is very
depressed and weeps into telephone. Feel depressed myself, and
completely useless. Reflect that have never done a thing to
justify having been born, and now am likely to be killed. We
haven't enough to do at office, since size of paper has been so
reduced. So during most of afternoon read Browning's "Ring and
the Book". Coming home through park, stand by fountain with
water lilies and for moment get feeling of something ageless and
enduring - earth and water, perhaps. Long to write a book, but
my mind is sterile, refusing to offer its children to destruction.

Friday, June 14, 1940

Germans enter Paris, which has been made an open town so that it
shall not be destroyed by bombs. Hitler orders victory-bells to
ring in Germany. So he's done it a day earlier than the promised
June 15. He promises London by August 15.
        Another large evacuation of schoolchildren from London,
but many parents keeping children with them, and Malcolm MacDonald
in broadcast admits that one place is not much safer than another.
To Stroud for my last Saturday.

Saturday, June 15, 1940

Allied Armies take up new positions south of Paris. Russia
uttering threats to Lithuania. Everyone hopes Russia will attack
Germany.
        Am very tired and do little else than top-and-tail goose-
berries, scrape carrots and potatoes, and lie on lawn in sun. In
evening it is cloudy and inclined to rain.

Sunday, June 16, 1940

Service full of foundations of the world being shaken, but we must not be dismayed. Wish they would not keep assuring us so vigorously in all the papers that the Allies will fight on whatever happens. Methinks they do protest too much.

Back to London. All names of stations on the line have been removed.

~~Saturd~~- Monday, June 17, 1940

David Roderick's third birthday.

Morning papers say French Government has resigned. Marshal Pétain has become Prime Minister instead of M. Reynaud. Pétain is 84. Then at 5 past one Mr. Thomas puts his head round door of office. He is very white. He says: "The French have laid down their arms. They've asked for terms". He repeats "They've asked for terms" as if he can scarcely believe it himself, and vanishes. Miss Playle feels in this hour of stress company of some kind she must have, and takes me off to lunch. She is convinced for some reason that should the Germans land in England, their first act would be to put her up against a wall and shoot her. "Of course, you'll be all right", she adds to me kindly. Cannot think why: unless she has been sending some of her famous memoranda to Hitler.

No one knows German terms. Evening news says very little. Churchill speaks for three or four minutes, merely saying the British Empire will fight on to the end. The evening is enlivened by the behaviour of two barrage balloons: one blows up and vanishes in smoke; the other is floundering about the sky like a wounded whale. I trust high wind is responsible and not sabotage. We have enough to put up with at present without that.

Suppose we may expect air raids pretty soon, when Hitler sees we have no intention of giving in.

Tuesday, June 18, 1940

Frightfully busy day at printers is crowned with news that Prime Minister may broadcast in 9 o'clock news: his secretary says he has no script, speech is not written, and he can give us no idea of length, but we stand by, and Editor seems to feel the occasion is one for a binge. So he invites Mr. Abraham and wife and me, and brings his own wife, and we have supper at the Escargot in Greek Street. Afterwards we all listen to Churchill on a set at Speaights. He speaks for thirty-one minutes - repeating very largely what he said in the House this afternoon: mostly to effect that we shall not give in. I go to Broadcasting House and collect script, which night stenographers are typing. Return to printers,

where the two wives are yawning their heads off.   At midnight
they go, accompanied by Mr. Abraham who has very bad cold.   Mr.
Thomas and I remain till 3.15, pulling the paper to bits to get
in 3,500 words.   In an interval we go out to Fleet Street and
I am edified by sight of my Editor sitting on a high stool in a
milk-bar drinking orange-juice (iced).   We cross the road and
drop in on the London office of the Manchester Guardian and see
James Bone (London Editor) and Evelyn Montague and wife.   E.M.
just back from France.   Says the French are very bitter against
us - think we didn't do all we could have.   Mr. Thomas says:
"What news?", and James Bone remarks placidly: "Well, just now
they're over Essex".
          Mr. T. remarks as we walk back to Speaight's, that he
supposes Hitler has caused more suffering than any other human
being who ever lived - except possible Jesus Christ.   I say:
well, he didn't do it in his lifetime.   No, admits Mr. T., it
was really the Church afterwards.   I add: And I don't suppose
Hitler will do it after he is dead.
          Arrive home in taxi at 4 o'clock, and walk through
grounds of Bedford College in eerie light, half full moon, half
approaching dawn - very beautiful.

Wednesday, June 19, 1940

I take afternoon off, in lieu of last night, and go to Hilary's
after lunch.   Last night 100 German planes were over the east
coast.   About 16 people killed and some injured.   Eight smallish
bombs fall in a pea-field a mile or so from Shirley, but on the
other side of a hill so that H. heard no great noise, only a kind
of whistle and something fell.   Eight German planes brought down.

Thursday, June 20, 1940

More raids on S. and S.E. coast this morning.   (Learn - though
it is not in papers - that 8 of the people killed yesterday were
at Cambridge.)   R.A.F. over Germany.
          Plans to send English children to the Dominions for
safety.   Mr. Thomas's two boys will go.
          Experts say Europe will be facing famine by next Spring,
and that in Germany conditions are comparable with those in 1918.
          Secret Session of Parliament, in which Mr. Lloyd George
is said to be taking a large part.
          French said still to be fighting, but Germans have pene-
trated to Brittany and the South and the news is obscure.
          Weather continues very fine and warm: there must be
danger of drought, but no one allowed to mention such a thing.
          B.B.C. passes now to have photographs of bearer on back.

Friday, June 21, 1940

Germans present terms to France: not yet made known.

Saturday, June 22, 1940

Armistice signed between France and Germany.   No conditions yet
known.
            After lunch, to Crowborough for weekend.   Brooklands
in ferment, trying to arrange for evacuation of school to Canada.
Government has no scheme at present for schools as such, but
only for individuals.   Surely better, though, to send children
in groups to which they are accustomed, than alone to strange
families in land where they know no one?
            Nurse's father was on duty as parashot night German plane
dropped bomb on Ashdown Forest.   There was trouble afterwards because no one had reported presence of aircraft.   He said frankly
that he'd seen an aeroplane and seen it drop 'coloured lights', but
apparently had not thought it his duty to do anything about it!

Sunday, June 23, 1940

Fighting still to continue in France until six hours after Armistice
has also been signed with Italy, where French delegates now are conferring.   By terms of Armistice, France is to be occupied on West
and North coasts, and north of line from Geneva to bottom south-west
corner (about four-fifths, I should think), France to pay for occupation.   All resources, arms, navy, etc., to be at disposal of
Germany to continue war against us, and France to facilitate communication between Italy and Germany.   Germany prisoners to be
freed, but French ones to be kept till peace signed.   If any part
of conditions is not fulfilled, Armistice comes to an end.   The
Bordeaux Governemtment has signed this, in spite of agreement with
British Govt. not to make separate peace.   One can only suspect
treachery.   It is impossible otherwise to explain this complete
capitulation on part of a first-class power such as France.
            But many parts of French Empire - Indo-China, Tunis,
Syria, Morocco, Jibuti, Sénégal, the Cameroons, etc., want to continue the fight, and General De Gaulle has invited all Frenchmen
who can, and who wish to remain free, to follow him and fight on.
Churchill reiterates determination of British Empire to continue .
            While these world-shattering events are taking place,
Phyllida and I go to morning service (which is very crowded and at
which we are assured that we have to go through the Furnace of
Affliction but are bidden be cheerful nevertheless); and after
lunch go for glorious walk through forest; tea at village; walk
back another way.   I decide not to return to town till tomorrow,
and sit on balcony in warmth of June evening, reading Helen
Waddell's "Peter Abelard", and feeldrenched in loveliness, and in
sadness that everything isn't as lovely as it looks.
            Phyllida is a kind of saint: one of the excellent in
whom is all my delight.

24
Monday, June 23, 1940

Rumours about Italy's demands from France: it is said she wants
all French territory which Germany has not taken, and most of
French Empire as well.   Have not heard truth of this, because in
evening David brings back two books and we go for walk round park,
so miss news.   He has registered as a Conscientious Objector, but
is willing to do R.A.M.C. work, and now has to break the news of
his decision to the Punch people.   Park looking glorious - all
overblown roses and beds of incredibly tall and blue delphiniums.
        Came back this morning early with "Peter Abelard" to
finish (have done so, and enjoyed it tremendously.   David says
Joyce regards it as almost "written in bed", but there's a lot more
to it than that), and tremen great sheaf of roses - not sheaf,
bundle _ which smell much sweeter than those in the park, and which
I reluctantly have to leave up at Listener office while I go down
to printers.

        Will type here a poem, which was conceived on May 4, as
I walked back from cowslip field, and came to birth about a fortnight later.   Afraid I shall forget it altogether if it doesn't
get recorded:-

                Have you not seen, saith the Lord,
                The trees put forth their green
                    Where lately stood
                    The starkest wood?
                How flowers abound
                For which I broke the ice-locked ground?
                    Look if these things be good.
                Have you not seen, my children, saith the Lord?

                Have you not heard, saith the Lord,
                The spring-returning bird
                   Filling with praise
                   Earth's silences?
                And young things cry
                Close to their mother where they lie?
                   Hark down my woodland ways.
                Have you not heard, my children, saith the Lord?

                Have you not known, saith the Lord,
                My spirit has been sown
                   In joyless hour,
                   And it shall flower
                Among your greed,
                Till peace and love come of that seed?
                   Then understand my power.
                Have you not known, my children, saith the Lord?

Am desolate to discover that from now onwards, the nights will
be longer.

Tuesday, June 25, 1940

At 1 a.m. awake to hear air-raid sirens. Have promised to take
to shelter one of the babies from the crêche, so leap from bed
and run length of building to their nursery, where I snatch up a
sleepy three-year-old and bear out of doors to building where air-
raid shelter is.   Discover he has tape round ankle saying he is
James Coote.   There are 17 children, all under 5, and they behave
beautifully.   Tea and biscuits are served, and passed round by
our resident M.P.   Men watch from roof, in case of incendiary
bombs, but report no plane to be seen, and only sound is roaring
of lions at zoo.   All Clear does not sound till 4 p.m., when we
go sleepily to our beds.
          Apparently there were raids in many parts of England,
including south-west.   In one town (probably Bristol) five killed.
          Very serious speech by Churchill in House, in which he
said: "The safety of Great Britain and the British Empire is
powerfully, though not decisively, affected by what happens to the
French Fleet".   I have not been at all convinced by the reiterat-
ed statements of politicians lately that whatever happens we shall
fight on, and though this speech repeats this assertion, it seems
to me to hint that if the French Fleet is not with us, we may make
terms with Hitler.
          Japan invades French Indo-China.
          Hard day at printers: work right through lunch-hour and
till 7.30.   Very tired.

Wednesday, June 26, 1940

Hilary has letter from Mother saying they had warning on Monday
night: and Molly Evans' Mother rings up from Painswick to say
they had one also last night, but no bombs.   Seven Nazi planes
brought down in England.   We had quiet night.
          Terms of Italian Armistice now made known.   Italy not
to have remains of France, but only part she herself has occupied.
All French colonies and Mediterranean bases to be disarmed. Fleet
to be handed over.
          In lunch-hour to Bach recital at National Gallery.
Hely-Hutchinson (piano), Alfred Cave (violin).   Audiences have
dropped considerably lately, I expect owing to war news.   Whenever there is another crisis, audiences become sparse, and when
people get used to the bad news they pick up again.

Thursday, June 27, 1940

Russia issues ultimatum to Rumania, demanding Bessarabia. Rumania
asks for discussions.
          Raids on north and north-east of England.   Not much
damage done, we are told.
          A small paragraph in paper denies that Sir Samuel Hoare,

who is in Madrid, is doing anything to negotiate a peace.   But
Leonard says (I go to H's to sleep, while he is on parashot duty)
his boss, asking loan from bank to extend works (they are doing
Government contracts) was told by Loans Expert at bank that it was
not expected the war would be long - they expected a negotiated
peace.
        Henry Ford says he won't make aeroplane engines for
Britain: he has very Isolationist and Pacifist views, which may
be the reason.

Friday, June 28, 1940

Rumania gives in to Russian demands.
        Home by 6.30, with Molly Evans (having Sat. in lieu of
overtime worked).   Find at Stroud they have had three warnings
this week, Monday, Tuesday and Wednesday.   Daddy's morning greet-
ing with Mother's cup of tea is now always
               "Through sleep and darkness safely brought,
               Restored to life and power and thought".
I have persuaded them not to sit in car in shed for shelter, but
to go in passage leading to kitchen, which has two walls on each
side.   One old man in Stroud tells Daddy he won't get out of bed
- "Bed's the right place to die in, isn't it?" and adds "And if a
bomb hits me I shall wake up in heaven and wonder how I got there".
        No letter from Roy for about three weeks, because Empire
air mails have been stopped.

Saturday, June 29, 1940

Miss Mearing told me yesterday her father (vicar) has been issued
with "Hints for Sermons" by the Ministry of Information.   Feel
if they are going to interfere in our spiritual instruction they
are as bad as the Nazis.   I know also that they have told the
newspapers not to give any prominence to news of air-raids.
Hear at Stroud that a bomb aimed at Temple Meads station, Bristol,
hit the station hotel and went through four floors without exploding.   Raids on Jersey and Guernsey last night, though they have
been demilitarised.   Probably intention to destroy food crops.
Many people killed.   German plane brought down near Bristol.
        Italian destroyer and two submarines sunk.   Marshal
Balbo, Italian air-chief, killed.
        I spend morning and some of evening painting colourless
varnish on to windows: supposed to stop their splintering.
Mother won't let me do French window, front windows, or her bedroom windows because it makes glass look a bit smeary, as if it
has rain on it.   So after air-raid, tell her she will have to
live in kitchen and back bedrooms.

Sunday, June 30, 1940

Very warm.   Hay is down in Rodborough fields.   The apples, which promised good crop, are dropping off through lack of rain.

In afternoon we essay to go to Beacon Tump on our petrol ration, but in middle of hill car stops as if all brakes have been applied. Fortunately we are going slowly or would have been thrown through windscreen. Friendly militiaman manages to start in reverse for us, but car makes strange noises, so we go on common instead.

Back to London with Molly Evans, who has heard that plague has broken out on the Continent because of the dead bodies lying in this hot sun - although Germans burn all they can as they go.

Garrulous old countryman in train says this is a War of Destiny, and adds that we shall be saved by Divine Intervention - not much Divine Intervention, because we don't deserve much, but just a little, which we deserve because we don't kill women and children.

Monday, ~~June~~ July 1, 1940

Still very hot and fine. Russia appears to be taking all the rest of Rumania - is landing tanks by aeroplane. Wonder what effect this will have on Germany.

Large area round coast to be militarised zone, prepared against invader. Rumour has it that invasion is to begin tonight or tomorrow.

Meet Kathleen Shuttleworth in Holborn, and her fiancé. They are to be married in a few weeks, and are going to China as missionaries, a prospect which they seem to view not only with equanimity but with pleasure. She says Mr. Hasler has been very ill.

(Go downstairs at this point to hear 9 o'clock news. It is slipped in casually in the middle that the Germans have occupied the Channel Islands, with which communication is now cut off. Apparently there was a rumour in Worcestershire that parachute troops had landed, but this is officially denied.)

Tuesday, July 2, 1940

Margarine and cooking fat manufacturers to pool their resources. Margarine to be in two qualities, 9d. and 5d. a lb.

Rumania has appealed to Germany for protection, and has renounced the guarantee of her frontiers given by Britain. No one knows yet whether Germany and Russia have agreed to partition Rumania between them as they did Poland, or whether each is trying to prevent the other getting too much territory.

Four Italian submarines sunk.

Letter from Joyce, who says bomb fell 1 mile from them in middle of village street at Westcote, at 2.15 a.m. last Wed. No warning, but though houses damaged, no one hurt.

Row on lake for ½ hour before dinner. No one to steer, so head turned backwards most of time. After dinner to film.

Wednesday, July 3, 1940

Paragraph from midday "Evening Standard", which was omitted from later editions:-

"Non-violence instead of war for the adjustment of relations between nations is urged by Mr. Gandhi in an appeal which he has addressed 'to every Briton wherever he may be'.

'I do not want Britain to be defeated, nor do I want her to be victorious in the trial of brute strength', Mr. Gandhi continues. 'British muscular bravery is an established fact'.

Asking Britain to fight with non-violent arms, Mr. Gandhi says: 'Let Hitler and Mussolini take possession of your beautiful island, your homes, and allow yourselves to be slaughtered, but refuse to owe allegiance to them'.

'I have been a lifelong and wholly disinterested friend of the British people', Mr. Gandhi concludes. 'Whatever happens, my love for Britain will not diminish. This appeal is prompted by that love'.

Mr. Gandhi revealed in his statement that he had informed the Viceroy that his services were at the disposal of the British Government should they consider them of any practical use in advancing the object of his appeal".

This paragraph makes Miss P. nearly foam with rage. And I am afraid if the British people laid down their arms it would be because they were afraid, and not for high and saintly motives such as Gandhi's.

Thursday, July 4, 1940

British liner, "Arandorra Star", sunk by U-boat, which does not realise that it is full of Germans and Italians being taken to Canada to be interned. Several hundred of them drowned, and our papers make great story of their bad behaviour - pushing to get into boats, etc. Am glad to see that "News-Chronicle" says also that one young German behaved like a hero and tried to rally the people to help themselves.

Germany has told Rumania she can offer her no military assistance.

Letter from Mother. They had German planes over on Monday night but no bombing. A letter has come from Roy referring to death of Gwynn Williams. Obviously one has gone astray. This one written before Italy came into war.

Lunch with Holy Aunt N.

Friday, July 5, 1940

"French Fleet No Longer in Being" (headline in News-Chronicle).
We have taken over two battleships, two cruisers, some submarines,
eight destroyers, and 200 smaller craft, which were in British
ports: have taken in charge also ships at Alexandria, including
a battleship, four cruisers, and a number of smaller ships: and
have fought with the ships at Oran which would not submit, so
that two capital ships have been set on fire, one sunk, and
another badly damaged, and a destroyer and seaplane-carrier have
also been sunk or burnt.
        Pro-Nazi Government has taken over power in Rumania.

Saturday, July 6, 1940

"Dunkerque", biggest French ship, bombed again by British, in case
it wasn't put properly out of action before. Churchill makes
speech in House describing action of Fleet against French and de-
ploring that we should have had to turn thus upon our one-time
friends, but we couldn't let ships be used against us by Germany.
He finishes in tears.
        To Hilary's after lunch. One day this week Leonard
was called out to deal with alleged parachutists, but whether they
were fictitious or not no one seems to know, least of all the
parashots - or perhaps they are pledged to secrecy.
        Moll, Margaret, and their 3-year-old Colin to tea - a
very pleasant small boy, who when we ask him to come again, says
agreeably "All right".

Sunday, July 7, 1940

Four German ships sunk by submarine off coast of Norway - where
no doubt they were lying in readiness for attack on England.
        Invasion of Hilary's in-laws to tea. I wash up vigor-
ously and mow lawns.

Monday, July 8, 1940

Seven German planes brought down over England last night, and six
during day.
        Tea is to be rationed - 2 oz. per week each. Also
margarine and cooking fats. Afraid rationing of tea and margarine will hit poorer people much more than the better-off.
        Charges here (Bedford College) have been raised by 10
per cent. All food very much dearer.
        Book just delivered which I have got for Hilary's birth-
day tomorrow: "On Being a Mother", which, together with the
"Mothercraft Manual", I boldly ordered in my own maiden name from
the Times Book Club.

Tuesday, July 9, 1940

"Richelieu", French battleship, put out of action by British Navy.
Reports that Reynaud has been assassinated, but no confirmation of
this.   He was recently in a motor-accident which most people
thought was an attempt at murder.   Hilary's birthday.

Wednesday, July 10, 1940

Duke of Windsor to be Governor of the Bahamas: America hopes for
brilliant social season centred round him and Duchess!
          Coast of Ireland mined.
          Lot of children of well-to-do parents have now arrived
in Canada and U.S. (Mr. Thomas's boys got there on Sat.): but the
Government now announces that the general evacuation of children
abroad will have to be drastically curtailed, because of the difficulties of sparing vessels for actual transport and for convoy.
This means, as usual, safety only for the rich, who, now their own
children are away, will not consider the scheme of such immense
importance.
          Eight German planes down in raids over Britain.
          Housewives asked to give up any aluminium vessels they
have, to help in manufacture of aircraft: Hitler's possession of
France means we have not the necessary raw materials for making
aluminium.
          Decide to take next week as holiday in cottage with Joyce.
          In evening find myself unexpectedly at party given by Dr.
Greaves, who used to be Lecturer in History at Bedford College and
is now in the Treasury but living in the residence.   Young man
called Bell there too - also living at Bedford - who came down
from Cambridge about two years ago, where he was at John's and knew
Roy.

Thursday, June 11, 1940

Letter from Mother.   They heard two bombs last Monday: aimed
probably at Quedgeley, but fell in middle of road.
          In lunchtime to National Gallery: Stratton String Quartet
(Haydn G major), and, with Moiseiwitsch, Schumann Quintet in E flat.
Both lovely.   Find myself sitting immediately behind Mr. Bell of
last night's party.
          Questions in House, particularly from Eleanor Rathbone,
on aliens over here, who are all being bundled into concentration
camps whether they are friendly to Britain or not.   Hear from Tina
Bruce in evening that some of the methods used are not much better
than those we deplore in the Nazis - people taken off in middle of
night without a chance to say goodbye to their wives, who are then
unable to get any news of their whereabouts.   Feel the whole thing
must be a kind of disease which has been attacking Europe and has
now crossed the Channel.   Lord have mercy upon us.

Paragraph from to-day's "News-Chronicle", reporting discussion in the House of Lords:-
"Viscount Elibank said that the Communist Party caused the collapse of the French military undertaking.
Lord Strabolgi: 'The surrender was made by Marshal Pétain and General Weygand, both Catholic Royalists; Laval, who has belonged to every Party in turn and is certainly not a Communist; Marquet, a renegade Socialist; and Baudouin, an international financier and friend of Italian bankers. Those are the people who sullied France's fair name'.
Viscount Elibank said those persons, when they found the extent of Communism in the State, went over to the Fascist side to save from the Communists what property they still possessed".

It is significant that The Times, in reporting the same discussion, omits Viscount Elibank's naive confession that the rich would rather give in to Hitler than risk losing their wealth in what might prove to be a Communist State.

Friday, July 11, 1940 (sorry, 12th)

Twenty-three aeroplanes (German) brought down round Britain yesterday. Miss Gladwin (B.B.C.), who was going for holiday to Looe, Cornwall, was last night rung up by proprietor of hotel to say that they were having raids down there daily.
Hear from Hilary that Phyllida spent yesterday with her, after adventurous journey. She had been reading detective story, and got into first train which came in. Discovered after a while that she was only passenger on it, and guard looked at her with deep suspicion and stopped train specially for her to get out at Three Bridges. Wonder she was not arrested.
Am told that unless Hitler invades England tonight, he has missed favourable tide, and will have to wait another month.
Take bicycle to Paddington in preparation for departure tomorrow.

Saturday, July 12, 1940 (no, 13th)

To Bould by 9.45 a.m., taking, besides sugar and butter rations for week, 3 lbs. tomatoes, and 2 lbs. cherries, in reply to J's appeal to bring 'all food I can lay hands on'. She meets me at station, and we have such a lot of conversation to make up, spend most of day talking both at same time on different subjects.
Go into woods to pick wild raspberries, but flies so thich we are driven into open. Meet Miss Bailey leading bull by nose; she says Joyce will have boy, and we feel she knows all about birth and is right.
J. says when bomb exploded at Westcote, a sentry supposed to be on guard at Kingham wakened up with a start and let off his rifle into the air, to everyone's surprise.
Rain in evening.

Sunday, July 14, 1940

Slept last night in J. and D.'s large, most married and voluptious
looking bed.   Feel it an outrage upon it for a thin virgin like
myself to lie alone in the middle and be cold.   Failing husband,
must get another blanket tonight.

Day is hot and cloudy alternately.   In afternoon cycle
to Westcote to see place where bomb dropped.   Back through Icombe,
where pause in churchyard to smell roses.   Vicar, who happens to
pass, asks if we'd like to go in.   Church is kept locked now in
case invaders get in and see where they are from brasses, etc., on
walls.   He looks like One of Old School, but does not blench at
my slacks, almost buttonless blouse, and J's stockingless legs.
She says "We haven't any hats", and he says "I am sure if you wear
reverence on your heads, no one will mind".   We like this so much,
decide to go tohis Evensong at six, so pedal home furiously, have
extremely hurried meal, make ourselves more respectable (J puts on
bandeau in which she cleans grate, 'the all-purposes headwear,
Modom'; and I wear floppy linen hat 12 years old), and return to
service, which contains nice prayer of thanksgiving for rain.

(In church during afternoon, we find book with list of
services.   Several dates say 'Prayer-fe 'Intercession for War',
and in the column called 'Remarks', one date has to confess to
Leopold's surrender, and another to the capitulation of France.
We hope the nice vicar is able to see answers to prayer even in
these untoward occurrences.)

On way home, meet extraordinary creature wearing feather
boa, best Sunday dress, wide straw hat, mounted upon immense tricycle looking as if made of iron.   She wears expression of fierce
determination, and no wonder.

In evening I am instructed in use of Primus stove.   J.
says the only thing to remember is: Who is to be master?

Monday, July 15, 1940

Letter from David hints that it is our duty not to go to Stroud
because cottage may be invaded and captured in our absence, which
upsets Joyce.   She weeps into her morning coffee, which we are
having in garden.   An hour later we have telegram saying he is
staying on at Reading for present and will phone at three.   He
does so - J. having to break into farm in absence at market of Mr.
and Mrs. Bull, while phone rings and rings, _too_ filmlike , and is
found by baker half in and half out in undignified and revealing
position.   Baby has not yet arrived but is on way.

I meanwhile have gone to Clapton-on-the-Hill, to get
strawberries from Strawberry Jim.   Start at 11.15, and it takes
till 1.15 toget there, and then find no strawberries left.   Lunch
on potato crisps bought at village shop and go home via. Burford,
where I buy bananas and apples.   Apples are 8d. or 9d. a lb.
Nice ride.   A little rain in the wind.   Arrive back at 4 p.m.:

two dogs here with Mrs. Monteith, who is assuring J. that I am
probablystill alive.   During journey I asked way of innumerable
people, none of whom, even when theywere soldiers, asked to see
my identity card, as they ought to have.

Tuesday, July 16, 1940

This place full of names like Happy Families: Mr. Bull the Farmer,
Mr. Gosling the Farmer's Man, Mrs. Lovegrove the Lavender-Grower.
        At 12.15, telegram announces arrival of Roger Green, 7lbs
6 ob.   All well.   We are very glad.
        See Mr. Bull's paper, which says submarine "Shark" lost.
Britain has rejected an ultimatum from Japan, I believe about trade
with China.   Italy's avowed intention is to keep our Fleet merry
in the Mediterranean while Hitler invades us.

Wednesday, July 17, 1940

Had intended to cycle to Stroud, but very high wind from south-west,
combined with expectation of visit from grocer, decides us to stay.
Ring up Daddy from P.O. at Bledington; on way meet 400 or 500
soldiers in groups of 50, who make osculatory noises to me as I
cycle past.   Every village now has post with printed notice inviting people to bring their scrap iron for war materials, and Bledington's heap is now quite a good size, though on Sunday there was nothing when we passed.   Villages also have barricades of posts and
barbed wire which are put across principal roads at nightfall and
guarded.

Thursday, July 18, 1940

To Stroud in high wind, but no rain except at lunch-time when we
are near convenient barn and eat reclining on warm straw.
        Through Chedworth and Daglingworth: at Park Corner, a
woman at cottage gives us tea and cake and we surreptitiously leave
behind 2/- because she is poor - her husband is shepherd.
        Cowcombe Hill and London Road, because way beside aero-
drome is closed from White Horse to Ragged Cot.   Try to take J.
over railway, but cannot lift bicycles over gate.   We push up
frightful pitch in Butterrow Hill, trying to take short cut.
Arrive home and find notice that two portions of duck, etc., are
in pantry, sowe warm them up and are eating hungrily when parents
arrive back from Beacon Tump.

Friday, July 19, 1940

Hitler makes speech in Reichstag saying this is his final warning
to everyone.   There is no reason for war to continue (of course
not, now he has got everything he wanted), and if it does it means
annihilation for Germany or Britain, and though Mr. Churchill thinks

it will be Germany, he knows it will be Britain.   (Mrs. Franklin's
comment: "No one takes any notice of what that old devil says".)
          Australian ship has sunk Italian fast cruiser.   There
is fighting in East Africa.
          It rains.   I mow only half lawn, and J. and I go to
film: Marx Brothers in "The Circus".   I have no glasses, and between short sight, arrival after film has started, and usual incom-
prehensibility of any Marx Bros. film, don't know where I am.   Besides, my mind is full of gypsy, who has come to back door at end
of morning.   Old Mother Lee.   Very queenly and tall, and by regal
manner and acute business sense, manages to remove 7/- altogether
from J., Mother and me, for some "lucky elephants": also gets pot
of tea and bread-and-butter (plenty of sugar, tea and butter, tho'
all are rationed), not to mention my bridesmaid's frock, which I
have only worn once, though it is true am unlikely ever to wear it
again.   In return she tells us our fortunes - not that any such
thing is mentioned, it is all worked in with the buying and selling.
J. is to marry One she Already Knows and have one son: is to make
a change in two months' time.   Mother to live to be 97, will not
end her days at Bryans (which is a good house and a happy house and
no bomb willever fall on it), and will see her son again.   Her
'old man' is one of the best and thinks the world of her.   She is
worried about one particular person.   This leads us to ask about
Hilary, and we receive information that she will have a son, and 6
years afterwards a daughter.   As for me, I am to be a Fine Lady,
rich and happy, to marry twice, once a widower and once a "single
gentleman", have no children, and to go abroad, where I shall end
my days: and "the sixteenth to the next month" I shall have a
change for the better.   Does she mean August 16?
          She desires greatly to relieve me of my old red jumper,
but though it is full of holes I ask humbly if I may not keep it,
and she regally grants my request.   What we give her we have to
assure her is "with a good heart", and I couldn't have done that
for the jumper.   She says the world is very wicked just now.
"There was a lot of wickedness yesterday" - bombing she means, I
gather in South Wales where her son is.
          Advice to me: Look up, not down: keep a gay heart and
a still tongue.

Saturday, July 20

Mother says in night voice said to her clearly: "Mr. Chamberlain
has resigned from the Government".   But nothing in this morning's
paper confirms this news.
          Back to Bould.   Strong wind with us all the way, so
journey very easy.   Butterrow, Brimscombe Hill, canal tow-path,
Frampton Mansell, Sapperton, and so on to main Cirencester Road.
Lunch behind haystack on way to Bibury when we have our only rain
of day; otherwise weather sunny with white clouds.   Tea beside
river at Bibury: afterwards through Coln St. Aldwyn and Westwell
(where we sit beside round pond with white ducks on it) to Burford.

Shopping, and then dinner at Highway Hotel. On to Bould through beautiful evening light. Postman has left message that all our letters are at Kingham P.O., so I cycle off and fetch them, and we have three from Joy and one from David, which we read with much interest. They are getting quite fond of Roger, in spite of his not being Sally.

Sunday, July 21, 1940

Back to London, reluctantly, but feel very well and as if I have been away a month.

Monday, July 22, 1940

Latvia, Esthonia and Lithuania ask Russia kindly to take them, and Russia does. Destroyer sunk. Several enemy planes down.
        Mr. Abraham assures me he got through in record time last week, with no one to play chess. Admits later to having missed me. Miss P. now on holiday. Halifax makes speech at 9, and I fetch bicycle from Paddington, cycle to Broadcasting House for manuscript and take it to printers to be our first article. On way home, every door and window is blaring forth this speech, the rehearsed copy of which I have just read. At 10.15, Mr. Thomas rings up to say it is not good enough for first article as intended, so must countermand order to printer at 8 a.m. tomorrow and get them to set it in 10 pt. only.
        Find eggs in London almost unobtainable: at Bould one just walked across field and asked Mrs. Bull for any number one wanted.

Tuesday, July 23, 1940

New emergency budget (Sir Kingsley Wood's first) raises income tax to 8/6 in the £, and puts more duty still on wines, tobacco and entertainment.
        Find to my immense chagrin that at least 4 pairs of stockings, probably more, and three of them new and expensive, have disappeared from my drawer, together with a new pair of green knickers. On reporting this, find other people have also had things stolen.

Wednesday, July 24, 1940

Rainy. Discover when I try to change wet coat and skirt, that woollen frock has disappeared; also my best blue petticoat and knickers. Very depressed at these losses, since prices are now so high.
        Hilary has bought flea-y, dirty and endearing puppy for 7/- in Old Kent Road.

Thursday, July 25, 1940

Turkey makes trade agreement with Germany.   Hitler has summoned
representatives of the Balkan States to confer with him in Berlin.
Germans sink French ship sailing from England to France with French
people who wish to be repatriated.   The boat was showing neutral
colours and ought not to have been torpedoed.

Friday, July 26, 1940

Hitler getting oil from Rumania.   British oil wells in Rumania
seized.

Saturday, July 27, 1940

To Hilary's after lunch.   Terrific thunderstorm when I am at
Victoria.   Leonard has given up L.D.V. duty, which was to be every
third night, because he usually works late and at weekends as well,
on Government orders.   (War Office has been giving him a lot of
extra work by supplying blueprints for one order numbered in one
way, and for another numbered on quite a different system.   He has
spent hours correlating the two.

Sunday, July 28, 1940

Billy Walters to tea.   She has a scholarship from Oxford to America
and is going this week.   Was at passport office, where were hundreds of refugees who had been waiting months for visas to go to
U.S.A.   She says they were being treated very discourteously, but
that the American people treated them better than the English ones.
When they knew she was British they treated her more politely.

Monday, July 29, 1940

Very busy in Mr. Abraham's absence.   Hilary has letter from Mother
saying German plane was brought down at Oakridge.   In evening go
to "Me and My Girl" with Tina Bruce.   Very light and entertaining.
        R.A.F. have brought down large number of German planes in
raids on this country.

Tuesday, July 30, 1940

Come down Oxford Street in bus, and notice large number of shop
premises To Let - not the big, established businesses, but small
dress shops, a home-made sweet shop, and some others.
        Hear August 16 is date when Council will decide whether
or not Bedford College people are to return to London.   If they do
return, shall have to make change.   The Gypsy warned me?

Wednesday, July 31, 1940

Invasion of Britain said to be imminent.   Neutral sources say
Germans are massing large numbers of troops on French coast.
          I buy blanket for Hilary's baby - Heal's, and it cost
19/6, but is guaranteed for 10 years.   At night to Beavans.   Had
p.c. for John last week, inviting me for Friday, Saturday, Sunday,
Tuesday, or Wednesday.   Was to have been Fun and Games, but turns
out to be trios, Edric being there and playing piano.   He invites
me to go back to Flask Walk to live in autumn, if I like taking a
friend with me.   Arthur back from Cardiff, where for three weeks
of his stay they had air-raids: they used to go to upper part of
house to watch from windows.   Schools do not start there now till
11 a.m., since children are so tired from being kept awake in the
night.

Thursday, August 1, 1940

To National Gallery Concert.   Kutcher String Quartet.   Mozart
in E flat major, and Brahams in B flat major.   Very lovely.
In evening, party in Dr. Greaves' room.   H. and L. decide to go
home for weekend, and I decide to join them.
          Sir John Anderson being asked lot of questions in the
House as to treatment of refugees who have been interned.   Sir
Richard Acland asks whether it is humane to put people in camps
where they cannot even get newspaper to read.   Sir John A. says
the whole question is being looked into.
          Germans last night dropped leaflet over Southampton -
extracts from Hitler's latest speech, "last appeal to reason".

Friday, August 2, 1940

To Stroud.   L. comes also, but 1st class, the snob, and H. has
already gone with puppy.   Sailor in my carriage says he was in
the "Havoc" which took part in the Narvik engagement.   They went
into the fjord three times, not expecting to come out alive.
When they went in the temperature was 12 below zero, and they all
had two overcoats, two suits, etc., each.   When the engagement
was over they were all stripped to the waist and sweating.   He
says in the middle of an engagement you are not frightened at all,
only excited.
          The plane brought down at Oakridge had four Germans in
it.   The parachute of one of them didn't open, and he was killed.
They buried him at Brimscombe.   They put a Union Jack on his
coffin (I suppose it was the only flag they had), and a girl at
the undertaker's worked a white Swastika across it for him.
The other three airmen came down by the schoolmaster's house, and
his 14-year-old daughter took them in and gave them beer and
cigarettes before they were taken into custody at the aerodrome.
The Hurricane which did most to bring the machine down was also
brought down and the pilot burned to death.

Saturday, August 3, 1940

Very tired. Weather turns out unexpectedly hot, and I have
brought nothing thin to wear.

We wonder whether Hitler, with his usual sense of the
dramatic, will invade England in the early hours of tomorrow,
August 4. So when, on going to bed at 10.15, I hear two immense
thuds which shake the house, think perhaps invasion has begun.
Three minutes later the sirens go and I join the family downstairs
As factory hooters are used in Stroud, one has to listen for a
long time to hear how long the blast is and whether what they are
sounding is warning or all clear, and as none of family stops
talking for more than two seconds, this very difficult. Daddy
insists on wandering round garden, replying to protests that if
he retires to outside lavatory he is quite safe bacause there is
no glass there. Naturally he keeps door wide open to get good
view. Three minutes later All Clear (as far as we can make out)
goes, and whole of Stroud emerges into its gardens talking excitedly. Two minutes later another noise sounds, whether belated All
Clear or new warning, no one seems to know, but we go to bed anyway.

Sunday, August 4, 1940

No bombs in south-west mentioned in to-day's news, but report of
leaflets in Scotland and south-east. Will swear what I heard was
heavier than a leaflet.

Back to London in great heat. Soldier and wife in
carriage, with 10-weeks baby which father has just seen. He and
wife so pleased with this unprepossessing infant, they can hardly
stop smiling. Private makes every excuse to nurse him, and is
very pleased when child goes to sleep on his arm.

Monday, August 5, 1940

Mr. Abraham, back from holiday, remarks that war seems temporarily
to have come to standstill. Feel this enough to make anything
happen immediately. More leaflets dropped, giving us a Last Ø/%
Chance to make peace, which we do not intend to do. Very hot day.

Tuesday, August 6, 1940

Plots to overthrow U.S.A. Government discovered: sabotage, etc.
Invasion from Germany expected within next few days, at any rate
within fortnight. Great activity on French coast. R.A.F. say
German bombing raids on this country have so far been only in the
nature of reconnaissance flights, not the real thing.

I celebrate these world-shaking happenings by washing
my white hat, which consists almost solely of a woollen net snood.
Alas, the halo around which snood is hung is lined with coloured
wool, I find, and it runs and hat is ruined.

Wednesday, August 7, 1940

Italians invade British Somaliland from Abyssinia. (French Somaliland has already been taken). Egypt is preparing for defence against immediate attack.

Germany Army leave cancelled, and large bodies of troops said to be moving towards coast. Britain is spending £10,000,000 a day.

Questions in House of Commons because Grace Fields (music hall artist) has been allowed to take large sums of money out of the country. M.P.s say other people, including members of the House of Lords, have also done so, and a full list ought to be supplied to Members of the House, with the amounts taken.

Sir Richard Acland, M.P., author of "Unser Kampf", has had some of his land in Devon commandeered by the Government, which has sent him money in recompense. He has returned the money, saying that he does not think it right to accept it, and if the Govt. takes more of his property, he will still accept no payment for it. This agrees with the principles which he propounds in his book. But most people think he is a revolutionary, an attacker of private property (although he possesses a good deal himself), and therefore very dangerous.

Thursday, August 8, 1940

Italians have taken 3 towns in Somaliland. We have brought down 8 or 9 German planes.

Miss Mearing to-day shows me the letters her father, as a clergyman, gets from the Ministry of Information. Also two booklets they sent out, one a sermon by Dr. J.D. Jones on the power to endure. Another is a pamphlet called "Cross into Swastika", with quotations from the German Press decrying Christianity. For example:-

"But I say unto you, love your enemies, bless them that curse you, do good to them that hate you, pray for them which despitefully use you and persecute you". According to Nordic feeling this is ethics for morons and idiots. It is an invitation to self-abasement without parallel, which would force anyone who agreed to it to feel the greatest contempt for himself. This teaching is so hair-raising that one cannot grasp the reason for its existence, unless one realises its mean intention of making humanity a crippled horde of slaves, which humbly obeys every gesture of the Jewish chosen people like an obedient automaton; to make of people a dull, standardised mush, such as the Jewish taskmasters have already made of the many millions of people in Soviet Russia. A man who does not hate as strongly as he loves has no power to assert himself in life or to take up arms for what is noble and worthy. The determination to des-

troy all opponents is just as indispensable a factor of human
worth and human dignity as the championship of everything
that is high and worthy of love".

(From "Bolshevism in the Bible", by
Hans Hauptmann. 1937).

There is much more in this vein: what seems to me far more dangerous for any opponents of Germany is the mysticism in the following
words of Hitler, as reported by Hermann Rauschning, one-time
president of the Danzig Senate. ("Hitler Speaks", - statements
made in 1933).

"The religions are all alike, no matter what they
call themselves. They have no future - certainly none
for the Germans. Fascism, if it likes, may come to
terms with the Church. So shall I. Why not? That
will not prevent me from tearing up Christianity root
and branch, and annihilating it in Germany. The German is serious in everything he undertakes. He wants
to be either a Christian or a heathen. He cannot be
both" ... ("Ye cannot serve God and Mammon" - and in connection with the fourth line, yesterday it was reported
that Germany was making peace with the Vatican) ... "You
cannot be b "For our people it is decisive whether they
acknowledge the Jewish Christ-creed with its effeminate
pity-ethics, or a strong, heroic belief in God in Nature,
God in our own people, in our destiny, in our blood.
"A German Church, a German Christianity, is distor-
tion. One is either a German or a Christian. You cannot be both. You can throw the epileptic Paul out of
Christianity - others have done so before us. You can
make Christ into a noble human being, and deny his divin-
ity and his role as a saviour. It's no use, you cannot
get rid of the mentality behind it.
"What is to be done, you say? I will tell you:
we must prevent the churches from doing anything but what
they are doing now, that is, losing ground day by day.
Do you really believe the masses will ever be Christian
again? Nonsense! Never again. That tale is finished.
No one will listen to it again. But we can hasten
matters. The parsons will be made to dig their own
graves. They will betray their God to us. They will
betray anything for the sake of their miserable little
jobs and incomes.
"We shall take the road back: Easter is no longer
resurrection, but the eternal renewal of our people.
Christmas is the birth of our saviour: the spirit of
heroism and the freedom of our people. Do you think
those liberal priests, who have no longer a belief, only

an office, will refuse to preach <u>our</u> God in their churches?
I can guarantee that they will replace the cross with our
swastika. Instead of worshipping the blood of their quondam
saviour, they will worship the pure blood of our people.
They will receive the fruits of the German soil as a divine
gift, and will eat it as a symbol of the eternal communion of
the people, as they have hitherto eaten of the body of their
God. And when we have reached that point, the churches will
be crowded again".

It is interesting to observe, in connection with the above, a
quoted statement of Goebbels, 1936:-

   "Our leader becomes the intermediary between his people
   and the throne of God... Everything which our Leader utters
   is religion in the highest sense, in its deepest and most
   hidden meaning".

Also the following, from "Westdeutsche Beobachter", 1936:-

   "We believe in our leader. We prove our faith through
   our deeds. Our body, our spirit, our possessions, our
   souls, belong to the Fuehrer. He has come out of us.
   He is the sum of our power and meaning and we live through
   him as God".

I find all this far more terrifying than the number of their
tanks and their aeroplanes.

Friday, August 9, 1940

Big fire in a London food storage depot where thousands of pounds
of tea and a great deal of canned fruit were. The suspicion of
sabotage is raised by the sentence in the "Evening Standard" which
suggests that the Police are investigating the possibility that
several fires started all over the building at about the same time.
        Number of aeroplanes brought down in yesterday's attack
on convoy now announced as 60. 400 German planes were in the fight.
16 of our planes lost. Five ships were sunk.
        To Stroud by 6.30.

Saturday, August 10, 1940

Hilda's wedding. Aunt Nina to stay for couple of nights, from Aunt
H's. She says the only pair of field-glasses possessed by the
South Cerney aerodrome is Aunt Tuttie's old pair. Also says a bomb
was dropped at aerodrome which contained only sawdust. It was
made in Czecho-Slovakia, where it is believed the workers, whose
labour is forced, put other things than dynamite into bombs when
they feel like it.

Sunday, August 11, 1940

15 German aeroplanes shot down.   Our losses not announced.
Albanians said to be revolting against Italians.
                        Bad behaviour of Daddy in chapel - on disapproving of
~~Monday, August 12, 1940~~ the sentiments expressed, or the way they
are expressed, in hymn 170, ("though He was charged with madness
here"), he sings words of hymn 171 throughout ("Awake my soul in
joyful lays").   I sing loudly to cover him up, but all the s's
come through.   More mutterings about Isaac Watts and his verse.

Monday, August 12, 1940

Miss Playle asserts that tale of sawdust-rum filled bombs is rumour
deliberated by a friend of hers, a Mrs. Fyleman, with the object
of cheering the population of England.
                        Big air battles in the Channel.   61 planes said to be
brought down.   Damage to ships not stated.
                        Party in Dr. Greaves' room in evening.

Tuesday, August 13, 1940

More air-raids - on Southampton, Portsmouth and Isle of Wight.
Everything peaceful in London, but all the balloons up.   Mother
and Daddy to Croydon for few days.

Wednesday, August 14, 1940

Extract from "Mein Kampf", quoted in booklet, "The Issue" (published Macmillan) which is among those issued to clergymen and others:-
            "Anyone who seriously wishes that the pacifist
        idea should prevail in this world ought to do all he
        is capable of doing to help the Germans to conquer
        the world.   The pacifist-humanitarian idea may indeed
        become an excellent one when the most superior type of
        manhood will have succeeded in subjugating the world
        to such an extent that this type is then sole master of
        the earth.   So, first of all, the fight, and then
        pacifism".
This should be compared with the broadcast in Hindustani which the
Germans recently put out to India, saying that the Germans held
Mahatma Gandhi in the same veneration as they held Adolf Hitler -
the aims of both were identical,   Fail to see what one can do
with such wrong thinking. (Have just found exact words as quoted
in Listener:- "The German people respect Mahatma Gandhi just as
much as they do Adolf Hitler.   Herr Hitler has the same principles
as Mahatma Gandhi.   National Socialism also teaches no violence,
and Herr Hitler tried his best to get German territories without
shedding blood".)
                        78 planes brought down in yesterday's raids.   13 of ours
missing.   I observe 17 empty shop buildings in Regent Street as I
go down in bus to National Gallery concert.   Back - not too good.

Thursday, August 15, 1940

About 20 German parachutes reported found in Midlands and Scotland.
No sign of parachutists.   Blitzkrieg, says the South Coast, where
bombers have been, has begun.   The English, Goebbels says, are
panic-stricken.   Have lunch with Mother, Daddy and Hilary, and
take them to see Bedford College (my table covered with beer-
bottles in preparation for tonight's party, and Mother on surveying
them says: "That I should live to see the day!"), and afterwards
to Rose Garden in Regent's Park, where people are sitting in deck-
chairs looking very peaceful and unworried.
            Edric rings asking me to Prom, but cannot go.   Kathleen
Hasler asks if I will sleep at Harman Drive next week in her absence
on holiday, because she is nervous of leaving Mr. Hasler with only
Alice after his recent illness.
            At 7.15 I am just getting out of bath when I hear sirens.
First reaction, "Can't be an air-raid: I'm having a bath".   We
go to shelter, but the All Clear goes half-an-hour later without
any noise of bombs.   Party takes place quite successfully.

Friday, August 16, 1940

169 planes down yesterday.   Hilary and Daddy saw German planes
coming from great height and diving on to Croydon aerodrome.   They
heard what H. describes as "pops", but nothing very terrifying.
Daddy insists on walking about during raids looking at sky and saying "O this is life, O this is joy!"
            We have two warnings to-day, one 12.45 - 1.15, the other
5.10 - 5.50.
            Confidential memorandum round in B.B.C. says Fascists,
Communists, conscientious objectors and pacifists are not to be
allowed at the microphone.   This is particularly aimed at pacifist
parsons and their sermons.

Saturday, August 17, 1940

Mother on telephone from Croydon: "I don't want to go home - it's
exciting here".
            Desmond MacCarthy brings copy (promised last Tuesday)
to office at 12.30, and then stays amending it till 1 o'clock.   So
I have to sub it and scale up his pictures after that, and take
stuff to printers at about 3 o'clock.
            At 9 p.m. to the Haslers at Golders Green, to sleep in
house in Kathleen's absence - because of Mr. H's recent illness.
It is very hot, but I have nice room with French windows and
balcony.
            Wrote yesterday's entry in early evening: after that
went to meeting addressed by Sir Richard Acland, M.P., whose idea
is that if we want to defeat Nazism, we must show the world some
better way of life and government, and must start reforms now, not

wait till after the war.   At the same meeting was Timperley of
the Manchester Guardian, who spoke about the Government's closing
of the Burma Road, and how it was against our pledges to China by
the League of Nations.   It cuts her off from war supplies, and
also from all Red Cross supplies.   Also he read figures of the
war materials supplied to Japan - well over 95 per cent. have come
from Britain and her Dominions, America, and the Dutch East End
Indies, who have all cried loudly against aggression in Europe
while apparently supporting it in the Far East.   Timperley referred to Halifax's recent broadcast, in which he said we were
fighting for Christianity: T. pointed out that however Christian
Halifax may be in his private life, it is not a Christian act to
close the road which takes China all her supplies, including her
medical supplies and toxin needed against cholera, etc., especially in the face of our pledged word to do nothing to hinder her
successful prosecution of the war.
          Did not realise all this and was very shocked.
          Have come to the conclusion that a very small percentage
of London's population goes to meetings: will swear that most of
the faces at any political meeting are the same, or very much of
the same ilk - Pacifist, Fabian, League of Nations, or Sir Richard
Acland's private following.

Sunday, August 18, 1940

Set off to Paddington at 10, go to a service at church called, I
think, St. Mary's, then see parents off at Paddington on their way
to Stroud.   Very crowded train but they have comfortable seats.
          To Bedford College for lunch.   Air raid warning just
as we begin, which last three-quarters of an hour.   Do not hear
any bombs, only a little machine-gun fire.

Monday, August 19, 1940

There are at least a dozen empty shop premises in Baker Street,
and another dozen in Wigmore Street.   Wonder what happens to the
proprietors and assistants?
          Gerald at breakfast, looking immense in Auxiliary Fire
Service uniform.   He will stay with his father tonight, so I have
evening off.

Tuesday, August 20, 1940

Mr. Abraham, pitying my plight as the guardian of the aged, kindly
takes me home to supper, so I don't get to Haslers till 10.30.

Wednesday, August 21, 1940

Letter from Roy, from Pretoria.   He thinks South Africa is ripe
for internal trouble, stirred up by unscrupulous people who are
encouraged by the Germans.   Smuts is pro-British and trying to

confiscate all arms, but there is i̶s̶ a great hatred of everything
British among certain sections, and there have been bomb explosions
round Johannesburg (like the ones we had in England from the I.R.A.
last year).   We don't get any news of this sort of thing in our
papers, which give us to understand the Empire is united as one man
against the common enemy.
   Evening with Mr. Hasler.   He is very old-looking now,
shuffles, and is deafer than ever.   I knit and am bored.

Thursday, August 22, 1940

Convoy of British ships bombed and shelled in the Channel, but news
says no sinkings.
   Go to see hotel near Marble Arch which is prepared to
accept large number of ex-Bedford College residents at reduced
price.   Would as soon be buried right away, with marble slab on
top, as go to live among such gilt and plush and stuffiness.   Tina
Bruce and I, who go together, have to have sherry to cheer us up
afterwards, and I am thereafter as whizzy as can be.   Feel almost
ill with tiredness.

Friday, August 23, 1940

Dover shelled last night.   I wake at about 3.15 a.m. and hear lot
of planes.   Get up and look out.   Very clear moonlit night - park
looks beautiful.   See searchlights following plane, but hear nothing.   Back in bed, hear distant crumps, and sound of guns.
Get out again, but can see nothing.   Back in bed, hear sound of
siren, and reluctantly arise.   In crêche find last baby - a nice
little boy who is crying because everyone else has gone and he
thinks he is abandoned.   He likes the bright moon.   By this time
all is perfectly peaceful, but we have to wait in shelter nearly
three-quarters of hour before All Clear goes. So tired all day
find it difficult to tackle with great rush of work occasioned by
absence of Miss Playle.   Can scarcely think.
   Arnold rings up from Manchester suggesting I spend week
with them, beginning next weekend - probably in Lakes.
   The Principal - Miss Jebb - is At Home for an hour in
evening, during which the residents present her, for the college,
a Dutch reproduction (Van Meer, "The Little Street") - a Nice
Thought, since members of Dutch Government have been living here.
The Netherlands Minister of Justice - who looks more like a bar-
tender than anything else - stands on platform and reads speech in
difficult English: invites us all to visit his country in happier
times.
   During lunch-time rush in taxi to Eaton Place, where look
at another potential abode with Tina Bruce.   Find it very depressing - surrounded by houses with "TO LET" or "TO BE SOLD" notices.

Saturday, August 24, 1940

Two air-raid alarms - one at 8.15 when I am in bath, and one at

3.45 when I am crossing Hampstead Heath to have tea with Mrs. Morris. Have already heard bomb in distance, and progress, to sounds of gunfire and more bombs. Soon after I arrive the noises cease, but All Clear not sounded for some time. Mrs. Morris tells me she is 79 years old, which I find it hard to believe.

Letter from Joyce, announcing her probable return to town, so I am to abandon all other thoughts and go and live with her at the Cundells. Try to ring Edric but he is apparently gone for weekend. Feel much more cheerful now this is settled - though it isn't till I can get hold of a Cundell.

Dover shelled from French coast: not much damage. But damage done near Ramsgate - gas works hit. And some aerodrome bombed and lot of buildings fired. There is tension between Italy and Greece - Ø Italy running a Press campaign against Greece, and troops said to be gathering on Greek frontier. Rumania and Hungary have been negotiating/ but with each other, but negotiations have broken down and representatives gone home.

Appeal to housewives to save not only waste paper - for re-making into new paper; waste food - for pigs; all metal caps to bottles; but also bones, which provide glue and all sorts of valuable products.

Sunday, August 25, 1940

Much air activity as I was about to get into bed last night - hum of planes, dozens of searchlights in play, sound of bombs and gun-fire. Warning came about 20 minutes later (11.30) and lasted till 1.30. Nothing near, but at midnight there was red glare all over sky in south-east. News to-day says it was fire in East London commercial buildings - rumour says Cheapside.

Cloudy warm day. Go to service at church opposite Lord's Cricket Ground in morning. Spend most of what remains of day washing and ironing, shortening skirt in preparation for holi-day, and washing hair.

Monday, August 26, 1940

Warning 10.30 - 11.30 last night, another for a quarter of an hour, and one this afternoon for about $\frac{3}{4}$-hour, while Mr. Abraham and I are at printers. We descend to machine-room, where Mr. Matthews kindly provides me with chair and Mr. A. sits on enormous roll of paper and we play chess. Feel quite whizzy in head and unable to think after disturbed night.

Tuesday, August 27, 1940

Warning last night 9.30 - 4 a.m., during which time I sit on chair in shelter, first reading book, then playing pentoon. At last, just before 4, after being forbidden by the Bursar to return to bed, I sneak back in the dark, groping my way through building, where lights have been switched off. Just as I reach a room which fumb-

lings lead me to believe is mine, All Clear is sounded.   The
babies are left to sleep in shelter.   Result of all this is that
today I feel incapable of coherent thought, am very cross, burst
into tears, and am rude to Mr. Thomas on telephone.   Edric comes
in to Speaights: I can go and live at Flask Walk again.

Wednesday, August 28, 1940

A good thing I _am_ going back to a private house I reflect during
night - warning goes at 9.30 while I amd rinking tea in Miss Saun-
ders' room - and lasts till midnight.   There is another at 12.30,
which lasts till 1 a.m.   Instead of going to shelter, I undress and
get into bed, but am unable to sleep: not only does siren sound on
each occasion, but authorities here also give electric warning on
each floor and blow innumerable very loud whistles.   Gradually the
tramp of people up and down the bare wooden corridor floors dies
away.   Then, when All Clear is sounded, back they all come, and at
least a dozen will visit the lavatory opposite my room, the door of
which squeaks horribly and the bolts of which make a terrific din.
At one time I imagine I am about to receive a heavenly vision, since
my room becomes filled with an unearthly sort of light.   But it is
only the searchlights, which play on an invisible hum somewhere
above the residence building.   When I finally get some sleep at 4
a.m, have nightmares that this week's Listener has appeared with
half of last week's issue mixed up with it, and a lot of blank
spaces.
        Feel so tired after this further disturbed night, tell
Editor at 3.30 that I cannot keep awake, and come back to the College,
where I spend several pleasant hours lying on grass in sunshine.

Thursday, August 29, 1940

Spend 9 last night to 4 this morning in air-raid shelter, going
there from a party in Bell's room.   Intended to escape to my own
bed at about 11, but one woman lent me a pillow, another a blanket,
and another offered me half of her mattress, so felt I was then
bound to stay.   Am very tired today.
        Party in the Devonshire at 6.30, given jointly by Roger
Wilson of Talks Department who has been sacked from the B.B.C. because he is a Quaker and will not fight, and Mr. Cockburn of Listener
Research who is joining the Air Force.   Roger Wilson is so nice,
and his occupation is supposed to be reserved.   The B.B.C. will only
have to get another man of military age, who is probably quite willing to fight.   Think they are wrong to sack him.

Friday, August 30, 1940

42 enemy aeroplanes down.   10 of ours missing.   Three warnings to-
day, the first while I am piling my luggage on to taxi to take to
Cundells, in a so-called long lunch-hour.   I go on nevertheless
and hear nothing but a distant plane.   Return to Bedford College,

and the All Clear goes as I walk through the rose garden on way
to Broadcasting House.

Two more warnings during afternoon, when I do not go down
to shelter, thus incurring deep displeasure of Miss Playle. No
sounds but one crump at what sounds like distance of several miles.
No warnings last night. This morning everyone very
cheerful after peaceful night.
Rumania has been forced to give Transylvania to Hungary.
Am writing in shelter (9.30 p.m.), another warning having just
sounded. Planes sound as if they are right overhead.

Saturday, August 31, 1940

All Clear did not go till 10 to 4 this morning. I return from
shelter to bed at 11 p.m., but do not sleep. There is a lot of
gunfire and many loud crumps. Get up once or twice and see shells
explode in the air. Another warning as I dress this morning at
about 8.30. This lasts till 9.15. I take train from Euston to
Manchester, leaving Bedford College reluctantly because it has been
so green and lovelyto live in, and has had nicest collection of
people I have ever met.
When train is about at Wembley, we hear sirens again.
Guard makes us draw blinds - suppose to afford slight protection
from flying glass. We are allowed to let them up again in another
half-hour or so. At Stoke see four German prisoners in charge of
enormous guards. They look very young and one is limping. Sorry
Stoke should be their idea of England.
Man in train says air-raid warnings are seriously inter-
fering with industrial output, which no doubt is intention of Hitler.
Reach Hale in great heat. Christopher and Richard
very much grown. M. says they have air-raid warnings every night
here too.

Sunday, September 1, 1940

Went to bed very early and at 11 had to get up for sirens. We go
below and lie on mattresses on floor of hall. All Clear at 2.50.
To-day we start out at 11.20, after great efforts. The
morning is dull, but as we run out of the dreadful Lancashire
cotton towns and into hills, sun comes out. Car is piled with
cot (on running board), pram, and incredible amount of luggage.
M. in front with Richard on lap, I at back with Christopher on mine.
Reach Mrs. Penny's, Eskdale, at 6. Most beautiful spot, where so
far only sounds are sheep ba-ing and hens clucking. Feel could do
with three months of it.

Monday, September 2, 1940

Spent beautiful night, though hear planes went over at 3 o'clock.
And beautiful day, though hear distant thumps and booms at, we
suppose, Barrow. M. throws newly-bought comb of honey to ground,

and we have to borrow soup-plate to take it home.   We improvise
carrier for Richard out of his father's shorts, slung on to frame
of haversack, which we take turns to carry on our backs.   With
this, and C. walking, we go out in warm afternoon sunshine and
peace.   Paper says they had six warnings in London on Saturday.
Shoppers in Croydon had dive-bomber above them, and many killed.
Hope Hilary was at home.   Evacuee ship has been torpedoed, but all
the children rescued.

Tuesday, September 3 - Sunday, September 8, 1940

Only news of outside world I gather is that America and Britain
have made defence pact, whereby Britain lends America air and naval
bases in Canada and Newfoundland;   that King Carol of Rumania has
abdicated and the Iron Guard are in power - which means that Hitler
and Mussoline have "won" in Rumania;   and that air attacks on this
country are fiercer.   Saturday (7th) seems to have been bad day
for raids on London.   Hear from home that Hilary is at Stroud for
a week.   Letter from Helena suggests I should live at cottage and
travel to London daily, but find this would mean getting to station
(3 miles still to go) at 9.45 nightly, even if not delayed by raids,
and leaving it at about 7 each morning.
          On Thursday night I am hot and restless, and on Thursday
stay in bed Wednesday with bad head and temperature.   On Friday
am better.   We have very pleasant walks with Christopher, who is
a darling.   Richard is a little terror and cries by night, which
seems too bad when we are far from sirens.
          Today (Sunday) I travel with Fuchs's by car to Lancaster,
where just catch 3 p.m. train.   No restaurant car, as had hoped,
but I get sandwiches at Rugby.   Soldier tells me 400 were killed
and 1300 injured in raids on London last night.   There is warning
when we are about ¾-hour from Euston, and we are made to put out
all lights.   However, lean out of window with three soldiers and
see searchlights in action, and later on see enormous red glow
over London.   We steam slowly into terminus an hour late (10 p.m.)
and I get to Hampstead and climb 321 steps with my luggage;   lifts
not working.   Nice little man helps with bag from halfway up.

Monday, September 9, 1940

No one at Flask Walk when arrived last night.   Settle down on
camp bed in basement at 11.45 or so, after looking out of top
window and seeing great fires somewhere near St. Paul's, which is
lit up by blaze.   At 1.20, amid much gunfire, Joyce arrives, after
perilous journey from Paddington.   We try to go to sleep, but the
bumps and bangs are terrific and at one moment windows seem on
point of blowing in.   All Clear at 5.20, which wakes me just as I
am falling asleep for first time.
          Today hear from Miss Playle that in Blackheath, where she
was, it was like front-line bombardment for 8 hours.   Two houses

in her road smashed.   Course (office boy) says evidence of bombs
all the way from Woodford Green to Liverpool Street.   Speaights
can do no type-setting because the gas main has gone in Holborn, but
at noon start improvising with blow-lamps.   They also have no
water.   The part of Holborn between Kingsway and Chancery Lane is
roped off and fires on both sides of the street are being put out.
        Warning at 5.55.   Mr. A. and I essay to go home in the
middle of it, and get to King's Cross before All Clear is sounded.
At Hampstead find Joyce has had enough and is returning to country
tomorrow, but the MacDonald family (Mrs. MacD. used to clean for
Cundells) turn up en bloc (Mr., Mrs and Mary aged 11).   Their house
(by 24 bus terminus) bombed at 5 this morning - when our windows
neatly blew in - and they are homeless.   Our promised char has not
turned up, so we welcome Mrs. MacD. with open arms.   She, Joyce,
Mary and I all settle down in basement for night, with Mr. MacD.
outside door, in middle of air-raid warning, which sounds at about
9 o'clock.

Tuesday, September 10, 1940

Joyce returns to Idbury.
        Bombs all night, but none very near.   This morning see
many shattered windows on way to printers, and one house demolished.
The Baptist Mission House, about 50 yards from Speaights, has had
bomb through middle of it.   Three warnings during day.   Watcher is
posted on roof as soon as sirens go, and he gives alarm if planes
are coming near, so except when danger is imminent we continue to
work.   Everything very much held up.   Still no gas or water.   We
can get no coffee with our lunch sandwiches, and no tea.   Mr. A.
sends me home at a quarter to 8, and I arrive in Flask Walk as alarm
sounds.   He leaves at about 9, and Mrs. A. rings up at 10 to say he
has arrived home safely.

Wednesday, September 11, 1940

Awful bombing last night.   One (said to have been in Fitzjohn's
Avenue) rocked the house.   Mrs. MacD. very nervous, and we have
night light.   Get no sleep at all till All Clear at 4.45, which is
an hour earlier than last night.   Telegram from home saying they
are anxious and asking me to ring up, but cannot get through by
telephone and though I send telegram, the girl in P.O. will not promise it will be delivered to-day.   Three warnings, one while I am
receiving receipt for frock I have just bought in D. H. Evans.   The
assistant hands over change with the words "There is an air-raid
warning, madam ... if you would like to go down to the basement?..."
But I walk back to Broadcasting House, passing shop walkers, who have
all put on tin helmets and stern expressions and become air raid
wardens.
        R.A.F. have been over Berlin and have bombed Reichstag.
Siren for night goes at 8.40.

Thursday, September 12, 1940

An absolutely terrific barrage of guns set up last night soon after
siren went - like nothing we have had before.   Some sound as if
they are in Flask Walk.   Three distinct sorts of gun: nearby one
goes Boom-boom, very deep; then there is one which makes noise like
shaking of lot of sheets of tin - it is a very staccato and impatient
gun.   There is also a baritone, which just fires and fires and
never seems to hit anything. Mary afraid, and I give her brandy-ball
which she thinks is kind of cure for air-raid jitters.   After a bit
she says "That brandy-ball has stopped my teeth chattering".   I
tell her "That's the brandy in it".   And a little later she says to
her mother "The brandy ball did make me feel better".   In spite of
nearness and loudness of guns, we feel much safer with them in
action, and sleep much better.   This morning find everyone else felt
the same - that they were being looked after.
          Last night Mr. Churchill broadcast, saying we must expect
attempt at invasion probably next week, and that the next weeks will
be the most fateful in English history.   Hitler has massed a fleet
down the coasts of Europe from Norway to Brest.
          Miss P. hears from John that yesterday's daylight raid did
great damage at Lewisham, where to-day they have no gas or water and
there is no traffic but only bewildered and homeless citizens wandering in the streets.   St. John's Wood had a good many incendiary
bombs, Buckingham Palace has had a time bomb which has now exploded
and done damage to some of the rooms and to a swimming bath.   I go
in lunch-time to see Marylebone Road, were where extremely powerful
bomb has gone right through middle of cinema next to Mme. Tussauds.
Glass is broken even in many of the shops away down Baker Street.
          Only one warning to-day, in the afternoon.   At time of
writing (9.15), alarm for the night has not sounded.
          Major Glendinning called last evening to see if any Cundells
Friday,-September-13,-1940 were here - had seen light under door.
Referred to last night's activities as "beautiful bit of barrage".

Friday, September 13, 1940

Great gunfire again last night, but few bombs that we could hear,
except one which appeared to whistle clean over the house and then
didn't explode.   I slept 7 - 8 hours, waking once for some more
very heavy gunfire about 3.30.
          Warning this morning at 7.30 - 8.15 and again from 9.40 -
when I am walking up Great Portland Street after getting lift from K
kind stranger from Camden Town station, where bus stop very crowded,
to G.P.S. station, to 2.10.   We sit for some time in shelter, return
to work, return to shelter again when we hear crumps.   Then Mr.
A., Miss Mearing and I get coffee in restaurant which is supposed to
be safe.   On return we look in on sandwich-bar, on lower ground
floor, in which light orchestra is rehearsing, and at concert hall,
which presents remarkable spectacle.   Mattresses are piled in
corners, charladies and typists and higher officials are sitting on

floor which is a sloping one, the atmosphere is thick with smoke
and sweat, and a dance band, with singer, is rehearsing on platform
amid buzz of conversation.   We grow tired of this and go back to
Langham Street, "at your own risk", the little man guarding the door
tells us glumly.   We get sandwiches, and, hearing bumps, retire to
shelter again till All Clear sounds.   Hear that a lot of incendiary
bombs were dropped in Kensington during this morning.   Mr. A. is
then rung up by his wife who says three delayed-action bombs are
near their house in Frognal and they must evacuate for three or four
days - this accounts for whistles over our head last night.   She
decides to come down to B.House for a bit.   Meantime a terrific and
quite unheralded whistle overhead causes us to fall on our faces.
2 delayed-action bombs, one in Little Portland Street, and no doubt
aimed at the B.B.C.   The plane came quite silently, gliding from a
height.   Afternoon finishes with sound of unperturbed barrel-organ
in Great Portland Street.
        Buckingham Palace bombed again: king and queen safe.

Saturday, September 14, 1940

More heavy gun-fire last night, not quite as much as night before.
3 or 4 bombs go screaming over the house, giving us rather a fright.
My chief fright, however, was waking up suddenly and sitting bolt
upright under impression that I was shut down in tube and could not
get out.
        To-day two warnings in morning, but no ~~bombs~~ sounds of
much activity.   One in afternoon as I am attempting to walk on the
heath with Mr. and Mrs. Abraham, and another at 6.15 or so while I
am at Flask Walk waiting for them to come to dinner.   One of the
bombs last night must have fallen on heath, where part by Ken Wood
is marked DANGER and is inaccessible - or this may mean guns are
there.   One is said to have fallen in Adelaide Road, killing about
10 people.   I find there is a gun on heath just at end of Well Walk,
so no wonder it sounds on top of house.
        The most pathetic sight these days is the people queuing
up for air raid shelters in the evening with babies and small children, carrying blankets and bundles of things for the night.   They
are outside the big stores in Regent Street, where the basements are
kept open, outside the public shelters, and especially they settle
down in the tubes, the platforms of which, particularly Hampstead
which is very deep, are covered with these pitiful objects of
humanity who are afraid to stay above ground.

Sunday, September 15, 1940

Much quieter night, which actually starts with All Clear.   At 1.30
there is tremendous gunfire, in middle of which the sirens quite un-
necessarily give the alarm.   All Clear again at 3.30.
        Beautiful morning.   I go to church, but come out before
sermon, in sudden need of lavatory, and anyway Sirens go almost at
once.   They go again in afternoon, when we hear plane but not much

gunfire.   Mrs. MacD. is very anxious to show me her bombed house, so in afternoon I go down to Kentish Town and have to look, first at the two houses completely demolished, then at her house, of which the ceilings are falling, the door frames thrusting out, etc. Finally, I have to look at the notice on the church opposite, of the funeral of the people killed.   "And what's it all for? Can you tell me that?" asks Mrs. MacD.   "What do they think they're going to settle like this?"

Am much impressed by the courage of Mr. and Mrs. King, to whom the house belongs and who, after a week of sitting all night in a public shelter, last night came back to their ricketty home, slept well in their own bed, and have been vigorously cleaning up the mess and putting things as much to rights as possible.

Monday, September 16, 1940

A noisy night, with at least one whizzer over the top of us, but I go to sleep about 3 O'clock and do not wake for the All Clear. 185 planes brought down in yesterday's raids.   Three warnings during the morning, which is spent mostly in the shelter; and I am caught on Kingsway platform on my way to printers at about 2 o'clock. They shut Chancery Lane station as soon as raid starts, and there are still no buses up Holborn.   I therefore sit on Kingsway station for $3\frac{1}{4}$ hours when, although All Clear has not sounded, I am so bored I walk to Speaights through Lincoln's Inn Fields - which looks very beautiful with sun shining through wet threes - and arrive in very bad temper.

People thick on platform of tubes on my way home at 7.30. The evening's warning starts at 8.15.   Hear from Stroud that Hilary is there, and get letter from South Africa which, in spite of Blitz-krieg, has taken only just over 3 weeks by sea.

Tuesday, September 17, 1940

Five bombs dropped all round the B.B.C. last night, so that from the printers we hear our offices are not habitable.   There have been a lot of bombs on Oxford Street and Regent Street, and a corner has been taken off the Langham Hotel.

Several warnings today, but no bombs near us.   We get the paper to press by 5 to 6, of which we are rather proud in the cir-cumstances, and do hope that Speaights won't be blown up tonight.

Have supper with the Abrahams at a restaurant in Hampstead: very kind of them, but should have had a better one from Mrs. MacD. The restaurant could not give us any meat, sausages or eggs, and we had to have beans on toast, or Welsh rarebit.   Neither did there appear to be any pudding.   My first real experience of food shortage, and that could not be regarded as serious.   The Abs. escort me to my door during a warning, and immediately a barrage sets up, so they comein and drink tea and wait for a lull.   Mr. MacD. comes in about 10, reporting great activity round Russell Sq.

He has been trying to cheer himself with a couple of pints, and
has succeeded in depressing himself.   He announces that we are
"beaten to a frazzle", "people can't stand it" he says.   "We might
as well give in".   I say he will feel better when he has had his
supper, but he is still gloomy.

There is a high wind, which we hope may be a bad thing for
the bombers.

Wednesday, September 16, 1940

Staff of Listener gathers in Concert Hall.   More time bombs have
fallen round B.B.C., and we are allowed nowhere near our offices.
We find temporary refuge in the two Portuguese news offices, which
are small and stuffy and have no rulers or pencils, and we have
none of our papers, but we are glad to be established somewhere.
There appears to be little I can do, so I go off for rest of day at
end of morning.   Hear that John Lewis's has been gutted, and go
and enquire about my dress that D.H.Evans's are making.   They are
open, although hoses are still playing on the next-door building.
They say my frock will be finished tomorrow, so I depart hoping no
bombs will fall on it tonight.   Bourne and Hollingsworth's have also
been bombed.   Comehome via. Swiss Cottage, in order to renew my
emergency food card.   Walk up Fitzjohn's Avenue, and see that No.20
has had a bomb in the front garden of the house opposite and the
windows are all out and the roof has holes in it.   Ring up "Punch"
office and find David was on A.F.S duty, not in the house, and no
one was hurt.

Walk across heath to Golders Green and come across bomb
crater.   Pick up conkers, which in the usual way would all have
been snatched at by small boys.   But there are no small boys, and
in Golders Hill Park there are no well-turned-out nannies with their
charges, only one or two old people wh and a whole lot of the grass
made into allotments.

In G.G. I go wild and buy blue silk pyjamas, thinking if
I am blown up the extravagance cannot matter, and if I am not they
will be very useful.   Warning as I return (they have been continuous all day) and I sit in the flower garden and look at the fountain
until it is over.

Write while guns bang above.   Have heard at least one bomb
go swishing past.

Mr. MacD. arrives home a little more cheerful than yester
day, but I hear him informing his wife that "the country is in a
terrible state: everywhere you go it is the same - chaos".   I understand him to say that if his advice had been followed some time
ago, such a thing could never have been.   His claim is gloom is
fortunately interrupted by Mary, who demands supper.   When she
comes in here again, I see that Mrs. MacD. has been crying.

We get no news of Egype, where the Italians say they are
advancing.   Neither are we told anything about shipping losses.   I
hope this does not mean all our food is going to the bottom of the
sea.

Thursday, September 19, 1940

A very noisy night in which I slept but little and got in a panic
when the night-light went out.   Feel ill to-day and am afraid I
am going to faint when train stops in tube tunnel.   Get horrible
shut-in feeling.   Miss Mearing invites me to her home at Amersham
for the weekend.   They have had no bombing near, though last night
could hear the guns in London.   Feel very fortified at the thought
of two possibly quiet nights.
        Find Listener is back in its own nice dirty offices, the
time bomb having yesterday been taken away on a lorry.   The building opposite our windows has had the corner taken off, and a demolition squad is enjoying itself hurtling down bricks all the afternoon, and sometimes papers which flutter down like a snow-storm.
In the lunch-hour I walk in Oxford Street - and on the way see two
of our office-boys very nearly decapitated by large pieces of glass
which fall beside them on the pavement in Upper Regent Street.
Oxford Street is a devastated area - no traffic, and the gutters
are full of broken glass.   Peter Robinson's has had the corner
taken off, and D.H. Evans are now shut, though a notice to staff on
the door says they may open tomorrow if the structure is safe.   So
I may get my frock yet.
        Hear there is great havoc near Marble Arch.   Daniel
Neill's is bombed, and there is a tale that Selfridges has a time
bomb, as yet unexploded, through the middle of it.   An enormous
land mine, which descended by parachute - it took four policemen to
take away the parachute - descended into Regent's Park, smashing
up some of the beautiful houses in the Outer Circle.   Hear also
that Kilburn has had heavy bombardment, and try to ring up Beavans.
Glad to find their phone bell rings, so presumably house still there.
But no reply, so hope they have gone to cottage.
        Cheered to get letter from Mother in evening, written
Monday and posted Tuesday.   My telegram of last Wednesday got to
them on Monday, but the letter posted the same same day arrived on
Friday.   Leonard has been down for short weekend.   They have had
incendiary bombs on his works, but fire soon put out, and in the
close at Shirley but not on the bungalow.   He is staying with his
Mother at Orpington; says it is impossible to get from East Croydon to Victoria.   Stroud full of refugees from London, who are some
of them sleeping in Bedford Street schoolroom.   They have had no
air raids near there lately.

Friday, September 20, 1940

Italians advancing in Egypt, and British have withdrawn from their
first positions.

Noisy night. I don't sleep, but keep saying "Amersham"
to myself, and finally get to sleep after the All Clear at 5.45.
Get wakened again by Mr. MacDonald's alarm clock. Mrs. MacDonald
has letter from Helena and decides to send Mary to cottage. Miss
Playle has telephone conversation with her brother during day, in
which he says that near their home at Lewisham a land mine has fall-
en and wrecked a whole road of houses. I get extraordinary scrib-
bled pencil note from Other Joyce asking me to get S.O.S. broadcast
for David's old nurse, because she is alone and ill and the telegram
she sent for the nurse was returned with "Compulsorily evacuated,
address unknown" on it. Of course can do no such thing. Feel no
one in this stricken city can help in such a case.

To Little Chalfont with Miss Mearing. Her father is
Vicar. Her mother has already got two schoolgirl evacuees, one
elderly lady from Lewisham, a son of 15, a large mongrel dog, only
one maid, a rummage sale tomorrow and a Harvest Festival the day
after. So am very sensitive of her kindness in having me as well.

Saturday, September 21, 1940

Slept beautifully, waking once or twice to gloat over my blissful
unbombed state. Stay in bed to breakfast and get up to lovely
sunny day. In afternoon to cricket match, where I sit in deck
chair in great comfort and watch Amersham Hill beat Chenies by 71
runs to 49. Mrs. Mearing comes in dead tired but triumphant, the
rummage sale having made over £21 for the building fund.

Sunday, September 22, 1940

Wireless says the outer suburbs of London were bombed last night,
and Mrs. M. reports having heard bombs and guns, but I slept very
well, waking only once at 4.45 to hear a distant All Clear. This
district is full of refugees from London. People arrive at the
Vicarage continuously asking if there is anywhere they can find accommodation. One couple offered 3 guineas each if someone would
let them have her back bedroom. All the houses are full up. One
woman said "I'm so tired. If only they'd let me stay for two
nights". I know so well how she felt.

I go to Harvest Festival at 11.30, after all the household
except me has been to Communion at 9 o'clock. "... and Ethel
thought what a good holy family she was staying with ..." Mr. Mearing, in effort to brighten service, has cut out Confession and most
of Te Deum, of which do not approve. T.D. best thing in Matins.
It rains after service and we get lift home. Walk in afternoon
after rain stops. Hear planes at night and see shells bursting
over London, but sleep well.

Monday, September 23, 1940

Back to London regretfully.   Alarm on the way, and when we, with vast crowds, essay to get out of tube at Oxford Circus, told the station is shut.   Feel quite ill and rush back into train and get out at Piccadilly where the queue for exit is so great feel shall never reach open air again.

Editor returns from holiday.   Mr. Abraham informs me he slept in my bed on Saturday night before going back to his own house last night, braving dangers of unexploded bomb.

Get home to find that last night a bomb fell about 50 yards from back of house in New End Square.   Only one of our windows broken, and no one hurt here, though a few broken arms, etc., in the houses hit.

Warning just gone (7.45).   Feel very tired.

A ship taking children to Canada has been torpedoed. Only about 7 children out of 70 saved.

Tuesday, September 24, 1940

Last night was really terrible - very noisy and lots of bombs. Once the house rocked on its foundations.   But the worst thing was that Mrs. MacDonald's nerve had quite gone and she gasped for breath after every explosion.   I almost order her husband to come in and get into bed with her (should not wonder at anything I find myself doing before this war is over), but he is almost no good: lies and drones on: "That's a heavy bomber ... There doesn't seem anything we can do against them ... It's really terrible ... There doesn't seem to be anything between us and what is falling on top of us ... Oh dear".   I try to hearten them, but am myself trembling in every limb.   Poor Mrs. MacD., after about 3 hours of noise, says "I can't stand much more of this, George, I shall go mad".   But they both go to sleep about 3 o'clock and don't wake till I say it is 8.30. I sleep only between 4.30 and 6.30, and resolve to try to get away next weekend for more rest if possible.

Hear many tales of bombing to-day.   Mr. Morgan had bomb in his road which demolished 14 houses.   Hear a land mine fell at the Angel and killed 100 people.   The furniture shop in College Creseent, Swiss Cottage, is there no more.   But, strangely enough, Hampstead looks much the same as ever.   The Woolworths near the printers has a bomb on it.   Tina Bruce rings me up and asks me to go and sleep with her, in Bedford College dugout.   But I return to the MacDonalds, and in the early evening, at any rate, Mrs. Mac-Donald seems less nervous.   Have tried to get a Thermos, to give us hot drinks in the night if we get a fright, but no vacuum flasks are to be had anywhere.   Letter from home.   There have been bombs near H's bungalow at Shirley, windows of which are broken.   L's works were bombed, but they were able to carry on.

Wednesday, September 25, 1940

When Mr. MacDonald came in last night, after I'd finished day's

entry, he reported fires at the back and side of us, started by
incendiary bombs.   Not such a bad night as the one before, but
Mrs. MacDonald again very nervy, and her husband's contribution to
the night was: "I don't know what we are coming to: there's no
resistance at all.   They call this a battle, but it isn't a battle,
there's only one side in it.   We can't do anything against them.
It's terrible".   At about 3 a bomb falls fairly near, but the
house scarcely trembles.   Mrs. MacD., waking suddenly at the noise,
declares it is practically on our doorstep and moans.   I assure
her it is not, that I was awake and heard what was happening, but
she does not think I know.

Try to persuade her to go to Cundells' cottage, or anywhere out of London, for a few days till she feels better again,
but she won't leave George - afraid if she does he will throw up
his job, and, I suspect, take toomuch comfort in the public house.

This morning have to go, through warning, to Swiss Cottage
to renew my food card, which is still a temporary one.   Young man
in dungarees, holding large tin cash box in one hand and small pot
of paint in other, walks alongside me and says, after commenting on
the horrid sound of the German plane above, that it is no use either
side praying for victory inthis war, because Jehovah won't listen
to them.   What we want is a righteous Government, instead of one
which, call it Democracy or Totalitarianism as you will, exploits
the people.   The only end of the present system is, according to
the Scriptures, Armageddon - "and that's what we are facing in
these times.   Good morning".   And with that he strikes off through
gateway and disappears.

Warning has caused all food card experts to go to hearth,
so have to wait some time in shelter opposite.   Then understanding
woman says she will pretend I am a school-teacher having holidays,
and gives me one to cover next 3 weeks.   See damage in College
Crescent, where the little draper's shop of "Merry Christmas"
renown, and the fruit shop next to it, have disappeared as well as
the furniture shop.   A blank wall is standing next to the Post
Office.   About 100 feet up a mantelpiece still is in place, and on
it a vase, apparently untouched by a bomb which has broken windows
all up the crescent.   St. George's Hall has had incendiary bombs
on it and is burnt out inside, with the theatre organ.   The B.B.C.
had one on the roof, but no harm was done.   Off Regent Street,
just south of Hanover Square, something very big and heavy has fall-
en and done great damage.   Half the windows in Regent Street are
blown out.

Through all this misery and muddle, it is a beautiful
sunny sharp autumn day, and ends with a glorious yellow sunset.

I type at 8.50: the warning went about half-an-hour ago,
and at the moment there is a German plane buzzing about in a nasty
officious manner.

Thursday, September 26, 1940

Not such a bad night, but still I don't sleep at all till the All
Clear. Feel very depressed at this, since all the other people
at the office can now sleep through bombs and guns. One gun (I
hope mobile and may it be moved before tonight) is so near and has
such a blast it nearly blows me out of bed, and knocks down black-
out. I sleep from 6 - 9.30 a.m. Then cannot get a bus at Camden
Town and so walk and am extremely late again. Come through the
edge of Regent's Park, where see the effects of land-mine dropped
recently. Windows shattered for hundreds of yards in the big
white houses in the Outer Circle, but in front of some of them,
where there is a strip of lawn, a little man is patiently pushing a
lawn-mower up and down. There is a big gap in the lovely crescent
of houses at the end of Portland Plaee. Am told eight bombs were
dropped in a row down Finchley Road last night, between Met.Station
and West End Lane - probably aimed at railway, which they missed.
Two B.B.C. waitresses, sisters, killed last weekend, together with
father and mother and two boys, when their house was hit.
          General de Gaulle, who attempted a landing at Dakar, in
French West Africa, with Allied Forces, has now withdrawn, it is
said in order'not to cause bloodshed of Frenchmen'. Another
successful evacuation!
          In lunchtime I buy stirrup-pump from Selfridges, part of
whose building is open again, and the office staff enjoys itself
practising publ pumping, unfortunately into umbrellastand which
leaks. Miss P. crawls with her nose the regulation 2 inches from
floor to show method of approaching fire, while rest of us make
floor very wet.
          Am now at home and find that in excitement at bringing
stirrup-pump, have left gas-mask and torch at office. Warning for
night went about an hour ago but so far little noise. Can hear
plane buzzing in distance and coming nearer.
          My new frock from D.H. Evans, which rather despaired of
ever seeing, has now come.

Friday, September 27, 1940

Japan has made military alliance with Germany and Italy.
          After last night's entry, things got very noisy, and Mrs.
MacD. very nervous as bombs fell. "Christ!" she says, as white as
a sheet, and adds "Oh George!" which makes me feel hysterical. I
knit furiously with shaking fingers. Extraordinary sound which
causes noise of breaking glass is said to have been land-mine at Mill
Lane, Highgate, which was blown up in the air by our guns. Only
sign of broken glass this morning is slightly more damage to window
already broken. These landmines create terrible havoc: they are
said to be, first, some of the stuff we left behind in France;
second, magnetic mines which are now no good to Germans for use in
sea because we know how to cope with them; third, our own mines,
fished out of the Baltic or somewhere. Spent very bad night and

feel a wreck.   My shoeman this morning says "What sort of night
did you spend, madam?"   I say "Rather noisy" and ask about his.
He lives at Lancaster Gate, he says, and adds, "For the last three
weeks, to put it plainly, madam, it's been Merry Hell".   Tells me
how he was blown down flight of stairs, how the bank at the corner
of his road was demolished at 9.20 last night, the bomb killing a
lot of people who were coming out of cinema, and how he turned on
gas-stove this morning and water came out instead of gas.
        Numerous warnings during day.   I only hope can manage
to get to Stroud.
        Letter from John saying Duque and Arthur are at cottage,
and he and Peter have an hour's music after the warning goes every
night, then go to bed in shelter.

Saturday, September 28, 1940

Did get to Stroud, though train was 2 hours late, and when I came
from restaurant car, found no lights either in corridor or carriages, and only by miracle ever found my carriage and luggage again.
Met by Daddy, cold from waiting.
        133 German planes brought down yesterday.   Hear there
was great raid on Bristol on Wednesday, when 100 people, mostly
young girls, were killed at the Filton aeroplane factory.
        Spent beautiful night and today stay in bed till lunch-
time.   Hilary and puppy both very much grown, former in girth,
latter in all directions.

Sunday, September 29, 1940

Another peaceful night.   Harvest Festival.   Hear Carey Kenred
Smith nearly killed when St.Thomas's Hospital was bombed.   His
best friend, Sir Bernard Spilsbury's son, was killed.   Carey has
been home but now gone to Guildford.
        Evening service at 6 o'clock because of blackout.   I
wash my hair instead of going.
        Mrs. Millard tells mother that the bacon factory at
Calne in Wiltshire has been bombed.   They were aiming at railway,
where troop train was due to pass, but it was five minutes late,
and they missed it and the lines.

Monday, September 30, 1940

Britain, having found its sops to Japan no good, thinks it will reopen Burma Road.   Leave Stroud at 8.6 a.m, and don't get to B.B.C.
till a quarter to one.   Bombs on or near line at Acton.   Paddington alive with children, all waving from tops of double-decker
buses, being evacuated with their mothers.   Chalk Farm has been
hit and Hampstead Tube out of action.   Double-decker buses running
from tube station to Camden Town, but these very crowded.
        Several warnings to-day but no bombs near.   Warning for

night has gone, but so far (8.30) not much noise.

Janet Adam Smith has had another baby, a boy: for few days had ∅ three under 3 years. Invites us to Cumberland if we want rest.

Tuesday, ~~Septembe~~ October 1, 1940

Beautiful autumn day, and feel quite cheerful in spite of poor and rather noisy night. Mrs. MacD., after bangs, says, "Are you awake Miss: did you hear that one?" which find rather wearing.

Letter from Marjorie Fuchs, and from Joyce: latter has had spill from bicycle. Several warnings during day, but we go triumphantly to press at 4.30. May Speaights not be hit during night. Go for walk on heath, which looks lovely. Very made-up woman asks if it is true the Messerschmitt which is on show has been hit. Did not know one was on show, but she assures me it was, in aid of Spitfire fund. Should explain that places, and firms, are giving money for Spitfire (£5,000) - but Hampstead, being rich, is giving Flight of Hurricanes. B.B.C. is giving Spitfire, and members of staff were asked to give 2 days' pay each - contribution to be spread over 6 months. At first did not fill in my form, feeling did not want to contribute to war in any way, but after one night of bad bombing lately, felt another Spitfire might have kept us quieter, and filled mine up.

Warning has gone about an hour ago (now 9.15). There has been sound of something dropping - seemed like incendiaries - and Mr. Abraham rang up to know if we were all right. Do hope shall be able to get some sleep.

Wednesday, October 2, 1940

Last night very noisy indeed, and at 4.30 something extremely big dropped not far off, which to-day we find was land-mine near Bull and Bush. J.D., who is air-raid warden, and whom I meet in the Walk, says casualties very few. Another bomb dropped on hard tennis court at University College School, and something else at corner of Arkwright Rd and Fitzjohn's Av. - Editor would have got this, but he was away for night. 7 warnings during to-day, and the night one is now on and planes buzzing about. Newspapers say we have a new way of dealing with raids, tried out successfully last night, but planes jettisoned bombs as they fled. Fear many jettisoned them in this district - they come in by a north-west route now. Hope they'll try the new weapon further out tonight.

Get bus this morning from Hampstead tube downHigh Street to Camden Town. Strange to see bus bowling down Heath Street from White Stone pond - find it comes from Edgware. Did not pay any fare, because ought to have got ticket at tube station but did not know this and afraid to confess delinquency to conductor who was not taking any money.

Extract from to-day's "Times": (headed Calvinia, October 1)

"The transparent Karroo skies satisfied the wildest expectations
of scientists to-day, when without the interference of a speck of
cloud, the great solar eclipse blotted out the daylight for 230
seconds.   A scientist told me that a.. this was the most perfect
eclipse ever known ... Dr. Redman of the Radcliffe Observatory at
Pretoria, was in the camp, operating the massive and delicate
spectrograph sent here from Cambridge.   To protect the sensitive
apparatus from variations of temperature, it was used in a pit 10
ft. deep.   Dr. Redman is recording the spectrum at the moment of
transition from partial to total eclipse".
              "Manchester Guardian" says the September shipping losses
~~Thursday, October 3, 1940~~   were very big, though not as big as in
the worst month of the last war.

Thursday, October 3, 1940

Last night was comparatively peaceful - there was almost silence
from 2 to 3, though a lot of noise from 3 to 4.   I doze several
times.   To-day wet and foggy.   Tina Bruce rings up and asks me
again to go and live with her in Manchester Street.   They have a
ground-floor to sleep on.   Peter also rings up and asks me to
come in for music and scramble and to sleep in their Anderson shelter.   Decide to go tomorrow.
              Mr. Chamberlain resigns from the Government, and Cabinet
changes are made as follows:-
       Lord President of Council, Sir John Anderson (in place
              of Neville Chamberlain)
       Home Secretary and Minister of Home Security, Herbert
              Morrison (in place of Sir John Anderson)
       Minister of Supply, Sir Andrew Duncan (in place of Herbert
              Morrison)
       President of Board of Trade, Capt. Oliver Lyttelton (in
              place of Sir Andrew Duncan)
       Minister of Works and Buildings (new job), Sir John Reith
              (also becomes First Commissioner of Works in place
              of Lord Tryon; also is to be made a Baron)
       Minister of Transport, Lieut.-Col. J.T.C. Moore-Brabazon
              (in place of Sir John Reith)
       Dominions Secretary, Viscount Cranborne (in place of Lord
              Caldecote)
Editor very disgusted with this announcement; says four of the
members of the War Cabinet want appeasement, and most of the others
have no gumption.   Sir Kingsley Wood and Ernest Bevin are now in
War Cabinet, which is increased to 8 members.
              Viceroy of India and Gandhi cannot agree on attitude of
Congress to war, but Gandhi says there must be no civil disobedience.
              Forgot to say at beginning of week that butter ration had
been reduced - 2 oz.   One gets 8 oz. margarine as well.   And no
cream is now sold.   I have had my income tax demand for 1941 and
amount I have to pay, in 2 instalments, is £92.11.6.   Much cheaper
to have no income.

- 225 -

Friday, October 4, 1940

All Clear at 9.30 last night, then alarm again at 10.30, and actually
the final All Clear at 2.30. Such a good night, can hardly believe
it. Editor says quiet was due to bad weather conditions, not to
our good defences.

Nine U-boats and one Italian destroyer sunk. Mussolini
and Hitler meet at Brenner Pass, one supposes to discuss plans for
winter.

In lunch-time to National Gallery concert, where see and
sit between Bob Greaves and Raymond Bell. Warning just before concert begins. It is given in the Air Raid shelter downstairs:
Isolde Menges and Myra Hess playing Beethoven sonatas. The adagio
of the C minor, Op.30, No.2, makes me weep, but I do so unobtrusively. Go back to B.H. through barrage of guns. One, in St.James's
Park, is so loud I jump violently in middle of Lower Regent Street.

To Beavans for night. Peter, John, and Betty Bryant
play Beethoven trio, and I knit, in a curious way oblivious of people
and hearing only Beethoven and barrage. Six of us settle down in
Anderson shelter for night. Peter is a Fire-Watcher Chief for
Oxford Road, and Florence an ordinary Fire-Watcher. They have put
out several incendiary bombs. Peter puts on a yellow oilskin sou'-
wester over his turbulent red hair, and on top of it a red-and-green
tea-cosy to act as a crash-helmet, and then apparently feels able to
cope with anything. I understand that he continues to sleep whatever falls, and others have to wake him and point out that he is
surrounded by incendiary bombs.

Saturday, October 5, 1940

Night began noisily but ended quietly, with All Clear at 3.35.
Nevertheless found it impossible to sleep in that shut-in place,
though they gave me the best bunk they'd built at the top, where I
lay feet to feet with John, with considerable amount of overlapping;
and J. brought me hot-water-bottle and was anxious for my comfort.
All the others slept and several snored, and I was very depressed
to think how others can sleep through things and not me. When they
have all got up this morning, and the opening is allowed to let in
some daylight, I sleep till 11 o'clock. Then return to Flask Walk,
snatch glass of milk and orange for lunch, and go to Bedford College to get my bicycle. Air Raid warning as I pump up tyres, and
sound as of dozens of planes going over behind clouds. I hope they
are ours and mount bicycle and ride to Oxford Road, and at 3.15 or
so, Peter, Florence and I set out up Kilburn High Road among all the
Saturday shoppers, in direction of cottage. Warning at Hendon, and
see 12 of our fighters, but they come back later and we have the All
Clear in about ¾-hour.

Miss way and unaccountably find ourselves riding into St.
Albans. By 6.45 I am ravenous, and at Hemel Hempstead we go into
place full of bus-drivers and soldiers, and get baked beans and chips,
tea, and new bread and margarine. Have rarely enjoyed meal so much.

After that it is dark and we wobble along through black-
out, and later through rain, and arrive at cottage at 8 or half-
past.   Florence does journey on man's bicycle, and she has scarcely
ridden for 10 years, and confesses when it is over to having been
scared stiff in Kilburn High Road.   Great flashes of light in sky
over London, and beautiful searchlights playing on a hum above us
as we cycle.   John arrives a little later - has been working all
day and then lost his way in dark.
        Sir Charles Portal has been made Chief of Air Staff in
place of Sir Charles Newall, who is made Governor of New Zealand.
Am told Sir C.P. likely to be much more ruthless.

Sunday, October 6, 1940

Slept beautifully.   Unfortunately to-day wet, so cannot walk to
Ivinghoe Beacon or cycle to Whipsnade, as suggested.   Eileen comes
for night.
        Woods very yellow and lovely.   Go down to look at village,
which is red-roofed and has stocks and a pond.   Beside pond is
structure intended to defend village to death against German invasion - full of holes for guns.   Also there is strange barrage of
tree-trunks across pond, set there, I suppose, in frail hope of holding up oncoming tanks.
        Read horrifying article in "New Statesman", by Kingsley
Martin, on plight of homeless in East End, and on conditions of Air
Raid shelters - large storehouse used still had margarine in it when
he saw it, and the lavatory provision was so meagre that tides of
urine flowed round cardboard packing cases.   Glad to say he had
margarine removed; but conditions people sleep in are such that if
not improved there will be frightful epidemics.

Monday, October 7, 1940

Rise at 6.30, after not much sleep, because Florence played cards
with boys till 12.30, and I was awake till after she came to bed.
Morning bright and beautiful after wild night.   John takes me to
station, last part of journey done on cross-bar of his bicycle -
new and rather enjoyable means of transport.
        Several warnings during day.   B.B.C. has new system -
red light shows downstairs (i.e. in restaurant or concert-hall) when
warning is on, and blue light when watchers from roof give warning
of immediate danger.   To printers in afternoon.   Mrs. Goldie comes
in with her copy and says "How brave of you to sit down in the City
like this", and says further that her huaband has just been on leave
from Air Force and is terrified at bombings - takes cover at once.
Type-n- Write now through barrage of guns at 8.15.   Last night was
very quiet in London, and MacDonalds appear to have had more sleep
than I had.
        German troops have entered Rumania, Hitler says to prevent
British sabotage of oil-wells.

Tuesday, October 7, 1940

Three bombs dropped in quick succession at about 10 oclock last
night.   Learn from Editor to-day that one was at bottom of Arkwright Road, on Hampstead Public Library.   Mrs. MacDonald went
very white when they fell, and when she had recovered her breath
and found she was still alive said several times "The sod!" - a
word I have never heard spoken before, and which is so bad that
our printers refused to print it when it came in one of our short
stories.   Apart from this, night was fairly peaceful - or at any
rate I slept pretty well, though All Clear did not go till 7 this
morning.
          To printers during warning.   See planes making tracks
of smoke in sky to cover their movements.   Down Gray's Inn Road
bus turns to left, just before Holborn.   "Where are you going",
someone asks Conductor, who replies nonchalently "Don't know;
never been this way before".   Am told on arriving at Speaights
that at 9 o'clock 2 bombs dropped at end of Gray's Inn Road, before anyone could obey roof-watchers' warning to go below.   About
30 people in a bus were killed.   Miss Evans was coming up Shaftesbury Avenue as 2 bombs fell at Cambridge Circus.
          Warnings without ceasing all day.   We are constantly
"whistled down" because planes are overhead.   Mr. Abraham on holiday, so am on my own.   Nevertheless, finish at 3 o'clock, and
remark extreme reds of creepers and yellows of trees as I go home
through Hampstead.
          To-day's Times announces that Mr. Lambert's mother went
down with "City of Benares", the ship from which so many refugee
children were drowned.
          E.M. Forster, in very good broadcast talk, says, apropos
of Nazi methods, "In this day, when so many brave plans have gone
wrong, and so many devices have jammed, it is a comfort to remember
that violence has so far never worked"... "Even when it seems to
conquer it fails in the long run".   This being so, I despair of
anything but evil resulting from our violent opposition to Nazi
violence.
          Get home to find Helena and Edric there, but they go again
Wednesday, before night.   Edric impressed by ruins he has seen on
way from Hampstead to Holborn, through Camden Town and Kentish Town.
I ask him what he thinks of people in tubes at night, and he says if
their idea is that it is necessary to maintain life even when life
consists of lying on a piece of concrete in an underground station
for 16 hours out of 24, then he can only regard it as a pity they
are not educated to something better.   Chances of being killed by
bombing are about 4000 to 1, and surely to live more like a human
being is worth this risk.

Wednesday, October 9, 1940

Slept well last night, though papers this morning say it was worst
bombardment of war.   Very windy, and at lunchtime see barrage

balloon blowing away.

Germans entering Rumania through Hungary.   Japan very
annoyed because we, with connivance of U.S.A., have opened Burma
Road to let supplies through to China.

Churchill made speech to House yesterday.   Says raids
have not caused as many casualties as expected.   Mentions Dakar
landings, and failure of this enterprise owing to the fact that 6
French warships were allowed to go through Gibraltar and were then
let escape.   1st Lord of Admiralty was never informed about these
ships.   P.M. says disciplinary action being taken, but people are
asking whether it was Fifth Column work.

Churchill adds that we cannot expect raids to be less
because of winter weather.   He ends: "Long dark months of trial
and tribulation lie before us.   Not only great dangers, but many
more misfortunes, many shortcomings and many mistakes, many disap-
pointments will surely be our lot.   Death and sorrow will be the
companions of our journey; hardship our garment; constancy and
valour our only shield".   Cannot help thinking he enjoyed rolling
out these words.

A.A. Milne, author of "Peace with Honour", has now written
a book called "War with Honour".   Among other writers who have withdrawn from the pacifist position are Beverley Nicholls, C. E. M.
Joad, and G. D. H. Cole.

Thursday, October 10, 1940

Last night very noisy, though I managed to sleep between whiles.
At 5.15 something very big dropped and Mrs. MacD., waking suddenly,
gets out of bed and puts on shoes and stockings and declares it is an
incendiary bomb, or alternatively it is a time bomb in the next
house.   She goes on to say it may have been a land-mine, and ends
feebly by remarking that it might have been a falling brick.   Is
upset because neither Mr. MacD. nor I moves.   Mr. MacD. loses his
temper, in fact, and repeats several times: "First you say it's an
incendiary, then you say it's a time bomb, then you say it's a land
mine, and now you say it's a brick falling.   Well, it can't be all
of them".   At 6.30 there is another tremendous explosion.   Mrs.
MacD. wakes and says "What, George?" and at once goes to sleep again.
The Editor had two fire bombs on his house at about 11 o'clock but
they did not harm except to a slate or two on the roof.   Mrs. Lines
had a bomb on the block of flats opposite her in Maida Vale, and her
front door, inside which, in the corridor, she was sleeping, blew
in.   The guns seemed to be doing very little.   Many people remark
on this, and the MacDonalds say gloomily that we have probably run
out of shells.

The day fairly quiet.   Go to lunchtime concert at National
Gallery: 1st anniversary of beginning of these concerts.   Stratton
String Quartet, all in Air Force Uniform, play Chacony by Purcell,
and then 3 of them and Myra Hess give Brahms' piano quartet, which
is broadcast.   Enjoy it very much, but heat so great, especially

after attendant has closed shutters because of air-raid warning,
do not stay to hear speech made at end by Sir Hugh Walpole.

Feel very depressed at thought of night. Even during
daytime feel cannot face twelve hours of bombing, but it is not
so bad if can sleep some of time. St. Paul's Cathedral has been
hit and the high alter wrecked, the Henry VII Chapel at Westminster Abbey has been defaced and some of the glass broken, there is
a great mess at the end of Tottenham Court Road too. One morning
paper says Germans are now in Bulgaria; as far as one can discover
the Italians are advancing in Egypt; Japan is very annoyed that
the Burma Road is being reopened. Things look anything but bright.
Yet there is a lovely golden sunset which I observe as I slowly
freeze waiting for half-a-dozen full-up buses.

Friday, October 11, 1940

Last night not quite so noisy, though hear quite a number of bombs.
Beautiful westher, in which I travel to Tring, catching the 4-
something train which leaves Euston at 5.10 and takes an hour to
get to Queen's Park; but after that we speed up, reaching Tring
at 7.20, and a kind American gives me a lift in his car into Aldbury. Boys were not to be there, but their weekend elsewhere cancelled, and soon after my arrival, in comes Peter, who had travelled on some train. He is rather wheezy with a cold, which means
he snores very loudly, and as we share second bedroom (two beds,
but what would Holy Aunts say? - Duque's reaction is that it is not
nearly as congested as an air-raid shelter), I do not sleep very
well.

Navy has attacked Cherbourg, without loss to itself, but
it is thought inflicting lot of loss on enemy.

Saturday, October 12, 1940

At 2.15 a.m. there was terrific noise and 2 bombs fall - we find
to-day about half-a-mile away. Village people very nervous. Many
of them get up and go downstairs for next few hours. Beautiful
morning, and Duque, Peter and I walk over common to Berkhamsted,
with golden sunshine and most heavenly autumn colours. We call on
friends of theirs, and do not have lunch till about 3 o'clock, and
then bus back. John arrives at 7.30. London had very quiet
night, warning ending at 2.30, but has had a lot of warnings today.

Sunday, October 13, 1940

Last night had John in other bed. "Men I have slept with", by
M.J.Redman. He does not snore like Peter, so I have better night.
To-day we have marvellous walk through red beech woods to Ivinghoe
Beacon and back. On top of the beacon was a plaque showing what
could be seen in every direction, but it has been removed in case
it should help invading Germans. Woods are beyond anything for
beauty: better even than last year. Return to very late lunch -

about 2.45, during which we listen to broadcast concert: Mendellsohn's "Fingal's Cave" Overture, Haydn's Cello concerto - played on viola by Lionel Tertis, Schubert's 5th Symphony.

Monday, October 14, 1940

The Germans are using fighters for bombing, because they find it easier to evade our fighters than the heavy bombers. They are having some success with them. And they have a bigger and more effective type of incendiary bomb.

Arthur, Peter and John go off early to catch 7.12, but I wait luxuriously till the 8.3. Even that means leaving house at 7.30. And it is so delayed, first by wreckage of train which had accident at weekend and is on line at Wembley, then by bomb on line between Harrow and Willesden, that I arrive at B.B.C. at 11.45. Am rather appalled by destruction in Holborn when I go down to printers by bus. There is a peculia smell peculiar to these bombed buildings - of dirt, decay and dissolution.

In evening to 10 Manchester Street for night, to see if I would like to go and live with Tina Bruce and party. There is a flat on 3rd/flo 2nd floor with 3 bedrooms - Tina's (she is Secretary to Sir Richard Acland, M.P.); Nancy Parkinson's (British Council - and I have to share with one of them); and Graham White's (Liberal M.P. for Birkenhead. Downstairs are 3 rooms - Raymond Bell's and Bob Greaves' (both Treasury), and Jack Child's (Ministry of Information, but once Master Navigator of The Discovery - I suppose the Research Ship, Discovery II). We eat upstairs with bombs falling all over the place, and then go downstairs and occupy ourselves playing chess, and performing infantile tricks like picking up a matchbox with our teeth without falling off a chair. We then go to bed, Graham, Tina and I in the corridor of the men's flat. It is true my horoscope for the year said I should be surprised at the things I should find myself doing this year, and indeed I never expected to spend a night in a corridor with my head two yards from that of a snoring M.P. He has to make a speech on the Purchasing Tax to the House tomorrow and does not seem to know yet what he is going to say.

Tuesday, October 15, 1940

Last night was dreadful. At least 30 bombs went swishing over the house, and the guns nearly blew me off my mattress. Did not sleep at all. Everyone anxious to assure me that this was the worst night yet and they often have it quieter. Paper says fires in three of the Rumanian oil-wells, I am afraid not big ones. H.M.S. "Ajax" has sunk 3 Italian destroyers.

Wednesday, October 16, 1940

Last night not so bad in Hampstead, though did not sleep till the

All Clear at 5.30.   But other parts of London apparently had a
dreadful time.   Mass raids, the paper says, for first time.   It
is full moon and they dropped incendiary and h.e. bombs everywhere.
Miss Playle had all her windows blown out; Miss Street-Parter had
to leave her flat in middle of night, and was nearly blown up by a
second bomb as she walked down road.   I find on arrival at Broadcasting House that a bomb went into the 5th floor, on the Portland
Place side, at 8.5 last night, and exploded at 9.2, killing six or
seven people.   Bruce Belfrage was reading the news when it went
off.   He paused, but continued - rather breathlessly - to the end.
There is a gaping hole in the side of the building, but except that
the telephones are not working, most people are able to use their
offices and get on with their jobs as usual.

In lunch-time buy boots for cold weather, which want to
get before Purchasing Tax is put on next week.

Churchill declines to make statement on our war aims.
Will only say we are fighting to survive.   Feel if, after nearly
14 months of war and after all the suffering of the civilian population, we do not know what we are fighting for, it is a poor do.

Thursday, October 17, 1940

Navy has sunk an enemy convoy.   Brookman's Park wireless transmit-
ters put out of action by bombing last night, and we still have no
telephones in B.H.   Take a walk down Great Portland Street and see
results of several bombs no doubt intended for us - one has reduced
Ryman's, the nice map shop, where I bought this typing paper, to a
heap of rubble; one has destroyed Pagani's, where officials enter
tained people at the expense of the B.B.C.; and another has smashed
up The George on the corner, where members of male staff of B.B.C.
could be found at any time during opening hours.

On the whole, night was not too noisy, probably owing to
heavy rain, though the house rocked on its foundations twice during
evening.   I did not sleep till the All Clear, and to-day feel a
wreck, and very depressed at hearing from everybody else how well
and long they slept.   We have no water to-day, and the Editor, going off duty at B.H., could not get a bath at any of his clubs and
so is very dismal all the morning.

Friday, October 18, 1940

Take belongings to 10 Manchester Street in morning, after tender
parting with Mrs. MacDonald.   Find the party is now all on ground
floor, so presumably shall be able to sleep in a bed.   Try to
phone Edric to remind him that I am coming for weekend, but find,
after I have queued for telephone box for some time, that his coming
to town has been so delayed he has telephoned School and gone back
to cottage.   Nevertheless, my enquiries cannot discover that there
is anything amiss on the line to delay me, so go forth by 5.20 from
Liverpool Street to Audley End.   It leaves only 10 minutes behind

time, but takes a circuitous route, with many stoppings.   It
begins in an air-raid warning, and soon the night one has begun.
No light at all in carriage, and conversation of fellow-travellers
consists of descriptions of bombing horrors.   It is past 11 when
I get to Audley End.   Walk 3 - 4 miles with heavy case.   Have
thoughts of sleeping under hayrick, of which there are plenty, but
it rains and I am very hungry, so I persevere, seeing neither vehicle nor any human being, but hearing very distant hum of planes
and still more distant gunfire.   I knock up Cundells at 12.30.
They have forgotten that I was coming, but rise at once and greet
me most kindly in darkness while a toothless Edric searches high
and low for box of matches.   I am given food, and a bed is prepared for me of two sofas, which is square and comfortable but not
really long enough.   Am very tired and glad to be in.

Saturday, October 19, 1940

America has introduced peace-time conscription.
        After not-too-good night, though my mind was at rest,
get up late and spend rural morning accompanying Helena on bicycle
as she tries to chivvy village into a desire to go and buy jam from
Women's Institute this afternoon, and to hear a man lecture on
Africa.   We meet mother and two children from London wandering in
a lane looking for billets, and she gives them lunch and lets the
youngest, who is only 3, lie on one of the children's beds to rest
while her mother gets fixed up.   The morning is dank and wet, but
after lunch becomes bbb bright and blue and I go for short cycle
ride before joining the Women's Institute (about 20 women) and
listen to someone from Saffron Walden talk quite interestingly
about Africa.   We have tea, with real farm butter, and even the
sound of bomb explosion not very far off does not disturb our
serenity.
        "Telegraph" says September 16 was intended by Hitler as
day for invasion of Britain - there was full moon and tide was very
high.   Suggestion is that R.A.F. bombings of French ports prevented
it.

Sunday, October 20, 1940

Such a marvellous sleep on a beautiful bed last night.   Absolutely
perfect day of warm sunshine.   Cycle and get berries in morning
and come back to listen to Haydn Quartet.   Fetch lunch beer from
pub. and hear that London had a bad time last night.   Visitors to
cottage have brought their own food, and after lunch I sit in sun
and knit, listening to Beethoven coming through window.   Mildred
Parry-Jones comes and talks to me and remarks that to be able to
say nowadays that you have not taken off your clothes for a fortnight shows that you are a woman of real sensibility - or so you
might imagine from the pride with which people give this piece of

information.   We ramble together through the lanes while she
picks autumn leaves and old man's beard, and come back for Beeh-
hoven and tea.   After that some Brahms before everyone has to go
because of the approaching blackout.   Edric, Helena and I take
an evening stroll through the blue twilight at the time when the
horror in London is just beginning.   Then Edric plays piano a bit,
and we go over the way to the converted cottage belonging to the
Bickleys, who are rich Jews from Hampstead and who will give Edric
and me a lift to London tomorrow.   We listen to the News and to
Priestley's last Postscript.   Two bombs, just after I get to bed,
make me jump more than anything in London, because wasn't prepared
for them.

Monday, October 21, 1940

Mr. Bickley's friend drives us so fast along the Essex lanes that
Edric's head often hits roof of car.   Hedges are bright with
colours.   At Palmer's Green we come upon a bomb crater with the
bomb still smoking in it.   It dropped 10 minutes before, and our
driver asks if we are not grateful to him for having started ten
minutes later than intended.
          Sorry to see in Oxford Street that Peter Robinson's, who
had been carrying on the women's part of the business in the men's
shop, and had even opened the ground floor of the other building,
have now had all windows of unbombed building blown in by bomb on
opposite side of street.
          Mr. Churchill broadcasts to French nation.
          In evening to 10 Manchester Street.   Tina has heard from
man at Evesham that they had an air attack last week on the B.B.C.
there, and that it felt very queer to be the enemy's sole target
and to have no defences except the Home Guard potting with their
rifles.   One man was killed.   Bob Greaves and Raymond Bell have
been bombed out of their offices at the Treasury.

Tuesday, October 22, 1940

Pretty quiet night, with All Clear at about 4.30.   Very trying day
at printers.   Telephone to Broadcasting House is working again, but
one gets cut off in middle of almost every conversation.   Editor
tells Mr. Abraham there is suggestion that whole Listener staff
should move to country, but not far enough into country to be
pleasant - probably place about as far off as Hatfield.   At
thought of impossibility of getting billets, and probability of
having to live with Listener staff all night as well as all day, become very depressed.   Strange that all staff should react violently
from idea of leaving this city of destruction: we are like the
slum mothers who refuse to be evacuated.
          Marylebone Station has been so bombed that it will not be
usable till next year.   St. Pancras, I was told yesterday, was in
the strange state of being able to receive trains but not send them

out again, which sounds extremely unlikely.   Great number of
Underground Stations are out of action.

Wednesday, October 23, 1940

Absolutely marvellous night - All Clear at 11.30, before I was in
bed, and though another warning at 12.30 or so, it lasted only
about half-an-hour.
        Churchill's broadcast to France takes on new meaning when
read in morning paper that Laval may be making pact with Axis against
us.   Graham remarks at breakfast in mildest of tones "One feels
that compared with Laval, Judas Iscariot must have been a pleasant
character".   The fact that Hitler says there is absolutely not a
word of truth in the suggestion that he is making a pact with Laval
against us leads everyone at once to feel that it must be the case.
        Hear from Mother that Stroud has 7,500 extra people in it
and the shops are bung full.
        In lunch-time to concert at National Gallery- Stratton
String Quartet playing Beethoven, C minor and G major.   We are in
different part of basement from last week.   This explained in the
middle of G major by terrific explosion - time bomb in other part
of gallery.   Think for moment that ceiling is coming in on us all,
and some people start to their feet.   But String Quartet does not
falter for one moment: plays straight on, and people not only sub-
side, but several by door say "SSSS-hhh", as if someone had talked
in slow movement of Eroica.   It was magnificent.   Afterwards discover that bomb was to have been removed in half-an-hour.   No one
was hurt but building damaged considerably inside.
        Learn that Priestley was removed from broadcasting mostly
by intervention of Margesson, Conservative Chief Whip.   Don't wonder - he said so many things that needed saying, such as that it
was disgraceful that people who had money but did no useful work
should be able to escape from London and book up all hotels, etc.,
so that people who were worn to death by bombing could find nowhere
to stay.   And other outspoken things.   Same man, Margesson, ob-
jected to Listener reviewing "Guilty Men", which indicted several
members of Conservative Party, eg.Chamberlain, etc., as being responsible for our being at war.   This may be why no one cares if
Listener is moved at once to wilds of country where there is no
possibility of bringing paper out
        Evening's warning starts earliest yet - about 6.35.
Almost at once hear sound of bomb in direction of B.B.C.   Hope it
is not hit, especially as Editor is on Home Guard duty.

Thursday, October 24, 1940

Hitler is going to the borders of Spain to meet General Franco,
presumably with hope of bringing Spain into the war.
We have another quiet night. Am told there was lot
of gunfire about 5 o'clock but was asleep. In lunchtime today
go to ballet at Arts Theatre, with Lesley Coad, which I enjoy
very much. There is the biggest crater I have yet seen in the
middle of Charing Cross Road. A lot of bookshops still open,
though there is considerable amount of destruction round Cambridge
Circus.
Tina says Liddell Hart, the military expert, is very
depressed about the state of the war - thinks we are being defeated, and that perhaps it would be better to make terms with Hitler
while there is still something left to safe. Other people think
that by next year we shall have all the materials we need, from
America and from our own output, and that we shall then begin an
offensive by making a landing in Holland.
I discover Jack is not in Ministry of Information - Tina
says I imagined this - but something to do with the Merchant Navy.
He was very concerned the other night because the men who ought to
have been repairing ships in the Docks refused to work after dusk.
The job can only be done at high tide, and high tide came too late
in the evening and too near the beginning of the night raid for
them. It is a job of national urgency, but they say, with justice,
that until a few months ago nobody cared anything about them and
their welfare, and why should they now put themselves out for the
people who ignored them?
A depressing day, very cold, and we have no heat in the
office because there is no gas. The project for transferring The
Listener seems to have been dropped for the moment, and though I
should have been very depressed if we had been going to move, am
also depressed that we are going to stay. Reflect on the stupidity
of human nature, particularly mine.

Friday, October 25, 1940

Another fairly quiet night. - All Clear about 2.30 - which leads
Nancy, who comes in to breakfast after sleeping at the British
Council, to remark that we shall soon all suffer from nervous
collapse under the strain of wondering what Hitler can be doing so
quietly. Someone suggested yesterday that he might be preparing
for big air attacks on Egypt, Greece and Turkey, and just be keep-
ing us occupied by sending over a few fighter planes with bombs.
Papers say that Spain is not coming into war at present.
Hitler is now trying to negotiate with Petain, to get unoccupied
France to unite with him against us.
In lunch-time am buying ticket from Polytechnic Travel
Bureau, when whistles go to show planes are overhead, and almost
at once two bombs come whizzing down. Sound very near, but find

on investigation they fell between Baker Street and Marylebone High Street, very near 10 Manchester Street, which has lost a window or two but not in our flats.

Get 4.15 to Stroud, which doesn't arrive till about 8.30. Chef from Dorchester Hotel, who travels in my carriage, produces cold steak pie from his suitcase and gives me large piece. The rest is consumed by three soldiers, who have been travelling all day and say Birmingham had a bad raid last night. Another man in carriage, one-time traveller in electrical appliances, shows me statement about his salary (£400 a year) and commission (one week £9) and tells me all about his firm, which was at Ilford and has been bombed, and his hopes for getting another job with a firm at Cheltenham.

Saturday, October 26, 1940

Fred and Phyllis to tea. They are staying at Amberley Inn for a week. Hilary worried about Leonard.

Hitler reaches agreement with Petain.

Sunday, October 27, 1940

Back to London by car with Phyllis and Fred. As we leave Stroud there is an air-raid warning, and I see Bert Beard, who has left the morning service, letting himself in to his mother's house, with a scared face. I understand they have a reinforced cellar there where doubtless he took refuge, but we speed on up London Road, and at Chalford a Constable tells us there is a warning and we proceed at our own risk. We thank him and continue to proceed. Lovely ride, and the trees are bright and beautiful. They drop me at Morden, where I get Underground, but have to get out at Tooting because the railway is not working, and take an Emergency Bus to Clapham North. Take it allthe way to the Strand, and discover as I arrive at Manchester Street, that there has been an air-raid warning, since the All Clear begins to sound.

Am expecting Greaves and Bell to appear for supper, but at present (8.45) am alone in the flat, with planes buzzing about and guns firing.

Monday, October 28, 1940

After writing last night's entry, found Jack wandering about, who advised me to proceed with supper. So did, and went to bed. Things pretty quiet and was asleep at midnight when there was loud sound of tramping down my corridor. Went out, expecting somehow to find stretcher party with casualties, but discovered the two absentees, who had missed buses and trains from country where they were walking. Assured me would have trodden like Agag had they known I was there, and I withdrew again.

Today Italy invades Greece, and Greece invokes aid of
Britain.   Question is, will Turkey fight, and will Russia then
honour her pledge to help the two of them.

Tuesday, October 29, 1940

Very cold, but fine.   Last night not bad, though some gunfire.
But did not sleep very well.   News today about Greece rather
vague.   Early morning broadcast says Greeks have pushed eight
miles into Albania.   Later, headline announces Italians advancing on several fronts.   Tina's Sir Richard has been seeing A.J.
Cummings of the News Chronicle, who says we cannot do much about
fighting Italy in Medi terranean, because between sinkings and demands of convoys, we are short of ships.   But he says the air
position is good.   We are geting 600 planes a month now.   Moreover we can stand bombing better than the Germans, whose towns
are built closer ~~together~~ - i.e. not as much open space in them -
and whose morale is not as good as ours because they have already
been under war conditions for three years.   Also he says there
is really a change of heart in the middle-classes in England, so
that a desire really does exist to build up something better for
the world once thisw ar is over.
         The question still is, what will Turkey do: and then
what will Russia do?
         On way home from printers, walk past end of Tottenham
Court Road, which has been very damaged by bombs - probably w eek
before last.
         "Empress of Britain", one of our largest liners, sunk.
         Have just remembered rather dramatic moment to-day when
sirens had gone, but we hadn't yet been whistled below, and I
looked out of window and saw everybody running, and there was a
loud bang, though not very near, and Mr. Ab. and I went downstairs
with great speed.

Wednesday, October 30, 1940

R.A.F. has attacked Italian naval base, and as far as one can as-
certain, the Italians are advancing, but news is very scanty.
Nancy comes in to breakfast with an evil rumour from Ministry of
Information that there has been naval encounter of which no details
will be given for a few days, which leads one to suppose it was not
successful.   Germany is threatening Turkey with what will happen
if she supports Greece.   Mr. Joseph Kennedy, late American Ambassador in Britain, has made speech in America supporting Roosevelt but
saying America will not go to war: she will give Britain all aid
short of actual fighting.   An article in the Manchester Guardian,
reporting Charles Boyer, the American newspaper correspondent who
was till lately in Berlin, says Germany is divided into two camps -
the Nazi Party and the others.   The N.Party have themselves admitted that Duff Cooper's speech in which he said the German people

must be exterminated has been more use to them than ten armoured
divisions.   The silly sausage.
        Joyce, in letter, reports bombs at Idbury and district,
probably incendiaries dropped with intention of lighting up surroundings for attack on aerodrome.   Project failed and no harm
done because they all fell in fields.
        Arnold appears - in London for 10 days relieving one of
the engineers here.   I invite him to Manchester Street for Friday
night and to cycle with me to Beavans' cottage on Saturday.   Later
discover from Peter cottage likely to be rather full, with bombed-
out charwoman and husband, etc., but this uncertain.

Thursday, October 31, 1940

Gibraltar attacked by Italians, unsuccessfully we are told.   News
from Greece still very scanty.
        Last night quiet.   Very long warning to-day from lunch-
time till about 4.30.   During this time I go to Hampstead to collect my mackintosh leggings for cycling and my rucksack.   The Wells
Tavern, in the middle of Well Walk, had a bomb outside it last night
and most of the windows around are shattered.   "Well End" escaped
injury.   Come back down Fitzjohn's Avenue in pouring rain and get
very wet.   At 4.30 go to Manchester Street and change into trousers
to go to fetch bicycle from Kilburn.   Jack comes in as I wait for
rain to abate a little, and makes tea for us both.   (He has lately
been down to Surrey Docks, where that disastrous fire was the first
night that bombing became really serious.   Says - and he is the
last one to exaggerate - that there are acres and acres which were
once timber yards, grain store-houses and workers' dwellings, which
are now like the battlefields of France, and the stench, which
appears to come from half-burnt bodies, is terrible.)
        I go forth in the rain and have difficulty in getting to
Kilburn - buses in Edgware Road are full, and they diverge from the
accustomed route so much that I walk to Paddington, where they
seem to have wandered, and a lot further before catching one, and
it then immediately goes off the track and I wonder where I am.   Am
upset by huge gap which was once couple of houses in Oxford Road,
almost opposite Beavans.   Cycle back in dusk, mist and rain, without a back light.   The exquisite Harry, our Wodehouse staff, screws
up his face in agony at spectacle I present, and averts his gaze.

Friday, November 1, 1940

Greeks say they have held Italians on every point and that R.A.F.
are helping them.   Italians say they have advanced quite a lot.
Last night fairly quiet.   To-day have lunch with Arnold and we get
our rations for tomorrow.   He comes to Manchester St. for night,
and first part of evening is very noisy.

Saturday, November 2, 1940

Not such a good night. All Clear at 2 o'clock and another alarm
at 2.30. Tina comes to bed at ~~2.30~~ a quarter to 2, after discussing the future of Europe with Raymond since 11 o'clock. I wake up
under impression that it must be morning and am astounded to find
her bed so far unslept in.
      R.A.F. have bombed Naples.
      A. and I set out at 9.30 for Aldbury. Call on some dis-
tant cousins of his - German Jews - at Cricklewood. The father,
aged 65, and son, who came from Germany because of Nazi persecution,
in 1932, were taken in June by our authorities to the Isle of Man
and interned for 2 months. 800 people went over on boat that
should hold 500. It rained and they were not allowed to go to
cabins. Because of heavy seas, ship stayed outside harbour all
night. They had no food or drink all the time. Now they have been
released, as enemy aliens, which means they have no wireless set and
their every movement must be reported to the police. The boy says
he does not feel an alien, let alone an enemy. Other friends have
been deported to Australia - fetched by police in middle of night
and allowed to collect only a suitcase full of clothes. Their
wives promised they should follow them, but many have not gone.
Feel ashamed when I hear all this, because we think ourselves better
than the Nazis, but these are like their methods we despise.
      Cycle on to Watford, where have lunch with two aunts.
A cousin also calls in (Stanley). Works at War Office. Was
recently buried when house in Bruton Street was bombed. Was dug
out: has something, probably glass, in one eye, and may lose sight
of it. After lunch it rains and ~~we~~ one aunt lends me mackintosh
hat. Enjoy ride in spite of elements, and keep pretty dry.

Sunday, November 3, 1940

Pouring wet day. Arnold earns Duque's love and gratitude by clearing out grate before she gets up. Hear from Beavans that eggs have
been "cornered", hence their price - 4d. They will continue to be
scarce, they say, till price is still higher. Arthur puts on Lord
Haw-haw, and I say the man's voice creeps with evil, and am rebuked.
A. thinks he may genuinely imagine the Nazi regime is best for the
world. Long argument results.

Monday, November 4, 1940

Rise at ~~4.30~~ 5.30 and cycle to London in pouring rain. We start
at 7, before it is light, but dawn comes greyly and imperceptibly
and is not exciting. Reach London about 10 in very wet state.
They had no air raid alarm at all last night - firsttime this has
happened for a long time, and it is put down to extremely bad weather.
      British have made landing on Crete. Americans say Ger-
many will soon have 300 - I think - submarines.

Tuesday, November 5, 1940

Gray's Inn bombed last night, so Mr. Abraham says, who reports
all windows broken when he comes down G.I. Road in bus. Tina
says there were bombs at Victoria - in South Eaton Place, not on
station. Night not too bad here.

Polling today for American President. Everyone hopes
Roosevelt will get in for the third term of office, and not Wendell Willkie, who represents Big Business.

Speech in house by Mr. Churchill, who says, among other
things: "There is no doubt that the full malice and power of the
enemy and his bombing force have been employed against us ...
14,000 civilians have been killed and 20,000 seriously wounded,
nearly four-fifths of them in London ... The weekly scale of the
casualties killed and seriously wounded was, for September 4,500,
and October, 3,500. In the first week of intensive bombardment
in September there were 6,000 casualties; in the last week of
Ocgober only 2,000. This diminution in the scale of the attack
is not entirely due to the weather ... there are other things going on which play their part". (Does this refer to the new weapon for dealing with air attack which has frequently been hinted
at in the newspapers?) ... "More serious than the air raids has
been the recent recrudescence of U-boat sinkings in the Atlantic
approaches to our islands. The fact that we cannot use the
south and west coasts of Ireland to refuel our flotillas and aircraft and thus prote ct the trade by which Ireland, as well as
Great Britain, lives, is a most heavy and grievous burden and one
which should re ver have been placed upon our shoulders"... "We
must expe ct that next year still heavier U-boat attacks will be
made upon us, and we are making immense preparations of all kinds
to meet them. We have to look a long way ahead in this sphere
of the war. We have to t hink about 1943 and 1944, and of the
tonnage programmes, and of what we shall have to move across the
oceans then". This does indeed sound depressing, and as if he
expects a long war.

Wednesday, November 6, 1940

A noisy night: the alarm began at 6.30 and did not end till 8.30
a.m.   At about 4 a.m., hear long and strange whistle, as of bomb
coming more slowly than usual. This may have been the land-mine
which Miss Evans had at the back of her block of flats at Hammersmith, or it may have been the s creaming bombs which were being used
in some districts.

Warnings on and off all day. In lunch time to National
Gallery Concert, where hear Beethoven and Brahms trio - latter
first played in this form in 1890, with same violinist as to-day,
Arnold Rosé.

Good news of to-day is that Roosevelt is elected U.S.
President. Imagine this will anger Germany, and rather expect
bad raids tonight. Warning has already gone and it is only 6.10.

Jawaharial Nehru, Indian Congress leader, has been sentenced to four years' "rigorous imprisonment", because he has made anti-war speeches. He was one of the two men chosen by Gandhi to make anti-war speeches as part of the Congress plan of limited civil disobedience. Tina opines there is no hope for us while we can do things like this.

Thursday, November 7, 1940

~~Last night very noisy again till after midnight.   Planes had different note: probably Italian.~~
Wrote last night's entry before dinner, when we all drank Roosevelt's health in aged and lovely port provided by Graham: with an American flag, improvised by Jack, stuck in an empty sherry bottle on the table. From 6 o'clock till midnight there was a constant succession of low-flying planes, and a great noise from A.A. guns. About 9, five or six bombs fell together - hear today they were in Great Titchfield and Great Portland Streets, and rocked the B.B.C., at which no doubt they were aimed. After midnight I sleep till 10 to 8, when am awakened by the All Clear. Learn that bombs last night damaged also St. Martin-in-the-Fields, but not irreparably, and the people sleeping in the crypt were not hurt.

A very low-flying plane over the B.B.C. startles us during the morning. And later, a member of a demolition squad we've watched working for weeks on bombed building at corner of Hallam Street, falls to street and is killed. During day there are five explosions quite near - probably time-bombs dropped last night somewhere between Broadcasting House and Tottenham Court Rd.

The day is full of rumours. Hear (1) the Stock Exchange is giving 25 to 1 that the war will be over by February. (2) That the R.A.F. is convinced all will be over, with British victorious, by April. (3) That the Greeks are retiring heavily, and that all stories of their temporary successes have come from Berlin, to mislead us - but that Ministry of Information will not shook us by letting retreat be made known right away.

General Hertzog has resigned, with his party, from South African Government. As he was anti-war and pro-Nazi, nobody here seems to care.

Friday, November 8, 1940

Last night very noisy again till after midnight. Planes had different note: probably Italians, since this morning paper says Italians have been taking part in air attack on London and that therefore we shall bomb Rome.

Eire has refused to let us have naval or air bases in Southern Ireland, since she is still technically neutral. Lord Craigavon, Governor of Northern Ireland, says it Just Shows, and that Ulster has now justified her existence a hundred-fold. Tina says he ought to be burnt and inhabitants of Ulster pushed into sea,

Saturday, November 9, 1940

Neville Chamberlain very ill.   Molotov, Soviet Foreign Minister,
going to Berlin to meet Ribbentrop.   Half of America's arms production to come to Britain.
            May I travel to Stroud for week's holiday by 9.15, which
is full of laden people unaccustomed to travelling, the women
clutching all their parcels and their handbags and their umbrellas
and their mackinstoshes and holding firmly on to all instead of
putting some of it on the rack.   Journey takes 4½ hours.

Sunday, November 10, 1940

Chamberlain died last night.   To-day a sermon by Rev.Hitchings in
which he goes to some trouble to explain that God is doing nothing
spectacular in Europe at the present time, is followed at 6 p.m.
by news that a tremendous earthquake has shaken Rumania, killing
hundreds of people in Bucharest and destroying many houses.   The
chief interest for Britain at present is whether the oil wells have
been affected: anyway communications have been upset.
            P. and I go for moonlight walk on common.   We hear
German planes going over but they drop no bombs here.   There are
searchlights from every hill trying to find them out.

Monday, November 11, 1940

Molotov on his way to Berlin.
            Lord Derby, at Rossall School speech day, told the boys
they must "fit themselves for the commercial battle for the world's
markets that will follow the war".   This has provoked furious comments from readers of News Chronicle.   Particularly unfortunate as
our rulers refuse to say exactly what we are fighting for, and one
cannot help feeling Lord D. was only speaking the unhappy truth.

Tuesday, November 12, 1940

News Chronicle very depressed about visit of Molotov to Berlin and
says the worst may be expected from it.
            Shopping in Stroud very difficult: the population has
increased by thousands because of evacuation, and goods are very
scarce.   One has to go to four or five shops and then get what one
does not want, at a very high price.   Daddy says he has received some
praces for which he would have been ashamed to ask for than 1/- a
little while back, and to get any provit on them at all he has to
ask 2/8, and says how can poor people afford that for a pair of
braces.

Wednesday, November 13, 1940

See in Times that Hurley and Barbara McCormick, and Barbara's father
have been killed by enemy action.

Nine ships of convoy sunk in Atlantic by German ship which is now f ree there.   It was engaged by an armed merchant trawler which accompanie d the convoy, the Jervis Bay, which thus drew off the attention of the warship so that 29 of our ships escaped.   The Jervis Bay was shop to bits.   A Swedish Captain who saw the encounter was so impressed with the courage of the trawler that he returned to pick up survivors instead of escaping right away.

The Fleet Air Arm has attacked the Italian Fleet in its own waters at Taranto, behind the coastal defences, and has done a great deal of damage: several s hips photographed by reconnaissance plane with their bows beneath water.   Also a submarine has sunk an Italian supply ship.

Sound of much gunfire in afternoon, and while P. and I are on common with Tramp, a German plane goes over, with all the guns in the neithbourhood going full blast.   At first, seeing all the puffs of smoke round the plane, I imagine it is 27 machines approaching. We lie in a ditch, holding down Tramp who is much excited. Mother (who has touch of flu) and Hilary get under stairs.   Daddy, and all shopkeepers and shoppers in Stroud, stand gaping in middle of street while panic-stricken population rushes to doors and gardens and gazes skywards.   Earlier, while guns were sounding, I had passed the Erinoid Works, where the entire staff appeared to be watching the heavens from outside the factory.

Thursday, November 14, 1940

Mother a little better but s tays in bed.   I accompany H. to doctor's, who pronounces her "fit as a fiddle".   In evening, H., P. and I take dog over hilli n brilliant full moon (the Lord gives clear full moon for bombers one night, and howling gales the next, when there is little air activity: Mr. Thomas said in the office one day that in his view God was neutral with a pro-Fascist bias). While we are on hill, many bombers go over, and searchlight s come into play.   A red light flashes from a distant hill, which seems to be a signal for the people at Rodborough Fort to set going the dynamo which works the searchlight.   We see a flare over the aerodrome, two flares over Brockworth, shells bursting in the sky in the direction of Coventry, and then there is heavy gunfire from Brockworth way.   We hover on edge of dilly, ready to plunge in and lieface downwards.   Tramp rushes barking in direction of guns: Phyllida is much more nervous of stray cows than of enemy aeroplanes.   It all seems wildly unlikely, especially with the evening itself so calm and bright.

Friday, November 15, 1940

The planes we heard last nightm ust have been going to Coventry, where there was v ery heavy raid, destroying the fourteenth-century cathedral and causing about 1,000 casualties.

Three more ships of convoy where Jervis Bay was sunk have now returned home.

Saturday, November 16, 1940

Heavy raid on London last night.   Our daily paper does not come
till midday.   On Friday night we bombed Hamburg.   The war, as
Clive Bell has said, is nothing but a bombing match.   One cynic
in letter in News Chronicle - I think it was ≯ suggested that as
both sides were short of petrol, we might bomb London and let the
Germans bomb Berlin.
            Greeks seem to be holding their own against Italians.
            Newspaper says we sent three offers to Russia during
October, but have received no reply.
            Mother better and gets up in afternoon.

Sunday, November 17, 1940

Have to return to London, the very thought of which gives me pains
in my stomach.   Phyllis and Fred, at Amberley Inn for another three
days, come in morning.   Delight Mother by gift of a week's rations.
She says she never thought that the present of a few ounces of
margarine, which she once so despised, would fill her with joy.
Fred takes me to station to catch 12.3, Daddy leaves chapel in
middle of sermon to see me off, and I start away in beautiful sunshine.   Arrive at Paddington at 3.45.   Am told Friday night's
raid here was worst since the first night I spent at Padd Manchester
Street.

Monday, November 18, 1940

Commander of Jervis Bay awarded V.C.   Number of casualties in
Comentry now estimated at 250 killed and about 750 or more wounded.
So the baker who met us and told us thousands had been killed was
exaggerating.
            Back to work.   Day turns out wet and foggy, and night
alarm does not sound till 8.30.   Hope it is too bad for much bombing.   Penberthy's in Oxford Street has been demolished, probably
last Friday; also National Gallery has been hit and a lot of damage
done at back of Westminster - not Abbey or H. or P., but mostly
blocks of flats.
            Shops in Oxford Street now closing at 4.30 p.m, to allow
assistants to leave in daylight.

Tuesday, November 19, 1940

Strange night of alarms and All Clears - four of them I believe.
I heard only two aeroplanes and they went over very quickly.   But
in spite of this quiet I did not sleep very much.   To-day we have
no warning at all until the evening, and wonder What They are Up to
Now.   What they seem to be up to is a plan to march through
Bulgaria and invade Turkey.   King Boris of Bulgaria is seeing
Hitler at Berchtesgaten.   The Greeks are still reported to be ad-

vancing. Koritza is said to have fallen to them. There still
is the possibility that the tales of their successes are put out
by our enemies so that our disappointment later on may be greater.
        I hear that the industrial damage in Coventry was very
much more than has been officially announced. Lord Beaverbrook,
Minister for Aircraft Production, has been visiting the city.
The B.B.C. news claims that the damage done by us to industrial
Germany is 20 times greater than anything they have done to us.
        Find that it was Swears and Wells which wasdemolished,
not Penberthy's, which, however, has all its windows gone, and so
has C.And A's, next door to it.

Wednesday, November 20, 1940

Night tolerably quiet - explained this morning by news that four
Midland towns have had heavy raids, and Birmingham the worst raid
it has yet had. A determined onslaught on our industrial output.
No siren yet to-day (6.30 p.m.).
        Leopold of Belgians going to visit Hitler. The Germans,
in broadcast intended for America, say that only the uncalled-for
interference of Britain prevents Europe from being one contented
and united state now. Does this include Russia, one wonders?
General feeling is that Russia is making terms with Germany now
only in order to gather strength to wipe her up later on.
        Tina shows me letter Sir Richard Acland wrote to Arch-
bishop of York, who is his cousin, about the Archb's recent broadcast talks. Ackland says he thinks the Church ought to preach to
people that the present order of things, by which most of our doings
are controlled by the private profit motive, is wrong: that it is
impossible for people to be real Christians in a society which by
its nature is non-Christian, which exists by making as much as
possible out of other people instead of by serving other people as
Christ taught. He thinks the Church ought not to say what ought
to be done instead - that is not its function. It ought merely
to say "This must stop", as it did about the slave trade, even
though hardships may be caused by the change involved, as no doubt
hardships were in some cases suffered by the slaves who gained
their freedom. The Archbishop in his reply seemed to go so far
but not all the way with Acland - agreed that the duty of the Church
was to point broad instead of particular lines of conduct, but said
that if the policy he'd advocated in his talks came forward at a
Church meeting, as a churchman he'd vote against it, because it was
not rightly within the Church's province. But as a man he supported it.

Thursday, November 21, 1940

Greeks daim more victories. Mother says the night of the Birmingham raids there were aeroplanes going over Stroud in a continuous
stream. Last night here not noisy except at about 4 a.m.

London buses are not to run after 10.30 p.m.

House of Lords has voted against publishing Lord
Horder's report on air raid shelter conditions.   Say it will
give a handle to the Germans.   Think this feeble, as last time
I heard Haw-Haw he was giving a talk about conditions in shelters,
and will now be able to say we dare not disclose what the real
situation is.

Friday, November 22, 1940

Greeks still having successes.   I ask Editor why he said the
other day the tales of their victories were not true.   He is
cross and denies that he said such a thing.   But he did.

Graham says in the bad raid last Friday the bombers
tried to hit the House of Commons but dropped eight bombs in the
Thames.   I go to National Gallery concert, and see new damage
done to Gallery and to Trafalgar Square, where Hampton's is gutted.
(All sandwiches sold at Nat.Gal., but nice woman gave me sandwich
bread which had not been used - about 8 pieces: so had rather dry
lunch.)

Saturday, November 23, 1940

Last night pretty quiet: some gunfire and three bombs about 4 a.m.
Today I cycle with Peter to Aldbury, in foggy morning which becomes sunny when we reach the country.   Evening is starry and
bright and I hear only one aeroplane.

Sunday, November 24, 1940

Shared the sitting-room floor with John last night.   Peter goes
off early today because he has to rehearse for Philharmonic Concert this afternoon and for Boyd Neel broadcast this evening.   We
have $2\frac{1}{2}$-hour amble over heath in clear sunshine and come home for
lunch at about 3.30.

Monday, November 25, 1940

Arise at 5 and at 6 J. and I start back on bicycles in dark.   He
has to leave me at Watford where he turns off for Teddington, but
by then it is light.   Get to London, have bath and change, and am
at office just after 10 - not bad.   Letter from Mother.   They
had disturbed night on Friday: lot of aeroplanes and gunfire.
West of England town - presumably Bristol - bombed last night.
Southampton had enormous fires on Friday and Saturday, so Mr.
Abraham learns from his father, who says the fires were visible
from the middle of Isle of Wight.   London, they tell me, was very
quiet last night.

Tuesday
~~Friday~~, November 26, 1940

No warning at all here last night.   Bob and Raymond spend some
time in evening ~~asking~~ arguing about solusists (spelling?) solipsists
people who think they are the only reality and all else is illu-
sion.   I have to go to bed while argument still rages, being
worn out with getting up at 5 and with intellectual effort.
        Papers say West of England town bombed again.   Nancy,
whose uncle has to take radium to places which have been bombed,
reports that Coventry is "like Pompeii before they cleared up the
mess".   The police cordon is 12 or 14 miles from centre of city,
and from then on it is impossible to tell what was streets, what
houses and what factories.   The factories there ~~are~~ were all in
middle of city, mixed up with houses, and all have suffered together.
        Greeks have made landing near Corfu, behind Italian
troops, cutting them off and taking thousands of prisoners.
Graham says it is a major defeat for Italy, the most important
effect of which will be in the minds of ~~G~~ Italian citizens who
probably didn't want war anyway.   Italians are explaining it by
saying they were not properly prepared, but since there was no
particular reason why the march into Greece should have taken
place when it did, this is not convincing.
        Bulgaria has refused to join Axis powers.

Wednesday, November 27, 1940

Very quiet night.   All Clear at 11 and nothing more till 7 a.m.
But we hear Bristol had raids again.
        A grand bust-up at B.B.C.   W.E. Williams, Listener
critic of "The Spoken Word" (talks, etc.), last week wrote dis-
paragingly of broadcasting manner and technique of Lord Lloyd,
who has complained to the D.G., and Mr. Ogilvie, who himself was
against Lord L. as a broadcaster, feels the noble peer will imagine
Williams was prompted to his remarks.   Accordingly, W's quite
harmless article for this week, in which he praises at length one
broadcast, but goes on to wish the "Dominion Commentators", High
Commissioners, etc., would see the opportunity they are missing
in not presenting their countries imaginatively to the public, is
suppressed.   Editor protests against this suppression of freedom
of speech, and receives reply that if liberty is not curtailed
thus, it will be removed altogether, and in fact paper for printing
of The Listener at all may be withheld.
        Williams comes up for interview today and is told that in
future he is not to criticise Cabinet Ministers, Members of Parliament
or Government officials.   Am glad to say he explodes with wrath,
but what the outcome is I do not yet know.
        Graham very depressed at supper because he has to go to
Manchester with the Committee on National Expenditure, of which he
is member.   Keeps murmuring disconsolately "Midland Hotel,

Manchester!"   Lets out the fact that at Birkenhead there has
been considerable amount of trouble in shipyards, whe re men have
sat down in ships and read newspapers, refusing to continue work
because they wish to be transferred to some othe r port where they
will receive higher wages.
        There are to be no bananas after Christmas: the ships
are to be used for transporting more essential goods.   One lot
of bananas will be paid for and then destroyed.
        B.B.C.'s bomb damage being very quickly put to rights,
and the whole building painted ugly grey like battleship - its
Portland stone was rather startling and distinc tive.
        There is to be no Bank Holiday on Boxing Day.
        Joyce, who sends me unstamped letter on which have to
pay 5d, reports bombs near cottage.

Thursday, November 28, 1940

House of Commons goes into secret session.   Seems likely they
discussed the shipping position, which is grave.   Ronald Cross,
Minister of Shipping, said in his broadcast talk on Tuesday that
since June our losses have been 60,000 tons a week, and our aver-
age for the war is the same as for the years 1914-18.
        W.E. Williams today sees Director-General.
        Closing-time for Oxford Street shops is now 4 p.m.
        I work rather late and go home through pitch blackness
lightened only by bursting of shells in sky.   Warning does not go
until I am nearly in Manchester Street, but planes are zooming
about and guns going.
        Raymond plays Hugo Wolf songs on gramophone , and Sibelius'
Fourth Symphony, during which I go to sleep in armchair.

Friday, November 29, 1940

Lot of planes about at beginning of last night, but papers say
bombers went over London and did not drop bombs here.   If they
use the way of over London as a route, fear barrage does not worry
them much.   Mother says when Bristol bombed last week, planes did
not go over Stroud but all came up Bristol Channel.   North-west
coastal town had heavy raid last night - probably Liverpool.
        Navy has pursued fleeing Italian ships and hit several.
        Office hours now 9.30 - 5.30 officially, but heads of
departments told to use their own discretion.
        To Stroud by 4.15.   Man in train gives his opinion that
Chamberlain died of a broken heart.   Fellow passenger disagrees.
        Bomb at Whotehhill yesterday night.

Saturday, November 30, 1940

Very cold and fine.   Wireless says heavy raid on London last
night.   Navy has encountered German ships in Channel: they go
away quickly and disappear in mist.

America making credit of several million dollars to China. Rumania full of internal disruption. Iron Guard has taken things into its own hands and is executing numbers of people. Greeks have sunk Italian submarine.

Sunday, December 1, 1940

Railway fares up again by 6½ per cent. Milk up ½d a pint. Is now 4½d. And supply has to be cut down by one-tenth. This is not to affect free milk for mothers and children.

Heavy raid last night on Southampton. Fires started, some serious. Hear when get back to Manchester Street in afternoon that Friday's night raid here was not bad. At time of writing (9.30), we have had evening's siren (at about 7.10) and since that an All Clear.

Monday, December 2, 1940

We did get another warning last night, but things pretty quiet except for some gunfire. Southampton raided again.

Tuesday, December 3, 1940

No warning at all here last night, but Bristol has heavy raid. Our shipping losses very serious. Britain makes trade agreement with Spain.

Williams has bowed his head and agreed not to criticise members of Government, etc. Very disappointed in him.

Wednesday, December 4, 1940

No air raid warning in London last night.

Bacon ration to be cut. It is difficult to buy sweet biscuits, chocolate bars, small electric torch batteries or toilet rolls. Eggs are almost impossible to get.

Thursday, December 5, 1940

Italians driven out of South Albania. Britain has made trade pact with Turkey.

Was so depressed yesterday, Tina suggested our going to film tonight. So we meet at Piccadilly Circus at 4.45, and - in spite of having first to sit through frightful crooning film and dreadful Ministry of Information film about air raid shelters which attempts to give impression that if people forgather in the warehouses the kind government has given them to shelter in, and are then prayed over by the Vicar, their night's repose will be sweet - in spite of these two, we really did enjoy "Our Town", and took no notice of the announcement from the stage that an air-raid warning was in progress. Took taxi home through wet, dark streets: impossible to see which way we were going.

<u>Friday, December 6, 1940</u>

It is announced in Daily Telegraph that Mr. Ogilvie, Director-
General of B.B.C., is resigning, and it is hinted that Sir Stephen
Tallents, his Deputy, is also going.   New appointment not announced, though hints dropped of "business man" and that Lord Lloyd
will have something to do with Corp.; the Foreign Broadcasting is
to come under the Foreign Office, and as he is Colonial Secretary,
this is not unlikely.
          Last night All Clear from midnight onwards.

<u>Saturday, December 7, 1940</u>

Telegraph this morning says Sir Walter Moncton or possibly Frank
Pick will succeed Mr. O.   News Chronicle, on other hand, says
there is not a word of truth in all these rumours, and that Mr. O.
is not r esigning.   Sir Stephen T. may go, but his successor is not
yet appointed.   (N.B.   News Chronicle's Editor, Sir Walter Layton,
is in America, and paper is being run by Vernon Bartlett, Cummings,
and Gerald Barry - all friends of our Mr. Thomas.   It is easy to
guess where they get their information.)
          I go to Aldbury by 12.15 and enjoyw alking from station
in sunshine.   Child in railway carriage stuffs her mouth so full
of chocolate (which is very hard to come by nowadays) she is sick.
          Boys not out here.   Arthur, Duque and I read bits of
verse aloud in evening, in quite unplanned and enjoyable way.

<u>Sunday, December 8, 1940</u>

Beautiful day.   We walk in sunshine in woods, but wind is cold.
Have long talk with Arthur about world affairs.   Dismal conclusions
we reach are that a new United States of Europe is necessary if
there is to be anything like peace for the coming generations:
that Hitler has by force achieved this in some measure: that none
the less we do not want him to win the war because his ideals are
repugnant to us: that if Britain wins, she is pledged to restore
their independece to all the little states of pre-war Europe, which
will lead us back to where we were before.   Arthur thinks if Hitler
wins the results will be awful; if we win they will be still more
awful.   In his work he meets lot of working-class people, among
whom he says there is no enthusiasm at all for the war, which they
feel, rightly, is being used to bolster up the profits of the present money-owning classes.   If we don't get socialisation of industry (which Hitler has pretty well done in Germany), the people
with pwoer in this country will naturally follow the way which pro-
tects their interests, which means short rations for the poor as
usual.
          "Haw-Haw", to whom A. listens every night - can't think
how he can, for the man's voice creeps with evil - has not yet
mentioned Italy or Greece in his English news.   To-day he satisfies

himself with trying to frighten us by descriptions of amounts
of bombs dropped on various towns in England, with promises of
more to come.   Accuses R.A.F. of indiscriminate bombing - like
our accusations against Luftwaffe.   Yesterday he gave talk on
our shipping losses.   Arthur Greenwood, I think it was, has
lately said in H. of C. that our losses are as great as in the
worst months of 1917.   In Lloyd George's Memoirs, Haw-Haw says,
it is admitted that the figure given to the public at this time
was only one-third of actual losses.   Well, Ronald Cross, Minister for Shipping, has just given us figures, which are not
nearly as big as those given by Ll.G. for 1917.   So presumably
we are not being told the truth now, either.   Aim of this talk
is to frighten us with threat of starvation.

<u>Monday, December 9, 1940</u>

At 11.20 last night, two great bombs bangs, and cottage shakes.
We do not find this morning where the bombs fell, because Arthur
and I leave house at 7.15 in the dark.   I approach Broadcasting
House through much broken glass, and find scene of desolation.
More gone from Langham, inside of All Soul's Church in a mess,
most of B.B.C. staff standing helplessly inf ront of main entrance,from which attendant is sweeping muddy water.   Landmine
last night in Portland Place, and building is flooded.   B.E.
Nicolls had ceiling descend on his head and is reported to be
badly hurt.   We go to printers and work there, five on one small
table.   Editor and Course get into office and salvage and few
things, but are not allowed to stay.   If nothing more untoward
happens we hope to produce Listener as usual.
        Raymond and Bob report very bad night in Manchester
Street - landmine in Marylebone High Street, three fires in Baker
Street, and sound of sweeping up broken glass all night.   All the
soot descended from Bob's chimney and covered him and room with
black.
        Tonight no alert so f ar, and it is 9.45.   Feel nearly
dead with exhaustion and depression.

<u>Tuesday, December 10, 1940</u>

No air raid warning at all last night, and nowhere else in country
seems to have had it either.   It is almost full moon, and as I
write (10 to 9) it is a bright, clear night, but so far no warning
again, which seems odd.   Sir Richard Acland had in his office to-
day man who had beeni n Southampton.   Says for area of 2 miles by
1 there is nothing left, and the people started putting all their
things onhand-carts, etc., and getting out on the roads, e xactly
as they did in France, and as they have been warned not to do here.
The man says moreover that the Portsmouth Fire Brigade was called
in to help the Southampton Brigade on the night of heavy bombing,

but none of the nozzles of their hoses fitted the Southampton hydrants.   In the raid on Sunday the House of Commons was hit.
Hear that the reason the papers have had to pipe down on Ogilvie's retirement is not because he is not going to retire but because they can find nobody to take his place - no one will take on the job.
At end of afternoon, Listener staff is able to get back to its offices.   I have not been up there yet, because spend day at printers.   Am still very tired and depressed, and make stupid mistakes all day, but clear my head a little by walking most of the way home - though after going for wome time in direction I imagine to be parallel with Oxford Street, am surprised to find myself at Euston Square.
We have attacked Italians in Libyan Desert, and according to reports have captured 1,000 men and occupied their first positions.

Wednesday, December 11, 1940

No alarm last night.   Go back to bed after breakfast, with pains and general lassitude, and remain there for rest of day.   On coming in and finding me thus, the party rallies: Tina gives me gin and Bob administers quinine.   It is a very cold day and I think I have an internal chill.
British advancing against Italians in Libya.

Thursday, December 12, 1940

Some intermittent gunfire, but most of last night's raid (in full moon) on Birmingham.   I get up for breakfast, but feel none too good and go back to bed.   Bob and Raymond provide me with many books to read.   Graham comes in with his secretary at 4.30 and gives me brandy, and goes to bed himself with brandy, with apparently the same ailment.   I get up for dinner.   Still very cold.
British still having successes in Libya.   Lord Lothian, British Ambassador to America, dead.

Friday, December 13, 1940

Contemplate going in to office, or alternatively going away to Joyce for weekend, but feel unlike either.   Graham isgetting a doctor friend to look him over, so he looks at me too, and diagnoses colitis.   Before this I ring Miss Playle at home, and find none of my messages to B.B.C. switchboard have been delivered (Listener still off the phone).
British have captured 28,000 Italians in Western Desert. Cannot imagine what they will do with them all, or how feed them.
Raid last night on Sheffield - not much on London.

Saturday, December 14, 1940

Still feel very inert.   Tina brings me flowers and fixes up Jack's
wireless, but I do not listen much.   Ring up Daddy and say I am
coming home for fortnight on Monday.   Letter from Joyce says
Cheltenham has been bombed.   No warning here last night.

Sunday, December 15, 1940

Very early alert (just after 6), followed by All Clear an hour or
two later.   Peaceful night.   Feel better and get up for lunch.

Monday, December 16, 1940

To Stroud by 1.55.   Feel rather done up after the journey, but
better than last week.

Tuesday, December 17, 1940

Over 100,000 tons of shipping lost last week.   No wonder Mr.
Pritchard says there is no meat in the West of Egnland;   and he does
not know whether there will be any for us tomorrow.

Wednesday, December 18, 1940

For short walk, but my knees still weak.   News on wireless sounds
exactly the same as all the news bulletins I have heard for the past
month.   Mr. Pritchard manages to let us have a little steak and a
little tripe.   The Waltons let P. have six eggs as special favour,
because they have heard I am on sick list.   These, even at 3½d
each, are treasure trove.

Thursday, December 19, 1940

Churchill makes statement in House of Commons: situation against
Italians is very satisfactory.   Chief difficulty at present is the
shipping losses in North Atlantic, a danger which a year ago we
thought we had successfully met, but which we must now bend all our
powers to overcome.
        Beautiful day.   We go for short ride, Daddy having got 5
gallons of petrol from a customer (who was allowed extra because he
is a farmer and has a motor tractor).   On the way down Cranham
Hill we essay to turn left, but find notice saying "UNEXPLODED BOMB"
so hastily return to main road.   All balloons flying over Brockworth, but 6 o'clock news says no air activity over country either
last night or today.

Friday, December 20, 1940

Bitterly cold, with east wind.   Cummings, in News-Chronicle, says
the high point in recent news is not our successes in Western
Desert, but Roosevelt's decision to lend materials which we may
pay in kind after war.   This gets round the non-intervention laws
of U.S.A.   Valona bombed by Navy and Air Force — it is the main
Italian supply base for Albania.   Submarine has sunk two Italian
supply ships.   Rumour that German troops are crossing Brenner
Pass into Italy.   In evening we have an Alert, which is still in
progress when we go to bed.   Hear aeroplanes going over, but no
bombs.   There seems no logic about sounding of Alert in Stroud:
we often hear planes going over at night, but get no warning.

Saturday, December 21, 1940

All Clear about 2 this morning but I do not hear it.   News reports
bombs on Midlands, but chief raid on Liverpool.   Discontent with
war reported ~~reported~~ from Italy.
        I am better and go shopping in Stroud.   No chocolates
obtainable in town, and canget only three oranges.

Sunday, December 22, 1940

Very cold again.   There is a post in spite of its being Sunday,
and H. gets letter from Leonard saying he has taken Miss Abbott's
furnished house at Ware.   We have already had a lot of Christmas
cards: were all asked to post early this year to avoid last-minute
rush for post office.
        Last night's raid on Liverpool and Merseyside.   A great
number of planes go over in evening, and on going to bed at 10.30
I hear an All Clear, though we did not hear warning.   But it is
ratherlike that here.   Leslie, who is in A.F.S., had to be fetched
the other night half-an-hour after warning had sounded, because he
had heard nothing.

Monday, December 23, 1940

Last night's raid was on Manchester, and very heavy.   Lord Halifax
appointed Ambassador to America in place of Lord Lothian, and
Anthony Eden becomes Foreign Secretary in his place.   Capt.
Margesson, Chief Government Whip, becomes War Minister.   Mr.
Churchill broadcasts at 9 o'clock.   Addresses his remarks to the
Italian people, and blames Mussolini for their plight.
        I make breadcrumbs for stuffing for turkey.

Tuesday, December 24, 1940

Bombs on Lancashire last night.   Here we do Christmas shopping.
Meat is so short in Stroud - we hear that it averages 2 oz. per

head for the whole of Christmas (i.e. 3 days), that there is a
long queue outside Hilliers, of people hoping to buy pigmeat.   I
manage to get 3 more oranges.   Boots haven't a handbag in their
shop.

Wednesday, Christmas Day, 1940

No air activity last night, either over this country or over Germany.
Beautiful weather, both clear sunshine and warmth.   Hilary, Phyllida and I go on common in morning.   Mrs. Franklin shows me the
miserable amount of foreign stewing beef (1s.1d.) which is all the
meat she has been able to get.   We are very lucky to have a turkey
though it will cost about 30/- for a 10-lb.one.   After dinner we
hear the King broadcast at 3 o'clock.   Vera brings in some confectioners' cream: assures us the Food Controller would put her in
prison if he knew she ate it, much less gave it away.   She brings
also big tin dripping, which is very welcome since fat is so scarce.
Leslie, Podge and Sal Prue Green call.   We open our presents,
which are under tree in drawing-room which H. has decorated with
tinsel, etc. from last year - there is none to be had in Stroud
this year.   Mother has several packets of chocolate, obtained with
difficulty.   In fact, if we have as much food next Christmas as we
have this, we shall have no cause to grumble.   We seem to have almost as many Christmas cards as usual. I have greetings telegram
from Listener.   Hilary has nothing from Leonard, which is rather
sad for her, and we have not yet heard from South Africa.

Thursday, Boxing Day, 1940

No air activity over this country or Germany last night.   This is
attributed to weather conditions rather than to desire for peace
and goodwill.   Tramp is very poorly,

Friday, December 27, 1940

No air activity again last night, but it is resumed today, and in
evening we hear German planes going over.   Bardia, in Libya, has
still not fallen to our Army, though we are bringing up supplies to
it.   Tramp still poorly and H. worried.   Announcement from Duggie
that Joan has had twins, boy and girl.

Saturday, December 28, 1940

Leonard (unexpected) and nurse (expected) arrive by same train.
Tramp better.   So Hilary, with nurse, husband, and recovering
puppy, is quite set up.
        I manage to get 4 pullets' eggs.   Phyllida has spent
whole day changing round bedrooms to accommodate everyone.
Mother, depressed, feels her home is being broken up irretrievably,
for there is great hammering of bedsteads and dragging of them to
other parts of house.

Sunday, December 29, 1940

Return to London, prospect of which depresses me exceedingly.
Find on arrival that everyone but Jack has been away since Christmas, and he is going out to supper.   There is a warning, and considerable activity, during which he cheers me with sherry.   A lot
of incendiary bombs are dropped: fire engines rush up and down
street.   Harry (waiter) makes me long speech telling me he is 65
and that we have been very lucky to escape bombs so far.   As I
write this there is sound of planes and of machine-gun rat-tat-tatting.   The deaf waiter, who lays my lone supper, tells me Hitler
ought to be flogged - and Goering too: destroying people's homes
like this.   It isn't what we do over there - we go for military
(which he can't say) objectives, n ot for churches, hospitals and
pubs.   The maid who makes up my bed says Lilley and Skinners, the
big Oxford Street shoe store, got a bomb just behind them the other
night.

Monday, December 30, 1940

When I went to bed last night there was a great glare in the sky
towards the City.   Today the papers describe great havoc.   St.
Bride's, Fleet Street, is only one of the Wren churches destroyed.
Guildhall is in ruins and Fenchurch Street Station out of action.
Some fires are still burning.
          I go back to work.   There is still a lot of mess in the
corridors of the B.B.C., and our room is very cold and damp because
of blown-out windows, though those in the room itself are all there.
No telephones still.

Tuesday, December 31, 1940

Last day of a bad year.   Lord Woolton says our food situation is
worse than in last war, which is rather depressing considering we
were very nearly starved into submission then.   Our shipping losses
not quite so bad in the last week, but still very high.
          At printers all day.   Hear horrifying stories of the
extent of damage in city.   Herbert Morrison says much of it might
have been saved if firms had followed regulations and kept firewatchers.   Our block-makers have one building gone destroyed and
another badly damaged.   A great many other block-makers have also
been destroyed, but they manage to park out our work somewhere.
Eyre and Spottiswoode's are gutted, and their work has been sent in
to Speaight's, who could cope with it if they had the machines.
          Very tired at night, but sit up with others till 12.   We
have sherry and port, and chocolates, and there is no Alert.   At
midnight am in midst of controversy on Christianity and Pacifism,
which leads into Bob holding forth on Hell.   The first words spoken
to me in 1941 are accordingly "Happy New Year: and don't forget the
worm that dieth not and the fire which is not quenched".

New Year's Day, 1941

No one has much heart to say "Happy New Year".

Morrison says fire-watching is to be compulsory on every building, and civilians may be conscripted for the purpose. General Smuts says America will come in on side of Britain and we shall win: Hitler has promised his troops full victory in 1941.

Miss Bayle's people, who were bombed out of their house on Friday, had it bombed still more on Sunday, and it is now uninhabitable, together with 2 roads of houses which suffered from the same land mine. But no one belonging to Miss P. was hurt.

The office is so icy, I have to wear my overcoat all day, and am still miserably cold. There are cracks in the walls of the corridors, holes in some of the outside walls, window panes are missing, and no one appears to have made any attempt to sweep up any mess. At 5.30 I am surprised that no one has come round to black out, and have just done the job myself when the electric light goes off. Miss Mearing, who is the only other person left, explains that since the land mine blew down so much blackout and made it impossible to black out many of the windows, they have done this daily. She lights two oil lamps which were brought in for illumination, but these do not help us as we stumble, torchless, along the complicated maze of corridors leading to the front entrance. When we reach it, we are surprised to find it still not ~~darj-iy~~ dark outside.

Am not happy all day till I get home and have glorious hot bath with beautiful new cake of Morny soap and huge clean bath-towel. Then we have steak and kidney pudding, and afterwards listen to a Schubert symphony on wireless, by a coal-fire. Although there is an Alert, feel we are very lucky to have all these good things in wartime, and begin to be a little less depressed about the prospects for the New Year.

Thursday, January 2, 1940

Say to Tina as I get up this morning "I feel as if that baby has arrived", and when I get home at night there is a letter from Mother. It begins as an ordinary weekly one, dated 31 December, but says Hilary has had pains. There is an addition at 12.45 a.m., New Year's Day, wishing me a happy New Year and saying the pains are getting worse. "Phyllida has phoned the doctor apprising him of state of affairs ... she is sleeping on settee with her clothes on in case nurse wants her to phone again. The little bed is ready and looks so pretty, and his first garments hanging over the back of a chair airing before the electric fire. Nurse making boracic for his eyes. I don't suppose I shall sleep. Wish the next 24 hours were over". At bottom of same sheet it says "New Year's Day". Martin is here... At a quarter to nine he began to cry lustily. We all rushed to the stairs and listened with rapture". This was written at 10.5, so everything was very new. H. pretty well. I phone L., but find he has gone to Stroud.

Peter going tonight to Glasgow to join merchant ship
bound for East or West Indies.

Friday, January 3, 1940

Bitterly cold, and I almost regret having promised to go to Idbury
to stay with Joyce, especially since Mr. A. is away and I am unable
to leave in time to catch 4.45.   The 6.5 is 2¾ hours late, and I
get to Paddock Cottage at 11.45.   House warm, though snow is on
hills outside.

Saturday, January 4, 1940

~~Last night~~ Three airmen in carriage last night, who were coming to
Great Rissington aerodrome, complained that what was the matter
with these parts was, there was too much countryside.   There was
also one soldier in carriage who talked to me when the airmen had
gone to get coffee.   He told me he was going to Evesham on two
days' "compassionate leave" because his father was ill.   He had
been doing what sounded like "manuring" but may have been "manoeu-
vuring", in some part of the country, and sleeping under hedges in
his great-coat, an exercise to harden the soldier.   I asked if
some did not go sick under this training, and he said that they
did.
        Today have breakfast in bed and get up very late.   There
is snow on ground and it is a little warmer than yesterday.
        Outlying defences of Bardia broken through.

Sunday, January 5, 1941.

Bardia penetrated two miles by Australians.   It has also been
heavily bombed by R.A.F.   We heard planes last night and are told
that there were bombs fairly near, but have no confirmation of
this.   J. and I to London: wait an hour on cold platform at
Kingham.   Warning about 6.30 this evening.

Monday, January 6, 1941.

Bardia taken by Australians, with great number of prisoners and
large amount of ammunition.   Biggest Italian stronghold in Libya,
and everyone very pleased it is captured, but Italians are be-
littling the victory.   Several warnings today.   It is so cold
in the office, for first time I am glad to go to printers as a
place more physically comfortable.   They are working under difficulties there too, because all Eyre & Spottiswoode's work has
descended upon them since E. and S. were bombed, and all their
apprentices sit in a cubicle next to ours, singing songs to themselves or playing chess.
        There is still a sprinkling of snow on the ground and
more falls in the evening.

Tuesday, January 7, 1941

No warning last night, but four today.   The general order of
events is (1) sound of guns, (2) sound of planes, (3) whistle from
watchers on roof, (4) printers all put out their lights and dis-
appear, (5) siren from outside.   Letter from home.   Martin John is a registered subject
of the British Empire, has an identity card and ration card.   They
have received parcel from South Africa with about 6 lb. sugar - Mothe:
says she "screamed with delight" when she say it - 2 lb. tea, and 4
pairs silk stockings.   All these are more precious than rubies.

Wednesday, January 8, 1941

To National Gallery concert with Tina, Raymond and Bob.   Their
friend Norman Tucker playing Beethoven piano sonatas, and a cello
sonata with Frank Phillips.   Very enjoyable.   At Hampton's, the
big furniture shop close by Nat.Gall., which-was-burnt-out-not-long
ago, a crane is hauling out of the wrecked building sodden masses
which were once beautiful carpets.   This sight occasions but little
interest and no surprise in the passers-by.   Australians and R.A.F. attacking Tobruk.

Thursday, January 9, 1941

Hearing from mother that there i s not enough meat in the Stroud district for customers even to have their meagre ration (1/2 worth of
meat each per week, including offal and everything except bacon
which is rationed separately, and sausages, tripe or game), I try to
get a chicken to take home with me.   The prices in Selfridges are
16/- for a medium-sized bird, or about 24/- for two very small ones.
Put off decision till tomorrow.   Miss Mearing complains their water is frozen and she cannot bath, so bring her to flat to bathe in lunch-hour.   Edric has
visited Flask Walk and found flood from bathroom to front door.   For first time for three nights there is a warning this
evening, with lot of gunfire, but hear no bombs.

Friday, January 10, 1941

Get duck to take home - 13/5.   Travel with carriage full of airmen
who give me mincepie through dark - lights are put out because there
is an air-raid warning, just before we get to Kemble.   Warning in
operation at Stroud, but no sound of planes or guns.   See my new
nephew, who looks healthy and yells hard for h is food.

Saturday, January 11, 1941

President Roosevelt has made speech asking Congress for extraordinary
powers to help Britain.   Air raid last n ight on Portsmouth.

Sunday, January 12, 1941

Back to town. News says big raid on London last night, but no new damage in Manchester Street, and a short walk round Selfridge's shows nothing new. Warning about 6.30 p.m. Lot of gunfire.

Monday, January 13, 1941

Vague rumours of a naval encounter off Sicely, in which Germans claim to have done great damage to our Fleet, though they admit losing one destroyer. No confirmation.

Graham White says the story which Lord Woolton, Minister of Food, is spreading, that meat is short because it is being sent to the troops in Libya, is quite untrue. The fact is that someone made a miscalculation about the amount of meat available: further that such meat as there is is not distributed.

Letters from Edgar Holt and Marjorie Fuchs both speak of the very great raid damage in Manchester. Marjorie says a quarter of the city was destroyed - think she must mean the centre. Edgar says "three or four more raids like that, and there just wouldn't be a Manchester".

Tina excited about Conference of bishops, clergy and laity at Malvern, called by Archbishop of York. It said practically what Sir Richard A. said in his letter to the Archbishop: condemned private ownership of the principal industrial resources of the community as being a stumbling-block to Christianity ... "It may deprive the poorest of members of the community of the essentials of life,.While these resources can be so owned, men will strive for ownership for themselves. As a consequence, a way of life founded on the supremacy of the economic motive will remain, which is contrary to God's plan for mankind. The time has come for Christians to proclaim the need for striving towards a form of society in which, while the essential values of the individual human personality are preserved, the continuance of these abuses will no longer be possible".

The News-Chronicle says about this: "Recommendations concerning the Church's attitude towards monetary policy, the rights of labour in industry, the revival of agriculture and other questions, are to be examined in co-operation with economists, men of business, and labour. The findings of the Conference will be submitted to the Commission of International Relationships and Social Responsibilities". *Raymond gets to his calling up papers.*

Tuesday, January 14, 1941

"La France Libre", the Free French journal, is going to press at Spaight's, since Eyre & Spottiswoode's are no longer able to publish it. Also journal for Free Holland.

Raymond going home tomorrow and has to report for duty at remote Welsh training station for Navy, on Monday.

Plymouth heavily bombed last night, but no warning here.

Wednesday, January 15, 1941

British report now on naval action off Sicely. Convoy was taking supplies to Greece and German bombers attacked it. Convoy got through safely, bringing down 7 dive bombers. Three of our ships hit, one an aircraft carrier, but one Italian ~~erui~~ destroyer sunk. News rather ambiguous. At least one of the vessels hit has reached port, but other two wounded ships may still be trying to get home.

To Beavans for night. It is snowing, so we hope for quiet night. No warning here last night.

Thursday, January 16, 1941

Several warnings last night in spite of snow, but we do not sleep in Anderson shelter, for which I am grateful. At 8 a.m. I rouse John and Florence, who are both still sleeping. Each must have been very late for work.

Another of the ships in the attacked convoy - the aircraft carrier - has reached port: it had on it a 1,000-ton bomb and is badly damaged.

To National Gallery, and hear Moiseiwitsch: Beethoven, including Moonlight Sonata - very enjoyable. Weather still bitterly cold and snow freezing on ground. Bomb near printers last night, cutting off their private line with blockmakers, and as Mr. Hale, who was in charge of blocks, has just been called up, things a bit vague. Editor away with flu.

Friday, January 17, 1941

Third damaged ship of convoy has had to be abandoned: when this is done by our enemies it is called "scuttling". Our shipping losses for first week of this year were only four ships: it is admitted this was probably due to weather.

Think it interesting to report that Graham says that if there could be found an honest man, one would feel like putting him in the British Museum - he was talking primarily of politicians. He added, however, that George Lansbury was such an one, and that nobody had ever doubted his sincerity.

Last night's raid on Bristol and other towns in that area.

Saturday, January 18, 1941

To Aldbury. There is still snow on the ground and it snows all the time I am on the way. A fat, youngish woman who shows me the Green Line bus station at Victoria, slips while she is crossing road but recovers her balance with remarkable agility. "I wasn't an acrobat for years for nothing", she says. Tells me she is on her way to see her husband who is in a military hospital at Dorking. He was hurt in the fire raid three weeks ago, has two or three bones

broken at the bottom of his spine and may never be able to walk
again.   No warning in London last night but bombs in South Wales.

Sunday, January 19, 1941

After I'd written yesterday's entry, John, Frank somebody, and
Essie McCormick arrived.   The last is Pat McC's daughter, and is
Sister-in-Charge of the Maternity Ward at King's College Hospital.
They had 420 windows broken in five minutes by two bombs, and once
lately had the gas and water mains broken, and for fourteen hours
had scarcely a spot of water for the mothers and babies.   She had
to go back this morning.   The rest of us go for walk in the slush,
for the snow is thawing fast.

Monday, January 20, 1941

Up and away in the half light.   It is snowing again and I much enjoy
walking to station.   At Euston it is pouring with rain and slush in
road is incredible.
            Very busy all day.   In evening Jack tells tale of how he
stood and watched house where police are investigating what, when I
enquire, he says was beer party, but Tina tells me it was a brothel.
I read Eliot's "Family Reunion", which is extremely interesting.

Tuesday, January 21, 1941

Pouring rain - which has merit of washing away remains of slush.
Grateful for my boots.   Most women in London now are wearing boots
and woollen or lisle stockings.   They look inelegant but are great
comfort on cold days.
            Terribly busy at printers.   Hardly have a pause till 6
p.m., just before which we discover, almost by accident, that one of
the talks in the paper has been suppressed by censor.   Hastily sub-
stitute something else and thank heaven for our delivery.   So tired
in evening, can do nothing but sit in armchair.
            No warning last night, but several today with sounds of
gunfire.   Joyce has made friends with naturalist whom the village
people of Idbury regard as spy.   He lies on back behind bushes with
field-glasses, and taps trees, which they suspect is sending out
messages in code.

Wednesday, January 22, 1941

Australians say Tobruk has fallen, but no official confirmation.
            Robert Boothby, Parliamentary Secretary to Ministry of
Food, has resigned his post after enquiry.   He appears to have been
accepting bribes to push through contracts.   Glad in this country
we are able to turn out such people.   But sorry that in this country
we have just suppressed the Communist papers "The Week" and "The Daily
Worker".   Since "Freedom is in Peril" and we are invited to "Defend

it with All Our Might", this appears to me unfortunate. Arthur,
at weekend, was wondering whether he will shortly be haled off to
prison as a Communist and Pacifist. He has had an interview with
the police, who called at cottage and required him to fill up form.
This may have been because he gave sanctuary to two German refugees
who were suddenly turned out of Cardiff when the city was made a
defence area, and had nowhere to go. Or it may have been because
of his anti-war poems. It is also announced in today's papers that
workers are to be conscripted for industry, in the war effort:
others are to be conscripted for fire watching.
          Much warmer, which makes life a good deal pleasanter.
A man called John Barlow comes to dinner, to inspect and be inspected by us, because he may take Raymond's vacant room.

Thursday, January 23, 1941

Tobruk really has fallen and we have taken 40,000 prisoners (again
I wonder how we shall feed them), and a lot of ammunition, etc.
Bob says there is a feeling that the Germans will make a gas attack
on us and it is as well to keep gas-masks in order.
          In evening we try to get a Beethoven concert, but wireless
is dead though there is no warning. Scarcely any air activity over
this country yesterday and we wonder what devilment the Germans are
up to that they keep so quiet.

Friday, January 24, 1941

Another quiet night. To Cundells' cottage for weekend. Train
very full and I get seat only because kind soldier gives me his.
Two A.T.S. girls talking in crowded corridor: one says "And all
those first-class seats empty ... it's a wrong system. And they
say we're fighting for freedom, my God!" Helen Bartrum and violin
get off same train and we have lift in Mr. Bickley's luxurious car.
Mr. B. is afflicted with violent hiccups which make him ill. Edric
And Edric play sonatas and I listen in great depression partly due
to tiredness. Remind myself that it is not everyone who can sit
by log fire and listen to Mozart, and this has some little effect.

Saturday, January 25, 1941

Cold grey day. "Telegraph" suggests air lull means concentrated
effort by Germans on some new enterprise. Undeterred by this, we
have string quartets from 11 a.m. to 6 p.m., with intervals for
food. Day outside very uninviting and it is pleasant to stay in
and listen.

Sunday, January 26, 1941

Garvin, in "Observer", says crisis of war will come in few days,
or at most few weeks. Meantime I knit, feeling rather like Mme.

Defarge, listen to Edric playing, help him paint fruit trees in
the cold cold paddock (cold as paddocks though I be), and go for
walk with Helen B. during which we discuss Time (Dunne), and the
astonishing fact that Helena, who seems so mature and able to deal
with things and to know a lot more than either of us, can ask quite
seriously such an immature question as "How can you believe in God
when you look round at what is happening in the world today?"

Monday, January 27, 1941

Entire Cundell household rises at 6.30.   Edric drives me to
station with Helen and we all catch 8 o'clock train - this all on my
account, as usually E. gets the third morning train.   I bear back
six fresh eggs, which I pack in my boots (not being worn) and give
as present to Miss Mearing, who chortles with joy at sight.

Tuesday, January 28, 1941

Daylight raids lately all come on Tuesday.   Again compositors go
below about 5 times when roof-spotters give alarm.   Mr. Matthews
explains that if the men are killed or maimed and have not taken
shelter, their dependants cannot claim compensation.   He remains
upstairs with us.

Wednesday, January 29, 1941

Letter from Mother who has been having flu.   She says no meat in the
district last week: they existed on sausage and bacon, but managed
to get fowl from Mr. Turner at weekend.
        Buy sanitary towels and belt at Selfridges.   Assistant
says their quota of towels for month is nearly exhausted, and that
both towels and belts are classed as luxuries and taxed.   Agree
with her when she adds that no doubt it was a man who made this regulation, and that she regards it as adding insult to injury.
        General Metaxas, Prime Minister of Greece, dies at age of
70, after operation on his throat.
        We have received instructions from Duff Cooper, Minister
of Information, that we are not to publish in Listener any talks
broadcast to German troops: I gather that they are full of rumours
and such news as is given receives a twist.   In this connection it
is interesting to quote letter signed "Fleet Street Journalist"
which Listener has received but will not published.   It says: "It
is to be regretted that the B.B.C. lent itself to rumour-mongering
by permitting the propagation of an unauthenticated story in a talk
by a trade union leader.   This story, which described the alleged
treatment of women in this country if Germany won, first appeared
in the British Press as a contribution from a neutral and anonymous
journalist who said that the information was given in a speech told
under conditions of prefound secrecy by the German Minister for
Agriculture and that he obtained his information from a source which

he was not at liberty to disclose: in short, the story should be
taken with the proverbial pinch of salt". Wording of this letter
appears to me rather strange. Here is extract from talk referred
to: it is by W.J. Brown, General Secretary of Civil Service Cleri-
cal Association...

"A week or two ago, there appeared in a well-known
Sunday paper a quotation of what was said to a British
General by an active Nazi agent in a country which has
since fallen under German rule. This, according to the
German agent, is how Germany would treat the British if
- which shall not be - the Germans were to be victorious
in this war:

'As soon as we beat England we shall make
an end of you English once and for all. Able-
bodied men and women will be exported as slaves
to the Continent. The old and the weakly will
be exterminated. All men remaining in Britain
- as slaves - will be sterilised. A million
or two of the young women of the Nordic type
will be segregated in a number of stud farms,
where, with the assistance of picked German
sires, they will during a period of ten or
twelve years produce nearly annually a series
of Nordic infants to be brought up in every way
as Germans. These infants will form the future
population of Britain. They will be partially
educated in Germany and only those who fully
satisfy Nazi requirements will be allowed to return to Britain and take up permanent residence.
The rest will be sterilised and sent to join the
slave gangs in Germany. Thus in a generation
or two the British will disappear'."

Feel we are coming to a pretty pass if our propaganda has to
fall back on such fantastic tales.
    Tina has been talking to someone who has just lunched
with ex-Editor of Yorkshire Post - Mann. He says Wendell
Willkie, who is over here from America, has come on behalf of
the Wall Street financiers to report to them whether we are worth
backing up or not. Willkie is Big Business, and was in running
for Presidency against Roosevelt.

Thursday, January 30, 1941

Brief air-raid warning last evening and a few guns.   Today a
series of short warnings and a lot of gunfire.   We moved our
offices yesterday to Brock House, where we are beautifully warm,
but whenever roof-watchers give warning of planes overhead we
are chivvied below to a basement where men are playing darts and
a loudspeaker is blaring jazz.   What the men's occupation is
when they are Going to It, I do not know, but someone remarks
that it is a pity Wendell Willkie can't see us.   Only two floors
of the building are occupied by B.B.C. staff, and there appears
to be no co-ordination between the roof-spotters of Brock House
and the roof-spotters of the B.B.C.   We are not only turned out
of offices, but locked out by a stern commissionaire – who unfortunately locks Molly Evans on to the inside with the rest of us
on the outside.   A printer's messanger appears and she pushes
the copy f or him under the door to us: she also views with pleasure several buckets of sand and hopes she will not have to deal
with incendiaries unaided.
          Hitler makes speech to German people but it is not re-
ported to us in any detail.

Friday, January 31, 1941

Day of warnings again.   We drag wearily up and down stairs.   At
lunchtime I am buying a duck in Marylebone High Street, to take
home for weekend, when several bombs whistle down.   One falls in
Devonshire Mews.   The High Street is filled with dust and everyone starts running – not to take cover but to see what has happened.
I go on buying rations, surprised that I am so unmoved.   Am able
to buy 1¾d. worth of cheese only (about 2 oz.) with my one ration
card.   Nine o'clock news says the Colonel Knox (American) says
invasion of Britain is imminent, and that gas may be expected to
be used on a wide scale.   Hope it will not be this weekend as I
have left my gasmask in London.

Saturday, February 1, 1941

Hardly any of our own aeroplanes have been s een over Stroud, even
during day, for some time.   Today I see only one, and hear one
going over about 9 p.m.   Try in vain to get oranges in Stroud.
Ball's have almost nothing in their shop but a few coconuts, celery
and (strangely) grapefruit.   In evening Mrs. Keene brings round
1¾lb. cheese which they do not want.   This received joyfully since
Daddy is wont to eat about that amount at one meal, and has lately
lost ½ stone, probably through its lack.
          Beautiful day, sunny and mild.   Begin to feel the spring.
I take Martin for walk to Manor end of King's Court.
          Wendell Willkie recalled to New York to give evidence
before some committee concerned with supplying arms to Britain.

Sunday, February 2, 1941

Edgar (milkman) very depressed.   Says milk will be short again, because of scarcity of feeding-stuffs.   From to-day on, every cow has a ration card!
Return to London, in company with Nurse, whose departure gives Hilary a pain of nervousness.   Mr. Mackenzie King, Canadian Prime Minister, has said that war on a scale which the world has never seen may be expected within a few weeks.   Phyllida says she has heard so much about this invasion, she will not worry about it ⌖ till it happens.
Have not been to a church service for months, and feel would like to, but on prowling around find that all e vensongs are now at 3.30 p.m., so am unable to indulge my desire.

Monday, February 3, 1941

Serious anti-British riots in Johannesburg.
Listener staff afflicted with flu.   Mr. Abraham, Miss Playle, Miss Mearing and Course all absent today.   In consequence I am very rushed.

Tuesday, February 4, 1941

So hectic at printers, should never have finished except for unexpected help from Mr. Ackerley, who comes down and reads about nine pages.   A very short alert last night, but fortunately no warnings to delay work today: perhaps because there is snow.   An air official has said that the lull in bombing may be entirely due to bad weather and does not necessarily mean German is planning coup.

Wednesday, February 5, 1941

Feel rather ill, since have been too overdone to sleep well the last two nights, and when I get letter saying Phyllida burst into tears on Sunday after Daddy had complained because joint was burnt, I burst into tears of sympathy with her.   (She had to take to bed with flu after the burning of the joint.)   Today Miss Playle and Miss Mearing are back, so things are better.   We have an enormous Professor Simey of the British Council to breakfast, and a little A.D.K. Owen of, I think, P.E.P., to supper.   Much interesting talk of affairs and I feel I am at heart of British Empire, which is, especially at present, centre of world.   Wendell Willkie is apparently not as dumb as daily papers might lead one to believe.   In a meeting of Rebecca West's group at the Dorchester Hotel, he said (according to A.D.K. Owen, who had it from a man who was there) that he thought Churchill was splendid - right man for the job - but he could think of circumstances where "he would be lousy".   Also he has met De Valera and told him his opinion of the lunatic way Ireland is behaving.
Lord Lloyd, Colonial Secretary, dies at age of sixty-one.

Thursday, February 6, 1941

David Owen and clergyman friend of Bob's who has been travelling all night from Northumberland, to breakfast, as well as nine of ourselves. We are indeed a large company, and have to form relays for breakfast.

Wendell Willkie has departed for America, first leaving message which he requests B.B.C. to breadcast to Germany. It says that he himself is pure German by descent, but, in common with almost all other American Germans, he has no use for Germany's present policy of "grab".

Snow last night, and I go down to National Gallery in lunch time through slush underfoot and with sunshine above. Stand within eating sandwiches and looking over Trafalgar Square, from very pretty under blue sky with its white covering, while rather trying woman I have never seen before makes banal remarks. Holst Trio, Haydn and Schubert (latter the one we have on records, and I enjoy it very much).

Friday, February 7, 1941

Tina shows me letter Sir Richard has had from Maxwell Stewart, of the American "Nation". It says there is a lot of misunderstanding between U.S.A. and Great Britain at present: causes are (1) hangover of distrust from the Chamberlain-Hoare-Simon era. Distrust has not been dissipated by choice of Halifax as Ambassador to U.S. Americans still bitter of Abyssinia, British betrayal of League, and British dishonour with regard to Czecho-Slovakia and Spain. (2) Very strong anti-British sentiment among Irish Americans. (3) Isolationists. (4) Distrust among Progressives of Britain's war aims, growing out of its treatment of India and half-hearted support of China, and recent attempts to appease Franco. Also attitude to Russia. Britain criticised on account of class distinctions in air-raid shelters and general slowness of reform.

Feel rather depressed by this, because our papers lead one to suppose that all Americans are 100 per cent. pro British.

Saturday, February 8, 1941

I write in Euston first-class ladies' waiting-Room, where I have no right to be because my ticket, which is third class anyway, has gone with John to Tring on the 5 o'clock train. He went on ahead to book (we had only just time to catch train) and I, being unused to the station, went a long way to find the barriers, only to find that platform six was an open one and I had been standing on it while train was moving out. We have been to Sadlers Wells ballet at New Theatre: very enjoyable, especally "Facade". The other items were "Les Patineurs" and "The Traveller".

This morning I spend having my hair cut infront and four bits "permed" so that it rolls back: this cost 25/-, and I don't know that the result does much but make me look just like everybody else.

British have taken Benghazi, main Libyan port, from
Italians. ~~Government has been~~ Cabinet has been changed. Mr.
Malcolm MacDonald going to Canada has High Commissioner, and
Ernest Brown, Secretary of State for Scotland, to be Minister
of Health inhis place. Scotland to have Tom Johnston.

Sunday, February 9, 1941

Had to buy another ticket yesterday, and travelled in deep gloom
feeling was inefficient idiot. However, was met at station by
John and Arthur, had very pleasant walk to cottage, and felt more
cheerful. To-day it is fine and warm. I cannot manage my new
hair style, but otherwise very pleasant day. We walk on common
and J. and I go up monument, 170 steps, and admire view. Height
makes me giddy. In evening Churchill broadcasts. Sums up our
progress in war so far, and says we must be ready to meet invasion
by parachute, by glider and with poison gas attacks.

Monday, February 10, 1941

Today, tomorrow or Wed. are most auspicious days this month for
invasion: moon and tides are full. There is only short alert
this evening, however, with All Clear at about 11 p.m. and no
sound of gunfire or bombs. Mr. Abraham returns from influenza,
but has to go to dentist in afternoon with raging toothache.

~~Wednesday,~~ Tuesday, February 11, 1941

Britain breaks off diplomatic relations with Rumania, where
Germany is planting large army.
            Very late going to press. Mr. A. has to go to Downing
Street to correct P.M.'s proof from original copy.

Wednesday, February 12, 1941

Mussolini and Franco meet and no doubt start hatching mischief.
            I buy very e xpensive jumper in Burlington Arcade (37/6)
and am overcome by thought of wicked extravagance. In evening
to Beavans, where we have Scramble and string quartets (Haydn and
Schubert), with Jean Layton, Betty, and Pauline. P. is working
in an aircraft factory where the hours are 8 - 6 and she gets very
tired. Jean says there has been good deal of delay and trouble
in industrial output because workers will ~~net~~ keep moving to other
places where they get better pay, and Government requires labour so
badly, it presumably dare not insist on people staying in any one
spot.
            There is a moon and no warning, so I return to Manchester
Street to sleep, t ravelling by Underground. There are now bunks
- rather rocky-looking ones - built in twos, for people who go to
Underground to sleep.

Thursday, February 13, 1941

Britons warned to leave Japan.   Australia preparing for trouble.
No doubt Hitler would be glad to divert its attention, and American supplies, to other side of world.
          Just before 1 o'clock am preparing to go to lunch when
there is knock at door of office and in walks Daddy.   They brought
H. back to Ware yesterday, and today he is trying to buy a few
things in the City.   Is very shocked at damage there.

Friday, February 14, 1941

Last evening one big bang and short alert.   Today newspaper reports considerable damage which I hear is at Hendon.   Must have
been aerial torpedo.   "Evening News" says Italians report British
papachute troops in extreme south of Italy.   This not official.
          In evening to Beavans.

Saturday, February 15, 1941

News of parachute troops now confirmed by Ministry of Information,
which is always last with news.   They tried to do damage to certain public works, and some have not returned to their base.   (NB
How do they return?   Certainly not by parachute.)   Result of
venture not yet announced.
          Beautiful day of sunshine and white clouds.   We have
sewing-woman to mend boys' socks, shorten skirts for us women, etc.
I go forth and order hat to be made, buy rations (very slow business), meet Bob, Tina and John (Catlow) for lunch at Barcelona, and
meet John (Beavan) for tea at Dutch Oven before going with him to
cottage.   Air-raid warning while we are at Euston, and lights go
out.   We get electric train and steam connection from Watford,
and all clear sounds as we journey.   After Dutch Oven we went to
film "The Edge of the World".   There was also very good propaganda one (G.P.O. Film Unit) called "The Spirit of Britain", which
upset me considerably.   Landscapes of Britain, then industrial
scene ... "These people still appreciate the best that was Germany"
... Malcolm Sargent conducting Halle Orchestra in Beethoven's 5th
Symphony against background of bombed Coventry (all this done very
well).   Then Huddersfield Choral Society singing the Hallelujah
Chorus ... "You can't break the spirit of people who can still
sing like this" ... But then, just when they got to the pianissimo
"The Kingdom of this world is become ... ", announcer was saying
"But this people has the power to hit back.   And they are going
to hit back" ... Pictures of bombing planes being assembled ...
and, as the last Hallelujah was reached, shot of one of our bombers taking off .   "And He shall reign for ever and ever.   Hallelujah."   Am thrown into despair for mankind.

Sunday, February 16, 1941

Cold, with drizzling rain. Lord Haw-Haw giving talk in memory
of Germans who died on Altmark. Churchill blamed for Altmark
action, which is described as act of savage piracy, against all
international law.

Monday, February 17, 1941

Barrows have appeared in streets with spring flowers - daffodils
and jonquils - just as in peacetime, only there are fewer and they
are very expensive: but they look lovelier than ever against background of bomb debris.

Tuesday, February 18, 1941

Bulgaria and Turkey making agreement which seems vague and rather
meaningless. Graham has cousin to supper who has been sitting on
food committee with Lord Woolton and representatives of catering
business, ship-owners, etc. Says catering establishments to be
cut down a good deal, especially in meat, which will be almost impossible to get in restaurants. Shipping space for sugar to be
reduced, so there will be even fewer sweets and sweet biscuits.
Private consumers' allowance will probably remain unaltered.
Cheese and eggs likely to be rationed. Shall have to live mostly
on carrots, turnips and oatmeal, he says. However, tonight we
have very good meal, followed by Napoleon brandy, 1860 or thereabouts, of Graham's, which everyone says is ambrosial, but I hardly
know how to swallow it.

Wednesday, February 19, 1941

Large force of Australians has landed at Singapore.
          Shops have no fruit except rhubarb. Graham says rhu-
barb is poisonous. Whenever it is on the bill of fare at the House
of Commons he crosses it off, thus giving himself the feeling that
he is saving the lives of many fellow-Members (he admits that this
may not be altogether desirable).
          To National Gallery: Blech String Quartet playing
Beethoven. It is so airless in the underground room they use for
concerts, I go into kind of coma and the music is rather wasted
on me.
          Some gunfire this evening, but no bombs.

Thursday, February 20, 1941

Bob in bed with flu.
          The concrete-enclosed sandbags round Broadcasting House
are being taken away and instead a brick wall is being built outside the building, with what look to me like holes for machine-
guns.

Friday, February 21, 1941

Very cold sunny day.   Swansea was town attacked by Germans yesterday, and it seems to have been bombed again last night.   We had
three warnings and some gunfire, but I heard no bombs.   We are
driven below once today by sound of gunfire and planes, though
there is no Alert.   During this time I start disastrous game of
chess with Mr. Abraham, who spends rest of day hoping Goering will
do it again so that he can beat me.

         On way to Paddington in taxi, see man cycling with orange
ball from top of Belisha Beacon under his arm.   Looks like some
exotic fruit.

Saturday, February 22, 1941

In spite of great talk of food scarcity, we have today in the house
half a cold chicken, half a steak and kidney pudding, and a little
joint of pork.   But this will probably have to last rest of week.
Mrs. Cook has not a single sweet in her window, only a few cardboard young women advertising cigarettes, and a notice STIRRUP
PUMP.   The Post Office is almost as denuded.   We are startled by
the information on the 6 o'clock News that the butter ration is to
be increased from 2 oz to 4 oz per week.   The whole fat ration -
8 oz - will remain the same.

         Rodborough has little bags of sand here and there (two
just inside our front gate) for use in case the enemy attacks the
district with incendiary bombs.   Swansea bombed again last night
- we could hear distant gunfire.   Tonight is quiet: weather probably too bad for bombers.

         Snow and sleet in afternoon.   I have short walk on
common in morning.   Enjoy sitting on grass and brooding over
King's Court (grass far too damp for any reasonable person to sit
on it).

         Everything set for formal German entry into Bulgaria.
Roads from frontier to Sofia have even German signposts on them.
The impudence of the creatures!

Sunday, February 23, 1941

Beautiful day: bright sunshine and layer of snow on ground. I
go short walk on common before getting 12.3 back to London.   The
Home Guard are lined up on the Bear road, with various of their
number standing at points about the common.   They are trying to
gauge how far away each person is and to train their rifles on
them: practice for catching parachutists, I imagine.   "Now",
says the leader, "Bert there, down by that bush".   "Two unred 'n
fifty", says one.   "Two unred", says another. "Two unred seventy
five", says a third.   Cannot stop to discover how wrong they are.

         On arriving at Baker Street, take my suitcase and go to
evensong at Marylebone Parish Church - a poor affair, with 10
people in the congregation, 9, like me, at the extreme back of the

large church, one old woman (deaf?) at extreme front, two old
clerics, and one or two hoarse choirboys. Feel report of the
Archbishops conference at Malvern was only too right when it said
the Church must alter its forms of service to meet the needs of
the present day. After this find Bob still confined to his room
in Manchester Street, and have theological discussion with him
during which he instructs me about the Mass, and says it is a
religious drama, and should be presented as such. (This does
not mean it signifies nothing more to him: he is very devout.)

Monday, February 24, 1941

Am afflicted with feeling that I am entirely useless and it were
better I were blown up by a bomb. Letter from Joyce from which it
seems that she also is depressed: she was glad to get my letter,
so perhaps I am a little use after all.
          See written newspaper placard which says "Italians Say
Musso Must Go", but cannot find any further support for this
statement.

Tuesday, February 25, 1941

Evening paper says it is to be a criminal offence to buy fish and
meat, or meat and cheese, or meat and eggs, at same meal. Am
therefore somewhat amused when Graham tells us at supper that he
lunched at the Carlton Grill where he had nine oysters, roast beef
and cheese besides other things.
          Wake up violently this morning out of dream in which I
was at least 12 years younger. Cannot remember where I am or what
has happened to me meantime, and have gently to reassure myself that
I know Manchester Street, and I know Tina who is in the other bed,
and that today I am going to the printers to help pass the Listener
to press, with Mr. Abraham, whom I also know. It is a horrible
feeling, rather like a nightmare. Depressed and inclined to weep
all day: am fortunately very busy but feel only just able to cope.
A beautiful clear day with glorious sky this morning and this evening. Am fortified by some of Graham's Napoleon brandy when I get
in, which is unpleasant but restorative.
          Kathleen McColgan, who has gone to Sir Charles Roberts'
place in Cumberland for a month, writes that she thinks the ritual
of the News has taken the place of family prayers. They assemble
in the South Drawing-Room at 8, at 1 (lunchtime has been altered
to allow this), at 6 and at 9 for the News, to which all listen
in reverent silence. After the 9 o'clock News, Sir C. reads Jane
Austen to them for half an hour before they go to bed. I had no
idea anything like it existed. Further she says that their idea
of winning the war is to be cheerful (they write letters to friends
in America saying how well "we" are standing the bombing - no one
there has ever heard a bomb or even a gun); and to make sacri-
fices (they have sacrificed a car and have now 3 instead of 4, and
have not had the drawing-room repapered this winter.

Wednesday, February 26, 1941

The Telegraph, and no other paper, carries surprising tale saying that Mussolini has sacked Graziani, who is now in prison:
that there was a great row in the Italian War Council, Graziani
being blamed for defeats in Libya, and countering this charge by
laying on table before his accusers plans which showed that the
enterprise was conceived by Mussolini against advice of Graziani.
        To dentist.   Poor Mr. Course, whom I have not seen
since the Blitz started, looks 10 years older.   (I dare say I
do too.)   He had been on Home Guard duty all night on Hampstead
Heath; his house was damaged by a nearby bomb last October and
he had to pay £400 to repair roof, etc.   Was sorry to see him so
thin and worried-looking.

Thursday, February 27, 1941

Reports in paper about disturbances in Holland at the Hague.
Graham had letter this week from friends at the Hague, which had
taken since November to come, through Geneva and Lisbon.   Writer
said her sons had come back from Army and were in ordinary occu-
pations, and husband also still had his job, so they felt themselves very lucky.   No comment, of course, on German occupation.
        Poor Mr. Abraham and wife have been having terrible
time with friend who parked herself on them and took leave of her
senses, declaring at times that she was the Virgin Mary, at others
the Scarlet Woman, and at others Queen Mary.   Feel pretty poor
myself and hope I shan't go off my head: it is whizzy enough.

Friday, February 28, 1941

Still feel whizzy.   Walk a little in Regent's Park after work
and see how lucky I was to live in Bedford College last summer.
Bob has had to have all his books removed from the College.   He
comes in very late for supper and immediately after finishing it
begins to arrange, with Tina's help, the piles of books in his
room and in corridor outside.   Fusses about so like a little
professor, can hardly help laughing.
        In Ms. of broadcast talk, Sir Walter Citrine says that
by 1942 we hope, with American aid, to have reached German air
strength.   This admission of present weakness deleted from talk
before broadcasting.

Saturday, March 1, 1941

Bulgaria signs pact with Axis; and Vichy Government has given in
to Japanese demands in French Indo-China.
        Feel a little more normal.   Walk across Hyde Park to
Gerald Road in morning and help Tina do some typing for Sir

Richard Acland.   In afternoon go out to buy rations with Bob's
ration card, and find halfway up Marylebone High Street that the
card has disappeared.   May have been due to shock on seeing a
cucumber in shop window priced at 4/-.   Also see English tomatoes, not priced.
         John, Jack, Bob, Tina and I dine at Chinese Restaurant
in Wardour Street.

Sunday, March 2, 1941

Bob takes Jack, Tina and me to High Mass at All Saint's, Margaret
Street, where we have Dom Bernard Clements preaching.   Much argument on way home about church procedure and contents of sermon.
Lunch in Baker Street, and Jack, Tina and I walk in Regent's Park,
where crocuses are coming up out of grass as golden as in days
of peace, and seagulls and ducks are very lively against blue-
and-white sky.
         With Tina to Gerald Road again, where Sir R.A., who is
Private in Army, has come up from Reading to do work.   His chief
interest at moment is in sketch, "How to Eat a Sausage", which he
has written for entertainment to be given by troops and broadcast.

Monday, March 3, 1941

German troops said to be approaching Greek frontier through
Bulgaria.   We have still not broken off relations with Bulgaria.

Tuesday, March 4, 1941

Cardiff has had worst fire raid of war - if it was worse than
the City of London's, it must have been bad.   Very hard day at
printer's, and am extremely tired but do not feel as whizzy as
last week.

Wednesday, March 5, 1941

Graham lunches with man from Russian Embassy, who doesnot enlight-
en him about Russia beyond saying that she is neutral and has done
nothing against British interests since outbreak of war.   The
Russian radio is said to be broadcasting its disapproval of
Bulgaria's action in allowing German troops through the country:
Germany said to be replying that she cannot but admire the frank-
ness of Russia, but that she does not agree that Bulgaria has
made it likely that the war will spread.
         Beautiful spring day, though a bit cold: not a day for
town.

Thursday, March 6, 1941

Find it encouraging that the five minutes "Lift up Your Hearts"
just before 8 a.m. News, usually given over to rather vague exhorta-
tions to kindness, today advises us to watch the coming debate on
Family Allowances in House of Lords, says the family is proper unit
for Christian Society, and urges us to make it possible economically
for people to have children without suffering hardship.
          Graham remarks at breakfast that the P.M. concentrates so
much on prosecution of war itself that some Ministers have not seen
him since they came into office: that he pays little attention to
the new scheme for the concentration of industry - i.e. for closing
down small factories not engaged on war work and putting the workers
into direct war production.   The flats here are very short of domestic staff because girls go into factories where they are paid very
much more than they can earn as servants.

Friday, March 7, 1941

British have made raids on Lofoten Islands off Norway and sunk German
ships.   Letter from Joyce asking me hopefully to take oranges, grapefruit and nuts when I go to Idbury.   Have seen none for a long time.
Last grapefruit I had, which was at Stroud, cost 1/-.

Saturday, March 8, 1941

Yugoslavs preparing against probable German invasion.   I have my
hair set.   Cannot disguise from myself that I look years older since
war started - haggard and tired and worried-looking.
          With Tina to Great Missenden (her brother's) for weekend,
where I play chess and beat brother's father-in-law, who whistles
under his breath to cheer himself whenever I put him in a difficult
position.   Walk in typical Bucks country.   Sleep on floor of sitting
room.   House rented furnished from Alec Waugh who was in films at
Elstree: two cottages converted.   Enormous gilt-edged French barometer which doesn't work, old prints, costume drawings, inefficient
and picturesque lighting, and all mod. cons.

Sunday
~~Saturday~~, March 9, 1941

Brother Frank on Home Guard duty till 2 p.m.   Holds forth at dinner
on iniquities of two local preachers who preached instead of turning
up for duty.   Announces intention of burning down their chapel as
soon as invasion starts.   News says heavy raid on London last night.
We heard lot of planes going over and distant guns.   Beat father-in-
law at chess again and he is sad, but he beats Elizabeth who comes to
tea, walking 10 miles from Chalfont St. Giles.

Monday, March 10, 1941

Bombs on Saturday hit Café de Paris where people were dancing and
killed good many.   There is a rope across end of Gray's Inn Road

when I go to printer's. Mr. Matthews says there is unexploded bomb
of terrific dimensions there. Mr. Abraham on holiday: am accordingly very busy.

Tuesday, March 11, 1941

Latest shipping losses are enormous. Roosevelt has signed Lease-and-
Lend Bill so that there is nothing now to stop American help to
Britain.

Editor says after our raid on Lofoten Islands, Admiralty
wanted to put out notice to effect that we had now stopped supplies
of codliver old to Germans (and were therefore giving German children
rickets): Ministry of Information censored it, as playing into
Hitler's hands. Am very upset by this and say that is why war is
wrong. Editor says he agrees: was there any other way of dealing
with Hitler?

Feel very done up when I get home from printer's. Am revived by Graham's brandy. In semi-stupor play rubber of bridge in
which I consistently get hands with no court cards.

Wednesday, March 12, 1941

About midday feel so queer, go home and retire to bed. Letter from
Mother, who is filled with rage because her favourite spot, Beacon
Tump, is having something built on it by Air Ministry, and the usual
road to it is barred. As she writes she says "Droves of planes going over", so there may be some sense in Air Ministry's precautions.

Thursday, March 13, 1941

Get in doctor (a woman) who says I am suffering from Fatigue and decides I had better go home for week. Miss P. dismayed on hearing
this, as she was going on holiday next week. Jack very depressed
because one of his company's ships has been lost with all hands - men
he know. Graham comes home from Secret Session remarking that he
thinks we shall all have to eat less. After supper he gets call
through to Birkenhead and hears that last night 30 landmines were
dropped there. His house appears to be standing amid ruins and is
giving shelter to numbers of bombed-out relations, including his
mother-in-law. This casts him into deep gloom.

Ring Hilary who says P. has today left for home: they had
lot of bombs at Ware two nights ago.

Friday, March 14, 1941

To Stroud by 1.55. Beautiful day, warm and sunny. Don't feel too
bad after journey. Met by Phyllida. Lots of German planes go over
in the full moon at night, and we have warning from 8 till 2 a.m.
And Daniels's Iron Works, and Erinoid (both now producing armaments)
had competition lately to see which could pierce the other's defences.
Erinoid won easily. Seven men got into Daniels's premises at back,

and one, dresses as woman, went in unchallenged and wandered all
over the works.

Saturday, March 15, 1941

We have chicken for dinner.   Daddy gets it from customer - people
are killing them off because of lack of chicken-food, so later on
there will be no chickens or eggs.   We also have a throat-piece,
which is supposed to be rationed but this one isn't.   A. V. Alexander
First Lord of Admiralty, says with American aid our victory will be
"certain and quick".
          Jam, syrup and marmalade are to be rationed.
          Stroll on common in sunshine and feel much better for it.

Sunday, March 16, 1941

Roosevelt makes speech promising all aid to Britain immediately.
Bevin, Minister of Labour, broadcasts: women of 20-21 and men of
40-45 are to register for war work.   Raids on London last night.
          Vera lets mother have cream and ½ lb. butter, which she
gets from her friend who works at a restaurant.   Joy, joy.
          We go to Beacon Tump.   Cannot take car down usual road.
Lie on grass beside Cromwell's Stone in beautiful warm sunshine.
Feel much better for it.

Monday, March 17, 1941

Cold.   Could not possibly lie anywhere on grass to-day.
          Hitler says Britain will be beaten within next year.
Raid on Bristol last night.   We had warning here but no sound of
planes - they go up the Severn.

Tuesday, March 18, 1941

Daddy gets another throat-piece and dozen eggs.   Mother sending
eggs to Hilary.   No letter from South Africa for three weeks.   I
do little but sleep, eat, walk a little, and read book of Bernard
Shaw's plays.

Wednesday, March 19, 1941

Beautiful day.   Walk on common in morning and to Aunt H's to tea in
afternoon.   Elsie announces intention of becoming fire-fighter and
wishes to join Home Guard.   She must be well over 50.
          Three German U-boats sunk.   Roosevelt has promised us
food as well as armaments.   Last night, warning at about 4 a.m.
and sound of gunfire.   Pop declares he heard bomb, and we learn to-
day there was one at Brockworth.   Air-raid casualties in Clydeside
and Merseyside last week were 500 killed on each of two days, and
total of 1200 badly injured.   Last night's raid was on Hull.

Thursday, March 20, 1941

London heavily bombed last night.

We go to Beacon Tump and have tea by Cromwell's Stone where all is sunshine andpeace. See man viewing Severn through field-glasses and Mother makes up her mind he is spy, but thereis so much mist that almost nothing can be seen: and Daddy often takes field-glasses to almost same spot. We climb over and look at what Air Ministry is building: looks like number of oblong water-tanks on tripods. They have ploughed in a good part of the land near the Beacon, which is National Trust.

Friday, March 21, 1941

Very tired, and stay in bed till dinner time. Raid on Plymouth last night: also small raid on London. We get no daily paper which we attribute to Hitler but find later it is due to carelessness of young woman who delivers for newsagent. Letter from Hilary: her charlady has six butchers living with her and says H. shall never want for meat or for bones for Tramp.

Saturday, March 22, 1941

Plymouth raided again last night. As we went to bed we could see 3 or 4 searchlights, not long rays of light moving about as usual, but splodges of light standing absolutely still. They stay thus till just before midnight. We have mysterious gift of parsnips put through kitchen window. I read more Bernard Shaw.

Sunday, March 23, 1941

Much colder. Day of National Prayer. Do not feel in right mood for it: am very dispirited at thought of returning to London. Per-haps what I need is change of job. Am certainly much better but do not feel bursting with health. Find John alone in flat. He says heavy raid last Wed. was mostly on East and South-East London.

Monday, March 24, 1941

No warning at all last night. Return unwillingly to work and get on quite well. Friend of John's to supper. Terrific theological argument rages most of evening. Friend is in R.A.M.C. and, I learn after he has gone, a pacifist.

By order of Minister of Information the following words are being deleted from version of "Three Men and a Parson" broadcast printed in Listener, though they were actually broadcast. "You have seen women wearing coats that cost hundreds of pounds, and some of these people have never done a day's work in their lives. You know that there are homes where the cost of one meal for these parasites would keep an underfed or sick family for a whole week". Too true to be good, I suppose.

Tuesday, March 25, 1941

Yugoslavs sign pact with Axis.   No air raids last night.
          Busy at printers.   We have cheese sandwiches for lunhh,
which is a treat, because cheese is very hard to come by now.
Mr. Matthews says one of his staff reports riots in West Ham, but
as the man is a Communist and talks wildly always, he does not know
if information is reliable.

Wednesday, March 26, 1941

First heavy rain for some time: the country needed it.   Have to
go to Marylebone Town Hall and have my National Registration Card
officially changed to the Marylebone Register.   Have "committed an
offence" in not doing this before. Young man I see is very polite
and on being told date of my birth apparently feels that all is well
          To doctor's in evening.   She says I am looking much better,
gives me new medicine which will "pep me up no end", and says I am
not to allow myself to get as near the edge of as that again without
going to her.   Suppose she means edge of insanity, because I told
her how my mind played tricks on me.

Thursday, March 27, 1941

Revolution in Yugoslavia: the regent, Prince Paul, flees, the two
ministers who arranged pact with Axis are imprisoned, and young King
Peter, aged 17, takes power.   Churchill says Yugoslavia has found
its soul.   British have successes in Abyssinia, so altogether everyone is rather cheered.
          Shopping in Selfridge's in lunch-time.   They have no dried
fruit except apple-rings.   There are no boxes of sweets left for
Mother, but manage to get 1 lb. box of chocolates in Oxford Street.

Friday, March 28, 1941

Yugoslavs say they have returned to complete neutrality.   They do
not denounce pact with Axis, but it will not be ratified.   Lunch-
time papers say German troops are advancing to Yugoslav frontier.
          Cheese rationed - 1 oz. per week per person, but farm-labour-
ersget 8 oz.   Meat ration to be cut to 1/--worth per person, per week
          Find I have not as much money in bank as I supposed, which
does not deter me from buying 2 expensive petticoats and 3 pairs
knickers in lunch-hour.   Also need pyjamas, since mine are falling
into holes, but put off their purchase for a bit. In Evans's meet Mr.
Nickelsberg, late of 20 Fitzjohn's Avenue.   He was there when bomb
fell opposite, and his report of happening was: "Next morning, there
we were, covered with dirt, but it was glorious, was glorious feeling
to be still there. I can't describe it".   He and wife living in
Bucks.   Small daughter in America.

Saturday, March 29, 1941

To Hilary's by Green Line bus.   Coming through North of London,
see roads lined with almond blossom, and forsythia bushes in gardens;
others where on both sides are huge gaps made by bombs, and windows
shattered for a half-mile round.
          Noah's Ark Bungalow very comfortable and in pleasant country
Find Martin very much grown.   He smiles and kicks at me and I take
him for walk, with Tramp.
          A naval engagement is taking place in Eastern Mediterranean
and one Italian battleship has been badly damaged.   The action still
continuing.

Sunday, March 30, 1941

Very cold, but patches of bright sunshine.   Walk again with Martin
and Tramp.   Latter has to be kept from chasing sheep, which are lambing.   We are grateful for joint of beef for dinner.   H. also very
pleased that she got $\frac{1}{2}$ lb. currants, $\frac{1}{2}$ lb. sultanas, 1 lb. dates and
some sweet biscuts from grocer this week.
          Six o'clock news says three Italian cruisers and two des-
troyers sunk with no British casualties.

Monday, March 31, 1941

Another Italian cruiser reported sunk in Eastern Mediterranean action.
Everyone very pleased, because to-day Matsuoka, Japanese Foreign
Secretary, is visiting Mussoline.
          Feel very much better and more cheerful than of late.
Letter from Arnold Foster, who writes from Whitbourne Hall, near
Worcester: "I joined Westminster School here in January" - he does
the music at the School - "after having had nothing to do for three
months, part of which time we spent in Sheffield and came in for its
blitz.   The School is divided into five country mansions each anything from two to five miles apart and I spend my time between two
music centres which have been formed.   One of them is a converted
stable.   We ourselves are housed in a place like an art gallery only
without heating.   We have a lovely room 35 ft. square and about 20
ft. high. .. I have managed to start a choral society here with ladies
of the district and elder boys of the school for tenors and bases".

Tuesday, April 1, 1941

Alas: feeling of wellbeing which I had yesterday has left me, and I
drag through long and arduous day at printer's with difficulty.   In
evening Sir Richard Acland to supper.   He holds forth with great
enthusiasm on the subject of his two books ("The Forward March" has
just come out).   The principal tenet is common ownership.   Feel
more and more as evening goes on that systems or changes of them are

no good without a change in the spirit of the people.   He admits
this, but thinks introduction of common ownership would help in
fostering right spirit of working for good of all rather than for good
of oneself.
    John, who is in Ministry of Health and so hears the figures,
says deaths in recent raid on Clydeside are now found to be nearer
700 than 500.

Wednesday, April 2, 1941

Feel none too good after yesterday's long session, but am cheered
by receiving letter from South Africa.   They haven't heard, at home,
for 5 weeks, though Roy writes regularly, but now perhaps will have
several letters at once.   This one was written on February 15.   He
says: "We get quite a guilty feeling when eating grapes, peaches, etc
to say nothing of meat and butter in as great quantities as we please,
but I suppose that if they are available here it is stupid not to eat
them.   We are distressed, however, to think of the restricted diet
on which the rest of you feed".

Thursday, April 3, 1941

Feel a little better.   Tina and I go for walk in park at 6 o'clock
and meet Greta, who tells us, to our distress, that Miss Proctor's
nephew, who came to supper with us a week or so ago, looking very
handsome in his officer's uniform, has been killed by enemy action -
ship on which he was sailing to India was bombed and machine-gunned
by Germans off Stornoway.   Miss P. and her sister brought up this
boy (he was only 19) and his sister, because their mother was dead.
    The Prime Minister of Hungary, Teleki, has died "in tragic
circumstances" the evening paper says, and the President, who has
taken over, is anti-Nazi.   Meantime Yugoslavs expect war within 24
hours.
    Virginia Woolf, essayist and novelist, went out from her
home lately and has never returned.   She left a letter for her husband, and it is thought that she has drowned herself.
    Letter from home.   Daddy very angry that a firm in Plymouth
which said he could have no more goods till June because he had already had his quota, now writes that owing to enemy action all their
stocks have been destroyed.   He has written to our M.P. on the
subject, and Tina tells me that Acland has had many letters about it
and is taking the matter up with the Economic Advisory Council, because if only such goods were distributed, at least some of them would
be saved.

Friday, April 4, 1941

Daddy's 65th birthday.   Feel very dim and queer all day, and end by
losing my temper with the trying Miss Playle, which makes me feel
ill worse than ever.   Have an incipient boil under my arm, which the
doctor says she will abort for me, which makes it sound like a baby.

Lunch with Joyce, going through London, who is wondering
what to do with her life, and advises me to leave this city for duration.   Everyone rather depressed, because our troops in Benghazi,
North Africa, have evacuated the town and Nazi troops have entered
it: the Germans have brought up reinforcements to help the Italians,
with plenty of tanks, etc.   People rather feel we have been taken
by surprise out there.

Saturday, April 5, 1941

Have heard that the Budget to be announced on Monday is an absolute
snorter, and that almost everything will be taxed.   So go forth in
morning and buy mother 3 pairs thick woollen combinations for next
winter, and myself pair of shoes.   Also have hair shampooed and set,
and really spend disgraceful amount of money - oh, and box of such
sweets as I can find for Phyllida's birthday, at cost of 10/6.
(Combs. were 16/11 each, and shoes 33/9 - and not as good leather as
the ones I got last winter for 25/6.)
        Bristol has been bombed for two successive nights.   We had
short alert here last night but everything was quiet.
        Raymond turns up exexpectedly for weekend, looking larger
than ever in bell-bottoms.   Much cheerful conversation.   As I bath
I muse in a steamy kind of way about relation between Tina and Raymond, which I lazily realise does not exactly fit into any particular
category.   Later T. comes to bed and says out of darkness and a
silence "Shall I tell you something?   Shall I tell you why I am
specially devoted to young Raymond? ... It's because he reminds me
of my brother.   And my brother committed suicide".

Sunday, April 6, 1941

Germany has declared war on Greece and Yugoslavia.   Belgrade and
Salonika reported bombed.   Germans advancing upon Greece and receiving strong resistance.   Russia has made non-aggression pact with
Yugoslavia, which seems to amount to little.   In North Africa we
have occupied Addis Ababa and are so far holding the Germans in their
advance from Benghazi.
        In the meantime, in spite of the disturbing news, we have
an enjoyable day.   T.,R and I go with Bob to All Saint's, Margaret
Street, to the Palm Sunday service, and Bob and I go up to altar and
receive palms.   The whole thing is like a well-organised ballet or
a complicated game.   The men go off to lunch with a friend of R.'s,
and T. and I go to Barcelona, where I eat kid - horrid but very
biblical - and see Stephen Spender and several people from B.B.C.
We then all four go to concert at Queen's Hall, programme including
Fingal's Cave Overture and Eroica Symphony.   Tea with Norman Tucker
and friend, and evening at home with addition of Jack to party.

Monday, April 7, 1941

Budget Day - there seems to be one every week or so now.   Income tax
up to 10/- in £, and I find I shall be liable for over £150.   This

seems to me so laughable cannot take it seriously.

It is announced that a British Expeditionary Force is in Greece, but has not yet met the enemy.

Tuesday, April 8, 1941

Very wearing day at printers, which lasts till 7 o'clock, is cast into even deeper gloom than mere tiredness would give, by constant trickle of news from Mr. Matthews of progress of Germans in Greece and in Libya.   They are advancing upon Salonika.

Come to conclusion that British workman is fundamentally dishonest.   When printers wanted to get home in daylight they worked from 4 - 5 on a Tuesday at such a rate that they all caught their trains.   Now that lighter evenings are here they get slower and slower as afternoon goes on, and after 6 o'clock when they begin to get overtime pay, become more and more cheerful and less and less quick.

Wednesday, April 9, 1941

Germans occupy Salonika.   They have cut off the Greek Army in Thrace Miss P. cast into deepest gloom all day about the military situation. The Editor hints at further bad news: we suppose it means that Turkey won't fight.   And there is no co-ordination at all between Greeks and Yugoslavs.   Graham very depressed when he comes home from hearing P.M.'s statement in House.   He goes so far as to say that he supposes the best we can hope for is another Dunkirk.

Raid on Coventry last night in bright moonlight.

Thursday, April 10, 1941

No news from Greek or Albanian fronts.   Midlands raided again last night.   We had warning in London but I slept.   Was just remarking to Tina that during worst nights of last September and October I derived considerable satisfaction from reflection that we, who had left other people to be bombed for years - in Spain, China, Czecho-slovakia, Finland, etc. - and done nothing about it, were at last getting our deserts - when sirens went.   Felt the Almighty had taken my remarks too literally.

To Stroud by 6.35.   Leave station with P. just as sirens are going.   We hear a good many aeroplanes going over during night, and some gunfire.

Friday, April 11, 1941

Aeroplanes last night were going to Birmingham.   Today cold and dull, and does not begin auspiciously because Daddy receives paper to fill up about accommodation.   Room has to be found in district for more workpeople.   Mother plunged into deepest gloom, and I call the whole family fools which produces umbrage.   Picnic at Randwick

Ash, after finding road to Beacon Tump stopped now at turning at top of Whiteshill.

        No news from Greece or Libya.

Saturday, April 12, 1941

Warm day, in which Mother and P. gather primroses and I sit on wall and watch them in sunshine.   Bristol badly bombed last night. Milk supply to be cut down.   Still no news from Greece or Libya.

        Aunt H. lately had man call at her house and warn her that in the event of invasion the Government would take possession and she would receive 24 hours notice to quit - or perhaps it was 48. Anyway, she will get no compensation, the man said, and as house represents her livelihood, she is put in great way.   After man went, saying what he had said was strictly confidential, she reflected that he was not in uniform, and showed her no credentials, and she wonders if he is a Quisling, preparing way for Germans to take possession if they land on the common.   She therefore reports the business to the Police, who know nothing of it but will take the matter up.

Sunday, April 13, 1941

Easter Day.   Daddy takes cup to tea to Phyllida in bed, with pious words "The Lord is risen!", catches teapot on corner of mantelpiece and overturns contents on to floor.

        As P. and I set out for afternoon walk, All Clear goes rather mysteriously, as there has been n o warning.

        In Libya, Germans claim to have taken Bardia.   Skirmishes in Greece, but no news of big engagement.

Monday, April 14, 1941

Return to London by early train.   Have pains all day.   In lunchtime find Oxford Street full of people wandering about, having the Bank Holiday, but apparently nothing to do.   Few eating places open and what there are very c rowded.   One of Peter Robinson's buildings taken over by government.

Tuesday, April 15, 1941

Still feel very strange in stomach, with a lot of pain.   News still very depressing though so wrapped up one is given to understand that we have withdrawn successfully and victoriously all over north of Africa and Egypt.

Wednesday, April 16, 1941

Heavy raid last night on Northern Ireland.   Nothing here, but as I write this (10.20 p.m.) there is big raid in progress - numbers of planes, plenty of gunfire and so far we have heard two bombs.   One

sounded as if it was near Marble Arch and the other in the direction
of B.B.C.

News from abroad all bad.   In Yugoslavia there appears to
be only guerrilla war now in progress - no concerted fighting.

My stomach still queer with lot of pain.

(Sound of fire-engines rushing past.)

Thursday, April 17, 1941

Last night's raid developed into the worst London has had, even worse
than those last autumn.   From 9.20 - 4 or after, streams of aeroplanes, all very low, were above us, with no interval at all.   There
were fires lighting up sky: screaming bombs: continual gunfire
except when our fighters were up, when noise of planes was re-
doubled.   No hope of sleep.   Greta slept in corridor - i.e. had
mattrees there - outside our door.   About 1 or 2, the men came
acrods from other flat and sat on floor in row, wrapped in eider-
downs.   Jack went out several times and came back from the inferno
with news, while Bob cheered the company by reading aloud from book
of limericks.   J. reported large fire at back of Broadcasting House
which as far as I could make out from description was either Brock
House or buildings opposite.

Today put on smartest hat in defiance of blitzes, and find,
picking way through broken glass and rubble, that it was indeed the
building opposite Brock House which got it last night.   Brock House
itself unapproachable.   When Editor arrives, he and I go through
barrier and get permission to enter.   Climb up stairs over much
debris, and successfully reach our offices, where desolation reigns:
windows blown out, one wall - once glass partition - gone, floors
in dreadful state.   However, staff musters, takes brooms, etc.,
from cleaners' cupboard, and sweeps debris into corridor.   Layers
of dirt over everything and we get filthy.   Fire still going in
building opposite, where a pub has completely vanished - 20-30
people killed there.

Printers unbombed, but have no gas, water or light for at
least part of day.   Charing Cross hotel burning, Waterloo and
Paddington hit, City Temple demolished, Selfridges, Peter Robinson's
building which Govt. had just taken over, Wallis's in Holborn, all
hit.

Hurried lunch with Joyce as she passes through London.

Friday, April 18, 1941

Jack brought home daffodils last night - his contribution to defy-
ing blitzes - together with gin and lime.   May have been drink,
or weariness after sleepless night and trying day: anyway, after
dinner I fall into somnolent state in chair, and am carried thence
and deposited on my bed and covered with eiderdown, where I sleep
from 8.30 - 10.30, when am partially roused by Tina, who comes to
bed and undresses me as if I were an infant.   No warning at

all, though many people expected another lively night.

Today walk from Tottenham Court Road to Oxford Circus, where lot of damage has been done. We work in gales of wind by reason of glassless windows. Every time I cut up proof, the bits blow away. Editor spends day in Home Guard overcoat and trilby hat. When I leave in evening it is raining hard, and water is coming into Brock House and running in stream down stairs. Was amused by two men who arrived at beginning of morning and asked if there was anything I wanted "adjusted"!

Next to bomb debris outside our window is green notice which says "Incident Officer".

Go across to Broadcasting House with envelope of stuff we could not replace, to put it in safe place for night. Leave it in news room, three - no, perhaps only two - stories below ground, where Senior News Editor, J.T. Clarke, is lying in bunk and requests me to place package on bunk above.

Germans say Yugoslavia has capitulated, which is probably true. They have also taken over French Morocco. We have sunk convoy of 8 ships, otherwise news very bad.

Saturday, April 19, 1941

To Hilary's. Baby very much grown: talks and crows at me and I take him and Tramp for walk. Later Martin has pain and I do floor walking with him, and soon after this we have warning and some fairly near bombs and gunfire.

Sunday, April 20, 1941

News says another heavy raid on London, with much damage. I take Martin in ppam. in afternoon, exploring down very muddy lane. Have come into open where there are no trees when terrific storm of hail gomes down. Tramp hides in hedge: baby, under his hood on which hail makes devastating noise, unperturbed. A little later there is forked lightning and tremendous crash of thunder. Tramp's hair stands on end, but Martin again unmoved and beams upon me. He is very happy baby, and if he cries it is because he is hungry or has pain.

Monday, April 21, 1941

Back to town. Office is worse than ever because one of our walls being knocked down with great enjoyment by two workmen.

Tuesday, April 22, 1941

Paper goes to press at 5.40, which is earlier than lately, and in view of difficulties last week, with Miss Playle away as well, feel gratified. Hear that Editor has glass put back into his windows, at which he is very pleased.

Wednesday, April 23, 1941

St. George's Day, and we hear part of Greek Army has surrendered and
Greek Government gone to Crete.   Army of workmen is busy all day in
and around our offices.   Have put back wall, and heating system is
in order again.   There is also towel in lavatory once more.   Civili-
sation is being restored.

Thursday, April 24, 1941

We are assured that British line in Greece still holds firm.   Workmen in office most of day, all very cheerful, singing from large re-
pertoire (Ave Maria to extracts from Rose Marie).   All Listener
offices now have beautiful panes of glass put into windows, so althoug
dust still thick on everything, we feel very fortunate.
        Lunch with Daddy (he and Mother went to H's yesterday for
2 days), and pass him copy of letter from Oliver Lyttelton, President
of Board of Trade, to Sir Richard Acland, about distribution of stocks
which says wholesalers are permitted, and indeed urged, to distribute
goods among retailers, though until they are allowed by law to release
the stuff under Govt. quota, it must not be sold to public.   This
would prevent large warehouses-full stocks of goods being lost if warehouses
are bombed.

Friday, April 25, 1941

To Stroud by 4.15.   Phyllida, who has springcleaned sitting-room in
parents' absence, is on point of accepting job with L.C.C. - mansion
near Malmesbury where 35 children (2 - 5 years old) are to be evacua
ted from slums.   She would help in teaching them.   Thing will start
from scratch, probably with no apparatus, so she feels there will be
scope.
        Germans say they have taken Pass of Thermopolae and Island of
Saturday, April 26, 1941   Lemnos.

In Stroud, tomatoes are 8/- a lb. and were lately 10/-, though I got
some at 1/6 in London for H. last Saturday.   Lettuce I buy is 10d.
        P. and I essay to pick cowslips but get only very few short
ones.   It is too cold for them yet.   The common quite dried up and
there is very drying north-east wind.   We need rain badly for seeds.
We meet rather wild-looking man who says he has just had telephone
message that 3 bombs have been dropped at Brockworth.   Looks as if
he is setting out to walk there at once, but it is 10 miles so perhaps
not.

Sunday, April 27, 1941

Germans say they have entered Athens.   Mr. Churchill broadcasts in
evening, but I am in train for London and do not hear him.   Flat full
of cowslips from Evesham brought by Jean.   Cold day, with nasty high
wind.

all, though many people expected another lively night.

      Today walk from Tottenham Court Road to Oxford Circus, where lot of damage has been done. We work in gales of wind through glassless windows. Every time I cut up proof, the bits blow away. When I leave in evening, it is raining hard, and water is coming into Brock House and running in stream down stairs.

      Germans say Yugoslavia has capitulated, which is probably true. They have also taken over French Morocco. We have sunk a convoy of 8 ships, otherwise news is very bad.

Saturday, April 19, 1941

Monday, April 28, 1941

Warmer.   Have to go to 10 Downing Street to check Prime Minister's broadcast with original script.   House is very big inside;   am taken along many corridors and given pleasant room to myself to work in. Then~h Think how trusting to leave stranger alone for $\frac{3}{4}$-hour: may have bomb in pocket.   But on emerging, find two men in corridor out- side, looking so much like detectives feel they can be nothing else. They look at me rather severely till I say I want to find way out, when they are only too anxious to show it to me.   Feel I am at heart of Empire, and have strange "I-have-been-here-before" sensation. Glad to observe that when P.M. quotes poetry, he does it correctly, down to last comma, which is more than can be said for other Ministers who have detestable habit of misquoting and even attributing the lines they quote to wrong poet.
    At lunch see Roger Wilson, who had to leave B.B.C. Talks Dept. because he is Quaker and Pacifist.   Glad to observe him looking very cheerful: he is organising Friends War Relief Committee which is doing good work for evacuees and in shelters in bombed districts, etc.

Tuesday, April 29, 1941

Not so late at printers, in spite of P.M. and other difficulties. Last night quiet - we have had very little since big raids fortnight ago.   B.E.F. trying to evacuate from Greece.   People remark sardoni- cally that we are getting quite efficient at evacuating troops.

Wednesday, April 30, 1941

Churchill announces in House that B.E.F. in Greece has already got 48,000 out of 60,000 men out of country.
    Raymond turns up unexpectedly to supper;   is only with us $\frac{3}{4}$ hour before catching train to Scotland to go on board destroyer Verdun. Is to go as ordinary seaman for three months, then if recommended by commander to have commission.
    Milk shortage beginning to show itself: we have no coffee tonight.

Thursday, May 1, 1941

Elizabeth and I go to Bedford College, where Miss Proctor, Bursar, has promised us a little patch of ground to grow lettuces, etc. Take large box of hop manure. Have to wait for Miss P. till it is nearly dark.   B.B.C. Fire Watchers, who had been offered four small beds and had done nothing with them, on hearing that one of beds was going to be given to us, hastily dig up ground.   So Miss P. promises to look for another piece for us.   She says I am shocking sight and need holiday, though I feel much better.

Friday, May 2, 1941

I go to Bedford College, where Miss Proctor and I interview gardener and he gives us small piece of ground.

Saturday, May 3, 1941

Have hair washed, which it needed badly.   Then to H's for weekend.
Baby grown and rather tearful in evening.   We hear warning as we
go to bed.   Clocks put on another hour (double summer time): first
time this has been done, and farmers don't like it.

Sunday, May 4, 1941

Warm and sunny.   Sit in garden and write.   L. borrows motor-mower
from Mrs. Parrish and plays with it happily all afternoon instead of
putting in potatoes.   H's grocer sent her three oranges this week.
Have not seen any for months.   Tiny little things, but I eat one
with great sense of luxury.   She also got 2 lb. apples, another
luxury nowadays.
        Martin sleeps all afternoon, so naturally willnot go to bed
at 6, and against all teachings of books I put him in pram and take
him for long walk, not returning till after 9 (7 by sun, so only
just getting chilly).   He sleeps $\frac{3}{4}$ hour, although I go over very
roughtrack exploring; and rest of time is happy watching trees go
by.
        Merseyside raided again for 2nd/ or 3rd night.   There is fighting
between our troops and Nazis in Iraq, where they want to capture
pipe line.

Monday, May 5, 1941

Graham returns from Birkenhead after almost no sleep for four nights
Raids on Merseyside very heavy and damage is terrible.
        Tina, Jack and I go to dig our plot at Bedford College and
put in hop manure.   J. loses signet ring.

Tuesday, May 6, 1941

Tiring day at printers and I therefore do not join digging party in
evening, but Tina and Greta go and find J's ring.   Merseyside raided again last night.   We have short alert but no noise.   British
fighting in Iraq.

Wednesday, May 7, 1941

Mr. Ackerley, who went to Liverpool for last weekend, says for two
nights there were worse raids than anything he has experienced in
London.   As if he had been actually in the City on the night of the
fire blitz there.   Raids on Merseyside again last night.

Thursday, May 8, 1941

Merseyside raided heavily again.   That means they have had a whole
week of heavy raids.

Friday, May 9, 1941

Letter from Joyce says that Sunday, May 11, is 'terrific' astrologi-
cally and may mean coming of New Messiah!

Saturday, May 10, 1941

To Hilary's, with small piece of veal-and-ham pie which she regards
as great prize.   Baby looks fatter than last week and greets me
with flattering pleasure.

Sunday, May 11, 1941

Some noise last night, H. says, though I slept well and heard nothing
Wireless today says very heavy raid on London: British Museum,
Westminster Abbey and Houses of Parliament among buildings hit. Here
it is warm lovely day, and I take baby and dog for two walks.

Monday, May 12, 1941

Taxi I ordered does not come, so I do not arrive at office till 10.55
passing on way the ruined Queen's Hall.   Printers and blockmakers
bombed, so paper has to be started all over again, with Waterlow's
of Park Royal printing it.   Blocks given out to three or four
different firms all over London.   Mr. Abraham and I travel to W's
by car from B.B.C.   It goes via Bedford College which received
direct hit on Saturday.   Residence appears to be unhurt but some
laboratories, now used by B.B.C. Photographic Dept., in ruins, and
photographs and valuable cameras have been destroyed.   Work till
8 o'clock and do not get home till 9.   Modern up-to-date works, but
last autumn windows were blown out so that compositors' room, off
which we work, is now lighted artificially, with greeny-yellow
light which makes everyone look on verge of heart attack plus/channel completed
crossing.
          Most pathetic sight of today was Mr. Matthews, foreman from
Speaights, who had been with firm about 40 years, coming in lost way
to Brock House with little gas-mask over his shoulder.

Tuesday, May 13, 1941

At printers till 9 o'clock.   Smallest Listener which has ever
appeared, only 28 pages.   Waterlow's overseer worked with us till
8 last night, went on 12 hours' Home Guard duty, and works with us
till 9 tonight.   New printers very good considering rushed job.
Radio Times staff, whose offices are in same building, take us to
pub for lunch   Lift from Miss Wynne in morning.   She picks up Mr.
Tristram, R.T. chief sub-editor on way: dirty old man with beard,
Buddhist, vegetarian and confirmed pessimist.   Waterlows lodged
official complaint because of terrible number of empty milk bottles
beneath his desk.   He assures me Park Royal will destroy me body
and soul.

Melodramatic news announced that Hess, Hitler's Deputy, has landed in Scotland by parachute from plane he piloted himself and allowed to crash. Germany had already announced that he had disappeared, and that he was suffering from hallucinations. Medical people over here report him sane. This extraordinary happening makes war more like H.G. Wells novel than ever - or, I suggest to Editor, comic opera. He is of opinion we could dispense with the Noises Off. Feel very disinclined to believe Rudolf Hess is New Messiah: it is interesting that Hitler is supposed to consult astrologers, and probably his followers also.

Wednesday, May 14, 1941

Hear from Mr. Ackerley ḥ½ that his flat was bombed on Saturday and he escaped with life only because he had gone to next street to stay with friend for duration of raid.

Lunch with Douglas who is very thin and has grown moustache. We meet at Bertorelli's, which has just escaped destruction: other end of Charlotte Street roped off. In evening to Sir Richard A's house at Victoria, where Tina gives supper to Jack, Greta and me, and we put cotton strands across lettuce bed we have made there.

Speculations as to motives of Hess in coming to England are made by everyone. It cannot be agreed whether he is escaping from Hitler's wrath after break in Nazi party; is somehow double-crossing us and is fore-runner of invasion; or is fanatic who somehow thinks he can save Germany from further trouble by making peace overtures through his friend the Duke of Hamilton, near whose estate he landed in Scotland.

Thursday, May 15, 1941

Mother very depressed by news that she has to receive 'a gentleman' - probably one of new war workers to be sent to Stroud district. John tells me they are going to build new war factories in Stroud valley and that there has been 'closure' order on the area, which accounts for notice received at home that only relations are to be allowed to come for visits longer than weekend, and they, I think, only for week at time without permission - but may be mistaken about last clause.

To National Gallery concert: Beethoven quartets. In evening to Bedford College with Greta and Jack to dig our plot, which was undamaged by bombs although next to building which has been destroyed. It remains to be seen, however, whether our little seeds have been blown out of ground by blast. We ignore notice which says we are not to approach along path where plot is because of danger of collapsing walls. Miss Proctor, bursar, who has already lost her nephew whom she brought up (his boat machine-gunned and bombed off coast of Scotland when he was just sailing for India) looks stricken by this new blow: old and bowed down.

French are giving Germans air-bases in Syria. America is holding French ships which are in U.S. ports, including <u>Normandie,</u> and threatens to occupy French colonies.

Friday, May 16, 1941

To H's by 6 o'clock bus, after very strenuous lunch-hour trying
to buy food.   Get lettuce at 1/-, radishes at 6d per bunch, ¼ lb.
somestrange unrationed meat and vegetable stuff set in a mould from
Selfridges: also chocolates and cigarettes for H. since she finds
it difficult to get them.   They are rare even in London.   It was
very cold night with sharp frost, but in afternoon becomes warmer.

Saturday, May 17, 1941

Very warm, but still frost at night, and Mrs. Johnson says blossom
has been cut off and there will be no fruit this year.   Am afraid
if we do not get rain many crops will be spoilt, which will be very
serious for us: the gardens are grey with dust.

Sunday, May 18, 1941

Hot.   Laze, weed garden, amuse baby, and feel far from war.

Monday, May 19, 1941

Letter from John (Beavan), who says Arthur, after severe mental
struggle, has decided not to register as a C.O. on Saturday, but
to say he will join A.F.S.   They are relieved things have turned
out like this.   Poor Arthur, who cannot bear physical pain and has
no nerve: how will he get on in a fire blitz?
            In evening Tina, Jack, John, Bob and I go to exciting film
in which French and we are still gallant Allies: funny too.

Tuesday, May 20, 1941

Germans make landings in Crete from gliders: men dressed in New
Zealand battle-dress, papers say (probably untrue).   But this news
quite overshadowed for me by working late at Waterlow's till 10 p.m.
They are supposed to be an up-to-date firm, but behaved in slowest
and most miserable manner all day.
            Editor says he hears from reliable source, but news not to
be passed on, that Hess is telling nothing to authorities over here.

Wednesday, May 21, 1941

Parachute troops in Crete rounded up, but sea landings now being
attempted.
            I meet Daddy for lunch.   Come up to try to buy stuff:
he finds Hine Parkers standing with two other buildings in otherwise
derelict street.   He falls over debris and lands on his nose which
is bleeding when I see him.

I buy (Vita-Weet' for Mother, which she cannot get in
Stroud: also hair-nets. Try to get side-combs for H. but fail:
told they were made in France and are now unobtainable. I look
complete wreck after last night's labours. In evening the flat
family goes to dine at "Chez Fillier", where we eat prodigiously and
drink moderately. Incidentally, there is plenty of meat to be had
in any Soho restaurant. We then go to film, 'Mademoiselle Ma Mère',
very French and improper.

Thursday, May 22, 1941

Big battle still raging for Crete. More troops landed by planes.
London having a "war-weapons week": trying to raise £100
millions in investments in war savings certificates, etc. Other
towns have raised enormous sums in this way. Cars with loudspeakers
go about the streets exhorting us to help win the war: but I have
done nothing about it, since cost of living has risen considerably
and my salary has not.

Friday, May 23, 1941

Home by 6.35: Mother has to entertain minister for Sunday School
Anniversary services and requests my help. Vera has given up week's
meat ration for week to feed man, eggs have somehow been procured,
butter has been forthcoming from I know not where, and Roy has just
sent 3½ lb. sugar from South Africa. So Mother's mind relieved of
anxiety. Feel it very good of people to give up rations for preacher'
sake.
Am horrified in train by openness with which soldiers and
sailors tell everyone where they have come from and where going. One
man even gives away to suspicious-looking character with foreign
accent that he is going on board ship tonight at Avonmouth.

Saturday, May 24, 1941

Wet. Glad, because gardens are so dry. The minister arrives after
6.30, having travelled since 8 this morning from Bangor where he is
Professor at Baptist College. His name is Williams Hughes and he is
very Welsh and amusing. Missed connection at Birmingham and is very
tired.
H.M.S.Hood lost in naval battle off Greenland, which is still
in progress. Feared there will be few survivors. Great battle
still going on in Crete.

Sunday, May 25, 1941

Minister sick in night (went too long without food yesterday and ate
too heartily when got in). Does not feel well, but preaches accept-
ably and sleeps on sofa between services. He has three sons, eldest
being Pacifist who got total exemption from Tribunal and is driving

mobile canteen through/Cardiff and Swansea.
air-raids in

Monday, May 26, 1941

Strong feeling at flat because management threatens to put up
charges 10 per cent by adding this as "service gratuity".   Rent
is already 11 guineas a week for two flats and one would imagine
quite enough.   To look for other accommodation is not easy, because
large blocks of flats have been taken by Government and others are
uninhabitable because of bombing.   Proprietors therefore know they
have advantage over us.

Tuesday, May 27, 1941

Great joy because we have sunk German crack battleship Bismarck,
which sank Hood.   But we have lost 2 cruisers and 4 destroyers off
Crete.
              At printers till 8.30.   At flat find no supper was ordered
for me, and Jack and Tina take me out to Canuto's and give me
delectable meal at 10 p.m. with wine which they share.   Am able to
have delicious mushroom omelette in spite of egg scarcity.   In fact
one can still feed very well if one can pay for it (or, as in this
case, if one's friends pay for it).   It is the poor who go short, as
usual.

Wednesday, May 28, 1941

Roosevelt has broadcast speech declaring state of national emergency
in America.   Says Germans are sinking our merchant ships three times
as quickly as we can build them, and twice as quickly as Americans
and British together can build them: but America intends to alter
that state of affairs.
              Hear from John (Beavan) that Peter has been home for 24
hours before sailing again.   He has been twice across Atlantic in
oil tanker, to and from West Indies, and is going again.
              David Green to supper.   He is in Auxiliary Fire Service.

Thursday, May 29, 1941

Germans landing more and more troops in Crete.   British also
making sea landings.   I go to film, 'Quiet Wedding', with John.
He is delayed at Home Guard drill, so we are too late for 'Kipps'
which we had intended to see.   Kipps reminds me that there is row
in progress because H.G.Wells wrote letter which we published in
Listener, saying that he invented the tank in story written about
1902, and that Sir Ernest Swinton (Major-General) who gave broadcast
saying more or less that he invented the tank, is wrong.   Swinton
threatens to sue us for publishing libel or calumny.

After film we eat at Corner House, which is even more
crowded than normally, since fewer places are open where one can
eat at such an hour.   There is the usual extraordinary mixed crowd
of people there, rather like dregs of humanity.

Friday, May 30, 1941

To Stroud by 6.35, with Bobby Large.   Hilary already there, having
brought Martin on an earlier train and in 1st-class carriage because
it was so full.   The man who rented bungalow to them has been posted to aerodrome few miles away, and he and wife and permanently in
house, and as they are at daggers drawn with H's help and hope, Mrs.
Johnson, atmosphere is tense with feeling.   H. gets upset and that
upsets Martin's food and he cries.   So she is home for few days to
recover.

Saturday, May 31, 1941

Hilda has son, 7¼ lb., born last night.
          Crete in very poor way.
          President of Board of Trade going to make important
announcement tomorrow morning at 9 o'clock.

Sunday, June 1, 1941

Martin is 6 months old today; Germans have conquered Crete;
President of Board of Trade announces that boots and clothes are to
be rationed as from tomorrow.   These last two announcements put Pop
into rather depressed state.

Monday, June 2, 1941

My 34th birthday.   Wash up singing "Days and moments quickly flying
Blend the living with the dead", especially when remember first time
I ever heard Aunt N's age she was 34, and looked upon her as senile.
          Details of clothes rationing announced.   66 coupons each
for year.   Woman's long coat costs 14 coupons; woollen frock, 11;
stockings, 2; vests, 3; shoes, 5; etc.

Tuesday, June 3, 1941

At Waterlow's till 10 p.m. when, very weary and hungry, I return to
London and try to get food at only place I can find open at 11
o'clock - i.e. Marble Arch Corner House.   There is queue waiting
to be admitted, and I have to wait about ¼-hour.   Sit opposite very
made-up woman who has argument with waiter because she wants sauce
with her fish as I have with mine, though her fish is not sort that
has sauce served with it.   She is ambulance driver from Kensington
and mutters to me that it is ridiculous - she wouldn't tell waiter,
if she picked him up wounded, that she couldn't take him anywhere
because he came from some other district.   Corner House is full of

revolting Jews and equally revolting Gentiles, and my feeling is, kfwe're fighting war to preserve people like this, God help us.
Arrive home at 12.30.

Wednesday, June 4, 1941

Very tired after yesterday's exertions.   Don't go to office till after lunch but spend morning going to Hampstead to get summer clothes which I've left at Cundells.   Distressed to find that though cotton frocks, e tc., in drawers a re still there, all things which were hanging in cupboard (two coats, 3 frocks and one suit) have gone.   Suppose that Helena thought they belonged to Dora (children's nurse) and has send them to her.   Hope to get them back, as impossible to replace them now, e ven were I rolling in money.   We find too the margarine coupons in ration books, which for obscure British reason have to be used for clothes, have been crossed out by Manageress of flats.
Very warm day and at end of ~~aftermppm-0-set-om-'arl-fpr~~ afternoon I sit in park for hour in deck chair and feel comforted thereby.

~~Thuzsdat~~&June 5, 1941

Last night there was air-raid warning in middle of thunderstorm, so that one hardly knew whether the noise following was guns or thunder. It wwas mostly God, not the Germans, and All Clear followed fairly quickly.
Receive telephone message to say Tina, Bob, Jack and I are dinging at Brasserie Universelle in Piccadilly Circus.   We meet and eat roast beef, potatoes and carrots; fruit salad and artificial cream.   Followed by s weet Turkish coffee and accompanied by sweet white wine.   The others have po t as well.   Restaurant very full and no apparent shortage of food.   We then go to film of H.G.Wells's 'Kipps' which we enjoy very much.   Jack takes us to Regent Palace Hotel for gin and lime afterwards.   Pleasant evening.
Letter from Helena.   She has been ill, and Edrick, commissioned to collect some of Dora's clothes from Hampstead, collected mine too.   So I shall get them back sometime.

Friday, June 6, 1941

With John to Philharmonic Concert at Coliseum, conducted by Malcolm Sargent.   Schumann's Piano Concerto (Moura Lympany) and Tchaikovsky's 4th Symphony, as well as 'La Boutique Fantasque' and other things. Malcolm Sargent tells us that Rossini originally wrote music of La B.F, as piano pieces for his young friends.   Later another Italian, Respighi, orchestrated them.   There is large and appreciative audience.   We walk home and find book stall in Oxford Street where a while back was a French patisserie.   Still open at 10 p.m., and we prowl around and buy booklets on Home Guard, novel by Rose Macaulay, remarkable clock which tells when to plant everything, e tc.

Saturday, June 7, 1941

Hairdresser has been bombed, but assistants housed in rival firm
opposite, where am able to have shampoo and set.   Manage to buy
at Selfridges ¾ lb. gruyère cheese, which is unrationed, at 4/6
a lb.   Feel this very immoral: it means people with money can
have as much cheese as they want; people with little can have
only 2 oz per week.   I visit Food Office and am relieved to learn
that margarine coupons are valid for clothes although crossed out.
          To Great Missenden with Tina.
          Sickened by news.   Hitler is saying great deal about
'New Order' in Europe, and though it must be obvious to everyone
of intelligence that a New Order will have to be formed somehow,
we are busy talking and writing it down as much as possible.   I
don't believe half of quarter of what we are told about Nazis' foul
intentions: authorities here just trying to ~~threaten us~~ frighten
us into fighting this war to bolster up capitalist system.
(Suppose this amounts to high treason.)

Sunday, June 8, 1941

Free French and Imperial Forces entered Syria early this morning.
They have delayed doing this till Germans, by 'infiltration' have
occupied all aerodromes.   Frank at Home Guard all morning.   Comes
home full of depression.   Says their company has 25 rigles and 30
hand grenades between 80 men: no tommy gun.   He asked one of men
training them, who had been in Greece, what Home Guard would do in
event of invasion, and received reply that they could do nothing, being unarmed, and that if Germans came to England in one-tenth the
strength they had in Crete, Home Guard would be absolutely useless.
Trust this is exaggerated, as heard from another quarter lately that
this country was defended magnificently.
          Listen to part of wireless talk definitely designed to
stir up hatred against Germans: there is singularly little hatred
among ordinary people.

Monday, June 9, 1941

Free French and British have so far met with little opposition in
Syria.
          Mr. Abraham and I at Waterlows.   Go by B.B.C. car.
Driver tells me B.B.C. petrol ration has been cut by 20 %.   But this
leaves sufficient for ordinary journeys.   Will not allow him to do
extra journeys for personal convenience of Radio Times staff.
Should think not.

Tuesday, June 10, 1941

Very wet day.   At Park Royal till 6.45: earlier hour appears to be
due to B.B.C.'s having told printers they will pay no overtime.
This throws me into pessimistic state of mind about honesty of work-

people.   Or perhaps system under which they work is to blame.
Pub where we lunch is able to give us roast beef and Yorkshire pudding, cabbage and potato, as well as plum pie.   Get supper at place
in Baker Street arcade called Vienna Café: waitress appears to be
Irish.
        Miss Philliston, of Bedford College, at flat.   She has
heard that Germans in France, contrary to everything we are told,
are behaving very well, so that French wonder what all the fuss was
about.

Wednesday, June 11, 1941

Mother's 65th birthday.   I sent her 1 lb. box chocolates, which I
managed to get at De Brys in New Oxford Street.   I receive two pairs
silk stockings from Roy in South Africa, posted May 13.   Do not
have to pay duty on them.
        With John and Florence to see film of 'Kipps' again.

Thursday, June 12, 1941

Receive my missing clothes from Helena.   Friend of Tina's has heard
from people in Denmark.   They refer to Germans obliquely as the
Salvation Army.   They think we shall win, and are waiting for the
day.   This conflicts with news of French people's attitude reported
by Miss Philliston on Wednesday. Tuesday.

Friday, June 13, 1941

To Stroud for week's holiday.   Met by Mother who reports Daddy in
bed, unwell.   Her birthday letter from Roy in S.Africa arrived on
the day: she was very pleased.

Saturday, June 14, 1941

Buy kettle in Stroud, with some difficulty.   Queues outside Hillier'
(pork and cooked meats), and West's and Tuck's (confectioners).   We
receive 1 lb. butter from girl who is cook at West's: she says
their allowance is being cut; there will probably be no more for us.
I register at Walton's for eggs.   Ration is to be 2 per week, but
many people who keep hens say they will give up: it is very difficult to get enough food for them, and if all eggs have to be sent to
a central depot the trouble involved is toogreat.   We shall therefore
be worse off with rationing than we were without it.

Sunday, June 15, 1941

Daddy tries to have bath and turns very faint.   Is afraid of heart
attack and goes back to bed.   Last night there waswarning here and
sound of guns.   Today Mrs. Wall says there was bomb at Painswick
which killed several people.
        Much talk of Sidon in news.   Or perhaps it is Tyre.
Anyway very like running commentary on Old Testament.

Very warm day after very cold dismal weather yesterday.
Sit on lawn and get quite sunburnt.·

Monday, June 16, 1941

Americans are going to close all German consulates, travel bureaux,
etc., in U.S.A., because they have been indulging in activities outside
their proper scope and anti-American in nature.

Doctor to see Daddy. Says he is suffering from over-work,
worry and food rationing, and must stay in bed. Adds that he is one
of many thus afflicted. Have come to Stroud for week's peace, and
on Saturday there were 6 bombs (number now confirmed) at Painswick,
my father has taken to his bed, Leslie reports that a man stole a
boiler suit from shop on Saturday, two or three shops have been
broken into and robbed, and man at cinema has been arrested for twice
trying to burn place down. He is from Channel Islands, said to be
anti-British, and local gossip says he was trying to light beacon for
German bombers. They flew over again last night but dropped nothing
near here.

Tuesday, June 17, 1941

News is of places in Middle East, and all sounds unintelligible to
me, but I gather we are gaining ground in Syria. Bombers flew over
here quite low last night but dropped no bombs.

David's fourth birthday. I do little but weed path and
sieve soil for flower border in front. Very warm.

Daddy seems a little better.

Wednesday, June 18, 1941

Doctor reports Daddy improving. We have 2 lb. sugar from S.Africa
for Mother's birthday. Postage costs far more than sugar, but of
course its value here is as fine gold. Tomatoes are still 3/- per
lb., and gooseberries, which are controlled by government, 5d. They
are hard to come by because people say it doesn't pay them to pick for
the price and they prefer wickedly to let them rot ont rees. Tomat-
ees are soon to be controlled, and greengrocer says they will then
disappear from market.

Thursday, June 19, 1941

Turkey has made pact with Germany.

Daddy not such a good night. Very feverish, counting
coupons, thinking he had to give up two for a "wee", and saying to
Mother "I am rather muddled: cannot quite remember what relation you
are to me".

I buy in town 2 small bundles of asparagus at 1/- each. To
Aunt H's, who sends me home with 8 eggs, lettuces and gooseberries.
Mrs. Franklin, who calls to enquire after Daddy, says she has had only
four eggs since last September.

Friday, June 20, 1941

Cummings, in News Chronicle, says great tension between Germany and Russia, and unless some agreement is reached quickly, there will be flare-up.

Doctor comes, and says don't give Daddy asparagus (bad for kidneys, and his are affected). Today we give him new carrots at 8d. for minute bundle.

Saturday, June 21, 1941

Longest day, which I find unpleasant thought because from now on evenings will be getting darker and nights longer. Daddy seems a little better. Leslie reports such busy-ness in shop as he has never known. He had to lock door. And it is so hot. He comes up to see Daddy after they are closed and gives me lift to Aunt Tuttie's. I walk back across common at about 10 o'clock. It is still very warm but there is pleasant breeze on top of hill.

Sunday, June 22, 1941

For no particular reason we all congregate to hear 9 o'clock News, Daddy coming down from bed for purpose. Very glad we did so, because it is announced that Germany has invaded Russia, in spite of her treaty with U.S.S.R.

In Chapel we have 'All Things Bright and Beautiful', which sing heartily, for it is lovely day. But feel it is very illogical, and compose for myself another verse:-

> All The mentally deficient
> And germs, and lice, and fleas,
> And men like Adolf Hitler -
> The Lord created these.
> All things grim and terrible,
> All creatures great and small,
> All things mad and miserable,
> The Lord God made them all.

Am sure no one is not spiritually minded who cannot sing this with as much fervour as he puts into Mrs. Alexander's pretty-pretty-isms.

Doctor comes: says Daddy <u>must</u> take things easy.

I return to London and am almost grilled in carriage. Bob is only person at flat, wandering about in shorts. We go for short stroll at 11 o'clock when it is still almost unbearably sultry.

Prime Minister broadcasts at 9 p.m.

Monday, June 23, 1941

Unwillingly back to work. Miss P. on holiday, and paper altered almost completely to get in Churchill and other weekend broadcasts. Persuade Mr. Ab. to go to 10 Downing St. instead of me to do necessary

checking because am wearing cotton frock, no hat and no gloves,
which feel is not suitable costume for visiting Prime Minister.
        Russian towns bombed.
        Not quite so hot to-day: last night almost unbearable.

Tuesday, ~~July~~ June 24, 1941

Germans have captured Brest-Litovsk.
        Very hectic at printers, which I leave at 8.30.   Get
quite good meal at B.B.C. restaurant.

Wednesday, ~~July~~ June 25, 1941

Daddy not so well.   Decide to go home for weekend.
        Flat party to dine with Kathleen McColgan, Graham's sec-
retary at Lawn Road Flats, Hampstead; we eat in garden, with
Wilfred Roberts, M.P., surrounded by extraordinary men with beards
and exotic women with shorts.   Drink gin and lime, and then some
very potent so-called cider-cup, which has an orange stuck with
cloves in it (first orange I have seen for long time) and strawberries, and tastes mostly of brandy.   We eat steak and onions,
another luxury, and asparagus, and rhubarb fool, and have coffee
and brandy after that.   Wilfred Roberts takes gloomy view of war,
and Kathleen, whom I suspect of having had much drink before we
arrived, tells us with much solemnity why we are not like two pennies
with which she is about to phone.

Thursday, ~~July~~ June 26, 1941

Buy charming shantung suit for Mother to give Martin.   Cash cheque
and am pleased to find I have 1s. 1d. in bank, so am still solvent.

Friday, ~~July~~ June 27, 1941

Germans and Russians bombing each other heartily.
        I find cleaners who will take my crumpled clothes: since
clothes-rationing was announced, so many people have decided to have
their old garments cleaned, that cleaners have been unable to accept
any.   The "6-hour" firm I find promises them back in a fortnight.
        Home by 6.35 p.m.

Saturday, ~~July~~ June 28, 1941

Daddy a little better.   Mother says on Wed. and Thurs. he seemed to
be in a coma, and she was very worried.
        No tomatoes to be had in Stroud because price is nowcon-
trolled, which always seems to have effect of banishing anything from
shops.   If we could get any, they would be 1/2 a lb.   I pay 9d. per
lb. for broad beans, which however are very nice.

Sunday, ~~July~~ June 29, 1941
Return to London.   Very warm.   Little news of note.

Monday, June 30, 1941

Paderewski, pianist and one-time President of Poland, dies.
        Great battle raging in Russia.   Germans trying their famous
pincer movement.   News rather obscure, but Germans advancing.

Tuesday, July 1, 1941

Terribly hectic day at printers.   Mr. Ab. not well and does not turn
up.   Editor seems surprised when I say I must have someone else out
there to read pages.   Miss P. comes and we are both at it as hard
with hardly a break until after 8.30.   Very tired.   Have strange
lump in my neck which looks like swollen glands.

Wednesday, July 2, 1941

Mr. Abraham has appendicitis.   His appendix removed yesterday evening.   I advise Editor that something must be done to improve position at printers or I shall be ill too.   Feel very done up and have
my breakfast in bed, with strawberries.   Spend rest of day grappling
with Listener half-yearly index which, owing to my holiday and then
Miss P's absence, is a fortnight in arrears and has now to go to press
        Germany seems to be making progress in Russia, but not very
quickly.   News still rather obscure.
        Eggs rationed.   For July we are to get one egg each a week.
Numbers of coupons for some summer clothes have been revised.

Thursday, July 3, 1941

Spend almost all day getting index to press and feel at end of it
almost incapable of coherent thought.
        To supper with David in garden of Lawn Road flats.   Very
pleasant.   He tells me that Joyce tried to commit suicide after her
baby was born.   We go to Daleham Gardens where he is living in very
pleasant room in house of film actress now in Hollywood.   He pays
only 10/- a week for it, and there is beautiful garden.   The other
two men in the house bring a succession of women home to sleep with
them.   We meet Miss Meagher, one-time housekeeper at 20 Fitzjohn's
Avenue, who greets us with great joy.

Friday, July 4, 1941

To Hilary's by 5.20 bus.   Walk to bungalow in warm evening.   Baby
very much grown and brown with sun.

Saturday, July 5, 1941

Very warm again.   Our bombers and fighters active over France but
little air activity over here.   We go for evening walk with baby
and see fighters coming back over aerodrome doing "victory roll"
which means they have brought down enemy machines.

Sunday, July 6, 1941

Visit to Lily and Ronald's cottage at Wareside.   Family tea: two
babies, two grandparents.

Monday, July 7, 1941

Rather kept awake by our aircraft going over last night.   Today get
lift to bus in butcher's van, which chases departing bus froms top
for 1½ miles and triumphantly overtakes it.   Very hot day, and am
angered by our supper, which costs us ₫ 2/6 each (plus the 10 per
cent they add on to everything), and consists solely of two sausages
each and some mashed potato.   Also we have been told that, since
coal is to be rationed, water will in future be hot on only half the
days in the week.   This determines us to look for other accommodation, and we are putting advertisement in New Statesman.

Tuesday, July 8, 1941

Hectic day at printers.   Leave about 8.30, and get, at Broadcasting
House, for 1/6, much better meal than I had last night for 2/6:
giblet hot-pot, new carrots, new potatoes, and green salad.   Feel
very tired.
                Heavy raid on Southampton in full moon last night.

Wednesday, July 9, 1941

Hilary's 29th birthday.   To doctor's, to show her lump which has come
up at side of my neck.   She thinks it is a cyst which ought to be
removed, and will arrange for me to see specialist.   Weather still
very warm.
                Russians claim they are holding Germans, but there seem to
be penetrations of German tanks for considerable distances at some
points.   Another poster says Germans have been "thrown back" across
a river.   Difficult to estimate true state of affairs, but most
people not very sanguine about ultimate victory of Russians.

Thursday, July 10, 1941

Yesterday evening to supper with Heimann at Putney.   Ernest has been
before Tribunal as Conscientious Objector, and is granted exemption
provided he does ambulance, A.R.P. or agricultural work.   Today very
hot again.   Spend evening trying to repair stockings.

Friday, July 11, 1941

Sir Cecil Graves, Deputy Director-General of B.B.C.,to supper.   Greta
is his secretary.   Very busy day.   Only just manage to snatch
moment to ring up hairdressers and make appointment for tomorrow.
N.B .   Tina reports Miss Oliver (our hairdresser) as saying that at
the place where we used to go for shampoos - now bombed - most of
clients were "kept" women from flats round Regent's Park.

Saturday, July 12, 1941

Still very hot. Hair washed. Then to H's, whose knees are knocking together because she has just pinned up her infant son with a safety-pin. She is much more affected by the occurrence than he is. Big thunder storm in evening.

Sunday, July 13, 1941

Stormy. Britain and Russia have made agreement to aid each other to defeat Germany. Neither is to make a separate peace. We go round beautiful gardens of neighbouring 'big house' in afternoon. In evening rush home from walk, with perambulator, in order to hear whether the Internationale is played along with other national anthems of allies. We hear only last few anthems and the Russian is not included to our disappointment.

Monday, July 14, 1941

Learn today that a Russian tune _was_ played last night, at begin- ning of anthems. Not the Internationale, which would have upset many, but a Russian military march. Churchill makes speech at L.C.C. luncheon, which is broadcast. He warns us to expect bad bombing again before long.

Tuesday, July 15, 1941

Trying day at printers again. Infuriated to discover that they have sent away index, which is being run off at their works in the City, when we have seen only galley proofs. Very angry and dis- mayed. Make appointment to see specialist about my neck on July 28 when he comes back from his holiday. Meanwhile lump is gettig bigger and more tender.

Wednesday, July 16, 1941

Spend lunch-hour buying two lots of chocolates, tin of stew, packet of Ryvita and some saccharine, all for Mother. Letter from home: Daddy has been very unwell again.

Thursday, July 17, 1941

Roy's thirty-sixth birthday. Graham says there is rumour that Duff Cooper (Minister of Information) is resigning. And another that Japan is about to invade Indo-China. Meanwhile Germans say they have taken Smolensk, an important Russian industrail town, and it seems only a matter of time before they reach Moscow.

Friday, July 18, 1941

To Stroud by 1.55, with Hilary, Tramp, Martin (last two should
have been mentioned in reverse order).   Work keeps Leonard from
coming at last moment.   We travel in 1st-class carriage marked
'Third class passengers use', and baby and dog both behave like
first-class infant and animal.   Try to buy Mother unrationed
cheese, but there is no more.   Take 2 lb. cherries at 3/- a lb.
and small basket of raspberries at 2/6.

Saturday, July 19, 1941

Stroud opens its "War Weapons Week", in which everyone is encouraged to invest money to win war.   It pours with rain all day
from morning to night.   We go on Vera's invitation to see procession from her window, and a Noble Lord takes the salute from
top of air raid shelter (suitably decorated with union jacks) at
corner of Wallbridge.   The procession quite imposing - soldiers,
airmen, home guard, air raid wardens, first-aid people, stretcher
parties, firemen, etc.   We enjoy spotting people we know trying
to look as if they were used to marching in step.   In evening we
go to film of The Ghost Train (Arthur Askey fooling most of time),
which we enjoy in spite of our sopping wet feet.

Sunday, July 20, 1941

Return to London, in 1st-class carriage, since there is no room
anywhere else.   John tells me he has primed Graham with question
to ask in House on the crazy egg-rationing scheme (which so far
has meant that eggs are almost unobtainable while they are going
bad in crates at railway stations):- In regard to the egg-rationing scheme, can the Minister say when the eggs are likely to come
home to roost?

Monday, July 21, 1941

According to John, many M.P.s very annoyed at new Ministerial
appointments just announced: Brendan Bracken, Parliamentary
Private Sec. to the P.M., is to be Minister of Information; and
Duncan Sandys, P.M.'s brother-in-law, is to be Financial Secretary
to the War Office.   They ask, will Vic Oliver, his other son-in-
law, and a comedian, be given the next juicy job?
        Jack, returned from business in Liverpool, takes Tina,
Motte (who happens in at right moment) and me to drinks and coffee
at Canuto's, and then to film 'Contraband' at the Classic.
        Germans said not yet to have caught up with their claims
in Russia.   Some of their tanks have penetrated where their troops
have not yet followed; and guerrilla fighters on the other side
have penetrated behind German lines and captured an aerodrome.   No
one will soon know where anyone else is.   What a war!

Tuesday, July 22, 1941

Another very tiring day at printers.   Editor goes to official
lunch for 3½ hours and is unobtainable during that time: and goes
out to dinner at 7 o'clock.   One day, when I am alone at printers,
shall adopt his formula: "I have to go out now", and leave the
paper to somebody else for a change.
        Moscow has had severe air attack.   Germans say much damage
done: Russians say planes did not penetrate city's air defences.

Wednesday, July 23, 1941

Very exhausted: breakfast in bed and do not go to office till
after lunch.   Sit in Queen Mary's Gardens in Regent's Park for an
hour after I leave, and feel a little better.
        Moscow has had another raid.   Accounts of it are much the
same, on both sides, as account of first one.

Thursday, July 24, 1941

Feel a good deal better, perhaps owing to brewer's yeast which Tina
brought home and made me take.   Peru and Ecuador are fighting each
other.   Japanese want bases in Indo-China, and Vichy Government
has granted them.
        Douglas Cooper, art critic now in R.A.F., who comes into
office today, says that in order to get information out of German
prisoners we treat them very badly, practically torturing them.

Friday, July 25, 1941

Very warm again and I feel poorly, but have an hour in Park on way
home in evening which makes me feel better.
        We have bombed Berlin, and no doubt London will get the re-
sult in a few days.

Saturday, July 26 1941

With Tina to Great Missenden, after breakfast in bed.   Very het
last night, but there was good deal of thunder rain in early hours
which has fortunately brought down temperature.   Today it rains
steadily.   T. and I go for enjoyable walk and get very wet.
        Britain and America have frozen Japanese assets, or British
and American assets in Japan (don't understand high finance): anyway it is said triumphantly that 90 per cent of Japan's war materials come from Britain, America and Netherlands East Endies - a fact
which was successfully disregarded, except by those classed as
dangerous revolutionaries, all the time we were supposed to be
helping China, under the League Covenant, but were really doing nothing for her at all.

In evening, Dorothy Thompson, American journalist, gives broadcast talk for which there is bound to be big demand in Listener (we always sell out when we have something by her).   Everyone here thinks her broadcast splendid; but when she praises Britain's heroism, the way we have 'stood up' to air raids, etc., all I can think is (a) the common people do not do these things because they are tough but because they have no choice; (b) and are the Germans, who are now puttingup with severe bombardment from us, therefore highly to be praised?

Sunday, July 27, 1941

Beautiful day of sunshine after yesterday's rain, and everything is green and refreshed.   Laze on porch all day till 6 o'clock, when Tina and I go for pleasant walk in corn fields, barley fields and wooded lanes for an hour and a half.   Have been reading Foster's 'Howard's End' with which am much impressed: also glanced at Ambassador Dodd's Diary, which Tina is reading (American Ambassador in Berlin, 1933-37).   He said in so many words that British and Americans could have stopped Japanese war with China in two months if they had tried, not by fighting but by cutting off supplies of war material, but business people who were making money out of the affair would not allow it.   So Hitler is right when he says we are ruled by financiers; and anything we get now we richly deserve for treachery to China.
        Both Reynolds News and New Statesman this week contain articles on Churchill and his refusal to delegate authority or to accept criticism.   John says when he is criticised, Churchill says 'Very well, I'll go', and that throws everyone into a panic, because who is there to take his place?

Monday, July 28, 1941

Raid on London last night, but mostly round docks.   Frank and Eve are goingup to town in car and give us lift.   At 12 I go to specialist in Harley Street, one Mr. Norbury.   I sit in his best armchair and springs of it immediately burst out and fall to floor. (Weighed the other day and am less than 8 stone).   The ice thus broken, we donverse amiably and it is decided that my lump must be removed and that instantly.   He thereupon rings up nursing home in Hampstead and arranges for me to go in on Wednesday and be operated on first thing Thursday morning.   Feel a little breathless at speed of these decisions: and go back to office and to printers in afternoon.

Tuesday, July 29, 1941

Long and arduous day at printers till 9 o'clock: very tired. Letter from Carl and Miriam in Victoria, B.C.   They say: "We listen to the B.B.C. news every morning ... We listen to Churchill whenever he speaks and get considerable enjoyment from his orations . I find his feeling for invective particularly pleasing and enjoyed his reference to Hitler this morning as a "bloodthirsty guttersnipe".

I must say" (it is Carl writing) "I get a certain amount of grim amusement out of the thought that certain gentlemen of well-known sympathies will now have to love the Russians in earnest. Mr. Churchill saved his dignity once for all in his speech this mornig and I suppose Stalin will similarly damn capitalism in one sentene and in the next extend the hand of friendship to a needed ally".

Shall have to keep notes as I am able and type diary for next week or two when I am well again.

Wednesday, July 30, 1941

Russians claim to be repulsing Germans and to have been making counter-attacks. But I am more taken up with my own personal affairs today. Go to nursing home in Belsize Grove, where am in private ward with three other people in it. Deaf nonogenarians: most depressing. They have washed my neck as it has not been washed in years, and tied it up. Appear to be going to remove the gland. Have pleasant dinner of chicken and feel slightly less miserable. The people from the flat sent gorgeous flowers which give me great pleasure.

Thursday, July 31, 1941

Well, I had a gland taken out this morning, and I must say, in spite of acute soreness of neck, I feel better than I have felt for some time. Of course this may be due to something they have given to pep me up, or it may be reaction after the worry before the opera-tion. Anyway I eat a good dinner. First thing I saw when I came round from anaesthetic was bouquet of flowers sent by David. Tina comes in evening and I dictate several letters. Feel rather tired with the effort of writing this. Slept hardly at all last night.

Friday, Agus- August 1, 1941

Fairly good night and good day. I eat a lot and feel so well, only hope it is not too soon to be so blooming. Perhaps bad gland is what has been matter with me for months. Am impressed by patience and cheerfulness of nurses under continual demands of noo-genarians. Tina comes again in evening and brings more flowers: also have more letters from kind friends.

Russians appear to be doing quite well.

Saturday, August 2, 1941

Do not sleep very well, owing to snores from nonogenarians, and hoarse demands for bed-pan from deafest of the lot. Mr. Norbury removes clips from my neck: by doing it thus early he hopes to get a neat scar. Have to keep head fairly still. David comes and brings chocolates.

front.   Paper says Russians are counter-attacking on all along

Sunday, August 3, 1941

Martin being 'dedicated' at Stroud today.   I do not sleep well,
but have good day.   Heimann comes at teatime and brings sweetpeas
which she grew on little slope outside her flat.
        Paper refers to great preparations by Germans in Norway - for
what, is not stated, but oneimagines for attempted invasion of this
country, or to meet threat of invasion from Britain.

Sunday, August 4, 1941

David comes, and returns in evening with pack of cards he has
fetched from flat.   Meanwhile Mr. and Mrs. Abraham call.   I am
rather tired after all these visits.   Heavy storms of rain.

Tuesday, August 5, 1941

Sleep well.   Mr. Norbury comes: is very pleased with scar, which
is still bleeding.   Phyllida comes in afternoon, en route for
temporary post at Crowborough.   Finds me sitting up, in single
room with newborn baby, who is undisturbed by our conversation.
In evening, Mr. Thomas comes bearing enormous bunch of phlox, and
at 9.15 Graham, Jack, John and Tina look in.   All comment on my
healthy appearance.   Graham has been making speech on India in
the House: was urged on the night before by Bob and John, who
pointed out that phrase "teeming millions" must on no account be
omitted.

Wednesday, August 6, 1941

Dies non: no letter or visitors, only bill from nursing home for
£10.13.2 for first week.   Have already had one from anaesthetist
for 5 guineas.

Thursday, August 7, 1941

Mr. Norbury and Dr. Turner come and break news that microscope
examination of gland showed tubercular condition, and I must take
at least 2 months to recuperate.   I go to Hampstead hospital for
X-ray of chest. Have to stand in thing rather like pillory, hollow
chest, lean forward, keep up chin, take deep breath and hold it.
Have difficulty in not letting it out immediately in guffaw.   Sit
in garden and write letters: David comes with beautiful mixed
bunch of flowers.

Friday, August 8, 1941

Too wet for garden.   Doctor Turner comes and chats, and in evening
Tina and Jack with 2 peaches and beautiful carnations.

Saturday, August 9, 1941

Paper says momentous decision by Vichy Govt. expected today.
Russians have bombed Berlin, where the poor people are now getting
attacked from two directions at once.
          Sit in garden in sun and John (Beavan) comes to tea.
Bob comes about 8.30.

Sunday, August 10, 1941

Mr. Norbury comes.   X-rayreveals no other glands are affected.   I
sit in garden and Bob comes again.
          Cannot discover that Vichy Govt. has made any decision of
note.

Monday, August 11, 1941

To Manchester Street in afternoon.   Very tiredm otherwise all right.

Tuesday, August 12, 1941

To Stroud.   Again tired.

Wednesday, August 13, 1941

Darlan has taken over great powers in France.   R.A.F. continues
heavy raids on Germany.
          Daddy's description of e gg rationing scheme: "They take
eggs from Mrs. Gardiner at Oakridge and send them to Canada.   Then
they send them all back, bad".

Thursday, August 14, 1941

Special announcement at 3 p.m. by Mr. Attlee, Deputy Prime Minister,
says that Roosevelt and Churchill have met at sea and discussed war
for three days.   Have issued manifesto saying that U.S.A and G.B.
seek no aggrandisement, territorial or otherwise, but want freedom
and economic security for all men.
          Hilda brings up her baby, nice little boy with brown skin
and dark eyes like hers.

Friday, August 15, 1941

Mr. Turner, greengrocer, brings 4 eggs to back door, in return for
which Mother has to listen to him spouting for at least 35 minutes
while he holds forth: three pearls of wisdom which I hear from bath
room are: "There's a lot of things as isn't right"; "If everyone
worked as hard as I do, the war would have been over long ago";
"If you got a million pounds and can't find nothing to spend it on,
you might as well have a million marbles to play with".

Saturday, August 16, 1941

Still very stormy.   MollyEvans and her sister to tea.   Afterwards
I go as far as the first seat - my longest walk - and feel well,
though very tired by 9 p.m.
        Germans said to be digging themselves in in their present
positions in Russia, which is taken as rather hopeful sign, showing
that they cannot advance quickly to new positions.

Sunday, August 17, 1941

Much rain still: I notice the weather now, when absence of sun and
presence of rain mean I cannot sit in garden.   Milk to be rationed:
probably about half pint each daily, though nursing mothers and babies
are to have a pint.   Mother very gloomy at prospect: we have always
had such a lot of milk.

Monday, August 18, 1941

Mr. Churchill back in this country after meeting with President
Roosevelt.
        Great dismay when Daddy leaves my week's rations in Rodborough
bus.   Mother says no doubt some woman from Kingscourt is by now
taking them home.   "I hope she will be struck dead", she adds
passionately.   "Oh, Mother!" I say, sanctimoniously.   "Well, she
deserves it", says Mother, working herself up about this entirely
fictitious miscreant.   As a matter of fact, the women of Kingscourt
have to be acquitted without a stain on their characters, for Daddy
discovers the parcels still on shelf of bus after it has journeyed
to Cirencester and back.
        Miss Royal sends us packet of sweet biscuits (great
treasure) and some tomatoes.   I have bill from specialist for £57.16

Tuesday, August 19, 1941

Weather better, with only occasional storms.   Mother gets four fresh
eggs from Mr. Turner, three from Mrs. Gardener, who have less than
the number of hens (50, I think) which makes it necessary for them
to send the eggs to central depot.

Wednesday, August 20, 1941

Germans still advancing on Leningrad, in spite of news that they were
"digging themselves in".   Daddy says despairingly that they are invincible.   Mr. Dowdeswell comes to dig garden, which he is supposed
to dig-regu do regularly, but cannot if he has bad rheumatics, or if
there is a funeral, when he has to be a bearer.

- - -

Thursday, August 21, 1941

Still very stormy, and in many fields around harvest is up in stooks.
Germans only 100 miles from Leningrad.
            Aunt H. gives Mother large piece of cheese and some little
pears from her tree.   Our apples have done so badly this year of all
years, that though we have plenty of little red eating ones, there
are no cookers, that generally there are so many of.   Usually we are
giving away baskets of fallers at this time of year.

Friday, August 22, 1941

Am able to sit out of doors most of day, and go for good walk in
evening.   We have chicken for dinner, from farmer Daddy knows: also
four eggs and ½ lb. butter from kind friends who had better be name-
less.   Have bill from doctor, which brings cost of my operation to
£64.15.7.

Saturday, August 23, 1941

Pouring rain all day.   Listen to broadcast of last night of Promenade
Concerts - from Albert Hall, whose acoustics have been improved, and
which of course holds much larger audience than Queen's Hall.   Henry
Wood's Fantasia on British Sea Songs, and audience roars "Rule
Britannia".   Not so much a musical occasion as an emotional orgy:
but very enjoyable.

Sunday, August 24, 1941

Fine: we can sit in garden.   Mr. Churchill broadcasts at 9 o'clock
and tells of meeting with Roosevelt.   His address, which is broadcast
to America, tries to tell Americans to come into war while there is
yet time.   He compares present conflict with age-old struggle between
right and wrong: describes how at morning service on board destroyer
where he met Roosevelt they sang "Onward Christian Soldiers", and he
felt that ours was indeed a cause to which a trumpet had called us
from on high.   I cannot see it in this way at all, and do not know
whether I am amoral and wrong or far-seeing and right.

Monday, August 25, 1941

British and Soviet troops have entered Iran.   Rain again in morning,
but fine afternoon.   Edgar says the trouble with the wheat is that
the Govt. encouraged farmers to apply artificial fertiliser to the
crop, and this made the wheat come up strong and high earlier than
usual, so that the July rains beat it down and in some places broke
it.   And it is ready for reaping now, instead of in September, but
we haven't got harvest weather.   "It's a terrible do", says Edgar.

Tuesday, August 26, 1941

Lord Woolton has a plan whereby we shall have to register for all

foods, rationed and unrationed.   Mother, filled with rage, declares
that Lord W., doubtless a very harassed man, lies in bed thinking out
what he can do which will be most awkward for everyone.   Further
expresses her opinion that he has a farm of his own and goes short of
nothing.

Wednesday, August 27, 1941

Laval and Deat shot at during parade of anti-communist volunteers.
            I go to see doctor and as a result am extremely tired.
He says I must rest a great deal and seems to think I am going on well

Thursday, August 28, 1941

Finer, after wild night.   Laundry man comes, which is now an event.
Before the war he collected on Mondays and delivered on Fridays.   Now
he calls about once in three weeks, and one hardly expects to see the
clothes again.
            Mr. Menzies, Prime Minister of Australia, resigns.   Govt.
of Iran resigns and new Cabinet asks for hostilities to cease.   No
doubt I am wrong, but there is not much difference in my mind between
our occupation of Iran and the German occupation of Norway.   The
answer given is that we do not intend to keep Iran after the war and
the Germans want Norway in the Reich.   But the method is the same.

Friday, August 29, 1941

Milk not to be rationed after all, except at discretion of retailers.
Edgar says: "It's what I always told you.   If we got milk you'll
have some: if we haven't, you wunt.   Stands to reason".
            Letter from Graham.   He says there will be famine and
pestilence in Europe this winter.   Russians have blown up their
beautiful Dniepestroi Dam in their retreat.   It cost, I think, £100
millions to built and was their pride and joy.

Saturday, August 30, 1941

Weather better.   Gas very poor.   Takes about $\frac{3}{4}$ hour to boil kettle.
This is due to Sperry's (munition works) using all the power.

Sunday, August 31, 1941

Really warm, settled-looking weather.   Perhaps harvest will be saved
after all.   But now there is the worry that it may be invasion
weather.   A broadcaster has told us we may expect invasion within
the next few weeks.

Monday, September 1, 1941
There is to be a big call-up of women for industry.   No men under
24 to be "reserved".

Tuesday, September 2, 1941

Mother goes shopping and returns with several lots of plums and
tomatoes, which she has had offered and does not like to refuse for
fear future favours will be denied.   End of second year of war.
Did not expect conditions of ordinary people to be as good as they
are, but neither did I expect Hitler would be in possession of most
of Europe by this time.

Wednesday, September 3, 1941

Appear to have lost entry for this date.

Thursday, September 4, 1941

Fierce fighting still for Leningrad.   Mother has 8 eggs from customer
of Pop's.   Joy, joy.   Very warm, and Mother not very well.

Friday, September 5, 1941

Mother a little better.   Warm.   Rain at night.

Saturday, September 6, 1941

Pouring rain clears up and in afternoon I go for walk and see children's
gymkhana in fort field.   Small boy of 11 is winning everything, and
when I am offered seat in car, find it is with his parents and that car
is hung with rosettes and cards saying First Prize.   After I have been
taken for child's mother by admiring strangers, and offered sandwiches
and stale cake by his father, I return.

Sunday, September 7, 1941

National Day of Prayer, and I go to chapel, getting up earlier than
since operation.   Read beginning of book called "Eternity of Time",
by A. P. Shepherd.

Monday, September 8, 1941

Mother and P. go off to Nancy Sollars' wedding and come back with all
the wedding flowers sent as present to me.   P. remarks that they
obviously think I am on my deathbed and that I had better not go into
town and let them see my sunburnt face.

Tuesday, September 9, 1941

Parliament reassembles and Churchill makes speech saying that our
situation, though not calling for easy optimism, is far better than it
was this time last year.   Germans, in 3 months' war against Russia, have
lost more men than they lost in any one year of last war.   Cummings,
in News Chronicle, is also very cheerful today.

Mother and Daddy to Ware to visit Hilary, taking wooden cat on wheels (5/6) and rubber ball (1/6). Toys difficult to get and very expensive. Celluloid ducks, etc., for sailing on baths, unobtainable.

Wednesday, September 10, 1941

Debate in Lords on Merchant Service. Lord Marchwood (with whom Jack has been in correspondence on subject) says more consideration must be shown for men of Merchant Navy, and their status and conditions of work must be improved. To doctor's, and he reiterates need for rest.

Thursday, September 11, 1941

New advances by Germans in Russia. Beautiful day. I laze on lawn most of day.

Friday, September 12, 1941

Roosevelt braadcasts to American nation saying in future American warships will fire on German submarines or warships at sight, in American waters.
Car trouble holds up parents' return.

Saturday, September 13, 1941

Mother and Daddy return, bringing plums at 8d, a lb. and pears at 1/6.

Sunday, September 14, 1941

Some of R.A.F. gone to help Russians.
P. gives us gramophone recital in evening. Enjoyable, but noise makes me very tired.

Monday, September 15, 1941

Col. Knox, Secretary of U.S. Navy, has announced that American warships will escort cargoes for Britain as far as Iceland.
Nice day, crisp and sunny. In eve. listen to broadcast of Shaw's "St. Joan", and cannot hlep sympathising with Dauphin when he says "If only she would keep quiet, or go home".

Tuesday, September 16, 1941

Shah of Persia (Iran) who was pro-German, has abdicated and Russian & British troops are advancing on Teheran.
Mother gathers tomatoes to ripen indoors. She has 6 plants, all with plenty of fruit.

Wednesday, September 17, 1941

Pop comes in at noon with bad pains, which we put down to pork pie he
ate yesterday.   Anyway, later he recovers.   Mr. Pritchard brings us
quite big piece of mutton with which we make Irish stew.   He brings
such meat as he can spare: there is no ordering of a joint or any
special cut dowadays.

Thursday, September 18, 1941

P. and I go to meeting in chapel, of Baptist Churches of district:
this to please Daddy who is playing organ.   We escape, however, from
the bun-fight afterwards to which parents go.   I have my hair washed
and set very nicely, and at much less cost than in London.   Feel all
this not what I should be doing in wartime: and I grudge every moment
spent out of sunshine.

Friday, September 19, 1941

Today, when I might bask all the time, it is dull and colder.   There
was a display of auorea-bor aurora borealis last night, but we didn't
see it.
          Germans have reached outskirts of Kiev in Russia.   "New
Statesman" very gloomy and throws P. into fit of depression.   Wardrobe
I ordered from Bowman's comes: despatched only yesterday.   It cost
£4.7.6d. with carriage, and is of plain unpainted wood and quite shoddy.
But Daddy says probably there is purchase tax of 30/- on it.   Whole
thing would have cost about 35/- before war.   Daddy and Mother to
Weston-super-Mare for week.

Saturday, September 20, 1941

P. and I to Enderly, but Aunt is out.   Returning, find telegram from
Tina saying she is coming on Sunday.   Did Dull day.   Germans claim
to have entered Kiev, capital of the Ukraine.

Sunday, September 21, 1941

Tina arrives at lunchtime.   My scar has begun to ooze again.

Monday, September 22, 1941

Russians admit evacuationof Kiev, news which depresses us very much.
"Tanks for Russia" week begins today, all war workers being urged to
work harder and to produce more and more tanks.
          I go to doctor, who is not at all dismayed at my leaking
neck.   Sun in afternoon and we laze on lawn.   Letter from parents:
Mother eating like an ox, they say.

Tuesday, September 23, 1941

Another dull morning which clears later.   Mr. Turner silently places
2 lb. tomatoes on our windowsill and vanishes, apparently undesirous

of payment.   British have sunk two large Italian liners taking troops
to Libya.

Wednesday, September 24, 1941

Col. Knox, American Foreign Secretary, has demanded immediate repeal
of Neutrality Act.
          I finish and post crawlers for Martin.   Warm thundery day.
Mr. Dowdeswell comes, and, taking no notice of request to prune
ramblers, digs up potatoes ag instead, which we feel sure will meet
with Pop's displeasure.

Thursday, September 25, 1941

P. buys Cox's Orange Pippins, at such a price that she refuses to
divulge it.   Walk too far in evening and am very tired.   Letter from
Roy: family got safely back from trip to Cape.

Friday, September 26, 1941

Ravings of News-Chronicle because we are not invading Continent, have
suddenly ceased, and certain small items of news, such as that in
France large rewards are offered for capture of parachutists, lead us
to suspect that something may be afoot.
          Minnie has 4 kittens: Mrs. Keene has letter from husband,
posted in Canada.

Saturday, September 27, 1941

Tina departs and parents return.   Disquieting news from Russia, but
detachment of R.A.F. helping them.
          Daddy annoyed because Mr. Dowdeswell has dug all potatoes and
onions in his absence.   I take beans and flowers for harvest festival.

Sunday, September 28, 1941

Germans declare martial law in Czechoslovakia because ofacts of sabotage.
          Harvest festival.   We find bundle of beans deposited on
sitting-room floor, and after hesitation, not knowing whether for us or
for the festival, have them for dinner.
          called round by Mrs. Keene to see Minnie's offspring, while a
grave for 3 of them is being dug at bottom of garden.   Such waste of
effort on poor Minnie's part.   Feel I am a waste product of nature too.

Monday, September 29, 1941

Leslie announces that he is going to join Fire Service fulltime.   Don't
know how Daddy can carry on: what is the use of doctor's telling him
to take things easy?   Girls up to 25 years in retail trade (except
food distribution) to be taken for war production.   When Miss Alder
(seedsman) asks what she can do with no assistants, she is told "Close

your business".   There is never any mercy, in our legislation, for the small, uninfluential people.

H.G. Wells, in Presidential Address to British Association, says general trend of humanity at present is towards decay and final extinction.

"Tanks for Russia" week has set up record in production: 25 per cent above previous best - in manufacturing weapons for our final extinction.

Letter from H. says Martin has flu.   Ring up in evening and find he is better.

Tuesday, September 30, 1941

Cummings (News-Chronicle) says German-occupied Europe full of unrest. Churchill's speech in Parliament rather encouraging.   Our shipping losses down and enemy's up.   Our food situation improved.

Wednesday, October 1, 1941

My scar still oozing, which makes me rather tired.   Doctor merely reiterates "Rest, rest, rest".

Leslie gets 4 eggs for Mother from customer: very welcome, since ration for October is 2 eggs each for the month.

Thursday, October 2, 1941

From mid-November, domestic rations are to be increased: fat, 8-10 oz, sugar, $\frac{1}{2}-\frac{3}{4}$ lb increase.   Joy, joy.   A "British Restaurant" to be started in Stroud - i.e. a communal feeding centre.

Friday, October 3, 1941

To Hale, Cheshire, to visit Fuche's.   By car with Pop to Gloucaster: F. accompanies me to Birmingham: Arnold meets me with car at Manchester. All the same, am very tired.

Saturday, October 4, 1941

Sit in garden in morning and go with family for drive in open car in afternoon, towards Peak District.   Still tired.

Sunday, October 5, 1941

Surprised that there are so many adults about, when I see perils into which young rush headlong. (i.e. Christopher, aged 5, and Richard, 2)

Monday, October 6, 1941

Arrangements being made for exchange of badly wounded prisoners between Britain and Germany.   Large offensive started on Moscow.

Take children to recreation ground, where my hair stands on end to behold young Richard climbing almost perpendicular 12-foot ladder and sliding down chute.

Tuesday, October 7, 1941

Hitch in exchange of prisoners.   Still feel very tired.

Wednesday, October 8, 1941

Germans prisoners who were to have been sent home, sent back to hospital,
poor things.   Fierce fighting in direction of Moscow.   Have notice
from B.B.C. of rise in salary to £545.   My income tax is already £155.
It will be about £180 on this, I imagine.

Thursday, October 9, 1941

Sit up till after 10 and finish blue suit for Martin, after which feel
quite exhausted.   Rain pours all day.

Friday, October 10, 1941

Richard's 2nd birthday.   We have 2 more small ones to tea, and there
is a little cake with 2 candles.
            Hitler has said battle for Moscow will be last desisive one of
year.   Germans advancing steadily.   News-Chronicle says can't we do
anything to help: it is surely our last chance.   I agree and feel so
depressed about this and my own exhaustion, lie in bed and weep.

Saturday, October 11, 1941

Feel better, though news still bad.   Vernon Bartlett says there are
miles of forest round Moscow, with trees so close no tank could get
through.

Sunday, October 12, 1941

Distinctly better, perhaps because weather, though still sunny, is
cooler and more seasonable.   Lizzie Foster arrives to tea, on bicycle,
with Hungarian doctor.

Monday, October 13, 1941

Feel better.   For walk to P.O., and see horst being shod in smithy.
Wakened about 11.30 last night by quite loud gunfire.   Rain on
Manchester, we think.   Germans'advance on Moscow said to be slowing
down.

Tuesday, October 14, 1941

Rainy.   Cannot sit out much.   Dreamt last night that I saw Cora
Hazard, who is dead.   I held out my hand and she came forward to shake
it, but then drew hers back and said: "No, not now: I'll see you
another time".   She gave me a queer look out of her shiny eyes and
went away.   Even in dream, I thought "It means I haven't to die this
time".

Wednesday, October 15, 1941

Much knitting of jersey for Richard.   Blowy day.

Thursday, October 16, 1941

Germans getting nearer and nearer Moscow.   High wind again.   Glorious
flaming sunset.   "Isn't it lovely?" I ask Christopher.   "No", he
replies, "I like it in rows".   Letter from Graham, written on back of
circular letter apparently written to Members of Parliament and containing following sentence:"Is it a matter for complacency that the
Government takes charge of new-laid eggs and sits on them till 17
millions stink?"

Friday, October 17, 1941

Russian Govt. has left Moscow.   The announcers read wireless news at
great speed, because lately there have been interruptions from the
enemy on the Forces wavelength - comments such as "Rot", "Good", etc.
            Pouring rain.   Chris. to birthday party with his friend
Barry.   I help him make coloured cut-outs for an offering.

Saturday, October 18, 1941

America has repealed Neutrality Act sufficiently to allow merchant
ships to be armed.   Wind: rain till late afternoon.

Sunday, October 19, 1941

Blustery day.   I have an orange.   M. got 2 lb. on the children's
ration books and insists on my having one.

Monday, October 20, 1941

Air-raid alarm at 8.30 or so, and a lot of gunfire.   Chris. brought
down from nursery to sleep on bed in passage (which when not in use
hangs on pulleys from ceiling), because he is nervous if he hears
"pops" and feels safe down there.   He does not wake up.

Tuesday, October 21, 1941

Chris. and I scrape inside out of rose-hips which he picked for his
father's birthday.   We intend to make jam of them, but progress slow.

Wednesday, October 22, 1941

More hips, and at night another warning and more pops.

Thursday, October 23, 1941

Cold.   C. develops temperature and has pain, but Dr. thinks it is not
serious.   Many executions in France because of attacks on Nazi officers

Friday, October 24, 1941

To Chester by train, where meet Graham and Mary and am transported by
car to Nant Twynant, beside Snowdon, where they have cottage. We go
right into sunset, over hills and moors, then come to a lake and the
mountains. Cottage white-washed and one-storeyed. Very charming.
Farm lets us have 1 lb. butter, a sight I had not seen for a long time.

Saturday, October 25, 1941

Last night heard two or three bombs - yes here, where one might imagine
news of a war was just percolating. Today sit in sun and go for walk
beside lake and write letters. Tired.

Sunday, October 26, 1941

Blowy and fine. Rest till 1 p.m., when we go little way towards
Snowdon - path goes straight up from back of cottage. Walk beside
stream and pass beautiful waterfall. Lunch 2.30 or so. Tot ea with
G.'s Uncle Sam, aged 97, who is living in house on other side of valley.
We are told planes on Friday killed 8 or 9 people at Bangor.

Monday, October 27, 1941

Leave Nant G. 9.30 a.m. in pouring rain and have wet tho' enjoyable
drive to Birkenhead. See a good deal of bomb damage, mostly blown-out
windows in sordid streets which form part of G.'s constituency. 'Mere
Cottage' on outskirts of Birkenhead is no cottage but a large house,
with a beautiful lawn and fan-tailed pigeons. I am very tired and
rest all the afternoon, then go to bed early.

Tuesday, October 28, 1941

Stay in bed till 11-ish. It is Betty's 22nd birthday, and I join her
and Mary in expedition to pictures: my first gaiety since my illness,
and I feel very daring. As it turns out, I am too daring, since I
turn faint after about 20 minutes and have to come out. Feel very
queer for rest of day. In evening G. answers letters, dictating to
Betty (his daughter) and I perceive that his constituents regard him
rather as a benevolent uncle, and approach him in all difficulties.
His constituency is a poor one, and this house is actually outside its
boundaries.

Wednesday, October 29, 1941

Beautiful day, crisp, sunny and windy. Go gentle walk and see things
looking like chicken or pig huts, which Mary says are camouflage for a
new kind of anti-aircraft gun which sends up chains, rockets and all
kinds of strange things. Houses round Mere Cottage are all big, with
large gardens, and they are just on edge of the country. Am able to

sit for hour or more in garden in sun.   Fan-tailed pigeons come on to
bedroom window-sill and want me to feed them.   Still feel tired.

Thursday, October 30, 1941

To Hale by 12.30 train, arriving 2.30.   Both children look to me grown
in a week.   Pouring wet day: I am lucky in having fine days for my
visits and wet days only for travelling.   Lot of letters awaiting me.
           Germans have captured Kharkov, very important Russian town.

Friday, October 31, 1941

Fine day but very cold.   Read Trollope's "Orley Farm" with much enjoyment.   M. tries to get sponge-bag for me to give Arnold for birthday,
but Altrincham has none.   Germans appear to be advancing in Crimea,
and outlook is dismal.

Saturday, November 1, 1941

Still fine and very cold: beautiful golden sunset with lowering clouds
Consumption of liquid milk to be cut by one-fifth.

Sunday, November 2, 1941

Bitterly cold with biting east wind.   Arnold and a carpenter spend day
putting up supports for ceiling in case of renewed air-raids.

Monday, November 3, 1941

U.S. tells Finland to stop war with Russia.   As I believe Finland is
largely run on American capital, this may have some effect.   Germans
advancing rapidly in Crimea.   Foggy, raw, drizzling day, and I am very
depressed.   Go with Chris. to Altrincham (about 1½ miles) on bus, and
try to buy mackintosh forRichard, but such a thing is unobtainable.

Tuesday, November 4, 1941

Back to Stroud.   Trains crowded.   Met by Daddy and P. at Gloucester.
Find myself very glad to be home.   Trees here still have leaves, and
are turning colour.

Wednesday, November 5, 1941

"Here is the 8 o'clock news for the Fifth of November: remember,
remember", said Frank Phillips on wireless this morning.   Beautiful
day and I walk on common.

Thursday, November 6, 1941

To doctor's.   He says I can go back to work on Jan. 1, not before.
Germans still advancing in Crimea.   Daddy gets 2 sacks of potatoes
and 4 eggs from a farmer.

Friday, November 7, 1941

Consumption of milk to be cut by another 10 per cent next week.
Stalin makes speech asking for another front against Germans.
        Sit in garden, as instructed by doctor, with rug, eiderdown,
hot-water bottle, woollen gloves.   Wear sunglasses because of lovely
sunshine, and P. says "You look like Greta Garbo on deck, returning
from a holiday in the Bahamas".

Saturday, November 8, 1941

From raids over Germany last night, 37 of our bombers did not return:
reason given is freak weather.
        Daddy has had boards made to black-out sitting room windows.
None fits perfectly and all take a good deal of putting up.   Leaves
have choked water pipe so that no water gets through to bathroom.
        Milder and foggier but still pleasant.   Have taken to waking
at 4 or 5 a.m. and am unable to sleep again unless I have something to
eat.
Sunday, November 9, 1941

After much effort by Daddy with rubber tube, water in bathroom now
available.
        See in "Baptist Times" that Mr. Smaje of Regent's Park
Mission has won the George Medal for bravery in attempting a rescue
during raids last winter.   He is leader of a stretcher party.
        We have annihilated convoy in Mediterranean.

Monday, November 10, 1941

Churchill says R.A.F. is now as strong as the Luftwaffe in numbers as
well as in quality.
        Have hair washed and re-permed.   Hairdresser says materials
for perms getting very scarce.

Tuesday, November 11, 1941

More sinkings by our submarines in Mediterranean.
        Mild day: I am able to sit outside.   We are reduced to one
box of matches.   They are very scarce.   Some weeks we can get one box,
and sometimes none.   Mother tries in vain to get a saucepan.   Stroud
can produce only one very small iron one.

Wednesday, November 12, 1941

P.M., in speech in Parliament, says German sinkings of our ships in
Atlantic are down by four-fifths.   They are still high, but Hitler's
hope of starving us out is not likely to be fulfilled this winter.
        Beautiful day: I sit in garden.

Thursday, November 13, 1941
Dreadful day of mist and rain.   By car to Cheltenham, where P. and I bo

London Symphony Orchestra concert, with Sammons in Beethoven Violin Concerto.   Also Mendelssohn's Overture to Mid. Nt's Dream, Arensky's Vars. on Theme by Tchaikovsky, and Brahms' 2nd Symphony.   Full audience, with lot of Cheltenham College girls and other children. Daddy and Mother shop, and Mother gets saucepan, which, owing to new regulation that only foods are to be wrapped, she carries in its glory down the Prom.   Return via Birdlip and get 4 eggs from a farmer's wife.

Friday, November 14, 1941

Aunt H's birthday and we go to tea with her.   On way meet woman carrying unwrapped washing-up bowl.   Instruction about wrappings is so far disregarded by Daddy (who has just paid £5 for a new lot of paper) and by most other tradesmen.
                Ark Royal, Britain's most famous aircraft carrier,sunk. America has repealed Neutrality Act sufficiently to arm merchant ships and to allow vessels in belligerent waters.   Seems as if U.S.A. will soon be at war with Japan.

Saturday, November 15, 1941

Beautiful day, but cold.   Fowl for dinner, which Mrs. G. let us have. Poultry difficult to get.   She also sent some fresh eggs.   And Aunt H. yesterday let me have some tinned butter sent from S.Africa.   So we are well provided for.   It is legal to let people have eggs when the poultry-keeper has less than - I think it is 50 - hens, and so does not have to send eggs to central depot.

Sunday, November 16, 1941

Wild wet day, which improves, so that I go to evening service, where I suffer from palpitations and wish I had not come.   Early snow and bad weather generally is holding up Germans in Russia.
                More women to be conscripted to make munitions.

Monday, November 17, 1941

Rain.   Germans have taken Kirche, important port in Crimea.

Tuesday, November 18, 1941

Mother and Daddy to Hilary's by train.   P. plays for Mother at Women's Meeting where she has to accompany solo about Sinner and Tempter, which ought to have beena quartet but was performed by one raucous lady. Perfect weather.

Wednesday, November 19, 1941

Mist and rain.   Fortunately Suttons cleared gutters round house of leaves yesterday.

Thursday, November 20, 1941

Britain has started another campaign in Libya, of which much is being made: our "second front". We have already in this war first gained and then lost vast expenses in Libya, and I am now entirely confused about the situation.

Friday, November 21, 1941

Mother and Daddy return, Mother in an excited frame of mind in which she appals P. by switching on light in unblacked-out pantry, declaring meantime that she is "agin the Govt." and doesn't care. I am very tired.

Saturday, November 22, 1941

Wet. Get flowers from Court and arrange for chapel. Germans claim capture of Rostov.

Sunday, November 23, 1941

American coal strike settled.

Monday, November 24, 1941

Milk rationing means no pots of tea will be served in restaurants, but only cups.
        Daily paper quotes this from Article 124 of the Stalin Constitution:-"Freedom of religious worship and freedom of anti-religious propaganda is recognised for all citizens". First four words of this were suppressed until Russia became our ally. Feel there is no honesty or integrity anywhere.
        Weather very mild which makes us all tired.

Tuesday, November 25, 1941

Battle still raging in Libya. Beautiful sunshine here.

Wednesday, November 26, 1941

It is reported by a News Agency that Hitler is preparing to raze Belgrade to the ground because Serb guerrillas are attacking Nazis.
        P. and I both have colds. P. collects bunch of winter flowers on common - daisies, colts foot and a few hips - and puts them in moss, making very pretty bowl.

Thursday, November 27, 1941

Hitler attacking Moscow in strength. Battle in Libya has reached no conclusion. I get impression that we are not having it as much our own way as we expected.
        To Cheltenham again by car, and hear Malcolm Sargent conduc

ing Ireland (London Overture), Elgar (Wand of Youth Suite 2), Holst
(Ballet Music from "Perfect Fool") and Beethoven (5th Symphony).   In
interval the Mayor introduces a Lieut.Gen, V.C., who makes speech on
behalf of Cheltenham's "Warship Week", so much like a parody of itself
that P. and I can hardly maintain gravity.

Friday, November 28, 1941

Aunt H. to tea.   She voices belief that the Lord intervened in the   .
war, turning wrath of Germans against Russia instead of against us -
an Old Testament view of the Almighty with which P. and I are somewhat
shocked.
          Mother presented with ½ lb. butter by Vera, and is greatly
pleased.

Saturday, November 29, 1941

Germans have 49 Divisions round Moscow, and only 2 in Libya about which
we are making such a fuss.   Mrs. Clutterbuck, collecting Mother's subscription to Nursing Association, remarks in mild voice that Hitler
ought to have red hot knitting needles stuck into him at 10-minute
intervals: further says placidly that he ought to be starved to death
with luscious and delectable-smelling food hung just in front of nose.
          Leslie (Daddy's assistant) gets summons to army medical exam.

Sunday, November 30, 1941

Russians have turned Germans out of Rostov.   Choir Sunday.

Monday, December 1, 1941

Cable from S.Africa to say Christopher George, 7½ lb.,born yesterday.
          We have sunk German raider in Atlantic.
          Mother buys presents for Hilary for Christmas, with H's own
clothes coupons.

Tuesday, December 2, 1941

Australian cruiser "Sydney" and another warship sunk.   Russians still
chasing Germans near Rostov.

Wednesday, December 3, 1941

To Aunt H. to tea.   Very depressed about state of world and about my
impending return to London, but see no alternative (a) to continuance
of war, (b) to my going back.

Thursday, December 4, 1941

We go to "thanksgiving" meeting in Sunday School, after which I am
very tired.

- 328 -

Friday, December 5, 1941

So tired, stay in bed till dinner-time.   My heart goes too fast.
        P. makes us beautiful salads for supper nowadays.   Foundation
is grated raw carrot, and there is also included (if we can get it)
lettuce, date, sultanas, celery, apple: but these things are all
scarce.
        Russians still chasing Germans in South: very heavy attacks
on Moscow.   Operations renewed in Libya.

Saturday, December 6, 1941

Roosevelt has sent personal letter to Emperor of Japan, one supposes
in hope of avoiding Japanese-American war.
        Feel ill and nervy, and hope I am not going out of my mind.

Sunday, December 7, 1941

Beautiful day: I go for long walk in sunshine and feel a bit better.
        Japanese have bombed American naval bases in Pacific.

Monday, December 8, 1941

Japan has declared war on Britain and America, so the conflict is now
world-wide.   At 6.30 (noon, American time), we hear President Roosevelt
asking Congress for declaration of war against Japan.   He sounds sober
and sane but Deputies hysterically excited and cheer madly.   At 9,
the Prime Minister broadcasts.   He has probably been up all night and
sounds tired out.

Tuesday, December 9, 1941

Thailand has surrendered to Japan.   About 3,000 people killed by
Japanese raids on Hawaii.   There is an invasion of N.Malaya, the West
Coast of America has had an air-raid alarm, and all the world is mad.
Meantime I am occupied in peaceful pursuit of taking my viyella frock
to Miss Greenwood to be let out - partly because of my increased girth,
partly because it has been washed and has shrunk.

Wednesday, December 10, 1941

News that H.M.S. "Prince of Wales" and H.M.S. "Repulse" have been sunk
off Singapore by Japanese throws us all into deep gloom.   P.of W. was
one of our best battle cruisers and regarded as almost unsinkable.
        I am very tired.

Thursday, December 11, 1941

2,300 reported saved from "Repulse" and "Prince of Wales".   Churchill
reviews war situation in House and speaks of heavy blow to our naval
resources.   We are progressing well in Libya, and in Russia the

Germans are retreating.   Germany and Italy have declared war on
America.   We have recordings of Hitler's and Mussolini's speeches
to their respective followers.   Each is cheered hysterically, just
as Roosevelt was cheered in the Chamber of Deputies.   The whole world
is a madhouse: and I am very tired again.

Friday, December 12, 1941

Aunt H. to tea.   She gives her opinion that Hitler is the devil in-
carnate, and that all the churches ought to pray "Come, Lord Jesus",
when Christ would come quickly (vide last verse of Revelation) and
reign for ever and ever.   She asks, if the last verse of the Bible
doesn't mean this, what does it mean?   A question which none of us
feels able to answer.

Saturday, December 13, 1941

We are still progressing in Libya, and the Germans are retreating in
Russia: we have sunk an Italian cruiser in the Mediterranean.   In
the Far East, Japanese progressing in Malaya.   Gardener at the Court
tells me we need to go about things more like the Russians do, instead
of having "a lot of civil servants who don't know nothing about it";
and says (a) onions have rotted all over the country because they were
stored in heaps, whereas everyone (except civil servants) knows that
onions have to be stored flat with plenty of air round them; (b) the
enormous factory which has been in construction at Edge for 18 months
is now being scrapped, since the site is found "unsuitable"; and
gives other instances of incompetence and stupidity.

Sunday, December 14, 1941

Wild wet day.   Mr. Starling from Frampton Mansell preaches.   He is
also padre at aerodrome and conducts communion and two services there
every Sunday, when he gets about 60 men.   He says there are a great
many flying accidents and deaths among the learners, but nothing is
said about them.

Monday, December 15, 1941

Russians still driving Germans back.   Situation in Far East serious,
and Singapore prepares for state of siege.

Tuesday, December 16, 1941

Phyllida has 30 replies to an advertisement she put in New Statesman
offering help with children.   Some letters very pathetic - from husbands who have to be called up and will leave invalid wives with
families; from people about to have operations, etc.   One wild
creature writes from middle of Pembrokeshire: says her husband's last
book was flop in America and they have no money: they live in a
derelict mansions with collapsing ceilings, are farming large tracts

of land, can offer her a hunter, but she does not say what her duties
will be (except for farming 68 acres, plastering ceilings and riding
hunter).
   I have x-ray at hospital. A woman (almoner?) says to me
"Whole or partial?" and I reply "Oh, only to the waist, I think", and
then find she is referring to fees, not bodies.

Wednesday, December 17, 1941

Have parcel from the Beals in Victoria, B.C., with dried milk, chocolate and box cheese - all very welcome. Shopping here very difficult,
and I try in vain for pair decent silk stockings. Mother makes 3
smallpuddings, which is all our suet ration (2 oz. each) will allow. No
candied peel, of course, and other ingredients not what they would be
in peace time. P. has many more replies to her advertisement.
   Japanese have landed in Borneo.

Thursday, December 18, 1941

Very cold and foggy. We go to carol service at Marling School and on
our return find 5 parcels from S.Africa put by postman through kitchen
window. All contain food - tinned butter, tinned meat, dried fruit,
tea, sugar, etc. P. has dozens more letters, many very heart-rending.

Friday, December 19, 1941

Japanese have landed strong force at Hongkong. To Aunt H's, where we
play laborious bridge. P. stays at home to answer the many more
replies to her ad.

Saturday, December 20, 1941

P. and I to doctor's. Former has her ears syringed. I receive my
x-ray report (very good: I am free of infection) and advice not to
return to London on Jan. 1, but to give myself another month. Feel
this probably right, as I still get very tired easily.
   Hongkong besieged by Japanese, but holding out.

Sunday, December 21, 1941

Carol service at Parish Church. Denis (Daddy's young assistant)
thinks he has shingles. If he has, we shan't be able to go to H's
till Christmas Day.
   Hitler has taken over supreme command of German Army.

Monday, December 22, 1941

P. goes off to H's by train to help her prepare for visitors.
There have been great warnings against rail travel this Christmas, because however big the crowds, no extra trains will be put on. But we
hope as this is rather early, P. will not have too bad a journey.
Mother has parcel from Mrs. Bancroft in Victoria, B.C., containing,

sugar, sultanas, prunes and onion powder.

Tuesday, December 23, 1941

It is announced that Churchill is in Washington, conferring with
Roosevelt.
          We stuff turkey ready to take to H's.   It is a small one and
we do not know price: 4/2 per lb., we think.

Wednesday, December 24, 1941

To Ware by car.   I am in bad temper and state of nerves before we
start, but feel better once we are en route, and weather becomes
beautiful.   Baby, of course, very much grown since I last saw him in
July.

Thursday, December 25, 1941

Christmas Day, and we feed well in spite of its being the 3rd of the
war.   King broadcasts at 3 p.m.   A fine day.   We are all depressed
in evening by news that Hongkong has to surrender to Japanese.

Friday, December 26, 1941

At 6.30 we hear Mr. Churchill speaking to U.S.A. Congress and House
of Representatives, and they cheer him uproariously.

Saturday, December 27, 1941

Manila, capital of the Philippines, after having been declared an open
and undefended town, has been bombed by Japanese.
          Two Evans's to lunch and five to tea.

Sunday, December 28, 1941

Bitterly cold, bright day.   Daddy and I to Church, met afterwards by
Mother with Martin in pram.

Monday, December 29, 1941

Return to Stroud by road in bright sunshine.   Frost has cracked water
tank of car and we have to beg can of water every 15 miles or so. P.
to London for interview.
          Mr. Eden returns from Moscow, where has been having conversa-
tions with Stalin - most important ever held between Britain and U.S.SR

Tuesday, December 30, 1941

Hear Mr. Churchill speaking to Canadian Parliament in Ottawa.
Russians pursuing fleeing Germans who are retreating in bitter winter
weather.   Japanese making progress in Philippines and Malaya: British
advancing in Libya.
          Warmer and not so fine.

Wednesday, December 31, 1941

End of an eventful year, for world in general and our family in
particular.

Thursday, January 1, 1942

Martin's first birthday. P. returns from H's, very tired. Has
accepted post at Uckfield. We all wonder what 1942 will bring forth.

Friday, January 2, 1942

P. stays in bed in exhausted state till tea-time.

Saturday, January 3, 1942

One result of Roosevelt's conversations with Churchill: it is
announced that General Wavell is to take charge of joing forces in
south-west Pacific.
          Our milk cut. We have 1 quart between 4, and that is a good
deal more than basic ration. But joy at dinner time when Daddy brings
home quart bottle of milk brought in to shop by a farmer's wife.

Sunday, January 4, 1942

Anthony Eden (Foreign Secretary) broadcasts about plight of poor German
soldiers in Russia. Only he doesn't call them poor. Many are so
young, and they are most inadequately protected against cold of Russian
winter, which has set in early.

Monday, January 5, 1942

Heaven sends us another quart of milk. As Edgar cut our regular
supply to ½ pint this morning, we are very grateful.

Tuesday, January 6, 1942

Roosevelt announces enormous armament schedule for America, and says
in order to strike at Germany, U.S. will have air, sea and land bases
in Britain.

Wednesday, January 7, 1942

P. stays in bed till tea-time, being very tired and very low. Beautiful day, sunny and crisp.

Thursday, January 8, 1942

P. has letter from Crowborough. John Haskins, now prisoner of war in
Germany, was caught with others making tunnel and trying to escape.
He got a month's solitary confinement.

Friday, January 9, 1942

R.A.F. has dropped leaflets from America over occupied France.
Cummings (News-Chronicle) says we know now that we shall win the war,
and we know roughly how, but we don't know when.

To tea with Aunt H., who has fallen down and blacked her eye.
Her milkman says steadfastly he "won't have nothing to do with them
cowpins", so we can't think how he gets on with the Ministry of Food.

Saturday, January 10, 1942

Mother is blessed from heaven with 2 more quarts of milk, which cheer
her a good deal.   P. buys ½ lb. tiny pears at 3/- a lb.   Am full of
aches and feel rather unwell.

Stroud News reports death of National Council of Social Service
official, who stepped out of London train at Stroud on Tuesday.
Train has overrun platform in blackout, and he stepped on to low
parapet and then fell through glass roof in brewery yard some way
below bridge.

Sunday, January 11, 1942

Bitterly cold.   P. and I hear pleasing performance of Bach's Christmas Oratorio (pts 3, 4 and 5) at Parish Church.

Rations of fats, cheese and sugar to be cut to summer rate -
owing, we rather gather, to shipping from America having to be used in
Far East.   Japanese have invaded Dutch East Indies.

Monday, January 12, 1942

P., in preparation for new job, has bought beautiful pair leather
boots, fleecy-lined, with thick crepe soles.   Refuses to divulge price
which she says is higher than we could ever guess.   There willbe no
morecrepe rubber soles because of war in Malaya.   Very cold.

Tuesday, January 13, 1942

Japanese have taken important oil-bearing island in Dutch East Indies.
Mr. Keene, home on leave, comes and tells us his experiences as gunner
in Merchant Navy.   Affirms cheerfully that the business will soon be
over, but the rest of us are not as sanguine.

Wednesday, January 14, 1942

P. very tired: stays in bed till lunch-time.   I am very depressed.
There has been Allied conference in London, and all they have so far
done is to declare their intention of punishing those responsible for
the war, when it is over.   "Hang the Kaiser" all over again.   It
seems we have not progressed one whit.

Japanese still advancing in Malaya.   Australia becoming
restive about situation there.

Thursday, January 15, 1942

Bitterly cold.   Letter from Roy telling how he had to go out at
midnight in torrential rain to get a nurse when Christopher George
was born on November 30.

Friday, January 16, 1942

No news about Churchill's return.   We are getting anxious.

Saturday, January 17, 1942

Mr. Churchill has got safely back: he came by flying-boat from Bermuda.

Sunday, January 18, 1942

A little snow last night, frozen over this morning, makes the hill
very slippery.

Monday, January 19, 1942

Phyllida departs for new job at Uckfield, and it snows all afternoon
and evening, so that we feel we have driven a poor orphan into the
blizzard - this feeling probably accentuated in my case by recent
re-reading of Dickens.
          Japanese have captured important aerodrome in Burma. Burmese
Premier, of the unlikely name of U Saw, detained by British for having
had negotiations with Japanese.   Not sure whether he was in England
or in America - he had recently been in both places.

Tuesday, January 20, 1942

Bitterly cold: snow lies on ground all day and pipes are frozen.
Typhus in Lithuania.

Wednesday, January 21, 1942

Russians retake Mojaisk.   Typhus in Algiers.   Archbishop of Canterbury resigns, "to make way for younger man".   Still bitterly cold:
no sign of snow thawing.

Thursday, January 22, 1942

Most terribly cold.   Japanese have made landings in the islands of
New Guinea north of Australia.   Australia preparing against invasion.

Friday, January 23, 1942

Germans in Libya have recaptured Jedabiya: weather there, as well as
in Russia, very bad.   Thaw sets in here, for which we are thankful
in spite of frightful slush at present underfoot.
          (Letter from P. yesterday announced safe arrival: first im-
pressions pleasant).   Failed to buy today: dish mop, saucepan.

Saturday, January 24, 1942

Australia has mobilised all civil defence workers in anticipation of Japanese invasion.

I paint bedroom cupboard (whitewood) green; also skilfully mend almost new pyjamas in which I burnt hole, by buttonholing round and making ornament of accident. Manage to get small dish-mop at Woolworth's, but no saucepan. No one could possibly setup house at present: the necessary goods are just not to be had. General thaw, with rain and wind.

Sunday, January 25, 1942

Very cold and windy, but snow almost gone. Big tank battle taking place in Libya. More foods to be rationed: dried fruits, cereals, etc.

Monday, January 26, 1942

Daddy has lost fountainpen and there is not a new one to be had in Stroud. Neither can one buy a rubber hot water bottle, and when P. tried to get an alarm clock she was laughed to scorn.

American troops land in Northern Ireland. Think it would be good thing if they occupied Eire.

Look at face in glass and have strange experience of seeing skull: then seevery old woman with hard countanance. Then become properly focussed and see myself, with very red nose because it is so cold.

Tuesday, January 27, 1942

Very tired. Go to doctor and he says don't return till weather is better,but I reply that I cannot keep telling people in London I am coming and then not come.

Debate in House of Commons. P.M. asks for vote of confidence. The Dominions to be represented in War Cabinet.

Wednesday, January 28, 1942

Debate in House stillcontinuing. Graham makes quite lengthy speech about control of industry. Much criticism of Government. De Valera protests against presence of American troops in Ulster. I feel very low and bad at thought of returning to London tomorrow. Weather better.

Thursday, January 29, 1942

Back to London. Feel quite illat thought, but better when I get there. Pleasant room, with electric fire, in Craven Hill Gardens. Very tired.

Friday, January 30, 1942

Benghazi recaptured by Germans. That is fourth time it has changed hands in this war.

       To dentist; to Hampstead to collect some of my books left at Flask Walk - house empty and desolate; to Town Hall to re-register; to Food Office; and shopping. Things much scarcer than when I left six months ago. Lose my way in rain and walk up and down roads around Craven HillGardens, all looking exactly alike.

Saturday, January 31, 1942

British in Malaya have retreated to Singapore where causeway connecting with mainland has been destroyed. To doctor's: she says I ought to have pint of milk a day, but finds on consulting list that I am not suffering sufficiently illto be eligible. If only I were really dying and never likely to be of more use to mankind, might get a quart. More shopping.

Sunday, February 1, 1942

Snow quite thick on ground. Go to church, passing the tabernacle of "Johovah's Witnesses" on way, about whom am rather curious but too nervous to go in. Ask way of lady who offers opinion that "we are getting on very well". It appears that she refers to conduct of war, and she expresses belief that we are letting Japanese all get on to islands because it will then be so easy to encircle them with our ships. Adds after pause, as if for first time she detects flaw: "Of course it depends on whether we have enough ships".

       In afternoon to Guildhall School of Music to try to collect some of my belongings left thre by Helena, but housekeeper, with keys, is not there. Streets now fullof slush, and not being swept up as usual. See only two sweepers, and while I am asking way of one of them, a bus spatters my coat and face with dirty slush, which road-sweeper kindly removes from my cheek with his finger as he directs me.

Monday, February 2, 1942

Ridiculously apprehensive and nervous about going back to iffice, but everyone kind and welcoming. Feel rather tired. Streets now covered with encrusted remains of snow.

Tuesday, February 3, 1942

To printers, where got on quite well. It has snowed again, and walking very difficult. By evening, thaw has set in, which makes everything nauseating. Tina has friend to supper, socialworker, full of statistics, among them that for every 5 babies born in this country, there is one abortion procured. At one time recently in Germany - perhaps during depression in 1931, I forget - the figure was one abortion for every baby. Can't think how they can check up such figures.

       Russians driving back Germans.

       Do not sleep well yet since returning to London.

Wednesday, February 4, 1942

Changes in Government. Lord Beaverbrook appointed Minister of
Production. Cold, icy and snowy: roads dangerous and I have difficulty in finding way home in half light.

Miss Morrison (proprietress of 19 Craven Hill Gardens) manages
to buy two smalltin kettles, a great achievement these days. In
spite of war difficulties, she feeds us very well.

Thursday, February 5, 1942

Snow and sleet. Roads still treacherous. Again I lose my way home
and feel very depressed, useless and miserable.

We get most strange messengers to and from printers, and to and
from Broadcasting House: all very old and gnome-like.

Friday, February 6, 1942

Heating system in office broken down again - we had no heat on Wednesday. I therefore leave after lunch and go to Hilary's. Walk
from bus (2½ miles) very slippery. She has been marooned for week
and is bursting with conversation.

Saturday, February 7, 1942

Still freezing. Baby and dog both pleased when I take them for outing along slippery roads.

Sunday, February 8, 1942

Soap and soap-flakes to be rationed from tomorrow. Feel sorry for
H., who has innumerable nappies and woolies to wash every day and
whose water is terribly hard. Beautiful day, still very cold.
Return to London.

Monday, February 9, 1942

Find everything weary, stale, flat and unprofitable. Glad thaw has
set in: sorry that the Japanese are managing their invasion of
Singapore with such success.

Tuesday, February 10, 1942

Japanese have mended Causeway connecting Singapore with mainland, and
way they are pouring on to island. Situation is grave. Everyone
very depressed - though I find them anyway much more depressed than
six months ago. To printers, which is a much more comfortable
business now, since we have new office (quitted by Radio Times) with
air, light and quiet, instead of the over-heated, aireless and noisy
box off the compositors room and backing on to the foundry, which we
had before.

Wednesday, February 11, 1942

Feel more cheerful, in spite of continued bad news from Singapore.

Thursday, February 12, 1942

My spirits definitely onup-grade, though war news does not warrant
it.   To concert at National Gallery: Ida Haendel (violin), Eric
Hope (piano): Mozart, (sonata which has slow movement reminding me
of hymn 'How Pleased and Blest Was I'), Bach Chaconne, and Poème by
Chausson.   There was more, but I couldn't stop for it and anyway was
very cold.   Thence went to Leicester Galleries to see Epstein's new
sculpture, Jacob wrestling with the Angel - a strange enough story
even without Epstein.   Immense statue, in alabaster, which gives a
translucent effect to angel's head, no doubt intentionally.   Great
feeling of strength and power.   Feel it hard to believe from it that
Jacob managed to prevail.   Feel, to see it properly, one needs a
stepladder, a telescope, and an immense vista.
          After this try to buy my soap ration for month, and have
great difficulty in getting any soapflakes at all.   Am appalled at
smallness of allowance, and cannot think how Hilary will manage with
the infant - there is talk of babies having special allowance.   When
I get home, find package of soap flakes from Marjorie Fuchs for H,
sent in kindness of her heart because she knows H's water is so hard,
and hers in Cheshire is from Lakes and very soft.
          (After outing, get back from lunch at about 4.15 or so.
Very disgraceful.   And everyone in London looks to me grotesque and
likean Epstein conception of humanity.)

Friday, February 13, 1942

There has been a terrific fight in the Channel between British and
German forces, and the two ~~British~~ German ships, the Scharnhorst and
Gniesnau, together with the Prince Eugin, which the R.A.F. have bombed
at Brest till we all hoped they didn't exist any more, have got away
up the Channel in a fog and managed to reach Heligoland.   Worse than
this, 40 or more of our bombers and other aircraft have been lost, for
20 or so of the enemy's. At the office everyone is very cast down by
this news.   And almost all the talks set up for this week's paper
have for one reason or another been cancelled: so this is indeed a
black Friday the thirteenth.
          To Hilary's for the weekend.

Saturday, February 14, 1942

A beautiful day, warm sunshine though the wind is cold.   I take the
willing baby and dog for 2-hour walk.   H. very perturbed about the
news, and nearly bursts into tears when I sing "If the dons sight
Devon, I'll quit the port of Heaven, And drum them up the Channel ..."
I feel as if we can never win this war: but it would not do to say so.

Sunday, February 15, 1942

Singapore has fallen, and the Japanese have overrun the whole of
Malaya.   This dismal news was announced by the Prime Minister in a
broadcast at 9 o'clock, which I hear after I return fromHilary's.
He introduced the information into the middle of his talk, and tho'
it was expected, I felt it as a blow.   (At any rate he has kindly
provided The Listener with a first article for its next issue.)
He tells us also of the advantages of having America, Russia and
China as our allies: and gets in a hit at the people who by their
criticism make the running of the war-machine difficult.
        Feel how pleasant - so far - to be Martin, who crawls
happily about the sitting room crooning to himself and smiling on
everything: and is entranced by the mere spectacle of a cow on the
walk I take him, and by the sound of an aeroplane which he in his
innocence does not associate with anything unpleasant.   I hope the
poor lamb will not find the world too intolerable when he grows up.

Monday, February 16, 1942

Miss Evans away for a fortnight with shingles.   There is a lot of
sickness about, which has increased since working hours have become
longer.
        Railings being removed by Government for scrap-iron.   The
effect round the parks is pleasant.

Tuesday, February 17, 1942

Official inquiry to be held on escape of "Scharnhorst" and "Gniesenau"
but Churchill refuses to allow findings tobe made public - decision
which rouses lot of criticism in House.
        The man at printers who usually brings our tea goes home
ill with flu, and we walk through miles of building to find canteen.
On way, see newly printed copies of Radio Times travelling along on
endless-looking belt, in enormous room, with huge machinery, in
traversing which I should certainly have got lost but for guidance of
Mr. Abraham.

Wednesday, February 18, 1942

Bitterly cold wind: Miss Playle away with bad cold.   Very depressed
most of day, untile vening, when have p.c. from John Beavan welcoming
me back and suggesting several dates: and there is interesting discussion at dinner-table on (a) English literature; (b) personal
relations.   Wish I could feel I had a niche in the scheme of things.

Thursday, February 19, 1942

All buses whizz by the bus-stops in the morning, as I stand in biting
east wind: but am given lift by motorist, who offers me Dr. Barnardo's
collection box into which I put my fare.   To National Gallery concert
with Mr. Abraham: two Brahms' piano quartets.
        Discussion in evening: Joan and Tina think people in this

country who have the money, and therefore the power, don't wish to
help Russia too much, and may try to make peace with Germany.
        The Australian mainland - Port Darwin in the extreme north
- has for the first time been bombed by the Japanese.

Friday, February 20, 1942

Ministerial changes, chief of which is that Mr.Lord Beaverbrook goes
to America, and Sir Stafford Cripps enters War Cabinet.   Am very
depressed indeed, and wish I could change my job.

Saturday, February 21, 1942

Have hair washed at Evans, where buy hank of knitting yarn, chiefly
because 8 oz. are offered for 1 coupon, and I have exactly one left
to finish before I can get my new card.   Carry this hank about unwrapped feeling as if I have been shop-lifting, and proceed through
snowstorm to labour exchange in Great Marlborough Street, where, in
company with other women born in 1907, I have to be registered.   If
anything had wanted to cast me into gloom, it was supplied by rows
of dismal looking females who, it pained me to remember, were all my
own age.   Lunch with Tina, who is so beset by enthusiastic helpers
(voluntary) for the Cause (Forward March), that she cannot get on
with her work and has to go back after the meal to clear up.   I go
on to Hampstead Heath, where walk with John Beavan, afterwards having
tea with him and returning to play 'Monopoly' at Oxford Road.   John
and I, who have taken the trouble to write to each other only once in
six months, fairly fall on each other's necks, which is somewhat
surprising.

Sunday, February 22, 1942

Bitterly cold.   Bob, who is only one of 'family' here for weekend,
takes me to Low Mass at a High Church, where we are aspurged with
holy water, and have incense shaken on to us.   In afternoon, help
him move his hundreds of books to a new room one floor higher than
his present one.   Historical and theological tomes.   My chief work
is to listen to him holding forth on them as he arranges them to his
satisfaction in the shelves.
        Forgot to remark yesterday that the Whitestone Pond at
Hampstead, where little boys used to sail their boats, is now walled
in, to give a deeper water supply in case of raids and fires.

Monday, February 23, 1942

More Ministerial changes, the most noticeable being that Captain
Margesson, Conservative Chief Whip, is out.   Lord Reith also out.
Still very cold.

- 341 -

Tuesday, February 24, 1942

P.M. , in House, reports big increase in shipping losses. Bitterly
cold again.

Wednesday, February 25, 1942

Letter from Joyce, who has been able to get, and is sending me, green
rubber hot water bottle .
          To doctor's.   Have gained 1 lb. since returning to London,
which is regarded as very meritorious in me.   I put it down to Miss
Morrison's good feeding.
          To National Gallery Concert: Franz Osborn (piano), Max
Rostal (violin): Schumann and Kreutzer Sonata.
          Sir Stafford Cripps makes his first speech in new role as
Leader of the H. of C.   Sounds business-like.   Tina says Cripps told
Sir Richard Acland that he would have gone in in opposition to the
Government, but that things were in far too bad a case for that, and
that our arms production, owing to individual control, is inhopeless
muddle.

Thursday, February 26, 1942

Dash around at lunch-time and get 4/3 worth of some extraordinary-
looking unrationed cold meat to take to H's; also ½ lb. rather mangy
petit-fours for 2/6.
          "Prinz Eugin" torpedoed - not sunk.

Friday, February 27, 1942

To H's, with goods bought yesterday, and 1 lb. very fat, very salt
American bacon, which is unrationed.

Saturday, February 28, 1942

Warmer: fine and sunny.   Walking out with baby inpram is pleasure,
not penance.   News of naval action off Java, which later turns out
to be dispersal of one of Japanese convoys, no doubt intended for
invasion of island.   There has been parachute attack by us on radiolocation station on north coast of France, near Havre.
          March 1
Sunday, February 29, 1942

Cold again.   H. has soaked American bacon for 2 days to get out the
sale, which has been done so effectively that L. reports there is no
taste left in it.   Cold meat from Selfridges a great success.
          We go to tea with some Czech refugees.   It turns out to
be high tea, and I have to leave immediately afterwards to catch bus
back to London.   Baby teething but pretty good and quite cheerful.

Monday, March 2, 1942

Bob, determined to do me good which no doubt I badly need, goes to
lengths of buying 18/- book to lend me: "Nature, Man and God", by
the Archbishop of York (Temple) who is about to become Archbishop of
Canterbury.
        Japanese have made landings on Java.

Tuesday, March 3, 1942

Pleasant day, sunny and not too cold.   Am becoming interested in
"Nature, Man and God", which is the Gifford Lectures of 1932-33 and
1933-34.   Just finished lecture 1, on last page of which was rather
pleased with: "'To thine own self be true' is a piece of high-class
ethical futility which Shakespeare appropriately puts into the mouth
of his own most priceless old dotard".

Wednesday, March 4, 1942

Milder: rain all day, which will be very welcome to farmers.   De-
fenders of Java have been told to hold out to the end, which presumably is not far off.   British have made big rain on Paris suburbs and
have destroyed armament works.

Thursday, March 5, 1942

Buy gloves (1 coupon because unlined), nosegay and feather (no coupons)
and feel I have smartened myself up a little.   Weather has turned
colder again and there is a little snow.   Letter from home - railings
and gate have been removed for Government scrap-metal to Daddy's rage
We spend evening bellowing hymns which Bob plays out of English
Hymnal: and this simple and innocent pastime we much enjoy.

Friday, March 6, 1942

Lunch with Lorna, who is leaving to become a V.A.D.   At Chinese
restaurant, where the five of us present over-eat on bowls of fried
rice and a lot of other messes.   4/- each.   Women B.B.C. employees
aged 20-30, unless engaged on special work, to be calledup.

Saturday, March 7, 1942

To Beavans at Aldbury by bus.   It is so cold that, walking from bus
to cottage, feel my hands will drop off.   Walk in woods with Duque.
John and Florence arrive about 9 p.m.
        Communication with Java now cut off.

Sunday, March 8, 1942

Lovely day of quite warm sunshine: we go for walk in woods, listen
to Beethoven's 7th Symphony and to Brains Trust, have another little
walk, and then hear programme on life of Jane Austen.   Very pleasant.
And meantime Java may be taken to have fallen to the Japanese, since
there has been no communication with the island.   Number of 'points'
required for many tinned foods has been increased.

Monday, March 9, 1942

Still milder and sunny.   Beautiful walk to bus in early morning.
But I have not slept well, am tired at getting up before usual time,
and have a cold.   These things not important compared with fact that
Japanese have taken Rangoon, capital of Burma.

Tuesday, March 10, 1942

Beautiful spring day.   I stream with a cold and sneeze a good deal.
In House of Commons, Anthony Eden reports great brutality by the
Japanese in Hongkong: reports - no doubt intended to stir us to
hatred and further warlike efforts - which must be very painful to
people who have relatives there.

Wednesday, March 11, 1942

Rain and fog.   My cold almost gone.   To National Gallery with
Audrey Mearing, who - In although her fiancé was likely to be in
Hongkong and she can get no news of him - keeps bravely cheerful.
Griller Quartet plus Denis Matthews(piano): Mozart's piano quartet
in G minor and string quartet in C major.   Very beautiful.
    In afternoon ring up Hilary and find parents have just
arrived there.   Leslie (Daddy's assistant) has had his calling up
papers and they are taking what they suppose will be their last
little outing.
    Stafford Cripps to go to India, which has been demanding
self-government, or the promise of it after the war, and has refused
to co-operate with the British unless the promise is given.

Thursday, March 12, 1942

To Beavans after supper.   John, just come in, says: "Room is rather
smoky, I'm afraid", which it is - almost impossible to see across.
He eats tinned fish on one corner of the table while Essie McCormick
and Frank play bézique on another: in an armchair a curious creature
(male), with long hair, looking rather dirty, sprawls with a book - I
find he is product of Dartington Hall, modern co-educational school:
from upstairs come sounds of a beginner's piano practice.   Think
what queer, though pleasant, friends I have.

<u>Friday, March 13, 1942</u>

To Hilary's.   Daddy has been unwell with upset tummy all day.   It
is announced that from the beginning of June there will be no petrol
for private motorists except in special cases.

<u>Saturday, March 14, 1942</u>

Beautiful warm spring day.   Take baby for walk.   Hilary and Leonard
take advantage of grandparents' presence to go out together.   They
buy bicycles, though they have not yet got money to pay for them, and
plan to have basket attached to one of them for baby.
          It is announced that in naval action off Java lately, 12
Allied ships were sunk, including 5 cruisers.   H. so upset by this
news, implores me not to walk about singing cheerfully, but to share
in general gloom.

<u>Sunday, March 15, 1942</u>

Parents return to Stroud - which today is having a mock invasion so
that there were no church services this morning.   I return to London
in very crowded bus: have first to stand and then to sit next to a
fretful baby.   Endeavour to forget physical discomfort in reading of
such "Nature, Man and God", e.g.: "The first and most conspicuous
feature of the free activity of mind is its detachment from successive-
ness"!   Learn that there are no isolated incidents (i.e. people
standing on one's feet), but only processes (i.e., I suppose, getting
eventually to Oxford Circus).

<u>Monday, March 16, 1942</u>

After horrible dream that Phyllida has died of tuberculosis and that
I was full of self-reproach because in some way I had not treated her
well, I receive letter from her asking me to lend her £5, which feel
compelled to despatch by return of post.
          Raymond has to go on board ship tomorrow.   He keeps saying:
'I must pack' and then sits down at piano and plays Chopin preludes,
very badly (usually he plays well).   Then he says again "Oh God, I
must pack" and thumps out a few more inaccurate chords.   He has to
take tropical kit, and that is all he knows about his destination.

<u>Tuesday, February 17, 1942</u>

Clothes coupons cut by a quarter, and coal, gas and electricity to be
rationed.
          Letters from Joyce Green and John Catlow.   Former says:
"I have decided it is no use trying to adjust oneself to the war.
The Marx Brothers attitude is the only one.   Either it is so
terrible that nothing is worth doing - as I held for some months - or
everything is so worth doing that it is not so terrible.   Presumably
the sense of proportion one was beginning to achieve in one's age in
peace time is still the standard.   War is outside all sense of

proportion and has to be considered separately. Not like religion
which is inside everything and must not be considered separately.
Good and evil. Is that sense?"
      Latter (John) says - after a few introductory sentences wherein
my letter-writing is compared with that of Mme. de Sévigné and Horace
Walpole, and my literary style with that of Jane Austen and E.M.
Delafield (this scatty diary is not a fair sample): "Nature is so
indifferent to what silly men do, isn't it? I often wish I were a
tree, or some other aloof impassive component of the natural scene."
He is now taking an officers' course at Torpoint and hating it.

Wednesday, February 18, 1942
         March

General MacArthur (U.S.A.) now in Australia. Here everyone is a
little depressed, mostly because temperature is mild and it is raining
      Read this to-day, from the Archbishop: "Will as the agent in
truly moral action is the whole organised nature of the person
concerned; it is his personality as a whole; and so far is it from
being an initial endowment of our nature, that the main function of
education is to fashion it - a process which is only complete when
the entire personality is fully integrated in a harmony of all its
constituent elements". Feel horribly afraid that if my entire personality were fully integrated in a harmony of all its constituent
elements, there would be left only something smaller than a grain of
mustard seed.
      Millicent Stowell, wife of Editor of Radio Times, comes in to
office today: very excited because, having been unsuccessful in
having any children of her own, she is going to adopt a baby girl.
It is much more difficult to adopt a girl than a boy, the demand is
so much greater. Why? Because when people have children of their
own they almost always want sons. Perhaps it is felt that a girl
of doubtful parentage will be more tractable than a boy.

Thursday, March 19, 1942

To Concert at National Gallery: Brahms cello sonata and clarinet
trio. On way back pay 1/9 for tablet of bath soap - 2 of my 4
coupons for the month. And get boracic powder, but am told it is
now very scarce.
      Feel rather unwell all day . Played 3 games of chess with
Bob last evening, which so exhausted me that I slept very badly.
      Herbert Morrison, Home Secretary, warns proprietors of
Daily Mirror that the paper will be suppressed if it continues its
present policy, which is likely to create alarm and despondency.
Allied naval forces have sunk large number of Japanese ships.

Friday, March 20, 1942

Feel in need of large meal and get at Bertorelli's in Charlotte St.:
calves head with vinaigrette sauce, sauté potatoes and sprouts;
enormous piece of bread and small piece of butter or margarine;
stewed dried apricots; white coffee (2 lumps of sugar). This costs
3/9, which I regard as excessive.

In evening to Beavans, where hear 2 Haydn quartets (pleasant) and sandwiched between them a Bartok (unpleasant). This is followed by spirited discussion on relative merits of Mendelssohn and Chopin, John opining that in 50 years Chopin will be thought little more of than Mendelssohn is now; Frank saying if he were on a desert island with a gramophone and nothing but Mendelssohn he would drown himself - though owning under pressure that Chopin would be not much better; Arthur Lawrence rising tumultuously from his seat now and then to say "Decadent", or "Morbid" in reference to Chopin; and the youngster from Dartington Hall talking of "technique" with many extravagant gestures and flicks of his cigarette.

Miss Morrison kindly gives me glass of milk, which is more to be desired than fresh nectar.

Saturday, March 21, 1942

To hairdresser's (where I acquire a side parting which is an improvement) - n.b. hairpins, hair combs, etc., now almost unobtainable; to dressmaker recommended by Tina, to have alterations done - n.b. almost impossible to find anyone who will do them now; the big stores, which when clothes rationing was instituted opened alterations departments, having now found that they have not enough staff to maintain them; and to Sir Richard Acland's, where I do a little typing for Tina. Am struck again by the desirability of having a Cause to work for, which makes you slave away in not particularly pleasant surroundings, on plain wooden tables, with colleagues who irritate you, and causes you to sink all thought of these things in the vision of the goal.

Sunday, March 22, 1942

Have I anywhere observed how many bus conductors are now women?

To exceedingly High church in this neighbourhood, where I am much distressed by the sermon, which I feel must have been distributed by the Ministry of Information and is concerned with London's Warship Week. What is the use of the Church if it doesn't lift up people's spirits to something above Warship Weeks? Come out early, not so much because of disapproval as because I have pains and feel faint. Spend most of remainder of day in bed with hot water bottle. Hear 9 o'clock News, and crashingly dull appeal by the extremely worthy Sir William Beveridge for a Total War Effort.

Monday, March 23, 1942

Joyce to supper, en route by night train to Newcastle, to try for job (commercial artist). She is lucky to have got a sleeper, since most are reserved for "Government".

London full of people carrying string bags such as old country women used to have, but these are brightly coloured and sold at about 5/- each, and are necessary because nothing is wrapped up and few shops are now able to deliver.

Tuesday, March 24, 1942

Joyce for night, on her return journey: result of interview not
known.   We go to Beavans and get nostalgic looking over happy pre-
war photographs with John.

Wednesday, March 25, 1942

Beautiful warm spring day.   Meet Joyce for lunch, and we go to film
of Walt Disney's "Dumbo" - a baby elephant who is ostracised because
of his enormous ears, but after many misadventures learns that he can
fly with them.   Then tea, at Fuller's, where we are allowed one cake
each, and I back to office while she takes train to Maidstone.
Much talk of probable invasion.

Thursday, March 26, 1942

With Bob and Tina to Shaw's "Doctor's Dilemma" at the Haymarket.   It
starts at 6 p.m., the usual time for theatres now.   Good performance
with Vivien Leigh as Mrs. Dubedat.   We have great difficulty in finding anywhere to eat afterwards.   Turn down the Brasserie Universelle
because it is so crowded, and we should have had to wait, and go hopefully from one Soho restaurant to another in ascending order of ex-
pensiveness as we get hungrier, finding them all shut.   Fortunately
it is moonlight.   Finally have to go to Lyons Tottenham Court Road
Corner House and wait in a queue.   Quite good meal when we do get
settled, but by this time I am so tired and hungry, can eat nothing.
Prime Minister says our Atlantic shipping position is more
serious, which I expect means food will be scarcer.

Friday, March 27, 1942

There has been attack by our Commandos on St. Lazaire, on French coast,
which appears to have been successful.
To Hilary's in evening.   Martin has had an inoculation
against diphtheria.

Saturday, March 28, 1942

Ralph and Marjorie (Leonard's brother and sister-in-law) come, with
adopted daughter aged 3.   Marjorie very peroxided and curled, a real
cockney, thoroughly honest, likeable and good-natured.

Sunday, March 29, 1942

Beautiful warm day .   We sit out of doors and enjoy the sunshine.
National Day of Prayer.   Hear broadcast sermon by Archbishop
of York (to be of Canterbury in a week or two), in which he says that
when the Europe of 1914 broke up in a cataclysm which is still continuing now, because men exalted possessions, then the Son of Man came
with power.   Which is the most cheering thing about the war I've so
far heard.

Monday, March 30, 1942

We go to press today instead of tomorrow, because of Easter.   Which
means I am at Waterlows till 8.50 and get no food until 9.50.   Tina
and I listen at 10.15 to Archbishop of York again.   He points out
that the World has a greater condemnation than the Flesh: it was not
the harlots who crucified Christ - they had no quarrel with him.   Nor
had the woman taken in adultery.   It was the respectable priests,
who, moreover, thought they were doing right.   "If the light that is
in you be darkness, how great is that darkness!"   He says the sins we
are conscious of are not the bad ones: the worst ones are those we
don't know we have, or think are allright.

Tuesday, March 31, 1942

Phyllida for night, en route for home.   She and I go to "The Nutmeg
Tree", with Yvonne Arnaud in principal part.   Very entertaining.
Afterwards we get food at Brasserie Universelle - quite pleasant, in
spite of all the harlots gathered round the bar.   We had had lunch
with the German Jewess who teaches in P's school, a very nice girl who
when she was in Germany woke up one night to find six or seven Storm
Troopers in her room.   They smashed up all the furniture among other
things, and she afterwards had a nervous breakdown.
        Today I saw a woman struggling up the steps of a bus carrying
an unwrapped slop-pail.

Wednesday, April 1, 1942

The first of April, and the weather is capricious.   I feel depressed
about my work: feel I am not doing a worth-while job now that the
paper is cut to about half its pre-war size.   In lunch-hour go to
collect dress, coat, and skirt, which have all been shortened.   Have
to carry them home unwrapped over my arm.   The charges are, dress,
3/6, skirt 2/6, coat 4/6, skirt 3/6, coat 5/6.   This seems plenty,
but is not as much as an Oxford Street store would have charged.

Thursday, April 2, 1942

Meet Phyllida at Paddington (she has Tramp with her) and we travel to
Stroud.   Whether everyone else is being good and doing what the Gov-
ernment tells them - i.e. staying put - or whether other people are
travelling tomorrow because they are working on Good Friday and having
Monday free, we don't know.   But we are glad to have a comfortable
uncrowded journey.   There is, surprisingly, an alert when we get to
Stroud, but no noise of bombs or guns.   Mother has got a kettle.   She
saw a woman in Stroud carrying one, and asked where she had got it.
"Two-and-nine", said the woman "it's a lot, but I had to have one".
"I'm desperate", said Mother, and galloped off to the Electric Co.
shop and bought one.   A dozen people asked her in the street where
she had bought it - and there was only one left in the shop.   Daddy
has fallen down in the hill and his face is covered with sticking-
plaster.

Friday, April 3, 1942

Good Friday.   Two aunts to tea. P. and I take the delighted Tramp
for a walk and find the hill very windy.   Rodborough has lost most
of its railings.   We have our stone parapet built higher instead, but
no gate.   We are promised a wooden one in time.

Saturday, April 4, 1942

Daddy's 66th birthday, and he has to work very hard with no Leslie.
P. and I to tea at Aunt H's.   She has a scheme for helping Daddy in
the shop.   Daddy declares nothing will induce him to have any woman
on the premises.   A daylight alert, and great sound of planes behind
low clouds - whether ours or the enemy's we cannot tell.   The nine
o'clock news says there were bombs at one town in the west, with some
casualties.   Spent 1/6 on a large cauliflower.

Sunday, April 5, 1942

I return to London, again travelling in great comfort.   Miss. M. has
glass of milk ready for me, as well as bread and butter and meat.
Tramp wants to come with me, to find Hilary again.   I read 60 pages
of the Archbishop in train, and suffer from mental indigestion.   Feel
rather like a spiritual outcast.   Miss B. at morning service played
the tune of "Christ is Risen" to the hymn "Alleluia, Alleluia", so
that when we got to the end of the first verse there were four more
lines of music to be accommodated.   Daddy, feeling he was saving the
situation, bellowed the first four lines of the verse again, and the
rest followed.   Then Miss B. was so surprised to find us all singing
unexpected words that she played "Amen" and finished it.

Monday, April 6, 1942

My 1/6 on a cauliflower on Saturday well beaten by Miss Morrison's 2/4
on a Savoy cabbage.   More foods to be on the "Points" scheme - including breakfast cereals.   Also number of points per month reduced.
Fine day with high wind.   Mr. Abraham and I to printer's in afternoon.
Cherry trees and forsythia are out, and though the strange smells of
the neighbourhood are still there, on the dirty canal little boys are
rowing boats because it is bank holiday.

Tuesday, April 7, 1942

At printer's all day: too tired in evening to go to string quartets
at Beavans.   To bed early.   Negotiations with India in full swing,
but no agreement reached.

Wednesday, April 8, 1942

Phyllida's 33rd birthday.   I go to Paddington in lunch-hour and help
Hilary to embark with Martin on 1.55 for Stroud.   Crowds much greater
than those P. and I encountered at Easter, probably because the
Services were not allowed to travel during the holiday.   Hilary looks

very tired.   To doctor's and get stomach powder.   In evening the
"Family" to a dancing class in Baker Street.   I find it an ordeal, and
am so tired by the end of an hour am almost in tears, while the world
appears a nightmare of nothing but moving legs and feet.

Thursday, April 9, 1942

Try to buy black leather handbag for Aunt N.   Find they are 4 guineas
or so each!   Bags at 25/-, which I regard as my limit, are unlined
and unfitted, and of very poor quality.   Shop assistant says "They
aren't making them any more".   Get for Mother 2 pairs ribbed lisle
stockings at 7/11 (and 2 coupons) each, and Whittier's poems for Aunt
H. to give Daddy - she was unable to obtain copy in Stroud, Gloucester
or Cheltenham.
            Bad news at night.   Japanese have sunk two cruisers, the
Dorsetshire and the Cornwall.

Friday, April 10, 1942

News is so consistently bad now that people don't even comment on it.
A British aircraft-carrier, the Hermes, reported sunk by Japanese,
but almost no one remarks on it.   Have joined fire party at B.B.C.,
and am to sleep at Broadcasting House on Sunday night.   To this end
I am issued with a tin helmet (rather thin and inefficient-looking)
and a boiler suit with a hole in it.   If I had a new boiler suit I
should have to give up 4 coupons.   Do not care for idea of sleeping
in the concert-hall.

Saturday, April 11, 1942

Plans for settlement with India turned down by Congress, and Cripps
returning home.   Might as wellhave finished The Listener make-up on
Friday, instead of waiting for weekend talks on the subject.
            To hairdresser's;   buy pair walking shoes for next winter,
price 57/6 and 5 coupons at Baber's.   Assistant says it will soon be
a case of taking not something that fits you, but the nearest there is.
Try to order fountain-pen for Daddy, but no one will take an order,
tho' Waterman's say they will have plenty on June 1st when their new
quota is delivered.   Buy very wide black felt belt for 6/6.   Sit
in Kensington Gardens in sun and read Archbishop's book.   Pleased with
this: "The conferring of spiritual quality upon inorganic matter, of
which the bare possibility is sometimes denied, is one of the commonest
experiences of life; the phrase is almost a definition of Art".

Sunday, April 12, 1942

To a Unitarian Church in morning (think, after reading some of their
hymn-book, they deny the doctrine of the Trinity); to Kew with Joan
in afternoon; to Beavans for music in evening; and at 9.30 I report
for fire-watching duty at Broadcasting House.   Am shown how to use
hose, which is almost too heavy to lift; how to take it apart to add
a piece to lengthen it - which I haven't enough muscular strength to

do; and how to report putting out of fire to Defence Headquarters,
which D.H. seems entirely uninterested in.   Then repair for night
to bunks in Concert Hall, which is below ground level and very stuffy
and warm, though it has a high ceiling.   Sleep very little.
        Today it has become law that where six or more people are
waiting for a bus, a queue must be formed.   All the way to Kew there
were rows of people at the bus-stops.

Monday, April 13, 1942

"Messiah" being broadcast in full this week, to commemorate bicentenary
of Handel, or of its writing.   Part I given this evening.   I listen
but am very tired after last night.   Could stand the Concert Hall no
more at 7.20 this morning, and got up.   After I had washed and dressed
in the dressing-rooms, returned to find the rest still slumbering at
8 o'clock.   Returned to Craven Hill Gardens for breakfast.

Tuesday, April 14, 1942

Budget Day.   No increase in income-tax, but luxuries - i.e. alcohol,
tobacco, cosmetics, etc. - taxed heavily.   Lady Graves (wife of B.B.C.
Director-General) to supper.   She, Greta and I to film, "Escape".

Wednesday, April 15, 1942

To first part of Contemporary Music Concert at Wigmore Hall: very un-
understandable.   Then to supper with Graham, who has been seeing Harry
Hopkins (from America) and is encouraged by accounts of American production.

Thursday, April 16, 1942

Laval in power in Vichy: everyone thinks that this means the Germans
will get French Fleet.
        Very depressed about job: trying to make up my mind to tell
Editor shall ask for transfer on grounds of not enough work, but feel
it will make him angry.
        Meet Phyllida for lunch: National Gallery concert: Schubert
trip and Trout Quintet.   Our dancing class in evening, which I quite
enjoy.

Friday, April 17, 1942

Home by 4.15, after depressingly idle day.   Laval forming new Cabinet
in France, composed, according to our News, of traitors.

Saturday, April 18, 1942

Tokyo has been bombed, probably from aircraft-carrier.   Push Martin
up hill in pram in warm sunshine: he is very heavy.   Leslie Darby has
been made store-keeper for Fire Service Divisional Headquarters, which
are in Stroud.   On first day he sorted up trousers marked "14" which
were larger than others marked "22", and made himself so useful that

he was asked to stay and see to storing of equipment.   Gives his
opinion, when he comes in this evening, that the whole thing may get
sorted out and arranged by the end of the war.

Sunday, April 19, 1942

Back to London.   Am lent "John o' London's Weekly" by amorous wife
of R.A.F. Sergeant in my carriage.   Note good quality of paper, large
number of pages, and absence of reference to war (on which am mentally
congratulating Editor), when observe that date of issue is July, 1937.
        There has been great attack on German works at Augsburg, where
U-boat engines are made, by 12 of our newest bombers which flew at
hedge-top height 500 miles there and 500 back, and hit their target.
Only 5 bombers returned to their base.

Monday, April 20, 1942

Tell Mr.Abraham that I have so little to do on 3 days in the week
now that the paper is so cut in size, that I want to ask for transfer.
He says I shall upset the apple-cart entirely if I make the reason a
lack of work.   After reflection, see that what would be done would be
that he would be removed to the armed Forces.   He advises me to produce masterpieces in office time, which he thinks would be justifying
being subsidised by B.B.C.   Am not sure that this is sound.
        Laval has made anti-British speech, saying Hitler has been a
considerate conqueror and France has no complaint against him.

Tuesday, April 21, 1942

At printers.   In evening Joan coaches us in our dancing, which is
entertaining but exhausting.

Wednesday, April 22, 1942

To David's to supper.   There is beautiful radiogram with numbers of
enchanting records, but I am so tired, feel unable to take interest
and can hardly make intelligible conversation.

Thursday, April 23, 1942

Feel very queer with my heart going too fast, and stay in bed till
midday.   After that, ¼-hour in sun in park revives me so much that I
go to office in afternoon, but do not join others in dancing-class in
evening.
        Much talk of our invasion of Continent, and reports of "Commando"
raids by our troops on French coast.

Friday, April 24, 1942

To Phyllida who is in bungalow in middle of wood in Sussex. Anemones
over floor of wood and primroses and violets in lanes. There is
high cold wind but bright sun.   Only other person in bungalow is 15-

year-old school-girl of such precocity that we find her in passionate
embrace of 20-year-old soldier whom she has known for 6 days.

Saturday, April 25, 1942

Precocious schoolgirl departs, rather to P's relief.   In spite of
sophistication is very likable and has made bungalow beautiful with
flowers.   I meet Mrs. Antoinette Sommaruga, half French and married
to Italian, who owns school and who says 10 day children may be coming
next term and willhave to have lunch.   Permit for food willbe obtained from Food Office, but it willnot be ready for fortnight.   Meantime
"We could open a tin, perhaps?" says she vaguely.   P. in state of
suppressed laughter at this grasp of practical difficulties.
    We walk and find place for tea where are so stunned at being
offered fresh boiled eggs and fresh salad, that we do not have them.
Do, however, have home-made scones and cakes, also very unusual at
present.
    P. says convoys have been pouring through Uckfield towards coast
the last week.   Bath had bad raid last night.

Sunday, April 26, 1942

Return to London laden ~~high~~ with wild flowers.   We haard bombs in
night, probably on coast.   Bath had another raid.   Today farmer's
wife calls us to see two newborn twin bullocks.

Monday, April 27, 1942

Still very high wind.   Charles Johnson to supper, who before war
lectured at National Gallery and is still employed there.   Find his
conversation on art very interesting.
    Heavy raid on Norwich.   Hitler has made speech which is regarded
in this country as encouraging because his threats of death to default-
ers in Germany show that morale there must be poor.

Tuesday, April 28, 1942

Terribly high winds still continue.   Feather from my hat is whisked
completely away and not seen again: dust is over everything.   So
afraid the fruit blossom willbe destroyed.
    Norwich had another bad raid last night.   David to supper.

Wednesday, April 29, 1942

There has been air-raid on York, with much damage.   Am told Germans
are now bombing everything in "Baedeker" (guide-book) which has three
stars to show it is of special historic interest.   Do not really
believe this.   "Daily Telegraph" is not correct in saying Bath is
not a military object.   A lot of the Admiralty and other Government
offices are there.
    Still very high wind.   Go with Heimann to theatre (7 p.m. this
time): "Blythe Spirit" by Noel Coward, very amusing.

Thursday, April 30, 1942

Fuel rationing scheme found impracticable and to be dropped, after
being opposed by all parties in House. Government has lost two seats
in by-elections. Tina pleased because one candidate (successful) has
Sir Richard Acland's ideas and was backed by him.
        To our dancing-class. Have resigned myself to idea of never
being successful dancer, but resolve to enjoy the exercise all the
same. To enjoyable, crowded National Gallery Concert: Myra Hess
(piano), Isabel Baillie (soprano): Bach programme.

Friday, May 1, 1942

Letter from home. Martin has had second inoculation against diphtheria, which seems not to have affected him. Mr. Shipway cremated
last Friday: Daddy rather upset by his death.
        I try to buy pair black shoes, and cannot get anything I like in
my size. Disgusted to find that my new expensive blue ones colour
my stockings when my feet get hot and perspire.

Saturday, May 2, 1942

Hair washed. Get 2 packets thin hairpins, at 4d. each (about $\frac{3}{4}$ $\frac{1}{4}$d.
a pin). Then buy pair black suède shoes, very comfortable, at 56/-
from the London Shoe Co. in Bond St. Have visited a dozen shops to
get what I want, i.e. plain black shoes, light-weight but flat with
wedge-heels, and well cut. These are American "Joyce" shoes.
        To Tina's at Great Missenden for weekend. Take veal and ham pie
from Selfridge's, at cost of 5/2½. New-born foal in field next to
house. Beautiful sunshine - which is pleasant, but the lack of rain
is becoming very serious.

Sunday, May 3, 1942

Bask in sun, go walk, and play chess with Mr. Dawkins. Enjoyable,
lazy day. Broadcast by Sir Stafford Cripps on his visit to India.

Monday, May 4, 1942

Fine and warm. On fire-duty at Broadcasting House. Before we
settle down to sleep in Concert Hall, we are taken tour of building;
on roof, 3 out of the six of us boggle at the idea of descending iron
vertical ladder on outside wall to next floor. Miss Mearing skips
up and down with no fear but much enjoyment. I feel imminent danger
of death from bomb or fire would be only sufficient inducement. In
other parts of building we are shown hooks where extra hose would be
hanging if they had not all gone to Alexandra Palace for some Fire
Contests. Will be back on Friday week. Meantime we are to hope there
willbe no raids, here at any rate. Last night Exeter was bombed
again

Tuesday, May 5, 1942

British have invaded Madagascar.   Sweets and chocolates to be
rationed: a move welcomed by most people, who at present get none.
        Here are extracts from talk on British Battle Schools, broadcast
on April 27 by Richard Sharp, which we are publishing this week.
When I began to read it, thought it must be about <u>German</u> training, and
must have been broadcast to emphasise brutality of Nazi system.   Was
nearly sick when I had to read proof: "We saw twenty men running slowly and heavily up a slope towards us.   They wore a kind of combination overall and battledress, black and shiny with water, streaked
with dull red, daubed with mud.   Some of their faces were purple
with extreme exertion, others white or yellow.   Round them, three or
four instructors pranced and skipped, gesticulating with short sticks,
and shouting hoarsely: 'Hurry, hurry, hurry.   On, on.   There are
Huns at the top of the hill.   Get at them.   Kill them, hurry.
They'll get you if you don't get them.   On, on"... This is what the
men had been through that morning.   First a lecture on hate, delivered in the Hate Room which was hung with photographs from occupied
Europe of starving people and sick people and dead people in ones and
in heaps.   The Commandant explained that you kill your enemy more
quickly and efficiently if you hate him, and it saves time if the men
go on the battlefield already hating.
        "After the lecture, the men, with rifles, bayonets and packs, had
run a sort of race.   First they'd lain on their backs and clawed
their way with bleeding hands under a nest of barbed wire ten yards
wide.   They had gone under and over low hurdles, throwing themselves
at them;   then through burning paraffin, wincing and screwing up their
eyes, but hurrying on;   then through deep water, under more barbed
wire with Bren-gun bullets cutting a crease in the grass just in front
of it.   And all the time there was an awful racket: instructors
yelling, themselves yelling, loudspeakers yelling: 'On, on; kill,
kill' ... Here and there in odd corners there were sandbags with bits
of meat on them.   An instructor would point excitedly to one of
these sandbags and say 'There's a German.   Kill him', and would
throw blood out of a tin over the soldier as he stabbed it".

Wednesday, May 6, 1942

We all forgather at Canuto's in Baker Street, for celebration of John's
passage through London on leave.   But we have telegram from Portsmouth, where he is held up till tomorrow.   The rest of us, including
Graham, Turnip and a man called Morgan Hewett, refresh ourselves and
have much pleasant talk.   Graham in good form: gives us all hints
for winning parliamentary election, ~~some~~ including: Go modestly to
the back of the platform at meetings, and have to be pulled forward
- this draws attention to you: stand about at a bus terminus or in
some other spot where citizens are coming and going all the time, and
let yourself be seen: when asked a very long and difficult question
at an election meeting, invite the interrogator to repeat it so that
you may get it quite clear - he will then be heartily sick of the
business before even the answer is begun.

- 356 -

Thursday, May 7, 1942

Madagascar has fallen. John arrives, looking inches taller and broader. We go to dancing class and tumble around in great heat but with considerable enjoyment.

Friday, May 8, 1942

Americans have sunk 8 Japanese warships. Colder. Lunch with Joyce who is still seeking suitable job. I buy salad stuff for Hilary at Shearn's: lettuces 1/- each, bundle radishes 8d., asparagus 2/-, 2 cooked beetroots 1/-. Enquire price of peaches and find they are 7/6 each! Arrive at bungalow about 7 o'clock.

Saturday, May 9, 1942

A great naval battle - "greatest since Jutland", News-Chronicle calls it, has been taking place north of Australia, between Japanese and Allied forces. At present there seems a lull, and the only news we have is that our losses are not as great as the enemy's, nor as great as the enemy has been proclaiming.

Martin can stagger a few steps alone. He takes them with beaming smile and much care, holding his arms out in front, ready to take the hands of the person he is approaching. If one takes his hand he can walk all round the garden looking at the flowers, and this he enjoys very much.

Sunday, May 10, 1942

Prime Minister broadcasts at 9 p.m. Reviews war situation since he took office 2 years ago today. Warns Germany that if she uses poison gas against Russia, we shall use it in bombing attacks against her, and implies that we must be ready to meet attacks by gas here.

The drought has at last broken and there is rain this evening. Hope it will rain all night.

Monday, May 11, 1942

Beautiful rain all last night: every green thing looks refreshed. Call for shoes, which are having spirit applied so that colour shall not stain my stockings.

Three British destroyers sunk in Mediterranean. Hear recording of P.M.'s broadcast of last night, taken at quicker speed than he spoke, so that pitch of his voice is raised. This destroys all oratory in his speech and makes him sound a ranting cad.

Tuesday, May 12, 1942

At printers, Mr. James tells us there have been very heavy air raids on Isle of Wight. Three families of his relations are homeless and two or three of the family have been killed. Weather colder.

Wednesday, May 13, 1942

More beautiful rain. National Gallery concert - Bach. Brandenburg
No.3 and suite in B minor for flute and strings. Very enjoyable.
Also a Church Cantata, not enjoyable, singer poor.

Thursday, May 14, 1942

Russians retreating at Kirch, advancing elsewhere. Hear recording of
broadcast discussion on India. There are 5 being given, with Indians
taking part, and they are the best thing broadcast for some time.
But the authorities are terrified about the subject - did not want us
to publish - asked whether we have any circulation in India. Have
impressed on us the need to follow the script exactly. I therefore
check our MS. with recording and find it is totally inaccurate.
    Buy pair suspenders - very difficult to get. Most shops tell
you they have no suspenders and no elastic, and when you enquire How
are we to keep our stockings up? reply that they are sure they don't
know. Cannot get saucepan scrubber: am told such a thing is of the
past. So we must have dirty saucepans and sloughing stockings.
    Dancing, at which I am too tired and therefore very bad.

Friday, May 15, 1942

To Hilary's, bearing 1 lb. cotton wool which she needs for washing
the infant's ears, nose, eyes, etc. Pay 3/6 for it. Could have got
an inferior unbleached brand cheaper, but thought his poor little face
would get scratched. Everything grown mightily round the bungalow
since the rain.

Saturday, May 16, 1942

Germans have taken Kirch; Russians about (one hopes) to take Kharkov.
One of them willcut the other off and we all hope the Russians will
cut off the Germans, not the other way about.
    Buttercup field next to Hilary's so bright one can hardly look
at it. Take baby on almost impassable track for pram, through wood,
where nearly upset him, but fortunately he is strapped in. He walks
alone and unbidden for first time and is very elated with his success.

Sunday, May 17, 1942

Leonard cycles with me to bus-stop, returning with two bicycles.
Tramp elects to stay behind with me, and I am afraid he will follow
the bus all the way to London. Ringup whenI get in, and find Leonard
has gone back and collected him: he was running about on the crossing
in a distracted way, surrounded by a crowd of sympathisers. He is
very like Hilary in the way he elicits friendly sympathy from all.

Monday, May 18, 1942

My watch refuses to go and a watchmaker tells me nothing can be
done to improve it.   I therefore go out to buy new one.   Selfridges
have one ladies' watch only, at £29.   Another shop has three, at
£14 each, but so vulgar-looking, with gold knobs on them, that I refuse.   At last I get a nice-looking one of £9.9.0. at a rather shady
little shop on the wrong side of OxfordStreet, which undertakes also
to repair my old one at a cost of 25/-.   Take shoes to be mended and
am told I cannot have them back for a month.

Tuesday, May 19, 1942

Graham to supper.   We all go to rather bad film, "Ball of Fire".
He asks me to cottage in Wales the weekend after next, but I am already engaged.   The new Archbishop of Canterbury, Dr. Temple, con-
demns as unchristian certain newspaper reports of our bombing of
Rostok which glory in destruction of ancient monuments and take delight in thought of suffering of civilians.   Says it is task of the
churches to maintain a Christian spirit through difficulties of war.

Wednesday, May 20, 1942

Spend very long time trying vainly to buy Martin open sandals: there
are none now being made, though we are told leather for uppers is
scarce and one might have thought a shoe with nothing but a couple of
straps above the sole was economical.

Thursday, May 21, 1942

As a result of having lost my temper with the Editor on quite an
matter, am filled with sufficient spirit to be able to tell him
that I would like to be moved, since there is too little work for
The Corporation is trying to cut down staff, but they want to cut
Ackerley, who does not particularly want to go, and as I do want
feel I might as well say so.   Editor very taken aback, and says
must think about it.

Friday, May 22, 1942

To Hilary's with crashing headache, owing to physical condition,
thunder in the air, and nervous reaction after losing my temper
terday.   Take her beautiful cos lettuce which costs 1/9.

Saturday, May 23, 1942

Headache most of day.   Take baby for walk, and let him and dog pull
hand or mouth fulls of straw out of haystack, both with much joy.
Mexica said to be about to declare war on Germany.

Sunday, May 24, 1942

Hailstorms (which excite Martin to great admiration) and sunshine.

Broadcast service for coming of Holy Spirit to Europe, in which
a Czech, Dutch, Norwegian, French and Englishman take part. Noble
speech later in evening by Duff Cooper, on occasion of Empire Day,
to which we cannot bear to listen.

Monday, May 25, 1942

At work, though it is a Bank Holiday.   But there are few crowds about.
I have following advertisement today in the Times personal column:-

> Woman (35), 10 years' experience sub-editor literary weekly,
> finds decrease in interest owing to paper restrictions and
> wishes change.

Sorry it went in today, when most people will be on holiday.   Don't
suppose I shall get any, or much, response, and it cost 31/- to put
in.   I have long talk to Editor during which he assures me it would
be a catastrophe if I departed, and asks me not to, at any rate for
the present.

Tuesday, May 26, 1942

Late at printers, because though we worked yesterday, they didn't;
so we get the worst of both worlds.   Tired.

Wednesday, May 27, 1942

Rommel on the move again in Libya.   I get shoes for Martin, which I
think are wide enough without being too long, but they cost 14/9 (and
1 coupon).   Nice soft leather.
        Dancing this evening instead of tomorrow.   I am very bad as
usual.

Thursday, May 28, 1942

Dreamt last night someone sent me six Canary bananas.   Not at all
pleased with Tina when she woke me up out of this pleasant fantasy.
Very bored all day with lack of work, and very tired as a result.
Ring up Times and find there has not been a single reply to my advertisement.

Friday, May 29, 1942

To Newell's at Potter's Bar, for weekend.   Surprised to find that
her older boy is 7½.   How old we are all getting.   I see queue at
station and, having a little time to spare, join it, to get a few
sweets for the children.   Then stroll to booking-office, where find
I am not at King's Cross as I supposed, but at St. Pancras.   Stop
strolling and begin to scuttle, and get train in time, struggling
between crowds of soldiers and airmen who are looking, in a bewildered way, for the platform they want.

Saturday, May 30, 1942

Am figure of great interest to Newell's two boys: the 3-year-old dashes into my room before breakfast, and when I say "Hello", dashes out again and reports triumphantly "She said Hello!" Both come and hold me up with guns. Their games are very warlike, and they rush around garden wearing tin hats and going "Bang, bang". Pleasant walk in what is part of London's "Green Belt".

Sunday, May 31, 1942

Biggest raid in history was last night carried out by R.A.F. over Cologne. Over 1,000 planes took part. Can't feel any jubilation over this horrible destruction. In evening go with Newell to Church of King Charles the Martyr at South Minns. Pleasant new building. Feel I am Roundhead and wonder if I ought therefore to abstain from attending.

Monday, June 1, 1942

Try to get fountain-pen for Daddy for his birthday last April. Waterman's were expecting deliveries at beginning of this month; but they had only one dozen in this morning, and of course by lunchtime they are all gone.

Tuesday, June 2, 1942

My 35th birthday: a grim thought. Have money contributions for my watch, a toothbrush from Martin. R.A.F. has made another 1,000-strong raid on Germany, chiefly on Essen. 35 of our planes lost. Very warm day. In evening we sit on my balcony listening to wireless.

Wednesday, June 3, 1942

To National Gallery concert: Mozart Trio and Piano Quartet, very pleasant. Band playing in Trafalgar Square and crowds of people listening in the sunshine; not at all as if we were at war. Meet Arnold for tea.

Thursday, June 4, 1942

Successful lunch-hour shopping in great heat produces slab chocolate from de Brys for Mother, and fountain-pen, 10/5, cheap-looking but one hopes it will write, for Daddy. Browse with 5/- gift-token in Boots, but cannot see anything to buy. Sit in park darning stockings in evening. Arnold for night: discusses the Forward March with Tina.
          Heydrich, head of Gestapo in occupied countries, dies of wounds received from assassin in Czechoslovakia lately. Hear one fat comfortable-looking matron impart this news to another in an A.B.C. café where I am buying cake. "Pity, isn't it", she says. "Why?" asks the other. "He ought to have been made to suffer more than that", she remarks, without malice.
          Have "airgraph" letter from Roy, the first I have seen. It

is a photograph, quarter size, of his original onesheet. The films
only, which are very small, are brought to England, which of course
saves a great deal of transport space. The charge for civilians is
8d. and for services less.

Friday, June 5, 1942

To Stroud at midday in immense heat. Very sorry for the soldiers
and airmen in battle-dress who are not allowed to remove their tunics
and look as if they will burst. Mother meets me. I spend the evening squirting greenfly on the roses. Daddy has had a success fou as
St. John the Divine in a performance at the chapel: dissuaded by
mother from either shaving off his moustache, wearing a white beard or
standing his hair on end to make himself look wild and prophetic. He
merely removed his spectacles, which gave him a myopic look of vision.
Obviously enjoyed himself hugely.

Saturday, June 6, 1942

Appallingly hot day ends in severe thunderstorm which reduces the
temperature. Arrange flowers for Mother at the chapel. Wonder what
I should do if suddenly granted a heavenly vision in the building.
Decide I shouldn't like it, and suppose that most people would rather
heavenly visitants left them alone, though Mother always longs to see
an angel.

Sunday, June 7, 1942

Return to London. Not so hot. Find Bob has written for me 12-page
treatise on Worship, because I said I knew nothing about the subject
and could not read a book on it by Evelyn Underhill which he lent me.
It has learned annotations. There has been a big explosion in London,
near the Elephant and Castle.
Monday, June 8, 1942

Miss Scott Johnston, who gets photographs for Listener, goes off
suddenly on leave because her husband has come home on leave from the
Middle East. Following my late conversations with the Editor, I am
detailed to do her work, about which I know very little. However, am
able with small difficulty to write captions for the "News-Reel" page.
Explosion at Elephant and Castle officially said to be unexploded bomb
which has now gone off heartily and wrecked a block of flats.

Tuesday, June 9, 1942

Germans making a great effort to take Sevastopol, but so far the
Russians have successfully kept them off. Very busy day at printers.

Wednesday, June 10, 1942

Send off birthday letter to Mother, but no present with it: have
failed to get her an ordinary comb, which she wants, or an enamel
colander - the only one I can see is of metal like the one she now
has which has gone rusty, but about 5 times as big: must have been
intended for an army kitchen.

Very busy day running around looking for pictures, which I enjoy.
Visit the Chinese Embassy, which has a waiting room with leather
chairs à la Anglais, and Chinese prints on the walls.

Thursday, June 11, 1942

Am doubly busy, because Miss Playle does not turn up, but instead
comes a telegram at mid-morning from Dumfries in Scotland, saying she
is unable to come today but willbe in tomorrow. Speculation is rife:
the general feeling is that in seeing off her nephew, who had a few
days' leave, she got carried away by accident.

Treaty announced between Russia, England and America, to last 20
years: each promises not to make a separate peace with Germany.

Friday, June 12, 1942

It was as we thought: Miss P. got carried away in the train by
accident. She left King's Cross at 9.15 p.m. and when she arrived
at Dumfries at 4 a.m., she was told the train had already stopped at
Rugby and Carlisle. Can only suppose she dined so well her sleep
was exceedingly heavy.

Saturday, June 13, 1942

To Hilary's at midday. Baby walking quite well now. Leonard goes
to hospital at Hertford to give pint of his blood for store. The
Americans report small Japanese landing on the Aleutian Islands off
Alaska.

Sunday, June 14, 1942

"United Nations" Day, which means as far as I am concerned that there
are a few Union Jacks hung from some houses. Return to town, where
John Catlow is up for day's leave from Portsmouth.

Monday, June 15, 1942

Four people away from office, so I cannot complain of no work.
Hardly know whether I am on my head or my heels. However, manage to
get through, but am very very tired.

Tuesday, June 16, 1942

At printers. Mr. Abraham, whose wife has gone to the Isle of Wight
to see her mother, is gloomy. Tells me crossly that the Editor is
bone-idle. Things not going too well for us in Libya.

Wednesday, June 17, 1942

Lunch with Holy Aunt.   Buy (because I see them and think it wise
to purchase while it is possible) small jar cream and small box of
powder, together costing over 11/-.   Dancing class in evening.
A Captain, R.N., about 45, who has a D.S.O. for bringing half a ship
back safely from Norway, and who we think is after Joan, comes too.
But he is too good for the rest of us and I do not think will come
again.   I am quite hopeless and never learn.   To B.B.C. to sleep
in Concert Hall - fire watching.

Thursday, June 18, 1942

Slept fairly well in stuffy Concert Hall, though it gave me headache.
Our troops have evacuated Sidi Resegh and El Adem.   Tobruk is
practically surrounded and the outlook is gloomy.
        Lovely broadcast in evening of Mozart's Nachtmusik and Dvorak's
New World Symphony.

Friday, June 19, 1942

To H's, with 2 lb. tripe, great treasure, and 3 salted bloaters.
She has got some liver (which is unrationed) so we feel we are lucky.

Saturday, June 20, 1942

It is announced that Churchill is in Washington for talks with
Roosevelt.
        Leonard barely avoids breaking his neck by pitching head-first
off his bicycle into a 6-foot ditch.   He is completely "winded" and
makes such noises that H. is terrified.   Martin very active and
charming.   I pick 8 lb. gooseberries for bottling from H's two small
bushes.

Sunday, June 21, 1942

Tobruk captured by Germans after 1 fierce attack.   We are now back
on Egyptian frontier.
        Very warm.   When I get back to London find 2 little tins of
tongue from S. Africa - my birthday present.   John Catlow to supper.
He has just been given a ship and has a few hours' embarkation leave.
        Letter from Peter Scott (Pilot-Officer in R.A.F.) who says it
all seems a dream, sleeping by day, having meals at wrong times, and
no Sundays free.   But he likes it.   Says "I always enjoy it, to
start off with it raining and dreary and suddenly to burst through
to a new sunny world of our own.   I always go high so we have to
use oxygen to keep us bright".

Monday, June 22, 1942

Miss Scott-Johnston back to do her own "News-Reel".   Cannot help

feeling relieved, since the news is poor: Germans reacing Egyptian
frontier, penetrating tne Sevastopol defences, etc.
    Warm summer weathe r.

Tuesday, June 23, 1942

Churchill and Roosevelt reported to be "in complete agreement", but
no details of their findings.

Wednesday, June 24, 1942

O alas, after today the evenings will get shorter.   Find paper
patterns are hard to get, but have ordered one for coat and leggings
for Martin.   H. intends to cut up an old green hockey tunic of very
good serge, for the material.   Have decided to give up dancing-class
which tires me dreadfully, and instead stay at home and write long
reply to Bob's paper on Worship which he composed on my behalf.   This
tires me very much too!

Thursday, June 25, 1942

Invasion of Egypt has begun, and Germans are advancing into the
country.   Miss Scott-Johnston's husband, just back from Cairo, is
very depressed about the situation: says we have no general as good
as Rommel, that the people in Cairo have been lotus-eating, and that
there is general inefficiency.   For instance, the job of looking
after the soldiers' mail for the desert was put into the hands of a
Wing-Commander's wife who had no idea how to do the job - merely so
that she should be occupied and not have to be evacuated to Cape Twon
with the junior officers' wives.   The result was that he walked into
her office one day.   "What do you want?" she said.   "To see if
there are any letters for me", he replied.   "Nothing for you at all",
she said very indignantly.   "How can you possibly know that?" he
asked.   "You don't even know my name".   He then went through the
mail himself, while she fumed and raged, and found 10 letters and 2
parcels addressed to him.

Friday, June 26, 1942

Another 1,000-plane raid on Germany.
To Hilary's, taking 1 lb. cherries (1/6, controlled price) and 3
haddock: also the 2 tins of tongue Roy sent me.

Saturday, June 27, 1942

Mr. Churchill back from his trip to America.
Give Hilary my old watch for her birthday, and my new one immediately
stops.   L. works on it with pin and needle unavailingly.   H. just
whizzes round the hands, probably dislodges piece of dust, and it goes
again.

Sunday, June 28, 1942

Our forces have met Axis forces in Egypt and big battle is raging.
Sir Cecil Graves' (D.G.of B.B.C.) son, aged 19, has D.F.C. for his
work as fighter pilot in Malta.
Long wait for Green Line bus back to London which has any room in it.

Monday, June 29, 1942

Axis doing well in Egypt.   We have evacuated Mersa Matruh.   Germans
also advancing in Russia.   And May sinkings in Atlantic by U-boats,
etc., said to be world record, and June's expected to be worse.
Hot, fine day.   Am reading some dialogues by Erasmus which are very
entertaining.

Tuesday, June 30, 1942

To Promenade Concert with Tina: Albert Hall, where sound is not as
good as in old Queen's Hall, and I do not like it as much.   Ida
Haendel in Elgar 'sViolin Concerto; Beethoven's 8th Symphony.   We
walk home across park in very hot evening with thunder rolling above
us.   Arrive on doorstep just as heavy storm breaks.

Wednesday, July 1, 1942

See in "Times" that nice George Mathieson, who came with us on our
ski-ing holiday just before the war, is missing.   He was in the Royal
Artillery.   His parents are asking if anyone has any information.
Buy pair sandals which hope will be big enough for Martin, whose feet
have gron so much since he started to walk that he will soon be unable
to wear the little shoes I got him.   These have not open toes, and
even this sort, the shopkeeper says, will soon go off the market because they are made by women who have been called up for war work!
House of Commons debating Libya, while Germans advance further into
Egypt.

Thursday, July 2, 1942

Germans calim fall of Sevastopol.   Censure motion on Government defeated by very large majority.

Friday, July 3, 1942

To Hilary's, with 2 lb. cherries, and paper pattern for coat and leggings for Martin.   Very slack again at office.

Saturday, July 4, 1942

Bath and bed Martin unaided while his parents try to go to cinema but
return - very surprised to find him sound asleep.   He is very good
and I know all his familiary songs to sing him off with.

Sunday, July 5, 1942
In London find letter from Roy posted May 3, so the airgraph beat the

ordinary mail by about 5 weeks.

Monday , July 6, 1942

News continues unaltered. We are holding the Germans at El Alamein
in Egypt, and they are advancing in Russia.

Tuesday, July 7, 1942

Letter from Peter Scott, asking me to have supper with him this evening at 6.30, on his way through London on leave, reaches me when I get
home at 6.45, so I do not see him.

Wednesday, July 8, 1942

Very tired and dispirited. So idle, with so much to be done: feel
there is no place for me anywhere.

Thursday, July 9, 1942

Visit Retta Acklam, who is in St. Mary's Hospital, Paddington, in preparation for operation tomorrow which she hopes will make it possible
for her to have a baby. She is nearly 39 and has been married nine
years or so. Hilary's 30th birthday.

Friday, July 10, 1942

.To Hilary's in rain, which continued all last night and refreshed the
countryside considerably. News placards say that Von Boch has taken
50 miles of railway in Russia.

Saturday, July 11, 1942

British have made small advance of about 5 miles in one sector in
Egypt and are so far holding it. Germans still advancing in Russia.

Sunday, July 12, 1942

Leonard called to Home Guard emergency action stations at 8.15 a.m.
Goes off in great hurry breakfast-less, and returns at 11 a.m., very
disgusted with the other men who rose at their leisure, breakfasted,
and turned up with half their kit.
    Mother and Daddy, on last of the petrol, arrive for 2 nights,
and we all go round gardens of Lord Crofts' house with the baby, who
is entranced with the car.

Monday, July 13, 1942

Take sandals for small repair, and find they will take a month, which
is very inconvenient in middle of summer. Reading "Cloister and the
Hearth", and find with much interest that Charles Reade has made full
use of Erasmus's Colloquies for his material, even to quoting whole

phrases for instance in his description of German inns.

Tuesday, July 14, 1942

After strenuous press day, when sudden French talk by General de
Gaulle is included, and there is not one printer who knows French
(so that every time one corrects something in a line and the line
is re-set, two more mistakes occur), I go to ballet at the New
Theatre, with Tina.   "Gods go Begging", "Hamlet", and "Facade":
"Hamlet" is very good - a new ballet by, and with, Robert Helpmann.
Come home to find John Catlow, called back from his ship which is a
minesweeper, for an interview at the Admiralty.

Wednesday, July 15, 1942

Tina and I to Promenade Concert: Handel and Bach, with Chopin's 2nd
Piano Concerto, played by Michal Hambourgh, thrown in as a make-
weight.   Walk home across park.   Observe that the Albert Memorial
has had a chip or two taken out of some of its many decorations by
air-raids.

Thursday, July 16, 1942

Retta's specialist very pleased with her progress, and says there is
now nothing to prevent her having a baby, and that if she is going to
have one it will be in the next six months.
       Am having an argument on paper with Bob, on the subject of wor-
ship.   Find it necessary to write down my faith, and find myself
being very shocking.

Friday, July 17, 1942

Wet and chilly.   In afternoon an air-raid siren, a very unusual
sound nowadays; and just as I take my departure to catch bus for
Ware, the "planes overhead" signal is given.   However, I see and
hear nothing untoward, and am more perturbed by the pouring rain than
by anything else.

Saturday, July 18, 1942

Very wet day, during which chief interest is that Martin get's his
head somehow stuck in his little wheel-chair and it has to be prised
apart before he can be extricated, screaming with fright.   Meantime
one of our statesmen tells us we are in a more serious position than
at any time since the Battle of Britain and that the next 80 days are
of vital importance.

Sunday, July 19, 1942

Weather clears; back to London in sunshine

Monday, July 20, 1942

Buy 16 oz. wool to make Martin a winter suit.   For this have to
give 8 coupons (total for the year is 60), but H. contributes 5 of
them.   In evening to Promenade Concert - Brahms 4th Symphony,
Variations on a theme of Haydn, and 1st Piano Concerto.   Mozart's
Overture to Magic Flute and Jupiter Symphony.   Albert Hallis packed,
and indeed Brahms does seem suited to the present state of the world.
Three promenaders faint and have to be attended to by nurses, and
one old man is so infuriated because his neighbour lights a match to
smoke a large cigar during one of the items, that three or four times
he leans forward and deliberately blows the match out.

Tuesday, July 21, 1942

Am much struck by the praise of Russia now being broadcast and
printed on every hand, in contrast to the silence or the bitter
criticism which was fashionable before we began to rely on her to
beat the Germans for us.

Wednesday, July 22, 1942

We all have a binge: dinner at Chez Fillier (food order says no meal
now to cost more than 5/-, but there is a "house charge" of 6d. and
wines are extra - my bill actually came to 5/9 which is moderate:
for this I had minestrone soup, fish and fried potatoes, and something called erroneously "banana trifle".   I now remember that my
sherry was paid for by Graham.)   Then we went to the revived film
of Charlie Chaplin in "The Gold Rush".   He himself does a commentary.
I had not seen the original and enjoyed it very much.   Graham has
promised at my request to ask a question in Parliament on the non-
arrival in Egypt of the men's mail.   We have heard from Raymond at
Alexandria, and he is obviously not getting all his letters.

Thursday, July 23, 1942

Germans advancing ominously in Russia.   John Beavan conveys joyful
news thatGeorge Mathieson is reported safe but prisoner in hands of
Friday, July24, 1942   Italians - taken in Libya.

To first half of Promenade Concert: Beethoven's Egmont Overture,
Violin Concerto, and 5th Symphony.   Emerge at half-time and hand
over seats to Mr. and Mr. Abraham, who are going to hear the newAlan
Bush Symphony in the second half.
        John Catlow has arrived in London from his minesweeper to
take a special course in Japanese at the School of Oriental Studies -
the course to take a year.   He has been at sea only one day, because
his boat had to put in to Middlesbrough for repairs.

Saturday, July 25, 1942

Remain in London for weekend in order to attend with Tina conference

of Forward March delegates.   This movement, founded by Sir Richard
Acland, is tomorrow going to amagamate with J.B.Priestley's 1941
Committee and 9-Point Group.   I have no official business among
these earnest people, for the meeting is private.   About 200 delegates from allover the country.   The sight of so many worthy creatures all sure they have the panacea for the world's ills, fills me
with gloom and despair.   While they talk and talk I knit sock for
Martin, and wonder if they are really constructing a new world while
I construct a bit of footwear.   "Must we really discuss these tiny
points?" asked Sir Richard patiently at one point.   "In a minute we
have got to decide what is our attitude to Winston Churchill".
When this weighty matter was being talked out, he suddenly addressed
an old man who had come in by the door at the back of the hall, and,
calling him Sir Ruthven Murgatroyd, or some other such Gilbert-and-
Sullivan name, requested him to leave the hall meeting forthwith, as
it was private.

I have high tea next to a little elderly man from Southampton,
to whom I confide that I am not really a member.   He asks me if I
haven't now made the Decision, and I feel I am at a revival meeting.
On going home; or rather while I wait for Tina, I behold a blind man
shuffling very slowly out of the building, and decide someone ought
to help him on his Forward March.   Discover he is a Unitarian Minister
from Birkenhead and has to get to the Eccleston Hotel at Victoria
although he has noidea of the route.   So I escort him thither, but it
is almost a case of the blind leading the blind, for in my usual way
I do not go by any means by the shortest route.   However, I deliver
him up to a lady with a bunch of keys, and wonder how on earth he can
undress in a strange room where he doesn't know the position of anything or how to get to the bathroom.   However, feel I cannot offer
to put him to bed, so bid him farewell.

Sunday, July 26, 1942

The Forward March and the 1941 Committee have a joint conference to-
day which begins at the iniquitous hour of 10 a.m. at the Caxton Hall.
On the platform are Acland, Preistley, Vernon Bartlett, M.P., Tom
Wintringham, Professor Macmurray, and other notabilities.   This day's
doings are to continue till 5.30, but I leave at 12.15, unable to bear
any more talk.   The new movement is to be called Common Wealth, because its basic principle is common ownership of resources.   Vernon
Bartlett makes an alarming speech which seems to indicate that he
thinks we are losing the war very rapidly.   Priestley becomes
emotional about the resistance of the common people in 1940 (the novelist and playwright coming out).   We are to go out to our fellows and
preach hope and faith.   Everyone applauds.   I feel more and more depressed.   The only concrete proposal made is that, when people find
that war production is being held up because private firms don't want
some invention, or some speed in production, to affect their after-
war profits, then the Common Wealth will take up the matter, even to
running a libel case and going to a court of law.   I foresee many
difficulties while we are so ruled by those with money, but this idea
is right.

In evening to service with Bob at All Saint/s, Margaret St.

Monday, July 27, 1942

This morning two air-raid alarms in quick succession at about 6 o'clock, but no sound of guns or bombs.

Tuesday, July 28, 1942

Last night, about 3, when the moon was very bright, there was great noise from guns in Hyde Park, and when they had stopped firing, an air-raid warning. Later guns started again and I could see bursts of fire inthe sky from where I lay in bed. Nevertheless, went to sleep and did not hear All Clear. Today's papers say that new secret guns were fired (they certainly made a strange noise; but that the main attack of the night was on Birmingham.
Russians evacuate Rostov.

Wednesday, July 29, 1942

To Promenade Concert with Bob: Bach mostly, including 3rd Brandenburg and 1st Suite. After interval, Falla's "Nights in a Garden of Spain" and Mendelssohn's Scottish Symophony (during which man on our right conducts imaginary orchestra and appears to play all instruments himself in turn, but with left hand).

Thursday, July 30, 1942

Last night a good deal of gunfire and 2 Alerts, but no bombs. Planes appear to be using London as pathway, inspite of great todo in papers about our wonderful new defence guns. Mother says in letter that there have been bombs at Cheltenham and Cirencester.
Sweets are now rationed (½ lb. per person per month) and result is that shops actually have sweets and chocolates in the windows, though until now I have not so much as seen a sweet for months.

Friday, July 31, 1942

A year ago today since I had gland taken out of my neck. Am certainly much better in health than I was then.
More gunfire last night: I see from my bed a firework display in the night sky. To Hilary's for weekend.

Saturday, August 1, 1942

Leonard off to Home Guard camp in broiling weather. Inhabitants of Wareside very scornful because they have to take clean pair of socks for 3 days. "Might as well take a clean shirt for 3 days" they say.

Sunday, August 2, 1942

Rain. Small girl, aged 6 or 7, from Mrs. Parrish's, for afternoon. She screams and shouts and is rough, and frightens Martin who afterwards will not go to sleep. Her stepfather has almost cut off his hand with circular saw which he is using, so we feel it is akindness

to have the child for a few hours. He has already been invalided
out of the army with an injury to the other arm.

Monday, August 3, 1942

Air raid warning, Hilary says, last night, though I hear nothing.
Return to London at midday (it is Bank Holiday) and have to work this
afternoon.

Tuesday, August 4 1942

To press late, 8 p.m. Very tired. Graham comes in, in evening,
and tells us of the case of Dr. Curtis which he has raised in speech
in house: a British subject, who at one time, through being born in
Germany, had also German citizenship. He came to this country with
his wife, a German jewess, when the persecution of the Jews began,
and has since held very high posts in the Ministry of Supply. Is
now given a fortnight's notice because, apparently, his credentials
have been questioned. As G. points out, either the man was never
fit to do this very confidential work and ought never to have been
appointed, or else he was fit, in which case he should not now be
summarily dismissed.

Wednesday, August 5, 1942

London crowded with holiday-makers - probably people up from suburbs
for the day because they are having "holidays at home" - which Hilary
says, after having her husband at home for a week, is no holiday at
all as far as the ordinary woman is concerned, but extra work.
        A great to-do in the newspapers because, it is said, we have
raided Congress headquarters in India and found papers showing that
Gandhi proposes to make terms with the Japanese and is determined to
drive British out of India. Feel (1) we had no business to raid
their private papers; (2) the facts as presented to us are probably
misrepresented. The general intention of the press is obviously
that we, and especially America, shall now believe Gandhi to be a
villain.
        To Bach Prom. with Miss Mearing. Double Violin Concerto and 2
Brandenburgs: very good.

Thursday, August 6, 1942

Glad to have letter from home saying Phyllida has arrived safely by
bicycle from Sussex, especially as Miss Street Porter told me the
other day that a young woman of her acquaintance was murdered by a
soldier who pursued her over a lonely Yorkshire moor after she had
been saying goodbye to her husband at a railway station.

Friday, August 7, 1942

Germans advancing at appalling rate in Russia. To Hilary's for
weekend. Try to get her earthenware pitcher to replace one she has

broken, but cannot get one.   Lewis's china department contains almost nothing: no pretty cups and saucers as usual, no dinner services.   Try also for side-combs for her, but without success. Only tortoiseshell (real) at 7/6 or 10/6 each comb.

Sunday
Saturday, August 6, 1942

Gandhi, and the Congress leaders in India, have been arrested.   I return to London.   In evening Bob reads T.S. Eliot to Joan and me: "East Coker", "Burnt Norton" and "The Dry Salvages".   Have read them before and been very impressed with them.

Saturday, August 8, 1942

Congress in India has demanded withdrawal of British.   Americans are attacking Japanese in Aleutian and Solomon Islands.   Hilary and Leonard go to cinema and I bath Martin and put him to bed.   He is very good.   End of double summer time.

Monday, August 10, 1942

To Promenade Concert with John Catlow: Schubert and Mozart (17th Piano Concerto, with Myra Hess).   Very fine performance of Schubert's C major Symphony conducted by Sir Adrian Boult in second half.   Hall very crowded.

Tuesday, August 10, 1942

Sweets ration to be increased to 3 oz per week instead of 2.   Notice this morning how very few private cars there are on roads even of London, since petrol ration except for business ceased at end of July.

Wednesday, August 12, 1942

Busy, because Miss Flayle is on holiday: which I enjoy.   In evening to "The Merry Wives of Windsor" with John Beavan.   Most enjoyable. We haven't seen each other for some time, and consequently are very friendly.   The evenings darker because of clocks going back. Theatre begins at 6.45, but afterwards we have meal and a walk across Trafalgar Square in the dark.   It appears to have an emergency water tank on it, and several soldiers courting on seats.   We avoid these obstacles with difficulty.

Thursday, August 13, 1942

Buy 3 dish-mops for Mother, who complains she cannot get one in Stroud. To Beavans after dinner.   Edgar Fuchs is there: and his cousin Elaine and her husband.   Haydn Quartet, with John playing cello, followed by difficult Dvorak which they cannot play.   We then have game of Scramble and leave about 11 in pitch darkness.

Friday, August 14, 1942

Home to Stroud for week's holiday.   Great Aunt Tuttie is staying, at
end of fortnight's holiday: 85 and eats and sleeps marvellously.   Her
memory not too good.   Mother already has one dish-mop, which Phyllis
managed to get at Smith and Lee's.   When she put it in her basket with
and end sticking out, the shopkeeper implored her to push it down to the
bottom, or he would be besieged by women clamouring for mops.
          Germans advancing into oil district of Caucasus.

Sa
Saturday, August 15, 1942

Rain nearly all day.   Letter from Roy.

Sunday, August 16, 1942

Fine and warm.   Aunt T. very anxious that we should all go to chapel.
She does not approve of my knitting on Sunday.   Daddy delights her
by turning up pages of his father's diary.   Although she cannot remember things that happened last week, she remembers clearly a visit to
Cheveril 70 years ago which Grandpa mentions.   She recalls that the
baker was at the door when she arrived, and she called out to tell her
cousins.   "A gallon", they said.   "No, the baker", said Tuttie, and
was surprised to learn that the gallon was a measurement of bread in
Wiltshire then, as the quartern is now.

Monday, August 17, 1942

Fine again.   Get food card transferred to Stroud for week, and collect
rations, except meat.   Butchers' shops are not open on Mondays.
Daddy gets his dinner in Stroud so that the rest of us may be able to
eke out the remains of the joint.   We hear distant gunfire in morning
and hear planes going by very high up.   Our fighters get active and we
wonder if there is trouble at Bristol.
          Russians have evacuated more towns in oil-bearing Caucasian regions.
They blew up oil wells before they left them.   It is announced that
the P.M. has been in Moscow consulting with Stalin about, together with
representatives of British and American forces.
          Aunt T. returns unwillingly to Brimscombe.

Tuesday, August 18, 1942

Walk on common in beautiful sunshine and take Mother to tea at the Bear.
Bread and butter, lettuce, cake and tea: 2/- each.   In pleasant
lounge.   Then P. and I to film of Kipling's "Jungle Book".   Not very
Kipling and probably not very jungle, but some fine shots of animals.
          P.M. has visited Cairo as well as Moscow.

Wednesday, August 19, 1942

Combined operations headquarters has announced that a raid is in progress on the region of France round Dieppe.   Its results are not yet
known.   The French people are warned in broadcasts that this is not

the invasion of the Continent yet, and they must not jeopardise
their safety by committing any anti-German acts at present.

Day is disappointingly wet. We all have lunch at West's. P.
and I to tea at Enderley, where Harold Humphries is staying: he was
called from his monastic vows to work in war factory and appears to be
in very nervy condition (for last 5 years has been suffering from
nervous breakdown). His sister is now sub-prioress of her community.

Thursday, August 20, 1942

Details of yesterday's raid on Dieppe: we lost 95 planes and the
Germans 80-odd for certain and about 100 more badly damaged. Heavy
casualties on both sides. We blew up gun-batter and munitions dump.

To baseball match between two teams of American soldiers, at Farm
Hill. It is like a glorified game of rounders, accompanied by shouts
catacalls, threats, etc. A great noise. No wonder they find cricket
dull.

Friday, August 21, 1942

Still more details about Dieppe raid. One of our landing parties
was surprised by German patrol and practically wiped out (these were
Canadians: there were also Americans, English and Free French in the
raid).

Germans advancing towards Russian Black Sea ports.

P. and I to film, "Blood and Sand": bull-fighting and amorous
interludes. If the public didn't care for adultery, what would films
be about?

Daddy is using at the shop paper with the names printed on it of
Madame Sawyer, hairdresser, who is further up George Street. This is
because Mr. Collins, the stationer, primed it, and when it was finished
the Govt. order about not wrapping things up was announced, and Sawyers
refused to pay for it. Mr. Collins was dying of cancer, and Daddy
bought it from him: so he daily breaks the law by wrapping up goods,
and at the same time advertises the hard-hearted Sawyers.

Saturday, August 22, 1942

Showery. Daddy and Mother to Weston; latter in deep gloom, in which
state she always sets out on a holiday. They get a taxi which takes
them to Bristol. This is strictly against the law, because of petrol
restrictions, but is much more convenient for them. Both very tired
and in need of rest. Hope they have good journey.

Brazil has declared war on Germany and Italy, which will mean
certain raw materials are made available to us.

P. and I visit Aunt Tuttie. Depressed by household.

Listen to finish of broadcast from Albert Hall of last Promenade
Concert of season. Terrific enthusiasm.

Sunday, August 23, 1942

Master from Marling School (music) preaches at morning service. Nice
and simple, but sometimes hard to hear because of (a) roaring of aeroplanes which inconsiderately do stunts over town during church-time;
(b) rumblings of Aunt Hermie's inside. Have not yet read Bob's
latest paper on Worship, in the controvery we are having, which he
gave me before I came away. Agree with Grandpa, who was very religious and whose diaries are full of references to the Almighty, but
who said to Mother once: "At the end of a long life and after giving
much thought to the subject, I have come to the conclusion that creeds
are of very little importance. What matters is that the mind should
be turned God-wards".
        Back to London with deep loathing. Bring 6 eggs for Martin,
which a farmer's wife brought in to shop.

Monday, August 24, 1942

Letter from Mother who says they had corner seats from Bristol; she
sounds quite cheerful, not at all as she looked on departure. P. to-
day has interview with the Land Army, which she wants to join.
        Work not so bad after all.
        Gather from gloomy conversation of Miss Playle that the Dieppe
raid met with more opposition than was expected. We lost a great
many men. But one can't make invasions without losses: anyway, Miss
P. always as gloomy and dramatic as possible.

Tuesday, August 25, 1942

At printers till 7 o'clock, partly because of late talk and pictures
included, and partly because we have 2 warnings of aircraft within a
radius of 10 miles. The works are in the middle of factories, many
of them making armaments, and they get a special warning, work stops
and the men stand at the entrance to shelters outside, ready to dive
in if necessary. The Editor went off in the middle of the day to a
luncheon of Canadian editors, at the Dorchester. He says the Canadian
eds. think the Dieppe raid was a great success, and say Lord Louis
Mountbatten who was in charge of the operation, was triumphant.
        Germand advancing on Stalingrad.

Wednesday, August 26, 1942

Duke of Kint killed yesterday in flying-boat which crashed in the north
of Scotland on its way to Iceland. In bus this morning a very French-
looking elderly man with a straw hat and a moustache with pointed end
said to his companion, "Did you ear the news? Duke of Kent a été tué"
She was suitably horrified.
        Have to go out to printers (on what proves to be a wild goose
chase and costs the Corporation 9/- in taxi-fare there). Meantime
Phyllida sends telegram asking me to meet her for lunch en route for
Hilary's, and I manage to do so. She found the house too dismal by
herself.

- 376 -

Thursday, August 27, 1942

Letter from Mother: they are enjoying themselves. The Congregational Chapel they attended last year is in ruins; so is the Baptist Chapel. They are being fed very well, chicken twice already, and meat three times a day. Very hot, and in evening John, Joan and I sit on my balcony till black-out time, John studying Japanese, Joan sewing, and I knitting winter woollies for Martin.

Friday, August 28, 1942

To Ware in very great heat, bearing for Hilary heavy earthenware pitcher I have brought from Stroud, because I couldn't get one in London, and she has broken hers. I also have 2 pork chops which were Miss P's meat ration and which she couldn't use; 4 smoked haddock, lard, margarine and sugar.

Saturday, August 29, 1942

Phyllida returns to Stroud. Another very hot day, which ends with a thunderstorm at night after we have transferred the sleeping Martin downstairs because the little upstairs room is so stuffy and hot. Russians doing a little better against the Germans; the Americans have recaptured most of the Solomon Islands from the Japanese.

Sunday, August 30, 1942

Cooler. Air raid warning while we sit in garden in afternoon, but no bombs or guns within earshot. Martin cutting hedge in imagination, in imitation of man who has been cutting it all the week. He then removes imaginary brushwood, saying "Wah, wah", which means "Fire", and presumably transfers it to an imaginary bonfire. They had a bomb at Ware last Tuesday, which demolished several cottages, but H. thinks killed no one. Martin now gets rather excited at the sight of an aeroplane.
          Japanese have landed on New Guinea. The Germans are still being held at Stalingrad, but have made progress somewhere else. Afraid my idea of the Russian front is extremely vague. Last night in full moon the Russians bombed Berlin and other places in Germany.

Monday, August 31, 1942

John brings home a fellow-learner of Japanese, who gives us the following clerihew:

> Palestrina
> Wrote a concerto for the concertina
> Which was orchestrated by Verdi
> For the herdy-gerdy.

Tuesday, September 1, 1942
A horrible day at the printers, complicated by the news that Rommel

has started an attack in Egypt, which means substitution of a new
block, etc., in News-Reel.   In bus which I take to printers are 2
poor women with a 9-months-old baby which has bronchial pneumonia.
They are taking her to hospital, and are glad the bus-fare is only
3d.   She is asleep in a shawl, but every now and then gives a
horrible little croak.

Wednesday, September 2, 1942

Stand in queue at Fortnum and Mason's for ½ lb. box chocolates, with
half my month's sweet ration.   Saving it for birthday or Christmas.
Germans advancing upon Stalingrad.

Thursday, September 3, 1942

National Day of Prayer.   Work stops at 11 for quarter-of-anhour.
I go down to All Saints, Margaret Street, which is packed with people.
Two women sitting behind me comment unfavourably on my hatless condition, though many others are also hatless.   In lunch-hour go to
20-minute service in church behind D.H. Evans, also packed with
people.   C.E.M. Joad, in "New Statesman", says all the factors are
present for a revival of religion and that if the energy is not
directed into the right channels it will mean an outburst of Fascism
and the setting up of a man-god for themselves by the people.

Friday, September 4, 1942

So depressed, eat my lunch with tears falling down my face, and even
trying on new green suit which Lewis's are just finishing and in which
I really look very presentable, does not cheer me.   Back from lunch,
am rung up by Peter Scott, going through London for week's leave, who
suggests a theatre.   We see "Quiet Weekend", pleasant play with no
reference to the war, good character-study, and I am quite cheered.
He is a Pilot-Officer, and is Observer in a bomber which goes on
flights before actual bombing raids, in order to make reports on
weather conditions.   One day his plane went off and a newly qualified
Observer asked if he might go instead of Peter: he did, and the plane
never came back.
         Learn, to my distress, that Mr. Abraham is to leave The Listener
in order to become head of the Gramophone Department, quite a big job
but I do not like the idea of the paper without him, especially if he
takes Miss Mearing too.

Saturday, September 5, 1942

Have hair washed, then at noon meet Joyce at Victoria.   She is en
route to Cambridge to discuss with a biologist the illustrations she
is doing for his book.   As her train draws in there is an air-raid
warning, which lasts however only about 20 minutes.   Lunch with her
and then join Tina and travel with her to Missenden for weekend.

Sunday, September 6, 1942

John, Joan and Greta arrive by 11 o'clock train and we have picnic
lunch on porch of cottage.   Then, in bright sun and white cloud we
pick about 10 lb. blackberries which in evening we take back to Miss
Morrison.   Joyce arrives for night and we talk a long time on all
sorts of subjects before going to bed.

Monday, September 7, 1942

Rommel being pushed back a little in Egypt and the Germans a little
near Stalingrad.   Every woman in country has to do 48 hours monthly
of fire-watching.   Lecturers say there is nothing one can do against
the new fire-bombs but go as far away as possible until they explode.
Brave people who try to tackle them get blown to bits.   I have had
£30 rise, of which I reckon I shall reap the benefit of about £12,
since £15 will go in income tax and nearly £3 in superannuation contributions.   My income-tax demand for this year is for 2 instalments
of over £80 each.

Tuesday, September 8, 1942

At printers.   Prime Minister makes speech to House which is on whole
an encouraging one.   Thinks situation in Libya "not altogether un-
satisfactory".

Wednesday, September 9, 1942

To dentist: one small filling.   He says rubber is used in making
false teeth and it is becoming increasingly difficult to get any.
     Others go to dancing-class but I mend my clothes instead.   In
lunch-time achieve 6 jars for fruit-bottling for Hilary.   These are
now very difficult to get.

Thursday, September 10, 1942

"Daily Worker" and "The Week" have now had the ban lifted from their
publication.

Friday, September 11, 1942

Decide at 5 p.m. to take next week as rest of my holiday.   Ring up
Hilary and tell her I am coming tonight.   In 3 minutes ring-up- Peter
Scott rings up on his way back from week's leave.   So ring up the
accommodating H. again and say not coming till Saturday morning.   Go
with P. to Emlyn Williams' play "The Morning Star", which is about
London air raids.   Only place open for eating after theatre (which
starts at 6 p.m.) is Lyons' Corner House, so we go there.

Saturday, September 12, 1942

To Hilary's on same bus as Margaret Dawson and 2 offspring, Colin (5),
Peter (1), who are going there for one night.   3 children play very
amiably and P. takes his first steps on lawn.   Beautiful day: feel I
did well to have holiday now.

Sunday, September 13, 1942

Cloudy and cooler.   Margaret happins and doctor is summoned: says h
she has little rupture.   L. hospitably says stay a week and recuperate.   I feel shall go mad if I have aweek with 3 children in this
small house, nice as they all are.   Fortunately she refuses.   H.
accompanies her to town while I put M. to bed.   He is very good.

Monday, September 14, 1942

Germans getting nearer Stalingrad.   H. and I go blackberrying
(alleged reason for this holiday was to gather blackberries), but we
find only so out ½ lb.

Tuesday, September 15, 1942

Very stormy early morn, then beautiful day.   H. and I take Martin to
Hertford, which means 2d. bus ride and is his idea of heaven.   Dom
Bernard Clements dead.   British have landed troops and made raid on
Tobruk.

Wednesday, September 16, 1942

Lovely day but very windy.   Japanese doing their best to recapture
Guadalcanar in Solomon Islands, which Americans took from them.   I
am stung by wasp.   We are surrounded all day by military manoeuvres
and have dive-bombers attacking troops at bottom of garden: most
exciting.   Tanks, lorries and armoured cars pass and repass each
other on road in front and lane at back of house.   Terribly haw-haw
young man on motor-bike says "I say, spread out all that stuff a bit,
will you?   It's frightfully congested down here.   If the Brigadier
comes along he'll raise hell".   We ask cheerful Irishman in lorry
which parks outside for 10 minutes whether they are advancing or retreating and he replies with grin that they haven't started yet.
Martin and I hang over front gate with great interest, and an Umpire
on motor-bike asks us if we will fill his water-bottle.   It is tea-
time and he comes in by the porch where we have been sitting, and has
cup of tea.   Makes great friends with Martin, gives him chocolate and
lets him sit on motor-bike and sound horn.   Says manoeuvres will
continue for 3 days and we are not to be afraid if we hear bangs in the
night.   At 7 or so, anotheryoung man on motor-bike comesand asks for
bread.   Assures us he has had nothing to eat since 4 a.m.   We give
him half a loaf and large chunk of cheese, some margarine and two
tomatoes, then ask him if he is attacking or defending, because if he
is the enemy we ought not to feed him.
           Such excitment that I have to sing "Ba-ba Black Sheep"about
15 times in succession to M. before he will go to sleep.

Thursday, September 17, 1942

Germans have reached suburbs of Stalingrad.   Lily brings David for

lunch and tea and has row on telephone with Fuel Office before she
can get permit to buy a gallon of paraffin a week to do her cooking.
Young clerk asks her if she knows there's a war on, and she replies
that she thought war was being fought for future generations, and all
she wants is something to cook her baby's food.   She gets the permit.

Friday, September 18, 1942

Street fighting in Stalingrad. More troops landed on Madagascar.
U.S. parachutists are in training in this country.   Pick blackberries
with Martin and tell him it is for a pie for Daddy.   He says "Oh,
dear Daddy!" at same time cramming intohis mouth as many as he can
lay hands on.   But sometimes he brings a little tight green one and
drops it sweetly into the tin.

Saturday, September 19, 1942

Pick 7 lb. blackberries, this time with Tramp.   Field full of cows
and a bull and am wearing scarlet jumper.   H. and L. go to film and
I bath M. and put him to bed.   H. seething with indignation because
Lord Crofts has a shoot and 4 high-powered cars are driven from place
to place, using the petrol which her milkman is unable to obtain for
delivering milk more than every other day even in hot weather.   Lord
Crofts is Under-Secretary of State for War.

Sunday, September 20, 1942

H. writes letter to A.J. Cummings of "News-Chronicle" on subject of
cars using petrol unlawfully, sending numbers of 4 cars seen yesterday.
I return to London unwillingly.

Monday, September 21,1942

Back to work.   Have sore stomach all day, which is not improved by
lunch at Greek Restaurant with Edgar Holt and wife, though it is
pleasant to see them.   Papers say "incredible slaughter" in streets
of Stalingrad.   And Greta has horrific tales of starving Greeks,
90 per cent. of whom she says will be dead by the Spring.   It pours
with rain, and between one thing and another I am very depressed.

Tuesday, September 22,1942

Joan's father, ex-Warden of an Oxford College, to supper and for
night.   He listens more than talks.   Tina hasbeen told by her doctor
she must work 2 hoursless per day because her heart is wonky.

Wednesday, September 23, 1942

Take frock to Danish Laundry to be washed, but they will not accept
it: lady in charge says she has no helpers at all.   Other hand-
laundry in Marylebone Lane is closed down and premises are To Let.
    Bob finishes at Treasury and is to start at Ministry of Production
as PrivateSecretary to the Minister, Oliver Lyttelton.

Thursday, September 24, 1942

While Stalingrad is a scene of dreadful slaughter, I go to National
Gallery Concert. Grinke Trio: Mozart. Don't enjoy it because
woman behind me knits throughout, and needles click, and I haven't
enough moral courage to ask her to stop. Letter from Roy, posted
Aug.24. As the letter from the P.M. to Smuts, inaugurating new Air-

Friday, September 25, 1942

graph Service, has taken 3 weeks,
feel this is very good.
Meet Mother and Phyllida for lunch, on their way to Hilary's.
Mother very nervous on moving stairs in Evans's. Utters small
screams of dismay and when the stairs become straight at the bottom,
leans back at an angle of 45 degrees. I endeavour to keep her perpendicular And but she declares she cannot help it. Onlookers very
amused. I join them at Ware about 7.30. Cold.

Saturday, September 26, 1942

Still cold. Pick blackberries with Martin, who beguiles his grand-
mother by saying "Dear Ganna" and leaning all across her lovingly.

Sunday, September 27, 1942

Suddenly warm and sunny again. L. to Home Guard manoeuvres. P.
escorts me to bus at 5, and we meet Daddy arriving before he is expected, carrying terribly heavy bag with apples and beans from garden
and, he says, a dozen eggs. As not an egg has been seen for weeks,
imagine this will be very welcome.

Monday, September 28, 1942

Russians still holding out at Stalingrad. As far as one can gather,
it is as if the British were making headway against the Germans at
Hampstead, the Germans were making an advance at Greenwich, and a
fierce battle were raging in theStrand. Cannot imagine what the city
must be like.

Tuesday, September 29, 1942

Tina arrives home and announces that Priestley and Vernon Bartlett
have resigned from Common Wealth, and also the Organising Secretary.
She needs cheering. So do I after very trying day at printer's. So
does John, who declares if he does any more Japanese today he will
burst. So we go to film "Palm Beach Story", which is very ridiculous and amusing and makes us all laugh and feel cheerful.

Wednesday, September 30, 1942

Warmer, and after wet morning there is beautiful sunset, making the
barrage balloons golden above Hyde Park, where the trees are turning
colour. Admire a jumper, price of which I find on enquiry to be 4
guineas! Try to buy marmalade jar as present for Edgar and Doris
Holt but cannot get anything pleasant.

Thursday, October 1, 1942

To National Gallery concert: Rosé Quartet, composed of aged men.
Mozart and Brahms.   Meet Margaret McLeod who used to be on Listener
and is now doing some sort of post-war planning with Sir William
Beveridge.

Friday, October 2, 1942

At Heal's get marmalade jar for the Holts.   Not very nice, 7/-.   See
there yellow and red ball, stuffed, material-covered, for 2/6, which
buy for Martin.   Green Line buses have now ceased to be, so have to
travel to Ware by train from Liverpool Street, which is more expensive
and less convenient and pleasant.

Saturday, October 3, 1942

Ralph and Marjorie Evans, with Jill aged 3½, for weekend, Ralph being
on leave from Army for week.   So all beds have to be changed round.
Nice day.   Misty morning clears.   Germans have not made any more
progress in Stalingrad.

Sunday, October 4, 1942

Most unfortunate day.   Jill has terribly swollen face and has not
slept.   P. has sick headache.   Martin will not go to sleep in morning and just as I have nursed him off with "The Three Bears", in come
Leonard and Ralph loudly and cheerfully from H.G., Tramp runs out to
meet them barking, and M. wakes up again.   To crown all, Leonard has
invited Ronald, Lily and baby along for afternoon, though knowing
that Lily and Marjorie E. are not on speaking terms.   H. makes him go
on bicycle and tell them not to come.   I return to London by 5 o'clock
train to go on fire duty at Broadcasting House at 6.45.   Attend to
many instructions about male and female hoses, and the need sometimes
to take one to the fire and sometimes the other, and understand very
little except that if I am on telephone duty and the bell won't stop
ringing I can make matters better by the use of a stout piece of
blotting paper.

Monday, October 5, 1942

Try to buy shoes, but they are all very uncomfortable and poor.   Do
buy beautiful jumper from Peter Robinson's for 47/6: golden cashmere

Tuesday, October 6, 1942

Mend stockings industriously.   Many of them I would have thrown away 3
years ago, but today their price is above rubies.

Wednesday, October 7, 1942

With Jina to "Bambi", Walt Disney's latest cartoon film, very charming.
Callfor her at new headquarters of "Common wealth", in room where

Tom Wintringham, who writes about a People's Army, is working.

Thursday, October 8 1942

Buy pair shoes by accident - am coming out of Lilley and Skinner's in
despair, and walk upstairs under impression that I am in basement.
Find myself on first floor in Juvenile Department, and get pair shoes
"Maid's" just what I wanted, 32/9 and quite good value, I think.   To
ask for plain walking-shoe in tan, flat heel, is like asking for the
moon.   In evening Jack gives us rum, which I have not tasted before.
It is ship's rum, in bottle in high wicker basket, and very potent.
Makes me feel vaguely amiable to all mankind, and John feels especially
amiable to me and presses me to lunch with him some time, which invitation I feel it is safe to accept whether he really intends it or no,
since tomorrow he is going on a week's leave.

Friday, October 9, 1942

Miss F. gives me her week's meat ration - 3 mutton chops - which I
take to H's.   Also some of her fat ration.

Saturday, October 10, 1942

Put Martin to bed while Le. and H. go to film.   Although he has been
naughty with eye-teeth all the week, he goes to bed as good as gold and
is fast asleep by 5.40.   Is very taken with story of Three Bears, at
end of which always says "More?"

Sunday, October 11, 1942

Value of some clothes coupons changed.   Fully-fashioned stockings are
to be 3 coupons instead of 2.

Monday, October 12, 1942

Day begins with phone call from representative of Postmaster General
who wants to come and see me and Miss Scott Johnston (Mrs. Melsome)
about my complaints to Graham that post to troops in Middle East never
reaches them.   He is annoyed that Miss S.-J. is in N. Wales.   Day
then continues in most annoying way possible.   I feel very dim and
do everything wrong, and Miss P. is no better.   Very depressed.

Tuesday, October 13, 1942

Prome Minister made speech yesterday on receiving freedom of City of
Edinburgh, in course of which says that in dealing with German
atrocities "no weakness will be shown".   This because Germans have
chained our prisoners taken at Dieppe, in return for tying of hands
of prisoners by us in small raid on Sark the other day.   Gov. says
treatment on field of battle is not same as treatment in captivity.
Anyway, we have now chained similar number of German prisoners here
and in Canada, and the whole thing seems likely to continue like the

idiotic retaliations of two groups of schoolboys.   Or so it seems to me.

Wednesday, October 14, 1942

Hair washed.   Meet Janet Adam Smith for tea.   Towels are obtainable only with clothing coupons.

Thursday, October 15, 1942

Read my diary for this day for past 3 years and become depressed: think my life not now as interesting as it was.   To National Gallery concert: 3 Brandenburg Concertos.   See Peter Beavan in audience, home on leave from Merchant Navy.   He gives me invitations for number of evenings, none of which can do.

Friday, October 16, 1942

To supper with David Green who is dispirited because he says everyone at his Fire Station gets promotion except him, and he does all the dirty work: filing correspondence for area, etc.   Tell him this is always so.   Useful people are left unpromoted lest someone else should have to do the work.   He gives me very nice supper of fried bread, tomato, baked beans and bacon and egg, and pears and splits into which he somehow gets cream and blackcurrant jam.   Also very good coffee. We gossip and listen to gramophone very pleasantly.

Saturday, October 17, 1942

Spend morning trying in vain to get hat to match new green suit. Only one which matches is £5.17.6 at Marshall & Snelgrove, and it is anyway too dressy for an all-purposes hat which this must be.   In evening to film "Moontide" with Tina.   Very obscure for some time: scene in low haunt thick with smoke or beside squalid wharf thick with fog.   Conversation consists of "Oh yeah!" "O.K.", "Sez you" and other such phrases, uttered nasally from corner of mouth.   At end decide film good, with some beautiful shots.   Walk back over park in October sunshine, and at 6.45 go to fire duty at B.H., where we do some ineffectual walking around with a stirrup pump.   Germans making some progress in Stalingrad.

Sunday, October 18, 1942

Whisked off to High Mass by Bob.   Very beautiful, though disagree with sermon.   In afternoon listen with him to orators in Hyde Park: A Communist, a Dominican friar, a negro with large coloured feathers in his hair who is waving four flags and apparently trying to lead community singing, a man in a red mortar-board whose mission is obscure (he says "The world is in a state of chaos; but when the world is in this state, every hundred years or so a man is born". Voice from crowd: "Can't anyone stop him?"), an ape-like creature who fixes Bob with a glare and asks if he is ready for eternity, and several ranting females whose voices are not powerful enough to be heard.

Monday, October 19, 1942

Germans still making some progress in Stalingrad.   Very tired.
Have cold and cough which cannot get rid of: and we cannot have
heating in offices until beginning of November.

Tuesday, October 20, 1942

Pouring wet day.   "Family" has meal at Canuto's, to which Graham
comes - says is founding movement called "Common Sense" in opposition
to Tina's "Common Wealth".   Meal with sherry and bone (don't know how
this is spelt, it is a Burgundy) is 11/7.   Some have brandy, which
is 5/- for minute quantity.   Good time had by all in spite of war and
in spite of vehement argument on divorce between Bob and rest of
company, the subject having wilfully been raised by Norman Tucker.

Wednesday, October 21, 1942

General Smuts is over here and speaks to both Houses.   Speech is recorded and broadcast at 9 p.m.   Very vigorous for man of 72 - goes on
for $\frac{3}{4}$ hour though it is true does not say anything new.   Lloyd George
who introduces him, sounds an old man.

Thursday, October 22, 1942

Buy new hat, 44/10, which is admired by everyone.   Strange that after
fruitless search on Saturday, this time I get one at once at first shop
I try.   Also get chocolate ration at Fortnum and Masons, which is
$\frac{1}{4}$ lb. for current month.   Price of mixed chocolates regulated at 5/-
per lb.   Germans new onslaught on Stalingrad said to be held up, partly by mud..

Friday, October 23, 1942

To National Gallery concert: the remaining 3 Brandenburgs, very good.
R.A.F. has bombed Genoa.   To Ware.

Saturday, October 24, 1942

Eighth Army has attacked in Egypt;   we have bombed Italy again - supply
bases for N. Africa.   And Moll Dawson rings up, on embarkation leave.
As he told Leonard 3 weeks ago that we would be getting this leave and
that it meant the beginning of the 2nd Front where he would be among the
first to land, we wonder if the new activity in Egypt in designed to
draw off attention from some other enterprise.   Stalingrad seems to
be holding off new German attacks.   There is glorious full moon.
            H. and I called upon by aged Catholic priest who addresses us
alternately as "Ma'am" and "Dear child", appears to have forgotten that
the woman living in the house who took "The Universe" left 2 years ago,
and departs on his bicycle in a great storm of rain leaving his card
which informs us that his name is "Macerone" - which convulses Hilary
who has hardly been able to maintain gravity throughout his visit.

Sunday, October 25, 1942

Gather late blackberries with Martin. Then leave for station in
squalls of rain. At Broxbourne have to change into crowded Cambridge
train, where stand next to messenger and commissionaire from S. Africa
House who says they had a great time last week keeping visitors from
Smuts and receiving presents and telegrams on his behalf.

Our men in Egypt have penetrated enemy's defences at some
points and enemy counterattacks have been ineffective. We have bombed
Milan.

Monday, October 26, 1942

Phyllida starts today as member of Land Army, in Fairford. Is billet-
ed in cottage, for which the woman gets 20/- a week. P. gets 10/- a
week, and 18/- after her month's training. Is possessed of well-made
uniform of good material: 3 pairs woollen stockings, farm breeches
and felt hat, green jersey, stout brown shoes. For wet days, an oil
skin and boots. And a milking overall. There is cold steady rain
all day, so the poor girl probably needs her oilskin. She is to milk
cows and drive pony and trap.

Tuesday, October 27, 1942

Government lifts ban on central heating, and within 2 hours of this
news coming through on the tape-machine, the hot water pipes in the
B.B.C. are beginning to function.

Wednesday, October 28, 1942

Enquire prices of toys, with view to Martin's Christmas presents.
Little unpainted wooden wheelbarrows are 17/6. Small wooden horse on
which he could sit (painted), 55/6. Listen to broadcast of Smetana's
"Bartered Bride", given in honour of Czech National Day - in very poor
English translation by Rose Newmarch.

Thursday, October 29, 1942

Reading and enjoying "Persuasion": can't think why I enjoy Jane Austen
so much. Her heroines are often fools and her heroes prigs. Frederick's impassioned letter to Anne contains the words "Too good, too
excellent creature!" and she is compelled to go away and tranquillise
her feelings for an hour after reading them. After any sight of him
she takes an hour or two to regain her composure.

Friday, October 30, 1942

See photographs of R.A.F. bomb damage on German cities, at Devonshire
House, Piccadilly. "Before" and "After". To my untrained eye nothing very much is apparent. On fire duty at B.B.C. A beautiful
member of our party informs the fire superintendent, with much flutter-

ing of her lovely eyelashes, that a friend is on leave and passing through London, and she wants to have a drink with him. So our exercise for the evening is cut down to 15 minutes, and the entire fire room helps the beautiful one to write up the log with which she is entrusted so that she shall meet her young man. She then departs, at about 7.30, ostensibly to the B.B.C. club, the only place to which we are allowed to go, but really to the Bolivar, and returns to her bunk at about 11.30. Learn in confidence that the "2 hours" really mean several days. But she really is very beautiful.

Saturday, October 31, 1942

To Hilary's with Tina. Germans have made sharp daylight air attack on Canterbury. It rains all afternoon.

Sunday, November 1, 1942

Chill relentless rain all day and I have bad cold.

Monday, November 2, 1942

Rise in time to catch 8.44 from Ware, which means leaving house about 8. Fortunately rain has stopped.

Tuesday, November 3, 1942

Come home during afternoon with appalling headache and go to bed. Others go to film to celebrate joint birthdays of Greta and Tina.

Wednesday, November 4, 1942

To doctor's. I have catarrh which gives me neuralgia. She tells me to stay in till Friday when she will come to see me, and gives me prescription for inhalant. Buy jug from Whiteley's to inhale from, 8/11. Will do for flowers when I have done with inhaling. Also get kettle to boil water, 2/11, which starts to leak immediately. Bob also comes home during afternoon with cold, his Minister being in U.S.A. so office being slack. We play chess and make toasted buns for tea.

Thursday, November 5, 1942

Axis forces in full retreat in Egypt. This beautiful headline so unusual, find it difficult to believe. Bob in uncertainty whether to go to office (because he has date he wants to keep tonight). Sits playing Bach preludes rather badly and muttering "I do hate these intellectual problems", and decides to stay and play bad chess with me

Friday, November 6, 1942

Complete change of weather to mild sunshine. Visited by doctor who

reports me better and allows me to go off to Ware in afternoon for
few days' recuperation.   Met by Hilary, Martin andTramp.   Country
looks very pleasant and like a different world from yesterday.

Saturday, November 7, 1942

R.A.F. bombs Genoa.   We are still pursuing retreating Germans in
Egypt.   Leonard held up, while working late in afternoon, by arrival
of two men from Quedgeley, calling for vehicle.   Beautiful afternoon
again after rain in morning.   B.B.C. broadcasts The Internationale
during a concert of Russian music to celebrate 25th Anniversary of
Russian Revolution.   We listen with wide smiles to this, since till
now there has been a ban on its broadcast.

Sunday, November 8, 1942

American expeditionary force has landed in French N. Africa.   British
reinforcements on way. R.A.F. bombs Genoa again.   Beautiful day.

Monday, November 9, 1942

Americans take Algiers and Darlan is a prisoner.   More landings by
Americans.
          All the bitches in the neighbourhood are on heat and Tramp
is in an excited state.   I take him into Wareside with Martin, and
we buy sweets, dog-biscuits and cigarettes at village shop, and Tramp
starts violent affairs with half-a-dozen bitches at once.

Tuesday, November 10, 1942

Americans have occupied Oran.   P.M., speaking at luncheon at Mansion
House, saysplainly that object of all this activity in N.Africa is to
make a jumping-off ground for invasion of Europe.   H. persuades me to
stay till end of week.   My catarrh better, but not gone.   Beautiful
day and warm in sun.

Wednesday, November 11, 1942

Day so full of news, can hardly remember it.   Germans marching into
unoccupied France and Pétain has protested against these violations
of the armistice terms.   Occupation of Corsica has also been ordered
German troops have made air-landings in Tunisia.   Yesterday Roosevelt
was stated to have asked the Bey of Tunisia for permission to march
through his territory.   French North Africa has capitulated and asked
Allies for armistice.   Axis troops driven right out of Egypt with
casualties said to be 59,000: ours, 13,000-odd.   Churchill inthe
House says great events are to be expected in the next few days, and
Hilary feels ill every time there is a news bulletin.   C. says Italy
will be bombed.   Next Sunday the church bells, which have been
silent since Dunkirk, because their ringing was to be warning of

invasion, are to be rung to celebrate victory in Egypt.

Beautiful mild sunny day after morning mist. Can sit in porch.
Following extraordinary conversation takes place as I hang out clothes
for H.:

    Lady on Bicycle: Goodmorning.
    Me (turning): Good-morning.
    Lady: Oh, I don't think you are you, I think you're your sister.
    Me: Yes, I am.

Feel better, but still a lot of catarrh.

Thursday, November 12, 1942

Foggy. It is reported in the House that our aid to Russia during
past 12 months has been 3,000 aircraft, 4,000 tanks, and 30,000
vehicles; most of these suplies reached their destination. Germans
have marched to S. coast of France in strength and have reached
Marseilles.

Friday, November 13, 1942

We have recaptured Bardia and Tobruk. Martin cutting teeth and rather
naughty. Falls off chairs, etc. When he is going to take up some
forbidden object, he says: "No no, Martin, No no", and then, looking
at it in his hand as if wondering how on earth it got there: "Oh
dear, dear , dear!"

Saturday, November 14, 1942

We still advance in Libya and the Americans in N.W.Africa. H. and
L. go looking for Christmas toys in Hertford,and the kitchen range,
which I erroneously imagine H. has stoked up, goes out while I take
M. for walk. In spite of many efforts with paraffin which interest
M. very much, I cannot light it. Neither canI discover the scullery
blackout anywhere. Am relieved when they return. It seems that I
had everything open which should have been closed and everything
closed which should have been open inthe range, and L. has a blazy in
3 minutes.

Sunday, November 15, 1942

Church bells are rung, for first time since June 1940. We hear them
through fog coming from Ware, and take M. to gate to hear them, after
Hilary has called out excitedly "Marjorie, they're ringing!" "Bells,
Martin", we say, and he replies intelligently "Big tick-tock". "No,
bells", says his fond Mamma, and he says "Bons" agreeably, looking
down the road where we are looking. When two cyclists emerge from
mist, he says joyfully "There bons!", glad to recognise something
familiar. "When you are grown up", says H., "I shall tell you you
heard the bells ring in 1942". "Bons", says M. proudly, and adds

inconsequently "Apple?" as we go indoors and he sees one on the dresser

Monday, November 16, 1942

Back to work, which is not too trying, but I am rather tired after it. Excellent broadcast by Commander Kimmins on the American landings in North Africa.

Tuesday, November 17, 1942

We have captured Derna. Latish at printers, owing to putting in Kimmins' broadcast at last moment.

Wednesday, November 18, 1942

British paratroops land in Tunisia. I buy myself another hat, black, for 27/6, since I am told output of hats is to be severely curtailed. It is of poor quality felt but quite becoming.

Thursday, November 19, 1942

Our parachute troops have captured important airfield in Tunisia.

Friday, November 20, 1942

In lunch-hour to Exhibition of Greek Art at Burlington House. Remember most clearly a blue velvet dress with gold embroidery which the women of Greece made for the Duchess of Kent when she was married in, I think, 1928; an exquisite silver dish, boat-shaped, with a dove on each end, about 7 or 8 inches long, dated A.D.1000; and a large earthenware-looking circular dish with a lid, B.C.450 or so. It was about a foot in diameter, and the lid had a dark pattern on it and a handle of two or three young horses. Come out into Piccadilly and look at all the people, thinking "Savages!" Go into Fortnum and Masons, and see bottles of fruit, such an unusual sight that I stop to look; find they are "peaches in brandy", "raspberries in gin", and other delicacies, the price of which I dare not even ask. But that there are some people who do buy them I discover by hearing a woman asking her elderly, dyspeptic husband if he could "fancy some". He does not appear to think he could.

Saturday, November 21, 1942

We have captured Benghazi and Rommel is nearly back to his original place of retreat. As you were. We have bombed Turin in the war's biggest air-raid on Italy. Cold, and I am very tired and depressed. Marvellous full moon.

Sunday, November 22, 1942

Return to London from Hilary's and in train near woman giving her small

boy wildly inaccurate information about the moon; but among dross is
this piece of rare metal:-

    Child: "Why do we go on seeing the moon, Mammy, after such
          a long way?"
    Mother: "It's the same moon everywhere, for all the world."
    Child: (shocked) "Not for Germany".
    Mother: "Yes it is; same moon for all the world".

- like the first line of a popular song. Felt it should have
continued "Until you came" or something like that.
    Reading C.A. Montague's "A Hind Let Loose". Why did nobody tell
me about him before? Enjoying it enormously. And have learnt by
heart Flecker's Prologue to "Hassan" about the Golden Journey to
Samarkand.

Monday, November 23, 1942

Changes in War Cabinet. Cripps goes out of Cabinet, ceases to be
Leader of House of Commons, and instead takes charge of Aircraft
Production, which the P.M. in aletter to him says is "stepping down"
but only to do a most important and necessary job. Russians advancing
at Stalingrad. Very cold.

Tuesday, November 24, 1942

Beautiful new typewriting ribbon. They are not sold on spools now,
but have to be wound on to the ones already in use, from a little
wooden round. Dakar and the whole of French West Africa have come
over to the Allies. This announced by Admiral Darlan, and exactly
what he is doing and whose side he is on, it is impossible to decide.
The whole business is extremely confused.

Wednesday, November 25, 1942

Receive tin butter, box wrapped cheese, and tin tongue, from Roy for
Christmas present.
    Russian relief force is has reached Stalingrad and the Germans are
being driven back both there and in the Caucasus.
    Fire-watching. I am the only woman who turns up with tin hat and
gas-mask. So when the man says "Gas warning", and all the firemen put
on their masks, I put on mine too, and the chief fireman says to two of
the women, without a smile, "You're dead" - "You're dead". He then
says "All clear" and we remove masks. Silly.

Thursday, November 26, 1942

Knitting furiously to try to finish for Christmas vest and woollen
knickers for Phyllida. Have promised to do set for Hilary as well.

Friday, November 27, 1942

Buy yet another hat, and feel so exceedingly wicked have stomach-
ache as I return from making this purchase.   Have spent £6.2.9 on
three hats in about three weeks.   But am told no more are to be made,
and this new one matched my blue suit, a difficult colour to get nowadays.   Shall have to go on wearing these for 5 years or so.   With
thoughts such as this I try all the afternoon to convince myself I am
justified in the extravagance.
          Germans have occupied Toulon, where most of the French Fleet is.

Saturday, November 28, 1942

The French ships at Toulon sank themselves at the approach of the
Germans.   Most of the Captains died on the bridges of their ships.
One submarine has escaped to Barcelona.   Some of the vessels will be
able to be raised, but it will take some months to do it.
          Martin has been sick with feverish cold, but seems better.

Sunday, November 29, 1942

Back to London, after a weekend when we ate toast with masses and
masses of butter on every slice - I took the tin which Roy sent me and
we opened it.   "Dear Oncle Roy", said Martin truly.   Talk in corridor of train with man who says he is liaison officer with Allied
Navies - he is certainly in naval uniform.   His references to the
Fighting French are most unflattering, and in my fiew most injudicious
in a crowded train, if his job is to promote good relations.
          Broadcast by Prime Minister, who hopes we shall stand success as
well as we have stood adversity, and quotes Kipling: "If you can
meet with triumph and disaster and treat those two impostors just the
same".

Monday, November 30, 1942

Christopher Redman is 1, and Winston Churchill 69, to-day.   The
Russians are driving the Germans back on all fronts.   On Friday I
got a map of Russia and looked at it, and at the map of Europe.   How
we have had the effrontery to continue cheerfully to think we should
win the war, with almost the whole of Europe, and most of the inhabit-
able part of Russia, occupied by the Germans, I can't think.   Hitler
himself said in "Mein Kampf", I believe, that the English never knew
when they were beaten and therefore ended by winning.

Tuesday, December 1, 1942

They have taken away the railings from Kensington Gardens.
          The "Beveridge Report" on Social Services is published: its aim
is to abolish want, and this it does by proposals for increased old
age and other pensions; health, unemployment and other insurances for
everyone; family allowances, etc.
          Very rushed day at printers without Mr. Abraham, whose father
has died suddenly.

Have lost entry for December 2.

Thursday, December 3, 1942

With David to ballet: "Gods Go A'Begging" (Handel - charming); "The Birds" (arr. Respighi - fantastic); "Hamlet" (Tchaikovsky - dramatic) Very good. We had stalls, 8/-.

Friday, December 4, 1942

Sick in morning, probably because had only two sandwiches instead of dinner last night. Crashing headache, but it goes off later. Get 1.55 to Stroud. Beautiful weather and good journey, not too crowded.

Saturday, December 5, 1942

Persuade parents not to attempt journey to Hilary's at Christmas, and feel a beast, as if I have denied a treat to two eager children. But do think it would be madness, especially as Daddy couldn't travel till Christmas Eve. Beautiful day.

Sunday, December 6, 1942

Phyllida's name read out at Communion Service, among others "serving their country", by virtue of her being in the Land Army. Bob Franklin has been called up and has gone into the Navy. Return to London: have to stand as far as Kemble.

Monday, December 7, 1942

Very tired. Knit with vigour and finish Phyllida's knickers. Buy pair woollen gloves. There is a hole in one of them, which shop darns for me and accordingly cuts down price by 3/- to 5/11. 1 coupon for unlined gloves.

Tuesday, December 8, 1942

Late to press (6.50), and I have to go straight from printers to Broadcasting House for fire-watching. We do another ineffectual exercise, during which I am useless, standing about in my men's dungarees.

Wednesday, December 9, 1942

Knit with enormous vigour while others are out. Terribly tired after fire-watching last night, though I slept most of the night.
    Progress in North Africa generally appears to be held up for the moment.

Thursday, December 10, 1942

Arnold to supper: he is up in town for a day or two. Brings, for H, 3 packets soap powder and ¼ lb. tea. Ring H., who says Martin has had what clinic thinks is suppressed whooping-cough, but is better.

Friday, December 11, 1942

To H's by 5.10.   Feel quite ill with tiredness.   We have beautiful
herrings for supper, a most unusual treat now adays.

Saturday, December 12, 1942

In addition to herrings last night, we have kippers for breakfast!
Feel better after good night.   Martin also has good night and he and
his parents are accordingly cheered.   Beautiful day, and I take him
for pram ride.

Sunday, December 13, 1942

Back to London.   Train, though crowded so that I stand, is punctual,
porbably owing to moon, whose phases we now watch with eagerness.

Monday, December 14, 1942

Joyful news that the 8th Army is again pursing Rommel, after their
advance had been stayed for about 3 weeks.   Manage to buy some thread
elastic, an event worth recording.   Work at printers till 6.15.
Browning waits for me with car for $\frac{1}{2}$ hour, and brings me home through
black-out.

Tuesday, December 15, 1942

Supposed to finish for press at midday, but in fact go on till 4.45.
I then come home and do my washing before dinner.

Wednesday, December 16, 1942

Oxford Street crammed with shoppers.   Shops short-staffed, so that it
is extremely difficult to get anyone to take any money for anything.
Feelhow easy is the shop-lifter's life compared with that of the honest
Very dispirited when, after taking 3 hours over lunch, have bought 2
Christmas cards and a coat hanger only.   To Beavans in evening - for
music, but it has been postponed till tomorrow, so play Monopoly with
Kohn and Frank.   Arthur's story has appeared in "Penguin Parade" 9.

Thursday, December 17, 1942

We have cut off part of Rommel's Army in N. Africa, and it is still
retreating.
     More shopping in lunch-hour, this time not quite so fruitless.
Collect up books in Bumpuses as I walk along, and find it difficult to
get anyone to accept money for them.   Finally discover old man standing in midst of crowd of people, with a bunch of notes in one hand and
coins in the other, saying "How much?" trustingly to customers, who
then pay him the right amount and walk out with the books.

Friday, December 18, 1942

Buy myself powder compact from Finnegan's, about the most expensive
shop in Bond Street.   It is very beautiful and cost £2.12.6.   The
family is giving me it for Christmas.   Feel dreadfully wicked at
this expenditure on a luxury.   There were others there, silver, at
six guineas, and one I admired, in plain black, was 8½ guineas.
          To Hilary's in pouring rain.   They have been having trying time
with Martin, who is still not well.

Saturday, December 19, 1942

Poor Leonard, after many sleepless nights when he has his son in his
bed (who is as bright as a button as soon asdaylight dawns and says
to his exhausted parent "Daddy, up.   Tea!"), rises this morning and
puts in the tea the milk H. was saving for cream cheese.   He goes to
his mother's for weekend, since he will not be seeing her at Christmas,
and M. is very feverish all the evening and does not go to sleep till
10 o'clock, when H. and I are quite exhausted too.

Sunday, December 20,1942

Russians have started another big offensive.   We are still pursuing
Rommel's army in N. Africa, though some of it was "encircled" but has
managed to escape.
          Find, on return to London, p.c. from Peter Scott, send from
Canada on Nov.9.   He said he might be going for six months, as R.A.F.
instructor.

Monday, December 21, 1942

This Post my Christmas parcels today, though Saturday was said to be
the last day for posting.   But I get letters posted yesterday, so
doubtless all my parcels will reach their destinations tomorrow.

Tuesday, December 22, 1942

Very busy at printers, where we are supposed to finish at noon this
week, but are actually done at 5 o'clock.

Wednesday, December 23, 1942

Have hair washed, and attempt a little more shopping, somewhat unsuccessfully.   Ask hopefully at a poulterers for a bird, but am regarded as semi-imbecile for making such an outrageous request.

Thursday, December 24, 1942

To Hilary's.   She actually has a small bird of unspecified breed from
her poulterers.   We suspect it is a partridge, and are gratefully
surprised at receiving it.   There are sprigs of holly on the kitchen

wall, and an artificial Christmas tree 18 inches high on the mantelpiece, with decorations from last year, and a few Christmas cards.
And a paper streamer in the sitting-room, and a real Christmas tree
in a pitcher, the total being about 18 inches again. Quite a lot of
decorations on it and a star at the top.

Martin still not very well. H. is to take him to Hertford hospital for examination on Monday.

Friday, December 25, 1942

Fourth Christmas of the war. I attain consciousness not long before
9 a.m., when I hear the Greenwich pips, followed by one verse of "O
Come All Ye Faithful", followed by Stuart Hibberd wishing everybody a
happy Christmas, followed immediately by the words "Darlan has been
assassinated". A put-up job, one supposes. But by whom?

We open presents after breakfast, beside the Christmas tree in the
sitting-room. There are presents from Leonard to "my little bundle
o' strife", to his "little lotus petal" and to his "blossoming rose-
bud", besides ones from Tramp to his dear mistress, from Pussy to her
dear master, and from everybody to Martin, who is very pleased with
his bus. Most surprisingly, the room seems to be about as knee-deep
as ever in paper and string when we have finished. Can't imagine
where it all came from. The bird turns out a great success, with
stuffing thrown together by H. in about 5 minutes from any ingredients
she happened to have handy; and Mother's pudding is almost pre-war in
quality. I take M. for short walk in his pram in afternoon, while
the King is giving his Christmas broadcast, and we meet no one - all
listening to their monarch or recovering from effects of dinner.

Church bells are allowed to be rung and we hear them thro' windows.

Saturday, December 26, 1942

Raw, foggy day. L. takes Martin for short walk, but he cries with
the cold and is brought back. The assassin of Darlan, a young French
national, is executed.

Sunday, December 27, 1942

Back to London. Journey takes 3 hours, and when I arrive it is so
black and foggy I do not know whether I am walking down Bayswater Rd.
or Queen's Road. I ask my whereabouts of a shadow, which replies in
despondent Canadian tones "I don't know". So ask of another, and an
old man with a torch kindly leads us both to our destinations. I cannot get a battery to fit my torch.

Monday, December 28, 1942

Ring up H. to find out how she fared at Hertford Hospital this afternoon, where she took M. to discover whether what he has is a tubercular germ. Relieved to hear that it is not, but what it is has not
been revealed. All the "family" in, except John, on holiday; also
Joan's brother John, Sandy, in the R.A.F. Furious argument about the
Church and its shortcomings, with Bob as defendant, rages all evening.

Tuesday, December 29, 1942

Sandy says he is working with a man who for four months went about
France observing things for the British Government.   He was dropped
by parachute.   Says there is plenty of food in the country, but they
are short in the towns.   He had conversation with German officers
about the bad driving of the Paris taxi-men.   He got free board and
lodging wherever he asked for it saying he was English.   He say no
atrocities and people are on the whole living normal lives.   They
want the Germans away and think we shall win, but meanting are carrying on as well as they can.

Wednesday, December 30, 1942

Very tired.   Cold and trying to snow.   Call for my sandals which have
been soled, ready for next summer.   The repair cost 14/6!

Thursday, December 31, 1942

Meet mother and convoy her across London to Liverpool Street en route
for Hilary's.   I get 2 No.8 torch batteries, most valuable and rare.

Friday, January 1, 1943

Feel sunk down to the earth with depression, a most inauspicious beginning to the New Year.   The Canadians, male and female, welcomed
in 1943 with shrieks and shouts and songs in Craven Hill Gardens till
well past midnight.   At 4.30 a.m. I awoke and heard French shoutings
going on, and a taxi hailed drunkenly.   It shounded as if the vehicle
ran over the hailer, to whose fate I felt completely indifferent.
        It is Martin's 2nd birthday and I go to Ware for weekend.   H.
reports that though he is still not good at nights, he is much better
and eating ravenously.

Saturday, January 2, 1943

Spent the night in double bed with mother and did not sleep much.
Bitterly cold day.   Martin certainly enjoying restoration of spirits.

Sunday, January 3, 1943

Return to London.   Tramp follows me to station and I leave him locked
in waiting-room.   Phone to H. who says she will fetch him - she is in
any case cycling in to meet Daddy, whose train arrives just after I
leave.

Monday, January 4, 1943

Ring up Ware.   H. says Tramp somehow escaped from waiting-room.   She
met Daddy in Musley Hill and was astonished to see Tramp with him - he
had run after Daddy and butted him joyfully in back as he left station
with crowd of people.
        Russians doing well, and making progress towards Rostov.

Tuesday, January 5, 1943

~~Pouring wet cold day~~ To printers with Mr. Pringle, who is not as
quick or as decided as Mr. Abraham.   In evening with Greta to Noel
Coward's film "In Which We Serve", about a destroyer of the R.N. and
the men in her.   Very good film, though a little too much of Noel C.
who as the captain is given to making noble speeches to his ship's
company on the least excuse.

Wednesday, January 6, 1943

Pouring wet cold day.   Go to Strand theatre in lunch-hour to try to
get tickets for "Arsenic and Old Lace", to see with Joyce on Friday.
Have to wait in queue of ticket-buyers for half-an-hour.   Had goose
for lunch, at D.H. Evans - goose with stuffing (very tasteless bird),
cauliflower and boiled potatoes; prunes and custard; white coffee.
This cost 4/11.   Still feel very depressed.   Have been doing some
interesting jobs which I took over from Mr. Abraham as far back as
August, and now have to give them up to Mr. Pringle.   Except for press
days, shall be practically unoccupied, and feel very depressed at prospect.

Thursday, January 7m 1943

John has a fellow student of Japanese to supper, who was in the
Lofoten Islands raid last ... whenever it was.   He said they were told
they were to occupy them for 6 weeks, but in fact left in a few hours.
They had expected to be welcomed by the inhabitants with open arms,
but the inhabitants were not at all pleased to see them.
       Buy 16 oz. wool for next year's winter woollies: really need 20
oz. but am told that is all I can have.   Have to give 8 coupons, but
it is real wool and a pretty colour.   Walk back to office with the
unwrapped hanks under my arm, looking too too like embryonic vests.

Friday, January 8, 1943

Bitterly cold day.   Joyce comes for weekend and we have lunch at D.H.
Evans's.   In evening to "Arsenic and Old Lace", a skit on murder, if
such a thing can be.   In the most tense moment of the play, when a
body is being brought through a window on to the darkened stage, someone below us in the stall has a fit or a seizure and has to be borne
out.   Thought at first the queer noises and cries for a doctor were
all part of play.   Theatre starts at 5.45 and we are home by 9 o'clock

Saturday, January 9, 1943

Bleak N.E..wind.   We talk, buy artists' materials which J. finds hard
to get in the country, see a Disney programme at the Polytechnic, have
tea at Quality Inn before the crowds start, and walk home to spend a
quiet evening knitting.
       Russians still doing very well and approaching Rostov, but we in
N. Africa appear to make little progress.

Sunday, January 10, 1943

Slithtly ... Slightly warmer but foggy and raw. We go to Friends'
House, Euston Road, to their morning meeting, knit and talk in the
afternoon, and I accompany J. to Victoria after tea (when we sit at
table with extraordinary old woman with straight long grey hair and
incredibly old clothes and cultured voice, who says "You can talk -
it's all right - I never listen to anyone's conversation" and then
proceeded to sympathise with Joyce at great length because her Welsh
Rabbit was such a long time coming). Quite like an old-time Sunday,
J. says, and very pleasant.

Monday, January 11, 1943

The "family" has a binge - supper at Canuto's, after which we get
taken by John and his friend Ian Watt to a pub. frequented by the men
who are taking J's Japanese course, because they most of them live in
a hostel just near it. My eyes smart and run with tobacco smoke of
others, and though I quite enjoy it I am conscious all the time that it
is not the sort of thing I enjoy doing most.

Tuesday, January 12, 1943

To press late. Editor and Deputy Editor discuss things irrelevant to
the paper we are trying to pass, which irritates me vastly and wastes
a lot of time. We leave about 6.45 in pouring rain which pretty well
ruins my new £2.10 hat.

Wednesday, January 13, 1943

In lunch-hour to Exhibition of 19th Century French Paintings at National
Gallery. Very crowded. Picasso, Seurat, Monet, Van Gogh, Corot -
these are the names I remember best. Think it was Monet who had done
a picture of Frost somewhere near Boulogne, which looked as if he had
had a lovely time squeezing Chinese white on to the canvas in fat blobs.
But when you stepped a little way off, there it was - Frost.
    Miss P. away and I am pleasantly busy. Buy pair woollen gloves -
                                        1 coupon, 7/11. Fawn.
Thursday, January 14, 1943

In lunch-hour, go with almost no forethought and order a thin suit for
next summer, from Lewis's. Not sure I care for pattern which is kind
of subdued check. They remove 18 coupons from me, which leaves 4 till
March. Price is to be 12 guineas! O my! Mother sends her and
Daddy's sweet coupons, hoping I can get some chocolates for them in
London.

Friday, January 15, 1943

Call for my sandals which Baber's have been repairing. They ask for

16/- for soling them and stitching in one place. Had not expected
anything like this, since sandals when new cost only 9/11 - though of
course unobtainable now - and have not enough money with me, so have
to leave them at shop. In evening to film with Greta, Tina and Miss
Ross who lives here. Complete waste of 2/6, since "Counter-Espionage"
which we go to see has almost finished when we get there, and what remains is a film with Clark Gable in it which is almost/one nothing but
one long embrace.

Saturday, January 16, 1943

Lunch with Tina and John at Der Vyaini's (spelling?) in Charlotte St.
Roast lamb, boiled potatoes and sprouts; apple charlotte; white
coffee. 4/6 with tip. But very nice and well cooked. John and I
afterwards essay to get into "Studio One" to see French film supposed
to be good, "Derrière la Façade", but seats left are at 7/- and 8/6,
which we deem too much; so we walk home to Craven Hill Gardens, and
later have tea together. I then have to go off to fire-watch at B.BC.
Our exercise over, play ping-pong at B.B.C. club till we turn in to
our bunks in concert-hall.   Iraq declares war on Axis.

Sunday, January 17, 1943

To Westminster Abbey in morning. Feel it a disgrace that I have
never been to a service there. Arrive at 10.45 and find Matins began
at 10.30. A lot of uniforms in congregation: I am next to Australian
soldier in cocked hat. Only men in choir - choir school has been
evacuated. On coming out, about 11.30, meet Bob going in and return
with him to Low Mass till 12.
        David Green to supper and about 8 or 8.15 there is air-raid warn-
ing and much noise of gunfire. He rings up his fire station and asks
if he shall return immediately on his bicycle, but they say it would
be dangerous and that he'd better wait till the All Clear - which goes
about 9.45. Graham also to supper. Very pleasant evening in spite
of noise without.

Monday, January 18, 1943

Another air raid warning early this morning, about 4.45. Great
barrage of guns. I see beautiful fire-work display from my window,
and then think perhaps it would be as well to get away from the glass
and from possibility of bits of shell flying through where window is
open. So go out on landing for half-an-hour. All Clear about 5.30.
Hear one plane but no bombs. Jack, who went out to supper last night,
has not slept in his bed and does not return to breakfast, but he
comes in just before I leave for office. Was in road with friend who
got badly hit by shrapnel and had to have 5 stitches. Jack, John,
Tina, Joan and I have very pleasant evening at "The Petrified Forest",
an American play, and afterwards eat at the Hongkong restaurant in
Shaftesbury Avenue, served by amiable Chinese - one of the few restaurants in London at which one can get a meal after 9 o'clock.

Tuesday, January 19, 1943

8th Army advancing along coast road to Tripoli.   Russians advancing
on all fronts.
      Letter from home: think it must be enquiry after my safety be-
cause of Sunday's raid, but find it is a request to get sweets or
chocolates, with ration cards enclosed.

Wednesday, January 20, 1943

Return from having hair washed in lunch-hour and find there has been
air-raid warning and considerable amount of gunfire.   Heard nothing
of this, perhaps because was sitting under drier, which is instrument
of torture almost as bad as bomb.   Evening paper says large force of
bombers came over, biggest since Battle of Britain, but only about 10
got through to London, and 11 were brought down.
      To supper with the Abrahams at Hampstead.   Whenever I try to
leave they say "Oh, don't go yet!" till at last there is an air-raid
warning which lasts till nearly 11, and then they say "Why don't you
stay the night?" So I do.

Thursday, January 21, 1943

A school was hit in yesterday's daylight raid, and 45 people - children and staff - killed.
      Spend considerable time in lunch-hour searching for sweets to
take home, with Mother and Daddy's ration-cards.   Manage to get - from
various shops - ½ lb. chocolates, ½ lb. toffees, ¼ lb. crême de menthe
Turkish delight, and ¼ lb. barley sugar.
      Meant to note yesterday that Gerald Abraham said the Programme
people (B.B.C.) had had an extraordinary but quite serious order that
Commando troops and grass-eating were never to be mentioned in the
same broadcast.   Rather like saying that no report on a raid over
Germany was to be mentioned at same time as Wesleyan Methodism.   Feel
there must be some exciting inner meaning to this.

Friday, January 22, 1943

Very crowded train to Stroud - Cheltenham College children returning
to school on the 1.55 which I take.   Welcomed by Martin with his
mouth so full of cake he cannot speak.   Has learnt to kiss, which art
he practises on his gratified aunt.

Saturday, January 23, 1943

Take Martin for long pram-ride in morning.   In afternoon meet Phyllida who comes by bus from Cirencester in her Land Army Uniform, in
which she looks very nice.   She brings us a large cockerel, price 10/-
and 18 eggs, O joy, O rapture, 5 of which are cracked en route and we
scramble them.

Sunday, January 24, 1943

Phyllida and I to chapel, which we find is in the Sunday school, the heating arrangements in chapel having failed. P., along with some man in the Services, is publicly welcomed by name. She points out to me with some amusement, that as I wear no uniform, it matters not how many air raids I may have to endure, I shall be neither prayed for nor welcomed in public. I return to London, carelessly leaving behind hot-water-bottle and spectacles. Christmas card from Peter Scott, in Canada, posted December 12.

Monday, January 25, 1943

Busy in Mr. Pringle's absence. His wife reports that he has been hit in the stomach by a Brussels sprout.
        There appears to be an epidemic of flu about.

Tuesday, January 26, 1943

Editor, at printers, lets fall belief, which appears to be general, that the Prime Minister is off on one of his trips again and that news about it will be announced tomorrow morning at 8. He also says that no further reference is to be made on the wireless or in the paper to the Beveridge Report, until the matter has been debated by Parliament And no in future any talk we print which is about a matter of current political interest, and which is taken from the Overseas programme, must be shown to Sir Richard Maconachie, Controller of Home Programmes.

Wednesday, January 27, 1943

8 a.m. news says Churchill has been having conferences with Roosevelt and chiefs of staff on both sides, for the last 10 days, at Casablanca in North Africa. Germany has been telling everyone that Churchill was in Washington. They say we are making plans to invade Europe, which they declare to be impossible, at same time announcing plans for calling up vast hordes of people to prevent it.
        German armies round Stalingrad all wiped out or captured. We are advancing from Tripoli to the west.
        I meet Hilary, Martin, Tramp and the pram at Paddington, with taxi all ready for them, and we go via. park and embankment to Liverpool Street, where we get a nice porter, catch a convenient, and Leonard promises to meet them at 3.10 at Ware. Martin very much better for change and very talkative.

Thursday, January 28, 1943

Letter from Graham enclosing one from Ass.P.M.G., stating, in very grandiloquent language, that something had been wrong with the organisation for dealing with post to Middle East, at the Middle East end, but that now things were put right. G. wrote a correspondingly grandiloquent accompanying note, and I have replied in a flowery

letter, full of long sentences with many subordinate clauses and un-
necessary adjectives.   Hope he will enjoy reading it as much as I
enjoyed writing it.

Thursday, January 28, 1943

We are constantly told to eat more potatoes and less bread.   Mr.
Pringle lunched at the Athenaeum to-day, and instead of bread, he and
host were offered basket of tepid jacket potatoes.   "A little suggestion of Lord Woolton's", said the waiter.   Lord W. (Minister of
Food) is member of Athenaeum, and consequently the club can have none
of the dealings with the black market other London clubs have.
        Have fitting for my new spring suit, with which am very dis-
appointed.   Will fit well, but colour is not right for me.   They
showed me such small piece of material for pattern, that I judged
wrongly which colours in the check would be most prominent in larger
piece.   Waste of 18 coupons and 12 guineas.

Friday, January 29, 1943

Molly Evans says she knows man at Ministry of Information who says
the many advertisements in the press for jobs at the B.B.C. are nothing but bluff.   The Corporation has been told it must give up so many
men unless it is impossible to replace them.   So their jobs are ad-
vertised, but no one who applies has the least chance of being considered, because they want to say no one suitable is available.   Do
not know how much truth there is in this.
        Fire-watching at night.   Hitler has cancelled his speech
for tomorrow, his anniversary date.   Only once before in 10 years
has he failed to speak on this day;   that was during one of his
"purges".

Saturday, January 30, 1943

To Jean Law's at Potter's Bar.   Her husband away till Sunday evening,
on Home Guard manoeuvres.   Her younger son, Timothy (3½ or so) has
fallen off bicycle and has enormous lump on forehead.   The older one,
Richard (8) is sick, with temperature.   He recovers in afternoon,
and at night Tim. is sick, twice, over his bedclothes.   It pours
with rain and blows a gale all day.

Sunday, January 31, 1943

Timmy in bed all day.   I read to him a little, and also "Wind in the
Willows" to Richard.   It still pours with rain and blows hard.   When
Bill comes in, soaked to skin, he says a hut was blown into the river.
        Yesterday, first when Geering and second when Goebbels were about
to make speeches at Nazi Party anniversary celebrations in Berlin, the
R.A.F. bombed the city in daylight, and the broadcast was postponed.
        Return home in storm and wind.

Monday, February 1, 1943

Still stormy and windy.   Tree down in Bayswater Road yesterday.
Have sore throat and incipient cold and am very tired.   Finish re-
reading "Sense and Sensibility", which have enjoyed very much.

Tuesday, February 2, 1943

Churchill has been to Turkey, having conferences with high officials
of state, and also to Cyprus.   To supper at Bertorelli's in Queen's
Road, with Jack, Graham, Tina and Greta.   Afterwards play bridge at
Craven Hill Gardens, when I get consistently bad hands.

Wednesday, February 3, 1943

Wonderful searchlight display last night which I see from bed - like
fingers of light across sky.   Sometimes they are concentrated on the
same spot, and make a big revolving wheel.
     Spend 19/3 on 1 pair shoes repaired, 3 pairs laces, 1 pair heel-
grips, and 1 pair shoe-trees.   Find newpair of shoes which I have had
for months but not worn are not quite long enough in one foot.   Lilly
and Skinners kindly change them for ½-size larger, in which have to
have chamois leather lining to keep heels from slipping.

Thursday, February 4, 1943

To film with Greta, "The Lady Vanishes" - an old one which I haven't
seen before, and enjoy.   We come out about 11 o'clock into Baker St.
and not a bus is left running.   G. flashes her torch unhopefully at a
taxi and we are surprised when it stops.   Driver agrees to take us to
Paddington, only adding as we plunge inside that he already has a naval
gentleman there.   Sure enough, a shy young naval officer is sitting in
the shadows, very startled at having 2 strange women diving in to his
taxi in the middle of London.   However, we talk to him about film to
try to show how harmless we are, and are dropped before cab goes into
Paddington, when driver tells us grandly we can pay him anything we can
afford when of course we feel compelled to give him twice the usual
fare so he, if not the naval officer, does well out of it.

Friday, February 5, 1943

Another fitting for my suit which I do not loathe quite as much.
     To Hilary's, where sleep in room with bed in it and not another
thing - no floor covering.   One of the parties whose furniture is in
the bungalow has removed its share, and what remains has not yet been
redistributed over the whole.

Saturday, February 6, 1943

Take Martin for walk, when we see beautiful rainbow.   He is much better
for his holiday.   Get ¼ lb. sweets, remains of his month's ration.
     Russians getting near Rostov.

Sunday, February 7, 1943

Churchill back in England.   Has visited Eighth Army in Tripoli.
        Leonard spends all morning with Home Guard, defending Wareside,
which is being attacked by Ware.   No one knows who has won, but a
good time was had by all.   L. sat in a hedge with a fire-rattle which
made machine-gun fire, and mowed down all oncomers, then rushed back
under cover of hedge to take up new position.   Both sides think they
were ~~vuetiruiys~~, victorious.   We see the Ware contingents (hundreds
of them against the village's 30) marching cheerfully home to Sunday
dinner.   They wave at Martin, so he enjoys the affair too.

Monday, February 8, 1943

Russians have recaptured Kursk, important town, and are advancing on
all fronts.

Tuesday, February 9, 1943

Very irritated by Miss Playle, who is so busy being something or other
to feed starving Europe after the war (which I am sure will be very
necessary) that she gives little proper attention to the job for which
she is paid, and makes numbers of mistakes which contribute to keeping
me late at printers.
        Was going to ballet with Miss Mearing, but she cannot get ticket.
Spend evening knitting knickers for Hilary.

Wednesday February 10, 1944

Air-raid warning during afternoon and sound of gunfire.   Buy pair
woollen ribbed stockings for Hilary, 8/4, at Dickens and Jones (3
coupons), and pair ribbed lisle (very difficult to get now), 7/6 and 3
coupons.
        Circulation of Listener goes up and up, and Editor is told to keep
it down.   Either that, or, if it goes up, the size will have to get
progressively smaller, because of paper shortage.   Rather odd for an
Editor to be told that his duty is to keep circulation down.

Thursday, February 11, 1943

Lunch-time concert at National Gallery: Griller Quartet - Haydn in
D major, and Fauré piano quartet.   Went off into haze in latter and
heard little, but enjoyed former.   Constable's "Hay Wain" being ex-
hibited (one of the Individual Masterpieces which is usually allthey
have now: they rush it to the vaults if there is an air-raid warning,
and each night as matter of course).   Was staggered at picture's
bright colours, having only seen black-and-white reproductions: blue-
and-white sky, green trees touched with yellow, horse with red trap-
pings on his harness, etc.   Like it very much.

Friday, February 12, 1943

Leonard has just been told he is to have £250 a year rise; so is
Ronald.   Moreover, Ronald, whose final reservation expires in April,
is to have the whole of his salary paid in his absence, and presumably same will apply to Leonard.   Beg Hilary to remember that £125
will go at once in income tax, so not to become too lavish.

Saturday, February 13, 1943

Have Martin sleeping in my room and he behaves perfectly, not stirring
till 7.30 a.m. when he stands up in cot and says "Cuckoo, Ahzah", so I
take him into my bed.   He seems very well and is full of conversation.
See about 40 Flying Fortresses going over in morning, and wireless reports later that the Americans have bombed targets in France and
Belgium.

Sunday, February 14, 1943

Russians seem to be cutting off Germans at Rostov.   Train to London
just sits on line for 15 minutes and so misses connection at Broxbourne and I am late for supper and therefore unpopular.   See magnificent sunset sky, and read Jeans' "Philosophy and Physics", of which
I dimly understand about a third.   It seems highly improbable that anything exists, except perhaps Mind.   Eddington, in "Science and the
Unseen World", which was a lecture to Quakers, says "Among leading
scientists today I think about half assert that the aether exists and
the other half deny its existence; but as a matter of fact both parties
mean exactly the same thing, and are divided only by words".   So where
are you?

Monday, February 15, 1943

Jack probably going to Algiers, to be in charge of a naval base of
some sort.   Is very pleased at the prospect.

Tuesday, February 16, 1943

Kharkov captured by Russians.   They may be doing glorious things, but
I spend whole evening knitting knickers for Hilary and then, finding I
have dropped a stitch miles down, taking out all I have knitted.
     Government has been debating Beveridge Report, and Graham has made
good speech, to effect that Government has chance for first time of
showing its good faith about social reconstruction.

Wednesday, February 17, 1943

In evening, with Miss Mearing to "Merchant of Venice", which starts at
6 p.m.   Frederick Valk, Czech actor, as very good Shylock.   First
time I have seen play and I enjoy it very much.

Thursday, February 18, 1943

Government trying to shelve Beveridge Report.   So annoyed, I spend

morning writing five letters to variouspapers, protesting. Try to
adapt in each case stype suited to paper I write to.   Use a nom-de-plume
for each: Elizabeth Stroud writes to the Herald, Joan Bryan to the Mail,
Cynthia Reed to News-Chronicle, Phyllida Stone to Express, and Joyce Evans
to the Mirror.
Friday,
~~Saturday~~. February 19, 1943

~~With Martin to village shop to~~ To Ware.   Lily going to have another baby,
and Mrs. Evans, faced with husband having operation, and the other little
boy to look after while L. is incapacitated, calls the news "dreadful".
Unless the Government takes steps to help people who are going to have
children, they will never get the increase in the birth-rate they are
supposed to want.

Saturday, February 20, 1943

With Martin to village shop in ineffectual effort to get soap-flakes.
Get only 1 small packet of soap-powder.

Sunday, February 21, 1943

Germans have captured 3 air-fields from Amer&ans in Tunisia.   Eighth
Army advancing.   Russians also doing well.   Regret to say that attitude
of most of English is not concern for our allies suffering reverses, but
pleasure that the Americans' haughty spirit is being brought low.
Prime Minister unwell with acute catarrh.

Monday, February 22, 1943

When I go to bed, am unable to sleep.   At 11.45, with strong feeling of
impending cold, get up and boil kettle to do some inhaling.
Tuesday
~~Wednesday~~, February 23, 1943

Late going to press.   Americans being driven back by Germans in Tunisia.
Certainly have cold.   Inhale again.

Wednesday
~~Thursday~~, February 24, 1943

Couldn't sleep last night.   Today have streaming cold.   In afternoon
go into park for about $\frac{3}{4}$ hour, feeling fresh air may drive it away.   At
night on fire duty.   British and Americans now repelling Germans in
Tunisia.   Am told that American newspapers are somewhat humbler than
they were.   They admit that at one time they thought one red-blooded
American equal to 3 British, and were uncharitable to us when we were
being defeated.   Say they are now learning their mistake and hope we
shall be more charitable to them in their adversity.

Thursday, February 25, 1943

Have hair washed.   Come home soon after 4 in afternoon, with very bad
cold.   Walk through park, where almond and other flowering trees are
already in blossom and crocuses are almost over.

<u>Friday, February 26, 1943</u>

In lunch-hour to concert at National Gallery - 2 pianos: Bach (good) but
rest ofprogramme dull.   In Trafalgar an aeroplane (bomber) is being
built, as incentive to people to invest money in war savings.   It is a
four-engined, enormous thing, and crowds watch it.
        They now tell us Prime Minister has had slight pneumonia.   Is now
better.   Sir Richard Acland has given his estates to the nation.

<u>Saturday, February 27, 1943</u>

Beautiful warm day.   To Claygate, to tea and supper with Pringles, who
have two amusing boys, 3½ and 1¾ years old.   Last night very heavy raid
by R.A.F. on Cologne, where 4,000 and even 8,000 lb. bombs were dropped.
The bomb which devastated the B.B.C. end of Portland Place was only about
2,000 lb. and that was one of the biggest London had.   Gandhi ill, from
a self-imposed fast in imprisonment.

<u>Sunday, February 28, 1943</u>

Go forth to morning service;   find St. Martin-in-the-Fields started at
10.30 with communion and does not have matins till 11.30.   Wander up St.
Martin's Lane, and after several investigations of bombed buildings, end
at Bloomsbury Baptist Chapel, which starts at the orthodox hour of 11.

<u>Monday, March 1, 1943</u>

Mild day for first of March, which comes in like a lamb.
        Madame Chiang Kai-shek ill.   Churchill better.   Still have cold and
am very snuffly.

<u>Tuesday, March 2, 1943</u>

Berlin given its heaviest raid of war last night, and we all expect one
on London in return.   Very late to press and am tired and depressed in
consequence.   Cold still rather bad.

<u>Wednesday, March 3, 1943</u>

Decide it is warm enough to leave off winter coat, then day turns out very
cold and feel have been foolish.   Gandhi has come through 21 days' fast
he set himself.

<u>Thursday, March 4, 1943</u>

Last evening after had made entry for diary, there was air-raid warning and
lot of gunfire for an hour.   Another short one in night, about 5 a.m.
Heard no bombs.   Today Hilary rings up to ask if raid was very heavy,
since the terrific gunfire round them rocked the house.   Buy pair shoes
for Martin and, great prize, get little pair rubber boots (sub-standard
and only 2/9) from Daniel Neal's.

Friday, March 5, 1943

Think I will take Hilary few mushrooms for treat , but on enquiry find
price is 12/6 a lb.   Also price of small bunch of daffodils is 12/6.
This is because there is ban on sending flowers either by rail or by
post.   So there are no barrows in streets with early flowers from the
Scillies and Cornwall.   One misses them: they are usually one of the
first tokens of Spring.

Saturday, March 6, 1943

Martin almost speechless with rapture over his little green boots, "like
Daddy's" - only Daddy's are black.   Leonard has heard he is on the
"permanent" list of reserved people - as permanent as anyone is nowadays.
If he is to be called up he will get 6 months' notice.   They have there-
fore sent for their furniture from Orpington.
     Beautiful day.   Take Martin to village shop to buy dog-biscuits for
Tramp, all of which he wishes to throw out on way home.

Sunday, March 7, 1943

Martin inmy room to sleep.   Has bad twinge of toothache at 1.30.   Even
magnificent offer of going into aunt's bed does not comfort him.   His
mother has to come up.   After twinge has passed he consents to come into
bed where he wriggles like an eel and tries to be very conversational for
two hours. After which we both sleep till 8.30. Beautiful day.   Sit
out of doors, in sun, on sheltered side of house.   Then go in and make
toast by kitchen fire for tea.   Combination which has disastrous effect
on face which becomes very sore.   Short air-raid warning during afternoon.
We wish for exciting dog-fight above, when our side shallwin, no one get
killed, and all German air-crew land by parachute in garden to be rounded
up by Leonard with Home Guard gun.   But nothing happens.

Monday, March 8, 1943

Miss Playle presents me with large basin of dripping from her sister's to
take to Hilary.   How her sister, on rations for two, gets large amounts
of dripping, cannot think.   Do not enquire but accept present gladly.
Short air-raid alarm last night, about 130.   Paper to-day says there was
only one enemy plane.   There was quite a bit of gunfire, but only for a
short time.
     Dreadful accident happened in air-raid shelter at Bethnel Green last
Wednesday, when people were going down at sound of air-raid alarm.   180
or so people suffocated to death, because - as far as one can make out - a
woman with baby and bundle tripped going down steps.   It seems incredible
that so many people should have been killed, and there is to be an enquiry.
Leonard's Home Guard colleagues had a tale that panic was deliberately
created by gang of pickpockets, who realised that the Bethnel Green people,
who have no confidence in Banks, etc., take all their possessions with
them to shelter.   Tina has story that very low pub. is near entrance to
shelter, and that people poured out of it half drunk and pushed the crowd
from behind.

Tuesday, March 9, 1943

Fire duty at night after heavy day at printers'.   There is new batch
of professional firemen, one of whom explains that one way of the hose
is the wap and the other way the wop (warp and woof?) and this must be
remembered because otherwise "it makes you look so foolish, don't it?"
- though of what use this knowledge is in putting out a fire he does
not say.   Also "Never call two lengths of hose 'hoses', it's 'hose',
just the same.   If you call it 'hoses' it makes you look so foolish,
don't it?"

Wednesday, March 10, 1943

No Alert last night.   Today to concert at National Gallery: Beethoven
Trio and Schubert's "Trout" Quintet.   Time of concert has been moved
to 1.30 for this week because "Wings for Victory" week is being held.
There is not only enormous Lancaster bomber in Trafalgar Square, but
bands, amplified through loudspeakers, and speeches urging people to
invest money in war savings certificates.   So after much communication
it has been agreed that if concerts start this week at 1.30, for the
last half-hour loudspeakers without shall be silent.   In return, we are
asked in short speech before concert to buy a few savings stamps.
      Elderly man next to me says after Trio: "This classical music is
dull though, isn't it?"   And then remarks loudly as they start the
"Trout", "This isn't so bad because of the piano".   I do not "show my
gratitude" by subscribing for bombs to be dropped over Germany.   The
papers today say that most of old Nuremberg has been destroyed, and
last night we attacked Munich.

Thursday, March 11, 1943

Strings of R.A.F. Orchestra at National Gallery.   Elgar's "Introduction
and Allegro for Strings".   Beautiful.   All young men playing: makes
one realise how all the orchestras one has heard lately have been made
up of old men and elderly women.
      John very upset at dinner time.   Does not speak at all.   We per-
suade him to come to film, from James Hilton's book "Random Harvest".
Good film which I enjoy.

Friday, March 12, 1943

Was awake for considerable amount of night worrying over sufferings of
hero and heroine in "Random Harvest".   To Ware, with basin of dripping
from Miss Playle's sister, which Hilary receives with great joy.
      Kharkov being re-attacked by Germans.

Saturday, March 13, 1943

There is fighting in streets of Kharkov; and we see 40 Flying Fortresses go over during morning - and count them all back in afternoon.
Meantime, in glorious sunshine Martin and I are engaged in such peaceful pursuits as having ride in farm-cart behind Bob, along with peelings
for pigs, and walking into Wareside.   Martin wears green boots so that
he can walk in water and splash.

Sunday, March 14, 1943

Beautiful day.   Help to dig garden in afternoon, and pick bunch of
violets to take back to London.   Hilary finds some wild white ones.
John's depression of Friday explained.   He had asked Nancy to marry
him and she had refused.   But he has not given up hope.

Monday, March 15, 1943

Kharkov evacuated by Russians, but they have taken Vyazma.

Tuesday, March 16, 1943

Still beautiful mild weather.   To film "Desert Victory", telling of
our attack against Rommel from Egypt to Tripoli.   Four photographers
were killed, four captured and three wounded in the taking of this
film.   It is a remarkable and terrible record of modern warfare. How
men can come out of it sane I don't know.   It all seems to me mad and
useless.   A horrible lascivious old man next to me keeps feeling my
thigh and trying to take my hand.   As soon as there is another vacant
seat I move intoit.

Wednesday, March 17, 1943

Foggy.   In lunch-hour to recital of 24 Chopin Etudes by Moiseiwitsch
at National Gallery, where I see Lesley Goad and absent-mindedly walk
off with 8/- of her change which she rings up and asks for in middle
of afternoon.   Go also to exhibition at Nat.Gall. organised by Royal
Institute of British Architects and other bodies, called "Rebuilding
Britain".   Wants planned towns, with houses separated from factories,
and shopping centre, civic centre, etc., all in not-too-big units.
And planned countryside.   Manage to buy 6 cups, saucers and plates for
Hilary - all plain white, cost of £1.1.0.   "Utility" cups have no
handles, but these are not "utility".

Thursday, March 18, 1943

Get vegetable dish for Mother who has broken lid of hers.   Fortunate
in getting same pattern - 9/6 from Lewis's.

Friday, March 19, 1943

Airgraph from Peter in Canada sent on 10th.   He appears to have won
the Air Force Cross, since A.F.C. is appended to name and address of
sender, but does not mention it.   Seems to be homesick: is staying
there for a while, lecturing.
     To Hilary's with crockery I got for her, which is very heavy to
carry, and quart of milk which she rings up and asks me to call for on
way from station.   She appears to have pretty well as much milk as she
likes at present.

Saturday, March 20, 1943

H.'s furniture comesfrom Orpington.   L. has put in all his Mother's
garden chairs by mistake.   Martin and I have ride beside driver while
he turns van round.   Many squeals of joy from H. as she opens old
boxes and finds what are now treasures of great price, i.e. old handbag, scarf, etc.   Go to village shop with Martin, who produces farth-
ing and reaches up to push it hopefully across counter.   Lady there so
touched that she gives him piece of toffee, which he will now expect ø
every time he goes.

Sunday, March 21, 1943

Back to London.   Train has broken down, so, øø in company of Sergeant
of Pioneer Corps, I take bus to Hertford and train from there to King's
Cross.   Now know almost everything about Pioneer Corps, A.T.S., and
the mud of Oxfordshire.   Prime Minister giveslong broadcast.

Monday, March 22, 1943

Listener pulled to pieces to get in four pages of Prime Minister.
There is criticism from many M.P.s about speech.   They think it ought
to have been made first to Parliament.

Tuesday, March 23, 1943

Long and trying press day.   Very tired.   Weather still beautiful.
Country beginning to look dusty and as if it needs rain.
        Eighth Army has pierced Mareth Line and is advancing in N. Africa.

Wednesday, March 24, 1943

Setback in N. Africa.   Germans have recaptured most of our gain in
Mareth Line.   P.M. says the struggle will be long and bloody.
        London looking more like itself in Spring, because ban on sending
flowers by train has been raised, and there are barrows with daffodils
about the streets.

Thursday, March 25, 1943

With Greata and 2 more women to supper at Paddington and to René Clair's
new film, "I Married a Witch".   Have to pay 5/6 to get in.   Quite good
but nothing like his old French films, "Sous les Toits de Paris", etc.

Friday, March 26, 1943

To Hilary's.   Leonard fire-watching.   He has made a little seat for
Martin to go on back of Hilary's bicycle.   It has curved back and two
arms, and M. sits strapped to it on a cushion, enjoying himself very øø
much.   H. has taken him twice into town and once into village on it and
find it a great saving of time and energy.

Saturday, March 27, 1943

Leonard looking very tired.   Has been working late all the week and
twice has dashed home for half-hour supper and immediately gone out to
Home Guard, on each occasion having to put on full kit and march four
miles to have rifle ø inspected and four miles back.   Then wasfire-
watching last night.   H. lets him off the gardening which is crying out
to be done and he snoozes most of afternoon.

Sunday, March 28, 1943

Warm sunshine disguises cold wind.   A little gentle gardening with
Martin and H.   Then M. and I pick violets from back of house, and it
is time for me to come away.

Monday, March 29, 1943

We have taken Mareth Line positions in N. Africa.
     With Tina and Audrey Mearing to Shaw's "Heartbreak House" (Edith
Evans as Mrs. Hushabye, Isabel Jeans as Lady Utterworth, Robert Donat
as Capt. Shotover, Deborah Kerr as Ellie.   Most enjoyable.   Not a dull
moment from ø/4ß/½ø/ 6.30 to 9.45.

Tuesday, March 30, 1943

Most irritating day, starting with my taking bundle of other people's
clothes to cleaners, only to be told they have exceeded their quota for
the week and cannot accept them.   Have to take them all back home which
makes me very late to printers.   The day goes badly and we do not
finish till 7 o'clock.   Have been given ticket for Vic.Wells ballet at
the New Theatre (opening night) which started at 6.45.   Arrive at 8
o'clock in middle of "Apparitions".   Meet Mr. McNaught, our music critic,
and sit next to Frank Howes, "Times" music critic, who shares my water-
cress.   See "Façade" which have seen before.   Sorry to have missed
"The Wise Virgins"; and my impressions of what was going on in the part
of "Apparitions" which I did see, differ widely from explanation I read
in programme notes when light goes up.

Wednesday, March 31, 1943

To supper with Abrahams.   Mosco Carner, conductor, there; and after
we have eaten a Polish artist and his Scottish wife arrive.   Enjoyable
evening.   Earlier in day had words with Editor on lateness of Listener
going to press and general slackness of us all.   Ask him to get rid of
a few of us, which will make for better work by those left; but this he
will not contemplate.

Thursday, April 1, 1943

R.A.F. Day, and broadcast programmes full of nauseating nobleness.

Friday, April 2, 1943

To Hilary's, where the wakeful Martin is standing up in cot declaring
his intention not to lie down and go to sleep.

Saturday, April 3, 1943

Very warm. Martin and I pick blue and white violets, and he jumps
up and down in 2 inches of water, wearing his green rubber boots.
Mrs. Parrish gives us 3 of her ducks' eggs. Clocks put on one hour.

Sunday, April 4, 1943

Daddy's 67th birthday. Bob is put out in field for first time this
year. He snorts with joy and thunders in rapturous circles and we are
warned to keep Martin from crawling through fence for day or two.

Monday, April 5, 1943

Fire-watching last night. We went on roof of Broadcasting Houseand
wewe actually allowed real water to play with. Our leader, with much
joy, directed flow from sitrrup pump into street, remarking that her
husband was somewhere about waiting for her.

Tuesday, April 6, 1943

Weather suddenly much colder, with north wind. Am knitting cardigan
for Martin with 11 or 12 different coloured stripes in it - from odd
bits of wool.

Wednesday, April 7, 1943

To dentist: 3 fillings to be done. He says there is much more dental
decay since war started - faulty diet, I suppose. Cannot make appoint
ment for second filling for anothermonth, and remarks as he drills
further and further into my head that he is working so hard, he acts all
the time in a dream: feel it may at any moment turninto nightmare for
me.
        Very high wind: cold. Eighth Army, and also Americans, advancing
in N. Africa.
        Mother has had flu. Daddy spent 67th birthday running up and
down stairs, cooking milk pudding with many instructions. She is a
little better.

Thursday, April 8, 1943

Phyllida's 34th birthday. To ballet with Audrey Mearing. "Gods Go
Begging" (music by Handel), a new one, "The Quest", from "Faerie Queene"
(Walton), and "Les Rendez-Vous" (forget whose music). Pay 5/- for
seats and enjoy it very much. New Budget, which will be announced
shortly, may put extra tax on entertainment. Buy plain tailored blue
silk blouse with long sleeves at iniquitous cost of £3.16.3.

Friday, April 9, 1943

Home by midday train. Mother still very weak and depressed after flu.

Saturday, April 10, 1943

Daddy glad to have someone to get his breakfast.   Mother's opinion
of Phyllida's friendship with airman, Arthur Place, has had three distinct phases, which, now she hears he is being transferred elsewhere,
run: (1) My poor daughter, no doubt being deceived by married man!
(2) Well, he may not be married, but anyway not half good enough for
Phyllida.   (3) Oh Poor Phyllida, now he'll probably go to North
Africa and she'll never see him again.

Sunday, April 11, 1943

Back to London.   Letter from Peter in Canada, which has come since
March 25.   Says people in Canada think they are suffering rigours of
war if they have to ask specially in restaurants for butter and cream.
Adds at end: "By the way I have altered to Flying Officer and added
an Air Force Cross to my tunic for some flying in England".   No explanation.

Monday, April 12, 1943

Budget puts extra prices on beer, alcohol and entertainments.   The
Abrahams to supper: glad to find the "family" here takes to them very
well, and they seem to take to it.

Tuesday, April 13, 1943

Very fine and warm.   The flowering trees round the printers building
are all at their best, so that the works look quite attractive.   Walk
beside the canal with Mr. Pringle in lunch-hour.   On his way to work
a man walked beside him and quite gratuitously gave him the information
that he was helping to make a new secret plane - the "Firefly", I think
he said.   Also said no one in his factory had done a good day's work
for two years.

Wednesday, April 14, 1943

To Newell's for night, to see her in Passion Play, in which she is the
Virgin Mary.   The caste varies from a very able and dramatic Judas (the
Curate), who much enjoys casting down his 30 pieces of silver and
taking rope from his robe to make dramatic exit for hanging, through an
able Pontius Pilate who, however, looks about 16, which he is, to a
perfect stick of a Caiaphas - he and Annas the High Priest obviously
being quite uneducated, whereas Peter the fisherman and Judas are equally obviously educated.   However, all actors throughly enjoy themselves.

Thursday, April 15, 1943

Before I get up, Timothy, aged 4, "reads" to me from one of the Moldy
Warp books - i.e. he knows it all by heart and turns over at right place
because of pictures.   Day turns out very hot and I am wearing winter
suit and long-sleeved woollen jumper still.

Friday, April 16, 1943

Miss Mearing has heard that her fiancé, from whom she has

not heard for about 2 years, is prisoner in Malaya.   Is going to try
to write to him - he may get letter, through Red Cross, in about 6
months.   But she is not likely to get letter back.   I have letter
from Roy written February 28.   He says mails to them take much longer
since the campaign in N. Africa started.   Refers to one Hertzsprung,
Director of the Leiden Observatory, who I gather is carrying on with
his work though the Germans have closed the University to which the
Observatory is attached.   Roy says: "... the sort kind of man who, if
the Germans took him out to shoot him one morning, would lecture the
firing squad on the vital necessity of observing variable stars regularly, and probably almost persuade them to do it!"

Saturday, April 17, 1943

Work in morning, because of oncoming of Easter.   In afternoon, to Kew
Gardens with Heimann.   Just the right time to go: pink, light and
deep, and white cherry trees in blossom, also magnolia and lilac, and
bluebells just coming on.   Very warm: we lie in sun for some time,
to detriment of my newly-cleaned suit.   In evening to Broadcasting Ho.
for fire-watching.

Sunday, April 18, 1943

We have made great raid on Skoda armament works in Czechoslovakia, and
on other targets.   600 planes, and 51 are lost.   I walk home from
fire-watching through park, which is full of blossom and fresh green in
early morning.   To service at St. Matthew's (I believe), Bayswater.
Low Church.   Like it.   In afternoon to Putney, to tea with Editor of
Radio Times and wife, to see their adopted baby (they had her at 5 weeks)
who has just had her 1st birthday.   Very attractive little dark girl.
Still beautifully fine and warm.   The lack of rain is becoming serious.

Monday, April 19, 1943

Mr. Pringle has flu.   At printers till 8 o'clock, going to press early
for Easter.   No need whatever for this late hour that I can see, except
desire of printers to earn a little overtime for the holiday.

Tuesday, April 20, 1943

Greta has sent home beautiful new coat and skirt which she bought ready
made for 23 guineas!   And her resident in this house told me recently
she had paid 25 guineas for a suit.   I go with Miss Mearing to get her
our parting present (she is being called up and sent into industry) and
she chooses "Revelation" suitcase (£3.19.6), well made but not leather-
none to be had - only fibre.   Weather cooler.

Wednesday, April 21, 1943

Buy new blue hat to go with my suit, 34/3 (value about 12/11 pre-war).
Difficulty in getting right colour, and Harrod's not at all anxious for
me to buy, since they have had their quota of hats and will get no more

until August.   Greta has had news during day that Jack has meningitis,
and has been very ill.   They have the new drug which cures the disease
in North Africa, so we hope he will be all right.

Cooler day, and in evening it is inclined to rain, which, in spite
of oncoming holiday, very much hope it will do, for the lack of it is
very serious.

Thursday, April 22, 1943

With Miss Mearing and Mr. Abraham to National Gallery concert in lunch-
hour.   Haydn's Seven Last Words from the Cross, played by Griller
Quartet.   Had not heard this before.   Written as music for small
orchestra to be played between arias at Cadiz Cathedral.   Later Haydn
arranged instrumental part for string quartet.

Friday, April 23, 1943

Good Friday but we work in morning.   Give lunch to Miss Mearing at
Viainis, 10/8, for each which we had beautifully cooked roast lamb,
roast potatoes, spinach;   minute amount of tinned fruit salad with real
cream;   coffee.   After this (her parting meal) go on to Ware;   met by
Martin (with Mother and dog) in mackintosh down to feet, with hood, and
little green boots.   He travels to Ark on his Mother's bicycle;   it
rains most of way.

Saturday, April 24, 1943

Eighth Army starts new offensive in N. Africa.   Mr. and Mrs. Evans
arrive about noon.   M. rides with them in taxi from station, event to
which he has been looking forward for days.   Mrs. E. brings many
provisions.   We now have in house, fish, joint of beef, two ½ lb. of
liber, cold lamb and knuckle bone of ham.

Sunday, April 25, 1943

Does not seem like Easter Sunday.   Ban on bell-ringing has been lifted
but we hear none.   Mr. White brings 6 ducks' eggs from Mrs Parrish's.
Hilary, Leonard, Martin and I for walk in afternoon.   L. very distressed
to see soldiers, with gun, on site which he and rest of Home Guard have
been preparing for their own purposes for weeks.

Monday, April 26, 1943

Very high wind which howls round unprotected Ark.   Gather firewood in
morning, of which there is any amount to be had for the picking up.
Return to London at midday, to work in afternoon.   However, leave
early and walk home.   Long queue outside Marble Arch Corner House
waiting for meal.

Tuesday, April 27, 1943

At printers till 8 p.m.   Much colder.   There appears to be tension between ~~American~~ Poles and Russians, between Americans and Finns, and between Germans and Swedes.

Wednesday, April 28, 1943

Still ~~no~~ knitting with much vigour my cardigan for Martin made out of wool remnants. Polesand Russians have broken off diplomatic relations

Thursday, April 29, 1943

Finish reading C. E. Montague's "Disenchantment" - enough to make one weep.   All the rottenness of the last war repeated in this one, and not one of the lessons (which he points out) learnt. Half the population still deluded with tales of atrocities which I for one do not believe.   Though Nancy Parkinson of the British Council, who comes to supper and has been talking to Poles, reports that they say: "But you wren't kept in prison by Russians from the age of 10 to 12, as I was, and told you were going to be put to death ... As a matter of fact I wasn't put to death" (said this woman) "but my father was shot instead". And anothersaid: "You weren't in our village when the Russians came and killed every man of fighting age. That was in 1939. It is not easy to forget".   But now the Russians are our allies it is only the Germans to whom atrocities are allowed, or the Italians or Japanese.

Friday, April 30, 1943

Lots of beautiful gentle rain which is just what the earth needs.   To National Gallery concert. Flute, piano, cello, violin. Haydn and Bach. Very pleasant.   But no one to go with now Miss Mearing has left. Fire-watching at night.

Saturday, May 1, 1943

To Ware with Tina, who brings ready-cooked meat pie with her.   Very cold wind.   H. says epidemic of measles in Ware.   She has cut up and washed old coat of hers which we begin to convert into dressing-gown for Martin.

Sunday, May 2, 1943

Cold again, but warm when one gets out of wind.   Go out for 2 hours with Martin, who walks for 1½ hours over fields. He pretends all time that he is Grandpa, and hits brambles out of way with walking-stick. I finish his little "Josepy" coat and Tina finishes his dressing-gown, which hasmany joins in odd places but of which he is very pleased because it is something like his Daddy's.

Monday, May 3, 1943

To London. Taxi to station.   Only hired vehicle left in Ware, so driver has to come early to fit in others catching same train. P.C. from Joyce who because of abscess has to have 2 front teeth out.

Tuesday, May 4, 1943

To press at 6 p.m..   In evening to film, "Shadow of a Doubt", rather exciting.

Wednesday, May 5, 1943

To dentist who does two fillings ¢¢ since he does not know when he could give me another appointment for ages.   In lunchtime meet Miss de la Mo Motte and have lunch with her.   Buy 6 fruit bottles (2 lb. size) for H., which, with metal caps and rubber rings, cost altogether 5/6.

Thursday, May 6, 1943

Americans and British in Tunisia are making large-scale attack.   I take clothes to be cleaned, but cannot find anyone who will receive them because they have all "exceeded their quota" for week already. Read John Steinbeck's "The Moon is Down", about the occupation of a town - presumably in Norway and presumably by the Germans.   Verywell written and rather heart-rending.   Jack, who has meningitis in Algiers, had been pronounced out of danger.

Friday, May 7, 1943

To Ware: call for quart milk en route (H. very lucky in amount of milk she can get).   Lift in car to door of Fanhams from one in V.A.D. uniform who, H. says, is Lady Anne Brocket.   Leonard on fire-duty.

Saturday, May 8, 1943

Air raid warning about 7.30 a.m., and sound of bomb at 7.45.   Just before 8, Leonard rings up from Hertford to say bomb has just burst about 200 yards from him, while he was shaving, and blown in window.   He is unhurt.   5 bombs altogether; not much damage and only a few minor injuries from broken glass.
    Tunis and Bizerta both captured by Allies.   Take Martin for walk ind readful wind and occasional rain, during all of which time he says he is the greengrocer.   Leonard gives pint of blood at Hertford hospital.   Blood is dried and sent in form of powder to front for use.

Sunday, May 9, 1943

L. supposed to go to Home Guard shooting competition, but is lethargic after yesterday's blood-letting and stays in bed.   Very high wind again but sunny in afternoon, and I take M. walk down overgrown lane where hedge-parsley is higher than he is: during all this time he is being the postman.

Monday, May 10, 1943

Back to London.   Ring up and manage to get car to fetch me to station, since morning is still very blustery and wet.

Tuesday, May 11, 1943

. Reading translation of Herodotus, in which it is said of Croesus, who was apparently a sort of Hitler about 560 B.C.: 'The Ephesians ... were the first Greeks whom he attacked. Afterwards, on some pretext or other, he made war in turn upon every Ionian and Aeolian state, bringing forward, where he could, a substantial ground of complaint; where such failed him, advancing some poor excuse'.

Wednesday, May 12, 1943

Mr. Churchill in Washington to discuss war plans with Roosevelt. We have turned Germans out of Bon Peninsula, last part of Tunisia they held.
    Peter Beavan, on leave from Merchant Navy, rings up, and I go with him and John and girl I haven't met before, to Shaw's "Heartbreak House": very pleasant. P. so pleased to be back in London. We go down and lean our arms on parapet of Thames and regard water with affection. He apparently founds string quartets wherever he goes - Bermuda, Halifax (Nova Scotia), etc. At Halifax he formed quartet, and on a second trip out took them music parts from England. Also once, on landing at Liverpool, found Philharmonic were giving concert, so went round to see them, found they had only 4 cellos, borrowed evening dress and instrument and played for them.

Thursday, May 13, 1943

Von Arnim captured. With Tina to Turgenev's "A Month in the Country". If Russians spend such hours laying bare their souls and handing the bits all round, how will they ever find time to win a war? Fire-watching in evening.

Friday, May 14, 1943

For first time during fire-watch of mine we have warning. Man comes and wakes us, saying "The red's up, ladies", which it takes me some time to understand. We stay up for hour, till All Clear. This morning have to wait in airless corridor for one of the dressing-rooms to become vacant, and feel very faint. Am revived by Matron with sal volatile and later with coffee. Take taxi home to breakfast. Feel very bad again on reading letter from David which begins "I expect you will have heard of the death, in an Ottawa hospital, of Peter Scott. We suppose from an air-crash". To Hilary's in hot sunshine. Have never seen fields so full of buttercups or hedges so white with hawthorn. Feel very tired and sad.
    Prime Minister broadcasts from Washington - only $\frac{1}{4}$ hour to celebrate Home Guard's third birthday.

Saturday, May 15, 1943

Martin wakes several times during hot night, and I am rather disturbed
and to-day very tired. Sit in warm sun, and go beautiful walk beside
hawthorn-laden hedges and feel a bit better.

Sunday, May 16, 1943

Still very tired.   Take Martin to see what I tell him are baby quack-
quacks, but find they are really goslings; so fluffy and pretty.   Back
to London by late train.   Take rhubarb for Miss Morrison with which she
is very pleased, for it is very difficult to buy it.

Monday, May 17, 1943

We have bombed some enormous dams which supply water for Ruhr, have
flooded miles of country and put much industry out of action.   Some
planes over here last night: 2 3 alerts and quite a lot of gunfire.
In evening Miss de la Motte to supper, when there occurs something which
I think is rather odd (especially as I am beginning to read Dunne's
"Experiment with Time").   I met her about a fortnight ago and referred
to Peter Scottwhom she knew.   Told her his brother had been killed and
that he was in Canada lecturing for R.A.F.   We had quite a little conversation about him, among other people.   To-day I show her letter
from David telling of Peter's death, and she says: "Yes, of course, I
knew he was dead. You told me".   And it appears she went away from
our former conversation (which I remember quite clearly) with impression
that Peter was dead (a fortnight before I heard the news).
       This evening we go to very bad film, "The Commandos Strike at Dawn".

Tuesday, May 18, 1943

To press late and I feel very exhausted.   Beautiful weather.

Wednesday, May 19, 1943

More alerts last night so that I get about 4 hours' sleep; there is a
full moon.   Churchill speaks to both Houses of Congress in America and
his speech is broadcast.

Thursday, May 20, 1943

To Beavans.   Peter still on leave and comes in at 9 o'clock after rehearsal with Boyd Neel Orchestra for broadcast on Sunday.   Arthur in
very nervous condition; is taking treatment from psychologist.

Friday, May 21, 1943

Very tired.   My eyes feel as if they have weights on them.   Am very
busy doing Listener centre spread, in lieu of Miss Scott-Johnston who is
on holiday.   Am doing pictures and resumé about all of Churchill's

- 422 -

journeys abroad since he became P.M.

     To Ware, feeling very exhausted.   Hilary has badly ulcerated
throat.

Saturday, May 22, 1943

H. goes to doctor.   Young assistant whose first patient she is, does
not even know where to find thermomeher, or which is the door to show
her out of.   Tells her to go to bed and later in day comes to see her.
Says she ought to have tonsils out.   The extraordinary beauty of last
weekend, when hawthorn, buttercups and the chestnut candles were such
as I have never seen before, has gone.   Take M. into village and we
get caught in rain.

Sunday, May 23, 1943

Coping with H. in bed.   It is difficult to know what is to happen next
week with nobody here.   L. tries to ring up his mother, but when I
leave at 7, to catch train, he has been unable to find her in.   Martin
feel s something is amiss and doesn't behave as well as usual.

Monday, May 24, 1943

Phone L., who says his mother is going to Hilary's till Thursday, when
she will have to return to collect her ration cards and new identity
cards for household.   They are being distributed alphabetically this
time, and her day for collection is Friday.   Greta making frantic
telephone calls to Lake District to book rooms for June or July;   can't
get in anywhere.

Tuesday, May 25, 1943

Dinner at Canuto's with "family" and Graham: very enjoyable.   He has
just come back from Ireland where he flew with Prince Bernhard of the
Netherlands, to speak at meeting of British Council.

Wednesday, May 26, 1943

To National Gallery concert.   Mozart: wind quintet and octet;   and
piano fantaisie in C minor, K 475.   Enjoyed last especially.   Fire-
watching at night.

Thursday, May 27, 1943

Cancel hair appointment at lunch-time and go to Ware to succour Hilary
who is still very unwell.   Mrs. Evans leaves Ware platform about 3
minutes before I arrive, and H. and M. are there to meet me, having
come down in her taxi and returning in mine.   Martin looks inches taller than last weekend.   I bear with me a ready-made fish pie in a dish;
about 1 ¾ lb. of tripe, 2 enormous cos lettuce at 1/- each and bunch
radishes also 1/-.   Paper today quotes from German broadcast which

describes (for benefit of its home listeners) panic of Londoners at
new and terrifying liquid-fire bombs.   This is complete fiction: have
seen and heard nothing of them in London.

Friday, May 28, 1943

Very warm.   Take M. short walk.   Go into town, but cannot get H's new
ration books because L. has gone off to London on business with his
identity card.

Saturday, May 29, 1943

Collect new rations cards, etc., to-day.   In spiteof stories in papers
that people have had to wait 5 hours in queues, have no waiting at all.
Very warm day.   H. better, but insists on working in garden and does
too much.   I pick the gooseberry crop, 5¾ 5¼ lb. this year.

Sunday, May 30, 1943

Strenuous day: begins with thunderstorm and ends with sunshine.   L.
brings us breakfast in bed, but after that I cope, and in afternoon pull
up enormous weeds from garden, very tall ones.   Feel as I pull them
that I am wreaking vengeance on all the tall arrogant people who have
ever made me feel small.   H. quite a bit better, and I return to London

Monday, May 31, 1943

Sixteen years ago to-day since I first came to B.B.C.   How middle-aged
and scrawny I am becoming.   Mr. Pringle away with temperature of 104.

Tuesday, June 1, 1943

Much colder than most of May has been.   Alert last night.   Am not
wakened by sirens, but by sound of guns, and after All Clear lie awake
for an hour.   Find Dunne's "Experiment with Time" very fascinating
reading.

Wednesday, June 2, 1943

My 36th birthday: how simply terrible.   Get tickets given me for
B.B.C. concert at Albert Hall: Elgar's "Falstaff" and Beethoven's 9th
Symphony, which an convinced would have been a better work un-choral.

Thursday, June 3, 1943

Mr. Pringle has chicken-pox and will be away a month.   Buy 2 pairs of
ribbed lisle stockings for Mother's birthday - 2 coupons each, un-
fashioned, and 6/10.   Sort of thing one would not have looked at before
the war but is now very glad to find.

Friday, June 4, 1943

Miriam's 4th birthday. To Ware. H. appears much better. There
has been a revolution in Argentina, and the pro-Axis president has
been turned out.

Saturday, June 5, 1943

Reading Dorothy Sayers' series of plays lately broadcast, "The Man
Born to Be King" - very good. Dig weeds out of garden. Martin
rather peevish, his last tooth coming through. American coal-strikers
have returned to work for fortnight, while further negotiations take
place. Paper says this is personal triumph for President Roosevelt.

Sunday, June 6, 1943

Prime Minister is back in England, having visited Gibraltar and Algiers
since his visit to America. Martin in better form to-day, though he
gave me a rather disturbed night. Day of alternating storms and sunshine. We all work in garden, while M. puffs up and down and is a
railway train.

Monday, June 7, 1943

French form new committee in North Afric called National Committee of
Liberation.
          At printers till 6.30 owing to approach of Whitsun.

Tuesday, June 8, 1943

Churchill tells House that "amphibious operations" on a large scale are
to be expected. It is thought the Germans may begin to use poison gas
(we practised Martin in wearing his mask on Sunday: he thought it was
a lovely game). Roosevelt and Churchill both threaten reprisals if
they do.
          Mr. Thomas comes to printer's. Full of woe about his mother
who threatens to leave Torquay where they had a sharp raid lately: a
trying old lady as far as I can see, whose life revolves round her
electric kettle - she must be where she can make tea in the middle of
the night. Is 82, so perhaps cannot be expected to realise state of
affairs in many parts of Europe.
          Fire-watching at night.

Wednesday, June 9, 1943

Very tired after fire-watching. Get 150 saccharine tablets! Miss
Mearing comes to see us: is training as inspector in aircraft factory
and has to measure aircraft parts correctly to the ten-thousandth part
of an inch.

Thursday, June 10, 1943

Meet Mother at Paddington, 12.45 and take her by taxi to D.H. Evans for

lunch.   Not a very good idea, because she has a bag which I can
scarcely lift (filled with provisions, I suppose), and after lunch I
have to carry it some way before we are able to get taxi to Liverpool
Street.   Have tried to put her on slow train which goes right through
but it has been taken off and she has to change at Broxbourne.   Can't
think how she will be able to lift case, but ring up Hilary's later
and find she arrived safely.

Friday, June 11, 1943

Mother's 67th birthday.   To Ware at midday.

Saturday, June 12, 1943

Mediterranean island of Pantellaria taken.   Biggest raid of war, so
far, on Ruhr.

Sunday, June 13, 1943

Lampedusa taken.   Daddy arrives by train.   We meet him at station.
He has a cake, 4 eggs, the weekly 'joint' - and his case, like mother's,
is almost too heavy to lift.

Monday, June 14, 1943

Back to London.   Another small island in Mediterranean taken.   Heavy
thunderstorms.

Tuesday, June 15, 1943

Terrific thunderstorms all day.   At printers till 7.15 or so.   Am
reading "The Jungle" by Upton Sinclair, about the frightful conditions
in the meat-packing industry in Chicago about 1906.   Believe they were
improved after publication of book.   Feel quite ill and converted to
the idea of work-people striking whenever they feel inclined!

Wednesday, June 16, 1943

The King in North Africa.   Still heavy thunder storms.   Very tired.
Get pleasant lunch at Wigmore Restaurant, which, however costs me 4/6 -
tomatoe omelette (made with dried eggs) and spinach, cherries and
custard, roll and butter, and large white coffee.   They actually give
sugar to sprinkle on fruit and 2 lumps for coffee.   I wait at Fortnum
and Mason's to buy shoes (having read in newspaper that no more leather
ones are to be made), but cannot get served and come away.

Thursday, June 17, 1943

Warm, and not quite so stormy.   Daddy, Mother, Hilary, Martin and
Tramp due to leave for Stroud today.   This is David Redman's 6th birthday.   Buy pair black "utility" shoes, quite plain, but which appear to

be real leather: 39/-(controlled price). The papers say that
leather will not be available for civilians' shoes and we shall have
to wear wooden soles. Get these at Marshall and Snelgrove's where
I do not have to wait long.

Friday, June 18, 1943

To Stroud by 4.15 train. Despaired of getting seat but after walking
almost as far as engine, found carriage and 3 with three capacious
nuns and one small girl. Arrive Stroud about 7.15 and Martin and
Daddy meet me on hill; the former having slept this morning, is still
very wide awake. . Very wet day.

Saturday, June 19, 1943

Stroud having its "Wings for Victory" week, when everyone is urged to
invest money in war savings sertificates. H. and I take Martin to
bottom of hill to see procession of Home Guard, Boy Scouts, First Aid
people, etc., with all of which he is much impressed. Mother has
.parcel from South Africa, containing 1 lb. tea, 1 lb. sugar, slab of
chocolate, tin of tongue, and box wrapped cheese. Sent for her birthday; one for me supposed to be also on the way.

Sunday, June 20, 1943

Rather expect parcel from S. A. to be waiting for me in London, but now
hear that Mount Pleasant (P.O. parcels depot) was bombed a night or two
ago; so I may never get it. Take back pinks and roses for my room,
and rhubarb with which Miss Morrison is very pleased. There is still
none to buy in London. New fast train from Stroud leaves 7.15 and
arrives 9.40, so I journey in comfort.

Monday, June 21, 1943

Longest day. Mr. Pringle returns from his chikkenpox bout. His wife
now has it but not the children yet. Fire duty in evening. We go
to bombed building in Suffolk Street (between Strand and Embankment)
and practise putting out incendiary bomb with stirrup pump. Have been
told there is cloakroom for changing, but fireman at fire headquarters
says in shocked tones that he is only person on premises and that therefore we cannot go in there and change. So we stand amid ruined building and don dongar dungarees behind wall. Afterwards three of us,
still wearing dungarees, eat at Corner House, where door-keeper asks us
respectfully which of the Services we belong to, and waiter treats us
with consideration. Filled with vainglory, we then swagger through
St. James's Park and look at ducks and at impregnable fortress built
next to Admiralty which is so secret no one will ever say a word about
it. We report late for duty at B. H.

Tuesday, June 21, 1943

Go to press somewhat late and am very tired after spending almost all
night lying awake in bunk in concert-hall. There were two alerts, but

only the woman who was on telephone duty was required to get up.
    The King has visited Malta.

Wednesday, June 23, 1943

My parcel from S.A. arrives safely after all.   It looks very battered
on the outside, but the contents (the same as in Mother's parcel) are
intact.   Weather has become warm and fine.

Thursday, June 24, 1943

To Prom. concert in Albert Hall with Mr. McNaught, our music critic, to
hear Vaughan Williams' new symphony (his 5th).   He conducts it himself.
It sounds very "same-y" to me, too quiet, though very pleasant, but the
critics think highly of it.   We leave after the symphony and go with
Gerald and Pat Abraham to the Piccadilly Corner House 'help yourself'
counter and have very pleasant meal together till 10 p.m.

Friday, June 25, 1943

The King is back in London.   Go with Tina to Prom. concert and this
time remain for all of it.   Beethoven's 1st symphony, Emperor Concerto
(with Moiseiwitsch playing), Leonora No. 3 overture.   Wish we had left
at interval, for rest of programme is "In Memoriam" for Rachmaninoff.
Begins with the Chopin funeral march for which we all stand (some few of
the packed hall try to applaud at end, but are "hushed" by their more
sensible companions) and goes on with R.'s 3rd symphony, for which I do
not greatly care.

Saturday, June 26, 1943

Brilliant morning.   Coffee with John.   Then to Audrey Mearing's, at
Oakley in Bucks.   Most pleasant country vicarage with large garden,
next to X 12th century church.   Walk up to Brill where there is a wind-
mill.

                        At Brill
                        On the hill
                        Is a rill mill.

Eat strawberries from garden and generally enjoy ourselves.

Sunday, June 27, 1943

To church, as befits guest of vicar.   Then for cycle ride.   In afternoon laze on lawn and at 5 have to start journey back by car, bus and
train, bearing rhubarb, lettuce and 6 new-laid eggs.   Many signposts
have been replaced in country, implying threat of invasion not imminent.
Monday, June 28, 1943

In park, lime flowers all out, smelling very sweetly.   Walk with Tina
and Bob, and look again for our singers (forgot to mention this last

Wednesday - went with Bob up to Marble Arch in evening, and stood on
edge of crowd engaged in singing fervently hymns of Moody and Sankey.
I joined in, singing loudly "O that willbe Glory for me", while Bob
stood silent, waiting for the reason for meeting to be made clear -
i.e. evangelistic sermon, invitation to attend Zion Chapel next Sunday - but to his surprise they were singing apprently for the sheer
pleasure of it) - this time we don't find singers, or only small knot
of them making not such a loud noise unto the Lord.   The leader, who
had a voice as huge as Daddy's, not there.

Tuesday, June 29, 1943

We have bombed Cologne again very heavily.   To press late.   Home at
8.30, very tired.

Wednesday, June 30, 1943

Call for suit which has been a month at cleaners: not ready.   Call
for shoes which have been being "heeled" for a fortnight and have to
wait 20 minutes for them.   Cannot think how people manage who have to
"clock" in to the minute at their jobs.
     In evening to Prom. concert with Audrey Mearing, who comes up to
town for purpose.   Beautiful 5th and 9th symphonies of Schubert.   And
2nd Piano Concerto and Préludes of Liszt (Louis Ketner at pinao in
concerto).   We then try to find somewhere to eat, and fetch up at
Greek Restaurant in Queen's Road, which charges 8/2 for not very much
food.   Audrey then comes to Craveh Hill G. and sleeps on divan in
lounge for night.

Thursday, July 1, 1943

Arise before 6 in order to get Audrey M. off to her aircraft factory
at Watford.   Feel quite dead for rest of day.   Joyce Green, up from
Shropshire for few days, rings me up and we lunch and talk.   She tells
me Peter Scott was not killed in air crash, but died of mumps - rather
ironic after completing enormous number of operationsl flights over
Germany without injury.   There seems to be outbreak of mumps all over
world, especially among adults - in Canada, here, and in S.Africa, where
Babe has been very ill with it.   Weather very fine and warm.   Collect
my new ration and identity cards, having to wait only 10 minutes for
them.

Friday, July 2, 1943

To National Gallery concert with Margaret McLeod - Mozart string quintet
and horn quintet, most beautiful.   I buy bottle of cleansing lotion
for face - for sensitive skins - at frightful and wicked price of 12/2
for quite small amount.
     Am glad to see that Dean Inge has said we shall regret this dread-
ful bombing of Europe.   He says we are all members one of another, in
bad things as well as in good, and we are destroying beauty which belongs to us all.   The "hate" propaganda - on our side as well as on
Germany's - is outrageous - this is my thought, not Dean Inge's.

Saturday, July 3, 1943

With Tina to her Mother's house at Dulwich, where I lie in hot sunshine on camp bed in garden and eat cherries (1/6 a lb.)

Sunday, July 4, 1943

Back to town after lazy, hot day.   On fire duty at night.   My turn
to be "on the book", which means that I have to be wakened if aircraft
cross the coast in - at any rate long before the official warning is
sounded in London.

Monday, July 5, 1943

General Sikorski, Polish Prime Minister and C.-in-C., killed in aero-
place accident near Gibraltar.   During lunch-time 4-engined bombers
in great numbers pass over London and we wonder whether the invasion
of the Continent has started, but no mention is made of them in the
news.   Quiet night on fire duty: no disturbance.

Tuesday, July 6, 1943

Germans have begun big offensive in Russia.   Heavy rain, for which
both Mr. Pringle and I (at printer's) unprepared.   At lunch-time we
'phone B.B.C. at Wembley and get van to drive us back to Waterlow's;
upon which it immediately clears up.   Very tired, though we finish at
about 6.   Wind 4 oz. of wool with Tina.

Wednesday, July 7, 1943

In lunch-time to concert at National Gallery by myself.   Buy scores
of the two works: Smetana's quartet in E minor and Haydn's in D major,
and much enjoy following them.   Thence to hairdresser.   After this
easy day, feel very exhausted, and depressed that I have not more energy,
and go to bed at 9.30.

Thursday, July 8, 1943

Meet Hilary and Martin, with Tramp, at Paddington at 12.45 and take
them by taxi to Liverpool Street.   Martin stands on seat and looks
speechlessly through little window in back of hood, breathless with
interest.   Have called for my suit which has been being cleaned for
the last six weeks.   The only spot which I remember is still there.
Cannot see that anything has been done for my 4/6.

Friday, July 9, 1943

Hilary's 31st birthday.   To Prom. with Tina: Beethoven's Eeonora
No.2, "Song of Penitence", and Eroica Symphony.   Then a Mozart piano
concerto and Berlioz' "Roman Carnival" overture.   Very enjoyable.
Hall packed.

<u>Saturday, July 10, 1943</u>

To Little Felcourt, to see Joyce, bearing 1 lb. cherries (1/6 a lb.) and my sweet ration for month (½ lb. chocolate creme-de-menthe and ¼ lb. fudge).   It rains and she assures me it is the worst weekend they have had for ages.   Lovely country: Montessori School among Sussex woods.   She lives in house where has beautiful sitting-room and woody small bedroom in which I sleep.   Weekend arrangements complicated by bomb which fellyesterday on cinema at East Grinstead, killing about 70 people.   This is 3 miles away: helper who was to have come to supervise children to-day has friend who suffered minor injuries, and so does not come. British have invaded Sicily.

<u>Sunday, July 11, 1943</u>

Get up late and have long and lazy breakfast with heaps and heaps of raspberries.   We wander wetly in woods where Canadian soldiers have camp, and into grounds of large house taken over by military where we are free to help ourselves to the flowers.   Gather beautiful bunch of roses for me to bring back to London.   Just laze and talk in afternoon, and wander up road for train soon after 8 o'clock.

<u>Monday, July 12, 1943</u>

We have captured 3 airports, as well as Syracuse and 9 towns, in Sicily. Are fighting on 100-mile front from south coast.   Invasion going well but we are warned it will get harder later on.
     Letter from Mother enclosing one from Phyllida.   Latter wants to marry Arthur Place, who was in midst of divorcing French wife when war broke out, and as she is in occupied France, it may not be easy to get the matter settled.   He is 50, P. says, and not intellectual but very intelligent and honest, and musical.   They are very fond of one another and she is willing to wait for him till after the war.   Mother - already in bed with what appears to be gastric flu - not cheered by the news. Thought of divorce very upsetting to the parents.   P. very happy and begs them to take tolerant view of the affair.

<u>Tuesday, July 13, 1943</u>

Feel very sad and worried, thinking of Phyllida so precariously happy. Go for walk in park in evening and feel better by reason of the trees which always look so stable and dependable.   In Sicily we are advancing.

<u>Wednesday, July 14, 1943</u>

With Gerald Abraham to National Gallery concert: French in honour of the day.   Kathleen Long plays some Ravel; Maggie Teyte sings songs by Fauré and others; and Kathleen Long and Eda Kersey play violin sonata by Debussy.   All very enjoyable.   Then accompany G.A. to Chesters where he buys music for Astra Desmond who is writing something for him (music becoming very scarce and difficult to obtain); after which have coffee

with him at Yarners, so that it is tea-time ½ when I sidle back into
the office.   At night go with Joan to Prom. concert - Mozart, with
piano concerto (Myra Hess); ending with Berlioz' Fantastic Symphony
which is tremendous.   Hall packed with enthusiastic audience.

Thursday, July 15, 1943

Letter from Mother who is a little better.   She and Daddy, like me,
cannot bear to dash Phyllida's obvious happiness, precarious though
they feel it to be.   I go to another National Gallery concert - R.A.F.
Orchestra, playing overture by Rossini, Elgar's Cello Concerto, and
"The Gods Go a-Begging" (Beecham's arrangement of Handel).   Very good.
See Leonard Isaacs in R.A.F. Uniform, who tells me since being called
up he is a total loss to the community, though he is making plenty of
music and has given ½½ two piano recitals, one at the National Gallery
and one in the City.   In the present concert he is Fourth Horn.
      Axis resistance in Sicily reported to be stiffening; but in
Russia the German offensive said to have fizzled out.

Friday, July 16, 1943

Russians have launched counter-offensive on the Eastern Front, I believe
near Orel.
      Beautiful day after night of rain which was badly needed.   I go
to Prom. concert with Miss Scott Johnston of The Listener: Beethoven -
Egmont Overture, Violin concerto (with Eda Kersey), and 4th Symphony with
which I find I am quite unfamiliar.   Enjoy Concerto especially.   We
leave after interval, when the works are to be by Frank Bridge and Ethel
Smyth, and I come home and eat dinner which has been kept for me but
not hot because I am late from pleasure and not from work.   This is a
rule of the house.

Saturday, July 17, 1943

Roy's 38th birthday.   In afternoon to see Mr. Hasler at Hampstead -
very old and thin and confined almost entirely to his room.   He is
extremely glad to have a visitor and totters forth with me to a tea
shop where I shout remarks into his welcoming ear.   At 7 to Albert
Hall to another Prom. Weber Overture, 3 songs by Vaughan Williams,
Liszt Piano Concerto, suite by Kodaly; and after the interval the
Siegfried Idyll and Enigma Variations.   Have to leave before last
are finished, just after the beautiful Nimrod variation, which the
programme says every orchestra in the country performed when they
heard of Elgar's death in 1934.   After this to B.B.C. for fire-
watching.   Must record following conversation overheard in park.
1st Lady: "Oh she ½½ Has been silly!   She has made a mess of things".
(I think sympathetically that the unknown has ruined her life.) 2nd
Lady: "Yes, she ought to have put it in a little dish!"

Sunday, July 18, 1943

Russians have regained all ground taken by Germans at beginning of the

recent offensive and have advanced 8 miles elsewhere.   In Sicily we
are advancing towards Catania.
        Last night quiet.   Today is Eileen (Irish maid here) 's wedding
day.   The 4 people in house who are now away for weekend (i.e. Bob,
Miss Morrison, Doris Crofts and me) swallow lunch hastily at 12.30 and
take ourselves to the ceremony at the Church of the Rosary, Marylebone
Road.   Eileen in great state of jitters, but looking very nice in white
frock with pink flowers on it which has been shortened from old evening
dress.   Service is wholly inaudible, since priest makes no attempt to
address it to any but the bride and bridegroom, and children at the
door of the church play and chatter all the time, and various people who
have been using the church for prayer get up and stump in and out at
will.   There is another wedding to take place in half an hour's time,
and the bride has already come to the church door before we are out.
Then an old man with an old-fashioned camera gets under a black cloth
which is in danger of being blown away by the wind and arranges the
group at the church door all the time the second ceremony is taking
place.   He gives the trembling Eileen a silver horse-shoe with a white
flower to hold while she is photographed, and meantime the high wind
blows his camera right over on to the ground.   The whole wedding party,
covered with confetti, crams itself into one taxi-cab and vanishes.
        This morning go to St. Matthew's, Bayswater, where a most earnest
curate tells us the hairs of our head are all numbered, and to illus-
trate the extraordinary care which this must involve, says there are
150,000 hairs in a head and that "we carelessly remove several every
day on our combs"!

Monday, July 19, 1943

Achieve a triumph in having accepted by the laundry a frock, a kimono
and a cardigan for washing.   But am much grieved by loss of gloves
which I leave in restaurant at lunch-time: rarely wear any except in
cold weather nowadays, but like to have some in case I want to appear
well-dressed.
        In evening to very bad film, "This Land is Mine", well acted by
Charles Laughton.   Same old theme - occupation of small country by
Germans and the sinfulness of the collaborators and the heroism of the
resisters.   The collaborators are called quislings if they ought to
be on our side.   On the other hand, the Sicilians who do not resist
our invasion are just sensible fellows, not quislings at all - this of
course not mentioned in film.   Very tired of heroines whose eyes brim
over with tears all the time, when they aren't turning to rend their
young men for having truck with the enemy (when really the poor young
men - whose looks turn to iron under the displeasure of the young
women, and of this also I am very weary - are the noble sabateurs.

Tuesday, July 20, 1943

Tales of mutiny of Italian troops in Sicily against their German offi-
cers, but these appear to be unauthenticated.
        Have just read with great enjoyment Lytton Strachey's "Queen
Victoria", inspired thereto by first reading the Rede Lecture, 1943, by
Max Beerbohm on Strachey.   Now reading Strachey's "Elizabeth & Essex".

Wednesday, July 21, 1943

Have copied this passage fro m "Elizabeth and Essex" (Strachey): "There is no respite for mortal creatures. Human relationships must either move or perish. When two consciousnesses come to a certain nearness the impetus of their interactions, growing ever intenser and intenser, leads on to an unescapable climax. The crescendo must rise to its topmost note; and only then is the preordained solution of the theme made manifest."

Thursday, July 22, 1943

Prom. com ert at Albert Hall: Bax's 7th Symphony which I don't like but which all the critics surrounding me obviously like very much.
        Things going well in Sicily and Russia.

Friday, July 23, 1943

Attempt to go to 1,000th National Gallery concert, where Myra Hess is playing 2 Mozart piano concertos, but the queue winds round corner into Charing Cross Road and I do not get in. Go with Margaret McLeod to her flat in Chelsea and sit on floor and try to listen to 2nd concerto which is being broadcast, on set which buzzes every time electric lift in building goes up or down. Also sit on some sort of fruit and make big purple stain on skirt and underclothes.
        To Ware with enormous green woodenengine for Martin, made by office boy's father, who is air-raid warden ahd I suppose has plenty of spare time. 30/-.

Saturday, July 24, 1943

Leonard in bed with cold. He has letter from Mother, to whom he tried to write cheering note on subject of Phyllida. Martin very pleased with engine.

Sunday, July 25, 1943

Very warm. Sit in garden and listen to Mozart on wireless. Huge harvest all round waiting to be reaped. Biggest raid of war on Hamburg

Monday, July 26, 1943

Astonishing news of Mussolini's resignation. Much excitement and specu-lation as to what the results are likely to be. Very warm. In evening to beautiful Prom. concert with David Green: Brahms' Variations on a Theme of Haydn, Violin & Cello concerto, and 4th Symphony. Have decided am very fond of Elgar and Brahms.

Tuesday, July 2 7, 1943

Still very warm. Churchill speaks in House on Mussolini's resignation. Tries to dispel any feelings we may have thatw ar is now over, or nearly over.

Wednesday, July 28, 1943

Read and am impressed by Henry James' "Turn of the Screw". Try to buy
pair of sunglasses but find they cost 17/6. A man who has been system-
atically stealing our review books by coming into office at lunch-time
and removing a few at a time, is sent to prison for 3 months.

Thursday, July 29, 1943

Have lunch in park in beautiful sunshine. Buy and much enjoy plums at
8d. a lb. In evening the flat "family", with Graham White and Norman
Tucker, have meal at "Mirabel" in Curzon Street - parting feast for John
whose course in Japanese is now finished and who is being sent to the Far
East. G. says Churchill's speech in House was aimed at Americans, who
have rushed to the conclusion since Mussolini's resignation that the war
is almost over.

Friday, July 30, 1943

Feel extremely ill before getting up this morning; think it a result of
unaccustomed plums yesterday, together with number of iced drinks I had
in evening. Well punished for my indiscretion.
     We have afternoon free but I cannot go away because of fire-watching
tonight. Meet Joyce who is up in town for afternoon, and we have meal
and go to Prom.: Beethoven. Most enjoyable in spite of great heat.
     Buy 2 yards knicker elastic in Oxford Street from man selling it on
pavement; almost pre-war quality - but at 1/6 a yard!

Saturday, July 31, 1943

No warning last night. To Ware. No crowds at station in spite of
horrifying stories of queues waiting for passenger trains. Martin has
enormous blisters on his leg, as if he has been burned. Leonard has
received bonus of £100, all in new pound notes. £50 will of course have
to go in income tax. Terrible heat which is broken in evening by
severe thunder-storm.

Sunday, August 1, 1943

Martin better. I take Tramp for walk through fields of ripe grain.
Sleep without pyjamas because of heat, which causes Martin to throw his
own off and lie naked on top of his bed, "like Auntie".

Monday, August 2, 1943

Back to London. Very busy with two people on holiday.
     Final offensive in Sicily said to have started.

Tuesday, August 3, 1943

Prime Minister says offensive in Sicily going according to plan.
Very busy at printers on very hot day.

Wednesday, August 4, 1943

In evening with Tina to Bach-Handel Prom. concert in packed Albert Hall.
6th Brandenburg Concerto, Isobel Baillie singing "Let the Bright
Seraphim" with Ernest Hall and his trumpet trying to behave like a burning row of them.   Very good.

Thursday, August 5, 1943

With Audrey Mearing to Prom. concert.   Schubert's Rosamunde Overture,
Rachmaninoff's Fantasia on a Theme of Paganini (Cyril Smith playing it),
and Elgar's 1st Symphony.   We leave at interval and try to eat sandwiches in park but it rains and blows and is very uninviting.   Audrey's
prospective mother-in-law has received p.c. from her fiancé after two
years' silence.   No address or date.   He is prisoner in Japanese hands
and is well.

Friday, August 6, 1943

To Ware with Tina.   Russians have taken Orel and we have taken Catania
in Sicily.

Saturday, August 7, 1943

We all go walk and find limpid river by which we sit in spasms of sunshine while Martin throws stones for Tramp to great danger of everyone.
In evening Hilary and Leonard to go to film, to celebrate their fourth
wedding anniversary earlier in week, and I bath Martin and put him to
bed.   He protests "I don't like Auntie", but gives in, and goes to
sleep almost as soon as he is in bed.

Sunday, August 8, 1943

It is discovered at tea-time that we have all eaten so heartily this
weekend there is scarcely any margarine left.   Tina and I, feeling we
have behaved like swarm of locusts, return to London.

Monday, August 9, 1943

Lunch in park again, where importunate sparrows and ducks wait for
crumbs.

Tuesday, August 10, 1943

We all eat dinner out, since Eileen is on holiday and Miss Morrison
very over-burdened without her help.   I eat alone at Sussex Court
restaurant because we are late going to press - mostly owing to Chinese
Embassy taking exception to our having cut Foreign Minister's MS. very
slightly.

Wednesday, August 11, 1943

Mr. Churchill in Canada and going on from there to the U.S.   Horrible discovery that caption in Listener makes it appear that Burma is still occupied by the British who operate from Rangoon: it passed by us all including Editor.   In evening to Haydn-Mendelssohn Prom., ending with Sir Henry Wood conducting Wedding March with all the brass in London at full blast.

Thursday, August 12, 1943

Buy small cake (1 coupon, 3 oz.) of delectable toilet soap at 2/6. Fire watching at night.   Russians advancing to Kharkov.

Friday, August 13, 1943

Did not sleep a wink last night, one of fellow-fire-watchers coughs so much.   Today work till 8 p.m., so my plan to take luggage to station tonight falls through.   Large daylight raid on Rome by American bombers.

Saturday, August 14, 1943

Rise, still very tired, at 6.30.   Miss M. gives me small breakfast at 7, and I go off in lowest spirits at 7.15 to Euston.   But there the steward of dining-car takes me under his wing, and I have another break- fast in dining-car and am allowed to stay onwhile a second meal is served.   Continue to sit and later have lunch and still remain while a second lunch is provided.   All the while the corridors are crowded and queues form for meals.   Change at Bangor into local train which is very slow but goes through pretty country, hills, streams, etc.   Change once more but do not have to wait, and arrive at Pwllheli, plus large part of Navy, or perhaps they are naval cadets, to find all Funchs family waiting to meet me.   We amuse ourselves until Eydern bus comes by going with the children on cars at a kind of fair, which bump into each other.   Bus 8 miles, and then walk across heathery common to farm on cliffs, while thunderstorm suddenly drenches us.

Sunday, August 15, 1943

Quite sunny.   Clocks went back an hour last night, but for some reason farm has not put its clocks back.   In fact clock in hall is two hours fast.   Meals, however, are about $\frac{3}{4}$ hour late on schedule.   Occasionally I hear pips from loudspeaker in kitchen.   My watch has broken.   All I can rely on is the ducks which can be guaranteed, it appears, to wake me up with their quacking at the break of day.   We go prawning and it takes a long time in evening to top and tail the catch, which then amounts to about 2 dessertspoonsful.   To get to beach we go down grassy slope. Grass extends right to narrow stretch of shingle.   Coast has few habita- tions and we see hardly anyone.   Christopher and Robhard quarrel at intervals.

We hear that Italians have declared Rome an open city.

Monday, August 16, 1943

Not so sunny, but wind less cold. Walk along coast to little bay, where the boys climb into two boats on beach and enjoy sailing to South America in them. C. makes me a pie of sand, which tastes, he says, of "chicken and duck and hot buttered toast".

Tuesday, August 17, 1943

A really hot day. Go some way to sandy cove, a little more inhabited than our usual one. Go in boat with delighted Christopher and Richard, lie on top of cliffs, and walk back through harvest fields getting very sunburnt.

Wednesday, August 18, 1943

Not so fine. Marjorie and I go walk oncliffs in morning while the rest energetically reap corn. In afternoon we lie on top of hay in barn where the sides are open to the sea, very cosy but not stuffy. For dinner we have duck and green peas. Richard says "Poor duck!" and does not want to eat it. We have as much milk to drink as we want - while in England the ration is ½ pint for 5 days in the week and nothing on the 2 remaining days - though Mother gets ½ pint every day and many people in uncrowded districts are even more fortunate.

Thursday, August 19, 1943

Wild wet morning which becomes warm and sunny in afternoon. We go blackberrying down lanes, lie on hay in barn, pick up shells on sea-shore and end day with a "wozzle" (demon patience or scramble).

Friday, August 20, 1943

Again very wild in morning. Mr. Powis (fellow-lodger and neighbour of Fuchs's) shoots 4 rabbits which we are to take home, three to distribute to friends and one to last till next week's rations are due. Much packing in evening.

Saturday, August 21, 1943

We travel 20 in a carriage for about 4 hours to Chester, where we can stand it no more and decide to change there instead of at Manchester. Literally hundreds are left behind at Rhyl and other places along the line, unable to get on the train at all. At Chester we have tea, buy a set of glasses and a jug to add to our already enormous amount of luggage, try to get the boys interested in the Wall - but they prefer the canal which they can see from the wall; and some interesting relics (pottery, armour, etc.) in a tower - but what they like is a fire-practice which they can see from steps of tower. Arrive home about 7 and Marjorie says how nice it is to be in her own house again.

Sunday, August 22, 1943

Gardening: Arnold has cabbages in his front garden now, though there
is also a bed of sweet-smelling antirrhinums - I spend lot of time pulling off the faded ones.

Monday, August 23, 1943

Germans have evacuated Kharkov.   Journey to Stroud: crowded train but
I have seat - next, first to woman who tells me with pride of her 6 step
sons and 1 stepdaughter (most of sons in Forces), and second to woman
of 78 who clutches all the time a largeblack bag which she tells me holds
the deeds of her house and which she never stirs without.   Entrusts it
to my care, however, while she goes to lavatory.   Mother squeals with
astonishment at sight of myunheralded approach.

Tuesday, August 24, 1943

Mrs. Gardener brings Daddy butter, eggs, and 2 quarts of milk.   It is
true milkman lets Mother have ½ pint extra because I have an emergency
ration card for week, but 1½ pints for 3 is not enough.   We go out to
lunch at West's since rations are short.   Biggest raid of war on Berlin.
58 of our bombers missing.

Wednesday, August 25, 1943

To tea with Aunt H., to whom I take windfalls.   She gives me blackberries in return.   Fox has killed 9 of her laying hens - a major
tragedy nowadays.   Mrs. Franklin gives us Victoria plums from garden.

Thursday, August 26, 1943

Mother jells blackberries.   I visit Mrs. Hawkins, and come away with
eating pears.   Country dwellers are most fortunate - in London one may
queue for fruit and apples are 8d. a lb.

Friday, August 27, 1943

Out to lunch again, this time to Tucks.   Visit Aunt Tuttie who says
"It's not a very nice Spring, dear, is it?"   Phyllida and Arthur come
for weekend.   Mother very wrought up.   A. small and seemingly inoffen-
sive; very quiet.   He is R.A.F. Sergeant, in charge of 40 men who go
around to newly constructed aerodromes, or dromes where construction has
to be done.   Says their food is so badly cooked, he can eat none.
Says Bomber Command and Fighter Command extremely efficient, but ground
staff and general organisation of R.A.F. very poor.   They were once
ordered to build a hangar, and though the man who gave the order knew it
had already been countermanded, yet becaused he had not yet received the
official document about it, he let the men complete it - they knowing
all the time it would have to come down again - and immediately it was
finished they set to work and demolished it.

Saturday, August 28, 1943

Raid on Nuremberg: over 30 bombers missing. King Boris of Bulgaria
dead, it is said from angina pectoris, but foul play is hinted at because he had lately been to see Hitler.

Sunday, August 29, 1943

Denmark put under martial law. I return to London. Blackout now at
8.15 which makes travel tedious.

Monday, August 30, 1943

Work not too bad. Russians retake Taganrog.

Tuesday, August 31, 1943

John, who now has his commission and looks beautiful in his new uniform,
says goodbye because he is to be posted to Far East. "See you in about
five years' time" he says somewhat sadly. Churchill makes speech in
America. Very disappointing - nothing to say. But Mr. Pringle decides (in Editor's absence) that it must go in paper, so 3 formes are
held open until tomorrow. Even so we don't finish at printers till 8
o'clock.
      Try on my two winter suits and find I have increased in girth so
much, shall have to have them let out. Mean to try to buy Mother some
brown boot polish, since there is none to be had in Stroud and she has
been using her fast waning and irreplaceable stock of furniture polish on
her shoes.

Wednesday, September 1, 1943

Big raid on Berlin last night: we lose 38 bombers. Joan's brother
Sandy, who has been in Middle East, arrives here at breakfast time,
after leaving Gibraltar last night. According to Joan, there are more
air-crews than planes and he has had nothing to do - so that our bomber
losses are serious. Miss Entract (in office) lost her brother in last
big raid over Milan, since when she has become completely listless. She
may hear later on that he is prisoner: it was to have been his last
operational flight - was just going to get ground job.
      Buy books for "family" to send John as parting gift. "Silence de
la Mer", a French long-short-story, just published; Lord David Cecil's
book on Hardy, and "Seven Years" (or Winters, or Summers) by Elizabeth
Bowen, a book about her childhood in Ireland.
      New Editor in Chief of B.B.C. announced, one Haley, Director of
Manchester Guardian, Evening News, Reuter's, Associated Press.

Thursday, September 2, 1943

Enquire price for re-making old suit of mine and find it will be 8 gns.
Do so much indexing and checking of index today, am reduced to state of
great depression and consciousness of utter uselessness.

Friday, September 3, 1943

Allied troops have crossed Straits of Messina and landed on "Toe" of
Italy.   This news given by B.B.C. at 8 a.m.   To Ware, with little
wooden boat for Martin to sail on his bath.   It is plain bit of wood
which before war would have cost 3d, but for which I gave 2/- in the
Burlington Arcade.   Have made enquiries about altering my winter suits
since I have grown fatter and they will need letting out.   Lewis's can
do them but are so short of labour cannot give any date for finishing
them.   For entirely re-making my oldsuit, the charge would be 8 guineas.

Saturday, September 4, 1943

Invasion of Italy said to be going well.   Martin pleased with boat but
even more pleased with shells I brought him fromN. Wales.   We go to
gather blackberries, but very few are ripe yet.   Get only 1½ lb. (N.B.
see in paper that pickers' price for wild blackberries is 4d. a lb.
maximum.   Sounds a lot but one could not get rich on such slow work as
mine.)

Sunday, September 5, 1943

Martin asks me "What God do?" and I say vaguely "Made the earth", and
he, thinking earth means the garden, says enquiringly "Have to wear his
old trousers?"   Return to London in gradually fading light and knit in
train till it becomes dark, when have to stop because there is no light
in carriage.

Monday, September 6, 1943

To spy film "Above Suspicion" in evening, not too tense but very entertaining.   Mr. Pringle tells me that in middle of night he found firemen
rushing into garden and spraying jets of water about.   A bonfire which
he thought he had put out had sprung up and set fire to the fence.   He
now fears he will have to pay large sums to Fire Brigade for putting it
out, and will be fined for showing light in blackout.   Moreover, he was
supposed to be on fire-watch last night!

Tuesday, September 7, 1943

At printers till 7.30 and then on fire-duty at B.H.   Very tired and
hungry by time I get meal about 9 o'clock.   Reading George Moore's
"Confessions of a Young Man" which find interesting though feel in real
life should not have cared for the Y.M.

Wednesday, September 8, 1943

Quiet fire-watch last night.   Take two suits to Lewis's to be altered
and find they have from this week made regulation that no work at all can
be accepted: they have no staff to do it.   Ring up several other shops
and they all give same answer - no labour.   In afternoon have hair

washed and on way back at 5 o'clock see little queue for evening paper and buy one. Nothing special in it. But at about ⅞ 5.45 Gerald Abraham rings up to say he is sorry he missed me whenI g∅∅ took over proof a few minutes ago, but he w.as "seeing about Italy". Upon my enquiring the meaning of this, he says that Italy has surrendered unconditionally. So we all go along to Radio Times office to hear six o'clock news, and Stuart Hibberd says "Here is the news - some of the best news of the war so far. John Snagge will read it to you". Then followed General Eisenhower's broadcast from United Nations radio at Algiers, telling of granting of armistice to Italy - which was signed last Friday but has not been made public until "a convenient moment for the Allies". At this we are all elated, except poor Miss Entract, whose brother is missing from raid over Milan about a fortnight ago, and who feels news is too late for her to rejoice in it.

At dinner, everyone's spirits very uplifted. I darn 8 pairs of stockings and listen to special programme of "Victory Music" - Beethoven No.5, a movement from Vaughan Williams' London Symphony, and 2 of Elgar's Pomp and Circumstance marches, Nos. 4 and 1.

Thursday, September 9, 1943

Papers full of wildest rumours: i.e. that Mussolini is in hands of the Allies. What is official is that the Americans, whose whereabouts since we landed in Italy have been cause of speculation, have sailed up west coast of Italy andmade landingsat Naples and elsewhere.

Miss Entract much cheered by news that one of the crew of her brother's 'plane is reported on German wireless as being prisoner. Air Ministry always warns people to take no notice of these announcements, but she cannot help being hopeful.

Friday, September 10, 1943

Americans have established bridgeheads in Naples area in face of severe German opposition. Germans said to be attacking Rome. Germans say they have occupied North of Italy. Rumoursagain rife. One says that Hitler has taken to bed with nervous breakdown, but on other hand report is given in 9 p.m. news of speech he has made. Mother assures me Mars ks in conjunction with Uranus (or something of the sort) so that it is not surprising if things are happening.

I feel very belligerent and have two furious but friendly arguments with Editor. Buy minute bottle of lavender water for Mother to give Mrs. H. - about 1" by 2" - for 4/-½d. Also 3 yards of web elastic 1" wide which I think may make braces for Martin, for 4/-. Miss White (at office) has found dressmaker who will alter my skirts, and she takes away one only, with measurements, to see if it gets done satisfactorily.

Saturday, September 11, 1943

Terrific thunderstorm last night. At first, on awakening, I think it is air-raid, then since it sounds unlike one, imagine it is naval engagement of great ferocity off coast. Then rain pours down on to balcony and bespatters my bed and face through open window. Last for

an hour.   Today beautiful, warm as summer, though trees in park look
like autumn after last night.
          Most of Italian fleet sails into Malta.
          Joyce, returning from Llandudno, arrives for night, brown
after holiday.

Sunday, September 12, 1943

Day of thanksgiving for capitulation of Italy.   I miztakenly take Joyce
to St. Matthew's, Bayswater, where she is so disgusted that with opinions
of preacher, she says she can't support that sort of thing, so puts nothing in collection.   He says, inter alia, that "Karl Marx, Voltaire,
Tolstoy"(and one other whom I have forgotten) "tried to strangle Christianity <u>at its birth</u>".   The poor Italians have made peace because they
can no longer face events, and things are worse for them than ever before
for their country has just been turned into battlefield.   If I were an
Italian peasant, I should say "These wretched English and Germans, always fighting their wars in other people's countries!"   However,
preacher we hear doesn't feel like this: is wholeheartedly able to thank
the Lord for "so kindly" giving us victory.

Monday, September 13, 1943

Another absolutely tremendous thunderstorm last night.   Today it is
announced by Germans that Mussolini and his eldest son are in Germany,
Musso.having been rescued by German paratroops.   Very fierce fighting
going on between Egnlish and Germans near Naples.
          I read "The Stricken Deer", Lord David Cecil's life of Cowper,
and feel almost that I am going mad myself after/the poor man's sufferings
                                        reading of the

Tuesday, September 14, 1943

At printers till 7.30.   Things not going so well for us near Naples.
Germans have very strong forces there.   Their tale of rescue of Musso.
gets more fantastic every minute.   Yesterday he was saved from a big
city where he was being kept, but today he was taken from a hotel high up
in the mountains, by planes which arrived almost silently.   He then
said joyfully "Ah, I knew my friend Hitler would send for me" - or something like that, and was silently borne away.

Wednesday, September 15, 1943

Buy "Utility" blouse, cotton, for 4 coupons and 18/5.   Also some un-
couponed yarn, yellow, for which I pay 8/- and which is enough to make
jumper with long sleeves.   Going into park in morning, see sheep which
has wandered into Bayswater Road and is bewildered by traffic. (There is
a flock in Kensington Gardens at present.)   It tries to leap low wall
back to safety and gets stuck on top with back legs kicking helplessly.
I advance upon it and with both hands begin to shove its buttocks, but it
is so alarmed at this that it falls off wall on top of me.   I then act
as sheep-dog and edge it gently through open gate, at all of which passing American soldier looks justifiably amused.

Thursday, September 16, 1943

No wonder Cowper wrote "God moves in a mysterious way His wonders to perform". When he wrote it, he was consciously moving into his second bout of madness. And it was after this, when he had lost the ardent faith which he had between the two bouts, that he wrote "O for a closer walk with God, a calm and heavenly frame", which goes on "Where is the blessedness I knew when first I saw the Lord". The poor man was convinced that he was eternally damned.

Friday, September 17, 1943

To Hilary's with four enormous kippers which have been on window-sill of office all the afternoon, smelling abominably. Also dish-mop for 1/3, with a wire handle which is too thin to support the mop properly when it is full of water.

Saturday, September 18, 1943

Blackberrying with Martin. We get 3½ lb. while H. is shopping in Hertford.
At Salerno in Italy, Allies' position is apparently now secure.

Sunday, September 19, 1943

Blackberrying again. Tramp disappears for about ½ hour with head down rabbit-hole. Milkman, who yesterday assured me he was coming, does not, and L. goes off in great fury to get milk from dairy for tea. He had been on H.G. exercise since 8.20 in the morning and felt this was too much. Says they will have to leave that house, and H. had better go home to Stroud and he into rooms. Milkman did not call this week between Monday and Thursday, and gave no warning of it: it is too bad. H. says work of the place and distance to go for everything is too much for her and she feels ill and tired all the time.
Prime Minister returns tot his country, from Canada.

Monday, September 20, 1943

Germans appear to have evacuated Sardinia and French are said to be taking possession of Corsica. I fire-watch at night, whiling away the evening by knitting woollenpants which I have been trying to finish for months. This morning Miss White brings back my skirt which dressmaker she knows has let out for me. She has completely ruined it and I send it back to be re-made.

Tuesday, September 21, 1943

Much colder. Sir Kingsley Wood, Chancellor of Exchequer, dies suddenly of heart attack. P.M. gives statement on war situation to Parliament. U-boat menace now well under control but says Germans about to launch new weapon for sinking our ships. I had quiet fire-watch last night.
Realise as I get into bed about 10.15 that I have forgotten to ring

up office and tell secretary on duty that we have finished at printer's, and hope she is not still there.

Wednesday, September 22, 1943

To National Gallery concert - Beethoven sonatas, Franz Osborn (piano), Max Rostal (violin). In evening to film of "Dear Octopus" with Bob, who expresses sudden desire for dissipation and for whom I can think of nothing more exciting than the local cinima. Film sentimental and snobbish but at least nothing to do with war.

Miss P. lately told me of many frightful horrors and atrocities committed by Germans: I now find source of information was a Mrs. Watson who says she was at Dunkirk, in starving Belgium, has spent years and years in China and knows every part of it, was in India, has divorced her husband, and generally seems to be dotty and to have too vivid an imagination.

Thursday, September 23, 1943

Apparently Allies had secretly armed thousands of Corsicans, who have now "taken" their own island. Russians progressing well. Last night we bombed Hanover. I manage to get bottle of "haliborange" for Martin, which unaccountably blows over on window-sill of office and smashes. I save about two-thirds of contents in a glue-jar, and the office-boy is despatched to same shop and manages to get another. Today and yesterday walk to and from office. Have practically nothing to do all day and feel very miserable and useless.

Friday, September 24, 1943

To Ware. No fish, no cake - one shop closed and the other empty when I go round after lunch. Hilary has been advised by doctor at clinic to send Martin to war nursery (really for war workers to send their children during day), because he "has too much imagination and too little to do with it". Cholera and typhus reported in Naples.

Saturday, September 25, 1943

Germans have evacuated Smolensk. Read copy of Churchill's speeches from 1938 in Free Trade Hall, Manchester, to end of 1940. Most interesting. Hope later to see next volume.

Blackberrying with Martin. Get 3½ lb. and H. bottles them. Martin overturns pail of soapsuds on to kitchen floor, I fear of malice aforethought, and then empties cocoa all over the floor and chairs.

Sunday, September 26, 1943

This is Battle of Britain Sunday, and also Harvest Festival in many churches. Hilary and I take Martin to Christ Church in Musley Hill and remain until the Te Deum. He is interested and sings his own words to "Come Ye Thankful People, Come". At home in afternoon he hurls reels

of cotton about sitting-room and generally shows need for robust
companionship.   Hope H. will decide to send him to war nursery.

Monday, September 27, 1943

Buy 8 press studs, 1/- (card of 40 would have cost 2d. or 3d. before
war) and 6 hair-grips, 1/-.   To film, very American, which I do not
enjoy much.   Cannot follow slick American slang.

Tuesday, September 28, 1943

At printers till8 o'clock.   Allies have captured Foggia in Italy and
last night made very heavy raid on Hanover.

Wednesday, September 29, 1943

Lunch with Aunt N. and then put her on train for Stroud.   In evening
to supper with the Gerald Abrahams who have received a brace of partridges and explain that they have to find someone to help eat them.

Thursday, September 30, 1943

Meet Mother at Paddington, have very poor lunch for 4/- each at Paddington Hotel, and then take her to Liverpool Street and put her on train
for Ware.   Grapes at 10/- a lb. and Cox's Orange Pippins at 1/- a lb.
on sale on barrows in streets.   Naples captured by Allies.

Friday, October 1, 1943

Go out to lunch at 1 o'clock and it is 20 to 3 before it is all served
to me.   To Ware, taking bottle of Haliborange for Martin and 2 cakes.

Saturday, October 2, 1943

Blackberrying: the blackberries here just at their best.   Bath Martin
while his parents go to cinema.   He is very good and goes to sleep at
once whenI put him to bed.

Sunday, October 3, 1943

Blackberrying again in morning.   Tramp goes into pond and gets himself
black on his lower half.   Return to London by 5 o'clock train for fire-
watching and so miss Daddy who arrives immediately afterwards   Am
told there wasAlert last night, but heard nothing.

Monday, October 4, 1943

There was Alert just as I was getting out of bath last night.   I was
"on the book" - i.e. on duty in Fire Duty Room at the telephone - and
had to dry in great hurry.   Alert for about 45 minutes.
    Have back one skirt from dressmaker, now wearable.   Glad to have

it because no central heating so far allowed in offices. The printers,
all the same, have it on. Probably their machinery generates it without extra power. Am enlarging Martin's winter outdoor knitted suit
which I made last year.

Tuesday, October 5, 1943

Russian campaign seems to be slowing down: autumn rains have begun.
Unfortunately they have not yet captured Kiev. David Green, in fireman's uniform, calls in evening. Very excited because he has just
bought cottage not far from Oxford. Most fortunate to get one nowadays
since housing shortage is acute and prices very high. Peter Beavan on
leave. His last trip was down West Coast of Africa and he had very bad
asthma.

Wednesday, October 6, 1943

To hairdressers, where casually and unpremeditatedly make appointment
for Nov.3 to have hair cut off and "permed". In evening settle down
joyfully with much knitting to listen alone to broadcast of "Eroica",
but there is Alert and transmission becomes very bad, so have sadly to
abandon the music.

Thursday, October 7, 1943

Meet parents for lunch at 12. Queue at Evans so tremendous, right
down past ladies' lavatories, that take them out to Wigmore Restaurant
where we feed more quickly (and expensively). In evening to Beavans.
Duque and Arthur up from cottage to be with Peter. String quartets
(Haydn, Beethoven), punctuated by loud gunfire because "Alert" has been
sounded. Man (Dick Gandy) sings Liebeslieder (Brahms, Schumann) very
beautifully, also with gun obbligato. Feel it strange and ridiculous
that we all sit there enjoying German music while Germans drop bombs on
us. Fortunately no bits of shell hit top of music room, for if they
had there is only a thin roof and nothing above us and we might have
been badly hurt. All clear at 11 before I go home.

Friday, October 8, 1943

Buy saucepan scrubber (wire) in Regent Street - on pavement - for 1/-.
In Bond Street meet Bob looking for birthday present for his sister.
He has been visiting the beauty salons and is surprised that they are
more like drawing-rooms than shops. With my aid he gets box of powder
(Chanel's) for 8/6 in Regent Street Boots, which I hope is right colour
for sister's complexion. I buy copy of Greek Orthodox Liturgy, with
intention next week of going to Greek Cathedral. It is full of
symbolism. i.e. Deacon says to Priest "Pray Father, slay", and the
priest with a sword "slays" the Lamb - i.e. pierces bread with sword -
and so on. Much of it very beautiful.

Saturday, October 9, 1943

Find on looking through diary that I forgot to enter about October 1
that I have received rise, making income £600 a year, and am informed
this brings me to maximum salary on my present grade.   But also a
notice came round lately about a cost of living bonus which we are to
receive at the rate of 11/- a week (half goes at once in income tax),
and this is to be retrospective from beginning of June, so next month's
cheque will have about £10 extra or more.
          To Joyce's at Little Felcourt at midday.   Wonderful warm sunny
October day and all trees at their best.   Walk with children by lake.

Sunday, October 10, 1943

Again bright sunshine.   Get beautiful roses and Michaelmas daisies from
grounds of big house where soldiers are in possession, and go for walk
by another lake, and later gather lot of mushrooms for supper which eat
with 2 real tomatoes and tin baked beans, very good.   Tedious journey
back, tho' black-out is not bad because there is bright moon, with long
wait on E.Croydon platform.

Monday, October 11, 1943

Mild.   In evening to "Mr. Brophy", play by James Bridie, with John.
Story of the devil's appearance in Scottish manse (Wee Frees), very amusing.

Tuesday, October 12, 1943

British midget submarines go into Alten Fjord, Norway, and damage battleship "Tirpitz".   Portuguese give us use of Azores for sea and air bases
Mr. Pringle says Americans are furious because facilities were not granted
to them.   Churchill tells house they have been given us under treaty
signed in 15th century.
          At printers till 7.40.

Wednesday, October 13, 1943

To National Gallery concert.   Myra Hess playing 2 Mozart concertos.   See
Peter's red head as orchestra comes in and speak to him afterwards as he
rushes off to rehearsal for concert at Wigmore Hall.   Ring Hilary, who
tells me Mr. Keene (our neighbour at home) has been killed.   He was
gunner in Merchant Navy, such a nice little man.   He and his wife ought
never to have had to be mixed up with a war.   She had been doing his
job to keep it for him till he came home, and to keep her home together.
In evening Miss Morrison has tantrum with Joan merely becaouselatter is
slow over her dinner.   Then Tina and I listen to wonderful broadcast of
Beethoven's Mass in D, and I think what a strange world this is, which
can contain Mozart concertos, and a young woman widowed as it seems quite
senselessly, and Miss Morrison's tantrums, and Beethoven's Missa Solemnis.

Thursday, October 14, 1943

Spend lunch-time trying in vain to get hair-nets for Mother; also buy
for Leonard's birthday Chinese lyrics translated by Helen Waddell; and
some Spanish poems translated by Stephen Spender (Garcia Lorca or somebody).
        There is terrible famine in India. Many people say it is our
fault, that it was foreseen two years ago and that we did nothing but
continued to export food and let people "corner" food and put up prices.
Others - such as Greta who has lived in India - say the States concerned
and under Indian control and it is not our responsibility because they
will brook no interference from British Government. Over lunch I
read Macaulay's "Lays of Ancient Rome" - Horatius - which reduces me to
tears of excitement.

Friday, October 15, 1943

To Beavans: Haydn and Beethoven quartets. Jean Layton there: she has
job, under Y.M.C.A., of driving van, with piano and gramophone, to lonely
gun outposts, and giving music recitals. Last week went round with
singer and pianist, and her own violin. Visits the same place 3 times,
giving them slightly "harder" music each time. Peter trying to get out
of Merchant Navy because of his asthma.
        At 8th attempt manage to get Mother some hair-nets.

Saturday, October 16, 1943

Lunch with Tina; then go with Bob to Evensong at Westminster Abbey and
walk home with across 3 parks and have tea near home. In evening on
fire duty at Broadcasting House.

Sunday, October 17, 1943

Had to get up about 1.45 last night for $\frac{3}{4}$-hour. Pouring wet morning.
I meet Bob at the Grosvenor Chapel, North Audley Street, for communion.
At least, I do not meet him because I am 5 minutes late, and sit at back
hatless, with rain trickling down my face and my feet wet, my suitcase
beside me. We manage to get taxi home. Then after breakfast go to
service at Greek Cathedral (Orthodox) just round corner, to which end I
have bought the Orthodox Liturgy - only in English unfortunately, and we
find it difficult to keep the place. Can recognise "Kyrie Eleison",
"Alleluia", "Maria", and "Amen", and nothing else. Most beautiful singing. We sit in the Strangers' Gallery. The Faithful stand for the
whole service, kneeling very occasionally. There are no proper seats
for them, only arms to lean on. Almost everyone lights a candle as he
comes in and kisses a picture - I think of the Virgin and Child, but I
cannot see it properly. The men are separated from the women. It does
not appear to matter exactly when one comes in. About 20 sailors arrive
together half way through the service. There is a man standing at the
back with an infant in arms who is on the whole very good.

Monday, October 18, 1943

Another Alert last night and heavy gunfire.   Joan's brother Sandy,
Flying Officer in Air Force, turns up unexpectedly for 3 days' leave,
and has hardly arrived before he is rung up to say there is telegram
requiring his instant return.

Tuesday, October 19, 1943

Three-Power Conference meets in Moscow.   At printers till 7.15.   Then
have to walk down dark track in pouring rain to get to station.   Editor
steps heartily into large puddle which makes him feel that such misery
and squalor cannot be endured and he must see if we can get car to fetch
us on Tuesdays.   Alert last night.

Wednesday, October 20, 1943

In Lunch-time to National Gallery concert: Brahms clarinet and piano
sonatas (Pauline Juler, Howard Ferguson) and songs by Jan van der Gucht.
Buy 1 lb. Cox's orange pippins from street stall for 1/3, which is 3d.
over legal price.   But in shop I saw they were picking out very worst
to sell to customers, leaving best to show in window.   Heating in office
suddenly comes on in afternoon: ban on central heating lifted.

Thursday, October 21, 1943

Admiral Sir Dudley Pound dies.   Another raid last night: bombs - I am
told - in Earl's Court.   To dentist who reports me sound.   Everyone
has bad cold and I feel rather queer with bad headache all morning.
Wish I could see any place for me in the scheme of things.   Reading "The
Pilgrim's Regress" by C.S. Lewis.

Friday, October 22, 1943

To Ware by 5.10, which has become 5.6.   Call for Martin's push-chair
which has been left at little shop by Ware station, which helps me in
transport of my bag, heavy with 3 bottles of Haliborange for him, and
books for his father's birthday on Tuesday.   One of them is copy of
Browning's poems, only one I could get for him, second-hand at 10/-.
About 7 we have warning and quite a lot of gunfire.   We stand in porch
and watch, but soundof piece of shell whizzing down drives us indoors.

Saturday, October 23, 1943

Martin, whom I put to bed, requests me to say "Jesus tender Shepherd",
and when I say "Bless Thy little lamb tonight", he says severely, "Not
say Little Lamb - Bob's Man" (which is character he has been most of day.
And when I end "Make Martin a good boy", he says "Not say Make Marty good
boy - I like to be naughty"boy".

Sunday, October 24, 1943

We

We gather mushrooms from field at back of house.   I return at 5.45 because evenings now getting dark early, and change at Broxbourne on to intolerably overcrowded Cambridge train.

Monday, October 25, 1943

Russians doing well.   Have learned whole of "Horatius" by heart (knew some of it from school-days) and enjoy it very much.   Tina has borrowed old copy of Moody and Sankey and we enjoy ourselves bellowing "Only an Armour-Bearer" and "Pull for the Shore Sailor".   Great robustness about most of them which is very refreshing, but others, "I Should like to Die said Willie", "Is there room for Mary there?" and "A drunkard reached his cheerless home" are so maudlin it is difficult to believe they were not written as burlesques.   P. has managed to get one week's holiday, though farmer was rather unwilling because the men get no holiday and they are already jealous of Women's Land Army.

Tuesday, October 26, 1943

Thick fog in evening.   Car comes to fetch us from Waterlows and gets a little lost in returning.   Very tired and depressed.

Wednesday, October 27, 1943

Buy one large comb for my hair at £1.1.0 (real tortoiseshell, but what a price!).   The other day enquired about some I saw in shop in Great Portland Street and found they were £4.10. and £5.10. each comb.   Still very foggy.   Russians advancing.

Thursday, October 28, 1943

Papers have been full of accounts by repatriated prisoners from Germany about low morale in that country.   Tucked away in corner of Telegraph today is paragraph saying American correspondents have complained that censorship has forced them to give very one-sided account of what these men have said.

Friday, October 29, 1943

Fire-watching.   We are shown 7 exits from Broadcasting House and also taken to control room which is now 2 floors below ground, and see the booster pump which has to be turned on as water supply if there is big fire.

Saturday, October 30, 1943

Had asked to be called at 7.30 but woman omits to do so.   I therefore miss 9.5 train to Ware and catch 10.5 in almost breakfastless condition, since I go innocently to A.B.C. only to find it is now cafeteria which sells only cups of tea and sweet cakes (at that hour of the morning!) roll and minute dab of butter.   Martin and I get mushrooms.   Hilary trying to have another baby to give him companion, tho' does not know how she will cope if she gets one.

Sunday, October 31, 1943

Mushrooming with Martin.   Take back about 2 lb. Very crowded, late train to Liverpool Street.

Monday, November 1, 1943

Russians still advancing.   Ring up Hilary, who has scalded her foot.   It might have been much worse if she had not been international hockey-player and done fast leap when she saw kettle coming.

Tuesday, November 2, 1943

Finish at printers at 7.   Car comes for us and there is warning as we drive back.   See flashes of gunfire in distant sky.   Knitting jersey for Martin from odd ounces of wool and it looks very pretty.

Wednesday, November 3, 1943

Spend whole morning having hair "permed", lots cut off, and rest turned up on top of head.   Feel rather as if I'm going to have head chopped off but like it very much.   Don't know how I am ever going to do it by my-self.   In evening take Greta and Tina, whose joint birthday it is, to Ben Travers' new farce "She Follows Me About", which starts at 7.15 and there is air-raid warning during first act.   All clear follows quickly. Very amusing and we enjoy it.

Thursday, November 4, 1943

Nearly everybody seems to like my new hair do.   Go at lunch-time to National Gallery with Mr. Abraham (who expresses approval of coiffure but says he feels as if I have lost a flying buttress at back).   Hirsch String Quartet play Haydn in F major (lovely) and Bartok's 'Mikrokosmos' (5 pieces - amusing), and with Joan Davies at piano, Cesar Franck's Piano Quintet.
        At last we seem to be advancing a bit in Italy.

Friday, November 5, 1943

To Ware with Tina who brings pigeon pie intended for Sir Richard Acland's supper last night, but which that high-minded man never even noticed among the other food.   Alert.

Saturday, November 6, 1943

Rain and wind.   Martin and I go to Wareside and get dog-biscuits for Tramp from village shop which is one of few places where one can buy any nowadays.

Sunday, November 7, 1943

Cold and windy.   Martin and I find a few mushrooms, he all the time pre-

tending to be either "little dicky-bird" or else "Home Guard".   Warning
as T. and I journey back, and All Clear as we walk along C.Hill Gardens.

Monday, November 8, 1943

To film, "My Friend Flicka", about little boy and a horse.   Pleasant
change from most films.   Last evening, during Alert while T. and I were
coming home about 9.30, a dance-hall and milk-bar were hit at Putney and
large number of people killed.

Tuesday, November 9, 1943

To press at 6.45.   Hitler has made speech rather on lines of Churchill's
1940 speeches, promising that Germans will never give in.   And today
Churchill speaks at Mansion House, saying bloodiest part of war for Britain
and America is yet to come: there is going to be great suffering and loss
of life.

Wednesday, November 10, 1943

Listen in evening to broadcast of Elgar's "Apostles", which have not heard
before and enjoy very much: "Alleluia" of angels near the end especially.

Thursday, November 11, 1943

No celebrations of Armistice Day, thank goodness: no two minutes'
silence (except by tomb of Unknown Warrior in the Abbey).   Fire-watching
at night.

Friday, November 12, 1943

Receive parcel from Helena with 3 handbags, one quite usable, 1 pair
wearable silk stockings, and 1 mildewed but cleanable pair of gloves,
which she has unearthed from among my belongings left with their furniture.   Great booty.
        Trouble in Lebanon and everyone looks to British to put matters
right.   French appear to be being very difficult.   To Ware, and walk
from station in brilliant moonlight, meeting Leonard walking into town
very rapidly for Home Guard lecture, his bicycle having got a puncture.
He is now a Corporal (cannot rise to be Sergeant because village has not
enough men).   Hilary says he has been out at Home Guard every night but
one this week.

Saturday, November 13, 1943

Very cold.   Heavy hailstorm while H. is at Ware shopping.   Nurse comes
and dresses her foot which has still not healed properly; but ointment she
is applying appears tobe doing it good.   Martin suddenly asks me if I
like "business men", which so startles me I am unable to reply.   He becomes very fond of me and demands that I shall put him to bed, which I do.

Sunday, November 14, 1943

Not so pleased with Martin's affection which he cries for his mother in
night (because I will not take him into my bed - it is only 11 o'clock).
I shout at poor child, but after a while tell him story instead, which
soothes him to sleep.   Next morning he walkes in half-light saying sweetly: "Is it morning-time yet, Auntie?" and being told that it is, comes
joyfully into my bed.   I walk back to station in frightfully cold rain
and wind, in coat borrowed from Leonard which comes down to my feet, and
he accompanies me most of the way.

Monday, November 15, 1943

Letter from Marjorie Fuchs.   Edgar (Arnold's brother) and wife borrowed
room from dentist in Manchester in which to borrow practise string quartets with another couple.   Took cello in perambulator which left outside.
There was much knocking at door: policeman stood there, and behind him
7 more policemen, who had seen empty pram. and heard such horrifying
noises within they thought baby was being murdered.   Knitting Martin's
Christmas jersey at night.

Tuesday, November 16, 1943

Miss Morrison returns my watch which has been cleaned at cost of 17/6,
and it stops six times during the day.   We go to press at 7 o'clock and
are fetched away in car.

Wednesday, November 17, 1943

To National Gallery concert, but find Griller Quartet, which was to have
played Haydn and Brahms, has one of its members ill.   So I go away and
shop: 2 yards of elastic from man on pavement at 1/- a yard; 3 toys for
Martin from Hamley's at total cost of £1.11.0½.   Very crude blocks with
pictures on two sides, 15/-; little 3-cornered 3-cornered blocks, plain
fawn, made of some kind of plastic and smelling rather nasty, 9/7½d; and
3 little sets of wooden curves in red-yellow and blue which make 3 little
men, 6/5.   Find on arriving home that elastic is 9 inches short of 2
yards - and the man only gave me 6d. change out of half-a-crown after I
had specifically asked for it, dishonest wretch.

Thursday, November 18, 1943

Continuing my wild career of expenditure, get £1-worth of books in lunch-
time, for Christmas and other presents, in addition to E.M. Forster's
Rede Lecture on Virginia Woolf, for myself (1/6).   Take mouldy gloves
to be cleaned.   Joan's brother Sandy for night, just flown back from
North Africa.   Brings 3 minute green bananas and 3 green lemons, which
cause some excitement.

Friday, November 19, 1943

By 4.15 to Stroud, in horrible drizzly rain and fog.   By standing in
short queue get Mother ½ lb. mixed chocolatesat controlled price of £ 5/-
a lb.

~~Sunday~~, Saturday, November 20, 1943

Visit Aunt H., in bed with remains of flu, and Aunt N.   Shop for Mother
in town and get ½ lb. tomatoes, 8½d. (from beneath counter).   Try to get
Optrex for Mother, but am told there is no witch-hazel to make it now
(tho' one can occasionally get a bottle).   Do get something in way of eye-
wash which Mr. Coley says is good.

Sunday, November 21, 1943

To chapel, where I perceive Pop stands to attention during the Gloria,
because, he says, why should he pay more respect to the National Anthem
than he does to it?   He is enjoying himself taking donations for parting
present for minister.   Comes home and turns coins and notes out of every
pocket and writes it all down in little red note book, often asking such
questions as "Mother, what's the name of that woman who stutters?   She
gave me 10/-".   A number of American soldiers in chapel: they are billet-
ed up at workhouse.   I travel back to London in comfort in first-class
carriage and guard does not reject my third-class ticket.

Monday, November 22, 1943 - complete blank, have made no entry.
(remember later, was sick on getting up in morning and felt queer all day)
Tuesday, November 23, 1943

Heavy raid on Berlin last night.   To press at 6 o'clock.   Fog clears,
but rain at night.

Wednesday, November 24, 1943

Feel rather unwell when I get up.   Take dress and skirt to dressmaker at
St. John's Wood with whom have waited for appointment for weeks and weeks.
She fusses with frock for 1½ hours so that I arrive at office at 11.15 or
so.   Another heavy raid on Berlin last night.   Fire-watching.

Thursday, November 25, 1943

Quiet fire-watch last night, though after our raids on Berlin I rather
expected to be disturbed.   Hilary comes up to have perm, and leaves Martin
with me in office for about an hour.   He amuses himself sharpening pencils and looking at books and is very good.   I take him to lunch at
Evans's where he eats tremendous amount.   Does not care for sight of his
mother with her hair drying.   In evening to "Hansel and Gretel" with Tina.
Very much enjoy it.   Many American soldiers there, including one in our
row with 5 'arrow' stripes on his arm, 3 rows of decorations, and a broad
khaki stripe.   Alert during performance, but it lasts only about ½-hour.

Friday, November 26, 1943

To National Gallery concert with Gerald Abraham, to hear London Wind Octet
in Mozart Serenades.   But owing to illness, probably prevalent flu, programme is changed.   We have Schubert Duo in A major for Violin and Piano.

and Brahms' Trio in E flat for violin, horn and piano. Dennis Brain is the horn and G.A. says he hasnever heard it better played. In evening to Ware. H. has had dreadful week, with incipient flu, and with gas, oil, and wireless batteries running out, and other miseries.

Saturday, November 27, 1943

Dreadful weather. Leonard to his mother's, to attend his niece's christening. He rings up Martin about 6 o'clock, but poor Martin can only sob out down telephone because cat has just slashed him across eye with her claw. At first, with blood, tears and fright, we do not know whether eye is touched, but mercifully the mark, which is quite deep, is one-eighth of an inch below eye. We bathe it with weak Dettol and give him warm sweet milk drink, and H. nurses him to sleepwhile I put hot-water bottle in his bed. No one but his mother will avail in this crisis, and when H. asks me to hold him for a moment, he gives me look of cold dislike and says "Auntie is horrible old thing".

Sunday, November 28, 1943

H., having said she was thankful last week was over and a new one begin-ning, arises this morning and, in taking down blackout board from kitchen window, drops it like a guillotine on her big toe, and nearly makes her-self faint. At which I, instead of succouring her, turn so faint and sick myself, am no use at all. Fortunately no bones broken, but toe is badly bruised. Also fortunately, though it is her scalded foot, board does not touch burnt part. Martin's eye no worse. He and I gather about 1½ lb. of mushrooms for dinner. Rather good for November 28. Back to London intotally unlighted railway carriage which have to myself.

Monday, November 29, 1943

Very cold. There is much influenza about, and I have cold myself. Dried egg ration to be doubled for next month.

Tuesday, November 30, 1943

Take Mr. Pringle to British Restaurant for lunch: it has lately been open opened near printers. For 1/4½d. each we have roast lamb, mashed swedes and potatoes, semolina pudding apparently made with eggs (dried?), bread, margarine and big piece of cheese, and cup of tea. The tea, I must own, is not very nice. Otherwise it is extremely good meal. Finish at printers at 6.45.
      Eighth Army attacking in Italy. Much talk (especially by Germans) of alleged meeting now taking place between Churchill, Roosevelt and Stalin. Our papers very reticent on subject.

Wednesday, December 1, 1943

Hair washed. Woman alarms me by putting little curls on top, quite without my connivance. Do not know how I shall manage them, but she points out that I have not yet tried.

Thursday, December 2, 1943

News at last published that Churchill, Roosevelt and Chiang Kai-shek have
met in N. Africa to discuss war in Far East.   There is much fury because
every other country in world has news before us.
        News from Joyce of death of Mr. Hasler.
        In lunch-time buy 6 plain white cups and saucers for H., at 2/9½
each, and pair bedroom slippers for Mother for Christmas, 21/5.   Velvet
lined and rather comfortable but seem a bit small in size.   4 coupons.
Also manage triumphantly to get 5 razor blades and some saccharine tablet.
Give 3 razor blades to Leonard and 2 to Gerald Abraham.   To dinner with
latter, who is befriending funny shy youth up from country to earn his
living by writing about music.   .

Friday, December 3, 1943

News now comes that Roosevelt and Churchill have moved on to Persia where
they are having meeting with Stalin.
        In lunch-time ask butcher in Great Titchfield Street whether he has
any tripe, which is unrationed.   He says no, but offers me liver.   Upon
my thanking him he says "You don't often get offered liver nowadays, do
you?   But I like the look of you!"   And on wrapping it up, shouts at
cash desk "A shilling's-worth of liver for the young girl"!   Miss Playle
also gets liver from her retailer, which she does not want, and a kidney;
so I take a quite heavy bag to Ware, with cups and saucers as well.

Saturday, December 4, 1943

Martin and I look for mushrooms to go with liver, but they are really
gone this time.   He has sniffly cold.   H. is better.   L. has been home
3 days with flu and looks a lot better for rest.   Last night our bombers
made feint attack on Berlin, then turned aside and dropped most of bombs
on Leipzig.

Sunday, December 5, 1943

Bright sunshine,and moonlight to come home in.   In spite of Martin's
cheering presence, feel irritable and depressed.

Monday, December 6, 1943

Buy tin kettle, 2/4, and am carrying it unwrapped through streets when
cabman leans from his seat and says "You've got a dent in that kettle.   I
should take it back if I were you".   So I change it.   Have also bought
2 night-dresses made of nunsveiling, at 46/- and 6 coupons each. Quite
plainly made.   Cannot afford pyjamas because they are 8 coupons each.
Declaration published from conference at Teheran of Roosevelt, Stalin and
Tuesday, December 7, 1943 Churchill.   Do not feel it says much.   There
are rumours that Turkey is coming in to war, that Germans are advancing
towards Turkish border from Rumania, and that Turkish President is now
in Cairo with Roosevelt and Churchill.

Tuesday, December 7, 1943

To press at 7, after which have to fire-watch. Fire-watchers' beds
have been moved to other end of concert-hall, where shift-workers' beds
are, which makes it more disturbed for us.

Wednesday, December 8, 1943

B.B.C. gives 21st anniversary lunch, to which about 200 of its 10,000
staff are invited. The Editor and Miss Playle (who has been here more
than 20 years) go from our section. Brendan Bracken, Minister of Information, to be guest of honour.

Thursday, December 9, 1943

H. comes up to have her new hair-do washed and set. Martin enjoys
moving staircases and lifts, and we take him to Lilley and Skinners'
children's department, where, although we do not get any shoes to fit, he
has ecstatic time on rocking-horse and looking at doll's house. Feel
very tired.

Friday, December 10, 1943

Buy extravagant 3-oz. piece of soap (1 coupon - we get 4 a month) at
2/10. Very nice. Also finish up my month's sweet ration ($\frac{3}{4}$ lb.) with
barley sugar stick for Christmas tree (2 out of the 12 oz.)

Saturday, December 11, 1943

Very cold: so cold that, after restless night, H. does not let Martin
come with me to village, which leads to great storm, in spite of his telling me to "go and burn myself up", that he will "cut me up in little bits
and eat me", and that he will "throw me out" - all of which threats
appear to give him great satisfaction.

Sunday, December 12, 1943

Still very cold. A little snow, which pleases Martin very much. He
brings handfuls into kitchen. H. thinks her efforts to have another baby
have been successful, and if so, she will in a few months give up the
bungalow and go home, since she really cannot cope with war-time shopping
at a distance of 2½ miles with Martin's 34 lb. weight always on back of
bicycle. Back to London in bright moonlight.

Monday, December 13, 1943

Work a little late at printers owing to approach of Christmas. Lot of
flu about. Newspapers say the epidemic, which started in north, is now
spreading to Midlands and London. So many people have it, it is hard to
believe it has not already arrived.

Tuesday, December 14, 1943

Very cold, busy press day. Tired and dispirited.

- 458 -

Wednesday, December 15, 1943

To dressmakers and to hair-dressers, which takes me all morning. Dressmaker has had flu and sits down to fit me. Come away feeling I am a
monstrosity, so far from "normal" do my measurements appear to be. Very
cold.

Thursday, December 16, 1943

Mr. Churchill ill with pneumonia in Middle East. Germans' "secret
weapon" reported to be bomb which destroys oxygen within radius of several
hundred yards of its explosion, thus suffocating everyone within that
area.
      Try to shop at lunchtime, a most disheartening task. Emerge from
Selfridges with 2 little "windmills" (to be held in hand), price 1/- each
(we used to give 2d for them when we were children). Feel very tired
and as if I am suffering from suppressed flu.

Friday, December 17, 1943

Queen Wilhelmina of the Netherlands in Broadcasting House. Buy necklace
for Hilary, 25/-. Salvation Army play carols on lawn of bungalow by
light of lamp: H. and I join in vocally.

Saturday, December 18, 1943

Take Martin to Wareside where he sits in very muddy puddle. Buy 2 lb.
dog-biscuits for Tramp (they are very difficult to get now) and some sweets.

Sunday, December 19, 1943

Home Guard exercises. Leonard's Wareside people are supposed to be
German parachutists who have taken the village, and the Ware people are
sent to relieve the inhabitants. H. and I act as 5th columnists and
ring up the parachutists at a farmhouse when we see their enemies approaching. I take Martin down muddy field track trying to get holly. Get a
few sprigs and some lovely haws and ivy. He trudges along with his boots
so covered with mud he can hardly lift them. Is so full of Irish stew
and suet pudding which he had for dinner, does not appear to mind at all.

Monday, December 20, 1943

Mr. Pringle has 2 children, father-in-law, mother-in-law and brother-in-
law in bed with flu, with unaided wife trying to cope. So he does not
stay late with me at printers (trying to get ahead before Christmas) but
returns at usual time to try to help her. I come forth in very dark
night and travel by train to Broadcasting House for fire-watching. We are
given lecture and shown one device for putting out fires when there are
electrical appliances about. The only trouble about it is that it is
highly poisonous when used in enclosed space, lecturer says, squirting it
all over floor in the underground room where we are gathered.

Tuesday, December 21, 1943

Alert at 2 a.m. Fireman comes into wrong end of concert-hall to wake us, cannot find us in dark, so shouts "Red's up, ladies", and all shift-workers wake up furiously and say "Sssh". Then he falls offplatform and someone puts on light to help him, and shift-workers all say "Put off that light!" Warning lasts for 30 minutes. Very tired today, and at printers till 7.30 or so, because just as we are finishing there is alert, and aircraft and gunfire right overhead, so we are sent to sit in damp dugout for 40 minutes. When we are told we can return, an officious printer, now in tin hat, rushes up and says, shall we want any revises (of formes), which, not having seen them, we are unable to say.

Wednesday, December 22, 1943

Shopping in lunchtime, during which, ladenwith parcels and having to search in bag for sweet coupons, I lose 5/- p.o. which Phyllida sent me this morning to buy myself Christmas present. Stand in queue for 20 minutes to get ½ lb. sweets. Little box which I think I will buy to put them in, is 2/3, and as sweets cost only 1/8, this seems to me out of proportion and I do not buy it. Get box mixed vegetable seeds for Fuchs's, 10/6. Christmas cards are awful price, very poor ones for 8d. and 10d.

Thursday, December 23, 1943

In lunch-time go to National Gallery concert - Fleet Street choir singing carols. "Lullay my Lyking" is best of them. Audience is asked to join in 7 well-known ones, which we do with great heartiness and enjoyment.

Friday, December 24, 1943

To Ware after lunch. Met about 20 yards from house by Leonard with very bad cold and Martin bounding with energy. We spend busy evening. I fetch cockerel from farm down raod, which we get for controlled price of 2/- a lb. (10/-). We are indeed lucky to get one, especially at a reasonable price. There is great "black market" in poultry: people pay fabulous prices for birds. Then we decorate 2 little trees with old decorations and a few paper new ones, quite pretty, which H. was fortunate enough to get for 4/6. Sheila (staying at Noah's Ark) brings Martin rubber boots which she has grown out of. They are unobtainable now, so H. is very pleased. I have to bath Tramp, who has rolled in manure.
   Eisenhower (American) has been appointed leader of forces to invade Europe.

Christmas Day, 1943

No bombing last night by either side. Very good, but I am afraid probably due only to weather conditions.
   Martin has stocking and is introduced to Father Christmas for first time. In it he has an orange, lucky boy, and a little "shop", a tiny cup and saucer with coat-of-arms of Ware on it and "Bold in God" underneath, a Christmas card, a little book, and a barley sugar stick. When he gets

up he has a crane made by his father, a garage with 3 little cars (2 made
by his father), a toy with aeroplanes, made by his grandfather, 2 jerseys
made by me, half-a-dozen books, , 2 pairs pyjamas from his grandparents
at Stroud.   The Mayes's to dinner and tea.   Father, Mother and Paul
aged 3½.   They bring mincepies (it was possible to buy bottle of mince-
meat instead of one's jam ration this month), cheese tarts, a few apples
(very difficult to get), milk, butter (real), and a cake iced.   The almond
icing is made from soya beans and is very good.   Also plasticine for
Martin, which is practically unobtainable nowadays.   So with the Christmas pudding made by mother, which we eat with custard made from a sweetened tin of condensed milk, and our cockerel and sprouts and potatoes, we
have good feast even in 5th Christmas of war.   Try to listen to King's
broadcast at 3 p.m., but hear very little with 2 children in room.   The
woman from whom we got cockerel arrives at tea-time with present of 2 eggs
for Martin and a rabbit which her husband has caught and killed.   Leonard
skins it for us.

Sunday, December 26, 1943

Not quite such pleasant weather as yesterday: mild but rather misty.
L. still has bad cold and stays in bed till tea-time.   M. and I go for
walk and play hide-and-seek round haystack; his energy is boundless.
He wants us all (he and Tramp and me) to "hide together" - though I point
out that that leaves nobody to find us.   But he thinks it is cosier that
way.

Monday, December 27, 1943

Back to work at midday.   London full of holiday-makers.   "Scharnhorst"
(German battleship) sunk when she attacked one of our convoys to Russia.

Tuesday, December 28, 1943

To press at 8 p.m.   Very tired indeed.

Wednesday, December 29, 1943

Too tired last night to sleep properly.   Today have hair washed and go to
sleep under drier.   2 3 more German destroyers sunk, this time in Bay of
Biscay.

Thursday, December 30, 1943

H. rings up to say that L. has been in bed again all week with heavy cold,
and Martin also has bad cold.   H. feels she could do with being in bed herself, but there is no opportunity of getting there.   I also feel very
heavy and unwell.   O dear!   Phyllida, in letter, says she get a number
of Christmas boxes when she took round milk just before Christmas, 1/- or
2/- from really poor people.   She was quite embarrassed by their genero-
sity.   Am kept awake by rowdy soldiers in streets after pubs. close at 11

<u>Friday, December 31, 1943</u>

Feel very seedy.   To Hilary's.   Last day of what I have found a very
depressing year.

<u>Saturday, January 1, 1944</u>

New Year's Day and Martin's 3rd birthday.   Parcel for him from Stroud
does not arrive and is not at Post Office in afternoon when I take him
into town to try to collect it.   Still feel very unwell and depressed
and have no pleasant hopes at all for the new year.   Daddy rings up.
Says Mother very dismayed about news, which she has just received, of
Hilary's expecting baby.

<u>Sunday, January 2, 1944</u>

To London early for fire-watching.   Alert at 11.45 while I am in bath,
which makes me late on duty.   Lasts till 12.30.

<u>Monday, January 3, 1944</u>

Very exhausted after last night's fire-watching and Alert.   To film with
Greta, "Flesh and Fantasy", rather unusual, on theme of determinism.
Berlin bombed very heavily.

<u>Tuesday, January 4, 1944</u>

Rush Davies rings up.   David now Vicar of church at West Dulwich.   Wants
me to go and see them.   To press about 6.50.   Very tired.

<u>Wednesday, January 5, 1944</u>

Russians advance patrols said to have crossed into Poland.   To Ruth and
David's.   See Rachel (whose middle name is Christiana) for first time:
11 months and rather attractive.   Diana, aged 7, is very tall.   David
now respectable Vicar with dog-collar, and author of best-selling books
on theology.   Looks happy and well, otherwise much the same.   House untidy but has modernconveniences.

<u>Thursday, January 6, 1944</u>

Change of outlook does not change Ruth, who does not wake me till 8.30,
so that I am rather late at office.   "I can't think how it happened", sh
remarks disarmingly, "I gave Rachel her orange-juice at 6 o'clock and I'm
sure I didn't go to sleep again, and then it was half past eight!"   '
(Babies get orange-juice in bottles, issued by Govt.)
     Polish Government in London getting agitated about Russia, and no
wonder!

<u>Friday, January 7, 1944</u>

Home to Stroud at 4.15.   Arrive about 7.30 in bright moonlight.   R.A.F.
have bombed Stettin.   Details announced of new jet-propelled aeroplane,

which Molly Evans' brother-in-law helped to build at Brockworth.

Saturday, January 8, 1944

Mother pleased because milkman lets her have 3 pints of milk (though he does not come tomorrow). Bernard's (Daddy's assistant) mother also sends bottle of milk. Bob Franklin (Navy) has been home on embarkation leave and now, having spent the leave in bed with flu, has departed, they think to the Mediterranean. Mother's bedroomslippers which I gave her for Christmas, nearly into holes already.

Sunday, January 9, 1944

To Aunt Hermie's. She gives me little old gold brooch (hunting-horn with fox on it) as Christmas present. Return home before tea, because at 4.50 Phyllida arrives, with pint milk, 6 eggs, and some cheese. To London at 6.15. Train very crowded: stand till Kemble.

Monday, January 10, 1944

To film, "49th parallel", with Greta - made at beginning of war, before America came in. Not bad.

Tuesday, January 11, 1944

Last night slept hardly at all but lay awake getting terribly worried about everything and thinking how useless and objectless and futile my existence is. Today we do not go to press till 8.40. Am very tired.

Wednesday, January 12, 1944

To dentist's for scaling. He finds a hole which must be filled but cannot give me another appointment for a month. Then to Paddington where meet Hilary and Martin, with dog, and also Joyce, and have sausage, beans and potatoes at snack-bar. J. and I then help tp put Hilary and baggage on train for Stroud. She has to pay half-fare for Martin because he is now three. Ticket-man says "I think I should have brazened it out a bit longer if I'd been you". J. comes for night to Craven Hill Gardens.

Thursday, January 13, 1944

In lunch-time with J. to National Gallery concert. Philharmonic Trio: Purcell, Haydn, Lennox Berkeley and Beethoven: v. enjoyable. Still very depressed, with a feeling that all is futility, and especially I am completely futile and useless.

Friday, January 41, 1944

Hair washed: assistant in despair because her drier has broken and will not be mended for a long time: she has to borrow other people's, which they keep coming and fetching away. Also says last week she hadn't a proper comb to do people's hair, and couldn't buy one.

Saturday, January 15, 1944

Spend morning washing clothes and typing diary. Meet Tina for lunch
and we then go to West End through thick fog to see film of "Jane
Eyre".   Queues are enormous for that and almost everything else.
So we go to Tatler and see programme of old films, Russian, the main
one being fairy tale "The Little Humpbacked Horse".   Adenoidal child
behind us asks questions throughout: "Daddeyh, whad are dhey goig to
do dow, Ad Daddeyh?"   We have optimistic thoughts of getting tea
afterwards but there is no chance of getting into a restaurant. So
we part and I go to Broadcasting House for fire-watching.   At 7.30
we are just settling down for lecture on new organisation of fire-
fighting when sirens sound and lecture is broken up.   Roof-spotters
say there is gunfire away to south.   All clear about 8.30.

Sunday, January 16, 1944

To Mass with Tina and Bob at All Saints, Margaret Street.   Mozart in
G, very enjoyable.   In afternoon, Tina, Marjorie Wise and I to concert
at Friends House: Handel overture, and Mozart Symphony in A major,
interspersed by lovely serenade for tenor só, horn and orchestra by
Benjamin Britten. Peter Pears singer, and Dennis Brain horn - both
most excellent.   We also have concerto for double string orchestra
by Michael Tippett, which do not like so much.   Very thick fog still
- can hardly see six yards in front of us.   We were not roused by any
Alert during night.

Monday, January 17, 1944

Fog has cleared.   Post brown cardigan to Martin.

Tuesday, January 18, 1944

Mr. Churchill arrives back in London and immediately attends War
Cabinet meeting.   To press at 6.30.

Wednesday, January 19, 1944

Russians have started new offensive in north, near Leningrad.   Listen
to broadcast of "Carmen" and - reverting to argument had with Tina on
Sunday - say I think Quaker state of mind, which she complains lacks
passion, is preferable to excesses of "Carmen".

Thursday, January 20, 1944

Molly Evans to supper. Have been trying to get blanket for Hilary's
new baby, but only one I can get - shop says it has been waiting two
years for delivery of this batch - is double thickness, very heavy and
horrible: feel poor infant would be extinguished.

Friday, January 21, 1944

Very heavy raid by R.A.F. on Berlin last night.   To Ruth's at West

Dulwich, in response to S.O.S. to effect that David will be away for
night.   So I go, but find he is to return - late - after all.   Nevertheless Ruth glad of my presence because we have raid at about 8.30
with extremely heavy gunfire.   She brings children downstairs and we
sit under extremely inconvenient "Morrison table" in the shelter room
- table with roof, so designed that one cannot sit up under it and
there is no room for everyone to lie down.   As we sit for hour and
half thus, I omit to point out that lighted gas fire in room is source
of great danger, being afraid we shall freeze without it.

Saturday, January 22, 1944

Another raid with tremendous gunfire ab 4.30 a.m. - by which time David
has returned.   As all family goes downstairs and under table, feel I
must too.   Most depressing.   To-day all get up late.   In afternoon
go with Ruth and Rachel (just one year old) to Sunday School children's
treat (3-8 years) where they are shown most unsuitable film, "The
Little Boy Whom Santa Claus Forgot", enough to make anyone weep, which
David discovers is shown because it is obtainable free from Gamages, be
ing a pre-war advertisements for their toys.

Sunday, January 23, 1944

We have made another landing in Italy, on West Coast below Rome.
To service and hear David preach, which he does very well.   He is to
preach in Westminster Abbey on 2nd Sunday in Lent, and take four lunch-
time addresses at Guildhall.   Moreover will probably give another
broadcast series;   has been invited to write his autobiography;   and
has more demand for articles than he can supply.   With all of which
success he is frankly and un-spiritually pleased;   and Ruth is pleased
to have for first time a comfortable house and enough money to live on.
Come to conclusion there is much to be said - especially in view of lack
of domestic help nowadays and awful muddle with children about - for
celebacy of clergy.

Monday, January 24, 1944

With Tina to film of "Wuthering Heights", very good and much øℤℤ#
enlivened by comments of American soldiers behind us.

Tuesday, January 25, 1944

To press about 7.   Very high wind.   Feel very tired. Airgraph from
John in New Delhi, written only January 5.
~~Thursday, January~~
Wednesday, January 26, 1944

Office receives box mixed chocolates from late Editor, R.S. Lambert,
now in Canada.   We have 3 each, and all eat them ravenously and at
once.

Thursday, January 27, 1944

Meet Marjorie and Arnold who are up for week, having parked children
at school, and go with them to Wilde's "Ideal Husband" at the Westminster, brilliantly acted by Martita Hunt and Roland Culver, Irene
Vanbrugh and Esmé Percy.   M. says she has lost all sense of adven-
ture, is now nothing but a skivvy and is tired all the time. All
the same she looks very well.

Friday, January 28, 1944

In lunch-time to Nat.Gallery concert to hear Schubert Octet. Max
Rostal (violin), Pauline Juler (clarinet), Dennis Brain (horn).
Very enjoyable. Gerald Abraham unable to accompany me - at home
with bad cold. Fire-watching in evening. Marjorie comes and stays
with me while Arnold visits Aunt, and we sit in club. Have just returned to Broadcasting House for coffee at about 10.30, when there is
Alert and I have to go on duty. When All Clear goes, at 11.30, they
have left for midnight train for Euston, so I do not see them again.
     Anthony Eden, Foreign Secretary, has spoken in House of ill-
treatment of prisoners by Japanese: says they are tortured and half-
starved. Very painful for those who have relatives and friends in
this plight.

Saturday, January 29, 1944

Remark at breakfast, apropos reports in paper of Eden's speech, that
the Japanese no doubt treat our people not much worse than they treat
their own, since standards are different. I mean standards of comfort and human endurance; but find this sort of remark always mis-
understood, and people always say, as Joan did this morning, "Yes,
they're not human - nothing but savages".
     No more alerts last night, but I did not sleep well, so many
shift workers were being called at all hours. During one doese, I
dream I see the name CARTARET all across front page of newspaper, and
on enquiry am told that he is actor: has apparently been murdered,
and paper I look at is full of photographs with place where body was
found indicated. To-day (the sort of thing Dunne quotes in his
"Time" book), I walk across parks to Westminster to go to Evensong
at Abbey, and find myself walking down funny back lane which, at end,
is labelled CARTARET STREET.   At Abbey am late for Evensong, having
mistaken time of service. They do not have sermon, so that I hear
only about half; but sit and listen to organ playing Handel afterwards, while many American soldiers, usually with female companions
when they are not in bunches of five or six, walk round wonderingly.
Female companions, mostly hatless, look - but not for that reason -
not at all at home in Abbey.

Sunday, January 30, 1944

Last evening was playing chess with Bob when (about 8.30) there was
Alert, and for about 1½ hours very heavy gunfire.   Today go with him
to High Mass at Margaret Street, and on way meet Mr. Pringle coming
away from fire-watching at B.B.C.   He was on duty as roof-spotter during gunfire last night and reports spectacular effects in sky.   Tina
returns from weekend at Southampton, standing for whole journey.

Monday, January 31, 1944

We have made another colossal raid on Berlin.   The city is reported to
be "slowly dying".   Play chess with Bob in evening, rather expecting
retaliation raid, but none comes.

Tuesday, February 1, 1944

To press at 6.30.   In evening accompany Greta to film by Orson Welles,
"Journey into Fear" (disappointing) and see also end of "Garden of Allah"
(most revoltingly bad and which I am glad to observe the audience finds
amusing rather than thrilling).

Wednesday, February 2, 1944

Have stiff knee.   Weather too mild and very tiring.   Spend lunch-time
trying to get soft soap flakes or powder.   Can get only 3 oz. (one
coupon's worth).   Audrey Mearing, now Govt. Inspector in aircraft
factory, comes in to office and talks about works she is in.   Says the
workers have no interests except to get 6d. more on their wages (to
which end they are prepared to sit down and strike any time), and the
wages are spent on cinemas, dance halls and pubs (quite mild drinking
on the whole).   Music, books and serious plays they never think about,
and the larger issues of the war are nothing to them.   Think probably
this is pessimistic view and that she has not "contacted" them.   Do
not, on reflection, think my own life is much superior in outlook.
        In evening listen to end of Elgar's "The Kingdom", which have not
heard before and like very much.

Thursday, February 3, 1944

Much colder.   Hair washed.

Friday, February 4, 1944

To Stroud at midday.   Hilary and Martin still there.   H. better for
her holiday.   I have won 2nd prize in "New Statesman" competition
(250 words from rather bad novel written in 2000 about England of 1940 -
plenty of local colour, mostly wrong.

Saturday, February 5, 1944

Take Martin and joyful Tramp for walk.   Crisp, cold day.   One of the

Slaughters (rumour varies as to whether Upper or Lower) has been
bombed, but villagers with buckets put out nearly all incendiaries.
Two barns with cattle food destroyed and school damaged.

Sunday, February 6, 1944

Phyllida and Arthur arrive about tea-time,   P. with bottle of milk,
12 eggs (including 2 ducks'), and some cheese.   Martin very thrilled
to be able to sit by real airman in uniform.   Back to London in very
crowded train.

Monday, February 7, 1944

Tina has airgraph from John (in India) written on January 16, and Bob
at same time has letter from him written on board ship in October.

Tuesday, February 8, 1944

Very windy.   To press about 6.30.   Russians re-capture Nikopol.
Miss Morrison rates us all soundly for not carrying plates to kitchen
which we point out that we are only too willing to do if we know it is
welcome.   Like everyone else she is overworked and terribly on edge.
Everyone is to have 1 lb. of oranges, and I have now got mine (4 small
ones).

Wednesday, February 9, 1944

Feed in evening with Tina, Audrey Mearing and a niece of John Gals-
worthy's.   Mr. Pringle says he has it on good authority that the "rout"
of the Germans in Russia is in fact an orderly withdrawal, in preparation for offensive in spring: or it may be in preparation for making
peace with Russia and returning its force upon us.   He says that nobody,
he thinks not even Churchill, knows what is intention of Russia when her
troops reach borders of Germany.

Thursday, February 10, 1944

To dentist who does small filling.   Meet Hilary and Martin at lunch-
time at Paddington and escort them to Liverpool Street.   H. has fixed
up with nursing home at Gloucester.   Daddy is air-raid marshall for
Stroud, and has received notice that within few weeks many evacuees
from east coast are to be expected: a sign no doubt that the invasion
of Europe is about to begin.   Weather has become very cold with biting
wind.

Friday, February 11, 1944

To Ware.   H. seems much better for holiday.   Take 1 lb. tripe (9d.)
which was in frozen splinters chopped off an iceberg;   and a half basin
of dripping, present from Miss Playle's sister.   In train are soldiers
talking of fighting in Italy.   One says "When you get out there you're
just a bloody number. Nobody cares anything about you".

- 468 -

Saturday, February 12, 1944

Cycle into town with Hilary's doctor's certificate saying she is
pregnant, and visit food office where I get food card for new baby.
This entitles her to 1 pint of milk a day, an extra egg whenever
there is an allocation, and half a meat ration a week.   Also gives
her 60 clothing coupons.   She has to renew the book every 3 months.
Then have to visit severally the butcher, grocer and dairyman, giving
each the appropriate form to fillup.   All this takes the best part
of the morning.   A far cry from the days when one did not mention a
baby till it was properly born.

Sunday, February 13, 1944

Back to London.   All lights in carriage go out when we are about 25
minutes from Liverpool Street.   Towards the station see a great splash
of flame coming up from ground over to our left, and then afire.
At station there is heavy burst of gunfire as I pass through barrier,
so that ticket-collector does not notice I have no ticket -have mislaid
my return half in darkness of carriage.

Monday, February 14, 1944

To film in evening: programme is not what we had expected.   It is
film about Russia made in Hollywood.   Idyllic village life broken up
by German invasion.   All Russians noble and handsome; all Germans
brutal and ugly.   Guerrillas with 1 rifle between 5 men recapture
village .   Fade-out as lovely heroine declares "We will make a world
in which there will be no more war.   Will will fight to make it",
which idiocy depresses me very much.

Tuesday, February 15, 1944

To press at 7 p.m.   We have bombed beautiful old Benedictine
monastery at Cassino which Germans had turned into fortress.

Wednesday, February 16, 1944

Hair washed.   With Abrahams and Audrey Mearing to Noel Coward's
"Blithe Spirit", which saw 2 years ago and enjoy again.   We eat at
Chinese restaurant in Wardour Street.

Thursday, February 17, 1944

To Abrahams to supper.   Alan Franck and wife come in, and a woman
composer who is married to a Czech author.   Very pleasant evening,

Friday, February 18, 1944

To Hilary's with 1 lb. of tripe which I leave on windowsill of office
in cold air all afternoon.   Snowing when I arrive.

Saturday, February 19, 1944
At 2 a.m. when I am asleep in downstairs bedroom wakened by H., who

asks if I willhave Martin in my bed. She says there has be en
great noise for half-an-hour and a big raid is taking plaover London.
She has just heard bomb drop and feels Martin would be safer downstairs. So I take him, sleeping soundly, a gunfire and sounds of
planes continue for another half-hour. I then attempt to take him
back to his own room and he says "No, not come into your bed till
morning-time"; so I try to get back into bed and he asks "Why are
you coming into my bed?" On being told it im mine, he is puzzled,
but agrees to go back to his own, and this morning remembers nothing
about it. Weather very cold.

Sunday, February 20, 1944

Back to London, and at 10 p.m. we have an hour's fire-raid, during
which houses are set on fire on every hand and the night becomes as
day. The planes drop long dotted lines of bright white light,
prettier than any firework show. We take bucket of water to top
floor and fill baths; and then do exactly what we oughtnot - run
from one window to another on top floor, looking at glows in
sky. One fire is immediately behind our house, where soldiers
are living. When all is quiet and I go to bed, I observea a large
barrage balloon flapping helplessly right past my window at rooftop
height, and think rather crossly "Killed by a barrage balloon. I
shall always pretend it was a high explosive."

Monday, February 21, 1944

Another short alert during last night, but no activity. Fires all
seem to be under control. Today, at printer's see that Heinz (Baked
Beans and sauces) factory has been hit. Whitehall had several
bombs, and it is said that Mortlake Brewery was among the damaged
buildings.

Tuesday, February 22, 1944

An alert, but no gunfire or bombs last night. I lie in bed and
watch strange activities of a searchlight - not a usual one but a
thin, pale finger of light pointing almost vertically, which is
obviously signalling, especially one word or phrase given by
Short - short- long - short. Today we go topess at 7 p.m. Churchill
makes statement in House on war situation. He warns us of bigger
raids to come.

Wednesday, February 23, 1944

Another noisy hour from midnight till about 1a.m. Gunfire tremendous.
The "rocket" shells sound like bombs coming down, but I do not hear
any real bombs. Anti-aircraft guns are sending up not only white
lights but red balls, designed, it is said, to counteract the
long ribbons of light which the aircraft drop; and these in turn
are said to aim at upsetting our radiolocation. This evening have

to fire-watch.   We are given lecture on new fire-bombs, and six of us
sit round table (with rest looking on) and play, with scale-plan of
Broadcasting House and environs, at deploying fire-parties.   Among
this distinguished company are Freddie Grisewood and John Snagge and
me.   During lecture we are told that lecturer himself saw lately in
Parliament Square, 23 incendiary bombs stuffed with iron filings.
Later we have real raid, and when "raiders overhead" signal is given,
I clear 3 floors of people and stand by for action.   Freddie Grisewood,
putting on tin hat, sets forth for roof-spotting, saying rather dismally,
"Well, here goes!"

Thursday , February 24, 1944

Wake up at 5 a.m. or so with frightful sick headache.   Am in darkened
concert-hall, far from any lavatory, no light or vessel available, and
know that if I stir I shall be sick.   At about 6.30, nature wins.   In
desperation I roll up sheet, which anyway has to be washed when I have
finished with it, and am sick into it.   Go forth and find First Aid
post and they succour me.   I lie down till about noon, in middle of
morning being transferred from stuffy basement Red Cross quarters to
upstairs surgery.   Feel it is rather much to go up in life at 10.30 a.m.
in pyjamas, but so it is.   H.H. has seen stranger sights.   Miss Playle
is taking holiday to-day, and I have theatre party in train for tonight,
so have to send for messenger from Listener and explain things to be
done.   At midday go home and retire to bed till dinner-time, when
headache has gone.   Another raid about 10 - 11 p.m.

Friday, February 25, 1944

Feel much better today.   Mr. Pringle arrives at work at noon, bombs
near Waterloo having held up traffic.   To Hilary's by 5.4, with Haliborange and hair-grips (six, bought from man in street for 1/-).   She
is completely out of coal and has been for two days.   Is burning very
wet logs which she has been fortunate enough to have delivered to-day.
This is for fuel and heat too.

Saturday , February 26, 1944

Into town, pushing Martin, and do enormous amoung of shopping.   Visit
coal-man, and/in/view interview his daughter, telling her of Hilary's
condition.   She says her father will do his best, and promises me paraffin.   So I return in afternoon, again pushing Martin, and get 2 gallons.
Have thus walked about 9 miles, besides wheeling logs from bottom of
garden for fire.   Coalman says new announcement that people can have
as much coke and anthracite as they like is ridiculous.   He has had
none since last August and hears from gas works that supply him that the
Government says they must burn it themselves.
     No raid last night.

<u>Sunday, February 27, 1944</u>

Leonard, who was stocktaking all day from 8 a.m. yesterday, has to rise
with the lark and go to Much Hadham to interview Home Guard colonel,
and is offered post as 2nd Lieutent, Signallers.   While Hilary is saw-
ing wood in garden, Mrs. Parrish takes pity on her and offers 2 scuttles
of coal, and just a few little lumps among the wood make all the difference between a fire and a dismal sizzle.
     Martin tells Hilary he thinks "God must have lots and lots of
matches because he has to keep on lighting up the sun", and he thinks
God must "bounce the sun up into the sky every morning".

<u>Monday, February 28, 1944</u>

No raid last night.   It is very cold, and I am so worried at thought of
Hilary, ring up in evening, and find Leonard has visited Fuel Officer,
who says Mr. Griffin, because he is a one-man business, is not getting a
fair deal; but he is trying to improve matters.   Meanwhile, he will
see that Hilary gets 4 cwt. of coal.

<u>Tuesday, February 29, 1944</u>

Very cold.   To press about 6.30.   Printers works being painted, so we
have working in our room a special accountant the firm has had to take
on to deal with staff's "pay-as-you-earn" income-tax.   He is believer in
Major Douglas's social credit scheme.

<u>Wednesday, March 1, 1944</u>

Short alert last night, some gunfire and sound of 'planes immediately
overhead.   But no bombs near us.   Two fires in distance.

<u>Thursday, March 2, 1944</u>

After writing to Roy yesterday, saying our Christmas parcels have not
arrived, hear today from Mother that Hilary's and Phyllida's have come.
Mine comes today too: 1 lb. sugar, ½ lb. tea, tin tongue, and same dried
fruit.   P. reports Fairford full of American soldiers who are "cheeky
beyond words".   One knocked at door of ordinary house and said "Do you
know where I can get a woman for the night?"
     Ex-member of Radio Times staff comes into office.   Her husband
captured bailed-out German airmen at Wembley the other night: reported
them very young and frightened and very nice   They say they bomb definite targets which are given them beforehand. Miss Playle full of fury at
implication that German airmen are no worse than ours.
     I buy two little shawls of mohair, 19/- each, which I think, sewn
together, will make pleasant covering for new baby, or for Martin.

<u>Friday, March 3, 1944</u>

To Ware with 2 bottles Haliborange, 1 lb. tripe, 2 Mohair rugs, and my
rations.   Find Hilary and Martin just retug from havingtea witth Mrs.

Mayes. Home Guard arrives and delivers up to Leonard a motor-bicycle
he is to have for his new duties.

Saturday, March 4, 1944

Most bitterly cold, and Hilary's 4 cwt. of coal decreasing alarmingly.
Leonard takes Martin for littleride, sitting on tank of motor-bicycle.
M. says with feeling: "It is nice to have a motor-bike". We have
great amount of food: 2 lots of fish, tripe, and weekly joint.

Sunday, March 5, 1944

M.,helping L. clean motor-bicycle, wears all-covering ancient pyjama
jacket of his father's. Bot enjoy themselves very much. Back to London
in bright moonlight.

Monday, March 6, 1944

Big daylight attack on Berlin by American Fortresses, of which 68 are
lost. Buy 2 more Mohair rugs and send home to Mother for knee-rugs.

Tuesday, March 7, 1944

Fire-watching at night: arrive half-an-hour late for it, from printers.

Wednesday, March 8, 1944

No alert last night: moon is still full. Nevertheless we continue to
attack Germany by night as well as by day. Hair washed.
        Having heard man relating to cloak-room attendant at Broadcasting
House horrific talks of air-raid damage round Kilburn Park station, I
ring up John, and find stories exaggerated as usual, and anyway Oxford
Road untouched. Peter has had bad asthma.

Thursday, March 9, 1944

Give lunch to Miss White, woman from office who has lined for me a lamb's
wool I bought, and interlined it with cotton-wool, which will make
beautiful cover for baby's pram. Pram covers, much inferior to this,
cost £5 at least in shops. See man selling side-combs on pavement in
Regent Street. Wildly buy 3 pairs at cost of 11/- (pre-war total cost
about 1/9). Think 2 pairs probably useless. Go to buy coat saw last
week at Jaegers, but it is gone. Everything goes if not bought at
once, but a "buy" costing 18 coupons and 15 guineas must be considered
a little.
        We have run out of coke at Craven Hill Gardens, and there will be
no more hot water for washing or baths till some is delivered, expt
what we boil up very slowly in small kettle on small gas-ring.

Friday, March 10, 1944

To Beavans, where are Peter, Duque and later John, besides Florence and

another girl.   Arthur fire-watching.   Duque seems depressed, in spite
of Peter's discharge from Merchant Navy and return to his cello-playing
which he does for E.N.S.A. AND C.E.M.A.

Saturday, March 11, 1944

With Greta to matinée of Emile Littler's pantomime at Coliseum, which I
enjoy very much.   To Ware.   Meet Leonard going into town to get petrol
for motor-bicycle, and I ride home on back

Sunday, March 12, 1944

Paul Mayes and his ~~father~~ mother to lunch and tea.   When I return to
railway station for London, take perambulator to leave at shop where it
is to be called for tomorrow to be "re-conditioned" for new occupant.   It
is only because the man who is to do it does work for Leonard's firm
that it is possible to get it done at all.

Monday, March 13, 1944

All travel to Ireland banned.

Tuesday, March 14, 1944

To film.   Later we have raid.   Fires in distance, and 2 very near-by
bumps which rock water out of jugs and cause books to fall off shelves.

Wednesday, March 15, 1944

St. Mary Abbot's church, Knightsbridge, hit in last night's raid.
To dressmaker's, who is turning and remaking my old grey suit.

Thursday, March 16 - No entry.

Friday, March 17, 1944

To National Gallery concert with Gerald Abraham.   Mozart String Trio and
Oboe Quartet.   To Hilary's at night.   Warning, but nothing happening
except very strange flares which we think are ours.

Saturday, March 18, 1944

Feel desperately tired.   Leonard buys 15 guinea paraffin cooker, hoping
to ease the fuel difficulites.

Sunday, March 18, 1944

Leonard, the spending mood having begun, buys car, price £60, to perform
his Home Guard duties, which involve supervising signals in are of 200
square miles.   His hope is to claim also a shopping allowance of petrol
for Hilary.   Still very tired.   Back to London.

Monday, March 20, 1944

Fire-watching. Time of dinner in restaurant changed to 7.30, and as
we have lecture at that time, we get very little to eat. Lecture is from
fireman, who by no means tells us to treat new incendiaries with respect, which is what we have been told till now, but says "If one ~~dot~~
drops on your bed, roll it up in the eiderdown and throw it out of the
window". I murmur that my window overlooks street, but no one thinks
prowling wardens are of any consequence.

Tuesday, March 21, 1944

~~Alert/about/1/a.m./last/night~~ No alert last night. Today we go to press
at about 6. Inside of works being painted, we learn, because there is
a factory act which says factories must be painted every 3 years, and
as - owing to the war - Waterlows have not been done for 7 years, they
are quoting the act in order to get materials and labour.

Wednesday, March 22, 1944

Alert about 1 last night and much noise but I do not hear anything fall
near. Am therefore surprised today to learn that No.6 platform at
Paddington has been hit. Hear also of damage at Elephant and Castle.
Hair washed.

Thursday, March 23, 1944

This evening, in order to create a little interest for ourselves, we run
a penny sweepstake on possible times for alert tonight. Eileen (Irish
maid) draws "No raid", and we all hope she has won.

Friday, March 24, 1944

Thought when I woke up that Eileen had won sweepstake, but find there
was Alert at midnight for which I did not wake.
     To Ware with Tina. She brings pigeon and steak pie and I bring 1/-
worth of tripe. New cooker has come, most beautiful object, green and
black, with 3 burners, and a detachable oven to go over 2 of them if one
if baking. Also new car - that is a second-hand one - Ford 8.

Saturday, March 25, 1944

Fine and warm. Raid on London last night, of which we hear distant
reverberations. Today Martin and I go little walk and meet Bob, the
farm horse, and ride back to stable in his cart all among the ashes.
He is put out in field for first time this Spring. H. takes car into
town with Martin, who says in deep awe "This is a very fine, big car,
Mamma". In afternoon, Henry Wood's jubilee concert broadcast from
Albert Hall. At 7, Leonard off for all-night Home Guard manoeuvre.

Sunday, March 26, 1944
Very fine and warm. Sit outside, pick violets, go for little walk.
Prime Minister speaks at 9 p.m. but we are in train returning to London.

Monday, March 27, 1944

Phyllida and Arthur turn up for lunch, which I eat with them at D.H.
Evans' - A. on leave, and P. has taken 3 weekends rolled into one.
I leave them on their way to Westminster Abbey.

Tuesday, March 28, 1944

To press about 3.30, in preparation for Easter.

Wednesday, March 29, 1944

Streets have barrows of daffodils, although weather has turned very
cold since last Sunday.   To Ruth's, for night.   David has become
Editor of "Church of England Newspaper", and is doing article for
"Sunday Despatch" for fee of 25 guineas.   He is not really a parson
but a journalist who has made a good thing for himself out of religion.

Thursday, March 30, 1944

To National Gallery Concert.   Three Brandenburgs (6, 4 and 2) played
by Boyd Neel Orchestra.   See Peter's red head as he arranges music
on platform, and then see him come down and talk to his Mother.   Get
up and speak to Duque who invites me to seat next to herswhich Peter
has saved.   Enjoy programme very much, especially No.6, for violas and
cellos only, with one double bass, Max Gilbert leading violas.   In
evening to Beavans; about 20 people present while a quartet tries out
new work by one Peter Gellhorn (married to one of Jean Layton's sisters),
who, when they have tried it rho through once, goes through it with them,
stopping them to say "Bring out the cello here", etc.   Very interesting,
and the work sounds to me good.   Peter Gellhorn obviously German, but
nobody so much as thinks about his nationality, since what is important
to him and everyone else is the music.   How right.   John, who comes
all over friendly, tells me George Mathieson, who was prisoner in Italy,
escaped from his camp in north, tracked to south and there joined the
British forces, and is now in this country.

Friday, March 31, 1944

To Ware.   Very cold again.   New Director General for B.B.C. announced -
present Editor-in-Chief, W.J. Haley.

Saturday, April 1, 1944

Bitterly cold.   Gift from Josephine's mother of 2 large eggs for Martin,
and daffodils and violets for Hilary.   Clocks go on another hour tonight.

Sunday, April 2, 1944

Fire-watching at night.   I arrive at 9.15 but find although summer time
(double) has already begun, later hours for fire-watching do not begin
until tomorrow, and I ought to have come at 6.45.

Monday, April 3, 1944

Three papers going to press simultaneously at printers. We finish at
7, leaving only 1 forme for tomorrow. There seems to be some appre-
hension about appointment of Mr. Haley as D.G. He is thought to be
"ruthless".
Quiet fire-watch last night.

Tuesday, April 4, 1944

Daddy's 68th birthday. Finish last forme at printers at 11 a.m., and
thereafter find it difficult to believe that to-day is Tuesday.

Wednesday, April 5, 1944

Hair washed. Full moon (or some reason) is preventing air raids this
week, at any rate over here.

Thursday, April 6, 1944

To National Gallery Concert. Griller Quartet: Haydn's "Seven Last
Words from the Cross", which theyplay beautifully but p pleave in so
many repeats I have to leave before the exciting Earthquake at the end.
Mrs. Morris writes that her furniture and belongings were all destroyed
in fire at one of Maple's stores during recent air-raid. Damage was
caused by water - no wonder we are told we shall not use fire hose unless there is very large fire indeed.
In evening to "Hamlet" with John. Robert Helpmann as Hamlet.
Very good production. Afterwards queue at Corner House for meal, and
are last but two to be admitted before that floor closes.

Friday, April 7, 1944

Good Friday. B.B.C. does not have holiday, but we work only in morning
because have to come in on Monday afternoon. Met/ To Ware. Met down
road by Martin, Leonard and Tramp, with Hilary following. Take Leonard
goose egg (off ration for wicked price of 3/-) as Easter offering. He
eats it boiled for supper and it quite fills him up.

Saturday, April 8, 1944

Phyllida's 35th birthday. Leonard takes Martin to his grandparents' at
Orpington. Crowds not large. They set out about 9.10 by bicycle for
station, and return at 7. Martin sleeps both ways for some of the
journey, and it is his father who is exhausted.
We have lot of food. I shop today and get ½ lb. liver: we have
small joint of pork; and today get chicken from Josephine's mother.
And Martin has present of 3 eggs, and Mother sends 4 or 5 more by post.

Sunday, April 9, 1944

Easter Sunday.   B.B.C. 9 a.m. News begins with record of one verse of "Jesus Christ is Risen Today, Alleluia", and the Announcer then proceeds to tell us what our bombers did during the night, and to inform housewives of new prices for rhubarb.
        Am reading Aldous Huxley's "Grey Eminence" with much interest. He says the mystics are the people who keep the entire world from going mad.   Where there is no vision the people perishes.   That politicians only keep within at least pretended bounds of decency as a concession to the mystics whose influence is in their midst, and if there are no more mystics, there will be no bounds at all set.

Monday, April 10, 1944

Martin enjoying himself being a farmer and raking up grass his father mows.   Back to work in afternoon.   Trains not full, but large crowds in Oxford Street queuing for tea still when I - having neither eaten nor drunk since 11.45 - leave office.

Tuesday, April 11, 1944

To press at 7 - not bad considering printers worked neither Friday nor Monday, and just shows what they can do if they try.   Reading "Introduction to the Devout Life" by St. Francis de Sales: very charming and, I think, helpful.
        Russians recapture Odessa.

Wednesday, April 12, 1944

This typewriter, which was sticking on every line I typed, and at the last did not move the ribbon at all but typed on the same spot - was saved by the resource of Tina who said it needed oil and applied a little castor oil on piece of cotton wool.   Poor thing was constipated.   Now quite recovered.
        Leave work early and go with Tina to Orson Welles' film "The Magnificent Ambersons", which, for a film, is very good; but I do not think that films are yet a very high artistic expression.
        We have had no coke and no hot water since the weekend, and are not likely to get any for several weeks.   .

Thursday, April 13, 1944

Editor discovers that my session at B.B.C. School (talked of for months and already put off four times) is to begin on Monday (a fact which he has known for several weeks but has forgotten) and that he has agreed to Mr. Pringle going on holiday one week of which willoverlap with my three weeks' course.   Moreover that Miss Evans's sick leave starts tomorrow. He looks so like a ruffled hen that I weakly agree once more to put off my school.
        We have bombed Budapest.

Friday, April 14, 1944

Am told can get tablet of Morny's sopa at Marshall and Snelgrove, and do so.   It is not on view but kept in background and only produced on request.   I then have bath at B.B.C., there still being no coke at home.
    To Ware.   Reading Michael Sadleir's biography of Trollope.

Saturday, April 15, 1944

Take Martin into town in push-chair in morning (Hilary now has two gallons of petrol a month allowed her, but to-day Leonard has had to take car to work in order to go on to Home Guard duties afterwards)½ We return triumphantly with ½ lb. liver (among other purchases) and having heard the cuckoo.   Can't buy comb anywhere in Ware.

Sunday, April 16, 1944

Eric shows Martin thrush's nest with two eggs in it in Mrs. Parrish's orchard; and chaffinch is building nest in hedge by Bob's field.   I take Martin for very long walk down overgrown lane.   I am Drum Major and go ahead waving stick, and he is a soldier.   He refers to himself in third person: "This soldier is slipping on this dirty path.   He must be careful".   He is so tired, goes to sleep immediately he is put to bed, instead of coming downstairs, wide awake and with borad smile, as he has been doing lately.

Monday, April 17, 1944

All the cherry and almond blossom is out at printing works.   From to-day there is to be no heat in offices, but at Waterlow's it continues warm, I suppose because the power has to be generated for machinery any-way.

Tuesday, April 18, 1944

Finish at printers at 7 p.m.   Foreman wants to know what we intend to do when Second Front opens, because he says 14 or 15 of his men will be called up for Home Guard duties.   We assure him that paper will have to be produced whatever happens, and whether it will be distributed or not. Everyone is of opinion that invasion of Europe is imminent.

Wednesday, April 19, 1944

Rather noisy air raid at 2 a.m. today.   Bombs were concentrated in north London, in direction of Walthamstow, and Miss White arrives very late at office - no water or gas at her home, and raid caused her sister to have a miscarriage.   In addition, today there is bus strike, which makes traffic confusion worse.
    I am lucky enough to get comb, for controlled price of 7½d.   Try to buy another from man in street who wants 2/- for it.   When I remind him that prices are now controlled, he looks round, sees two policeman in distance, and makes off quickly.
    In evening to Vic-Wells performance of "Rigoletto" with Tina and

Denis.   Good performance, but have general impression that all opera
is ridiculous - such things as a scene on wild moor in thunderstorm
where (apparently) conversation is inn, door of which is shut, is plainly audible from without.

Thursday, April 20, 1944

Everyone thinks invasion of Europe is very near.   Nevertheless decide to
go home for weekend, since I somehow do not expect it till next week, so
regard this as a last chance for some time to come.   This evening an
enormous number of heavy bombers, in groups of about 60, are going over
London for about 3 hours, very high up, with the evening sun lighting up
one or two of them like silver, and the rest just grey shadows and a
far-off humming.

Friday, April 21, 1944

London bus strike has grown, and Army has been put to drive and conduct
buses on routes affected.   Private who is conducting my bus does not
take any fares, and when I press 3d. into his hand, expecting 1d. change,
he pockets it as a tip, tactfully looking away from size of coin.   To
Stroud by 4.15 in ~~order to~~ bright sunshine.   Everything green and lovely.

Saturday, April 22, 1944

To tea with Aunt H., who gives me 3 eggs.   Three of her guests have
been staying at guest-house at Blockley which is attached to café, and
they found that part of house, and all of café, was run for delectation
of American soldiers and their women.   They constantly had American
soldiers, drunk, coming into their bedrooms and, when ordered out, sitting on bed and preparing to argue the point, with "Now, see here, honey",
and - when pressed to go - "Now I call that very unfriendly".

Sunday, April 23, 1944

Another day of brilliant sunshine, and the country is crying out for
water.   Phyllida - bringing Audrey- comes over from Fairford in afternoon.   They have had an exciting time - 2,000 parachute troops arrived
in village on exercise overnight, provisions, bicycles , etc., being
dropped as well as men.   We are also told by Mrs. Wall of friend of
hers not far from Stroud who awoke one morning to find regiment washing
ans shaving in stream in her garden - all arrived by parachute during
night. She was most indignant.   Coming back to London in train this
evening, I see large succession of gliders flying over us - being trailed
on ropes.

Monday, April 24, 1944

On the patch of green opposite my window three Companies of A.T.S. are
assembled after breakfast.   This obviously a rehearsal, for at 7.30 p.m.
they congregate again, this time with a band, and are inspected by a male

"red-hat", who solemnly parades up and down their ranks with their full-bosomed, bass-voiced officers. He then reads them an address and presents certificates of some sort to three of them. The whole thing fills me with horror, and with gratitude that I am not called up to be an At.

Tuesday, April 25, 1944

We go to press at about 6.30. In Michael Sadleir's biography of Trollope are some letters. In one of them Trollope wrote (in 1862, about the American Civil War - letter to an American):-

"This conscription is very bad. Was it absolutely necessary? My feeling is that a man should die rather than be made a soldier against his will. One's country has no right to demand everything. There is much that is higher and better and greater than one's country. One is patriotic only because one is small and too weak to be cosmopolitan. If a country cannot get along without a military conscription, it had better give up - and let its children seek other ties".

Chancellor introduces new Budget - for once no taxes for ordinary consumer, only 1d. on beer at manufactuerd end.

Wednesday, April 26, 1944

Have at last found cobbler who mends shoes himself and mends them properly. Very pleased with pair he has just soled and heeled (8/6, as far as I remember). Most are now done very badly with unskilled labour.

Thursday, April 27, 1944

Hair washed. Also call for my grey suit which has been turned and re-made. Done very well indeed, at cost of 5½ guineas. For this I have what is virtually a new suit, at no coupon charge and of much better material than one can get now.

Friday, April 28, 1944

National Gallery concert with Gerald Abraham: London Wind Players - Serenade for Wind Octet (Mozart), which is original form of String Quintet in C minor; and Octet in E flat major (Beethoven) which is original form of String Quintet in E flat major. Very pleasant indeed. Fire-watching at night - now the evenings are light we do not begin till 9.15.

Saturday, April 29, 1944

We were awakened once last night for a "purple" - i.e. last warning before a general Alert (red). But I had only just struggled into my dungarees when we were told the All Clear had sounded. To Ware by 9.10.

Ring up from station, and after a bit Martin starts out to meet me, very proud of coming alone. But as soon as the poor mite sees me rounding the corner he starts to run joyfully, and at once falls, so I am greeted by pathetic figure with tears streaming down its cheeks and blood streaming down its legs, and its hands grazed. Streams and streams of aeroplanes going over all day.

Sunday, April 30, 1944

Very warm and sunny. Martin, after short night - wouldn't go off last evening and woke at 5.45 - goes to sleep in garden for 2½ hours. We pick cowslips while the 'planes zoom over and there is a distant rumbling and we wonder whether the invasion has begun and whether I shall get back to London safely. Train service appears to be normal, however, and I arrive at about usual time. .

Monday, May 1, 1944

Very fine and warm again: rain badly needed. Manage to buy 2 small-size combs, one at 1/- and one at 1/6. I thought controlled prices were less than this, but as this was a respectable chemist's shop, do not question them.

Tuesday, May 2, 1944

Take 2 fly-papers to printers, because last week we were pestered by flies. Find not only Waterlows but many factories round had complained to Municipal Council about rubbish dump which must be cause; sanitary inspector has been round; and poison has been provided which, when put in saucer in drop of milk, causes flies to fall dead all over place, so that I am told canteen floor is covered with them in morning. Certainly things are better and I do not have to use my fly-papers, which I give to Editor for his wife, because apparently they are hard to come by. Am told Ministry of Health (1) had ordered rubbish to be put on dump instead of being taken to country as before war, and that bulldozer had gone wrong.

Wednesday, May 3, 1944

Have onerous task of buying maternity skirt for Hilary, who says her present waist measurement is 31 - at least, the place from which her skirts depend is 31. Get a very nice grey one but it costs 92/11 and 6 coupons, and I feel rather nervous about it.
　　Still beautiful weather, but high wind. At lunch-time, when am still in office, hear cries of "Stop him!" and whistles being blown, and policeman chases man, catches him and gets on top of him, and another policeman comes up and helps. Crowd immediately collects, and man struggles violently but does not get away.

Thursday, May 4, 1944

Buy maternity skirt for Hilary: 92/11 and 6 coupons.   In evening to
supper with Abrahams.   Mosco Carner there, now British subject - ex-
Viennese conductor and music writer.   Also man from British Museum and
his wife from Board of Trade.   Latter talks about new process (for
which firm concerned has taken out 15 patents) whereby any material of
any sort can be in some way sprayed or impregnated with a metal so that
to all intents and purposes it is that metal: e.g. silk stockings can
be given the durability of gold while retaining their flexibility and
lightness.

Friday, May 5, 1944

Much colder, and wet.   To Ware, where H., who has brought car into
town to do shopping and has stayed to tea with Mrs. Mayes, meets me at
station, I suppose strictly an illegal proceeding.

Saturday, May 6, 1944

Tramp on rampage.   Goes off into gale, returning apparently after fight
with rival, with onepaw badly bitten, blood all over his coat, and able
to walk on only two legs.

Sunday, May 7, 1944

Fine and calm again.   Leonard spent last evening making a miniature
switchboard to help on the Home Guard communications.   Martin is running about before breakfast, and has put it on a ledge where it cannot
be found until after his father, fuming, has had to leave to meet his
sergeant.   The Mayes family comes to tea.   They arrive with American
soldier with whom they have got into conversation on the road, who is
with an 8-year-old girl.   So they come to tea too.   It appears that
the girl has an older sister on whom the soldier called - one Celia -
but Celia was washing her hair, and the young Pat was told to take the
young man out for walk.   He discusses his love affair openly with room
full of people.   Says his name is Lee.

Monday, May 8, 1944

Buy comb for Mother, 3/6, and pocket comb for myself, 1/9.   Feel sure
am being swindled, since price of combs is supposed to be controlled,
but lack courage to tell chemist so, and am glad to find comb at any
price (which he no doubt knows).

Tuesday, May 9, 1944

B.B.C. Home Guard has to guard Regent's Park every night, in case of
parachutists attempting to land - a most fantastic idea in my view.
Surely they would land somewhere less inhabited.

Wednesday, May 10, 1944

Buy materials for winter coat.   Utility cloth, about 14/6 a yard as far
as I remember.   With Gerlad Abraham to B.B.C. concert at Albert Hall.
Hear Stravinsky's "Sacre du Printemps" for first time, and am very impressed.   We sit among the critics, Edwin Evans, Dyneley Hussey, and F.
Bonavia, and in interval we eat sandwiches by Albert's calves.

Thursday, May 11, 1944

To supper with Mary Stiles, whom have not seen for about 10 years.   She
was evacuated from London at beginning of war, (works at Lloyd's Bank
head office), and has now been sent back.   Finds she now knows hardly
anyone in town, and bethinks of me; rings me up at B.B.C.   She has flat
in Willow Road, Hampstead.   We walk on Heath, much changed from its
peace-time aspect by reason of many allotments and some guns.

Friday, May 12, 1944

Go to buy Hilary two winceyette squares, called dusters, for cot-sheets,
ans succumb to temptation whenwoman offers me pair of sheets (which are
coupon-free), which she points out are of beautiful pale-blue linen and
can be made into summer dresses.   So buy pair for 5 guineas, but very
much doubt whether I shall be able to get them made into anything this
year.
        Fifth and Eighth Armies in Italy start newattack.
        Very hot.   To Ware.   Leonard at Home Guard until midnight.

Saturday, May 13, 1944

Very hot, until late afternoon when there is thunderstorm, and weather
then becomes colder and windy.

Sunday, May 14, 1944

Fifth and Eighth Armies'attacks seem to be going well.   Weather has become cold and blustery.   Martin and I go for walk.   Spend some time
typing instructions for Leonard, for Home Guard.

Monday, May 15, 1944

At end of last week saw some stockings I thought Mother would like.   So
wrote to her at once.   But by today, when I have her ration book, none
are left.   Mr. Pringle back from holiday, very brown.   There are
American soldiers even at Penzance.   In evening to Albert Hall concert
with Tina: Beethoven's 7th Symphony and Bliss's "Morning Heroes".
Very cold in Albert H.
Tuesday, May 16, 1944

Ban on central heating removed.   To press about 6.45 in works infested
with flies.   Rubbish dump nearby has not been dealt with adequately.

We are told that by order of Ministry of <u>Health</u> and because of lack of transport, rubbish is dumped instead of being taken into country; and that the bulldozer which normally covers it with earth has gone wrong. So that now there is negotàation between Ministries of Health and Supply about bulldozer.   Meantime I h̶a̶v̶e̶ a poison has been put about the works in saucers, which causes flies to drop dead when they take infumes.   So I read proof about wonders of modern science while dead flies fall on to blotting-paper in front of me and I have to keep teacup covered with one hand for fear of drinking poisoned fly.

<u>Wednesday, May 17, 1944</u>

To National Gallery concert: Strings of R.A.F. Orchestra - all young and full of zest - playing H̶a̶n̶d̶e̶l̶'̶s̶ ̶W̶a̶t̶e̶r̶ ̶M̶u̶s̶i̶c̶ Mozart's "Eine Kleine Nachtmusik", Elgar's Serenade in E minor, a Rhapsody with Piano (Leonard Isaacs) by Turina, and Warlock's Capriol suite.   Exceedingly pleasant.

<u>Thursday, May 18, 1944</u>

Am suffering from sore throat and cough, withcold on chest - a very common complaint just now.   With Bob to hear sermon by Archbishop of Canterbury at St. Michael and All Angels, Ladbroke Grove.   They are having an Evangelical campaign.   Very simple - am impressed that author of "Nature, Man and God" can be so simple.   Says (he is speaking, of course, to the Faithful), that people outside Church take no notice of parsons.   Parsons are to strengthen faith of the converted, and the converted are to talk of their faith to outsiders, who will take more notice of lay people.

<u>Friday, May 19, 1944</u>

To Ware.   The American soldier of last week calls - which he was invited to do if he felt so inclined - but says too long, and I am bored. His name, we find on enquiring more deeply, is Levi Strohl, and his mother was Irish.   He never reads a book.   Is "tough".   His love affair not going well, he says, - the girl "gets mad at" him.   So we (Tina also with us) all offer him advice and sympathy.

<u>Saturday, May 20, 1944</u>

Things appear to be goimg well in Italy.
    Mayes family to tea.   American comesagain and saays hours talking about himself - also scythes grass for us.   Lady on bicycle calls because she has puncture and wants pump.   So our remote spot is full of bustle.   Present of 7 ducks' eggs from Mrs. Parrish.

<u>Sunday, May 21, 1944</u>

Colder.   Take Tramp for Walk and he tears his ear; but when I return find Leonard's H.Guard seageant present, who before war trained greyhounds.   He therefore knows about dogs, and bathes ear, which Tramp allows him to do with great docility.

Monday, May 22, 1944

Mr. Browning (car driver) says convoys have been going south all day.
Mr. Pringle of opinion invasion still far off.

Tuesday, May 23, 1944

Still very pestered by flies at printers.   Representatives of Ministry
of Health visit works.

Wednesday, May 24, 1944

To National Gallery concert in beautiful sunshine.   Griller Quartet:
Schubert in A minor, Mozart in G major.   Very beautiful.   Fire-watching
at night.

Thursday, May 25, 1944

With Mary Stiles and Tina to film at Academy: "The Forgotten Village"
(Mexico) by John Steinbeck.   Very good and moving.   Also French film
with Jean Gabin, "Underworld".   Get peanut butter for Hilary, who rings
up to say she has found recipe for making marzipan, main ingredient s being peanut butter and soya bean flour.

Friday, May 26, 1944

Away at lunchtime.   Sultry, dull day which becomes sunny later on.   Do
 shopping for Hilary and get her new food cards.   Heavenly walk with
Tramp in evening, beside sweet-smelling bean field.   Reading Virginia
Woolf's "The Voyage Out".

Saturday, May 27, 1944

Leonard distempering kitchen.   Fortunately weather very hot, and we eat
meals in garden, and go round outside of house when we want to get to
scullery from other parts of building.   American soldier comes again,
this time with Spanish American from Porto Rica.   We sit in garden and
talk to them.   They obviously cannot understand how we can enjoy being
in such a quiet spot.   They have great idea of "having a good time", which
means never being at home but always rushing about somewhere else.   And
it would seem from their conversation that all Americans get divorced and
take to themselves new partners.

Sunday, May 28, 1944

Very hot.   Martin and I go for walk and find wonderful clover field -
blazing with blossom - not pale purple but a deep crimson.

Monday, May 29, 1944

Back to London in intense heat.   Working in afternoon.   In evening do
fire-watch for Greta who is on holiday.   Just before I set out for duty

- 486 -

there is freak storm - much thunder and hail stones like lumps of sugar.
At Lancaster Gate half the road is flooded.   Temperature not reduced at
all by hail, but most unbearably sultry.

Tuesday, May 30, 1944

Airgraph from Roy, written May 12.   He says, re invasion, that surely
never was a secret military operation talked about so openly before.
He begins to think the whole affair is a gigantic bluff.
        To press at 8 p.m. (late because of Bank Holiday on Monday). Flies
still very troublesome.

Wednesday, May 31, 1944

To National Gallery concert.   Aeolian String Quartet, and Jimmy Whitehead, in Schubert's Quartet in E flat major and Quintet in C major.
Not quite so unbearably hot: try to buy frock.   At Lafayette's, there
seems to be no price between 29/6 and 8 guineas, which seems/as I feel
is absurd.

Thursday, June 1, 1944

Birthday letter (by ordinary mail) from Roy, written April 2.   Also
one from Joyce, who is never sure whether the date is June 1, 2 or 3.

Friday, June 2, 1944

My 37th birthday.   Have letters from Marjorie Fuchs, Mother and Daddy
(who send £1 and 1 gn. respectively), and Phyllida (who sends 7/6).
In lunchtime I buy myself nail-file, the only one I can find, which is
5/-,and some cream for my face, 7/6.   In evening to Ware, where H.
gives me book token for 10/6.

Saturday, June 3, 1944

Martin has sad accident in bed which causes me to strip him and take
him into mine at beginning of night.   He says with shame: "It were a
accident", and adds sadly: "I were so comfy in my bed till this
arrived!"   This morning he presents me with birthday card with pink
asters and a yellow butterfly on it and the words "Wishing you a Happy
Birthday Auntie Dear.   May this your Birthday prove to be The best day
of the year".   We walk into village and buy dog biscuits, some sweet
ration, soap flakes, and soap powder which proves later to be nothing
but soda and almost useless.

Sunday, June 4, 1944

Martin and I go long walk in morning over fields and through woods, and
in afternoon he enjoys himself helping his father plant cabbages.   As
result he is tired and asleep before I leave.   Weather cooler. Rain,
sorely needed, at night.

Monday, June 5, 1944

Allied troops enter Rome, and we hear on radio the bell of St.
Peter's tolling out musically against background of tanks.
    I begin course at B.B.C. staff training school: 3 weeks. Among
my 9 fellow students are a Madame Belina Brzozowska of the Polish
Ministry of Information, a Mr. Chen of the Chinese service, a Gaelic-
speaking Scot with a most beautiful Highland voice, a Welsh-speaking
Dr. Thomas (who comes, surprisingly,from North Region), and 4 young
Canadian soldiers.

Tuesday, June 6, 1944

On 8 o'clock news we quote German reports that Allied troops have
landed near Le Havre and at other points in France. Our first class
this morning is interrupted for us to hear announcements, being put
out on all B.B.C.'s wavelengths, including a bulletin from General
Dwight D. Eisenhower, Allied C.in C., and warnings to all enemy
occupied countries on west coast of Europe. French are told by E.
not to rise at present but to await word from him. This is obviously what they call "D" Day - i.e. invasion day. Much excitement, and
when we return to lecture on internal organisation of B.B.C., the
speaker (one-time actor) says "Well, this seems rather a come-down:
I'm sure all our thoughts are with the boys on the job. And as we
have several representatives of the United Nations with us, I think
it would be rather nice if, as a gesture, we all stood for a moment
as a kind of salute to them". This slightly theatrical gesture somewhat embarrasses my Anglo-Saxon nature, but the Canadians think it is
all right, and the Welshman next to me mutters "Splendid! Splendid!
That's right!" King broadcasts at 9p.m. and calls us to prayer.

Wednesday, June 7, 1944

After technical lectures this morning, we spend afternoon at our
largest studio, at Maida Vale (it used to be skating rink), learning
about studio acoustics. And we all speak in turn into microphone
in studio while everyone looks at us through glass panel and listens
on loudspeaker next door. Very nerve-racking, and I am much worst
in class. I become quite strangled in reading, owing to not taking
any breath through nervousness. Good thing I never thought it
possible to turn myself into Beautiful Female Announcer.

Thursday, June 8, 1944

We have captured Bayeux in France. There is not a great deal of
news, but things seem so far to be satisfactory. Churchill warns
everyone against over-optimism. Was so worked up at having had to
speak into microphone yesterday, could not sleep last night. Four
interesting but straight lectures to-day, which find tiring.

F̶r̶i̶d̶a̶y̶,̶ ̶J̶u̶n̶e̶ ̶9̶,̶ ̶1̶9̶4̶4̶

Hilary rings up at breakfast time to say Petrol rationing people
have given her allowance to go by car to Stroud, and Leonard is
so anxious to get her off before - perhaps - he has to go out all
night for several days on Home Guard duty, that he says she is to
go on Saturday.   So he is taking the family down then.   My weekend Ark has thus left me for the time being.

Friday, June 9, 1944

Progress reported on all fronts in France.   Heavy rain in afternoon and evening, which may not be so good for landing supplies and
reinforcements for our troops, but which will be very welcome to
the farmers.

Saturday, June 10, 1944

There is certainly a decrease in number of American and Canadian troops
one sees about streets.
        In morning to Listener office to do some indexing.   In evening
Bob and I, with Listener press ticket, go to first night of Promenade
season (Jubilee year).   About 6,000 people at Albert Hall, and all
not already standing rise to feet when Henry appears, and cheer.
Everyone feeling a bit worked up just now, and sings National Anthem
with great heartiness.   And at end of concert all bellow "Land of Hope
and Glory".   A great wallow.   See Edric and Helena Cundell, who have
returned to their Hampstead house: and Mosco Carner who introduces me
to his wife.   Frank Howes, the Times critic, sitting just behind us.
In Handel's 7th Organ Concerto (as Albert Hall-ed by Henry), he says
to companion in voice thrilling with agony "Let us go!" Very mixed
programme: Berlioz' Roman Carnival overture, Delius' Cuckoo in Spring,
Grieg's 2nd Piano concerto (Moura Lympany), etc.

Sunday, June 11, 1944

Mother's 68th birthday.   I go in morning to All Saints, Margaret St.,
and hear a Mass by Dvořák.   In evening go with Bob to a very "High"
church in a poor Paddington neighbourhood, where they are having a
special service in honour of Corpus Christi.   They have a great procession, led by the tiniest children with their hands devoutly folded
before them and long veils down to their feet at the back, and then
the bigger ones coming behind with the adults last, all of them carrying lighted candles.   And then came the Blessed Sacrament, preceded
by six little girls in white who scattered rose-petals before it.   It
was borne by a priest, in festal robes, supported by two lesser priests
and in front (coming next after the little girls with rose-petals)
went a man swinging incense.   We all knelt down as the Sacrament
passed down one aisle, and turned slowly round as it went by the back
of the church, so that we did not irreverently turn our backs to it -
after all, we should do as much for the King - and then knelt again as
it went up the central aisle.   Many people in the congregation had
lighted candles too.   It was all very picturesque and they all enjoyed
it very much; so did Bob and I.   We sang a long hymn by Thos.Aquinas.

Monday, June 12, 1944

Things going well in France.   But my thoughts more on my course.   We
hear "Itma" programme played over and have discussion on its construction.   Also have lecture from John Snagge on news announcing and
hear records of how not to do it.

Tuesday, June 13, 1944

In afternoon we read through MS. of feature we are going to record
tomorrow.   I am to be small boy (with Devonshire accent) of about 9.
Am practising speaking in piping treble.
        In evening to Promenade Concert with Tina.   Schumann's Piano
Concerto in A minor (Solomon) and Dvorak's 4th Symphony.

Wednesday, June 14, 1944

Spend all day in airless studios in Broadcasting House, first rehearsing and then recording "The Stones Cry Out - The Barbican, Plymouth",
by Louis MacNeice - which we all enjoy even when we do it very badly.

Thursday, June 15, 1944

Nerve-racking day.   First hear recording of our effort of yesterday
- not bad considering circumstances of production, and my effort at a
9-year-old not as ludicrous as I expected.   Have to listen to criticism of show from Director of studies - fortunately he does not get
personal but criticises production.   In fact it turns into argument
between him and Mr. McConnel who produced, on how it should have been
managed.   Then later on I sit on tenterhooks because we have a Talks
session for which we have had to prepare a script each for delivery
through microphone to rest of class.   But Mr. Harding does not get
as far through alphabet as R so I am spared.   But Then the Promenade
Concert ticket which has been sent to me through our Post Room, does
not arrive.   Have arranged with Greta to meet me there, so have to
go and smile ingratiatingly upon man in Box Office, who lets me in but
gives me to understand it must never happen again.   Concert makes up
for all these agonies - notably Elgar's Violin Concerto played by
Albert Sammons.

Friday, June 16, 1944

Air-raid warning lasted all last night.   One plane sounded as if it
would take off our chimneys; it made a noise like an express train
coming through the window.   To-day we are warned that the Germans
have started to use robot - i.e. pilotless - planes against us, and we
are told to take cover when they come.   We can distinguish them by
a little trail of fire behind the tail, which just before the bomb is
to explode, goes out.   Then the sound ceases, and within 15 seconds
at most the bomb has fallen.   All very comfortable.
        Glad to go home to Stroud on the 6.35, in which travel without
inconvenience.

Saturday, June 17, 1944

We hear there have been more pilotless aircraft over London.   I take
Martin for walk on common in morning, and in afternoon sit on lawn
while he plays in hammock (tying himself up in it and pretending he's
a parcel for Daddy).   He looks inches taller, and Hilary has grown
in girth.

Sunday, June 18, 1944

Martin and Hilary meet us in fields on way home from morning service.
I take former for another long walk over common.   At about 5, Phyllida arrives, very sunburnt from haymaking, bearing 9 eggs and a
bottle of milk.   Says the first airborne invasion troops went from
the aerodrome near Fairford.   For several days before the event no
one was allowed in or out of the aerodrome.   A baker who did go in
was kept there.   And all post leaving the village was censored.
        Return comfortably to London. Find they have had two disturbed
nights and that pilotless aircraft have been going over all day.
Tyburn Convent hit, also (during 11 a.m. service today) the Guards
Chapel.   And, I am told, Charing Cross Bridge.

Monday, June 19, 1944

Slept very badly, with an Alert all night and at times these wretched
robot machines going over.   When they are about to land, the engine
stops, and when that happens one turns over and waits for the bang.
We have warnings off and on all day today, and I need the two gins
and lime which Mr. Eld, a fellow-student, gives me on my way home.
        Fire-watching at night. Parcel from S. Africa: 1 lb. tea, 1 lb.
sugar, tin beef and some chocolates.

Tuesday, June 20, 1944

Very tired after fire-watching last night.   There was an Alert from
11.30 onwards, but we werenot kept up all the time.   On whole slept
pretty well for 6 hours.   Today have to deliver a talk, through the
microphone, to the class.   Am so nervous that I can scarcely speak,
but find to my great surprise that I have been enormous success.
Yesterday when I suggested subject - National Gallery concert audience
- to Mr. Harding (supervisor), he said dubiously that Max Beerbohm
might manage it.   Today he congratulates me on having "brought it off
triumphantly".   After which I am completely exhausted.   Go into
Kensington Gardens with Greta in evening, and we childishly and enjoy-
ably play with wooden toy made by her uncle, which might almost be described as pilotless aircraft.   We then talk to friends of hers who
have allotment in the park and are picking green-peas from it.

Wednesday, June 21, 1944

Talk to Mr. Chen, our Chinese, who tells me that 400-500 years ago

there was novel in China, of Jules Verne or H.G. Wells variety,
which foretold use of underwater craft, air machines, etc.; and it
seems the anonymous author even included the pilotless plane in -
the countermeasure for which, in the book, was to devise method of
deflecting plane back on to its originators.

Several of the aircraft over last night - someone in the house
counted 15. One exploded fairly near. On 3 occasions when I hear
plane stop and stutter, and see flash of its tail light on my ceiling,
I leap out of bed and into corridor almost in one, feeling that I had
better in future go to bed in my slippers!

Allied troops said to be entering Cherbourg, and Americans said
to have captured one or two sites of pilotless planes - now generally
called doodle-bugs, buzz-bombs, or P-planes.

Hand over identity card to Miss Morrison who, taking it to Food
Office together with old ration card, can get new ration card. She
is allowed to do all household together.

In evening to beautiful Promenade Concert with Tina: Haydn-
Brahms. "Philosopher" Symphony of former, and 2 songs. Of latter,
1st Piano Concerto, Variations of Theme of Haydn, and 2nd Symphony.
Two poles in front have a red and green light on left and right hand
respectively, to give us air-raid warning if one occurs. But none
does occur. There is slightly depleted audience. Music most lovely
and consoling.

Thursday, June 22, 1944

More buzz-bombs, but sleep not too badly. One of the walls of
Buckingham Palace, in Constitution Hill, has been knocked down. This
evening Tina and I sit on my balcony and have Italian lesson with Miss
Johnson. If we speak as she does, we shall talk Italian with stutter.
She is very nice indeed. Forty or fifty bombers, shining high up in
evening sunshine, go over us.

Entertaining story from Gordon McConnel about early days of
broadcasting. About 20 years ago (when everyone listened on crystal
sets), Cardiff station was going to put out 2-hour show, written by
the Station Director, on the history of the Great War as seen through
eyes of 3 privates - including one "gentleman" private of rather
mystical nature who saw visions while scrubbing canteen floors.
They had only one studio - with one extra one as alternative, from
which all sounds could be heard in first studio. Had engaged local
Welsh choir, and roped in all local British Legion (primed with beer)
who were to do a glorious battle in lane outside broadcasting premises
which was to be broadcast. It opened all right, with the mystic
seeing visions on Salisbury Plain. While engaged on his menial tasks
he said "Hark! I hear the sound of distant music!" and this was to
be signal for orchestra in other studio to start up "The Banner of St.
George". Unfortunately conductor had lost his cue-sheet and nothing
happened. Mystic repeated his line. At which the conductor burst
into the second of the two pieces he had to play, which happened to be
"Tipperary". That, unfortunately, was signal for Welsh Choir to begin, and they sang with great heartiness. And that was the cue for

the ex-Service men to start their battle - and they'd been so primed
and were enjoying themselves so much, they couldn't be induced to
stop.   So all in one, the scene had shifted to France, and half-an-
hour of the script had been left out.   Well, they let an entertainment for the troops in the trenches, which occurred later on, go on
for 15 minutes longer than it should; and meantime the distracted
author write another scene (w̶h̶i̶c̶h̶ in which the mystic got shot), which
was broadcast even as he wrote it, with no rehearsal at all.

Friday, June 23, 1944

A lot of bombs over between 2 and 4 a.m.   This morning, about 9.30,
we have warning, and I hear later that bomb fell near Waterloo Station,
disintegrated a bus, and badly cut a lot of people on the platform.
This contradicted later by Doris, whose people were called to do First
Aid.   She says 2 were killed and about a dozen hurt, and the bus was
not disintegrated.   Broadcast programmes are somewhat altered - the
Promenade broadcasts not given, but an alternative programme of
symphony music put on on gramophone records.   Sorry our School is over

Saturday, June 24, 1944

Midsummer Day and very fine and warm.   Slept quite well last night
until about 6 a.m. when we had a number of bombs over.   In morning
to office to do some indexing, and in afternoon to "Patience" at
King's Theatre, Hammersmith, with Greta.   Afterwards we see queue for
cherries in greengrocer's, and each get 1 lb.   No Alert all day.

Sunday, June 25, 1944

Not as fine as yesterday - in afternoon it cloudsover.   Awake from
2 till after 4, with bombs going over intermittently.   It is an uncomfortable moment when engine stops.   This morning to service at
Friends House, Euston Road, and afterwards walk home.   Am now typing
onbalcony.   Two balconies away are a number of babies put out to
sleep - a few of the illegitimate ones who appear to be being born in
great numbers at present.

Monday, June 26, 1944

Night not too bad.   Back to work rather reluctantly.   In afternoon
to printers, where Mr. Pringle and I find them all in outside shelters.
We are obliged to join them; but when signal is received that aircraft are outside the 35-mile limit, we can go in.   Have to go down
several more times.   In evening meet Arnold who has come up for meeting tomorrow.   Feed with him at Park Hotel Restaurant.   Marjorie has
said he is to sleep in deepest vaults of B.B.C., for as much safety
as possible, so about 10 oclock Tina and I walk with him to Marble
Arch through park, and there part.

Tuesday, June 27, 1944

Not a good night. At least 9 bombs round about. Get tired of
hopping out of bed into corridor, so that when the nearest one drops,
which rocks house, have not got out but only turn over with face in
pillow and put fingers in ears. Find today that this bomb fell near
restaurant where Arnold and I satlast night, saying how pleasant it
was to look at trees. Now windows are gone and there are boards instead. We spend all day at printers rushing in and out of dugouts,
and finally finish at 7.30.

Wednesday, June 28, 1944

Better night. Only distant bombs. But warnings all day, When we
are chivvied into inside corridor by Editor. Letter from Joyce.
Ruth Meyer had bomb on house where she lives at West End Lane. Some
people killed and some injured. She was fire-watching and so escaped
it. Letter also from David, pressing me to go for weekend to Church
Hanborough, and even saying they will adopt me by deed-poll if I want
to get out of London away from bombs! Letter from Mother written
June 20 arrives only this afternoon.
        To Promenade concert with Bob. No alert while we are there.
Handel: "Comfort Ye","Every Valley", and also the overture, from
"Messiah"; and the Plague Choruses from "Israel in Egypt"; besides
oboe concerto and Firework music. Then Elgar's "Music-Makers".
Good.

Thursday, June 29, 1944

Too tired to go to Prom. concert. Am passionately anxious to survive
till the weekend, because it will be so lovely to be away from bombs.
More over in lunch-hour, in fact most of day. I manage tosleep quite
a lot. Arnold has taken back to Hale with him Marjorie's sister Mary
and her two children, aged about 5 and 8 eight months, for some rest.

Friday, June 30, 1944

People beginning to look very tired. Have several loud reports near
us today; Bush House has bomb just beside it - some of our offices
are there. And annexe of Regent Palace Hotel hit. In evening by
crowded 6.55 train to Stroud. Feel my equilibrium restored by sight
of cows and horses peacefully grazing in fields. And further restored on arriving and picking up local paper and reading account of
how one woman was prosecuted by another for attacking her with a bucket; the magistrate, dismissing the case and saying the evidence was
conflicting and there were doubtless faults on both sides, said "The
state of affairs at Nag's Head Village is deplorable".

Saturday, July 1, 1944

Sleep blissfully for undisturbed 8 hours. Wet day; Martin plays

with bubble-pipe I brought him.   He, Hilary and Tramp all looking
very well.   Mother has been worried by tales of damage in London;
Mrs. Thomas from top of hill made point of leaningover garden gate
specially to inform her that Paddington was completely devastated.
Had letter from Phyllida once this week where she said in Fairford
it was generally believed that most of London was demolished; and
it was said that the flying-bombs were going over every minute and
people were reduced to nervous wrecks.

Sunday, July 2, 1944

Another beautiful night.   To-day it rains a lot, and I take Martin
for wet afternoon walk.   In morning to chapel with Mother and
Daddy, where the hymn "How firm a foundation ye saints of the Lord"
is announced "by request".   Would bet anyone any sum that the request was Daddy's, for my benefit, several lines running

> "When through fiery trials thy pathway shall lie
> My grace all-sufficient shall be thy supply.
> The flame shall not hurt thee; I only design
> Thy dross to consume and thy gold to refine.
>
> When through the deep waters I cause thee to go
> The rivers of grief shall not thee overflow;
> For I will be with thee in trouble to bless
> And sanctify to thee thy deepest distress."

and also somewhere there is the line "As thy days may demand shall
thy strength ever be".
        In spite of this assurance I feel rather dismal at having to
return to London, in a train so crowded that I stand all the way to
Swindon.   Then get seat, and woman in carriage describes not only
without shame but with pride, how she bought some clothes coupons
from someone for 21/-, an illegal procedure, and when she bought
something in Oxford Street, produced a pair of nail-scissors and pre-
tended she had just cut them out herself from her book "just to help
you out", she told the assistant who protested at her action.
        Have to fire-watch at Broadcasting House.   So many people sleep-
ing in its safe vaults that there are no clean sheets or clean towels
left for fire-watchers.   I do at last get a clean sheet from man at
Egton House, as reward for listening to story of how his sister,
buried under debris, was dug out, and what she looked like.

Monday, July 3, 1944

We were left in peace last night, and though sleep was in stuffy and
airless concert-hall, was glad to feel safe.   To-day we have alert
continually from about 11 a.m. to 8.45 p.m., with many "blues".   One
bomb goes over house just before dinner, and one, or two, went over
printers, where we were this time allowed to go under stairs instead
of to dugouts.   Men had to go outside, however, and work is dreadfully
behindhand.   Promenade Concerts at Albert Hall have been suspended for
Security reasons.   Too many people in one vulberable spot.

Tuesday, July 4 1944

Not at all a bad night.   I go to Waterlows, but am turned out of
train at Willesden, two stations before Stonebridge Park, because
of bomb on line.   Finish journey by bus and arrive late.   "Imminent Danger" signal 16 or 17 times during day - it is given by a
foghorn which goes off outside our room, it is true, but not many
yards away, and is quite deafening.   Printers go to dugouts and
we go under stairs.   To press at 8 o'clock, very tired.   Browning
brings us back by car, assuring us all the way that, though there
is an Alert on, no bomb ever falls in the Harrow Road - a most
dangerous generality as it seems to me.   But we arrive scatheless
none the less.   Reading Gerald Heard's two pamphlets "Training
for the Life of the Spirit", with which am impressed.

Wednesday, July 5 1944

Again a quite good night.   I am awake between 3 and 5 and hear a
number of distant plonks.   East a spam roll left over from printers
yesterday and thereafter go to sleep.   All clear most of this morning, but warning at lunch-time and at end of afternoon several near-
ish bombs.
     The enormous balloon barrage set up in countryside to stop
coming of bombs said (by someone coming from Tunbridge Wells) to be
stoppong 7 out of 8 bombs.   All balloons have disappeared from
London.
     In evening listen to Brahms' 4th Symphony (being played at
Bedford, since Proms are cancelled), and read Gerald Heard's "Training for the Life of the Spirit".   It has now been decided that all
the works which would have been broadcast from the Proms shall be
given "live" at Bedford and broadcast from there.
     Alert is still in progress and it is raining.

Thursday, July 6 1944

Again not too bad a night, though this morning at about 8.30 a loud
report shakes the house.   To supper with Abrahams.   Learn that
early yesterday morning bomb fell at Hampstead, where 24 bus stops,
and broke all windows in South Hill Park.   It dropped on edge of
pond and fishes were found as far off as Willoughby Road, and people
were collecting them for their cats.   Many alerts during day.
Churchill makes speech in House on flying bombs.   About 3,000 people
have been launched in a month, and deaths have been about 3,000 too
- but as he adds that a large number of bombs are stopped before they
reach London, the proportion per bomb is higher than would at first
appear.   He says the battle may be a long one, and deep shelters
are being built.   Adds that nothing must interfere with the fighting
in France and Italy, and utters a veiled threat of reprisals whenhe
says that this beginning by the Germans of indiscriminate bombing may
be not be without its results.

Friday, July 7, 1944

Loud reports which shake windows at about midnight.   Thereafter I
sleep pretty well.   Today Miss Entract upset by news that (about
12 last night) a school friend had her entire family wiped out.   The
friend herself is in hospital, unconscious, suffering from injuries to
spine.   Not so many bombs over today.   Travel by crowded 6.5 train
to Hanborough, and thence by taxi (needless to say previously booked
for me) to Greens' grey stone cottage at Church Hanborough.   In
large whitewashed attic I settle down luxuriously for peaceful night.
Am very very tired.

Saturday, July 8, 1944D¢¢¢

Doubtful morning turns into sunny afternoon, and I am taken into woods
by the starry-eyed 4-year-old Roger.   We get lost and return to late
tea after 2 hours.   Garden ¢¢¢¢¢¢ of cottage slopes to quiet graveyard
of grey church.   Many of our own aeroplanes flying but it all seems
very peaceful and cottage gardens are full of madonna lilies.   Feel
very relaxed and drained of all energy.

Sunday, July 9, 1944

David, on bicycle, arrives 10.a.m. from Oxford, where he is now
stationed in National Fire Service.   Brings great sheaf of bulrushes
he has gathered on way.   Rain nearly all day.   Clears up after tea
and I go for walk with D. by river.   Hilary's 32nd birthday.

Monday, July 10, 1944

Rise early and ride Joyce's bicycle to station, while David walks
through woods.   He comes with me by train to Oxford on 8.17 and I
travel on to London.   Yesterday there were 16 hours free of flying
bombs.   British have captured Caen.

Tuesday, July 11, 1944

Quiet night.   No bombs on London area.   But a good many alerts to-
day.   One as I walk from station to printers.   Something drones over
which I take to be bombs and I steel myself to likelihood of having
to throw myself face downwards in bed of nettles with old rusty saucepans from rubbish dump hitting me on head.   But drones turn out to be
Fortresses going out.   To press about 7.30.   See mess created about
3 p.m. today off Harrow Road as we return.   Miss Morrison says our
house was shaken by explosion.

Wednesday, July 12, 1944

Again a quiet night.   Some activity today.   Gerald Abraham says "A
bomb was coming down Portland Place as I went up, so I cut it dead".
Buy Arthur Waley's translation from the Chinese "The Way and its
Thought", and Neitzsche's "Thus Spake Zarathustra", which I have

impression is account of Zoroastrianism, but find it is nothing of the sort, but ideology peculiar to Neitzsche and (I should say) the Nazis.

Thursday, July 13, 1944

Still a quiet night: too good almost to be true. Russians advancing rapidly, and Editor writes leader (for next Thursday) beginning "Now that the Russians are on the soil of East Prussia" - which it seems likely they will be by next week. Tina and I have Italian lesson from Miss Johnson. Her brother's Irish housekeeper thinks the reason everyone is so busy nowadays is because the Government has taken two hours off the clock, which amounts to "fourteen hours a week and a week a month" - rather strange arithmetic on top of her "give-us-back-our-nine-days" mentality.

Friday, July 14, 1944

Quiet night again. Alert as I am approaching office, and bomb in Regent's Park. One or two more alerts during day. The siren at Oxford Circus, which yesterday had gone wrong so that while other sirens gave Alert it gave All Clear and continued to give it for 10 minutes, today seems to be mended. To National Gallery concert - held because of bombs in the basement. French Independence Day programme: Chausson's "Chanson Perpetuelle" with Maggie Teyte, Griller Quartet, and Howard Ferguson (piano); and Faure's Piano Quartet in G minor.

Saturday, July 15, 1944

Again a quiet night. Sit on my balcony and knit while air raid warning is on, and when both anything seems to be coming over, go inside on to landing. There is one crash not very far away. Walk in park with Bob, again while Alert is in being - and we see "imminent danger" signal on top of distant building. Strollers in park, and people rowing on Serpentine, and those sitting on grass, appear unmoved by thoughts of any danger at all. Fire-watching at night.

Sunday, July 16, 1944

An Alert from midnight till about 8 this morning. I am on duty from 4.30 - 6, when I get up. A bomb in Regent's Park during my watch. Fireman brings me watery cup of tea from canteen. To Victoria to catch 8.28 to Dormans to see Joyce. There is still an Alert and the tubes are crowded with sleepers who have not gone up to the air yet. The only way to get to Victoria during air-raid (buses being almost non-existent at this hour on Sunday) seems to be to go from Oxford Circus to Piccadilly and then change and go to Hyde Park Corner, and then get out and walk. Catch train with ease. Journey enlivened by bomb stories from other occupants of carriage. I am given general impression that EastGrinstead has been heavily bombed, but find from

Joyce that it has had only one bomb.   Balloon barrage is now being
moved further out so that it seems as if very soon J. will have about
three balloons on her doorstep, with prospect of doodle-bugs falling
in every direction.

I have brought her 1 lb. cherries, and she has enormous dish of
raspberries and beautiful tomatoes.   Day turns out fine and we gather
mushrooms for breakfast and wander peacefully while now and then the
flybombs go over our heads.

Monday, July 17, 1944

Noise of buzzbombs going over last night, a few towards morning very
loud.   Travel back to London during All Clear.   On platform is
Army officer who last Wednesday was in Caen.   Says there is nothing
at all left of it.   We sent 450 bombers over and blew it to bits.
Even the roads out of the town are destroyed. Population is completely dazed; they cannot understand why we, their allies, should bomb
them so terribly.

Day becomes very hot and I wishI had a thin frock with me.   Buy
grape-fruit squash (synthetic) for 2/6.   Roy's 39th birthday.

Tuesday, July 18, 1944

Trying press day, fortunately with very few bombing interruptions, or
we should never have finished.   As it is we leave at 8 p.m.

Wednesday, July 19, 1944

A very noisy, disturbed night.   No sleep till 3, and then constant
noises to reawaken me.   Many crashes, house shakes.   One goesover
very low, and then apparently turns and begins to come back, but drops
before it reaches us.   I put my head under two pillows and wait.
Today warm and fine again.   A number of bombs over during day.   Buy
cherries from barrow at 1/6 a lb.   Hear from Ruth Davies that she
and children have gone to Aberystwyth till bombing is over.   She is
going to have another baby in February.

Attend B.B.C. meeting about buzz-bombs.   Seven types have been
used; their range is about 120 miles; they fly at about 1,000 feet,
but may be anything between 2,000 and 200 feet up.

We have captured Leghorn and Ancona in Italy; and General
Montgomery says he is satisfied with situation in France.

Thursday, July 20, 1944

Another bad night, but not quite as horrible as Tuesday's.   Block-
makers (back of Fetter Lane) have had their windows blasted.   Papers
tellus that although we have bombed flying-bomb sites on coast,
Germans have now been able to move them inland.

Friday, July 21, 1944

Last night counted 34 bombs exploding. Slept a little in between whiles;   not

as bad a night as Tuesday.   This morning's newspapers say attack
has been made on Hitler's life, and later in morning we hear wild and
wishful rumours that revolution has started in Germany.   Listen to
1 o'clock news which does say Hitler has broadcast about "revolt" in
army, and several officers, including General Beck, have been put to
death.

In evening to Brill, to see the Mearings;   met by Mr. Mearing
with car and we go to Oakley Vicarage.   There are two little girls,
evacuated from Wembley.   Settle down happily for peaceful night all
among the elms and the little grey church and the grassy fields.

Saturday, July 22, 1944

More rumours from inside Germany.   It seems that one "camp" is held
by rebels, and they are being bombed by the S.S.

At lunchtime Audrey arrives from her war factory in Oxford, and
we go after lunch for walk to Brill, returning to pick and eat raspberries and blackcurrants in garden.

Sunday, July 23, 1944

Loud explosion some time towards beginning of night.   Weake up, think
"They ought not to come here", and go to sleep again.   This morning
walk across garden and churchyard and go to matins, which like very
much.   At lunch-time schoolboy arrives for day (German refugee, came
to this country in 1939).   He and Audrey and I go for cycle ride.
To evensong.   Also have conversation with Vicar when I find myself
holding forth to him about religion, and am rather overcome and almost
stop in middle of sentence when I realise what I am doing.

Monday, July 24, 1944

Start back early this morning for London, after another peaceful night.
Arrive about 10.45 at office, and am extremely busy, with Miss Playle
away.   Have not time even to extract roses from case and put them in
water.   Quiet day;   only 3 "imminents".

Tuesday, July 25, 1944

Busy press day;   fortunately doodle-bugs leave us alone.   Not finished
till 8.15.

Wednesday, July 26, 1944

One extremely loud explosion last night - didn't even hear engine of
buzz-bomb, it must have glided some way.   House rocked to its foundations, but windows held.   In evening to coffee with Miss Scott Johnston of The Listener (Mrs. Melsom);   her husband coming back tomorrow
from Ireland.   He is in Air Force.   They have been married 5 years
and have been together only 9 months.   She would like a baby but must
be about 40 now, if not more.   Nice Polish airman there, and American
girl.   Polish airman tells us of beautiful sentence in French booke he
read: "There was a silence like 300 pianos with nobody playing on them'

Thursday, July 27, 1944

Tina and I have another Italian lesson, but we are all so sleepy we can scarcely keep awake, and end in philosophical discussion about "actives" and "contemplatives".

Friday, July 28, 1944

Not a bad night - a few distant bangs.   Nevertheless, feel so tired can hardly drag myself about.   At lunch-time Tina has windows of restaurant in which she is, blown all over her herring, and goes back to find several office windows missing.   Fire-watching at night.

Saturday, July 29, 1944

To Ware by afternoon train, arriving about 5 o'clock.   Ring up L. who has just returned from Stroud, and he meets me in car - illegally, of course.   Also gives lift to Mrs. Steele, friend, and two children, so car is crowded.   Learn that L. went home by car, because he had to take the pram for H.   He dismantled it and started his journey about 4 a.m. so that he shouldn't be stopped.

Sunday, July 30, 1944

Peaceful night.   Hear none of the "hundreds of bombs which go right over the house" referred to by Mrs. Steele yesterday.   Get dinner for L., the potatoes turning out a queer colour because I enthusiastically boil quantities of mint in the water before putting them in. Devise sweet of powdered milk and rice, with a few sultanas thrown in for variety, and the whole - on Leonard's suggestion - thickened with custard-powder.   We eat it with quantities of apricot jam on top.

Monday, July 31, 1944

Up at 6.45 and leave house at 7.30.   Again a peaceful night, and only about 3 "overheads" all day.   Not only the Editor, but Miss Playle and Miss Scott-Johnston away to-day.   Very busy: work late at printers in anticipation of bank holiday and am very tired.

Tuesday, August 1, 1944

Quiet night;   hear only 2 explosions.   Very busy day: weather has become warm.   3 "overheads" during day.   Once I go under stairs and twice outside where we sit in bright sunshine on edge of dugout. Multiplicity of alarms and whistles of one sort or another from the factories all round.

Wednesday, August 2, 1944

Dull morning turns into fine day.   Everyone seems very tired.   Buy comb (after some difficulty) for Phyllida who cannot get one in Fairford: price 2/6. Mother and Daddy's 40*th wedding anniversary. I send them card with large wedding-bell on it. Have already sent Daddy box of chocolates to give mother - the box alone cost 2/3 and the ½ lb. of chocolates 2/6. I wrap up each one separately and pack for posting.

Only 2 alerts during day. Mr. Churchill makes speech in House: very encouraging. In France we are breaking out of Cherbourg Peninsula; in Italy we are at gates of Florence; in the Far East the Americans have made such good progress that he thinks war there may not last much longer than war in Europe; Red Army is only 10 miles from East Prussia. Flying-bombs have caused deaths of more than 4,000 people. 1,000,000 people have left London and he advises any others who can to go. We have to be prepared for possibility of use by Germans of new rocket projectile, and the London area will be the main target.

Thursday, August 3, 1944

Very warm. Italian lesson on balcony in evening. Last night very noisy everywhere, as if the Germans were determined to make a reply to Churchill's speech. This morning plenty of "alerts" and "over-heads" - one bomb very low over office.

Friday, August 4, 1944

Last night not too bad. Very hot day. Leave office at midday and get 1.45 for Hanborough. People 4 or 5 deep on platform, but I get corner seat by walking to very front of train. Have to wait nearly 2 hours at Oxford, and again get corner seat. 3 small children in carriage, one nor more thana year old, in white satin frock, whose Mother gives her large piece of chocolate to manage by herself. Results - on a sultry day - may be imagined. Roger in bed when I arrive at Greens. David at home for past fortnight, enjoying light attack of tonsilitis and slightly sprained ankle.

German wireless early this morning said that 10 one-man torpedoes have sunk 40,000 tons of our shipping in mouth of Seine. No mention of this on our news.

Saturday, August 5, 1944

Very pleasant, lazy day, thought I do not sleep well during night in spite of absence of bombs. With David and Roger to river. Small boys bathing there. No sign here of war except that the farm-hands, one observes, are occasionally dressed in khaki and have olive skins. They are Italian prisoners. And our own aeroplanes zoom overhead all day and quite a lot of the night.

Sunday, August 6, 1944

Again very hot. Picnic in hayfield. David builds Roger house of hay in which he determines to sleep all night. The only flying menace here is the wasps. War news good: we arecutting off the Breton peninsula.

Monday, August 7, 1944

Catch 9.55 a.m. for London. Travel in Guard's van as far as Oxford and then in 1st Class Pullman. Very warm and fine. At Craven Hill Gardens find letter from Mother, written Saturday, saying "Martin's sister arrived this morning at 4 o'clock. We took her - H. - to nursing home Thursday eve, so evidently wasn't so quick as we had been led to expect ... M. a good boy tho' not exactly transported at the news. Got under the bed at first, then relieved his feelings by stripping himself stark naked in the bathroom and was found washing himself all over in cold water" - a sort of vicarious purification rite, I suppose.

We are expected to be at office at about 2.30, but Mr. Pringle waits 2¼ hours for train on Guildford platform, and so does not arrive till 4.30. Hence, since Editor is away, our afternoon extends till 6.30, and messenger who has come in specially to take stuff to printers fumes and frets. Keeps saying "It's my day off", till I get cross and say "It's our day off too".

Tuesday, August 8, 1944

Another fine day, and the doodle-bugs leave us alone to go to press. A few bombs at about 6 this morning, but nothing very near.   War news continues good.

Wednesday, August 9,1944

Again hot and fine.   A few fly-bombs at dawn, but nothing very near. Postcard from Mother says Hilary's baby was 7 lb. 14 oz. - heavier than her brother was - and gave more trouble than Martin.

Thursday, August 10, 1944

Italian lesson in evening, to which I am unable to pay much attention because I am packing for my holiday at the same time.   And at 8.15 I have to leave for fire-watching.   Alert about 9 p.m. but All Clear soon afterwards.

Friday, August 11, 1944

No Alert last night: one at about 7.30 this morning with a "blue". Travel to Stroud by 4.15.   Crowded trains but I get a seat, and listen to tales of bombing by doodle-bugs, from family of father, mother and one boy.   300 families lost their homes from one bomb which fell on block of flats.   But many people were in a shelter and only 3 were killed.   Martin in bed when I arrive: Mother very tired.

Saturday, August 12, 1944

Take Martin to Gloucester to see his Mother and new sister in their

nursing home. Baby won't take to breast and has lost weight. · H.
very well except that her breasts are sore because the child nibbles
instead of sucking. In evening, when M. is in bed, water-tank in
roof bursts, floods lavatory, and larder beneath, and every vessel
in house is brought into use to catch water. We let tank drain,
and Pop and I bale out. Mother thrown into despair.

Sunday, August 13, 1944

After yesterday's upset, Mother persuaded to stay in bed till dinner
time, so no one goes to chapel. Daddy and I go at night and he plays
organ. Wally Collier has died as/result of wounds received in
Normandy. Take Martin for walk beside stream at bottom of fields.

Monday, August 14, 1944

Go over to Gloucester to see H., alone. She is still having great
difficulty in getting the baby to feed. Letter from Joyce who has
lost - or had stolen - her handbag, with 8 weeks' pay and bonus, 8
weeks' emergency food cards, her ration book, an incredible number
of clothing coupons, her P.O. savings book, and a book of valuable
addresses for her work.

Tuesday, August 15, 1944

One o'clock news announces landings by Allies in south of France.
Says initial stages are going well. In evening, 5.30, we all visit
H. in Mr. Bingham's car and see the baby, whose grandparents declare
her to be extremely beautiful and intelligent. Nevertheless, she
will not feed from the maternal bosom, which is "chewed to ribbons",
H. says.

Wednesday, August 16, 1944

Progress of in south of France good. In afternoon take Martin to brook
again, where he paddles and the dog swims. Still very hot.

Thursday, August 17, 1944

Cloudy for first time for about a fortnight. News of invasion troops
continues good. Advances also in north of France as far as Orleans
and Chartres. We are within 40 miles of Paris. The To Gloucester
to see H. The strife has had to be abandoned and Christine put on a
bottle. Poor H. taking masses of pills to drain away her unused
milk. She has a headache and temperature. It is very sad. I see
the baby having her bottle, and even over that she goes to sleep.
Daddy to Bristol to buy goods, but does not get all he wants. He
feels he cannot carry on much longer, and is making arrangements to
sell the business. Letter from Roy (enclosing photograph of Miriam)
posted on July 9.

Friday, August 18, 1944

War news very good. Says Battle of Normandy is over and Germans

have no more power to resist in France but can only fight delaying
actions.   We lunch in Stroud, having no more rations, and I essay
to take Martin to see Miss Greenwood, but he falls and cuts his
knees in Folly Lane, immediately after remarking with a swagger that
he is "past the crying stage".   Not true: an awful hullabaloo, and
I have to lead him home.

Saturday, August 19, 1944

Fine weather has broken.   Very heavy storms during night, and from
3 - 6 a.m. Daddy and I are coping with more floods in lavatory and
larder.   As result we are all very tired today, and Mother so worn
out I relieve her of Martin's presence and take him to Gloucester to
see his Mother in afternoon.   She is up for first time.   The milk
has gone.   Christine seems to be satisfied now she has a bottle.
        War news still good.   Americans approaching outskirts of Paris.

Sunday, August 20, 1944

First Sunday of new minister at chapel, Mr. Robinson.   We take Martin
to service (up to sermon) and he is very good.   P. comes in afternoon, very sunburnt after helping in harvest.   On Wednesday she had
to tell the farmer she could do no more overtime: had been working
side by side with a man in fields in blazing sunshine and felt she
could not keep it up.

Monday, August 21, 1944

Fetch Hilary and baby home from Gloucester.   Try to register the
child on the way - it has to be done by a parent.   I guide H's somewhat feeble steps up a flight into registrar's office.   As 4 people
already waiting (and all looking as though they are come to register
deaths) and no one takes any notice of any of us.   So after 5 minutes
H. begins to feel queer and we leave, the baby still unnamed.

Tuesday, August 22, 1944

Great penetrations being made in south of France.   Germans say we
have landed at Bordeaux.   Sir Henry Wood has died.
        New baby fairly good.   Much spoilt by her grandmother.   I walk
on common with Martin.

Wednesday, August 23, 1944

Paris falls to French Forces of the Interior, who have been fighting
in the streets for 4 days.   At 1, 6 and 9, when the news is given,
the Marseillaise is played.
        Martin and I for long walk on common.

Thursday, August 24, 1944

Rumania asks Russia for Armistice.   Fighting hasbroken out again

between German forces and French in Paris.   In meantime American
troops are approaching suburbs.   Rumours of risings in Hungary.
        Baby cries a bit and we all get rather het up.   Daddy washes
car, aided by a delighted Martin, and destroys wasps' nest on lawn.

Friday, August 25, 1944

Phyllida arrives midday for week's holiday, bearing bottle milk,
2 dozen eggs, and fat chicken.   A letter from Arthur awaits her,
saying he is coming for 48 hours' leave; which throws Mother in a
turmoil, but P. calmly gets on with the work and goes to meet him
at 5 p.m., when they contrive to miss one another and he comes home
first.   Aunt Nina meanwhile turns up to tea, and Mrs. Franklin calls
to see the baby.   Baby is very good until evening when she cries so
much, and is evidently so hungry, H. says timetable or not she will
not have six adults disturbed, and gives her food, whereat she goes
peacefully to sleep.   Arthur has to spend night on sofa in drawing-
room, and Phyllida sleeps on floor of my room.

Saturday, August 26, 1944

War news continues good, and there has been a 24-hour lull in doodle-
bugs over London.   After dinner, horrible discovery is made by the
nauseated Hilary that flies have laid eggs on chicken, in spite of
its being wrapped up, and grubs have hatched out in to-day's heat.
She and Mother clean it up, inside and out, with vinegar, and decide
to cook it this evening instead of tomorrow.   I take Martin to
Enderly.   Aunt H's comment on baby and her feeding is that "of course
she knows better when she needs food than any label on a tin", which
seems true.   Because when H. wakes her this evening to feed her at
the appointed hour, she is reluctant to leave her sleep, and throws
the lot up.   I have been trying to get teats for Hilary in Stroud,
with no result.   Had difficulty in buying feeding-bottle with any
teats attached - they at first handed me one with open ends, and con-
fessed when I burst out laughing that of course it was no good without
something to suck through.

Sunday, August 27, 1944

Martin again comes to chapel and is very good.   The baby looks to us
bigger and has not given us a disturbed night since she came home.
Mr. Franklin brings up beautiful Victoria plums.
        Back to London in great heat.   Get seat for most part of
journey.

Monday, August 28, 1944

No Alert last night.   I return rather unwillingly to work this morning.   Tina says some firms have left London because of the Germans'
threat of rocket missiles to be used against us.   Common Wealth head
office is moving out too.   Wet day, not so warm.   I buy comb (am
always buying combs) for Phyllida to give her colleague who is leaving,

as welcome parting present): only one I can get is of poor quality
and costs 2/-. Try to buy teats for Hilary for baby's feeding-bottle
but can get none.

Tuesday, August 29, 1944

Much cooler. To press at 7.45. Find that Waterlows are making
plans for printing the paper in north of England if the rocket bombs
really come. No flying-bombs last night.

Wednesday, August 30, 1944

We have taken Rheims and Rouen, and, what is more important, the
Russians have taken Ploesti, the Rumanian oil centre.
        Try at least a dozen chemists for feeding-bottle teats, but can
get none, except from 2 chemists at St. John's Wood who let me have
one each. Miss Hall begins my winter coat. I have left with her
also maetrial for summer frocks, but they will have to be for next
year.

Thursday, August 31, 1944

Try more and more places for teats, and at length sit down and type
letter to Mr. Willink, Minister of Health, asking him what, as the
person responsible for the health of this country, he is going to do
about it. Add that I have looked in "Who's Who" and find he is the
father of a family, so that he will not need to be told that a three-
weeks-old baby will not wait for her food while Government departments
work their slow wills. After this do manage to buy one teat, for 1/-.
        To Abrahams to supper. We listen to news: we have reached
Amiens and Russians have taken Bucharest. Germans have occupied
Hungary.

Friday, September 1, 1945

Lunch with Miss Playle, her nephew (Sub-Lieutenant in Navy) who has
just come back from West Africa, and his fiancée to whom he hopes to
be married in a fortnight's time. He brought back the material for
her wedding-dress from W. Africa, so that the coupon difficulty need
not worry her.
        We have reached Verdun, Americans have reached Belgian frontier,
Canadians have captured Dieppe. Many flying-bomb sites captured.
(We had no raid last night). Germans have been shelling across
Straits of Dover - say they are bombing invasion ships, etc., but it
is more probable that they are letting off ammunition before it is all
captured. Goebbels has said, in article in "Das Reich" (so reports
say) that perhaps after all they will have to use their new secret
weapons for defence instead of offence; moreover that miracles must
not be expected of them and that although of course they will change
the course of the war, this may not be accomplished overnight. Find
this very encouraging.

Saturday, September 2, 1944

Very wet day. Want strap of my sandal stitched, and walk into
shoemaker's in little mews near Craven Hill Gardens which has notice
on window "No more work can be accepted this week", and another on
door "Sorry I can take no new customers". Undaunted, I go in, and
the man nails the strap for me then and there, for cost of 3d.
      In evening to "Cosi fan Tutte", by Sadlers Wells Company, at
Prince's Theatre, with Marjorie Wise and Bob. Marjorie W. knows
Margaret Ritchie, one of the leading ladies, and after the performance - a very good one - takes us round to her dressing-room. We
then - Bob feeling very extravagant - go to booked table at the
Majorca and eat minestrone soup, lobster and salad, and mixed fruit
salad, and coffee. This comes to about 7/1,7/-, and Bob does not
let us pay for our drinks - cocktails and cider cup. As he also
gave me gin and lime before the theatre - to which we rolled affluent-
ly in a taxi, being waved at hopefully by all the American soldiers
in London, who have no idea of going anywhere except in a cab - feel
I have had very alcoholic and enjoyable evening.

Sunday, September 3, 1944

Fifth anniversary of outbreak of war, and national day of prayer.
To All Saints, Margaret Street, with Bob, where we sing the complete
National Anthem, with that very unchristian verse saying "confound
their politics, frustrate their knavish tricks. The Rev. Prebendary
Ely does go so far, in his sermon, as to tell us that we all, indivi-
dually, and Britain and the British Empire, had our share of responsibility for bringing about the war: at which naval officer immediately in front of me fidgets rather uncomfortably.

Monday, September 4, 1944

Brussels and Antwerp taken by Allies. Mr. Browning, our chauffeur,
in state of un-chauffeur-ish excitement when he picks us up at printers at 5.45, saying we have taken Calais, Boulogne and Dunkirk.
This, however, merely a proof of the way people read the papers: the
news being quite unofficial and unconfirmed reports. S.O.S. from
Hilary. Stroud now has no "Cow and Gate" and the baby is thriving
on it. I am asked to send some quickly, which I do.

Tuesday, September 5, 1944

Extremely strenuous day at printers. At lunchtime Mr. Pringle still
writing his leader, and I am still writing captions for the spread.
In middle of afternoon I get phone message that there is rumour that
Germany has capitulated and that there are cheering crowds in West
End. Editor arrives about 3.50 with "Evening Standard". Stop Press
news gives in large type this tale, put out by British United Press,
they say from a Brussels broadcast. Home News Department of B.B.C.
inundated with telephone calls. As far as one can discover there is
no foundation for rumour, and when printers excitedly ask Editor

- 508 -

what he will do if Germans give in tonight, he growls "I shall do
nothing: I shall be very surprised". We do not finish until 8.30,
and I then come straight to Broadcasting House for fire-watching.
Have supper with Arnold, who is up for a meeting. We had no Alert
last night, but a few flying-bombs came over, some of I am told, at
Ware.

Wednesday, September 6, 1944

In lunch-hour buy gramophone record for John Lyne and Elizabeth Stut-
field who are getting married next Tuesday. A 12-inch record (6/-
pre-war, now 9/11) of a Mozart rondo played by a chamber orchestra
and pianish (Fischer). Almost everything I choose from catalogue is
out of stock, but I enjoy playing this record to myself, and Mozart's
"Petits Riens" which I do not buy. Ring up Leonard, who says of the
few flying bombs which came over the other morning early, one passed
over the bungalow and crashed in a field the other side of War. "I
thought the war was over until I heard this thing going past", he
said. This evening the Minister for War says the Home Guard need
not now do compulsory parades and drills, and thanks them for services
they have rendered, in last 4½ years, in freeing some units of army
for other duties. Fire-watching at night also to be discontinued in
some areas, but not in London.

Thursday, September 7, 1944

Daily Express gives figures of road accidents in Great Britain since
war began. They are over half a million, and more than the total of
killed during the war for the whole Empire. A large proportion are
children. Duncan Sandys gives facts about flying-bombs. Eighteen
months ago our agents reported experiments by Germans on new weapon.
Reconnaissance photographs showed strange structures at Peenemunde on
Baltic. It was decided they were for jet-propelled aircraft, but
whether for offence or for target practice was not known. In November
the Germans began structures along Channel coast, pointing in direction of England. 100 were sought out and destroyed. It took the
Germans until June to rebuild, on simplified scale; and they did not
begin to attack until after our invasion had started, so that some of
the guns and balloons which had been guarding embarkations ports
could then be used for defence of London. 80,000 launched and 8,000
people killed.

Friday, September 8, 1944

Home by 4.15 train. Only get seat by kindness of man who gives me
wooden folding stool to sit on in corridor. Martin and baby look
much grown and Hilary stronger. Weather has become cold.

Saturday, September 9, 1944

Brought Hilary 3 tins of "Cow and Gate" yesterday. Baby pretty good.
Crisp day with bright sunshine. With Martin and Tramp on common.

Sunday, September 10, 1944

Fine and warm.   Martin to chapel and afterwards for walk with me:
we collect conkers.   Daddy alarms us in afternoon by feeling ill,
rather, he says, as he did seven yearsago whenhe had his heart
attack.   Lies down, but insists on getting up again for tea, with
far too high a colour.
        I return to London in very crowded train, in which I am fortu-
nate to get a seat.   Paddington platform covered with perambulators
and bicycles,probably belonging to returning evanuees who cintinue
to come in spite of Government warnings that danger is not yet over.
Learn that guns from France have been audible in London all day:
people have been sitting on my balcony listening to them.   Greata
rings up from Worthing, where crowds are so tremendous she cannot get
back for her fire-wa ching this evening.

Monday, September 11, 1944

Buy new torch, 3/11, quite ordinary.   Fine but cold and I take to a
woollen jumper, but find that the printers have central heating on when
we go down there this afternoon.

Tuesday, September 12, 1944

Le Havre captured.   Americans invade Germany.   About 6.30 this
morning there is tremendous explosion at some distance.   No explanation of it given.   Woman in train to Stonebridge Park says it is "V.2"
(HItler's second secret weapon) and that there was an explosion of
like magnitude on Friday evening: that the official story is that a
gas-main burst at Chiswick - "but what hit the gas-main?" she asks in
sinister fashion.   And further conversation reveals that she has a
friend who is a Leading Fireman, who has had orders to stand by for
action because "V.2" is now being used; that "V.2" is a rocket-bomb
which flies up to the stratosphere and down again, making a large
crater but not causing as much blast horizontally as the flying-bombs,
This story somewhat corroborated by Tina who knows of someone who was
killed at Chiswick on Friday.   Still no official explanation, but
evacuees again warned to stay away from London.
        To press at 7.15 in spite of Miss P. allowing for extra "ad."
page and our having to put in an additional article while she is enjoying herself at her nephew's wedding.

Wednesday, September 13, 1944

To have new coat fitted.   Remark on leaving that I suppose it will
be impossible to get hat of same colour; and even if it is, it will
be hideous shape and cost about 8 guineas.   Whereupon Miss Hall
meditatively lays piece of material on my head and surveys it, and
says she thinks she can perhaps make me a hat of the odd bits left
over.   Which I gladly commission her to do.   In lunch-time ask the
watch-maker in South Moulton Street if he has been able to look at my
watch, and he says it needs a new hair-spring which cannot be obtained

until after the war, and the balance is anyway all wrong and asks
if someone hasattempted to clean it lately.   Alas, I paid 17/5 for
it to be cleaned, and it hasnever gone since.

    Miss Johnson (of the Censorship) says the Press are to say
nothing of "V.2" for five days, and that such as have been launched
have been sent off from Groeningen in Holland.   It is hoped that
we shall soon have captured the sites.   Meantime American troops
are fighting inside Germany, and the Rhineland is being subjected
to such severe attack that I imagine a few rocket-bombs are nothing
to it.   General Eisenhower has warned the people of Rhineland and
the Ruhr that extremely heavy air attacks are coming, and told them
to move away.   Poor creatures.

    My fountain-pen gives up - nib acts like a loose tooth and
waggles.   It is almost impossible to get a new one, but Bob lends
me a second one he has - a Swan - in fact says he will give it to
me - and Miss White tells me of an address in Leominster which may
possibly be able to supply one if her name is mentioned, so I write
off hopefully.

    Forgot to say last Friday that I had a reply from Minister of
Health about babies' teats.   He says the shortage is fully realised
and the Board of Trade and Rubber Control have arranged for rubber
to be released to make some, and that soon stocks should be available all over the country where there is now a shortage; but of
course this will all take time ... (Query: can one explain all this
to a hungry baby crying for food?)

Thursday, September 14, 1944

About 10 days ago people were talking as though thewar would last at
the mostonly a few moreweeks.   But Graham White gave it six months.
Now Bob says he knows from official documents that the Government is
planning to switch over its production from war to peace time neces-
sities at the end of this year (the date having been brought forward
six months from where it previously stood).   He has also seen evidence that the supply of teats for babies' bottles is to be hurried up.

    Letter from Mother: doctor says Daddy's indisposition is not heart
but an intestinal complaint that is about.   Martin also has had tummy-
ache.

    Keenes (next-door) leaving to run guest-house at Clevedon.

    Hear that last night there were 3 large explosions (but none
audible at our house).   Miss White, who comes up from Essex, says they
were near her, and is later rung up by doctor friend of hers at
Walthamstow who says a missile fell in middle of shopping centre,
causing many deaths and - since these new things penetrate deeply -
breaking the gas and water mains.

Friday, September 15, 1944

Another very loud distant bang about 4.30 a.m.   Bob says the trouble
about these new "rockets" is that we don't know yet what they are,
though Tina has it from a soldier that they don't contain as much
dynamite as the ordonary bomb, but a lot of compressed air.   Don't

know whether this is technically ridiculous.   In parts of Essex
large notices have been put up advising people to sleep in shelters
again.   Hear at lunch-time that this morning's bomb fell at Richmond
or thereabouts.   Chiswick - Walthamstow - Richmond - it sounds as if
the wretches are straddling their target.   Miss Playle comes in with
tale, alleged to be from someone at Ministry of Information, that the
whole thing is sabotage.   Miss White asks if sabatage is capable of
creating a crater 30 feet deep and 40 feet wide.
        Buy lining for my coat, 3½ yards at 2/11½ a yard, and 7 coupons.
        Am weighed: 8 stone 12 lb., more than I have ever been.
        Joyce comes for weekend.

Saturday, September 16, 1944

One loud bang during night and a few doodle-bugs in distance.
Beautiful crisp day.   Joyce buys Jaegar short coat in morning and I,
having tried in vain two days ago to book seats for "Richard III", go
down to New Theatre to get 2 of the seats only available on the day
of performance.   Join queue at 9.45 and after some minutes, woman I
am talking to ventures timidly to remark that I have attached myself
to front and not back of it.   Get almost last 2 seats at back of
upper circle (3/6) and we very much enjoy performace in evening at
6.15, with Laurence Olivier asRichard III and Ralph Richardson as
Richmond.   When latter speaks noble piece about foul and bloody
deeds of tyrants turning upon themselves, there is feeling of complete
approval throughout house, and voice in stalls says "Hear, hear!"
        Clocks go back 1 hour tonight.

Sunday, September 17, 1944

Again beautiful day.   J. and I to Unitarian service in morning.   In
afternoon we sit on my balcony when we hear someone else's wireless
talking of landings somewhere, and on switching on ourselves find that
we have made large parachute descents upon Holland, behind German
lines.   Blackberry-pickers returning from Bucks. say they saw great
numbers of trailer-planes going out.   This evening blackout restrictions are relaxed somewhat (but not in London), and we have just be-
for 9 p.m. a very brief alert and one doodle-bug, the engine of
which stops, with subsequent bang.

Monday, September 18, 1944

Am told that last evening's buzz-bomb fellin Regent's Park.   There
were no casualties but 2 swans took flight and haven't been seen
since.   Callfor fountain-pen which has been mended for cost of 2/-.
Base of nib was cracked, and nib is now very short but does write.
This evening have to report for fire watching at 6.45 instead of 9.15,
because of darker evenings.   In most part of England it has ceased
to be obligatory, but not here.
        Landing in Holland appears to be going well.   R.A.F. have bombed
very intensely large "gun-site" on coast of Holland which may be sourc

of our latest explosions. Last night dreamt I was in Berlin, the
streets of which, in the poorer quarters, were littered with people
dead or dying from starvation. I was weeping bitterly, and to the
reproaches of the people could only say, "I could no more help this
than you could help my being bombed with doodle-bugs".

Tuesday, September 19, 1944

Am told by naval officer that Germans have behaved very well in
Denmark - where of course they met no opposition to their invasion -
and, strangely, in the Channel Islands, where, he added, we should
find it difficult to live up to the same standard when we arrived
there. Later today Greta tells me of lecture she has just been to
by man who has come from Greece, and the frightful tales of reprisals
and savageries by the Italians as well as the Germans, chiefly to the
Jews.
        Raymond Bell home on leave from Alexandria after 2½ years. We
have supper at the Majorca at 8.45. Afterwards in the dimness of
Regent Street a drunken American soldier tries to attach himself to
us, but R. deals effectively with him. Piccadilly Circus swarms
~~holds/all~~ with half-drunk people and is most objectionable.
        Understand that there was Alert and three doodle-bugs over last
night, within earshot of here, but we were not roused from our sleep
as fire-watchers ought to have been. A p.c. from Joyce Green in
Church Hanborough says: "They say it's bad in London again", and
invites me for weekend, but have promised to go to Ware.

Wednesday, September 20, 1944

It occurs to me that it is 27 years ago to-day - 27 - since Florence
Franklin and I, in new gym slips, went timidly off down the hill to
the High School for the first time, while our two proud mothers stood
outside our gate and watched us go. Reflect on this as I sit in
National Gallery at concert of Brahms cello music (James Whitehead
and Kathleen long), and decide I am not greatly changed from myself
when 10 years old, not in essence that is: which leads me further
to philosophical reflection on what makes a personality and whether
it can ever in essence be changed: I don't think it can, but can
only be directed.
        In evening hear broadcast of first performance in England of
Bartók's Violin Concerto, played by Yehudi Menuhin. Am sufficiently
uninformed to find this very strange, and prefer him in Bach.
        To dentist who finds nothing wrong with me. Evening paper
says spectacular news may be expected within next 12 hours.

Thursday, September 21, 1944

Morning papers do not give any "spectacular" news, though British
troops have reached the Rhine and are obviously trying to cut off
the part of Holland not yet occupied, from the Germans.
        Hair washed. Coat and two dresses cleaned for cost of 17/6.

Friday, September 22, 1944

The airborne troops landed in Holland are in difficult position near
Arnhem.   If we could get through to them and take this place, Mr.
Pringle says, we should have cut in at back of Siegfried Line,
should be over the Rhine, and there would be no more rivers or hills
of any account between us and Berlin.   But meantime Germans are
fighting very hard.
        To Ware with Tina, who brings large tin of Gumption, 2/-, bottle
of liquid soap (2/3), a meat pie, ~~bottl~~ 4 sausage-rolls and a teacake
for toasting.   I bring ½ lb. tea (sent by Roy), tin of sardines
(bought with some of my holiday "points"), our margarine and sugar
and a little lard and tin of meat Miss Morrison lets us have.

Saturday, September 23, 1944

Great cleaning operation begins at the Ark.   We sweep down cobwebs
and scour bath, etc.   I gather 12 mushrooms and about 1 lb. blackberries.   About 2 p.m. we see lots of gliders being towed to south-
east: L. says not as many as last Monday when the whole of the sky
was filled with aircraft.   We heard 3 buzz-bombs explode last night,
and he thinks Hilary had better delay her return for a few weeks.

Sunday, September 24, 1944

More scouring.   I discover that "Gumption" cleans paint on doors,
but have only time to tackle two black surfaces.   A wild, ~~wet~~ wet
day.   To tea at the Mayes' on our way to station.   Pick up a lot
of "conkers" for Paul.
        News says supplies dropped yesterday to airborne troops at
Arnhem.   A few of our tanks have made contact with them, but position
still very serious.

Monday, September 25, 1944

Cold, blowy day.   Spending mood upon me.   Buy Shaw's new book
"Everybody's Political What's What?" (10/-) - probably for Leonard's
birthday.   Cleansing lotion, 7/6; 2 coat-hangers, 1/- each (reduced,
and I think on getting them hom, not much good); 3 yards white
ribbon, 2d. a yard.   Refuse bottle of scent, 13/6 for about 4 drops,
at which assistant is offended, since it is a great honour to be
offered any.

Tuesday, September 26, 1944

Finish at 6.15 at printers.   Suspect it is because now evenings are
darker, men find it pleasanter to make effort to end earlier.   Get
angry with Mr. James, and as result feel very worn out and tired.

Wednesday, September 27, 1944

Hear from Hilary that she has already got Shaw's book for Leonard, so

- 514 -

Tina offers to buy ½ my copy, since she was going to get one anyway.   Also Miss White's woman sends me fountain-pen, 12/10, but as
Bob has now given me his Swan, I sell it to Miss Playle.
        One bang last night.   News says our men withdrawing from Arn-
hem pocket.   But Germans say they have taken about 8,000 prisoners.

Thursday, September 28, 1944

The broadcasts last night, and the newspapers this morning, are full
of the "glorious heroism" of our men at Arnhem, who fought to the
very end.   I am glad that Mr. Pringle this morning voiced my own
views when he said he was disgusted at the maudlin sentimentality
launched on the public about these troops, in comparison with the
accounts of the German soldiers who held out in the Channel ports
until the very end, under the most terrible bombardments: they are
called "Nazi fanatics" and are sneered at.   I am thrown into despair at the stupidity of the human race, and can see no hope for it
at all.   To-day am reading Virginia Woolf's posthumour book of
essays.   In "Thoughts on Peace in an Air Raid" she says: "We must
help the young Englishmen to root out from themselves the love of
medals and decorations.   We must create more honourable activities
for those who try to conquer in themselves their fighting instinct,
their subconscious Hitlerism.   We must compensate the man for the
loss of his gun".
        Churchill makes war statement in House.
        Buy short jacket, rust colour to go with my viyella frock, 8
coupons (would have been 12 if it was lined),(98/2).

Friday, September 29, 1944

Churchill's remark in House, that war might possibly last into next
year, has thrown some people, who had high hopes of a quick end, into
gloom.   People are very easily inflated with optimism or crushed
with despair.   On the whole his speech was cheerful.
        To National Gallery concert with Gerald Abraham: Czech Trio
playing Smetana and Brahms.   Audience asked, if it can, to remain
behind while film is made for Czech Government.   We stay for about
15 minutes, while rest of audience goes, and while 1st movement of
Smetana is played again.   Are then requested to stay longer if
possible while close-ups are taken of audience; but feel we ought
to go.   All the same get back very late to office because we go to
Yarner's for coffee.

Saturday, September 30, 1944

Very pleasant day in Epping Forest with Miss White: pick blackberries and return with beautiful beech-leaves (told later that I
have broken law in removing them from what is a public Park).   One
would not imagine there was war anywhere, and yet this part has been
badly damaged by bombs, and in the forst itself there are occasional
rings of trees bare and blasted as if a witches' rite had been practised there and had killed every living thing.

Germans in Calais have asked for armistice while they send civilians out of the town. So an armistice has been granted until noon to-day, and 25,000 civilians who have been bombed so heavily the last few days, leave - or at any rate some of them. At noon the bombardment is resumed. It all seems so silly to me. Hitler has told the Germans to hold out to the last man.

Sunday, October 1, 1944

With Bob to a High Church service at which an ex-Bishop of Colombo preaches; and there is a procession with 5 banners round the church, but so much incense is used that I find it difficult to make out what they all represent. One, which I see says "Laus Deo", has long white, bridal-looking ribbons attached, and looks so much like a wedding car, think it must have something to do with the hymn we are singing, about the Church being espoused to Christ. Since the celebration is of the church's foundation day, think this most probable.
Calais has surrendered.
Fire-watching at night.

Monday, October 2, 1944

A quiet night: but it seems that now we are not to be wakened up even if there is an Alert, and even if there is an "imminent danger" signal; only if there is an "incident". I said to the fireman in charge last night, "Then what is the use of being here?" "Money for jam", he replied with a wide smile, handing me 4/6, our meal allowance, as if I enjoyed coming to earn it. Weather has become cold. We are fortunate in having heat we can turn on in the office, although strictly speaking it is illegal to use it. Greta is in a huge room with no heat and no proper glass in the windows, only flapping canvas, and is bitterly cold all day.
Go in lunch-hour to collect seats for Sadler's Wells ballet which I have booked by telephone, but there is crawling queue and I have to leave without them.

Tuesday, October 3, 1944

Again cold and stormy. To press about 7.15. Mr. Howes, the foreman, brings us some beautiful apples from his tree, something like a Cox's Orange Pippin and something like a Blenheim, but in any case the most delicious thing I have tasted for a long time.

Wednesday, October 4, 1944

Turn out every item in my wardrobe and look it over, and dust the cupboard thoroughly, because Greta says she has seen a moth in it, and one cannot afford to give clothes to the moth nowadays. Find no trace of any depredations - or of the moth.

By going to lunch very early, manage to collect my ballet tickets.   In evening Italian lesson, punctuated by discussion during which Tina gives opinion that Rousseau was quite justified in having 6 children and then leaving them if by acting in this un-social manner he was able to write "The Social Contract".

Loud distant explosion, unheralded, about 11 last night.

Thursday, October 5, 1944

Take ancient coat to be cleaned, in hope that later it may be turned into dress; also short jacket.   And my umbrella to be recovered - yesterday, in pouring rain, the wind nipped the old cover half away. Also take 2 pairs of shoes to be mended, and feel I am doing my best with my wardrobe even if I have no coupons for many.additions.

S.O.S. from Hilary for more teats.   A question has been asked in the House of Commons about supply, and more are to be made, but meantime those one can get are of such poor quality as to be of little use.   I may say that Bob was offered contraceptives by his hairdresser the other day - things made of rubber, of which there appears to be no shortage.   Upon saying "No thank-you, he had nouse for them", the hairdresser said in surprise, "Everyone uses them now, sir".   Yet the policy of the Government is supposed to be to encourage people to have children, not to help them to prevent it and then to make it difficult to feed them if they do get born. (N.B. Do not mean to imply that growth of population should be encouraged among the unmarried.)

Christine has been promoted to orange juice , which one can obtain, for infants, in bottles from the welfare clinics.

Friday, October 6, 1944

Send 3 teats to Hilary and manage to buy a fourth.   To National Gallery concert with Gerald Abraham, and to supper with Abrahams, where Mosco Carner also is.

Saturday, October 7, 1944

At noon to Dormans to see Joyce.   Because somebody's baby is arriving ahead of schedule and prospective aunt has had to go to aid of prospective mother, J. has to sleep at school, so I am alone in The Pines - in fact, alone in the wood, because the other houses, once occupied by soldiers, are now empty.   Do not mind once I am in bed, and in middle of night look out of window on to beautiful moonlit scene.   Two Alerts last evening.

Sunday, October 8, 1944

Pick blackberries, which I put in kettle J. has given me (given to her by soldiers as they abandoned camp), to take back to London. Also gather roses, Michaelmas daisies and bright-coloured leaves from garden of deserted mansion.   Listen to Yehudi Menuhin again playing Bartók's violin concerto, and also the Mendelssohn.

Monday, October 9, 1944

Get up early, have pleasant walk through morning, and travel back
to London with my roses and my kettle of blackberries.

Queen Wilhelmina of the Netherlands has given pathetic broadcast in which she says her country is being flooded and destroyed
(I am afraid by us as well as by the German, though she does not say
so) and in a fortnight the people willbe starving.

In evening to film of "Rebecca" with Greata: very well done.

Tuesday, October 10, 1944

Ought not to go to /s/l/o/d/r/a/m passionate melodramas - cannot sleep
after it.   At midnight drunken soldier - sounds like French
Canadian - rolls slowly down road singing at top of voice.   At 4 a.m.
a taxi with a cough in its exhaust goes slowly up and down looking
for its destination, and stopping and starting again with many jerks.
About 5 there is soundlike demented screech-owl, or it might have
been amorous cat with bass voice, or it might have been a soul in
agony.   I stand on balcony in moonlight, but can see nothing.
Later fall into uneasy slumber and to-day feelvery tired.

Allieshave encircled Aachen and now have delivered ulitmatum
that unless it surrenders it will be destroyed.

Telephone message from Leonard.   Hilary proposes to drive her
family back, unaided, on Saturday, and Tina and I have promised to
go and help prepare bungalow against their arrival.

Wednesday, October 11, 1944

To Miss Hall who has finished my new coat and hat, which are rather
good.   For making coat she charged £3.18.6, and for hat £2.5.0., and
altogether, with cost of materials I have therefore got a hat and
coat for £8.12., which for to-day is extremely cheat.

At 11.10 a bus takes females B.B.C. workers to hospital at
Kentish Town, where we submit to "mass radiography", which is to de-
tect any flaws in our lungs.   The taking part in the enterprise
was voluntary.   Women are provided with modest chest-coverings to
be photographed in.   The men are to go tomorrow.   Editor is cross
that he has agreed to it, and persuades Mr. Pringle, who had not put
his name down for the test, to go too.

Thursday, October 12, 1944

Tina and I take Miss Johnson to ballet, beautiful 9/- seats in
middle of 5th row of stalls.   "Patineurs" and "Giselle", which we
enjoy very much, especially the latter with Margot Fontaine.

Germans in Aachen have replied to American demand that they
should surrender, "Surely even the Americans do not expect us to
surrender without a fight a city in which 37" - or 27, I forget which
- /e/m/p/e/r/o/r/s German emperors were crowned".   Was very upset yesterday
to read that many citizens laid white sheets on roofs of their houses

vainly hoping I suppose, poor things, that somehow the bombs would not fall upon them.   The city is now reported to be burning.

Friday, October 13, 1944

To National Gallery concert with Gerald Abraham.   Beethoven sonata recital by Franz Osborn and Max Rostal.

Tina and I to Ware, to prepare house once more for H.'s coming. We have to walk to Ark through most frightful rain and wind.   Two hard-hearted men with empty cars pass us on our 2 dreary way without offering a lift.   L. passes on bicycle, and has lights on when we arrive, but the place looks very desolate.

Athens taken by British paratroops and Greek forces.

Saturday, October 14, 1944

Fortunately a warm, sunny, blowy day.   We scour, and wash innumerable towels and shirts, and when I can only find about 8 dirty pegs strewn about the garden, I commission L. to buy 3 dozen more for future use on the baby's nappies.   H. and family arrive at 5.10, after a good journey with the baby asleep all the time, and Martin very well-behaved.   Both children larger.   The tidy house becomes strewn with belongings in 5 minutes and Christine has immediately to be given food.   Air-raid warning last night but I heard no bombs.

Sunday, October 15, 1944

Am told there was warning last night and 3 distant bumps, but heard nothing.   H. nervous of the flying-bombs.   To-day all very busy. Martin, off with his father to works, since L. has to go in to see about a special order, says grandly: "We men are going out: you girls can get on with the work".   Take him mushrooming in afternoon. Find the line he now takes, perhaps because of baby's presence, is one of swashbuckling masculinity.   Has on pair of gumboots much too big for him, and new knickers very large to allow for growth, and, with striped jersey, swaggers about throwing and kicking a ball, like a little schoolboy.

Tina and I back to London by train which is $\frac{3}{4}$-hour late on what should be only a 1-hour journey.

Monday, October 16, 1944

Wet, wild day.   Three alerts in night, I am told.   Heard only one.

Tuesday, October 17, 1944

Wet and wild again.   Have to borrow umbrella from compositor at lunch-time and even then get feet and legs soaked.   The printers now have an enormous bell, looking like a bicycle bell about 18" across, on stairs.   If a rocket approaches, we are to have warning on this bell, given by a central control for the whole factory area, but it will not give us time to do more than fall to the ground.

Wednesday, October 18, 1944

Hair cut and washed. My usual assistant back, after an operation.
Come in in evening, wishing there would be something nice by post,
and find parcel of Blenheim apples from the Mearings. Italian
lesson in evening.

Thursday, October 19, 1944

To exhibition of Royal Oil Painters to see Graham's portrait: good.
And his daughter Betty's: bad. In evening to supper with Mary
Stiles in Willow Road, Hampstead. She has only half-windows, the
glass having been blown out for the third time only last week, when
a bomb fell on the heath off Well Walk. We eat spam and lettuce
and burnt mashed potatoes, and baked apples.
    Letter from Mother contains rather joyful sentence: (re.
Christine): "She is a dear, darling little thing, isn't she? But
oh, when she is bad she is horrid. I find "Jesus shall rein" to
"Duke Street" has a soothing effect".

Friday, October 20, 1944

To another concert of Beethoven sonatas by Franz Osborn and Max
Rostal. Pouring wet day, and I am rather late and have to sit in
outer chamber, where pattering of water on the corrugated iron which
has been put over broken glass skylights adds an obbligato.
    In evening to Ware.

Saturday, October 21, 1944

Hilary still nervous of flying-bombs. Gets up during each Alert.
Fortunately they are short. When a bomb falls, however distantly
- and sometimes out of human earshot - the partridges from the nearby fields all rise up with a whirring and chattering. But for a
thunderstorm, however noisy, they remain mute. Mushrooming with
Martin, but find only about 10.

Sunday, October 22, 1944

Leonard in bed with bad cold. Mushrooming again and this time get
1½ lb. in ¾-hour. In afternoon take baby out in pram. and Martin
collects acorns. He says, "Oh, come and see this little rumming-
commentary stream", and has a conversation with me beginning "What
is a Mother?", continuing to ask if I am too old to have a baby, and
ending by advising me to return to London to marry a husband and
have one as quickly as possible. He shone a torch through his
fingers under the bedclothes this morning, and said: "It's as red
as a blacksmith's shoe".
    Back to London, where find new short jacket I have bought, with
which am pleased.

Monday   23
~~Thursday~~, October ~~5~~, 1944

Raymond returns to live with us again for a time, while he takes a
course - or, he says "does odd jobs", at some outpost of the Admiralty's
at Wimbledon.

Tuesday, October 24, 1944

Nearly driven to despair at printers by indecision of Editor and Deputy
Editor, in this case over discussion, "What Shall We Do with Germany?",
our MS. of which was from a recording (corrected by broadcast version),
and through which, long after pages have officially been passed, they go
with fine-tooth comb, querying commas. Sentiments of most of people in
the discussion deplorable. Barbara Ward, of "The Economist" the only
one who is willing to concede that Germans ought to be treated like
human beings.

Wednesday, October 25, 1944

Letter from Mrs. Morris, who is in town attending to her furniture
(damaged when Maple's was bombed); and seeing an eye-specialist.
        To-day spend 16/6 on umbrella which has been recovered, 3/6 on
mended shoes (heels and toes only), 9/6 on cleaning of two jackets, 10/6
on books for Leonard's birthday (translations of poems from Chinese), besides 28/- on 4 theatre tickets for "No Medals" by Esther McCracken -
but 14/- of this I hope to have repaid. In evening to film with Greta.
We walk along beside park in moonlight. There is Alert and a buzz-bomb
suddenly whizzes overhead. In middle of film, full of picturesque
Hungarian peasant costumes, young Lieutenant in romantic uniform appears
on screen, and G. clutches me and remarks "You see that young man?
That's the one who climbed in through my bedroom window when I was in
France"-- an episode, she explains later, rather troublesome than romantic

Thursday, October 26, 1944

Buy hat in lunch-hour for only 22/6 - nowadays a most moderate price.
Several shown to me where 4 guineas. In afternoon go to private showing
by Ministry of Information, for B.B.C., of American film about T.V.A.
The Tennessee Valley is an area almost as large as Great Britain, where
rains and unwise farming washed away soil until farmers were ruined and
land worthless. By building series of great dams down river and its
tributaries, and by persuading farmers to try ploughing to contours of
country instead of straight, the whole valley has been made fertile.
Looking at the film, and listening to the commentary about everything
being done for the people as a whole, I thought of the poor Dutch, whose
dykes have been bombed, so that their country is flooded and made sterile
by salt water; of the Russians who had to blow up their great power
dam when the Germans were advancing; and of the Germans whose Rhine
dams we have bombed and burst.

Two other films were thrown in by the American Office of War
Information, for Overseas audiences, obviously designed to show that
the Americans, too, suffer inconvenience from the war - workers going
to new areas for ship-building, etc., have had to live in caravans.

Death announced of Princess Beatrice, aged 87, last surviving child
of Queen Victoria, and of the Archbishop of Canterbury, William Temple,
who was only 63, a good man with wide sympathies and interest, who will
be much missed.   A very great loss to the nation just when they need
leadership.

In evening Italian lesson with Miss Johnson, who produces Italian
illustrated papers, captured lately in Italy, one for July, 1940, with a
map of England and of the West of the Continent, showing all the air
bases from which Axis could attack us.   And diagram of barges coming
across the Channel, landing at Dover, Folkestone, and, surprisingly,
in Cornwall (from Brest)

Friday, October 27, 1944

In lunch-hour to National Gallery concert with Gerald Abraham.   Henry
Holst and Frank Merrick (violin and piano): Brahms, Sibelius, Schubert.
Fire-watching in evening.   Fireman says, after I have signed on, that I
may go to the pictures if I like, as there will be nothing for me to do,
and I am sorry to think of my curtailed weekend apparently for no purpose.

Saturday, October 28, 1944

Conversation between attendants in B.B.C. cloak-room this morning:
1st Woman: "I'd shoot the lot of them.   Didn't ought to live".
2nd Woman: "There was a piece in the paper the other day said, Would
             you bring up a German child with your own".
3rd Woman: "No, might contaminate them".
1st Woman: "No, shoot them all".

To Ware after lunch.   Take Martin and Christine for walk.   M.
nearly knocked down by bicyclist, which probably accounts for his being
sick at about 9 on bedroom floor.   It is arranged for H. to have him
in her room for night, and Leonard takes the baby.

Sunday, October 29, 1944

Christine quite good with her father.   Martin better to-day and we
manage to find a few mushrooms.   He called his mother his "Dear little
goilet-roll" one day this week, probably because she had said such
articles were precious and almost unobtainable nowadays.

Monday, October 30, 1944

In evening Bob finds note on his mantelpiece from Raymond, announcing that
he has been married at 12.30 today, to the girl we all knew he might
marry some day, but this was rather sudden.   They told nobody, not even
their parents.   Bob somewhat taken aback.   To film, "The Seventh Cross"
grim but good, with an anti-Vansittart bias.

Tuesday, October 31, 1944

At least three "rocket" explosions in night, and a warning and flying-bomb early this morning. More bangs during day. Prime Minister, in H. of C., says war may last into spring, or even into summer of next year, so I suppose we must be prepared for a winter of bombardment, we do not know on what scale.

Wednesday, November 1, 1944

In evening to extremely good production of "Arms and the Man". Come out in bright moonlight, which makes return home much more enjoyable than it would otherwise have been. A few unhearalded explisions today.

Thursday, November 2, 1944

Arnold in London: comes for night, bringing ½ lb. fea for Hilary.   In Manchester they do no fire-watching now.

Friday, November 3, 1944

Get book, 3/6, and send to Colin Hitchings, in hospital, on behalf of H. Also get 8/6 book for Fuchs boys. To Ware.

Saturday, November 4, 1944

Martin and I look hopefully for more mushrooms, but find only two rather dilapidated remains. He has a cold. In afternoon goes shopping by car with his father and mother, and I take Christine for long walk between russet hedges. High wind.

Sunday, November 5, 1944

Gale all day until late afternoon when it suddenly veers from west to north and becomes a gentle breeze - at same time rain begins to come down steadily. About 100 Flying Fortresses come very low over house. I am very depressed and irritable all day.

Monday, November 6, 1944

Rocket fell at Highgate yesterday afternoon, causing - on dit - 200 casualties. There has been another near Tina's mother's house at Dulwich, also causing immense damage. It is now said that there are two bombs in one, the first causing deep penetraiton, and the second, on top, causing surface blast. Still feel very depressed. Many people, including Editor, appear to be unwell.

Tuesday, November 7, 1944

Editor has succumbed to germ and does not come. Ribald comments, since B.B.C. Home Guard last night had a dinner to celebrate its disbanding.
    Death of Queen's father, Earl of Strathmore. Mr. Browning, once chauffeur to Duke and Duchess of York, says the earl was "a very eccentric man". Goes on to say that in Court circles there is jealousy and intrigue from smallest scullery maid to highest lady in waiting. Matters are

complicated because each new king brings his own retinue and domestic staff, and feelings between the old staff and the new run high. Also tells us how he used to go to Glamis Castle for the summer, and they used to have concerts, cinema entertainments and dances provided for them.

Wednesday, November 8, 1944

Roosevelt returned for 4th term as President of U.S. Germans have now put out announcement about "V2", their rocket bomb, which they say has been used (true), has been far more effective than the flying-bomb (so far untrue), and that Euston Station has been totally destroyed by one of these missiles (also untrue).

To Old Vic performance of "Peer Gynt" at New Theatre, which enjoy very much. Ralph Richardson as Peer Gynt.

Thursday, November 9, 1944

Hitler did not speak at annual Munich beer-cellar celebration this year. Miss P. asserts that he is dead - killed by the bomb attempt on his life lately. National Gallery Concert: Griller Quartet. Fire-watching at night.

Friday, November 10, 1944

Buy wool for socks for Daddy, 10 oz. for 2 pairs - 5 coupons. And 4 needles for Hilary which cost 1/11 - ivory. To Ware by early train.

Saturday, November 11, 1944

Hilary got up during Alert in night and saw flying bomb fall. Papers full of revelations, now released by censor, about rocket-bombs, which travel an incredible height into stratosphere and down again. The reason we hear 2 explosions is that one is the bomb going off and the other is the noise of its flight through the air catching up on it, since it travels faster than sound. So if one is to be killed, one hears nothing. H. and L. oversleep till 8.30, and H. drives her break-fastless husband to Hertford, where he arrives at 9.10, only 10 minutes late.

Sunday, November 12, 1944

Martin's good remarks this weekend: "When you see pictures in the pillow, is that dreaming?" "When I hold sticks in my hand for a long time, my fingers feel rusty". We go wooding, getting "kindling", with which word his is so delighted he keeps using it. "Here's another piece of kindling, Auntie", "This will be good for kindling, won't it?" etc. The baby likely to be as talkative as her brother: lies on my lap "talking" to me for 20 minutes at a time.

Train back to London very cold and very late. Trains in general better heated now, but the line to Hertford is the exception. Carriages also incredibly dirty. Two or three times lately I have been in L.P.T.B. buses with plain wooden seats - no upholstery. Thought these were old vehicles revived, but am told they are the new ones.

Monday, November 13, 1944

"Tirpitz", Germany's last big battleship, at last sunk by aircraft, in Tromsoe Fjord.

Tuesday, November 14, 1944

To press by 6.30. Churchill back from Paris, where he has been receiving acclamations from the people.

Wednesday, N6666666615, 1944

A most disturbed night. Two rockets and 4 buzz-bombs within earshot. Two alerts. And I have pains, owing, I think, to the accident of sitting in a room last night for five minutes with the gas-ring full on and unlit.
To-day call for my 2nd umbrella which has been recovered (17/6). In evening, Tina, Greta and I take Graham to "No Medals", by Esther McCracken. Amusing. G. takes us afterwards to dine at Monseigneur, where we have beautiful meal of pre-war character: very good sherry, soup, masses of chicken, baked apple and custard, and coffee. Most pleasant.

Thursday, November 16, 1944

Tina, Bob and I all receive airgraphs from John in Ceylon, written Nov.3 Very good going. Hestill seems very depressed. I write him an air-letter, and, discovering that one can send air-letters to South Africa, write them one also. Buy 25/- montaineering book for Daddy forChristmas. Also ½ lb. chocolates to put into box with ½ lb. from last month's ration, for Mother. Have managed too to get two beautiful stalls (at 15/6 each) for Hilary and Leonard for matinee of "Arms and the Man" on December 16, which I hope nothing will prevent their using.

Friday, November 17, 1944

To Stroud by 1.55. A couple in my carriage, the very first one in train, have taken 1st-class tickets but cannot get a 1st-class seat. And I am mean enough to stop the man from smoking in my non-smoker. Poured with rain all last night and the whole of to-day until I arrive, and is much warmer.

Saturday, November 18,1944

Pouring wet day again, and the milder weather makes everything within the house run with moisture too. There are lights in the streets in Stroud. Great smell of gas as I came past Wallbridge last evening, and to-day two people were taken to hospital unconscious, suffering from coal-gas poisoning, and a fire starts where the leak is. Repairs are put in hand at once. Mother hasbought beautiful Rodex coat, 17 guineas, coat and skirt, blouse and hat - in all nearly £30. After

which expenditure she says she felt so wicked that she was constrained
to put 10/- into the missionary box.

Sunday, November 19,1944

Again very mild and wet.   Have to stand allthe way back to London,
and train is 40 minutes late.   Arrive at 10, bearing, as well as my
weekend case, a large bag of apples with which Miss Morrison is very
delighted.

Monday, November 20, 1944

General offensive on western front; things seem to be going well.

Tuesday, November 21, 1944

Very tired after hard day.   Leader has to be scrapped, or almost entirely re-written, at 5.30.   This wouldn't have been so bad, but two
Editors exasperate me almost beyond belief by not getting on with what
is in front of them, but chatting comfortably about interesting irre-
levancies.
     Jack at Craven Hill Gardens for two nights, back from Mediterranean

Wednesday, November 22, 1944

Gather at breakfast that Jack arrived back and kissed all withing reach
including the embarrassed but pleased Miss Morrison.   In spite of
having taken part in the preliminary stages of several invasions (was
in Athens before British troops arrived), sweetly remembered to bring
hairpins and hairgrips for his female friends.
     Very loud report from rocket explosion last night.   This
evening have to fire-watch.   Very warm and damp.   Go for breath of
air to Oxford Circus and back at about 10 p.m., and find there is lighting now all the way down the street.   It is, as the Editor says, the
sort of illumination which in peace-time would lead one to ask "What's
gone wrong with the lighting", but never the less a great improvement
on nothing at all.

Thursday, November 23, 1944

Feel very headachy and faint when I get up in stuffy concert-hall, and
dress in stuffy bathroom with no air in it.   But recover after breakfast.
     To-day buy tools for Martin's Christmas present.   A box of toy
tools was 15/-, so I get from Woolworth's a lot of odd things, such as
a wooden mallet, spirit level, screw-driver, some screws, screw-gauge,
a door-hinge, as well as thing for filing off rust, for about 3/6.

Friday, November 24, 1944

To Ware with Tina.   Martin's latest good remark - putting a tea-cosy
on his head - "Aren't I a monologue!"

Saturday, November 25, 1944

Take Martin and baby wooding.   He asks resentfully, "Why do you have
to take thepram? Why can'twe go across the fields?"   Calor gas
gives out.   Also car won't start when H. tries to go into town, and
Mr. Chapman the greengrocer tows her up and down the road for ½-hour,
I suppose while customers are waiting for vegetables.

Sunday, November 26, 1944

Ware has its Home Guard "stand down". H. takes M. to see procession.
Air Force band plays with such vim that it bursts big bass drum.   H.
impressed with plainness and determination of our fellow citizens -
such a nasty-looking lot she never saw.   Isconvinced Germans wouldn't
have had a chance against them.   L., who has to conduct military
traffic, has squad of six to assist him.   They are marched up to him
and corporal says "Halt", when they all stop with such suddenness they
fall on top of one another.   Are told "Right turn!" and two turn left.
Then are told "Stand at ease", and the confusion is complete.

Monday, November 27, 1944

Feel very tired and dispirited.   Audrey Mearing calls to see us.
Has been having nervous trouble and is to be sent away from her aircraft factory, probably back to B.B.C.   She says 50% of girls cannot
stand the factory and have to leave.   And conditions are such that
very few of the people - only the violent ones, the Communists - have
the energyenergy for thinking at all after work.   There is complete
apathy.
        Rocket at New Cross fell, I am told, on a Woolworth's on Saturday
morning at about 11 when it was full of people.   There was also one
at the Holborn end of Chancery Lane.

Tuesday, November 28, 1944

News desperately depressing: There is mutiny in B.C., Canada, over
decision to send soldiers abroad.   Government in Rome has fallen.
There are riots in Belgium, and in Brussels streets barricades have
been put up.   Poles cannot agree on any government, and relations
between them and Russians are strained to breaking point.   All this
in the name of "liberation".   Secretly I feel these countries may not
feel more happy under us than they did under Germans.

Wednesday, November 29, 1944

In evening to Ruth's.   Go all the way to Crystal Palace terminus in
the dark and have to come back a tuppeny ride.   She says Young People's
Fellowship is having social there this evening.   Young P.F. seems
devoid of shyness.   Come into bedroom where I am reading bedtime story
to Diana, and take away the chairs.   Come into kitchen where I am
eating and take away the crockery.   David is now writing for all 3
Church of England newspapers, High, Low and Middle.   Hear 3 wumps
during evening and early night.

·

Thursday, November 30, 1944

Christopher Redman's 3rd birthday.   Buy several things for Martin's
Christmas stocking in lunch-hour - little magnet, 1/3, ~~some~~ a magnify-
ing glass, 2/6, stick of sealing wax, 6d.   Cannot anywhere buy pack
of ~~cards~~ which is what Aunt H. wants.

Friday, December 1, 1944

Wake with an appalling headache, and am sick.   Go back to bed, take
aspirin tablet, and fall into coma.   Get to office about 12.30.   In
evening catch 6.5 from Paddington to Handborough.   It does not leave
till 7.25, long after 6.35 for Cheltenham, into which, when it steams
in, we all climb hopefully, only to be ~~told~~ turned out again.   Taxi
which Joyce has cleverly managed to get to meet me waits an hour and
then has to go for another job.   But I am met by Doe Lockley (wife
ofR.M. Lockley , author of "Island Farm", etc.) who carries my bag all
the way on the 2-mile walk from station.   Am administered gin and
orange on arrival (synthetic orange, of course, and the gin has been
obtained because David's family has a wine business in the City.)

Saturday, December 2, 1944

Feel a little better after peaceful night.   Lie in bed in morning
and look at beautiful bare elm tree with sun shining on it and moon
coming through branches.   Give Roger a magnet, and at tea he stares
fixedly at me, and sais lovingly in explanation, "I'm looking at you
because you brought me that lifter".   David arrives from Oxford and
we go for walk in bright sunshine.   He tells me Doe Lockley's husband
told her he never wanted to see her again (this after about 15 years
of marriage), so she went to London and ~~hoped~~ helped run a club in
Hoxton.   Her husband now tells everyone that his wife has left him.
They have a daughter, Ann, aged 14.   Much entertained by David's
account of a fire at a shop which sold R.C. priests' robes.   After
the fire had been dealt with, one member of the Fire Service was playing poker ina a biretta, and there was a game of cricket with allthe
XI wearing this holy headgear.

Sunday, December 3, 1944

Continue to feelbetter.   Today is very wet.   Roger takes Doe and me
into wood and sturdily leads us in what we consider the wrong direction.   But the 4½-year-old turns out to be right.
        King takes salute at "Stand-down" of Home Guard, in Hyde Park.

Monday, December 4, 1944

Up at dawn and walk to station through breaking dawn and moonlight.
Kind Doe comes with me again.   Train ½-hour late at Paddington.
Colder, and beautiful day of sunshine.   Everyone at office seems very
tired.
        Martial law in Athens.   Raymond has been demobilised from Navy
and restored to his job in Treasury.

Tuesday, December 5, 1944

Americans have bombed Berlin in daylight and had battle over city.

To press at 6.50 after busy day. Mr. Howes, the foreman, holds forth to me on trouble there now is in so-called "liberated" countries, and on attitude of our Government, which he, a skilled workman, can see is not good. He says "These countries may have moved to the Left since the war began, and who are we to say that this is not as it should be".

Wednesday, December 6, 1944

State of Civil War in Greece, with British troops involved. America has protested at our behaviour both in Italy and in Greece, saying that we have interfered in what was purely a domestic affair and ought not to have influenced their choice of governments.

To exhibition of wonderful paintings by Epstein at Leicester Galleries - flower studies and studies of Epping Forest, a room of each. Very colourful. All paintings, at 30 guineas each, sold on opening day of show. So some people stillhave some money.

In evening Bayswater Road has lights down its whole length: not very bright lights, it is true, but appearance of road is so changed that I think I have got off bus at wrong stop and dither to and fro before I am sure I am at the right place.

Thursday, December 7, 1944

Sound of rocket about 11 last night. Did not think it was very close, in spite of long rumber afterwards. But this morning find all Self-ridge's windows are blown out, and most of glass at that end of Oxford Street. The rocket fell in Duke Street.

At lunch-time buy 2 dozen rough wooden blocks, the size of child-ren's building blocks, un-sandpapered, from little wood shop in D'Arbley Street off Berwick Street. 1½d. each.

This morning's paper says 50 million people in Germany are homeless because of our bombing. But in post-war plans, when everyone says savagely that the Germans must be set to repair and rebuild the damage done in this and other countries, no mention is ever made of damage we have done to them or how it is to be repaired.

Write following poem:-

How can I adequately write
The piling-up of such delight?
An attic-window looking where
The church's steeple strikes the air;
The full-moon shining where I lie -
Shining from out a quiet sky;
And spread about my country bed
Apples of gold, apples of red.

The naked elm-tree meets the sun
Returning when the night is done.
(How can I adequately write
The piling-up of such delight?)

> The sun upon her branches glowed
> But through the boughs the full-moon showed.
> And I could see it from my bed
> While all around me there were spread
> Apples of gold, apples of red.

In evening to "The Scandal at Barchester", play from Trollope's "Barchester Towers" - this, and dinner, being our wedding present to Raymond and his wife. Very pleasant time, dinner at the Majorca.

Friday, December 8, 1944

To Ware by early train: miss Leonard, who looks for me in rain, and have to walk to bungalow with very heavy case containing Christmas presents (1st instalment).

Saturday, December 9, 1944

Beautiful day. German prisoners of war working in fields other side of road. "Working" may not be right word. They take 20-30 minutes to assemble from their lorry when they arrive, and ½ hour later re-assemble from distant corners of field to make coffee, for which they come to house for water - one Englishman to ask, and one German to carry Fair-haired youngsters, most of the. H. says that any morning when she is looking out of window she can see rows of Germans relieving themselves by the hedge. Martin is intrigued beyond words to discover that they speak another language. He asks at intervals, "Do they know chair?" - meaning, have they got a word for it; "Do they know table", etc.

Sunday, December 10, 1944

Very wet again. Forget to bring sandwiches for my supper and go to bed a little empty. Alert as I am leaving, before 7 p.m., He and Hilary sees 3 fly-bombs fall in distance. We also have noise of rocket during day, but not very close.

Monday, December 11, 1944

Very busy. Work till 7.30 in anticipation of Christmas.

Tuesday, December 12, 1944

To press about 6.45, after which go to King's Theatre, Hammersmith, with Doris Crofts, to see Sadler's Wells ballet. Arrive in first interval, and see "Nocturne" and "A Miracle in the Gorbals" (new". Enjoy both, especially latter. Alert during performace. We feed at Greek Restaurant in Queen's Road, which even nowadays is open till midnight. At 11 p.m. a very loud rocket explosion makes us all jump.
    Hilary has had several application for her jodhpurs (which I advertised for her in "Horse and Hound")- three actually enclosing cheques; but no offers of child's bicycle in exchange, which advertisement mentioned she wanted.

Wednesday, December 13, 1944

Am told last night's rocket was in Lancaster Road, about 1½ miles away. Molly Evans was within ¾ mile of it, and when explosion was over, masonry and glass fell all round her.

Today go into Selfridges, where assistants are wearing coats, because the shop has no heating and the windows have no glass. Very foggy. Editor, returning from funeral of Managing Director of Waterlow's, reports that in the country there is crisp, bright sunshine.

Thursday, December 14, 1944

Hair washed. Fog has cleared. Rocket explosion about 5 this afternoon. Very tired after trying day and much packing of Christmas parcels. Ring Hilary, who continues to have cheques sent her for jodhpurs. Has also had letter from someone in Devon saying writer has child's bicycle for sale, suitable for child 4 - 7 years, £6, no offers. She has sent off money, which apparently now flows about the country with the greatest ease, since goods are so much more valuable.

Friday, December 15, 1944

Tina and I to Ware. Feel very tired and depressed. Too much rushing about getting presents. Tina has ½-bottle of gin for Christmas, most triumphant achievement.

Saturday, December 16, 1944

Hilary off early by 10.10 train to London, there to meet Leonard for lunch and both to go to matinee of "Arms and the Man" - my Christmas present. Goes off in high spirits leaving Tina and me to cope. I bath baby with much success. Children are very good until after tea when Christine bellows and Martin, not to be outdone, just shouts. I thing "What _are_ a few rockets, after all". H. and L. return after enjoyable time. Almost missed first act of play because, without a qualm, I told them matinee would begin at 2.30, whereas it began at 2, and it was only by great good fortune that they arrive at 2.5, Hilary having miraculously persuaded a taxi-driver to take them there from the Majorca where they fed. Martin lies awake to hear them come in and greets them with broad smiles. Tina and they have great argument on Greece in evening.

Sunday, December 17, 1944

Rocket as I begin to take Martin and Christine for walk. We gather fire-wood.

Monday, December 18, 1944

To press today instead of tomorrow, because of approach of Christmas. Receive pair fully-fashioned stockings from Marjorie Fuchs, and gift token for 7/6 from Aunt N.

- 531 -

Tuesday, December 19, 1944

Get 2 utility dresses for Christine, 4/5 each.   Receive box of hand-
kerchiefs from Aunt H.
        Germans have launched big offensive and have driven good many
miles into Belgium and Luxembourg.   Luftwaffe has appeared in more
strength than for some time.   Our H.Q. have clamped down on news, but
no one pretends that it is a small matter.   It may be we were all too
optimistic about end of war.
        Joyce's 40th birthday.

Wednesday, December 20, 1944

Germans 20miles into Belgium.   Fog all day.   Hilary rings up saying
Leonard has been givena turkey, and a bottle of whiskey.   It is impossible to convey greatness of this news.   Have started knitting pair
socks for Daddy (just finished Martin's 3rd vest), since those one can
buy are hardly more than anklets.

Thursday, December 21 - forgot to make any entry.

Friday, December 22, 1944

Leave work at lunch-time - that is, would have, but office boy does not
return with my train tickets till 1.20.   I then find have lost B.B.C.
pass, and to get lunch at B.House have to sign chit at entrance saying
I am seeing restaurant cashire.   Stamp with impatience, and after waiting in queue in canteen, overturn whole of my lunch on floor.   Manage
nevertheless to meet Tina at Liverpool Street in time to catch 2.20.
Very crowded.   Hilary meets us at station and car returns packed with
4 adults and 2 children.

Saturday, December 23, 1944

Martin and I look for holly.   Find none with berries, but gethips and
haws to make up for it.   In afternoon Tina and I decorate tree, under
Martin's instructions, while L. and H. go shopping.   In evening all
wrap up parcels and fill row of stockings which are slung hung in
kitchen - we have decided to make tomorrow our Christmas Day, or Tina
and I will have to leave almost before festivities have begun.   Three
nurses come carol-singing, with a collection box that is a little man
on whose hand one puts a coin, presses a handle, and he then ingeniously
throws coin into his mouth.

Sunday, December 24, 1944

Our Christmas Day, heralded by Leonard with cup of tea, and noise of
rocket.   There is joyful shout up stairs from Martin, "Mamma, it is
full", and all stockings are brought in and opened on Tina's and my beds
Presents under Christmas tree afterwards.   Martin has beautiful little
chair and table, oak, made by carpenter at L.'s works.   But he is most
entranced by tools I give him.   He and I go wooding, and he slips down
muddy bank into stream, so we have to return through bright cold morning

and get another coat and change his trousers.   Go out again and return
to find turkey cooked and dinner laid.   After all is cleared, Leonard
and Hilary go for short walk to callfor duck we had ordered from
Josephine's mother, which Pat's mother is now going to have.   M. is
making mud pies in garden.   I suddenly become aware that he is there
no longer.   Decide he has gone to join Pat and put on coat to make
sure.   On way, glance at baby, in her pram in porch, and find her
wallowing in sick.   Snatch her up and have to strip and wash her.
Am then alarmed by return of H. and L. who have just seen Pat's mother
and report M. not there.   Leave baby to Tina and we allgo out to look
for him.   Go down by stream where we were this morning, calling all
the time, but there is no sign or sound.   By 5.30, when it is getting
very misty and dark, we are stillsearhhing.   I return to house where
baby is yelling screaming, and hold her while Tina makes her food.
In midst of this, am extremely relieved to see his father coming,
carrying him in.   He had tried to follow his father and mother, and
while they were in Josephine's house, must have passed it.   Went on
to Wareside, at least 1½ miles, where two little boys, he says, told
him it was getting dark and he'd better go home.   Was found by
visitor of Mrs. Parrish's sitting on bank, saying "I know I mustn't
cry, but I can't help it!"   He begins to cry again on coming in, and
whenI lay down baby to comfort him, she yells too.   Hilary still out
looking for him but returns in about 10 minutes, having abandoned her
bicycle in the mud of a field.   Leonard then has to go out and retrieve bicycle.   Martin now begins to be full of conceit and vainglory at thought of everybody scouring countryside for him.   Goes off
to bed at last saying "Father Christmas brought me some tools and
everything I wanted".   We are all quite exhausted in evening.

Monday, December 25, 1944

Everything covered with hoar frost which remains all day, and in afternoon mist comes down.   After large lunch of cold turkey (it really
was a magnificent bird), and after enormous efforts, we all, except
Tina, and plus Pat, go for walk, during which baby is again sick all
over pram, and goes placidly to sleep in middle of it looking picture
of healthy contentment.   Pat comes to tea, and she and Martin have
pink ribbons going from their plates to a treasure which each finds.

Tuesday, December 26, 1944

Rise early, and, after awful ¼-hour when ignition key of car cannot be
found, are driven thro' crisp, white morning to station by Leonard.
Train is cancelled and we wait an hour and freeze in unheated waiting-
room, then for 15 minutes sit in Guard's room where there is a stove.
Do not arrive at office, after journey in unheated train, till 12
o'clock.   Work till 1.30, then lunch and return home.
        Mr. Churchill and Mr. Eden in Athens.   Bright weather has
helped our flying forces, who seem to have stayed German advance somewhat.   (N.B.   Our 'crisp, white morning' turned to horrid grey dank
fog when we got near London.)

Wednesday, December 27, 1944

To press all day.   In morning find Bakerloo tube at Paddington closed: there was a fire there on Saturday or Sunday, and damage has not yet been repaired.   Still bitterly cold and hoar-frost unmelted. Telegram to say Mother's visit to Hilary postponed because of weather.

Thursday, December 28¼, 1944

Not quite so bitterly cold.   Have headache all day.

Friday, December 29, 1944

Very foggy and raw.   Hoar frost still unmelted, andbeginning to be covered with London grime.   Go to catch 5.6 train for Ware.   It is cancelled.   Get a so-called 5.26, which leaves at 6 and gets to Ware at 7.50.   H. says they have had crisp clear days here all the week. Martin's bicycle has come, a strong little machine, though shabby.

Saturday, December 30, 1944

Hilary and Martin to children's party at Fanham's Hall, all among the County.   H. says her child behaved as well as, and was quite as good looking as, the elites' offspring, and as for the babies, Christine is much better looking.   There is Christmas tree as high as the room, with coloured lights, and Martin has from it a money-box, a spinning top, a colouring book with 3 pencils in loops attached, and a wooden pistol.   We think he was invited by an amused County, because he happened in to Mrs. Parrish's drawing-room when some elegant ladies were present, and, on being asked how his little sister was getting on, wagged his head solemnly and replied: "When she was on the nipple she scweamed and scweamed, but now she's on the bottle she's all wight. But of course it was much better when you could just clap her onthe nipple".   Which reduced elegant party to state of hysteria.
    Leonard joyfully takes M's bicycle to pieces and makes adjustments

Sunday, December 31, 1944

Feel rather unwell but better as the day goes on.   Still frosty but not quite so cold.   L. and M. spend rapturous morning making altera-tions to bicycle, adding wooden blocks to pedals to make it easier for M. to reach them.   In afternoon I take him up and down the road, hold-ing the saddle.   Very exhausting.
    King George of Greece has appointed Archbishop of Athens tobe Regent - firstfruits of Churchill's and Eden's visit.

Monday, New Year's Day, 1945

Did not see the New Year in and have no expectations from it.   Mr. Nicolls has C.B.E. in today's honours.   2 rockets last night, one very loud.

Tuesday, January 2, 1945

More rockets last night.   To press about 7.50.   Very tired.

Wednesday, January 3, 1945

Loud rocket at breakfast-time.   Hear later it fell on Chelsea
Hospital (where the Pensioners live.)   2 Alerts during evening.
        Call for 2 pairs of gloves which have been cleaned most beauti-
fully, for cost (for 2) of 2/9.   Also have fitting with Miss Hall,
who has made me handbag out of snippets left from my coat, for which
she charges £1.16.   She has finished frock made out of summer one of
Mother's, which she gave me, for which Miss Hall charges £4.4.0.

Thursday, January 4, 1945

Feel very depressed with new year already, but perhaps this is not
giving it a fair chance.   Mother and Hilary both unwell.   Rather
upset by phone-call from H. who says they have had a good many bangs
near them this last week, one very loud one just as Martin was going
to bed last night. He had never been frightened before, but when two
more went off in night, woke up screaming.   Asks searching questions
about reason for explosions, which Hilary is loath to answer in full.
One rocket here last night, and several during day - last night's
said to be at Muswell Hill.

Friday, January 5, 1945

Buy 4/- tin Ovaltine for Hilary - she can only rarely get it in Ware.
Also Miss P. gives me 2 boxes of matches for her, which I take.

Saturday, January 6, 1945

Several rocket explosions, one while I am wooding in fields with
Martin.   He does not seem frightened in daylight.   First there is
the double explosion, very loud and unheralded.   Then long low rumbling, then for 15 seconds sound of an express train rushing through
the air, which is noise of rocket's flight catching up with it.

Sunday, January 7, 1945

Christine holds long and rather grumbling conversation with me all
through her 2 p.m. feed, till at last I say to H., "Did you put the
sugar in this feed?", and she says, "Oh no, I forgot it".   So sugar
is added, and the 5-months-old then takes it contentedly.

Monday, January 8, 1945

A good many rockets during day, and in evening Mary Moore arrives:
was travelling from Hereford to Amersham, but at Baker Street is told
bomb on line has put railway to Bucks. temporarily out of action.
Stays for night.   Spend evening composing, with Tina's help, letter
from Daddy to Minister of Labour, asking about Leslie's position, and
whether it is possible that he might be released to take charge of

shop, since Fire Service is closing down, he is C3, and Daddy, who is nearly 69, feels he cannot carry on any longer.

Tuesday, January 9, 1945

Arrive at printers in snowstorm: more snow at lunch-time. No rockets last night or today.

Have just read article which appeared recently in "The Economist" and which yesterday's "Telegraph" reprinted. It comments very un-favourably on American's criticisms of this country. Americans are furious about it, and incapable of understanding how anyone - especial-ly a paper which is of considerable standing and has been very pro-American in sympathies - should criticise them. Everyone I have spoken to is highly delighted that a few home truths have at last been spoken, and that by a reputable authority.

Finish one of Daddy's socks.

Wednesday, January 10, 1945

No rockets again last night. More snow. Streets very slippery. Walk through Park in morning; the trees very beautiful with the black bareboughs lined with white. To National Gallery concert. Mozart quartet in F major and quintet in C major. Enjoyable, but Gallery unheated and draughty. Hear one rocket during day.

· In evening listen to play by Louis MacNeice about the Roman Saturnalia, their mid-winter festival (pre-Christian Christmas): world then in as bad as mess as it is now - perhaps we are due for another Messiah? The Saturnalia was taking place on the night of Christ's birth.

Thursday, January 11, 1945

Meet 12.45 at Paddington - it is 32 minutes late. Take Mother by taxi to Liverpool Street and put her on 1.50 for Ware. Still very snowy. Daddy returns draft of letter to Mr. Bevin for me to make fair copy. Feel very depressed and tired. Cannot see the use of myself. Everyone very war-weary. Judging by broadcasts, other countries are feelingthe same. Was depressed too by reading old volume of Listener - 1934 - article by William Plomer on the Japanese, among whom he lived and whom he liked. Now, of course, everyone thinks they are all devils. When I ventured one evening to remark that my brother had been to Japan and found the people very pleasant, I was regarded, I felt, as an outcast for having such misguided rela-tions. Letter from Joyce, whose coalman told her that there were 40 rockets in an hour round Westminster way. This fortunately not so far true. Nine in 24 hours is as much asI have heard, and they were not all in one district by any means.

Friday, January 12, 1945

Thaw has set in, but there is bleak raw wind which blows my hat into mud in Oxford Street. Am extremely depressed: nothing to do at the office. Wish I could think of any sphere in which I could be useful. Buy breakfast cup, 11d. to replace H.'s breakage last week. Also wax tapers from Woolworth's, 4 a penny. Then spend ¼ lb. of my sweet ration on some liquorice allsorts (5d.) which I guzzle.

     To Ware. L. has made beautiful little toboggan for Martin, but as soon as it was finished snow melted.

     Fighting in Athens is to stop. Settlement seems probable.

Saturday, January 13, 1945

Altho' snow has gone, very raw and cold. Out wooding with Martin, and in afternoon with him and baby. Mother quite enraptured with Christine. Several rockets during day.

Sunday, January 14, 1945

More rockets, one 4 milesaway. Still cold but some sunshine. Still tired and depressed. Can see no point in existence. Daddy arrives from Stroud, after slow journey. Full of cheerfulness as usual, seeing lots of point in existence, and with enormous bag containing inter alia some eggs and pot of cream. Chicken which Phyllida posted from Fairford last Wednesday has not yet arrived. Back toLondon in evening

Monday, January 15, 1945

Tired and irritable all day, and cross to the office on telephone when I speak to them from printers.

Tuesday, January 16, 1945

Russians have begun new big offensive.

Wednesday, January 16, 1945

To Miss Hall, who is making me 2 summer dresses out of 2 blue linen sheets, has altered old coat, and offers to make hat. At lunchtime to beautiful concert at National Gallery: Boyd Neel Orchestra playing Symphony by   , Soliloquy for string orchestra, 2 horns and cello, by Edmund Rubbra, and piano concerto (Myra Hess), No.5 (Bach). Very good. Peter among orchestra. Officer next to me (not young, and next rank above major) says tohis lady friend "Do you like your hand held during playing?" To which she says "I really don't mind". So he does it. After this, to Leicester Galleries, exhibition of pictures by John Piper, of Renishaw Hall, home of Sir Osbert Sitwell, commissioned by Sir O. as illustrations to his autobiography, which is to come out in 4 vols. at 15/- each, the first in March. Wildly put my name down on subscription list for this publication.

Thursday, January 18, 1945

Cold, and very high wind.   Meet parents for lunch at Paddington
Hotel and see them on to not-too-crowded train for Stroud.   Molly
Evans has to go on sick leave again: her pulse is 140 all the time
- a war casualty!

Friday, January 19, 1945

To Ware.   Leonard yesterday had narrow escape.   Was driving car
on main road where army vehicles were parked in left-hand outer
traffic-lane, and met car with glaring headlights now allowed which
so blinded him he went into traffic 'roundabout' without seeing it.
Man advises him not to report accident, since place is "death-trap"
and people run into concrete pillars there every night.   Seems to me
this is better argument for reporting existence of death-trap; but
he follows advice, and crawls home very slowly and very late, arriving about 1.30 very chilled.

Saturday, January 20, 1945

Take Christine out in pram in snowstorm whichshe appears to enjoy.
Snow shows no sigh of thawing.

Sunday, January 21, 1945

Take Martin toboganning.   Beautiful day - bright sunshine on unmelt-
ing snow: more like Switzerland than England.   Moonlit walk over
snow to station at night; most beautiful.   A few droning aeroplanes
to keep one reminded of things earthly.

Monday, January 22, 1945

One heavy bang during day.   Feel a little more cheerful, perhaps
after refreshing weekend.   Snow still lying.

Tuesday, January 23, 1945

Still snowing.   American soldier aged 22, and Welsh girl aged 18
both condemned to death for murder of taximan, whom they appear to
have shot in cold blood in order to rob him - they got £4.   After
verdict delivered, Judge reveals that they have been on several raids
of the same kind already, attacking people viciously without thought
of whether they took life or not.   Feel rather sick at thought of
girl of 18 being hanged

Wednesday, January 24, 1945

With Miss White to British Drama Leage exhibition at Burlington House.
Far more interesting than photographs of old theatres, plans for new
theatres and designs for national theatres - or so I thought - were the
"penny plain and twopence coloured " sheets of theatrical characters

made famous by Robert Louis Stevenson.

Thursday, January 25, 1945

Great Russian offensive doing well.   To National Gallery.   Piano
and violin: Beethoven, Bach, Mozart.   Intensely cold.

Friday, January 26, 1945

With Greta at lunch-time to mysterious exhibition in Oxford Street
with which both had been privately intrigued for months: "bearded
woman", "sea monster", etc.   We spend 6d. each and are most disappointed to find only photographs of these interesting phenomenon.
     To Ware.   Snow still lying on ground as it has for past week.
Intensely cold.   Minister of Fuel and Power tells us we must economise, and to that end switches off the electricity in some neighbour-
hoods just whenpeople are cooking their breakfasts.   We are warned
of a serious potato shortage - said to be because of lack of labour
for lifting, and not for lack of potatoes - and told they may be
rationed.

Saturday, January 27, 1945

Not quite so bitterly cold.   Loud rocket when I am out in afternoon
with Martin, toboggan, Pat, Christine in perambulator, and Tramp.
Mrs. Parrish's water-pumping apparatus gives out: she asks if she
can come for bathtomorrow.   H. consents, though hot-water position
in bungalow is precarious and there is great difficulty in getting
Christine's washing dry.

Sunday, January 28, 1945

Leonard triumphantly mends Mrs. Parrish's pumping engine, which an
expert yesterday failed to do any good with.   Sunshine on snow (a
little more fell last night).   Leonard and I take Martin tobogganning.

Monday, January 29, 1945

Bitterly cold morning, but a little milder in evening, and at about
10 o'clock more snow falls.   Deliveries of fuel are held up, and in
Harrow Road see women struggling with little sacks of coal which they
have fetched themselves, sometimes in their arms, sometimes in perambulators.   Told they are allowed to fetch ½ cwt. each.
     I go to bank and enquire whether B.B.C. haspaid in our monthly
cheques yet.   Onbeing told "Not till tomorrow", I say, "I think I'd
better have something transferred from my deposit to my current account".   "Oh no!" says the assistant, "that doesn't matter".   "But
I'm already overdrawn", I say.   She goes away, comes back and says
"That's all right".   So though I am already overdrawn by £7 (not yet
having got over the expense of Christmas presents), I am trustingly
given another £3.

Tuesday, January 30, 1945

Restrictions announced on coal to be supplied to householders. There are 3 - 4 inches of snow on ground, but on my way to printers it begins to rain. Held up for 20 minutes or more at Queen's Park. Mr. Pringle so held up he does not arrive until lunch-time.

Wednesday, January 31, 1945

Snow almost gone. Much milder. Leaking pipes everywhere. In Lewis's in Oxford Street water has come through to ground floor. Hear also that there was flood in Selfridge's. In latter shop I examine material which assistant tells me in succession (having doubts at first as to my wants) is winter-weight, spring-weight, and summer-weight. In evening to rather melodramatic film called "Dark Waters", with Greta.
    Russians still advancing in Germany, and there have been no rockets for 48 hours.

Thursday, February 1, 1945

Very loud rocket at 4 a;m. and several during day. Amso depressed I could die. Mother reports burst pipes and floods.

Friday, February 2, 1945

Great change in temperature - now very mild. To Ware with Tina. Still extremely depressed.

Saturday, February 3, 1945

Very mild, spring-likeday. Martin and I get 4 basketsful of wood , and in afternoon I get another one while I take Christine in perambulator. Ralph, Leonard's brother, an army driver, for tea. He has been driving one of the amphibious vehicles called "Ducks", which can do about 50 m.p.h. on land and 8 p.h. in water. He drove out 6 miles into Channel one pitch-black night. Navigator thentold him to switch on all his lights and describe a circle. They then went a little further to left, put on lights and described another circle. This time they got signal from ship, which they approached. Stretcher with sick seaman was then lowered on to "duck", which drove him over water and land to hospital. Ralph brings edition of "Star" with him - our only source of news, since wireless batteries have given out - which reports enormous raid on Berlin, which, it says blatantly in large headlines, is packed with refugees. Of course it's all right when our side does it! ...

Sunday, February 4, 1945

A number of rocket explosions in distance. Martin draws a car. When I suggest putting in a door, he gives me a most severe look and says "There isn't any door: you just pop out through a hole in the roof". Christine absolutely refuses to open her mouth to admit a spoonful of sieved vegetables which the clinic says she ought now to take.

Monday, February 5, 1945

Mild, spring-like day. My stomach upset - a common weakness just now. Mr. Pringle's 4-year-old son is very sick and can keep down no food.

Tuesday, February 6, 1945

Most hectic day at printers. Churchill, Roosevelt and Stalin holding conference in some place not made known to public.

Wednesday, February 7, 1945

Audrey Mearing, whose health has brokendown in her aircraft factory, comes up for interview and rejoins Corporation in Radio Times. Has to begin on Monday, but has nowhere to stay, so I ask Miss Morrison if she can put her up for a week, to which she agrees.

Buy ream of typing paper (which am now using). Have been trying to get some for days. Assistant says it is 6/9, then an overseer comes up, remarks that he is testing it for me by taking out one of my beautiful sheets, crumpling it up in his hand and throwing it away, and then says the price is 7/6.

To Annie McCall nursing home to see Ruth (in Stockwell), who had a son last Saturday week. She had one hour's labour and he was 6 lb. Is called Richard Temple - Temple after late Archbishop. House in which she is lying is only one in road with its windows complete.

Thursday, February 8, 1945

Offensive has started on western front and so far seems to be going well. To National Gallery concert with Audrey Mearing and Gerald Abraham: trios (clarinet, cello and piano) by Brahms and Beethoven, and piano sonata by Schubert. Very pleasant. In evening to Sur-Optimists' Club, to which am invited by my dressmaker who is secretary. Women's equivalent of Rotary Clubs. Only one person of each profession allowed. Informal discussion on kitchens, during which someone remarks commonsensically that it is no use starting on the frills until the essential are there, and gives statistics of houses in country districts which have no water laid on. It is suggested that this should be made an issue at next Election, and meeting decides to get in touch with Women's Institutes which are agitating on matter, and back them up.

Get home and find telephone message to ring up unknown Stroud number: fly to conclusion that disaster has overcome family, but find they are trying out new telephone which has been installed - they got it put in in war time, because District Nurse, next door, had to have it, so it meant little extra labour.

<u>Friday, February 9, 1945</u>

To Ware, bearing basin of dripping and two boxes of matches.

<u>Saturday, February 10, 1945</u>

Temperature drops in afternoon. Take Martin, Pat and baby out.   M.
insists on taking his tricycle and yells with rage if I will not stand
in blizzard and wait for him: if I do wait for him, freezing to the
ground as I do so, Christine complains from pram because I have
stopped. <u>Not</u> an enjoyable walk. We come back in teeth of gale
with driving snow and hail. Pat, the little Cockney, much the best
behaved of the trio.
    It seems as though the war in Europe is expected to end soon,
for Leonard, and other firms engaged on war work, have orders to pack
everything in special water-tight packing-cases. He has to go up to
London to arrange for firm to do this, as his small firm has not the
facilities.

<u>Sunday, February 11, 1945</u>

Frost, but it becomes wet and warmer. Manage to persuade Christine
to accept several spoonfuls of mashed potato and sprout. Martinde-
clares there is a little aimal, "like a rat", fighting with his legs
in bed, reminiscent of Hilary and the worms she used to be afraid of.

<u>Monday, February 12, 1945</u>

Joint declaration by Churchill, Stalin and Roosevelt, after their
meeting in Crimea: broadcast programmes interrupted at 9.30 to give
this news.   N.B. Pyramid, which is supposed to foretell future,
gives March 9 as vital date in war. Has already given two dates -
Pearl Harbour was one, and invasion of Russia by Germany the other.
    Oranges about. Actually see pile of them in shop in Harrow Road:
but one has to show ration book to get any.

<u>Tuesday, February 13, 1945</u>

P. to Ware. Budapest finally captured by Russians.   "Listener"
this week full of miseries of "liberated" Europe.

<u>Wednesday, February 14, 1945</u>

Very loud report from rocket - said to have exploded in air. Everyone,
wherever situated, declares exactly above their heads. 5 p.m. And
another at 10 p.m. When latter goesoff, Bob and I are at Notting Hill
Gate, after supping very pleasantly with Charles Johnson, an Assistant
Keeper at National Gallery.

<u>Thursday, February 15, 1945</u>

There is terrible picture of Cleves in this morning's paper, a town
we have now captured with hardly a house left standing. I recall
Hitler's words that if Germany was defeated she would go down into 1,000

years of barbarism, into which, he added, he would bring also the
whole of the rest of Europe.   (N.B. I only know this in an English
report, and the accent may be wrong - he may have meant, if he didn't
manage to start his New Order going, that was the fate confronting
Europe.)   Perhaps after all the man is a prophet.   Except that "by
their fruits ye shall know them", and his fruits appear to have been
persecution of minorities, I would say thatwe have been fighting
against the inevitable setting up of a new order, and were wrong.
As it is, the "liberated" countries in Europe are, at any rate at
present, in far worse state than they were under German occupation.
One hears conflicting reports but so far as I am able to judge, their
conditions under the Germans were, except in Poland and except for the
Jews, not very dreadful.

    I buy myself material for spring coat.   2¾ yards (12 coupons)
at 41/8 a yard, i.e. £5.14.7.   Feel very wicked all the afternoon at
having spent so much.

    In evening to Abrahams, where meet Alec Robertson of Music Dept.,
B.B.C., and Evelyn Hardy, who has written book on Donne.   Very
pleasant time.

Friday, February 16, 1945

Ridiculously tired after two evenings out - neither of them late.
To Ware, where Phyllida is staying.   Hilary and Leonard to Red Cross
dance organised by L's firm.   Terrific amount of dressing in order
to leave about 8.45.   Martin gets wind early that something unusual
is happening, decides he is being abandoned by everyone, and falls to
yelling at top of voice.   P. has to sing him to sleep, which takes
until just before his parents depart.

Saturday, February 17, 1945

H. and L. returned about 12.30 and had dreadful night with naughty
little Christine, who is today as smiling and lively as can be, while
her parents feel wrecks, and so do I, since I also heard the tumult
from afar.   P. leaves, to meet Arthur at Paddington, and misses her
train.   Christine rolls on to her stomach unaided for first time.

Sunday, February 18, 1945

Mild, sunny, spring-like day.   Crocuses and violets in garden, and
catkins and celandines in hedges.   Several distant explosions last
night.

Monday, February 19, 1945

Cherniakhovsky, one ofRussia's generals, dies of woulds.   Aged only
37, and remarkable in my mind chiefly because B.B.C. news announcer
3 or 4 weeks ago made a solemn pronouncement about "Cherniakhovsky's
fosces", and then hadn't slightest idea what he had done wrong.

Tuesday, February 20, 1945

Reading biography of Albert Schweitzer by George Seaver.   Schweitzer

said, according to Seaver, that "personality develops as it learns
to love more widely and more deeply, but withers as it attaches itself to groups" - which is rather consoling for one like me who has
never been able to attach herself to any group in spite of urgings of
many friends in many directions. Unfortunately feel have not been
able, either, to "love more widely and more deeply".

Ridiculously mild weather; everyone feels tired, and trees are
beginning to think it is time to come out.

Wednesday, February 21, 1945

Take my beautiful coat material to Miss Hall. Pay for two linen
frocks, which, together with cost of stuff, work out at 6 guineas
each! This dreadful figure is, however, quite as much as one would
pay for ready-made article nowadays. And for altering old, acnient
coat, £1.15.0 (more than its original price); and for altering small
jacket, 25/-. No wonder I have had to ask bank to put £12 from my
deposit to my current account. Neither they nor I can find my pass
book. If I have it, it must be in trunk, which has six other trunks
or cases, very dusty all of them, on top of it, in the attic.

When Miss White tells me her mother has had to take to her bed,
she has been so upset by number of rockets near their home at Ching-
ford, and especially by one very close one last night, feel I must be
entirely without heart to be able to fuss with clothes while people
are losing everything.

In evening with Audrey Mearing to "King Lear" - incredibly silly
old man. Brilliant performance by Donald Wolfit; rest of caste not
good.

Thursday, February 22, 1945

In evening call upon Jehovah's Witnesses, who have their headquarters
near here. Knock at door of house with their literature in window.
Little man with north-country voice rather staggered that anyone should
go in and buy anything. Get a book which he says tells me everything,
at 1/6, and 3 pamphlets at 3d. each. Make mistake of giving him my
name and address, which I imagine is to send more literature, but he
suggests someone should call on me. Hastily go into reverse and say
I am away all day, away every weekend, and away practically all night!
As far as can see, they are harmless anarchists, if such a thing can
be. Believe in government direct from God and no other. Are somehow descended from Judge Rutherford's movement - "Millians Now Living
Will Never Die" - and have worked out exact number of souls who will
be saved. (So why bother with anyone, since it is all settled?)

Friday, February 23, 1945

Turkey declares war on Germany and Japan - only because we have said
if she does this she can be represented at the San Francisco conference
in April. Declaration to take effect from March 1. Very odd.

Home sto Stroud by 1.55 for weekend. Phyllida there, but has
to report at farm near Chipping Campden on Monday. Arthur probably
being moved to Paris.

Saturday, February 24 1945

Daddy has heard from Ministry of Labour that he is not nationally
of any importance and that therefore Leslie, who is doing nothing
at all in Fire Service, cannot be released to help him. He is
therefore going to sell the business outright and live on what is
realised, which he says will last him and mother as long as they
are likely to live. Is very tired and feels cannot continue much
longer, and is impatient to get the whole thing settled. He and
Mother both looking older.

Sunday, February 25, 1945

Daddy looks old and worn when he takes up collection in chapel.
Says he is a bit dizzy and will stay in tonight - an unusual decision for him - and then Miss Brinkworth says she has gastric trouble
and asks him to play organ tonight, so he has to go out after all.
        Egypt has followed Turkey's lead and declared war on Germany,
and her Prime Minister has at once been assassinated.
        Back to London. Get seat in train: very stuffy carriage full
of soldiers who all smoke without so much as "by-your-leave", though
it is a non-smoker. On Friday travelled with three mothers going to
see their daughters at Cheltenham College. Discussing difficulties
of clothing daughters on present coupon allowance. One mother says
"These shoes I've got on are a pair Betty has grown out of; and I've
only got one coat and skirt now - I've had to have the other altered
for her".

Monday, February 26, 1945

American reported only 13 miles from Cologne and on the main motor
road. Cry of "oranges" goes up just when I am leaving for office
in morning, and I seize four ration books and get 1 lb. for each
person.

Tuesday, February 27, 1945

Lloyd George (recently raised to the peerage - everyone surprised
he accepted a title) seriously ill. We have pictures ready against
his death, but he appears to be rallying. N.B. Prayers said for him
in churches on Sunday, in Welsh and English!

Wednesday, February 28, 1945

Marjorie Wise has friend who has come back from Arnhem with great
hatred of Germans. Says they came across man who was tortured by
having fingers of his 9-year-old son broken, one by one, in his presence. On other hand, Mr. Pringle has friend who has come back from
Arnhem with great admiration for Germans. Says they were meticulous
in their care not to fire on or bomb Red Cross vehicles; and when
wounded were being helped they always held their fire.

Americans advancing on Cologne.   In evening with Joan to
Albert Hall.   Concert in aid of Polish children, chief item being
Michael Tippett's oratorio "A Child of Our Time".   He wrote words
himself - story of persecuted Jew - and has used Negro Spirituals as
chorales.   Very moving.   Michael Tippett, who is Music Director at
Morley Working Men's College, is pacifist who at beginning of war was
put into prison as conscientious objector who refused to take up any
alternative work suggested by Government.   Owing to intervention of
influential people, he was released: it was argued - with letters
about it in the Press - that a gift like his should not be locked up
in prison, to loss of nation's music.

Thursday, March 1, 1945

To National Gallery concert.   Max Rostal and Franz Osborn (violin
and piano): Brahms.   But am rather tired and do not take in much.

Friday, March 2, 1945

Very tired.   To Ware.   Rocket fell on outskirts of Wareside one
night this week, making one house uninhabitable and blowing out some
windows but injuring no one.   Hilary reports no deliveries of calor gas
matches or paraffin to dealers.   Wonder if another big invasion
(perhaps of Norway?) imminent, since this is state of affairs which
existed just before "D-Day".   Leonard thinks it may be beginning of
large convoy to Far East.

Saturday, March 3, 1945

Sirens to-day, and flying-bomb right over house.   After so long with
no warnings but only unheralded explosions, we feel quite nervous, and
take children into lane in chill sunshine, to get into ditch if another
comes.   L. has borrowed 3 gallons of paraffin from works.   Baby's
leggings which I knitted, and a towel, blow off airing-rail on to
cooker.   Former burnt to cinder and latter has its end removed.
Chimney of one of oil-lamps cracks.
    Germans before Cologne appear to be in state of chaos.   Americans
have reached Rhine.   During a great deal of morning we see gliders being towed south, but wireless gives no news of any airborne landings.

Sunday, March 4, 1945

Get up with bad head, am sick and have to return to bed.   Up again
for dinner.   Hear one flying-bomb and one rocket in early morning.
Wireless reports attacks down East Coast from piloted aircraft last
night.

Monday, March 5, 1945

American tanks in Cologne.   Two Alerts this morning, and hear two
flying-bombs explode.   Everyone seems very tired.   I hope the war
will end before we are too tired to go on any more.
    Paddy Howatson (whose name I do not at first remember) arrives in

office unannounced.   Think object of visit is to get free lunch.
She looks wild, and gives no coherent account of herself, but I
rather gather she is perpetually out of a job - odd nowadays when
labour is in such demand.   Give her lunch at B.B.C. canteen, since
I am in hurry, where when man accidentally bumps against her she
jabs him viciously in leg.   Says you can't trust anyone nowadays.
Am glad she goes before she creates a scene about anything.   Miss
Playle rings me while I am at printing works to say she came in to
office again in afternoon and hung about for some time: Miss P.
did her best to get rid of her.   O dear! do not wish to be harassed
by the semi-mad.

Tuesday, March 6, 1945

The 15 per cent. of Cologne, including cathedral, which remains, now
in allied hands, together with the 85 per cent. of ruins.   One or
two rockets and one or two flying-bombs during day.   Two of Waterlow's
readers away, and only one able to work after 5 p.m., so we do not
finish till 7.45.

Wednesday, March 7, 1945

Several loud reports during night, but was more disturbed by rowdy
soldiers who at midnight paraded street singing loudly and drunkenly.
Today to St. George's Hospital to see Molly Evans.   Take her eggs
from Editor and Audrey Mearing, grapefruit which Mother sent (first
consignment for years which has just reached England), etc.   She has
so many eggs and so much fruit from kind friends, can hardly deal with
it all.   Has ½ lb. butter which grocer let her Mother have for her.
In bus as I go, there is sitting opposite me an old determined lady,
rather like the late Dame Ethel Smyth, in ancient fur coat, loud tweed
suit, uncompromising felt hat, very thin stockings with thick knitted
anklets, and through thin stockings I can see, tattooed on her leg, a
skull-and-crossbones.   She has educated voice and explains to someone
that she cannot get into her own house because it has been taken over
by the Yugoslavs.
        Lunch-hour concert at National Gallery: Baroque Ensemble, playing
Gibbons, etc.: settings for recorder, viola da gamba and viola d'amore,
etc.

Thursday, March 8, 1945

Most excited to hear on 9 p.m. news that Allies have crossed the Rhine
near Bonn.   Didn't expect it for about 2 mmonths.   Meantime we have to
put up with rather a lot of rockets.

Friday, March 9, 1945

Of course news of Rhine crossing is splashed across front of newspapers,
so I do not hesitate to point out that Pyramid, which people allege in
some way foretells future, gave March 9 as turning-point in war.   The

Editor points out that the crossing took place on the 7th.
By 4.45 to Handborough, and arrive at Greens about dusk, rather tired.   Joyce meets me on edge of wood.

Saturday, March 10, 1945

David arrives from Oxford for day.   He has lately had small articles published in Manchester Guardian, and long one in Country Life - reminiscences which he took down from butler who was once pantry boy at Blenheim.   Beautiful day.   Gather primroses in wood with D. and Roger. Latter, starry-eyed as ever and now 4½, can read quite well, and no one has set out to teach him.   There is a plenitude of eggs in the house such as I haven't known since pre-war days.   We have custard with two eggs in it, fish in egg and breadcrumbs, and I had boiled duck's egg for supper last night.
Papers say of Rhine crossing that it happened 10 minutes only before bridge was to have been blown up by Germans.

Sunday, March 11, 1945

Another beautiful day.   Sit on sunny bank and pick white violets with Roger.   D. has gone back to Oxford (he does 24 hours on and 24 off in Fire Service there).   Meditate on the way I don't plan my life at all, whereas D. and J. are always comfortable and provided for because they plan everything.   Back to London under starry sky.   Have heard drone of bombers all weekend, but no bombs of course.

Monday, March 12, 1945

Another beautiful day.   Almond and forsythia out at Waterlows.   In evening to Wigmore Hall with Audrey Mearing, with press tickets given us by Gerald Abraham, to hear first performance in this country of Poulenc's violin and piano sonata.   Frank Howes, music critic of "The Times", after discovering he is sitting in seat for which lady has bought ticket, asks Audrey if weare "press", since he and Scott Goddard of the News Chronincle are coveting our seats.   We reply firmly "Yes", much to his annoyance.
More rockets.   When Arthur got up to Darlington on leave last Monday, to stay with his aunt, he found house empty because they were away, and on letting himself in, discovered much debris and a shell embedded in his aunt's room.   Result of raid by "live" planes the other night.   Two more grapefruit from Mother.

Tuesday, March 13, 1945

Mr. Pringle tells me his Mother-in-law has heard from a cousin of hers in Paris who appears to have lived comfortably while Germans were there (letter came uncensored).   Sends snapshots of himself and family on German photographic paper - here one can rarely buy films.   There was no food shortage till the Allies entered Paris.   Another friend, boy of about 21, in southern France, was not sent to forced labour or otherwise ill-treated.   Indeed, I have not heard at first hand of any of these alleged atrocities, and much disbelieve the whole lot.

Wednesday, March 14, 1945

A cold sunny morning which turns to a mild spring day.   I feel so
unsettled, leave the office at 4 and walk home through park, where
there are crocuses on the grass, and forsythia and almond trees in
flower.   An Alert about 9.30 a.m., and one flying-bomb.   To concert at National Gallery in lunch-hour, with Audrey Mearing.   Max
Rostal and his Chamber Orchestra playing Mozart.

Just finished Virginia Woolf's "The Waves" - second attempt at
reading it.   Glad I persevered.   Think very highly of it.

Thursday, March 15, 1945

Papers report with glee that we are now using 22,000-lb. bombs on
Germany, 11 times the size of the one which fell opposite Broadcasting
House during London blitz and did so much damage.   One cannot imagine
what they are like.   I cannot feel any pleasure at thinking of the
destruction they are wreaking.   Feel very depressed altogether, and
at the futility of the war and of everything else.   Glad I see something young and cheerful at weekend.

Daddy has sold his business.   He asked £3,000 for it, premises
and all (stock extra), and firm who bought it did not demur at all.
He was determined not to haggle: that was his price, they could take
it or leave it.   I think he could have got twice as much for it at
present-day prices, but he says Mother and he will be able to live on
their capital for 12 years and he doesn't expect either of them to last
much beyond 80, and what is the use of haggling and haggling and then
leaving it behind?

Friday, March 16, 1945

To Ware.   Beautiful sunny day.   Several rockets in night, I am told.
Heard only one.   Hilary says there have been great many within her
earshot, day and night, for past week.   Buy ribbon for my hat, 2/6 a
yard.   This extravagance pales into nothing beside Leonard's news -
that his firm has been issuing him with war savings certificates for
some time past, and now say they have not, as they ought, deducted the
cost of them from his monthly cheques.   So he now owes the firm £88,
and will have to sell back all the certificates to pay it.   This, as
H. says, is a blow, when for first time they thought they were saving
some money against the end of the war, when L. may not have a job.
Monthly cheques bear so little relation to one's supposed earnings,
with income-tax and what-all taken off, that this is quite understandable - from L.'s point of view.   He can't complain because his brother is the firm's accountant and so finally responsible, and Ronald
can't ask the firm to be generous to this wronged man because it is
his brother and would look like a suspiciously put-up job.

Saturday, March 17, 1945

Aeroplanes going over in great numbers all day.   Take children out
picking white violets, and the distant rockets we hear seem quite remote and unreal.

Sunday, March 18, 1945

Heard one warning in night, followed by immediate All Clear. Am told
there were two more, and several rockets, and that Christine was very
wakeful, so that her parents had a most restless night. While I am
Wooding with Martin, he says suddenly and soulfully, "I just heard God
singing a little song"; and follows this with the suggestion that I
shouldn't go to Ware next weekend, "because you always take me for
walks and then I don't see what Daddy's doing" - this because his father
is making him a pedal-car. Both children very rosy-looking from the
sun lately. Christine full of winning ways.
     Berlin has its heaviest raid of the war.

Monday, March 19, 1945

On arriving back last night, was told rocket fell at 9.20 in the morning at Marble Arch, just inside gates of park where orators always
stand. Walk through park in morning and see crater. Editor had one
at end of his road on Saturday morning early, which blew out some of
his windows and covered one of his son's beds with glass - but fortunately the boy was away at school.

Tuesday, March 20, 1945

Still very sunny and warm: early blossom out everywhere.

Wednesday, March 21, 1945

To Cundells to try to retrieve my evening dress and coat, left at their
house in early days of war. But since then their things have been
stored, and both are missing. They lost several things from the store
including horn belonging to Edric. In evening to Ruth Davies, who is
in terrific muddle as usual. 7-weeks-old baby not beautiful but very
wide-awake.

Thursday, March 22, 1945

Between crying from (a) 2-year-old Rachel, and (b) 7-weeks-old Richard,
and 3 rockets, sleep hardly at all, and to-day have cold and feel
dreadful. Everyone is very tired and can hardly drag around.

Friday, March 23, 1945

H. says on phone she heard 10 rockets in night and they have been having many in the day too. Martin is getting nervous about them, and
L. wants H. to take children to Stroud, but she thinks she cannot till
Daddy has settled up his business and is less harassed. I go early,
having bad cold, and they met me at station. Tramp has been chasing
lambing ewes, and H. has to tie him up. The bitch at the farm is on
heat so he whines all the time to be off. Leonard at Birmingham for
night. Mother has touch of flu, which is another reason for postponing visit to Stroud, but L. thinks Germans will be sending over all they
can in next week or fortnight, and is anxious for his family to get
somewhere safer.

- 550 -

Saturday, March 24, 1945

One loud rocket about 11 last night, and warning and couple of flying-bombs in early morning, but otherwise night peaceful. H. says the bombardment always stops when I arrive. Beautiful day. Take children, and the erring Tramp, on lead, for walk. Told by young girl as I return that a Soldier has been seen prowling round our house. This, however, is Ralph, who is expected for weekend, In morning we see number of gliders assemble in heavens, and broadcast news says Rhine hasbeen crossed by Montgomery's forces at 3 points, and also by Americans.

Sunday, March 25, 1945

~~News continues very good, and rockets continue to go off.---Lloyd George dies at age of 82, and upsets make-up of Listener.---Miss Morrison says in irritation, "Now why did Lloyd George want to die like that, it will make Miss Redman late for supper!"~~
A little rain in night, and not so brilliant today, but very mild. During night, Tramp (shut in scullery) scrabbled under door coconut matting from passage, and ate large pieces from the sides. The matting doesnot belong to Hilary, and one can get no more of it.

Monday, March 26, 1945

News continues very good, and rockets continue to go off. Lloyd George diesat age of 82, and upsets make-up of Listener. Miss Morrison says in irritation, "Now why did Lloyd George want to die just then, it will make Miss Redman late for supper!"

Tuesday, March 27, 1945

Noisy night. Very tired today. Everyone is very tired. The news continues excellent. Montgomery's troops have broken out of their bridgehead across Rhine. Most trying press day, with much late copy.

Wednesday, March 28, 1945

Quiet night, but I was awake for two hours. Newspapers have headlines to effect that German front at Rhine has collapsed. Eisenhower says there may still be hard fighting, however, but everyone is very optimistic. To dentist and have one tooth filled.

Thursday, March 29, 1945

Mother seems to be very limp. Decide to go home for Easter and not to Ware. Receive copy, which I had ordered, of Osbert Sitwell's autobiography, "Left Hand, Right Hand". Hilary, on phone, reports their hot-water boiler has fallen literally to pieces. There was flying-bomb over house as she was speaking, and she says though past few nights have not been so bad, as soon as I left there was a positive bombardment of rockets.

Friday, March 30, 1945

Home by 1.55. Long queue for train at Paddington, but I get a seat.
Mother and Daddy very pleased to see me. Former still tottery after
flu but on the mend. Letter from Roy which arrived about Wednesday
was only posted on March 4. They are almost sure that they are going
to have another baby in late October, and hope it will be a girl this
time. Miriam says "There are ~~enough boys~~ too many boys on this hill".

Saturday, March 31, 1945

Daddy's last day serving at the shop. We feel as we wait for him to
come home that we ought to have laurel wreaths to hang round his brow.
He has told Mother beforehand (who tells me) that he will feel very
sentimental when he locks up for the last time, but that he won't
waste time in sentiment, but will kneel down and say a prayer before
he comes away. He arrives home tired but pleased with himself and
says, "We went through fire and through water, but Thou broughtest us
out into a wealthy place", and adds that fire and water was what it
sometimes was. Says he now feels like a boy let out from school.
Has been touched and surprised at the number of people who have said
how sorry they are he is giving up - one man nearly wept, and one said
it would be like a landmark going.
Mother has beautiful presents of flowers from Miss Churchman and
Retta.

Sunday, April 1, 1945

Easter Day. Go to two services and a Communion. Mother comes down t
morning service but is rather shaky. Wild, wet day. The wireless
this morning started the 9 a.m. news with "Jesus Christ is risen to-
day", and continued with information about our bombing of Germany.

Monday, April 2, 1945

Daddy on his first free day (though he still has to take stock for
the incoming people) is hit in the eye by a piece of coal, while he
is chopping some for the fire. Back to town: train at Stroud not
too full. Much brighter morning that any during the holiday. Nine
o'clock news says Dortmund-Ems Canal crossed by Montgomery's troops.
And there is a hint that there may be no more rockets! First weather
broadcast since before the war - warning to farmers and fruit-growers
about ground-frost.

Tuesday, April 3, 1945

To press at 9 p.m. At 7 we are taking corrections for broadcast by
Vernon Bartlett which has only been broadcast at 6.15. Montgomery's
forces have certainly gone into north Holland, and there is great hope
that rocket attacks are at an end, though flying-bombs are still a
possibility.

Wednesday, April 4, 1945

Daddy's 69th birthday.   To National Gallery concert.   London
surging with people, all apparently having nothing to do but block
up the pavement in Oxford Street.

Thursday, April 5, 1945

Much talk going on about "V-Day", which, since it will be difficult
to say when the war is at an end, is to be announced arbitrarily by
General Eisenhower.   We are told that then everyone will "down
tools" for the remainder of the day and the whole of the next day.
So that it appears that although when Broadcasting House was bombed
and we could not get at our needed material, The Listener came out
at the proper time; when there were fires all down Holborn and we
spent most of press day sitting in a basement amid enormous machines
with bombs falling around us, still we came out to time; when we had
no windows in the office and no heat, and had to climb up the stairs
over piles of rubble, we came out to time; when the printers and
blockmakers both were laid in ruins over the weekend, still we went
to press on Tuesday as usual; and when we spent nearly all day taking
enforced cover from flying bombs, still we appeared on the right day -
yet when the war is over, we may be faced with the inevitable prospect
of appearing two days late.

Friday, April 6, 1945

Joyce appears for lunch, having escorted 7 children to London for the
holidays.   Thinks she will become full-time artist and give up school
at end of next term.   To Hilary's.   Hot water system out of order,
calor gas given out, H. looks white and tired, but children are flourish
ing.   Christine has cut a tooth.

Saturday, April 7, 1945

Leonard returns from business trip to Edinburgh.   Hilary manages to
get cylinder of calor gas, but then two wicks of oil cooker suddenly
go out of action, and L., rising suddenly, knocks to bits one of the
calor gasmantles.   Martin and I pick horse-mushrooms which are very
good.   Christine naughty all evening.   At 10 p.m. is sitting up
brightly and making conversation while theadults are dropping with
fatigue.

Sunday, April 8, 1945

Phyllida's 36th birthday.   We ring her up at home.   Leonard spends
most of day unavailingly endeavouring to get hot water tap to run.
There are yards of hosepipe in scullery, and Martin has enjoyable time
rushing in and out and stepping in the pools of water on the floor.
I return to London somewhat gratefully.   Bring bits of rhubarb for
Miss Morrison with which she is very pleased.   Hilary has not enough
sugar to use it.

Monday, April 9, 1945

Europe is in ruins, and I spend evening trying to re-furbish an old hat with a bit of pink veiling. New hats of any quality are £5 or £6.

Tuesday, April 10, 1945

Morning paper says our pilots report that from the air the whole of north-west Germany appears to be ablze - may be ammunition dumps fired by Germans themselves. "It looks like the end of the world". One town was "wiped off the face of the earth" in 25 minutes by waves of our bombers. It is plain that another big war would wipe out the whole of Europe. This one is leaving nothing but ruins everywhere.
And meantime, Joan spends a lot of the evening making up my face, with eyelash black, rough and lip-stick. Declares result is an enormous improvement, but I am not entirely convinced that it is. Will buy some cosmetics tomorrow and experiment.

Wednesday, April 11, 1945

To National Gallery and hear Adela Verne (piano) play Bach, Beethoven (Moonlight Sonata) and Chopin. Very warm and I feel very tired.
Edward Ward, B.B.C. War Correspondent who was captured by Italians in N. Africa and has now been rescued from prison camp in Germany, has been back in this country. He offered to Pat Ryan (B.B.C. Controller of News) "a very good talk on the terror raids". "Terror raids!" says Ryan. "Yes - you know, the R.A.F. terror raids. I could do you a good piece on them". "I presume", says Ryan, "you are referring to the R.A.F. pin-point raids on industrial targets. Of course if a few civilians were actually sitting on the roof of a war factory at the time, that is very unfortunate. I am afraid we know nothing about any 'terror raids'". And the public takes for Gospel truth everything it sees in the papers and hears on the wireless.
In evening receive S.O.S. by telephone from Leonard. Hilary in bed with temperature. Say I will go over tomorrow.

Thursday, April 12, 1945

To Ware by 10.6 train. Find Leonard coping. He gets lunch - sausages, and the paraffin stove flares and covers them with a greasy black layer but we eat them tho' I am not surprised that Hilary does not. L. then goes to office. H. has very heavy cold and awful head and sore throat. Children very good. I work very hard, and even then L. gets dinner, which he makes with dried egg (omelettes).

Friday, April 13, 1945

Full of domestic duties and no time for anything but nappie washing, etch. H. a little better. Weather perfect and children very good. I am constantly interrupted in arduous labours by Martin who wants water in vessels to play with in the garden. Tina arrives in evening like angel from heaven.

Grievous news on wireless at 8 a.m. that Roosevelt has died suddenly of cerebral haemorrhage.

Sunday Saturday, April 14, 1945

Ralph turns up and wehave no bed for him so he goes away to Ronald's for night, after helping Leonard with motorcar he is making for M. Woman actually comes for interview re. work. Agrees to come at some vague future date, but H. does not expect it to last long anyway.

Sunday, April 15, 1945

Aeroplanes going over all day. Germany nearly cut in half by Americans, and government and military control to be divided, Kesselring in south and Busch (spelling?) in north. Leonard takes Martin to Orpington to see Grandma Evans. Perfect weather. We have tea in garden and Christine is out all day in sunshine. Gather mushrooms. Back to London. Hilary considerably better, though not really fit to be left to cope alone.

Roosevelt's funeral in New York. On return to London find the Polish Officers who occupy house next door have put a flag out of their window specially to honour Roosevelt by putting it at half mast.

Monday, April 16, 1945

Receive air Altho' price of combs is supposed to be regulated, it is usually impossible to buy one except at exorbitant prices from men on pavement in Oxford Street. Today I get 3, one for Mother, one for Phyllida, one for Hilary, all by request, and have to pay 3/6 each for them. And even while I am handing over the money, the man mutters to his companion, "Look out, Bill, here's a policeman", and the tray is hastily folded up into a suitcase, and Bill and mate fade back into what I observe is a Salvation Army hall. I then proceed down pavement towards Selfridge's, and presumably policeman passes by, because I become aware that out of all the dark doorways and little alleyways on my left, men and gently oozing forth bearing trays full of combs and once more taking up their stand on the pavement.

Tuesday, April 17, 1945

Receive air-letter from John in Ceylon posted only on the 12th. "V"-Day, Eisenhower says, is not to be yet; reminds us that Norway is still to be cleared. Papers are full of horrors of the concentration camp at Buchenwald, where Germans kept what appear mostly to have been foreign internees in dreadful conditions, and, the reports say, there treated them with the utmost cruelty and barbarism. As much hate as possible is being fostered against all Germans, and people are very angry if one tries to keep cool in the matter.

Wednesday, April 18, 1945

Weather very hot, most unusual for April. To Ruby Thompson's (née

Cobley) in evening.   She asks me to have meal before I come, and I
wait in queue for half-an-hour at Lyons Corner House to get a salad,
and then, being still nowhere near getting it, return to B.B.C.
canteen which begins evening meals at 6.30. Ruby and husband coach
backward and difficult boys, or such as need special help in one
subject.   Their house full of coming and goings, and very alive.

Thursday, April 19, 1945

National Gallery concert: string trio, and piano quartet.   Arnold
for night.   Get 1 lb. oranges in morning.

Friday, April 20, 1945

Get Hilary pair nail-scissors, 2/9 (a great find, poor though they
are).   Cannot get her any films for her camera.   Neither can I buy
copy of Trevelyan's "Social History", which since end of last year
has only this month gone into new edition and sold out again.
        Martin has fallen on his face and banged his lip which is very
discoloured.   Very hot day.

Saturday, April 21, 1945

Not quite so fine.   Aeroplanes in great numbers going over all day.

Sunday, April 22, 1945

Quite cold.   Russians in outskirts of Berlin and passing the city on
each side.   Goebbels says death to everyone in any house putting up
a white flag.

Monday, April 23, 1945

Across park with Greta - it is bright with red hawthorn - to visit her
two elderly aunts (one of 76) who are very nice and full of good works.

Tuesday, April 24, 1945

To press at 7.   Very tired, and depressed by Editor's leading article
about German atrocities.   Feel in 10 years' time he will not think
very highly of what he has written.   Atrocity stories still continue.
Graham White has been with party of M.P.s to Buchenwald and other camps
and they are to make official report.   But I feel our attitude of
"revenge on all Germans" is allwrong.   And we keep saying they must
make good the bomb damage here, but no mention is made of their own
hundred times greater bomb damage caused by us.

Wednesday, April 25, 1945

Hilary to Stroud.   Meet her at Liverpool Street and get taxi to

- 556 -

take her and children and suitcases, etc., to Paddington.   This not
too difficult.   Had not expected it to be as easy, and on way asked
taxi-driver in Great Portland Street if he would take me to L.S., wait
perhaps 5 minutes, and transport us to Paddington.   He explains frankly that he can get commission - he means tips - on four or five fares
while he is doing that, so I must make it worth his while.   I ask
how much would make it worth his while, and he says 12/- to 15/-.
Fare from L.S. to Paddington (excluding extras which he knows nothing
about) is 4/6, and from Oxford Circus to L.S. could not be more than
2/6 at most, so he wanted 100% tip, and I refused and went to L.S. by
tube for 3d.   Daddy comes to Paddington to help H. on second half of
journey.
        Letter from Roy, posted March 24 while they were on holiday.
My last one to him vented my irritaion with America and the Americans
He says, "Don't judge the U.S. by young and irresponsible G.I.s, any
more than you would recommend the French to judge England by the behaviour of our soldiers over there.   On the other hand their bragg-
ing can be very vexing, although it is only their peculiar way of
keeping up their own morale.   Historians will no doubt straighten
out things later on.   We owe the U.S. a lot - they saved the shipping
situation for us when the submarine campaign was at its worst and they
are now taking the greater part of the burden on the western front.
On the other hand they lost Singapore for us at Pearl Harbour by
criminal carelessness and I suspect the Ardennes trouble back last
December was as much due to their carelessness as to German efficiency
But it is too early yet to argue over these things".
        Russians say Berlin is entirely encircled; and we are now try-
ing to encircle Munich (or perhaps that is the Americans).   Germans
say Hitler himself is in command in the capital, 90 per cent.of which
is reported to be destroyed.

Thursday, April 26, 1945

We have rent away from the office windows the netting which has been
over the glass ever since the building was blasted in 1940.   (The
blackout ended officially last Monday.)   The office-boy spends most
of the afternoon clearing off the dirt and glue, and now we almost
feel we are sitting in the street, it is so bright and clear.
        Bremen captured.   Risings of Patriots in North Italy.   Russians
take Brno.
        In evening to Miss Scott-Johnston's (Mrs. Milsom), whose husband
states emphatically that people who steal things from railways ought
to be shot, as looters; and that the Italians are most unpleasant
people, as bad as the Germans.   This does not in the least agree
with the verdict of Miss Johnson who lived there and who thinks they
are charming people.
        The Editor's leader of to-day, to which I took exception, says
among other things: "'Cold fury', according to one correspondent,
was the feeling engendered among the British troops by what they
saw and experienced" (in the concentration camps in Germany); "it is
a feeling that is as fully shared as it can be by the people of these
islands - reinforcing our determination that justice shall be done
and that the perpetrators of these crimes against humanity shall be

sought out and visited, if not with the punishment they deserve (for
that would be impossible) at least with punishment as exemplary as
we can make it.   Nor must the perpetrators, direct and indirect, of
these abominations be the only ones to feel the attentions of the outside world;   the German people themselves, they who have allowed these
~~abominations~~ things to happen within their borders, must somehow or
other be made aware - as far as they are capable of being made aware
- of the extent to whichthey have permitted the name of humanity to
be disgraced".   And, "Germany is part of Europe and will remain part
of Europe;   at present she may be regarded more as a plague-spot than
as a country;   but as she is part of Europe, Europe owes it to herself
that this plague-spot shall be so 'treated' that the cause of the
plague may be restored".   All this gives room, it seems to me, for
us, in our attitude and treatment of Germany, to become as sadistic
and bad as the Nazis themselves.

Friday, April 27, 1945

American troops link up with Russians.   Mussolini reported to be
captured in North Italy, "yellow with fear and hatred".
        Much colder: I travel to Felcourt for weekend.   Country look-
ing wonderful after rain yesterday, but temperature about half what
it has been lately.

Saturday, April 28, 1945

Reports, which seem to have foundation, that Germany has offered unconditional surrender to Britain and the United States, but not to
Russia.   Downing Street issues statement that no offers can be
considered which are not made equally to the three Powers.
        Fantastic weather, especially considering that a fortnight ago
we had midsummer heat.   Scurries of snow and hail all day, with icy
winds, and bright sunshine in between.   Walk to East Grinstead (3
miles) through unbelievably green trees, to try to buy Trevelyan's
"English Social History" (London cannot produce one copy), but the
bookshop is closed.   So we wait in snowstormfor bus, while elderly
lady explains to elderly man how an unconscious friend lay for an
hour in the cemetery, "and she has a companion and a housemaid and a
nephew and must needs go out alone".   The deaf man, puzzled, says,
"Why did she lie in the cemetery", which shows he does not hear properly because the reason was that she had fallen and broken her leg.

Sunday, April 29, 1945

Allied air fleet on its way to Occupied Holland with cargo of food
to drop.   Wake up ~~up~~ in early hours and there is layer of snow on
ground, which has gone this morning, but it is still very cold.
Beautiful colours - one part of sky blue with sun shining: in opposite point of heavens is purple thundercloud, and aginst it, ~~with~~
lit up by the sun, a very green beech tree next to a dark pine.
Near the station is cottage with long straggly garden path, and down
it on each side are little union jacks, and over the garden gate are
lots of little flags sewn together to make a big one, and in strag

letters, "Welcome Home" - probably for a returning prisoner, of whom
there are a good many just now.

Monday, April 30, 1945

Still very cold. Fantastic rumours circulating all day. Himmler
says Hitler is dead; Himmler says Hitler is dying; Himmler says
Hitler is mad - he is said to be making speeches to an empty room and
constructing a model of London. Goering said to be mad, dressing up
in a Roman toga and painting his finger-nails pink. (It was Himmler
who made the offer of unconditional surrender to Britain and U.S.)
We wish we knew when "VE"-Day (Victory in Europe) is likely to be
announced, it would be very much more convenient for the paper.
The uncertainty has as bad an effect on my stomach as the outbreak
of war and the beginning of the blitz. Even the weather continues
to be fantastic, and there is 4-hour snowstorm in Straitsof Dover.
    To one of the Baptist May Meetings - enormous building packed
with animated Baptists who look as though they don't know yet that
there is a war in progress.

Tuesday, May 1, 1945

Rumours still rampant, but there is nothing definite, until at 10.45
p.m. the German radio announced that Hitler is dead. This news con-
veyed to me by Nancy as she rushes downstairs to take a telephone
call. Listen, therefore to Forces News at 10.45,which says he has
died in action, "of a stroke", whatever that may signify. This after
an announcement earlier in the day that the last pocket of resistance
in Berlin has Hitler as its core. Count Bernadotte of Sweden, who
seems to be a go-between in peace moves, has returned to his country
from Germany, it is said with no further offers from Himmler.
    We go to press as usual, with an "interim" leader, written at
the last moment by the Editor, neither an ordinary leader nor special
"Victory" leader appearing suitable at the moment. Mr. Pringle,
surveying general situation, says that Europe will be faced next
winter with the worst food shortage for centuries.

Wednesday, May 2, 1945

Morning papers splash "HITLER DEAD", and I go into office to see what
steps Listener will take about breaking up formes to get news into
paper. Mr. Pringle has matter in hand, and I go off to Bloomsbury
Baptist Church (for another of these May Meetings - was asked by Mr.
Millard of Stroud to be a delegate), where they start with reading
"In the year that King Uzziah died I saw also the Lord. Meet Vera
Beard for lunch, which is served so slowly it takes 2 hours. In
evening "Missionary Rally", packed with people, and very hot, which
goes on far too long. Get meal at convenient place near Paddington
which is open very late and where I eat real lamb chop. When I get
home Tina says German armies in Italy have surrendered unconditionally
and we have a million prisioners; and that Berlin has fallen.

"Horror pictures" of captured German concentration camps are being shown in London, and I observe a long queue waiting to go in and see them.   A woman from Manchester tells me she heard two boys talking, and one said, this time a propos of the film of the camps, "Hast seen horros, lad?"   "Eh, I've seen them twice," said the other,"theyre champion".   "Come on, let's have another go", said his companion.

Thursday, May 3, 1945

Letter in Telegraph from Lord Birkenhead protesting against pictures of Mussolini being published - he was hanged by his own countrymen or shot first and then hanged, along with his mistress, and photographs have been in all the newspapers.   Russians are now saying that Hitler and Goebbels committed suicide.   On 1 o'clock News, which I hear while I am lunching at Peter Robinson's, surrender of Hamburg is announced.

Friday, May 4, 1945

Weather has improved a little.   To Handborough.   Likely to be one of the most dramatic weeks of war, and I must needs go where there is no wireless set.   After 9 o'clock news a neighbour tells us that Denmark, the enemy-occupied part of Holland, and the rest of North Germany is to be surrendered to Montgomery as from 8 a.m. tomorrow.

Saturday, May 5, 1945

In evening we are told that more "pockets" in south of Germany have given in.   Helen, the girl who informs us, has young cousin back after two years as prisoner in Germany.   He is very thin and his face twitches.
      It pours with rain almost all day.   In evening I go for stroll down lanes laden with hawthorn, very sweet-smelling.

Sunday, May 6, 1945

Still windy and wet, and still no definite news of end of war.   I go out just before lunch, and lanes smell of wet warm earth, hedge parsley and again hawthorn.
      Back to London.   Paddington Hotel has hadbarriers round door (to keep in light and keep out bomb blast) taken away.   The swing door is visible, with lights shining out and people coming and going.

Monday, May 7, 1945

Suddenly it is very mild, muggy and thundery, though at lunch-time the sun shines and flags have begun to appear in Oxford Street and the smaller roads round it.   We are given a copy of the speech the King is to broadcast, but no one knows when so it is Highly Confidential;   and the Prime Minister is to speak, no one knows when or for

how long. We go to printers, who seem in great muddle as to whether
they are going to continue working all night, or normally, nor not going to work at all. We hear 6 o'clock news which merely says that
the Germans say they have surrendered. Am an hour late for dinner,
and listen to 9 o'clock news, which announces that the Prime Minister
will broadcast at 3 o'clock tomorrow, which is to be regarded as "V"
Day - or "VE"-Day, because it is only the end of the European war -
and the King at 9 o'clock. It is all very flat, even though my
balcony is bedecked with all the little flags which Miss Morrison
got out and washed last autumn. I see I shall have to work very
late tomorrow, though officially it is a public holiday. Feel very
cross, which is not the right feeling for the end of the war. Then
read the 40th chapter of Isaiah and go to bed. At 11.15 am got up
to go down to lounge and drink glass of sherry from bottle which
Miss Conby has been saving for three years for this occasion.

  Not very much excitement in streets. A house at back has
managed to get a "V" sign in electric lights over its door, flanked
by two Union Jacks, whichis rather effective.

Tuesday, May 8, 1945

There was tremendous and dramatic thunderstorm last night, reminding
me of the one on the night of Sept. 1 - 2, 1940, when Cabinet was
meeting to decide about declaration of war. Lie in bed listening
to cracks of thunder and watching brilliant flashes and wonder how
an Old Testament prophet would interpret it: Jehovah saying, this
is the end of war, tomorrow will be peace; or saying, you imagine
you've achieved peace, do you? - well, look out!

  General holiday, but I have to go to printing works, where do
not achieve much because printers are engaged in getting out special
emergency number of Radio Times. Am full of fury at way we are always to be subordinated to another paper and express strong views to
Editor who agrees with them heartily.

  Mr. Pringle and I eat sandwiches for lunch, sitting on bank of
canal in sunshine, and reflect that one might spend "VE-Day" in worse
surroundings - probably West End of London is unbearably crowded.
Try to get drink at Abbey Arms - restaurant part is shut but bar
open - but there are about 200 people, and apparently the place has
about 30 glasses, so there is no hope. Rowdy house - knot of
Canadiansoldiers singing songs (quite harmlessly) to themselves,
glasses in hand; one couple dancing; some people playing darts;
altogether a great noise and I prefer the canal.

  In evening At 3 o'clock listen to Prime Minister's broadcast,
in which he officially announces end of war in Europe, ending drama-
tically "Advance Britannia! Long live the cause of liberty! God
save the King!" Take it down for printers to set up.

  In evening have drink of gin and grape fruit, which far-seeing
Constance has been hoarding, and listen to King's broadcast at nine
o'clock, which check with proof I have,already set up. Then four of
us say we will go for little stroll in park in warm evening, to get

some air.   Guns are firing victory salvoes - great mistake in
London, we think.   Some boys are lighting bonfire in Kensington
Gardens and piling wood on it.   We stroll on down Serpentine and
across Hyde Park Corner and down Constitution Hill.   More people
here, but not too crowded.   See from distance that Buckingham
Palace is flood-lit, and just when we are approaching hear great
wave of cheering spread over crowds assembled before it.   So we
hurry last bit of way, and on balcony are King, Queen and two
princesses waving to crowd.   Am too short-sighted to see them, but
am told King is wearing naval uniform, Queen is in blue with tiara,
Princess Elizabeth in A.T.S. uniform, and Princess Margaret Rose in
blue dress.   Coloured lights are being sent up from St. James's
Park and they appear to fall in front of flood-lit palace, with
very pretty effect.   We then wander home, having without trouble
seen what many people struggled through dense crowds down the Mall
to see, and then waited for a long time before it happened.

Wednesday, May 9, 1945

The Cease Fire sounded on all fronts at 1 minute after midnight,
and today the Russians are rejoicing.   We go to press today instead
of yesterday, owing to Radio Times, and printers are to have tomorro
off, so that paper will not be machined till Friday, and won't reac
readers till Saturday, when allthe news we have sweated to get in
will be out of date.   Am very tired and dispirited.   This is the
end of the war in Europe and also the end of this diary.   As far
as the family is concerned, Daddy has had his wish and has lived to
see the defeat of Germany.   He has sold his business and thinks he
has enough to live on.   He and Mother have naturally aged a good
deal in the last five years, but they are still both very fresh and
young in mind and spirit.   Roy has had two more children since the
war started, and a fourth is on the way.   Phyllida has returned
from South Africa, given up her job - in fact changed several times
gone intothe Land Army and got engaged to Arthur Place - for if and
when he is free to marry her.   Hilary has had two children since
the war started, and has had the blitz at Croydon, and the rockets
at Ware - where she has had a very inconvenient house to live in,
but has had her family with her all the time, and is fortunate to
have a whole house at all, even temporarily.   I have done nothing
worth doing since the war started; have had a 6-months illness,
feel I have got old and tired and cross and crotchety, and have
stuck in the same job (not that I was at liberty to move, under the
Ministry of Labour regulations).   Do not feel I have improved in
any way, but have become worse in almost all respects.   Have made
some new friends and let drop some old ones, but none of the old
ones I really cared most about.   Am very depressed to think of all
the destruction and sorrow there is all over Europe, and do not
see how the job of "building a better world" can even be contemplated
until we all have a new heart and spirit.